Dictionary of Literary Biography

Dictionary of Literary Biography Documentary Series

Dictionary of Literary Biography Yearbooks

1980 edited by Karen L. Rood, Jean W. Ross, and Richard Ziegfeld (1981)

1981 edited by Karen L. Rood, Jean W. Ross, and Richard Ziegfeld (1982)

1982 edited by Richard Ziegfeld; associate editors: Jean W. Ross and Lynne C. Zeigler (1983)

1983 edited by Mary Bruccoli and Jean W. Ross; associate editor Richard Ziegfeld (1984)

1984 edited by Jean W. Ross (1985)

1985 edited by Jean W. Ross (1986)

1986 edited by J. M. Brook (1987)

1987 edited by J. M. Brook (1988)

1988 edited by J. M. Brook (1989)

1989 edited by J. M. Brook (1990)

1990 edited by James W. Hipp (1991)

1991 edited by James W. Hipp (1992)

1992 edited by James W. Hipp (1993)

1993 edited by James W. Hipp, contributing editor George Garrett (1994)

1994 edited by James W. Hipp, contributing editor George Garrett (1995)

1995 edited by James W. Hipp, contributing editor George Garrett (1996)

1996 edited by Samuel W. Bruce and L. Kay Webster, contributing editor George Garrett (1997)

1997 edited by Matthew J. Bruccoli and George Garrett, with the assistance of L. Kay Webster (1998)

1998 edited by Matthew J. Bruccoli, contributing editor George Garrett, with the assistance of D. W. Thomas (1999)

1999 edited by Matthew J. Bruccoli, contributing editor George Garrett, with the assistance of D. W. Thomas (2000)

2000 edited by Matthew J. Bruccoli, contributing editor George Garrett, with the assistance of George Parker Anderson (2001)

2001 edited by Matthew J. Bruccoli, contributing editor George Garrett, with the assistance of George Parker Anderson (2002)

Concise Series

Concise Dictionary of American Literary Biography, 7 volumes (1988–1999): *The New Consciousness, 1941–1968; Colonization to the American Renaissance, 1640–1865; Realism, Naturalism, and Local Color, 1865–1917; The Twenties, 1917–1929; The Age of Maturity, 1929–1941; Broadening Views, 1968–1988; Supplement: Modern Writers, 1900–1998.*

Concise Dictionary of British Literary Biography, 8 volumes (1991–1992): *Writers of the Middle Ages and Renaissance Before 1660; Writers of the Restoration and Eighteenth Century, 1660–1789; Writers of the Romantic Period, 1789–1832; Victorian Writers, 1832–1890; Late-Victorian and Edwardian Writers, 1890–1914; Modern Writers, 1914–1945; Writers After World War II, 1945–1960; Contemporary Writers, 1960 to Present.*

Concise Dictionary of World Literary Biography, 10 volumes projected (1999–   ): *Ancient Greek and Roman Writers; German Writers; African, Caribbean, and Latin American Writers; South Slavic and Eastern European Writers.*

Seventeenth-Century French Writers

Dictionary of Literary Biography® • Volume Two Hundred Sixty-Eight

Seventeenth-Century French Writers

Edited by
Françoise Jaouën
Yale University

A Bruccoli Clark Layman Book

GALE®

THOMSON

GALE

Detroit • New York • San Diego • San Francisco • Cleveland • New Haven, Conn. • Waterville, Maine • London • Munich

THOMSON

™

GALE

Dictionary of Literary Biography
Volume 268: Seventeenth-Century
French Writers
Françoise Jaouën

Advisory Board
John Baker
William Cagle
Patrick O'Connor
George Garrett
Trudier Harris
Alvin Kernan
Kenny J. Williams

Editorial Directors
Matthew J. Bruccoli and Richard Layman

Senior Editor
Karen L. Rood

While every effort has been made to ensure the reliability of the information presented in this publication, The Gale Group, Inc. does not guarantee the accuracy of the data contained herein. The Gale Group, Inc. accepts no payment for listing; and inclusion in the publication of any organization, agency, institution, publication, service, or individual does not imply endorsement of the editors or publisher. Errors brought to the attention of the publisher and verified to the satisfaction of the publisher will be corrected in future editions.

LIBRARY OF CONGRESS CATALOGING-IN-PUBLICATION DATA

Seventeenth-Century French writers / edited by Françoise Jaouën.
    p. cm. — (Dictionary of literary biography ; v. 268)
"A Bruccoli Clark Layman book."
Includes bibliographical references and index.
        ISBN 0-7876-6012-4
        1. French literature—17th century—Dictionaries.
        2. French literature—17th century—Bio-bibliography—Dictionaries.
        3. Authors, French—17th century—Biography—Dictionaries.
        I. Title: 17th-century French writers. II. Jaouën, Françoise.
        III. Series.
PQ241 .S48 2002
840.9'004'03—dc21   2002032524
[B]

Printed in the United States of America
10 9 8 7 6 5 4 3 2 1

Contents

Plan of the Series

The advisory board, the editors, and the publisher of the *Dictionary of Literary Biography* are joined in endorsing Mark Twain's declaration. The literature of a nation provides an inexhaustible resource of permanent worth. Our purpose is to make literature and its creators better understood and more accessible to students and the reading public, while satisfying the needs of teachers and researchers.

To meet these requirements, *literary biography* has been construed in terms of the author's achievement. The most important thing about a writer is his writing. Accordingly, the entries in *DLB* are career biographies, tracing the development of the author's canon and the evolution of his reputation.

The purpose of *DLB* is not only to provide reliable information in a usable format but also to place the figures in the larger perspective of literary history and to offer appraisals of their accomplishments by qualified scholars.

The publication plan for *DLB* resulted from two years of preparation. The project was proposed to Bruccoli Clark by Frederick G. Ruffner, president of the Gale Research Company, in November 1975. After specimen entries were prepared and typeset, an advisory board was formed to refine the entry format and develop the series rationale. In meetings held during 1976, the publisher, series editors, and advisory board approved the scheme for a comprehensive biographical dictionary of persons who contributed to literature. Editorial work on the first volume began in January 1977, and it was published in 1978. In order to make *DLB* more than a dictionary and to compile volumes that individually have claim to status as literary history, it was decided to organize volumes by topic, period, or

genre. Each of these freestanding volumes provides a biographical-bibliographical guide and overview for a particular area of literature. We are convinced that this organization—as opposed to a single alphabet method—constitutes a valuable innovation in the presentation of reference material. The volume plan necessarily requires many decisions for the placement and treatment of authors. Certain figures will be included in separate volumes, but with different entries emphasizing the aspect of his career appropriate to each volume. Ernest Hemingway, for example, is represented in *American Writers in Paris, 1920–1939* by an entry focusing on his expatriate apprenticeship; he is also in *American Novelists, 1910–1945* with an entry surveying his entire career, as well as in *American Short-Story Writers, 1910–1945, Second Series* with an entry concentrating on his short fiction. Each volume includes a cumulative index of the subject authors and articles.

Since 1981 the series has been further augmented by the *DLB Yearbooks*, which update published entries, add new entries to keep the *DLB* current with contemporary activity, and provide articles on literary history. There have also been nineteen *DLB Documentary Series* volumes, which provide illustrations, facsimiles, and biographical and critical source materials for figures, works, or groups judged to have particular interest for students. In 1999 the *Documentary Series* was incorporated into the *DLB* volume numbering system beginning with *DLB 210: Ernest Hemingway.*

We define literature as the *intellectual commerce of a nation:* not merely as belles lettres but as that ample and complex process by which ideas are generated, shaped, and transmitted. *DLB* entries are not limited to "creative writers" but extend to other figures who in their time and in their way influenced the mind of a people. Thus the series encompasses historians, journalists, publishers, book collectors, and screenwriters. By this means readers of *DLB* may be aided to perceive literature not as cult scripture in the keeping of intellectual high priests but firmly positioned at the center of a nation's life.

DLB includes the major writers appropriate to each volume and those standing in the ranks behind them. Scholarly and critical counsel has been sought in deciding which minor figures to include and how full their entries should be. Wherever possible, useful references are made to figures who do not warrant separate entries.

Each *DLB* volume has an expert volume editor responsible for planning the volume, selecting the figures for inclusion, and assigning the entries. Volume editors are also responsible for preparing, where appropriate, appendices surveying the major periodicals and literary and intellectual movements for their volumes, as well as lists of further readings. Work on the series as a whole is coordinated at the Bruccoli Clark Layman editorial center in Columbia, South Carolina, where the editorial staff is responsible for accuracy and utility of the published volumes.

One feature that distinguishes *DLB* is the illustration policy—its concern with the iconography of literature. Just as an author is influenced by his surroundings, so is the reader's understanding of the author enhanced by a knowledge of his environment. Therefore *DLB* volumes include not only drawings, paintings, and photographs of authors, often depicting them at various stages in their careers, but also illustrations of their families and places where they lived. Title pages are regularly reproduced in facsimile along with dust jackets for modern authors. The dust jackets are a special feature of *DLB* because they often document better than anything else the way in which an author's work was perceived in its own time. Specimens of the writers' manuscripts and letters are included when feasible.

Samuel Johnson rightly decreed that "The chief glory of every people arises from its authors." The purpose of the *Dictionary of Literary Biography* is to compile literary history in the surest way available to us—by accurate and comprehensive treatment of the lives and work of those who contributed to it.

The *DLB* Advisory Board

Introduction

To label literary periods according to certain ideological criteria established for the most part by literary historians of the nineteenth century has become traditional practice. Although these criteria have recently come under scrutiny and are now being questioned, former labels die hard. The *Middle Ages,* the *Renaissance,* and the *Enlightenment* are still key words in periodization. Such is also the case for the French seventeenth century, long called "Siècle classique" (the classical century) or "Siècle de Louis XIV" (the century of Louis XIV). The label "classical" was applied in reference to the renewed interest in Greek and Roman authors and the imitation and rewriting of many important works of antiquity by such luminaries as Pierre Corneille, Jean Racine, and Jean de La Bruyère. It also referred to a set of rules, both technical and ideological, refined and put in place during the period—such rules as the three unities of time, place, and action for tragedy; rules of grammar and style; and verisimilitude and propriety of subject matter. Although these rules played a key role in the literature of the period, to apply the label "classical" indiscriminately to a whole century is misleading for two reasons: many important writers, including so-called classical ones, did not obey those rules and did their best to break them; furthermore, "classical" refers for the most part to writers of the second half of the century only. Still today, many works and writers of the first half of the century are called "pré-classiques" (pre-classical). The name "Siècle de Louix XIV" is even more reductive, since Louis XIV did not come into power until 1661 at the age of twenty-three, well after the death of René Descartes (1650) and well after most of Corneille's major plays (*Le Cid,* 1637; *Horace,* 1640; and *Cinna,* 1642).

What perhaps best defines the literature of the period, however, is revealed by what these two former titles imply—a certain type of political order and the growing awareness of literature as a separate domain, in need of rules and regulations. "Le siècle de Louis XIV" may in fact be an apt label insofar as the Sun King came to embody absolutism, a form of government practically "invented" and put into place by Armand du Plessis, cardinal de Richelieu in the 1620s and 1630s. The rules of French classicism were developed at the same time and hotly debated in countless treatises. What is perhaps difficult to understand today is that both absolutism and the imposition of aesthetic standards were to a large extent embraced by many as the means to an end—political and artistic independence and stability after a long period of turmoil begun several decades earlier. In 1559, during the festivities celebrating the marriage of his daughter Elizabeth to King Phillip II of Spain, the king of France, Henri II, was wounded during a joust: his opponent's lance pierced his helmet, broke off, and lodged in his brain through the eye. He died after several days of intense agony. This famous tragic episode (recounted in Marie-Madeleine Pioche de La Vergne, comtesse de Lafayette's 1678 novel *La Princesse de Clèves*) was interpreted by some as an ominous sign for the monarchy. The sudden and brutal death of the king coincided with the beginning of one of the bloodiest chapters in French history, marked by civil and religious strife and large-scale massacres. The political turmoil was exacerbated by feuds between princely families vying for power. In 1589 the assassination of Henri III, the last scion of the Valois dynasty, further weakened the monarchy almost to the point of extinction, since the next in line to the throne was a Protestant prince, Henri de Bourbon-Navarre, and the fundamental laws of the kingdom demanded a Catholic king. After many negotiations and renewed fighting, Henri de Navarre converted to Catholicism and became Henri IV, the first French Bourbon king, founder of the last French royal dynasty and grandfather of Louis XIV. Henri IV is best remembered today for the 1598 edict of religious toleration called the Edict of Nantes, which granted Protestants the freedom to practice their religion in specific places of worship. The edict, often wrongly assumed to be a universal treaty of religious tolerance, in fact, had many restrictions and was established for political reasons: forced conversion of the Protestants had failed, and to put an end to civil wars and restore some measure of order was imperative. No longer demonized, the Protestants were simple heretics "by mistake" to be converted by persuasion and not repression. The edict effectively put an end to civil strife and brought peace back to the kingdom. Stability was short-lived, however, and Henri IV was assassinated in 1610. The death of a king is a momentous event under any circumstances, but this assassination was especially significant, for it marked the third time in fifty years that a French king had come to a brutal end. The assassinations of Henri III and Henri IV put in serious jeopardy the notion of the divine right of kings, since the last three had apparently not been blessed with special protection from above. Furthermore, Henri IV's assassin, François Ravaillac, claimed that he was the instrument of divine justice befalling the tyrant king, guilty of protecting heresy. The claim was taken seriously, since far from being the isolated decree of a madman, it had been put forth in a series of anonymous pamphlets emanating from extremists of various religious and political hues. The gravity of these accusations was compounded by the invoking of the Scriptures and such authorities as Aristotle and St. Thomas Aquinas in support of the legitimacy of regicide in cases of tyranny. Confronted with yet another threat, the ruling powers of the kingdom rallied; the Sorbonne, the highest spiritual authority of the kingdom, convened and declared heretical any attempt against the sacred person of the king. A few days later, the French Parliament issued a decree condemning regicide and establishing the absolute legitimacy of the king. From then on, civil peace became the goal to be achieved by any means necessary. The half-century between 1559 and 1610 was seen restrospectively as a nightmarish episode, best buried in the collective unconscious. This view may explain in part why so few works of the period deal with recent French history, or even contemporary history. Unlike William Shakespeare, neither Corneille nor Racine wrote "historical" plays. They chose their subject matter from the works of antiquity, among the Greek and Roman playwrights, or found inspiration in Roman historians and poets. Not until the 1660s did recent French history find its way into fiction, in novels and novellas.

The impulse toward Antiquity should not, however, be construed as escapism. The Greeks and the Romans provided an excellent template for political and artistic reflection. Ancient Greece was the birthplace of philosophy, literature, and the arts; Ancient Rome, that of politics and history. The history of Rome, from its mythical beginnings to the fall of the Roman Empire, provided endless fodder for investigation into the nature of political power, providence, and historical relativism. Inspired by Niccolò Machiavelli's work on the art of politics based on his commentaries of Roman historians, the French followed suit in countless works, both fictional and nonfictional, and manufactured their own brand of political critique, at once extolling the virtues of absolutism and showing its pitfalls under cover of famous ancient histories.

Curious though it may sound, the interest in Ancient Rome was in fact a modern move, for it was, paradoxically, a way to break with tradition and to overcome the hurdle that writers of the previous century had faced. During the sixteenth century, political and religious turmoil fostered a vast inquiry into the origins of French language and culture, as well as its political roots, in order to provide stable historical foundations for the emerging nation-state. The history of the Franks and the Gauls became a favorite focus of research and a typical motif in national histories. These investigations soon reached an impasse, however, for the evidence pointed to a mixed Frankish and Germanic origin, with the unavoidable traces of Roman invasion. French historians then rewrote in part the history of origins and added some mythical elements in order to build a seamless, unbroken record of evolution. The name France was no longer a derivation of "Frankish" but the name left to the nation by its founder, Francion or Francus (the hero of an epic poem by Pierre de Ronsard), a Trojan hero who had, much like Aeneas, escaped from the ruined city of Troy and wandered off to establish a new state. The myth, based on Virgil's *Aeneid* (circa 30 B.C.), was not new; it can be traced back to the seventh century and was popular elsewhere in Europe. In the sixteenth century this legend of Trojan origins provided a convenient shortcut, bypassing centuries of doubtful or controversial historical records and going all the way back to what was at the time considered the first "history," Homer's *Iliad* (circa ninth- or eighth-century B.C.?). No one actually believed in the myth; its popularity was born out of the impulse to find incontrovertible evidence of pristine national roots in order to claim political and cultural independence, if not supremacy.

The search, however, produced significant results. Scholars developed an interest in little-studied languages such as Arabic and Hebrew as well as forgotten ancient languages such as Aramaic. The Reformation and the Counter Reformation further encouraged research on ancient texts, as scholars from all faiths studied the origins and authenticity of both scriptural and doctrinal documents. Methods of research were also devised; treatises written; and concepts developed. The French language was also affected. Grammarians and philologists devoted their efforts to the creation of a technical apparatus that would give their language the tools it needed to become an instrument of national unity. Until late in the sixteenth century and even into the seventeenth century, grammar, spelling, and syntax were not standardized. They varied not only in different regions but also according to the printer, since different printers used different character sets. In a telling anecdote, Michel Eyquem de Montaigne claimed he chose to write his *Essais* (1580; augmented in 1582 and 1588) in French (instead of Latin, his "native" tongue) because he did not expect his work, intended for a close circle of family and friends and not for an actual public, to survive. Whether true or not, the claim, also made by other writers of the period, reflects the shifting quality of the French language as well as its rapid evolution. John Calvin's *Institutio Christianae Religionis* (Institutes of the Christian Religion, 1541) went through several translations in a few years as each translation rapidly became obsolete. Poets and authors became similarly involved in this process of linguistic and aesthetic "nationalization" and produced important treatises on poetics, the most famous of which is the *Défense et illustration de la langue française* (Defense and Illustration of the French Language), published by Joachim du Bellay in 1549.

The effort of these authors and scholars was carried into the seventeenth century, but the spirit in which it had been undertaken was lost. Many scholars of the Renaissance thought of national unity as a concept that would promote the notion of citizenship over that of religious obedience, and therefore as the means to overcome civil disturbance. Once the Edict of Nantes had been put into place, and after Henry IV had been assassinated, national unity became the diminished by-product of an enforced civil order.

Richelieu's avowed goal was to centralize power, quell rebellion in any and every form, and put an end to the political pretentions of the high aristocracy whose military and economic power was still considerable. The shadow revolution known as the Fronde (1648–1653), fomented to a large degree by these noble families, nearly succeeded in unseating the monarchy. The adolescent Louis XIV, forced to escape the Louvre palace in Paris and take refuge in Saint-Germain, is said to have based his politics of absolute rule on this episode, which proved the need to protect the monarchy once and for all from the threat of feudalism.

To find traces of serious dissent in the texts of the period, however, is difficult. Most authors rallied to absolutism as the means to ensure civil peace, which was, as Blaise Pascal wrote, "le plus grand bien" (the greatest of goods). Political critique, when it existed, always targeted "les grands" (the aristocracy) or ministers, seldom the king or the form of government. Similarly, libertinism was directed against the Church, not the State, and most seventeenth-century *libertins* (free-thinkers) held politically conservative views. Subversion did exist, but it took on subtle and often misleading forms. Descartes, credited with the invention of modern metaphysics, based his new philosophy on reason because, he said, it is the one intellectual gift shared by all mankind and therefore the only solid foundation on which to build a truly universal system. Paradoxically, this belief resulted in an "absolutist" philosophy

in which the ego is the sole ruler and judge of its world, seemingly belying its universal purpose. But Descartes's method, as expressed in his *Discours de la Méthode pour bien conduire sa raison, et chercher la verité dans les sciences* (1637) and other works, was also revolutionary in that it presupposed the dismissal of all previous knowledge as useless and false. The new method did away with established opinions and paved the way for novel inquiries into the nature of truth. In Descartes's system, reason became the weapon that covertly undermined all previous belief systems to such an extent that Cartesianism was censored in many countries, including France, in one form or another.

The emphasis placed on reason, not only by Descartes but also by many of his contemporaries, was similarly a double-edged concept based on Latin etymology. The Latin word *ratio* is both the word that defines the capacity of the mind to understand and analyze, and the word for proportion. It thus evokes the multiple and coterminous meanings of order, ordering, judgment, propriety, and clarity. Only by derivation has *raison* becomes equivalent with its modern acceptation of rationality. *La raison* was therefore the instrument for imposing order on the world, as well as the means to transcend contradictions, whether political, philosophical, or religious. Early in the century, many philosophers began looking for a "universal" scientific method of inquiry that would bring together all areas of human knowledge in a perfectly logical system. This endeavor also included the search for a "universal" language that would not only bridge the gap between scientists and nonscientists but also simply abolish linguistic diversity. Descartes and Gottfried Wilhelm Leibniz were among those philosophers who believed the task, although difficult, was not insurmountable. Religious differences were similarly placed under the magnifying lens of *raison*. Since variations between beliefs were mostly a matter of faith, some Christian thinkers tried to reconcile various convictions by putting the emphasis on their commonalities rather than their differences, as a matter of common sense. Others, such as Pascal, argued for belief from a purely logical perspective: the demonstration of the existence of God having failed, one could not argue that belief was rational. But that it was *not* irrational could be argued, based on apagogical reasoning or reductio ad absurdum logic.

Reason, in all its multiple meanings, is indeed a key word for the period. Among its manifest applications are the countless *traités* and *discours* (treatises and expositions) on a variety of subjects—ranging from ethics and politics to rhetoric and poetry, as well as literary genres—which have a common purpose, whatever the subject matter: to establish rules and impose order. The desire to find practical definitions, to establish criteria, and to build a system is omnipresent. The theater is perhaps the first major genre to undergo a critical examination, beginning with the "pre-classical" playwrights of the early period, who inaugurated the practice of publishing their plays with forewords in which they discussed various rules, explicit or implicit, technical or theoretical, in order to defend their own poetic practice. The first French treatise on the theater, commissioned by Richelieu before his death in 1642, appeared in 1657, authored by François Hédelin, abbé d'Aubignac, shortly followed by Corneille's own *Discours,* published in 1660.

By then, another genre, the novel, was coming into its own after undergoing some significant changes. The first half of the century was marked by long novels published over several years, such as Honoré d'Urfé's influential pastoral romance *L'Astrée* (1607–1627), or heroic novels, such as Marin Le Roy, sieur de Gomberville's *Polexandre* (1629–1637) and Madeleine de Scudéry's *Le Grand Cyrus* (1649–1653) and *Clélie* (1654–1660). These novels were extremely popular, so popular that they immediately became the focus of many satires and parodies deriding their length, their improbable settings, and their lovelorn characters. The word *roman* (romance) applied to these novels described then a particular genre with specific characteristics—remote or fabulous locales, heroic characters of noble birth, countless episodes and digressions, and a happy ending reuniting the star-crossed lovers. The critics of these novels, therefore, used the same term as a synonym of "fiction," that is, affabulation. Several parodic novels are titled *roman* with a deliberate sarcastic intent: the title of Antoine Furetière's novel, *Le Roman bourgeois* (1666), is a contradiction in terms since, by definition, *roman* characters cannot be of low extraction. This tug of war between "serious" romance writers and their satirists resulted in a flurry of theoretical texts exploring the nature of the genre and the nature of fiction, first in epistles and prefaces to the novels themselves, then in treatises proper, the first of which, *L'origine des romans* (The Origin of Novels) by Pierre-Daniel Huet, bishop of Avranches, appeared in 1669. The novella developed during the same period, and several important collections were published throughout the century. Often called "histoires" (histories), most of them purported to recount the "true" stories of ordinary people, in opposition to the "fables" told in *romans*. The convergence of these two genres, along with a renewed interest in recent history, resulted in the emergence of the *roman court* (short novel), the most famous of which is Lafayette's *La Princesse de Clèves.*

In addition to treatises dealing with specific genres, the seventeenth century also produced several important works on the French language, leading to the imposition of the first linguistic standards under the rules of order and reason. The landmark *Remarques sur la langue francaise* (1647) by Claude Favre, seigneur de Vaugelas, quickly became the reference work for proper usage. In 1660 the Jansenist Claude Lancelot published the first French grammar of the seventeenth century. Several French dictionaries appeared shortly thereafter: César-Pierre Richelet's (1680), Furetière's (1690), and finally the dictionary issued by the Académie Française in 1694.

This feverish effort was doubly symptomatic of the overt nationalism prevalent during the period, as well as of the need to give definition to the concept of literature. The seventeenth century is arguably the period in which the notion of French literature as an autonomous artistic domain, existing in its own right and free from outside influence, begins to emerge. The phrase "Republic of Letters" is frequently invoked in works of the period; it is a key notion that undergoes a significant shift from its Renaissance meaning. Initially used to represent the intellectual community across Europe, it acquires political undertones in the seventeenth century. No longer applied to the exchange of ideas, it is used to define French *Belles Lettres* as a republic—that is, a community whose members are of equal standing and in which legislative power rests with usage, reason, and public success.

The famous "Querelle du Cid" (Quarrel Concerning *Le Cid*), which developed around Corneille's play in 1637, was a landmark episode in this respect. What had begun as a dispute launched by rival authors jealous of the unprecedented success of the play quickly turned into a major controversy. The newly formed Académie Française was ordered by Richelieu to examine *Le Cid* and to issue a formal "censure." Although the publication in 1637 of the *Sentiments de l'Académie sur la tragicomédie du Cid* (Opinion of the Academy on the tragicomedy of *Le Cid*) put an end to the dispute, the episode was remembered and frequently cited afterward as an example of tyrannical rule over the Republic of Letters. The Académie Française and its members became the object of many satires. Many authors, however, lobbied actively for election as *académiciens,* for the title conferred undeniable prestige. Literary history of the period is in fact defined to a large extent by the uneasy alliance between state control and artistic independence. The creation of the Académie Française was the first instance of official state involvement in artistic matters, treading the fine line between protection by the institution and censorship. Other royal academies (for example, painting and sculpture, and history) were created under Louis XIV, ostensibly to promote the politics of the reign.

The reign of Louis XIV, the longest in French history, marked a period of military victories abroad and unprecedented colonial expansion. The title "Sun King" referred both to Louis XIV's mythical double, Apollo, and to the new French colonies in India and the Americas, thanks to which the king could claim that "the Sun never set" on his kingdom. The power and glory of the reign, however, came at a heavy price, both human and financial. The cost of maintaining an army and a fleet to fight constant wars abroad and the lavish court expenses compounded by the construction of the Versailles palace drained the resources of the state in spite of increased taxation. Several popular rebellions were brutally repressed. The Revocation of the Edict of Nantes in 1685, after decades of gradual erosion of the rights it had granted the Protestants, forced the emigration of countless French nationals of the middle and upper classes, draining the kingdom further of many of its craftsmen, merchants, and intellectuals. One of the unforeseen and paradoxical results of the Revocation of the Edict of Nantes was the creation of a French intellectual diaspora, which increased the influence of French culture abroad. One of its best-known figures is the Protestant Pierre Bayle, considered by many the precursor of the French Enlightenment. Forced into exile in Holland after the Revocation, he published the first modern encyclopedia, the *Dictionnaire historique et critique* (Historical and Critical Dictionary, 1696), in which he applied his vast erudition to discrediting historical falsehoods. His serial *Nouvelles de la République des Lettres* (News from the Republic of Letters, 1684–1687) was widely read and circulated throughout Europe.

For many, 1685 marks symbolically the end of the seventeenth century and the beginning of a slow and difficult transition into the Enlightenment. Molière dies in 1673; Corneille in 1684; François de La Rochefoucauld in 1680. Racine's last secular play dates from 1677. "Classical" standards were gradually abandoned, and the last decade of the century for the most part belongs to pre-Enlightenment writers such as Bayle, Bernard Le Bovier de Fontenelle, and François de Salignac de La Mothe-Fénelon, as well as to several women writers long ignored by literary history, such as Marie-Catherine Le Jumel de Barneville, comtesse d'Aulnoy, and Catherine Bernard. The last years of Louis XIV's reign were a period of political decline. The hegemonic pretensions of France were stopped by the European coalition known as the League of Augsburg. After decades of spectacular festivities, austerity prevailed at the court as the aging king turned to religion. The burden of war, several famines, and excessive taxation left the population in a state of misery. The centralization of power and its attendant increase in censorship and repression further aggravated social and political sclero-

sis. When Louis XIV died in 1715, having survived two generations of would-be heirs to the throne, he left to his great-grandson, Louis XV, a depleted country in dire need of resources and social reform.

–*Françoise Jaouën*

References:

Antoine Adam, *Grandeur and Illusion: French Literature and Society, 1600–1715,* translated by Herbert Tint (London: Weidenfeld & Nicolson, 1972);

Hans Bots and Françoise Waquet, *La République des Lettres* (Paris: Belin, 1997);

Gerald R. Cragg, *The Church and the Age of Reason, 1648–1789,* The Pelican History of the Church, volume 4 (Harmondsworth, U.K.: Penguin, 1960);

Giovanni Dotoli, *Temps de préfaces: Le Débat théâtral en France de Hardy à la querelle du "Cid"* (Paris: Klincksieck, 1996);

Claude-Gilbert Dubois, *Les Conceptions de l'histoire en France au XVIe siècle (1560–1610)* (Paris: Nizet, 1977);

Nannerl O. Keohane, *Philosophy and the State in France: The Renaissance to the Enlightenment* (Princeton, N.J.: Princeton University Press, 1980);

Bernard Magne, *Crise de la littérature française sous Louis XIV: Humanisme et nationalisme,* 2 volumes (Paris: Champion, 1976);

Roland Mousnier, *L'assassinat d'Henri IV* (Paris: Gallimard, 1964); translated by Joan Spencer as *The Assassination of Henry IV: The Tyrannicide Problem and the Consolidation of the French Absolute Monarchy in the Early Seventeenth Century* (London: Faber & Faber, 1973);

Peter Rickard, *The French Language in the Seventeenth Century: Contemporary Opinion in France* (Cambridge & Rochester: Brewer, 1992);

Mary Slaughter, *Universal Languages and Scientific Taxonomy in the Seventeenth Century* (Cambridge & New York: Cambridge University Press, 1982).

Acknowledgments

This book was produced by Bruccoli Clark Layman, Inc. Karen L. Rood is senior editor. Penelope M. Hope was the in-house editor. She was assisted by R. Bland Lawson and Michael Allen.

Production manager is Philip B. Dematteis.

Administrative support was provided by Ann M. Cheschi and Carol A. Cheschi.

Accountant is Ann-Marie Holland.

Copyediting supervisor is Sally R. Evans. The copyediting staff includes Phyllis A. Avant, Caryl Brown, Melissa D. Hinton, Philip I. Jones, Rebecca Mayo, Nancy E.

Smith, and Elizabeth Jo Ann Sumner. Freelance copyeditors are Brenda Cabra and Alice Poyner.

Editorial associates are Michael S. Martin, Catherine M. Polit, and Amelia B. Lacey.

Permissions editor and database manager is Amber L. Coker.

Layout and graphics supervisor is Janet E. Hill. The graphics staff includes Zoe R. Cook and Sydney E. Hammock.

Office manager is Kathy Lawler Merlette.

Photography supervisor is Paul Talbot. Photography editor is Scott Nemzek.

Digital photographic copy work was performed by Joseph M. Bruccoli.

Systems manager is Marie L. Parker.

Typesetting supervisor is Kathleen M. Flanagan. The typesetting staff includes Patricia Marie Flanagan, Mark J. McEwan, and Pamela D. Norton. Freelance typesetters are Wanda Adams and Rebecca Mayo.

Walter W. Ross did library research. He was assisted by Jo Cottingham and the following other librarians at the Thomas Cooper Library of the University of South Carolina: circulation department head Tucker Taylor; reference department head Virginia W. Weathers; reference department staff Brette Barron, Marilee Birchfield, Paul Cammarata, Gary Geer, Michael Macan, Tom Marcil, Rose Marshall, and Sharon Verba; interlibrary loan department head John Brunswick; and interlibrary loan staff Robert Arndt, Hayden Battle, Alex Byrne, Bill Fetty, Marna Hostetler, and Nelson Rivera.

Dictionary of Literary Biography® • Volume Two Hundred Sixty-Eight

Seventeenth-Century French Writers

Dictionary of Literary Biography

Antoine Arnauld
(6 February 1612 – 8 August 1694)

Thomas M. Carr Jr.
University of Nebraska–Lincoln

SELECTED WORKS*: *De la fréquente Communion* (Paris: A. Vitré, 1643);

Apologie de M. Jansénius (N.p., 1644);

Considérations sur l'entreprise faite par maître Nicolas Cornet (N.p., 1649);

Apologie pour les saints Pères de l'Eglise (Paris, 1651);

Réponse à la lettre d'une personne de condition (N.p., 1654);

Seconde Lettre à un duc et pair (N.p., 1655);

Grammaire générale et raisonnée, by Arnauld and Claude Lancelot (Paris: P. Le Petit, 1660); translated by Dale Allen Myers as *A General and Rational Grammar* (London: J. Nourse, 1753);

La Logique, ou l'Art de penser, by Arnauld and Pierre Nicole (Paris: C. Savreux, 1662; revised and enlarged, 1664, 1683); translated as *The Logic; or, The Art of Thinking* (London: H. Sawbridge, 1685);

Apologie pour les religieuses de Port-Royal (N.p., 1665);

Défense de la traduction du Nouveau Testament imprimée à Mons (N.p., 1667);

Nouveaux Essais de géométrie (Paris: C. Savreux, 1667);

La Morale pratique des Jésuites (Cologne: G. Quentol, 1669–1695);

La Perpétuité de la foi de l'Eglise catholique touchant l'eucharistie, 3 volumes (Paris: C. Savreux, 1669–1674);

Le Calvinisme convaincu de nouveau de dogmes impies (Cologne: P. Binsfelt, 1682);

Antoine Arnauld (Musée national du chateau, Versailles)

Traité des vraies et des fausses idées (Cologne: N. Schouten, 1683); translated by Stephen Gaukroger as *On True and False Ideas* (Manchester & New York: Manchester University Press, 1990);

Le Fantôme du Jansénisme (Colgne: N. Schouten, 1686);

Réflexions sur l'éloquence des prédicateurs (Paris: Delaulne, 1695);

---

*Only major book-length works by Arnauld are listed; lost works, letters, and most pamphlets have been omitted. Jean Laporte enumerates more than three hundred items in his useful chronological list of Arnauld's writings; see also his detailed list of the table of contents volume by volume in the 1775–1783 *Oeuvres complètes,* pp. xli–li.

Règles pour discerner les bonnes et les mauvaises critiques des traductions de l'Ecriture sainte (Paris: C. Hugnier, 1707);

Mémoire sur le règlement des études dans les lettres humaines, edited by A. Gazier (Paris: Armand Colin, 1886).*

Editions and Collections: *Les Oeuvres de Messire Antoine Arnauld,* edited by Noël de Larrière, 43 volumes (Lausanne: Sigismond d'Arnay, 1775–1783; reprinted, Brussels: Culture et civilisation, 1964–1967);

La Logique, edited by Pierre Clair and François Girbal (Paris: Vrin, 1965);

Des vrayes et des fausses idées, edited by Christiane Frémont (Paris: Fayard, 1986);

Réflexions sur l'éloquence des prédicateurs, edited by Thomas M. Carr Jr. (Geneva: Droz, 1992);

Grammaire générale et raisonnée, edited by Jean-Marc Mandosio (Paris: Allia, 1997);

Textes philosophiques, edited by Denis Moreau (Paris: Presses Universitaires de France, 2001).

Editions in English: *The Perpetuity of the Faith of the Catholic Church on the Eucharist* (Dublin: J. Coyne, 1834);

The Port-Royal Grammar, translated by Jacques Rieux and Bernard E. Rollin (The Hague: Mouton, 1975);

The Logic; or, The Art of Thinking, translated by Jill Vance Buroker (Cambridge: Cambridge University Press, 1996).

OTHER: "Carmen in laudes libri cui titutus Le Prince," in Guez de Balzac, *Le Prince* (Paris, 1631);

"Objectiones quartae," in René Descartes, *Meditationes de prima philosophia* (Paris: Soly, 1641).

The Jansenist theologian of grace, known as the Great Arnauld to distinguish him from other members of his family, was a tireless worker with encyclopedic interests. Although his point of view was always moral and religious even when treating nontheological issues, his work in such areas as philosophy and rhetoric, rather than his incessant defense of Augustinianism, is most alive today. The defender of theological tradition is most relevant in fields he considered peripheral. While his importance to philosophy is generally recognized, his contributions to many of the literary debates of his day dealing with grammar, theories regarding translation, and eloquence have been less appreciated because of the fragmentary way in which he treated them.

Antoine Arnauld's companion in exile during his last years and first biographer, Pasquier Quesnel, divides Arnauld's life into four periods: from his birth until the publication of his first major polemical work in 1643; from 1643 until the Peace of the Church in 1668–the period of Jansenist controversies, when he was often in hiding; the eleven-year period of the Peace, when he moved openly in Paris; and the period of his self-imposed Belgium exile, from when the persecution broke out in 1678 until his death in 1694.

Arnauld was born on 6 February 1612 in Paris, the last of twenty children of Catherine Marion and Antoine Arnauld. His father, who died when he was seven, had earned the enmity of the Jesuits for his demands for their expulsion in the 1590s. By the time Antoine the son entered the Collège de Calvi for his study of the humanities, his mother had committed herself to the convent of Port-Royal, which Antoine's sister Angélique had returned to strict observance of the Rule of St. Benedict in 1609. But although more attention was given to Antoine's spiritual formation than to that of his elder brothers Robert and Henri, Antoine did not immediately discover his vocation. By age sixteen he had not only read the best of the ancient authors, but he had also committed to memory large extracts from them, which he could still recite fifty or sixty years later. This influence is seen in his 1631 Latin poem on Guez de Balzac's *Le Prince* (1631).

After studying philosophy at the Collège de Lisieux along with his nephews Antoine Le Maistre and Louis-Isaac, Le Maistre de Sacy, Arnauld studied law for a short while, but in 1632 at his mother's urging he entered the Sorbonne to devote himself to theology. While he was enrolled there, he seemed at first chiefly interested in displaying the pugnacious debating skills of his father. Only later did he come to deep commitment to the penitential theology of Jean Duvergier de Hauranne, better known as Saint-Cyran, favored by his mother. His progress through the various university degrees toward his doctorate in 1641 (the same year he was ordained a priest) was slow for several reasons: his gradual conversion under the guidance of Saint-Cyran; his initiation into the theology of St. Augustine, which brought him into opposition with influential teachers such as Jacques Lescot; and his work on other projects.

Chief among these projects was his critique of René Descartes's *Méditations,* published as the "Objectiones quartae" (Four Objections) when the treatise appeared in 1641 under the Latin title *Renati Descartes Meditationes de Prima Philosophia* (René Descartes's Meditations First Philosophy; translated by John Veitch as *Meditations,* 1863). The value of Arnauld's "Objectiones quartae" can be seen in their being the only ones that provoked Descartes to make modifications to his text. If Descartes considered them the best of all the objections he received, it was because, as he wrote to Marin Mersenne (4 March 1641), that they were the only ones that entered into the spirit of his thought. Indeed, Arnauld was a more sympathetic reader than other

DE LA FREQVENTE

COMMVNION.

OV' LES SENTIMENS DES PERES,
DES PAPES, ET DES CONCILES, TOVCHANT
l'vfage des Sacremens de PENITENCE & D'EVCHARISTIE,
font fidelement expofez : Pour feruir d'addreffe aux perfon-
nes qui penfent ferieufement à fe conuertir à DIEV; & aux
Pafteurs & Confeffeurs zelez pour le bien des ames.

PAR M. ANTOINE ARNAVLD, PRESTRE,
Docteur en Theologie de la Maifon de Sorbonne.

SECONDE EDITION.

SANCTA SANCTIS.

A PARIS,
Chez Antoine Vitré, Imprimeur ordinaire du Roy, & de la Reyne
Regente Mere de fa Majefté, & du Clergé de France,
Ruë des Carmes, au College des Lombards.

M. DC. XLIII.
AVEC PRIVILEGE, ET APPROBATIONS.

« Un très bon livre... »

Title page for the second edition of Arnauld's book, based on Jansenist doctrine, in which he recommends frequent
communion to maintain a state of grace (Bibliothèque Nationale, Paris)

authors of objections, such as Thomas Hobbes and Pierre Gassendi, because he saw an affinity between Descartes and Augustine, and thus repeatedly cites parallels between Descartes's proofs in the *Méditations* and the beliefs of Augustine. Arnauld's study of Augustine under the tutelage of Saint-Cyran had concentrated on the theological questions of grace, justification, and predestination. His contact with Descartes's writings allowed him to appreciate better the metaphysical dimension of Augustine, the bishop of Hippo, making Arnauld in turn a lifelong Cartesian. Unlike most other Jansenists, he believed Descartes's dualism and method were not only compatible with Christian doctrine but could also support it. His support did not prevent him, however, from honing in on the weak points in the *Méditations*. He noted the circularity of Descartes's arguments about clear and distinct ideas and the existence of God. Finally, Arnauld questioned the

compatibility of Descartes's view that sensible qualities are not modes of bodies with the doctrine of transubstantiation in the Eucharist.

At the same time, Arnauld was preparing his *De la fréquente Communion* (On Frequent Communion), which he finished in 1641 but which was not published until 1643. In 1639 Saint-Cyran, who was imprisoned in Vincennes on the orders of Cardinal Richelieu, delegated his disciple Arnauld to reply to an opinion given to Madame de Sablé by her Jesuit confessor, recommending frequent communion even for persons not withdrawn from a worldly life. Arnauld applies to practical moral questions and ecclesiastical discipline the ideas on grace included in the posthumous *Augustinus* (1640) of Saint-Cyran's friend, the theologian and bishop of Ypres, Cornelius Jansen.

Jansenism, which claimed to be the true interpretation of Augustine's doctrine of grace, is notoriously difficult to define. It stressed that as a result of original sin humans could only love themselves. Without grace given by God, the will could not be freed from this concupiscence; grace alone enables humans to love God and attain salvation. While the Jesuits emphasized the need of the will to cooperate with grace for it to be effective, Jansenist efficacious grace irresistibly reorients the will and is unmerited by those predestined to receive it; however, it can be withdrawn, unlike the Calvinist doctrine of the perseverance of the saints.

In *De la fréquente Communion,* Arnauld stresses the need for this reorientation of the will by grace. External piety and mechanical reception of the sacrament cannot be allowed to replace a penitential spirit. Arnauld formulates the issue around this question: Is it better for persons who feel themselves guilty of mortal sins to receive communion as soon as they have gone to confession, or to take some time in order to purify themselves by penitential exercises before receiving the Eucharist? He answers that interior renewal is the prerequisite to the reception of the sacrament—true repentance and contrition before absolution in confession, a period of penance before reception of communion. In the case of public or habitual sinners, a delay before granting absolution may be necessary, and a period of renewal and preparation is advisable before receiving communion. Frequent communion is reserved for those who have no affection remaining for venial sins and have entirely eliminated the appeal of mortal ones.

While Arnauld saw himself as calling for a return to the penitential discipline of the early Church, recently restored by Charles Borromeo in Milan, the Jesuits accused him of cutting off the faithful from the nourishment of the sacrament. In their eyes, the Jansenists reserved the Eucharist for a spiritual elite. Attacked publicly in sermons preached against him by the Jesuit Jacques Nouet, and threatened with referral to the Roman Inquisition, Arnauld found it prudent to go into hiding in March 1644; of the remaining fifty years of his life, thirty-one were spent in exile or concealment.

The style of *De la fréquente Communion* increased its impact and resonance. In its effort to be the definitive refutation of his opponent, the book is ponderous. Arnauld first cites a short proposition from the recommendations of the Jesuit confessor (whom he never identifies) of Madame de Sablé and then refutes him at length. But the book also has appeal for the general reader. Arnauld heaps his irony on the faulty scholarship of the Jesuit and destroys his credibility by detailing his many errors. Arnauld makes theological debate accessible to the general educated public for the first time through his clear, nontechnical French. He avoids the terminology and divisions of the scholastics in favor

of conclusions based on exhaustive lists of proofs drawn from Scripture, the Fathers, and the deliberations of the councils.

In the next decade the enemies of Jansen's theories of grace managed a campaign that eventually resulted in the condemnation by Pope Innocent X in 1653 of five theses that were held to sum up the doctrine of grace in the *Augustinus.* After the death of Saint-Cyran in 1643, Arnauld, as his chief disciple, took charge of the defense. Because of Arnauld's tireless energy, immense learning, and inability to resist the pleasure of refuting an opponent, the dispute remained constantly before the public without a possibility of compromise or calming spirits. In 1644 he published the *Apologie de M. Jansénius* (Apology for Monsieur Jansen). In 1649 in the *Considérations sur l'entreprise par maître Nicolas Cornet* (Considerations on the enterprise of Cornet) he attacked Nicolas Cornet's request that the Sorbonne condemn the five theses. In 1651 the *Apologie pour les saints Pères de l'Eglise* (Apology for the Holy Fathers of the Church) appeared. The strategy of defense adopted by Arnauld was the distinction between *le droit* and *le fait,* that is, the distinction between the truth of the propositions themselves and whether they were included in Jansen's book. This strategy allowed the Jansenists to submit to the authority of the pope in doctrinal matters while contesting whether or not the propositions indeed summed up Jansen's teaching. Since the enemies of Jansen realized how effective Arnauld was as chief of his party, they quickly tried to condemn him along with the *Augustinus,* and his personal fate came to be tied to that of the five propositions. He had already had to wait two years after receiving his doctorate from the Sorbonne until Richelieu's death in 1643 to be admitted as a member of that theology faculty; now his enemies wanted his expulsion.

This quarrel became the occasion of Blaise Pascal's *Les Provinciales* (Letters Written to a Provincial, 1656). In February 1655 the duke of Liancourt was refused absolution by a priest of his parish for refusing to break relations with Port-Royal. Arnauld published two letters attacking this position, the most important of which is the *Seconde Lettre à un duc et pair* (Second letter to a duke and peer), addressed to the duke of Luynes. Arnauld's enemies decided to condemn the letters as a pretext for expelling him from the Sorbonne, thus depriving him of a major forum. After trumped-up debates that lasted from 1 December 1655 to 31 January 1656, at which Chancellor Pierre Séguier was often present to strengthen the party against Arnauld, Arnauld was excluded.

Realizing that to battle in the Sorbonne was hopeless, Arnauld turned to public opinion. Aware that his own pugnacious theological style was too ponderous for the occasion, in January 1656 he induced Pascal to enter the fray. What began as a defense of Arnauld soon became a more general attack against the Jesuits and casuistry. Every few weeks during the course of the year, Pascal, consulting constantly with Arnauld and Pierre Nicole, produced a short pamphlet. While Pascal was far from the simple "secretary of Port-Royal" that the Jesuits claimed, he relied greatly on documentation furnished by the two theologians, who also assisted in the preparation of the manuscript for publication. In addition, Arnauld could well have written parts of the third and sixteenth of the *Provinciales,* the style of which differs greatly from the lighter approach of Pascal in the rest of the letters. Arnauld's recourse to Pascal was inspired. Pascal's concision in the letters won over an even wider public than Arnauld had with *De la fréquente Communion.* Pascal's gift for the telling example, properly dosed irony, and dramatization of his opponents, coupled with occasional bursts of indignation, made theological debate not just accessible to the general public but also a delight to read.

During all these years polemics was hardly Arnauld's only activity. He was a confessor and director of conscience at his sisters' monastery of Port-Royal. He published many translations of St. Augustine's works, his contribution to a broad campaign by the solitaries of Port-Royal to make the works of the Fathers, the Bible, and key liturgical texts available in French not just to the clergy but also to the devout laity.

Although Arnauld was not significantly involved as a teacher in the "little schools of Port-Royal," which flourished from 1637 to 1660, he played a major role in three textbooks that came out of them. The classes at the primary and secondary level taught by the solitaries offered a more personalized program and innovative methods than the schools of the Jesuits. Arnauld's *Grammaire générale et raisonnée* (A General and Rational Grammar, 1660) was written with Claude Lancelot, and *La Logique, ou l'Art de penser* (The Logic, or The Art of Thinking, 1662, usually called the *Logique* of Port-Royal), was written with Pierre Nicole. *La Logique* achieved immense success by reworking the post-Renaissance hostility to Aristotelian logic and the syllogism in terms of a Cartesian emphasis on clear and distinct ideas and an Augustinian appreciation of the consequences of the Fall. *La Logique* is organized around four operations of the mind—conceiving, judging, reasoning, and ordering—but reinterpreted in light of Cartesian self-evidence. The book is important for its analysis of how words signify. While Arnauld and Nicole maintain that were it not for the necessity of communicating thoughts to others, ideas could be considered in themselves without attaching any exterior

LA LOGIQVE

O V

L'ART DE PENSER:

Contenant, outre les Regles communes, plu-
fieurs obferuations nouvelles propres
à former le iugement.

A PARIS,

Chez

IEAN GVIGNART le pere; au pre-
mier Pillier de la grand' Sale du Palais, au
Sacrifice d'Abel.

CHARLES SAVREVX, au pied de la
Tour de Nôtre-Dame.

IEAN DE LAVNAY, fous le Porche
des Efcoles de Sorbonne.

M. DC. LXII.

AVEC PRIVILEGE DV ROY.

Title page for a textbook written by Arnauld and Pierre Nicole for use in the "little schools" of Port-Royal (1970 facsimile edition; Thomas Cooper Library, University of South Carolina)

linguistic sign to them, they admit that language is a practical necessity. They analyze the figures of speech in terms of accessory ideas that adhere to principal ones. Such accessory ideas communicate the speaker's subjective reaction to the principal ideas. While recourse to figures of speech is inappropriate for speculative topics, it is required when presenting religious truths that are meant to be loved as well as known.

The *Grammaire générale et raisonnée* interprets the grammatical parts of speech in terms of the distinction in *La Logique* between the two major operations of the mind—conception and judgment. Nouns, articles, prepositions, and adverbs are assigned to the first operation, while verbs, interjections, and conjunctions are assigned to the second; rhetoric is aligned with this second operation, which corresponds to the site of the speaker's subjectivity, the personal way in which ideas

The monastery at Port-Royal, where Arnauld's sisters were nuns and where he served as confessor and director of conscience; engraving by Jeremias Wolf, circa 1700

are conceived. Noam Chomsky saw this attempt to describe language in terms of the operations of the mind as a precursor to his theory of deep structures presented in his *Cartesian Linguistics* (1966). Arnauld also produced a new method for presenting Euclid's geometry, the *Nouveaux Essais de géométrie* (New Essays in Geometry, 1667).

The textbooks were published just when attacks against Port-Royal began to threaten the existence of the monastery. King Louis XIV wanted unity on the religious as well as the political front and was highly suspicious of Jansenism because it advocated rigorous personal moral values and mortification along with the subordination of political interests of the state to those of religion. Moreover, its most fervent followers practiced a disengagement from the world. Thus, in 1661 he required that all priests and nuns sign a formulary condemning as heretical the five propositions said to summarize the doctrine of grace in Jansen's *Augustinus*. When royal and ecclesiastical authorities refused to accept Arnauld's distinction between the questions pertaining to doctrine and whether or not they were included in Jansen's book, matters came to a head. Most of the nuns at Port-Royal refused to sign the formulary without reservations, and in hopes of making them submit, the leaders of the monastery were sequestered in 1664 in other convents by the archbishop of Paris; when that measure failed, the archbishop ordered that all nuns who would not sign be gathered at Port-Royal des Champs, where they were deprived of the sacraments and where authorities tried to prevent contact between them and their supporters and advisors, such as Arnauld. During this period Arnauld himself

continued in hiding but published many defenses of the nuns as well as works designed to place the monastery and its constitution in the best light. He also defended the translation of the Bible sponsored by the solitaries, Sacy's *Le Nouveau Testament de N.S. Jésus-Christ* (The New Testament of Our Lord Jesus Christ, 1667)–known as the Bible of Mons for the city in the Spanish Netherlands where it was published–against attacks by the Jesuits.

Only with the arrival of Clement IX, a pope more favorable to the Jansenists, and the desire of Louis XIV for national unity in preparation for war with Holland was an accommodation reached in 1668. Arnauld was amenable to compromise and played an active role in the negotiations between the authorities and the nuns. Under this so-called Peace of the Church, the nuns signed the formulary in early 1669, and the interdiction that deprived them of the sacraments was lifted; Arnauld had even been presented to the king in October 1668 at Saint Germain.

The Peace of the Church allowed Arnauld to circulate in public for the first time in years and facilitated links with the Parisian literary world. He met Nicolas Boileau, who wrote his third *Epître* (Epistle, 1674) in Arnauld's honor and who began a reconciliation with Jean Racine. Although the story reported by Racine's son Louis, according to which Arnauld read and approved the main lines of *Phèdre* (first performed in 1677), is probably apocryphal, it is the source of the persistent reading of the play as Jansenist. The reconciliation had to await the dramatist's renunciation of the theater, condemned unequivocally by the Augustinians, which took place after September 1677 when Racine was named royal historiographer. In the last months of his life, Arnauld defended Boileau's tenth satire, on women, in a May 1694 letter to Charles Perrault, who had written against Boileau.

The Peace of the Church also allowed Arnauld to bring to the forefront his attacks against Calvinism. This result was particularly opportune, since Louis XIV had intensified his campaign against the Protestants; in 1685 the king revoked the Edict of Nantes that had allowed them limited toleration. Jansenism had been attacked by the Jesuits as a sort of crypto-Protestantism, and the Arnauld family had ties to the movement. Arnauld's grandfather had been a Huguenot, and some of Arnauld's aunts, uncles, and cousins had remained in the reformed faith. Arnauld chose a point on which the Jansenists were unquestionably orthodox–their defense of the priesthood and eucharistic transubstantiation. His sister Angélique had dedicated Port-Royal to the Blessed Sacrament and instituted its perpetual adoration. In January 1669 the first volume of what was called the "great" *Perpétuité de la foi de l'Eglise catholique touchant l'eucharistie* (The Perpetuity of the Faith of the Catholic Church on the Eucharist, 1669–1674) appeared, to distinguish it from a shorter version written by Nicole, which had appeared in 1664. The general belief is that Arnauld furnished the outline and main arguments of this latter text, even if Nicole did more of the actual writing. The *Perpétuité de la foi de l'Eglise catholique touchant l'eucharistie* was written to refute–by an appeal to historical probability, not by theological arguments per se–the Calvinist charge that belief in Christ's real presence in the Eucharist was an innovation that introduced itself imperceptibly sometime between 890 and the eleventh century. Even Arnauld's Calvinist opponents admitted that belief in the real presence was general in the Latin Church in the eleventh century. Arnauld argues that since even the Protestants admit that a consensus concerning the real presence existed by the eleventh century, such an enormous shift in belief is impossible on so central a doctrine. Another of the collaborative fruits of this period is the first edition of Pascal's *Pensées* (1670), known as the edition of Port-Royal, which was the text known for the next hundred years until the marquis de Condorcet's 1776 edition.

This period of Arnauld's open participation in the intellectual life of France and of prosperity for Port-Royal proved short. After the death of the king's cousin Anne Geneviève de Bourbon, duchesse de Longueville, who had protected Port-Royal in spring 1679, Louis returned to his policy of restrictions against the Jansenists. The pensioners were expelled from the monastery, and the recruitment of new nuns was forbidden. To maintain his independence, Arnauld left in June of

that year for the Spanish Netherlands and Holland, where he lived in secrecy for the rest of his life.

Even though his letters and manuscripts had to be smuggled into France, the self-exiled Arnauld remained a force to be reckoned with in France, much as Voltaire (who enjoyed much more favorable conditions abroad) was a force in France from Geneva in the next century. Arnauld was first accompanied by Nicole and later by Quesnel, as well as by devoted secretaries, and supported by a network of Jansenist sympathizers.

Attacks against the Jesuits now took precedence over polemics with the Calvinists, but Arnauld also reemerged as a significant player on the philosophical stage. *Traité des vraies et des fausses idées* (On True and False Ideas, 1683) is the most famous book in the Malebranche-Arnauld debate, which went on until well after Arnauld's death in 1694, since Nicolas Malebranche was replying as late as 1709 to texts Arnauld's friends published posthumously. Although this first book by Arnauld attacks Malebranche's theory of knowledge, known as vision in God, first set out in the *De la recherche de la vérité* (On the Search for the Truth, 1674), Arnauld was less offended as a Cartesian than as an Augustinian. What raised Arnauld's ire were the theological consequences of Malebranche's *Traité de la nature et de la grâce* (Treatise on Nature and Grace, 1680), which limited divine intervention in creation in the name of the simplicity of means by which God acts. According to Malebranche, the divine will operates even in the domain of grace by general acts. In Arnauld's eyes such a theory renders problematic such doctrines as miracles, a particular providence, predestination, and efficacious grace. Although Arnauld showed clearly that Malebranche had departed significantly from his initial Cartesian inspiration and created a new system that in many ways betrayed Descartes, he could not stem Malebranche's influence. Much as Arnauld had feared, the oratorian Malebranche's most lasting impact was not on Christian philosophers but on deists such as Voltaire or atheists such as David Hume, who secularized his concepts such as a general providence or occasional causality.

Besides philosophical and theological polemics, Arnauld also dealt during this period, especially in the last year of his life, with issues involving translation and rhetorical theory. In the *Règles pour discerner les bonnes et les mauvaises critiques des traductions de l'Ecriture sainte* (Rules for Discerning Good from Bad Critiques of Translations of Saintly Writing), written in April 1694 but published posthumously in 1707, he continued his defense of the Sacy translation of the Bible. Arnauld is attentive to the need to convey the simplicity of New Testament style while avoiding both too worldly a delicacy and a hyperliteralism that would make Scripture appear crude

LA
PERPETUITÉ
DE LA FOY
DE L'EGLISE
CATHOLIQVE
TOUCHANT
L'EUCHARISTIE,
DEFFENDUE
Contre le Livre du SIEVR CLAVDE,
Ministre de Charenton.

Quod apud multos unum invenitur, non est erratum sed traditum. Tert. de præsc. cap. 28.

AMANS SPE NEXA

A PARIS,
Chez CHARLES SAVREUX, Libraire juré, sous la Tour de N.Dame,
du costé de l'Archevesché, à l'Enseigne des trois Vertus.
M. DC. LXIX.
Avec Approbations, & Privilege du Roy.

Title page for a work in which Arnauld argues for the Catholic doctrine of transubstantiation (from Jean Lesaulnier, ed., Port-Royal Insolite, 1992)

and barbarous. This aim led him to reflect once again on the issues of connotation and usage that had been raised in the treatment of accessory and principal ideas in *La Logique*.

One of Arnauld's last works was a defense of traditional rhetorical values, published posthumously as the *Réflexions sur l'éloquence des prédicateurs* (Reflection on the Eloquence of Preachers, 1695). This position is not surprising when one considers his earlier *Mémoire sur le règlement des études dans les lettres humaines* (Memorandum on the Organization of Studies in the Humanities, not published until 1886), which shows the progressive nature of his ideas about rhetorical instruction. This memorandum was probably written in the last decades of his life at the request of an unidentified professor in one of the Parisian colleges, who had solicited Arnauld's advice about the reform of the discipline. Arnauld rejects the common practice of instructors dictating lectures to their students in favor of the explica-

tion of the rhetorical texts of the masters of antiquity–Aristotle, Quintilian, and Cicero. His recommendations for organizing the school day envisage an hour of theory in the morning, alternating between the textbook of the Jesuit Cyprien Soarez and the ancient treatises.

In his *Réflexions sur l'éloquence des prédicateurs*, Arnauld undertook to set straight an old friend, Philippe Goibaut du Bois, who had sought to restrict to a minimum a preacher's recourse to rhetoric. Although du Bois invokes the authority of St. Augustine for this view in his preface to the saint's sermons, his hostility to rhetoric can also be seen as a reductive version of Saint-Cyran's advice that prayerful meditation of a scriptural text is preparation enough for a preacher; likewise, it reflects a reductive view of the Cartesian preference for pure intellection over the imagination. Du Bois maintained that the preacher should avoid initial recourse to the imagination but should aim for the heart through the intelligence. The art of rhetoric is useless; a preacher who is touched himself by the truths he proclaims will infallibly persuade his audience. Arnauld replies that Augustine himself taught that the precepts of rhetoric could be used to persuade truth or falsehood and that the preacher had every right to avail himself of them. Likewise, du Bois's attack against the imagination is based on a faulty view of that faculty, which has, according to Arnauld, a legitimate role to play in teaching Christian dogma. Finally, the ability to persuade is independent of knowledge of the truth or being touched by it, and thus a knowledge of the art of persuasion–that is, of rhetoric–is useful.

Arnauld saw himself as a defender of tradition rather than a theologian whose mission was to produce a new synthesis or understanding of the truth of the faith. This view in part results from his position as practitioner of positive rather than speculative theology. Propositions must be constantly tested against tradition and scripture as well as against reason. The implications of this stance are multiple.

First, it would be difficult to locate a work in the forty-two volumes of his complete works that is not meant to refute an opponent or set a friend straight on some point. With friends the tone is firm, correction softened by gentle dismay, as with du Bois. With enemies whom Arnauld considers impervious to correction, such as the Jesuits, he does not hesitate to denounce their errors and indict their bad faith in the strongest terms. This impulse to refute also determines the structure of his works. His turn of mind is not to write a systematic treatise on a topic but to go straight for the source of error. At his simplest he writes a series of remarks correcting the errors as they appear in the work being refuted. More often he identifies early on in his refutation the faulty definitions that serve as premises to his opponents' errors; by correcting them with what he considers solid premises concerning the issue, he sets out the fundamental principles involved, but without going on to produce a comprehensive overview of the issue. The works that do supply such an overview, such as *La Logique* or the *Grammaire générale et raisonnée,* were as often as not written in large part by such collaborators as Nicole or Lancelot.

Second, his view of himself as a defender of a living tradition meant that his method of work was highly collaborative. He was not an isolated intellectual working alone. Arnauld needed an opponent whom he saw as betraying the tradition and who served as a sort of negative collaborator to stimulate his thought, and he usually produced his refutation while working closely with others who shared his vision of the truth. He animated a group of scholars, theologians, and writers whose core was formed by the solitaries of Port-Royal, but he could call on others—such as Racine—who were sympathetic to the ideals of the monastery without being as closely identified with it as he was. Members of the inner circle collaborated on the research and composition of books. Arnauld was, however, almost always the leading figure. When he did not furnish the outline or inspiration, he was the arbitrator of disputes, the authority who gave final approval to texts.

Finally, Arnauld's distrust of human nature because of his extreme view of the consequences of original sin or his belief in the superiority of pure intellection over sensate ideas, which was reinforced by Cartesianism, did not blind him to the beauties of literature or to the ways in which the corporal faculties, such as the imagination, passions, or even pleasure, could be harnessed in the service of truth. If he was an eloquent defender of traditional views on rhetoric, it was because he saw the need for effective preaching. If he was attentive to the need to balance usage with accuracy in translation, it was because he wanted the sacred texts in the hands of the faithful. If he developed a particularly rich theory of how words signify, it was to interpret Scripture and dogma and to communicate this doctrine to the faithful. Language, like philosophy, must serve religion.

Antoine Arnauld died on 8 August 1694 in his clandestine lodgings in Brussels and was buried surreptitiously in a nearby parish church with the connivance of a sympathetic priest. Arnauld's heart was interred at Port-Royal des Champs a month later.

Bibliography:

Denis Moreau, "Un essai de bibliographie arnaldienne," in Antoine Arnauld, *Textes philosophiques,*

edited by Denis Moreau (Paris: Presses Universitaires de France, 2001), pp. 287–319.

Biographies:

Pasquier Quesnel, *Histoire abrégée de la vie et des ouvrages de M. Arnauld* (Cologne: Nicolas Schouten, 1697);

Noël de Larrière, "Vie de Messire Antoine Arnauld," in *Les Œuvres de Messire Antoine Arnauld,* volume 43 (Lausanne: Sigismond d'Arnay, 1775–1783), pp. 1–319;

Emile Jacques, *Les Années d'exil d'Antoine Arnauld* (Louvain: Publications universitaires de Louvain, 1976);

Alexander Sedgwick, *The Travails of Conscience: The Arnauld Family and the Ancien Régime* (Cambridge, Mass.: Harvard University Press, 1998).

References:

Noam Chomsky, *Cartesian Linguistics: A Chapter in the History of Rationalist Thought* (New York: Harper & Row, 1966);

Chroniques de Port-Royal, special Arnauld issue, 44 (1995);

Dominique Descotes, "Force et violence dans les discours d'Antoine Arnauld," in *Antoine Arnauld: Philosophie du langage et de la connaissance,* edited by Jean-Claude Pariente (Paris: Vrin, 1995), pp. 33–64;

Marc Dominicy, *La Naissance de la grammaire moderne. Langage, logique et philosophie à Port-Royal* (Brussels: Pierre Mardaga, 1984);

Jean Laporte, *La Doctrine de Port-Royal,* volume 2: *Exposition de la doctrine d'après Arnauld* (Paris: Presses universitaires de France, 1923);

Denis Moreau, *Deux Cartésiens: La polémique entre Antoine Arnauld et Nicolas Malebranche* (Paris: Vrin, 1999);

Steven M. Nadler, *Arnauld and the Cartesian Philosophy of Ideas* (Manchester: Manchester University Press, 1989);

Aloyse-Raymonde Ndiaye, *La Philosophie d'Antoine Arnauld* (Paris: Vrin, 1991);

C. A. Sainte-Beuve, *Port-Royal,* 3 volumes, edited by Maxime Leroy (Paris: Gallimard, 1952);

Leonardo Verga, *Il pensiero filosofico e scientifico di Antoine Arnauld,* 2 volumes (Milan: Pubblicazioni della Università Cattolica del Sacro Cuore, 1972).

Papers:

Antoine Arnauld's papers are in the Bibliothèque Nationale de France, Paris, and the Utrechts Archief, in Utrecht, Holland.

Marie-Catherine Le Jumel de Barneville, comtesse d'Aulnoy

(1650 or 1651 – 1705)

Allison Stedman
Bucknell University

BOOKS: *Histoire d'Hypolite, comte de Duglas* (Paris: L. Sevestre, 1690); translated as *Hypolitus, Earl of Douglas. Containing some Memoirs of the Court of Scotland; with The Secret History of Mack-Beth King of Scotland. To Which Is Added, the Amours of Count Schlick* (London: Woodward, 1708);

Mémoires de la cour d'Espagne, 2 volumes (Paris: C. Barbin, 1690); translated by Tom Brown as *Memoirs of the Court of Spain. In Two Parts. Written by an Ingenious French Lady* (London: Horn, Saunders & Bennet, 1692);

Relation du Voyage d'Espagne, 3 volumes (Paris: C. Barbin, 1691); translated as *The Lady's Travels into Spain* (London: Samuel Crouch, 1691);

Histoire de Jean de Bourbon, Prince de Carency, 3 volumes (Paris: C. Barbin, 1692); translated as *The Prince of Carency; A Novel* (London: W. Wilkins, 1719);

Nouvelles Espagnoles, par Madame D***, 2 volumes (Paris: C. Barbin, 1692)—comprises volume 1, *Histoire du Marquis de Lemos et de Dona Eléonor de Monteléon, Le Marquis de Leyva,* and *Dona Camille Darellano;* volume 2, *Histoire du Marquis de Mansera et de Dona Teresa de Castro* and *Lettres de Dona Teresa de Castro au Marquis de Mansera;* translated in *The Diverting Works of the Countess d'Anois, Author of Ladies Travels to Spain* . . . , 4 volumes (London, 1707);

Nouvelles ou mémoires historiques contenant ce qui s'est passé de plus remarquable dans l'Europe tant aux guerres, prises de places, et batailles sur terre et sur mer qu'aux divers intérêts des princes et des souverains qui ont agi depuis 1672 jusqu'en 1679, par Madame D***, 2 volumes (Paris: C. Barbin, 1693);

Mémoires de la Cour d'Angleterre, par Madame D***, 2 volumes (Paris: C. Barbin, 1695); translated by J.C. as *Memoirs of the Court of England. In Two Parts, by the Countess of Dunois . . . Now Made in English . . .* (London: Bragg, 1707);

Les Contes des fées, 4 volumes (Paris: Veuve de T. Girard, 1697)—lost edition; volume 1 translated as *Tales of*

Marie-Catherine Le Jumel de Barneville, comtesse d'Aulnoy
(from Madame d'Aulnoy, Contes I, *1997)*

Fairies (London: 1699); volumes 1 and 2 translated in *The Diverting Works of the Countess d'Aunois,* volume 4 (London: J. Nicholson, 1707); volumes 3 and 4 translated as *A Collection of Novels and Tales of the Fairies,* 2 volumes (London: J. Brotherton, 1721);

Les Contes nouveaux ou les Fées à la mode, 4 volumes (Paris: Veuve de T. Girard, 1698);

Sentiments d'une âme penitente, sur le pseaume 50, Miserere mei Deus, et Le Retour d'une Ame à Dieu, sur le pseaume 102, Bendic anima mea. Accompagnées de Reflexions Chrétiennes. Par Madame D*** (Paris: Veuve de T. Girard, 1698);

Le Comte de Warwick, par Madame d'Aulnoy, 2 volumes (Paris: Compagnie des Libraires Associés, 1703); translated as *The History of the Earl of Warwick, Sir-nam'd the King-Maker: Containing His Amours, and Other Memorable Transactions. By the Author of the Memoirs of the English Court* (London: J. Woodward & J. Morphew, 1708).

Editions: *Sentimens d'une âme pénitente, sur le pseaume Miserere mei et Retour d'une âme à Dieu, sur le pseaume Benedic, anima mea par Madame D*** Augmenté des Prières du matin et du soir, de celles à dire pendant la sainte Messe, avant et après la Confession et la Communion; des Vêpres et Complies du Dimanche, des Hymnes des principales Fêtes de l'année et des Antiennes de la sainte Vierge* (Avignon: J.-A. Fischer-Joly, 1829);

La Cour et la ville de Madrid vers la fin du XVIIe siècle . . . par la comtesse d'Aulnoy, edited and annotated by Mme B. Carey (Paris: E. Plon, 1876);

Relation du voyage d'Espagne, edited by R. Foulché-Delbosc (Paris: Klincksieck, 1926);

Histoire d'Hypolite, comte de Duglas, facsimile edition, introduction by René Godenne (Genèva: Slatkine, 1978);

Le Nouveau cabinet des fées, 18 volumes (Geneva: Slatkine, 1978); reprint of *Les contes des fées* in volumes 3 and 4; reprint of *Contes nouveaux ou les fées à la mode* in volumes 4 and 5;

L'Histoire d'Hypolite, comte de Duglas, edited, with an introduction, by Shirley Jones Day (London: University of London, Institute of Romance Studies, 1994);

Contes I. Les Contes des fées, reprint of 1697 edition, introduction by Jacques Barchilon, edited, with notes, by Philippe Hourcade (Paris: Société des Textes Français Modernes, Edition du tricentenaire, 1997)–comprises *Gracieuse et Percinet, La Belle aux Cheveux d'or, L'Oiseau Bleu, Le Prince Lutin, La Princesse Printanière, Le Rameau d'or, l'Oranger et l'Abeille, La Bonne Petite Souris* (volume 4); *Don Gabriel Ponce de Leon* [includes *Le Mouton, Finette Cendron, Fortune*], *Don Fernand de Tolède* [includes *Le Nain Jaune, Serpentin Vert*], and *Babiole;*

Contes II. Contes nouveaux ou les Fées à la mode, reprint of 1698 edition, introduction by Barchilon, edited, with notes, by Hourcade (Paris: Société des Textes Français Modernes, 1998)–comprises *La Princesse Carpillon, La Grenouille Bienfaisante, La Biche au Bois, Le Nouveau Gentilhomme Bourgeois* [includes *La Chatte Blanche, Belle-Belle ou le Chevalier Fortuné, Le Pigeon et la Colombe, La Princesse Belle-Etoile et le Prince Chéri, Le Prince Marcassin, Le Dauphin*].

Editions in English: *Memoirs of the Court of Spain. In Two Parts. Written by an Ingenious French Lady* (London: Horn, Saunders & Bennet, 1692); reprint available through Wing English Books 1641–1700 (Microfilm, 80:5);

The Fairy Tales of Mme d'Aulnoy, translated by Annie Macdonnel and Miss Lee (London, 1912);

Memoirs of the Court of England in 1675, edited by George Gilbert, translated by Lucretia Arthur (London: Routledge / New York: Dutton, 1913);

Travelers into Spain (London: Routledge, 1930);

Hypolitus, Earl of Douglas, introduction by Josephine Grieder (New York: Garland, 1973);

Beauties, Beasts and Enchantment: Classic French Fairy Tales, edited by Jack Zipes (New York: New American Library, 1989).

Although Marie-Catherine Le Jumel de Barneville, comtesse d'Aulnoy, did not begin her brief, thirteen-year literary career until the age of thirty-nine or forty, she rapidly became one of the most popular and influential authors of the turn of the eighteenth century. Her literary corpus is extremely diverse–three historical novels, six Spanish novellas, two pseudomemoirs, three devotional meditations, two epistolary novels, three short stories, one contemporary history, and twenty-five fairy tales–and boasts, among other innovations, the first literary fairy tale of the French tradition.

In France, d'Aulnoy's original plots, quick-witted heroines, sensitive heroes, and lively, conversational style attracted the attention of the popular publisher Claude Barbin and afforded d'Aulnoy the protection of King Louis XIV's two daughters, the duchess of Bourbon and the princess of Conti. Most important, however, her innovative talent for fairy tales sparked a vogue of publication in France that lasted from 1690 until 1715–sweeping up prominent literary figures such as Charles Perrault; Catherine Bernard; Henriette-Julie de Castelnau, comtesse de Murat; and Charlotte-Rose Caumont de La Force.

Born in Normandy, in Barneville-La-Bertrand, in 1650 or 1651, Marie-Catherine was the only daughter of Nicolas-Claude Le Jumel, seigneur de Barneville and Pennedepie, and Judith-Angélique Le Coustelier de Saint-Pater (Madame de Gaudanes, by remarriage). After losing her father at a young age, Marie-Catherine was educated in part by her maternal aunt, who instilled in her niece both a flair for "préciosité" (the refined speech of mid-seventeenth-century Parisian society) and a love of Norman folktales. Proficient in

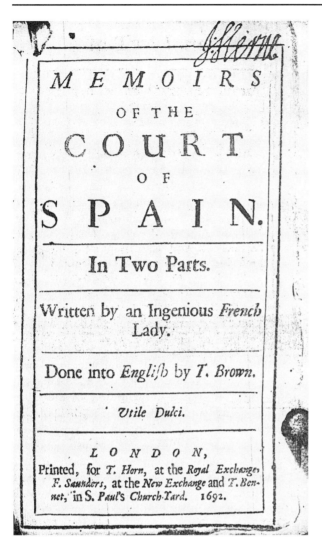

*Title page for the first English edition of d'Aulnoy's 1690
Mémoires de la cour d'Espagne, based on the
mysterious death of Marie-Louise d'Orléans
(University of Chicago Library)*

Spanish and English, Marie-Catherine was also well versed in classical and medieval French literature, Renaissance poetry, and Spanish baroque drama–a knowledge she later incorporated with great success into her literary creations.

On 8 March 1666, at age fifteen or sixteen, Marie-Catherine wed the forty-six-year-old François de La Motte, baron d'Aulnoy, in the Church of Saint-Gervais in Paris. La Motte was the estate manager, and possibly even lover, of the Duke of Vendôme. He was also a notorious gambler, and the marriage was a failure. Shortly after the birth of the couple's second child, the widowed mother of Marie-Catherine and three Norman accomplices tried to gain control of La Motte's fortune by framing him for high treason. The baron was imprisoned

in the Bastille for several months. But the plot was eventually discovered; the Norman gentlemen were executed; and Madame de Gaudanes emigrated from France, first to England and then to Spain, where she worked for many years as a double agent, serving both the French and the Spanish governments. Madame d'Aulnoy's role in the scandal was never determined, but she and La Motte separated after his release from jail. He died in Paris in 1700, at the age of eighty, having completely excluded his estranged wife from his will.

Aside from the baptismal records of her last three children–dated Paris 1668, 1669, and 1676 and marked "père absent" (father absent)–not much is known about d'Aulnoy's activities between 1668 and 1685. In her *Sentiments d'une âme penitente, sur le pseaume 50, Miserere mei Deus, et Le Retour d'une Ame à Dieu, sur le pseaume 102, Bendic anima mea. Accompagnées de Reflexions Chrétiennes* (1698), she alludes to a sojourn in a convent, a long illness, and a profound religious transformation. She also likely spent much of this time traveling extensively in England, Holland, and Spain. As Raymond Foulché-Delbosc and Shirley Jones Day have pointed out, d'Aulnoy's memoirs of the Spanish and English courts include accurate details about aspects of life in those countries not found in print elsewhere.

In 1685, after d'Aulnoy received permission to return to Paris, she bought a house on the Rue Saint-Benoit, which became the site of one of the most stimulating literary salons of the period. Madame Déshoulières, the marquise de Sevigné, Saint-Evremond, and Marie-Jeanne L'Héritier de Villandon–in addition to Perrault, La Force, and Murat–were on her list of regulars, and in this intimate, conversational environment d'Aulnoy began her authorial career.

In 1690 d'Aulnoy published her first novel, *Histoire d'Hypolite, comte de Duglas* (translated as *Hypolitus, Earl of Douglas,* 1708), a romanesque story of love and adventure set in England, France, and Italy between 1538 and 1557. In addition to including "L'île de la félicité," the first published literary fairy tale of the French tradition–published in translation as *The Story of Adolphus, Prince of Russia; and The Princess of Happiness* (1691)–*Histoire d'Hypolite, comte de Duglas* introduces several important stock characters who resurface throughout d'Aulnoy's subsequent fictional works. Julie–the virtuous, orphaned, aristocratic heroine placed in the power of a tyrannical, adoptive family–announces the fate of countless fairy-tale heroines who, isolated from their parents at birth, must rely on their own wit and ingenuity for survival. Hypolite–the devoted, valiant, sentimental hero prepared to die for his love—is reincarnated, not only in future fairy tales but also in subsequent novelistic characters, notably Jean, the Prince of Carency, in the *Histoire de Jean de Bourbon, Prince de Carency* (1692; translated as *The Prince of Carency*, 1719).

Most important, however, in *Histoire d'Hypolite, comte de Duglas,* d'Aulnoy first introduces her vision of marriage as an empty signifier, a mask of false virtue designed to serve the interests of a patriarchal ideology described as corrupt and often irrational. Whether set in medieval France, Renaissance England, seventeenth-century Spain, or "once upon a time," in d'Aulnoy's works the tyrannical dynamics of parental control within the nuclear family present a microcosm for the political oppression perpetuated by an absolute monarchy. The fate of her romantic heroes and heroines, powerless to assert their individual desires in the face of constant parental opposition, evokes the ongoing frustration of late-seventeenth-century aristocrats forced to comply with the increasing demands of Louis XIV. Beneath the surface of romantic intrigue thus emerges the beginnings of Enlightenment philosophy, as d'Aulnoy's heroes and heroines problematize their own lack of individual freedom in a world where sovereign rule is often irrational.

Following the success of *Histoire d'Hypolite, comte de Duglas,* d'Aulnoy turned toward realist fiction with the *Mémoires de la cour d'Espagne* (1690; translated as *Memoirs of the Court of Spain,* 1692). Focusing on the years 1679–1681, the work utilizes the interest aroused by the mysterious death of Marie-Louise d'Orléans, the young and sensitive French queen of Spain, victimized by a political marriage to the weak Charles II during the Spanish succession. Republished six times in France between 1690 and 1693 and translated into English, these memoirs were d'Aulnoy's first international success and launched her career in the English literary arena.

In early 1691 d'Aulnoy composed her first epistolary novel, *Relation du voyage d'Espagne* (translated as *The Lady's Travels into Spain,* 1691). This collection of fifteen letters addressed to a cousin in France describes a voyage through Spain and a sojourn in Madrid between September 1679 and May 1681. Replete with digressions about geographical surroundings, historical curiosities, administrative details, entertaining fictional anecdotes, and even an interpolated fairy tale, the frank, conversational style of the novel played an important role in the development of epistolary fiction. In England in particular, *Relation du voyage d'Espagne* was so successful that by 1697 it had already gone through four editions.

Overwhelmed by her success, d'Aulnoy paused midyear in 1691 to devote her literary talent to God's service with the composition of two devotional meditations. In the first, on the *Miserere,* d'Aulnoy repents her libertine past and thanks God for his eternal mercy. In the second, on the *Benedic anima,* d'Aulnoy asks God to guide her in her new *carrière* (undertaking) and expresses regret for not having used her literary talents to glorify him sooner. Both pamphlets were approved by the Sorbonne theologians in 1691 but were not published until 1698, along with thirty pages of Christian reflections.

At the insistence of the duchess of Bourbon and the princess of Conti, d'Aulnoy returned to romance fiction in the fall of 1691, hastily composing the *Histoire de Jean de Bourbon, Prince de Carency*. Set in late-fourteenth-century France, Spain, Italy, North Africa, and Turkey, *Histoire de Jean de Bourbon, Prince de Carency* illustrates d'Aulnoy's familiarity with medieval history, chivalric romances, and the chronicles of Jean de Froissart. As in the *Histoire d'Hypolite, comte de Duglas,* the plot of *Histoire de Jean de Bourbon, Prince de Carency* depicts the plight of two chaste lovers, Jean de Bourbon and Leonide de Velasco, who, faced with their family's disapproval, embark on a series of adventures that lead them across Europe and Arabia. Unlike the lovers in *Histoire d'Hypolite, comte de Duglas,* however, the lovers of *Histoire de Jean de Bourbon, Prince de Carency* do not live happily ever after. No sooner do they begin plans for their long-awaited wedding when Leonide's rival, Casilda, strikes the heroine dead in a fit of jealousy. Stunned and bewildered, Jean returns to France where, at the insistence of his parents and King Charles VI, he marries Catherine d'Artois. Highly controversial, the ending outraged d'Aulnoy's contemporaries to the point that the anonymous English translator changed it, omitting the scene in which Leonide is stabbed, thereby permitting the hero and heroine to marry. In France, however, the nontraditional ending proved a lucrative selling point, and *Histoire de Jean de Bourbon, Prince de Carency* went through three editions the year it was published.

D'Aulnoy showed her varied talents once more in 1692 with the publication of the *Nouvelles Espagnoles,* a collection of three short stories, a two-part novel, and a seventy-letter epistolary novel that illustrates her familiarity with the picaresque novels of Miguel de Cervantes as well as with the *Lettres Portugaises,* a collection of letters published in 1669, now considered fictional but thought at the time to be genuine letters written by a Portuguese nun. Situated in contemporary settings, the tales portray love as a game that often ridicules noble personages and court personalities. The following year, perhaps in an attempt to diminish the political critique underlying the *Nouvelles Espagnoles,* d'Aulnoy

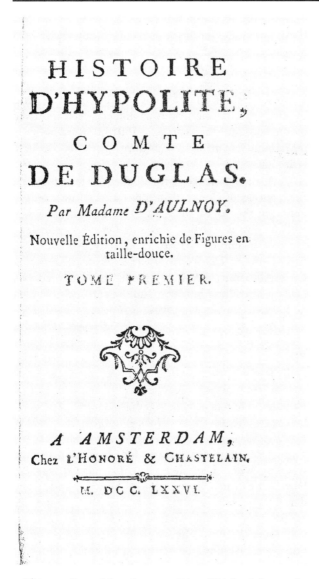

HISTOIRE D'HYPOLITE,

C O M T E

DE DUGLAS.

Par Madame D'AULNOY.

Nouvelle Édition, enrichie de Figures en
taille-douce.

TOME PREMIER.

A AMSTERDAM,

Chez L'HONORÉ & CHASTELAIN.

M. DCC. LXXVI.

*Title page for an eighteenth-century edition of d'Aulnoy's first novel,
a romance set in England, France, and Italy during the
sixteenth century (Sterling Library, Yale University)*

composed the *Nouvelles ou mémoires historiques* (1693), a
meticulously detailed, adulatory account of the wars of
Louis XIV against Holland.

Then d'Aulnoy turned her attention once again
to foreign characters, capitalizing on the curiosity surrounding the depression of the English monarchy.
The *Mémoires de la cour d'Angleterre,* (1695; translated
as *Memoirs of the Court of England,* 1707) is a chatty,
first-person account of a six-day sojourn at the
English court in 1675. This collection of romantic
intrigues, which describes the amorous exploits of historical characters such as Lord Arran and the dukes
of Monmouth and Buckingham, includes a series of
twenty-six letters, an informational pamphlet titled

"Conseils pour bien écrire" (Tips for Good Writing),
and the lively interpolated story "L'amant travesti"
(The Cross-Dressed Lover).

In 1697 d'Aulnoy applied her talent to yet
another genre much in vogue, the fairy tale, a genre
she had popularized in her salon. *Les Contes des fées*
(Fairy Tales) is a four-volume collection replete with
clever heroines and sentimental heroes; it once again
demonstrates d'Aulnoy's penchant for diversity. The
first two volumes, published together in April 1697,
are a short collection of nine fairy tales; the next two
volumes are made up of two Spanish novels that
include six fairy tales and are framed by a narrative
called "Le Récit de Saint-Cloud" (The Narrative of
Saint-Cloud). These fairy tales, for which d'Aulnoy
is best known today, became immediately popular,
and d'Aulnoy, attuned to public taste, published
another similarly diverse four-volume collection the
following year, *Les Contes nouveaux ou les Fées à la mode*
(1698). The first volume is a short collection of three
fairy tales, followed by a three-volume novel, *Le Nouveau Gentilhomme bourgeois* (The New Bourgeois Gentleman), into which are inserted other fairy tales.
The novel, which describes a bourgeois gentleman's
devious efforts to secure a marriage contract with the
daughter of one of the local barons, plays on the rising insecurities of the French aristocracy during a
period of economic decline.

In 1698 d'Aulnoy was elected to the prestigious Accademia dei Ricovrati of Padua (one of only
nine women to receive this distinction), by whom
she was awarded the title "Clio l'Eloquente," the eloquent muse of history. The following year, however,
another scandal broke out that threatened her reputation. Madame Tiquet, an intimate friend and regular at d'Aulnoy's salon, was indicted for having
orchestrated the murder of her husband. Claiming
she could not have committed the crime, Tiquet
cited her presence at d'Aulnoy's salon on the day of
the murder. Suspicion surrounded the now-famous
author; Madame Tiquet was executed; and d'Aulnoy retired into semiseclusion.

In 1703, just two years before her death, d'Aulnoy published the last of her historical novels, *Le
Comte de Warwick* (translated as *The History of the Earl
of Warwick,* 1708). Set in the second half of the fifteenth century (1461–1471), the novel connects love
and power more directly than any of d'Aulnoy's previous works, describing a secret love affair as the
true motive behind Warwick's most influential political decisions. For d'Aulnoy scholars, *Le Comte de
Warwick* is also notable for a signed preface by d'Aulnoy, in which she gives a list of her works with the
intention of clearing up misattributions associated

with her pen name, "Madame D***." This list, which includes only the works mentioned above, is unfortunately not respected by most library catalogues today.

D'Aulnoy died in 1705 in her home on the Rue Saint-Benoit, but her popularity and influence did not die with her. Her works were republished dozens of times in France between 1690 and 1785. More than sixty-five editions appeared in England and more than ten appeared in Germany, Holland, and Spain. In France she inspired such writers as Madame de Villeneuve and Rétif de la Bretonne, who, like many others, imitated d'Aulnoy's trademark interpolation of fairy tales into novels. In England the sentimental realism of her memoirs and epistolary novels influenced mid-century novelists such as Samuel Richardson, while her pseudohistorical romances and gloomy Spanish novellas contributed to the late-eighteenth-century Gothic revival, inspiring works such as Ann Radcliffe's *A Sicilian Romance* (1790).

Although d'Aulnoy's novels and memoirs continued to be republished sporadically throughout the nineteenth century (*Histoire d'Hypolite, comte de Duglas,* the most popular of her novels, was republished twenty times), today her literary reputation rests almost entirely on her fairy tales, most of which are now read separately or in simplified form in children's collections. While scholars have recently begun to reassess the intellectual and political content of d'Aulnoy's fairy tales, her novels and memoirs are still in need of rehabilitation.

Bibliographies:

Raymond Foulché-Delbosc, "Madame d'Aulnoy et l'Espagne," *Revue hispanique,* 67 (1926): 1–152;

Nancy Palmer and Melvin D. Palmer, "English Editions of French contes de fées Attributed to Mme d'Aulnoy," *Studies in Bibliography: Papers of the Bibliographical Society of the University of Virginia,* 27 (1974): 227–232;

Melvin D. Palmer, "Madame d'Aulnoy in England," *Comparative Literature,* 27 (1975): 237–253.

References:

Jacques Barchilon, "Madame d'Aulnoy, reine dans la féerie," in *Le Conte merveilleux français de 1690 à 1790. Cent ans de féerie et de poésie ignorées de l'histoire littéraire* (Paris: H. Champion, 1975);

James R. Beeler, "An interesting use of genealogy in historical romances (*Jean de Bourbon*)," *Renaissance and other studies in honor of W. L. Wiley* (Chapel Hill: University of North Carolina Press, 1968), pp. 31–40;

Ruth Carver Capasso, "Madame d'Aulnoy and the Comedy of Transformation," *Papers on French Seventeenth Century Literature,* 14 (1987): 575–588;

Henri Coulet, *Le Roman jusqu'à la Révolution,* volume 1 (Paris: Colin, 1967), pp. 290–291;

R. A. Day, "Madame d'Aulnoy on the *Lettres Portugaises,"Modern Languages Notes* (December 1952): 544–546;

Anne DeFrance, *Les Contes de fées et les nouvelles de Madame d'Aulnoy (1690–1698)* (Geneva: Droz, 1998);

Amy Vanderlyn DeGraff, *The Tower and the Well: A Psychological Interpretation of the Fairy Tales of Madame d'Aulnoy* (Birmingham, Ala.: Summa Publications, 1981);

Joan DeJean, *Tender Geographies* (New York: Columbia University Press, 1994);

Teresa Di Scanno, *Les Contes de fées à l'époque classique (1680–1715)* (Naples: Liguori Editore, 1975);

Anne E. Duggan, "Feminine Genealogy, Matriarchy, and Utopia in the Fairy Tales of Marie-Catherine d'Aulnoy," *Neophilologus,* 82 (1998): 199–208;

Michèle Farrell, "Celebration and Repression of Feminine Desire in Mme d'Aulnoy's Fairy Tale: *La Chatte Blanche," L'Esprit Créateur,* 29 (1989): 52–64;

René Godenne, "Présentation," in *Histoire d'Hypolite, comte de Duglas,* by Marie-Catherine d'Aulnoy (Geneva: Slatkine, 1979), pp. i–xxvi;

Patricia Hannon, "A Politics of Disguise: Marie-Catherine d'Aulnoy's 'Belle Etoile' and the Narrative Structure of Ambivalence," *Anxious Power: Reading, Writing, and Ambivalence in Narrative by Women,* edited by Carol J. Singley and Susan Elisabeth Sweeney (Albany: State University of New York Press, 1993), pp. 73–89;

Renée Riese Hubert, "L'Amour et la féerie chez Madame d'Aulnoy," *Romanische Forshungen,* 75 (1963): 1–10;

Hubert, "Poetic Humor in Madame d'Aulnoy's Fairy Tales," *L'Esprit Créateur,* 3 (1963): 123–129;

Hubert, "Le Sens du voyage dans quelques contes de Madame d'Aulnoy," *French Review,* 46 (1973): 931–937;

Shirley Jones, "Examples of Sensibility in the Late Seventeenth-Century Feminine Novel in France," *Modern Language Review,* 61 (1966): 199–208;

Shirley Jones Day, "Madame d'Aulnoy's Julie: A Heroine in the 1690s," in *Writers and Heroines: Essays on Women in French Literature,* edited by Jones Day (Bern: Peter Lang, 1999), pp. 71–88;

Jones Day, *The Search for Lyonesse: Women's Fiction in France 1670–1703* (Bern: Peter Lang, 1999);

Jean Mainil, *Madame d'Aulnoy et le Rire des Fées: Essai sur la subversion féerique et le merveilleux comique sous l'ancien régime* (Paris: Editions Kimé, 2001);

Catherine Marin, "Plaisir et violence dans les contes de fées de Madame d'Aulnoy," *Narratology* (1998): 263–272;

Jane Tucker Mitchell, *A Thematic Analysis of Mme d'Aulnoy's Fairy Tales* (University, Miss.: Romance Monographs, 1978);

Melvin D. Palmer, "Madame d'Aulnoy's Pseudo-Autobiographical Works on Spain," *Romanische Forshungen,* 83 (1971): 220–229;

Raymonde Robert, *Le Conte de fées littéraire en France de la fin du XVIIe à la fin du XVIIIe siècle* (Nancy: Presses Universitaires de Nancy, 1982);

Jeanne Roche-Mazon, *Autour des contes de fées* (Paris: Didier, 1968);

Roche-Mazon, *En Marge de l'oiseau bleu* (Paris: Livres de l'Artisan, 1930);

Lewis Seifert, "Marie-Catherine, Le Jumel de Barneville, Comtesse d'Aulnoy," *French Women Writers: A Bio-Bibliographical Source Book,* edited by Eva Martin Sartori and Dorothy Wynne Zimmerman (New York: Greenwood Press, 1991), pp. 11–20;

Seifert, *Nostalgic Utopias* (Cambridge, Mass.: Harvard University Press, 1997);

Maya Slater, "Madame d'Aulnoy and the Adult Fairy Tale," *Newsletter for Seventeenth-Century Studies* (1982): 69–75;

Mary Elizabeth Storer, *Un épisode littéraire de la fin du XVIIème siècle: La mode des contes de fées* (Paris: Champion, 1928);

Gabrielle Verdier, "Comment l'auteur des 'Fées à la mode' devint 'Mother Bunch': Métamorphoses de la Comtesse d'Aulnoy en Angleterre," *Marvels and Tales,* 10 (1996): 285–309;

Verdier, "Plaisir et Violence dans les contes des fées de Madame d'Aulnoy," in *Violence et Fiction jusqu'à la Révolution,* edited by M. Debaiseux and G. Verdier (Tübingen: Narr, 1998), pp. 263–272;

Marcelle Maistre Welch, "Le Devenir de la jeune fille dans les contes de fées de Madame d'Aulnoy," *Cahiers du Dix-septième: An Interdisciplinary Journal,* 1 (1987): 53–62;

Welch, "La femme, le mariage, et l'amour dans les contes de fées mondains du XVIIème siècle français," *Papers on French Seventeenth Century Literature,* 10 (1983): 47–58;

Welch, "Rebellion et resignation dans les contes de fées de Mme d'Aulnoy et Mme de Murat," *Cahiers du Dix-Septième: An Interdisciplinary Journal,* 3 (1989): 131–142;

Adrienne E. Zuerner, "Reflections of the Monarchy in d'Aulnoy's Belle-Belle ou le chevalier Fortuné," in *Out of the Woods: The Origins of the Literary Fairy Tale in Italy and France,* edited by Nancy L. Canepa (Detroit, Mich.: Wayne State University Press, 1997), pp. 194–217.

Guez de Balzac
(1597? – 1654)

Michael Taormina
Columbia University

SELECTED BOOKS*: *Harangues panégyriques, au Roy sur l'ouverture de ses Estats, et à la Reine sur l'heureux succez de sa régence* (Paris: T. du Bray, 1615);

Lettres du sieur de Balzac (Paris: T. du Bray, 1624; revised and enlarged, 1625; revised and enlarged again, 1626);

Apologie pour Monsieur de Balzac, by Balzac and François Ogier (Paris: C. Morlot, 1627);

Les Œuvres de Monsieur de Balzac, 2 volumes (Paris: T. du Bray, 1627; revised and enlarged, 1 volume, 1628; revised and enlarged again, Paris: P. Rocolet, 1642);

Le Prince (Paris: T. du Bray, P. Rocolet et C. Sonnius, 1631; revised, 1632); translated by H.G. as *The Prince* (London: Printed for M. Meighen & G. Bedell, 1648);

Lettres de Mr de Balzac, seconde partie (Paris: P. Rocolet, 1636);

Discours sur une tragédie de Monsieur Heinsius intitulée Herodes infanticida (Paris: P. Rocolet, 1636);

Recueil de nouvelles lettres de Monsieur de Balzac (Paris: J. Camusat, 1637);

Lettre de Mr de Balzac à Mr de Scudéry sur ses observations du Cid, et la Response de Mr de Scudéry à Mr de Balzac: Avec la lettre de Mr de Scudéry à Messieurs de l'Académie françoise, sur le jugement qu'ils ont fait du Cid et de ses observations (Paris: A. de Sommaville, 1637);

Les Œuvres diverses du sieur de Balzac (Paris: P. Rocolet, 1644; enlarged edition, Paris: C. Barbin, 1658);

Lettres choisies du sieur de Balzac, 2 volumes (Paris: A. Courbé, 1647);

Le Barbon (Paris: A. Courbé, 1648);

Guez de Balzac; engraving by Guillaume Vallet

Ioannis Ludovici Guezii Balzacii Carminum, Libri tres: Eiusdem Epistoae Selecae (Paris: A. Courbé, 1650);

Socrate chrestien, par le sr de Balzac, et autres œuvres du mesme autheur; Dissertation, ou Diverses remarques sur divers escrits à Monsieur Conrart, conseiller et secrétaire du Roy (Paris: A. Courbé, 1652);

Lettres familières de Monsieur de Balzac à Monsieur Chapelain (Paris: A. Courbé, 1656);

*Only major or book-length works of Guez de Balzac are listed above; short pamphlets, short epistles, and lost works have been omitted. An exhaustive bibliography of works, including those now lost, has been published by Bernard Beugnot (see back rubric).

Les Entretiens de feu Monsieur de Balzac (Paris: A. Courbé, 1657);

Aristippe, ou De la Cour, par Monsieur de Balzac (Paris: A. Courbé, 1658); translated by R.W. as *Aristippus; or, Monsr. de Balsac's Masterpiece: Being a discourse concerning the court: With an exact table of the principall matter* (London: Printed by Tho. Newcomb for Nat. Eakins & Tho. Johnson, 1659);

Lettres de feu M. de Balzac à M. Conrart (Paris: A. Courbé, 1659);

Les Lettres diverses de Monsieur de Balzac, dernière édition (Paris: C. Barbin, 1659);

Les Œuvres de Monsieur de Balzac, divisées en deux tomes, 2 volumes, edited by Valentin Conrart (Paris: L. Billaine, 1665).

Editions: *Œuvres de J. L. Guez, Sr de Balzac*, 2 volumes, edited by Louis Moreau (Paris: J. Lecoffre, 1854);

Lettres de Jean-Louis Guez de Balzac, edited by Philippe Tamizey de Larroque (Paris: Imprimerie Nationale, 1873);

Les Premières Lettres de Guez de Balzac: 1618–1627, 2 volumes, edited by H. Bibas & K. T. Butler (Paris: Droz, 1933, 1934);

Œuvres de Monsieur de Balzac en deux tomes, 2 volumes (Geneva: Slatkine, 1971);

Les Entretiens: 1657, 2 volumes, edited by Bernard Beugnot (Paris: Marcel Didier, 1972);

Apologie pour Monsieur de Balzac, edited by Jean Jehasse (Saint-Etienne: Université de Saint-Etienne, 1977);

Epistolae selectae: 1650, Epîtres latines choisies, edited and translated by Jehasse and Bernard Yon (Saint-Etienne: Université de Saint-Etienne, 1990);

Œuvres diverses, edited by Roger Zuber (Paris: H. Champion, 1995).

Editions in English: *The Letters of Mounsieur de Balzac*, translated by William Tirwhyt (London: Printed by Nicholas Okes for Richard Clotterbuck, 1634);

New Epistles of Mounsieur de Balzac, translated by Richard Baker (London: Printed by T. Cotes for F. Eglesfield, J. Crooke & R. Serger, 1638);

A Collection of Some Modern Epistles of Monsieur de Balzac (Oxford: Printed by Leonard Lichfield for Francis Bowman, 1639);

The Roman: The Conversation of the Romans and Maecenas, in Three Excellent Discourses Written in French by Monsieur de Balsac (London: Printed by T.N. for J. Holden, 1652);

Letters of Mounsieur de Balzac: 1. 2. 3. and 4th parts, translated by Baker and others (London: Printed for John Williams & Francis Eglesfield, 1654).

Jean-Louis Guez de Balzac was widely acclaimed during his lifetime as a master of French prose. His var-

ious writings successfully balance the demands of a native French aristocratic public against those of the humanist legacy, wherein Latin was the basis of a European Republic of Letters. He was the quintessential man of letters: he, in fact, wrote primarily letters, a genre that then served as a vehicle for the public expression of ideas, opinions, and taste. He was actively writing in a period that, strictly speaking, had just witnessed what Alain Viala has called *La Naissance de l'écrivain* (The Birth of the Writer, 1985)—that is, someone who earns his living by writing. Such a profession was not only considered vulgar by his peers, but also his letters earned him little or no compensation, apart from wide popularity and authority in literary matters, though not without controversy. His letters fill several volumes; of particular note is his massive correspondence with such luminaries as Jean Chapelain and Valentin Conrart, founding members of the Académie Française and considered by many as the architects of French classicism. These private letters, most probably circulating prior to their integral publication, established Guez de Balzac as a preeminent literary critic, making and breaking the reputations of writers and poets for generations to come. A talented polemicist, Guez de Balzac also wrote literary and political libel, satire, and longer works of "practical" philosophy on the political and religious issues of his day. Of his various and prolific publications, however, one may single out his *Lettres du sieur de Balzac* (Letters of M. de Balzac, 1624), *Le Prince* (1631), *Les Œuvres diverses du sieur de Balzac* (The Divers Works of M. de Balzac, 1644), and *Socrate chrétien, par le sr de Balzac, et autres oeuvres du mesme autheur* (The Christian Socrates by M. de Balzac and Other Works by the Same Author, 1652).

Jean-Louis Guez was born to a well-to-do family in the province of Charente. The actual year of his birth is unknown, but most critics agree on 1597, based on the date of his certificate of baptism (June of that year). His father, Guillaume Guez, served as secretary to Jean-Louis Nogaret de la Valette, Duke of Epernon, before retiring to his lands of Balzac near Angoulême in 1588. Jean-Louis Guez was named after the duke, his godfather, and later added the title "de Balzac" to the family name. Relatively little is known of Guez's life; the only biography known, published by his friend Claude Girard, has now been lost. Guez's early schooling took place in Angoulême; he then spent two years at the Jesuit Collège de Puygarreau in Poitiers before joining the Collège de la Marche in Paris in 1619 to study philosophy. He traveled to Holland around 1613 with the libertine poet Théophile de Viau and may have spent some time in Amsterdam, where both were registered as students at the University of Leyden in 1615. For reasons that have remained obscure, Guez and Théophile ended their friendship soon thereafter. Guez then returned to Paris and may have taken a second trip to Holland. In 1618 he was back in Angoulême, where he had assumed his father's post as secretary to the duke of Epernon. Through his relationship with the duke, Guez was introduced to various important personages of the time, among them the Queen Mother, Marie de Médicis, and the bishop of Luçon, the future cardinal of Richelieu, as well as an obscure character in Richelieu's entourage by the name of François Le Métel de Boisrobert. Boisrobert later became an important member of the Académie Française and was instrumental in the publication of Guez's early works. During that time Guez developed an interest in politics and wrote several polemical letters that, without causing him any serious trouble, nevertheless gained him notice as an undiplomatic writer.

In the fall of 1620 he was sent to Rome in the service of Cardinal Louis de la Valette, the youngest of d'Epernon's three sons. Little is known of Guez's actual mission to Rome—there is some speculation that it had to do with the promotion of Richelieu to the post of cardinal—but his correspondence from Italy describes an easy and fairly idle life. Several critics have deplored the lack of information about this period since likely he found in Rome the inspiration not only for his later work on antiquity and ancient eloquence but also for the genre for which he is best known—the letter. His letters from Rome were circulated and mark the beginning of his reputation as a writer. He returned to Angoulême in 1622, complaining of ill health.

The youthful rashness evident in his early polemical letters, which developed into masterly polemical talent, might have cost Guez de Balzac the political career to which he could rightly have aspired, considering his education and his family connections. Instead, he mostly remained in Angoulême for the rest of his life, trading politics for the title of *unico eloquente* (unique man of eloquence), a title he enjoyed until his death in 1654. His retirement in his province of Charente, at a time when life away from the capital was considered a sort of exile, also won him the title of "hermit." Throughout his life he resisted various attempts to lure him to Paris or to provide him with gratifications in the form of pensions or sinecures, praising instead his quiet life in the "desert." Elected against his wishes to the Académie Française shortly after its foundation in 1635, he even declined to travel to Paris and give the obligatory "compliment" and speech. However, his physical seclusion from public life, perhaps resulting also from poor health and a propensity to melancholy, was offset by an extraordinarily active, and sometimes controversial, involvement in the intellectual life of his time and an uninterrupted flow of correspondence.

Shortly after his return to Angoulême in 1622, Guez de Balzac, with the help of Boisrobert, published *Lettres du sieur de Balzac,* a collection of the various letters he had addressed to the most powerful personages in the French Court and Church, to an overwhelmingly positive reception by the French aristocracy. Thanks to the diversity of addressees, the letters explore a vast terrain of contemporary problems and touch upon politics and ethics. In the eyes of his contemporaries, moreover, the frank and lucid style of the letters encourages both an "ethical" portrait of the addressee, or some third party, and a self-portrait. From this collection, then, emerges a profoundly irreverent Guez de Balzac with conservative politics, a "Roman spirit" in whom antiquity and modernity coexist, but who is at the same time unabashedly French.

Guez de Balzac manages to capture the majesty and authority of Latin for his native French by selecting as his model Justius Lipsus—a man from the "Moderns" rather than the Ancients. Lipsus was a man whose style, depth of learning, and wide circle of powerful correspondents had earned him an unparalleled rank among humanist writers. It is a stroke of genius on the part of Guez de Balzac to have transposed the style, authority, and prestige of Lipsus's letters into a French aristocratic arena. Guez de Balzac thus captures for himself the persona of Lipsus, a man who from the privacy of his library exercises public influence on ethical, political, and linguistic debate.

Occupying an envious territory shared by Rome and Paris, Latin and French, humanists and aristocrats, Guez de Balzac nonetheless shows himself in the *Lettres* to be a staunch modernist. In one letter he claims "to have discovered what the Ancients have never seen, and encountered, with new glasses, new stars in the heavens of Eloquence." The independence and originality that Guez de Balzac reserves for himself probably held an irresistible attraction for his aristocratic peers. They must have thrilled in his pride when he wrote, "I learn from the Ancients what they would have learned from me had I been first in the world, but I am not slavishly dependent on their thinking, nor am I subject exclusively to their laws and example." The success of the *Lettres,* their sudden authority in French eloquence, thus could not fail to provoke a controversy between rival camps.

Shortly after the publication of the *Lettres,* Guez de Balzac became involved in a bitter dispute with his former friend Théophile, whom he had criticized both as a poet and as a *libertin.* Some critics have taken a dim view of this episode of Guez de Balzac's life since Théophile was at the time involved in a long, drawn-out trial for atheism that nearly cost him his life. Shortly after his release from prison, and a few months before his death in 1626 at the age of thirty-six, Théophile replied to Guez de Balzac in a letter published in 1629, accusing him of intellectual sterility and plagiarism of ancient authors.

This episode marked the beginning of a series of attacks on Guez de Balzac by humanists in 1625. One pamphlet in particular, *La Conformité de l'Eloquence de M. de Bazac avec celle des plus grands personnages du temps présent et du passé* (The Conformity of the Eloquence of M. de Balzac with the Eloquence of the Greatest Writers past and Present, 1627), circulating in aristocratic circles, renewed the accusation of plagiarism. The author, Frère André de Saint Denis, argued that the so-called eloquence of the *Lettres* originated simply because of translated citations from unacknowledged ancient and modern Latin sources, which Guez de Balzac had acquired in his humanist education. In 1627 François Ogier, probably with the help of Guez de Balzac himself, launched a counterattack in *Apologie pour Monsieur de Balzac* (Defense of M. de Balzac), defending the author's willful "forgetting" of ancient and modern sources on the grounds of creative imitation, or emulation, which is imitation as rivalry. It is difficult to overestimate the virulence of these polemics, in which many intellectuals took part. One anecdote has it that Guez de Balzac, enraged by the critique of an aristocratic peer, actually hired an armed band of men "to correct" the literary upstart's views. In any event, the significant effect of this long-winded literary polemic was to divert the critical debate once confined to the erudite circles of the Republic of Letters into a native French arena dominated by Guez de Balzac's aristocratic peers. Critical debate on the best style was being conducted in French on a French writer. The real sense of Guez de Balzac's modernism is the adaptation of the Latin sources to a contemporary context, not their abandonment. His triumph over the humanist opposition authorized him to act as the humanist educator of the aristocratic public.

The ongoing success in literary matters had to be some consolation to Guez de Balzac, who, prior to the publication of *Le Prince* in 1631, still nourished political ambitions. In 1619 he had participated in a military operation led by the duke of Epernon to liberate Marie de Medicis from her imprisonment at Blois, whence she took refuge in Angoulême at the home of the Balzacs. But this occurrence was the closest that the young Guez ever came to the inner circle of power. The Balzacs had aided the weaker political faction, and the cardinal de Richelieu, hostile to the Queen Mother and soon to become a formidable political figure, never forgot the incident. Guez de Balzac, however, tried to win the patronage of Richelieu by sending him the manuscript of *Le Prince,* which is an idealized portrait of King Louis XIII rendered in a potpourri of religious, historical, and political reflections. Richelieu read it and disapproved. The book was published anyway; the second and third parts were abandoned, however, and the episode marked the end of Guez de Balzac's political ambitions.

Furthermore, the perceived lack of coherence of the book as well as its idiosyncratic exposition of certain religious and political ideas current in the seventeenth century touched off nothing but negative reactions from every quarter. In *Le Prince,* Guez de Balzac takes up the cause of Louis XIII's monarchy, with its string of recent military victories, against what he considers to be national disintegration in the form of political factionalism. However, Guez de Balzac's ideas somehow managed to alienate every single political faction—the powerful nobles, such as the duke of Epernon, nostalgic for an aristocratic feudalism; the Queen Mother's entourage, hiding its pro-Spanish or Roman agenda behind Catholic piety and devotion; the university theologians and savants, who valued speculative truth over the practical wisdom of action; the Queen Mother herself and her youngest son, Gaston d'Orléans, whom an authoritarian king necessarily excluded from the decision-making process; and the Protestant minority, feeling increasingly marginalized in their Catholic motherland. In preaching a harmonious unity organized around an idealized monarch, Guez de Balzac attempted to combine the best of the Roman and Christian traditions. His ideal was an authoritarian monarchy that derived its legitimacy from divine will but limited its power to a national territory, where reason and the rule of law reigned. Still, Louis XIII did not appreciate the idealized portrait. As a foil to this picture, moreover, Guez de Balzac detailed the vices of princes from antiquity to the present. The king found the work embarrassing, if not ridiculous. It is perhaps no surprise that the Spanish had *Le Prince* burned in public when everyone realized that the portrait of tyranny was drawn after the Spanish monarchy. The English, too, swore revenge for the unflattering portrait of their queen. The French ambassador to England had to intervene on Guez de Balzac's behalf. Given such a negative reaction at home and abroad, Richelieu was perhaps justified in characterizing Guez de Balzac the political writer as *un étourdi* (reckless and naive). Richelieu never offered Guez de Balzac either employment or pension.

Guez de Balzac had to console himself with a literary career. He reportedly enjoyed the company of François Maynard, Honorat de Bueil, Seigneur de Racan, Nicolas Faret, Jean Chapelain, and Valentin Conrart, but he knew them mostly by correspondence. Chapelain, an erudite humanist who frequented the Hôtel de Rambouillet and was a founding member of the Académie Française, first introduced Guez de

Frontispiece for Balzac's 1631 idealized word portrait of King Louis XIII; engraving by M. Lasne
(Dickinson College Library)

Balzac to Madame la marquise de Rambouillet and her literary salon in 1638. But Guez de Balzac's reputation had well preceded him. The style of his *Lettres* announced certain sympathies with the Malherbian poetic reforms that had penetrated the Hôtel. Guez de Balzac's literary criticism, moreover, having first gained exposure in his private correspondence with Chapelain as early as 1627, was warmly received by the Hôtel. After the founding of the Académie Française in 1635, when Guez de Balzac's correspondence with Chapelain intensified, the Hôtel de Rambouillet became the privileged forum for the views of Chapelain, Conrart, and Guez de Balzac. These pioneers of classicism were attempting, in Guez de Balzac's words, "to civilize doctrine"—that is, to introduce the aristocratic public to an erudition traditionally accessible only to the literati. In touch with the Académie and the Hôtel de Rambouillet, Guez de Balzac became one of the most important literary critics of his day.

From 1636 to 1637 he was instrumental in pioneering an aesthetic that sets the stage for classicism. Most of his views appeared first in private correspondence, were later refined, and were then published separately—for example, in the sixteen *Epistolae* appended to his *Recueil de nouvelles lettres* (New Collected Letters, 1637) or later in his 1644 *Les Œuvres diverses*. The literary quarrels following on the heels of his *Lettres* and *Le Prince* had spurred Guez de Balzac to formulate a theory of style based on an explicit critique of writing practices current in the Republic of Letters.

Guez de Balzac's modernist strategy of creative imitation, or emulation, against mere citation of ancient sources is in fact a consequence of his literary classicism. If the language and thoughts of the best authors from antiquity are timeless, then the contemporary writer need only adapt them to his own context. This belief is what Guez de Balzac means when he writes, "Whatever shall be eternal is always new." Of course,

Guez de Balzac argues, a writer must then observe a double criterion of eloquence–on the one hand, his own judgment as formed by his liberal education; on the other hand, the approval of his audience. Gone are the days of erudite obscurity and elitism. Guez de Balzac attacks Pierre de Ronsard and La Pléiade (the poets of Ronsard's circle) for their obscure diction–a hybrid of Greek, Latin, and French–and for their disdain toward the French-speaking public. He denounces not only affected diction but also far-fetched metaphors and inept imitation of models resulting in a kind of obsolescence. Instead, the writer should secure the approval of those speakers of a native, pure, and beautiful French. The aristocrats of the Hôtel de Rambouillet could not fail to assign themselves the role of privileged audience. Moreover, Guez de Balzac has nothing but praise for the poetry of François de Malherbe, which had already taken a step in the right direction. Guez de Balzac only adds the proviso that the writer must display a certain seriousness tempered by playful wit. Elegance, studied negligence, and a frank simplicity that one associates with refined conversation–these criteria of style, though borrowed from humanist rhetorical theory, were so successfully civilized in the Hôtel de Rambouillet that the tide of taste definitively turned against the Republic of Letters. Later, even the work of Guez de Balzac himself came to seem too pedantic in the eyes of the aristocratic public.

Guez de Balzac's literary criticism, obliquely connected with the Académie, exhibits both erudition and originality. In 1636, criticizing *Herodes Infanticida* (Herod, Murderer of the Innocents), a Latin tragedy by Daniel Heinsius, renowned scholar of the Republic of Letters, Guez de Balzac takes pains to track down the Latin sources of the allusions in order to praise the author's creative imitation. What Guez de Balzac values in a tragedy, however, is not so much the culture and erudition as the internal coherence of the work, as well as *bienséance* (decorum). In 1637, however, Guez de Balzac defended Pierre Corneille's *Le Cid* (first performed, 1637), which was then being censured by the Académie on the grounds of lack of verisimilitude and *bienséance,* and in 1642 applauded the playwright's bigger-than-life Roman characters in *Cinna* (first performed, 1641). Guez de Balzac clearly had no use for the dogmatic literary theory of the Académie.

The encounter of the triumvirate of French letters–Chapelain, Conrart, and Guez de Balzac–with the Hôtel de Rambouillet furnished Guez de Balzac with the occasion for the publication of *Les Œuvres diverses.* This eloquent and ambitious work brings the literary preoccupations of the Hôtel to the larger Republic of Letters. It comprises eighteen *discours* (conversations), written monologues addressed to a particular interlocutor who never speaks but to whom Guez de Balzac responds. The addressees include members of the literary salon at the Hôtel, such as the marquise herself; celebrated savants of the Republic, Préfacier Buchard and Pierre Costar; and a personal friend, such as Maynard. These carefully chosen addressees constitute a relay system whereby larger groups of readers are invited to eavesdrop, as it were, on the conversations that the Hôtel has inspired. Guez de Balzac is thus able to create a certain intimacy while maintaining the aristocratic ideal of disinterestedness, or detachment from worldly honors, even as he discourses on worldly topics such as virtue, prudence, or beauty. The aristocratic tenor of the work–that is, the pride that Guez de Balzac must have taken in it–is attested to by its lack of dedication to a powerful personage: it was usual to dedicate the work to a Maecenas, or patron, so as to procure a monetary compensation. With this publication, Guez de Balzac transcends mere consolation for his political failures: he enters the realm of the creation of values.

In *Les Œuvres diverses,* Guez de Balzac reports on the higher preoccupations of the Rambouillet salon while reflecting on his own tastes and values. *Discours* 1 through 9 present the ideal portrait of the "Roman," reflect on his urbane conversation, and explore the consequences of a humanist education for the taste and sensibility of the aristocrat.

The "Discours premier, A Madame la marquise de Rambouillet" begins almost in the middle of a conversation: "What they have told you, Madame, is quite true . . . it is beyond doubt that the great souls, of which we have spoken so many times, were housed in bodies of mediocre size." Guez de Balzac thus opens the question of moral virtue, or excellence of soul, which the Romans–in Guez de Balzac's opinion–possessed more than any other nation in history. What distinguishes them is not their physical force but their heroic spirit. "The spirit is the sovereign artisan of the great works: military actions as well as civil affairs." Guez de Balzac knows that his addressee, la marquise, is of Roman origin and that she will appreciate a reflection on how the moral superiority of her ancestors has survived in the aristocratic spirit, confronted by the tyranny of Richelieu.

The second text, "Suite d'un entretien de vive voix, ou de la conversation des Romains" (Sequel to an Actual Discussion, or On the Conversation of the Romans), defines the concept of urbanity, one aspect of the Roman spirit that lives in the Hôtel, and gives examples of the urbane conversation of the Romans. Urbanity is "a certain air of high society," "a courtly tincture that colors not only words and opinions, but the tone of voice and the movements of the body." Nothing of this air or color should appear studied. It exhibits "neglected grace and artless ornaments, of which scholars are ignorant, and which are beyond rules and precepts." Above all, urbanity is witty conversation—"the skill of pricking the spirit by I do not know what kind of sting, but which is agreeable to the one who receives it, because it tickles and does not wound." The Roman who best exemplifies this quality is Cicero, but in his letters to Atticus, not in his orations or rhetorical works. Still, the concept owes just as much to the Rome of Popes Leon X and Urbane VIII, whose Ciceronian orators Guez de Balzac studied while in Italy. For the remainder of his maturity, Guez de Balzac pursued the ideal of urbanity in his writing.

The second half of the work, *Discours* 10 through 17, comprises a belated defense of Guez de Balzac's prose style. While this defense beautifully displays Guez de Balzac's talent for polemic, it is nonetheless a virulent personal attack on Père Goulu, a Jesuit who had aggressively criticized the eloquence of the *Lettres* of 1624. Perhaps the most interesting aspect of this literary broadside is Guez de Balzac's intellectual autobiography in *Discours* 16. Guez de Balzac insists that his attacks, in the 1627 *Apologie,* on the language and style of Père Goulu were not meant for the clergy in particular but were aimed at "those people who, abusing the abundance of their free time as well as the convenience of the printing press, dishonor our century every day with the publication of what merits nothing but censure, and is good but not for reading." The social rank of the writer does not determine the quality of his prose. Explaining how he came to formulate his own personal style, Guez de Balzac nods to the influence of Malherbe, "France's foremost grammarian," and the Latinist Monsieur Bourbon, "who remade me and reformed my thinking." From the latter, Guez de Balzac learned of the majesty and grandeur of Rome, so that, after visiting Italy, he was able to distinguish true from false eloquence. Guez de Balzac learned how to judge the virtues of an author's style and how to distinguish one style from another. Once again, Guez de Balzac is reconciling French and Latin, Paris and Rome, the aristocratic and the humanist audiences. The extended self-portrait of the second half of *Les Œuvres diverses* is essentially a justification for his literary taste and judgment.

The prose style of *Les Œuvres diverses,* addressed to such a variety of interlocutors and touching on such a variety of topics, exemplifies a judicious mix of tones and levels of language in accordance with the ideal of urbane conversation. In rhetorical theory, this prose style is called *varietas* (variety), which is obliquely evoked by the adjective *diverse* in the title of work. With this work, Guez de Balzac mastered an ideal of style that had been the subject of a long-standing, if intermittent, debate in France from the time of Desiderius Erasmus's *Ciceronianus* (1528) on. It is not just a question of the nature of "right" imitation but a question of how to define the Attic style and who merits this highly sought-after distinction. Cicero first raised the question in his *Brutus* (46 B.C.) and *Orator* (46 B.C.), criticizing writers who reserved the title "Attic" for the plain style, which closely resembles polite conversation, more from meticulousness and fear of error than from any real virtue or excellence of spirit. Instead, Cicero wrests away the title "Attic" for his own prose style—*varietas.* For Guez de Balzac, the concept of urbanity subsumes both polite conversation and Ciceronian variety—honesty of character, naturalness of style, gaiety of wit, and even light irony, qualities that neatly synthesize the Hôtel with the Republic of Letters. The flamboyant originality so in vogue prior to the arrest and imprisonment of Théophile in 1623 and still perceptible in Guez de Balzac's *Lettres* has entirely disappeared from view.

The literary quarrels at the Hôtel de Rambouillet finally relegated Guez de Balzac to the rank of humanist pedant, but this position only further spurred him in his efforts to reconcile conflicting literary currents—always in the interest of his own reputation. After using the Hôtel, where the classical humanist tradition had taken hold in a civilized version, to broaden the audience of French letters, Guez de Balzac used it again to reconcile the newly "humanized" aristocrat with the truth of Christianity, especially since the accusations of pedantry, casuistry, and lax morality leveled against the Jesuits, the schoolteachers of aristocratic youth, reflected badly on the Church. Guez de Balzac needed to adapt the persona and style of *Les Œuvres diverses* to a wider set of interlocutors on the topics of pagan philosophy and Christianity. With the publication of *Socrate chrétien* in 1652, two years before his death, he assembled in one persona a philosopher, a Christian, and a noble. He thus managed to embrace at the same time members of the Republic of Letters, the humanist magistrates of Parlement and the clergy, as well as members of the Rambouillet salon, frequented for the most part by *la noblesse d'épée* (the old aristocracy). In *Socrate chrétien* Guez de Balzac's modernism evolved into what it perhaps had been all along, an ultraconservatism that advocates the peaceful enjoyment of what the pagan philosophers and the Christian tradition had bequeathed to the privileged classes.

Socrate chrétien is Augustinian in inspiration, which means that it makes the heart, not reason, the access to God. "It was necessary," writes Guez de Balzac, "that the Truth be made flesh, in order to make itself perceptible, and become familiar, to mankind, in order to make itself seen and tangible." This Truth is the incarnation of the Christ in Jesus, son of God and of Man.

Because human reason cannot fathom this incarnation, the language of the Bible "leads us to the truth" through figures that "advance things which are unbelievable, in order to make us adjust our faith." In other words, the figures of the Bible are designed to humiliate reason in order to make mankind submit to faith. Guez de Balzac argues that reason in the realm of "divine things" becomes "strangely equivocal." In the sacred realm, "our endeavors are out of all proportion to our forces." In theological matters, therefore, reason "should be more discrete and reserved . . . sheer ignorance is much better than this science of error." However, the visible universe falls well within the jurisdiction of reason, as the pagan philosophers have shown. In this respect, Guez de Balzac exhibits a dogmatic rationalism. Thus, the only responsible intellectual position is one of learned ignorance. The science and ethics of the pagan philosophers have been completed by Christ, the truth of the Christian faith. The moderns should respect this double limit to their knowledge. "Let the modesty of the Ancients be a lesson for us Moderns, that by their example we cure ourselves of the desire for Novelty . . . and prevent ourselves from penetrating any further into a Country which they have discovered." In the hands of the Christian Socrates, religion is enriched by the humanist legacy, disciplined by reason, and refitted to the values of aristocratic society. The Christian Socrates proposes to live off an ancient intellectual heritage tempered by Christian faith—just as the old nobility lives off its private income. This late work of Guez de Balzac did not achieve the success of Pascal's *Lettres provinciales* (1656), which also seeks to reconcile the aristocrats with the Church, but it wields Socratic irony to much greater effect.

In 1648 Guez de Balzac's health worsened considerably. He nevertheless continued to write, complaining of his ruined body. During a brief respite in 1652 he considered leaving France in order to escape the troubles of the Fronde but never realized his project. By late 1653 he was contemplating his approaching death, which occurred a few months later.

The change of taste for which Guez de Balzac was partly responsible surpassed his taste and judgment in the pursuit of ever more prescriptive formulations of eloquence. Clearly, Guez de Balzac is a pivotal figure in the ulterior developments of French classicism. Some critics even go so far as to speak of the existence of a classicism specific to the reign of Louis XIII. In any event, Guez de Balzac is the victim of his own "classicizing" narrative, which circumscribes in space and time an ideal period of literary production. Whether it is the Rome of the Emperor Augustus, Pope Leon X, or Pope Urbane VIII, this ideal of taste and style ascends into an atemporal realm of eloquence to be imitated by those subsequent writers who joined the canon. This sort of narrative, deftly exploited by the next generation of French writers—for example, Jean La Fontaine, Jean Racine, and Jean de La Bruyère—was taken literally by later literary critics, beginning with Voltaire. However, they ascribed this ideal of literary production to the now mythical generation of French writers that flourished between 1660 and 1680, not to the generation of Guez de Balzac.

In the eyes of the public of the later seventeenth century, Guez de Balzac came to seem too flamboyant; too erudite; too Baroque, in a word, for their ideal canon. What his contemporaries applauded time and again in his prose was an acute sense of decorum—that is, sensitivity to the particular expectations of his audience. Later seventeenth-century readers felt that the idiosyncrasy of his persona solicited their admiration too much and blamed the *amour-propre* (self-love) emerging from his prose, which aspired to win nothing less than universal approval. By then, Guez de Balzac, whether the aristocratic hermit by the fire in his library, the erudite "Roman" genius, or the Christian Socrates of the Hôtel de Rambouillet, dazzled more than he pleased.

Bibliographies:

Bernard Beugnot, *Guez de Balzac: Bibliographie générale* (Montreal: Presses de l'Université de Montréal, 1967);

Beugnot, *Guez de Balzac: Bibliographie générale, supplément I* (Montreal: Presses de l'Université de Montréal, 1969);

Beugnot, *Guez de Balzac: Bibliographie générale, supplément II* (Saint-Etienne: Université de Saint-Etienne, 1979).

References:

Antoine Adam, *Histoire de la littérature française au 17e siècle,* 3 volumes (Paris: Albin Michel, 1997), I: 213–284;

Bernard Beugnot, "La figure de Mecenas," in *L'Age d'or du mécénat (1598–1661),* edited by Roland Mousnier and Jean Mesnard, with an introduction by Marc Fumaroli (Paris: CNRS, 1985), pp. 285–293;

Mathilde Bombart, "Représenter la distinction: Comédie et urbanité chez Guez de Balzac," in *Littératures Classiques,* 37 (Autumn 1999): 117–140;

Bernard Bray, "Critique et forme épistolaire: Le dialogue de Jean Chapelain et de Guez de Balzac," in *Critique et création littéraires en France au XVIIe siècle,* edited by Fumaroli and Mesnard (Paris: CNRS, 1977), pp. 103–113;

Fumaroli, "Sous le signe de Protée, 1594–1630," in *Précis de littérature française du XVIIe siècle,* edited by Mesnard (Paris: PUF, 1990), pp. 19–108;

Gaston Guillaumie, *J. L. Guez de Balzac et la prose française: Contribution à l'étude de la langue et du style pendant la première moitié du XVIIe siècle,* 1927 (Geneva: Slatkine, 1977);

Jean Jehasse, "Guez de Balzac et l'art de la critique littéraire," *XVIIe Siècle,* 159 (1988): 129–139;

Jehasse, *Guez de Balzac et le génie romain* (Saint-Etienne: Université de Saint-Etienne, 1977);

Christian Jouhaud and Hélène Merlin, "Aristippe ou les équivoques de la publication, I & II," in *Ordre et contestation au temps des classiques,* 2 volumes, edited by Roger Duchêne and Pierre Ronzeaud (Paris, Seattle & Tübingen: Papers on French Seventeenth Century Literature, 1992), I: 155–178;

Littératures classiques, issue devoted to Guez de Balzac, 33 (Spring 1998); edited, with an introduction, by Beugnot;

F. E. Sutcliffe, *Guez de Balzac et son temps: Littérature et politique* (Paris: Nizet, 1959);

Alain Viala, *La Naissance de l'écrivain* (Paris: Minuit, 1985);

Zobeidah Youssef, *Polémique et littérature chez Guez de Balzac* (Paris: Nizet, 1972);

Roger Zuber, "Atticisme et classicisme," in *Critique et Création Littéraires en France au XVIIe siècle,* edited by Fumaroli and Mesnard (Paris: CNRS, 1977);

Zuber, *Les "Belles infidèles" et la formation du goût classique* (Paris: Armand Colin, 1968);

Zuber, "Guez de Balzac et les deux antiquités," *XVIIe Siècle,* 131 (1981): 135–148;

Zuber, "Le temps des choix: 1630–1660," in *Précis de littérature française du XVIIe siècle,* edited by Mesnard (Paris: PUF, 1990), pp. 111–209.

Pierre Bayle

(18 November 1647 - 28 December 1706)

Gita May
Columbia University

SELECTED BOOKS*: *Lettre à M.L.A.D.C. Docteur de Sorbonne: où il est prouvé que les comètes ne sont point le présage d'aucun malheur,* anonymous (Rotterdam: Leers, 1682); republished as *Pensées diverses écrites à un docteur de Sorbonne, à l'occasion de la comète qui parut au mois de décembre 1680* (Rotterdam: Leers, 1683); translated as *Miscellaneous Reflections, Occasion'd by the Comet Which Appear'd in December 1680: Chiefly Tending to Explode Popular Superstitions,* 2 volumes (London: Printed for J. Morphew, 1708);

Critique générale de l'histoire du calvinisme de M. Maimbourg, anonymous (Amsterdam: P. Le Blanc, 1682);

Ce que c'est que la France toute catholique sous le règne de Louis le Grand (S. Omer [Amsterdam]: Jean Pierre, l'ami marchand libraire, 1686);

Commentaire philosophique sur ces paroles de Jésus-Chrit: Contrain-les d'entrer, 2 volumes (Cantorbery [Amsterdam?]: T. Litwel, 1686);

Addition aux Pensées diverses sur les comètes (Rotterdam: Leers, 1694);

Dictionaire historique et critique, 2 volumes (Rotterdam: Leers, 1697; enlarged edition, 1701); translated, with additions made by the author, as *An Historical and Critical Dictionary,* 4 volumes (London: C. Harper, 1710);

Continuation des Pensées diverses écrites à un Docteur de Sorbonne (Rotterdam: Leers, 1705).

Editions: *Oeuvres diverses de Mr. Pierre Bayle, professeur en philosophie et en histoire, à Rotterdam: contenant tout ce que cet auteur a publié sur des matières de théologie, de philosophie, de critique, d'histoire, et de littérature, excepté son Dictionnaire historique et critique,* 4 volumes (The Hague: Compagnie des Libraires, 1727);

Choix de textes, edited by Marcel Raymond (Paris: Egloff, 1948);

*All major works are included; works of disputed authorship and short works have been excluded.

Pierre Bayle; portrait by Louis Elle-Ferdinand (Musée National du Château, Versailles)

Bayle polémiste; extraits du dictionnaire historique et critique, edited by Jacques Solé (Paris: R. Laffont, 1972);

Ce que c'est que la France toute catholique sous le règne de Louis le Grand, edited by Elisabeth Labrousse, Hélène Himelfarb, and Roger Zuber (Paris: Vrin, 1973).

Editions in English: *Selections from Bayle's Dictionary,* translated and edited by E. A. Beller and M. du P. Lee Jr. (Princeton: Princeton University Press, 1952);

Historical and Critical Dictionary; Selections, translated, with an introduction and notes, by Richard Popkin, with the assistance of Craig Brush (Indianapolis: Bobbs-Merrill, 1965);

Various Thoughts on the Occasion of a Comet, translated, with notes and an interpretive essay, by Robert C. Bartlett (Albany: State University of New York Press, 2000).

OTHER: *Nouvelles de la république des lettres,* edited by Bayle, 1684–1687.

Pierre Bayle plays a singularly important role as a precursor of the philosophes (deistic or materialistic writers and thinkers of the Enlightenment). Many of his ideas, as set forth in the *Dictionaire historique et critique* (Historical and Critical Dictionary, 1697) and other works, were utilized to great effect by such writers as Voltaire and Denis Diderot. The French Enlightenment is difficult to fathom without taking into account Bayle's enormous impact on Diderot's encyclopedia.

The body of Bayle's works does not belong to any of the traditional classical literary genres. As an historian, theologian, philosopher, and moralist, he is what today is called too interdisciplinary to be confined to a single literary domain. Moreover, he was never an elegant stylist, in the manner of such writers as Bernard Le Bovier de Fontenelle and Francois de Salignac de La Mothe-Fénelon, for content and ideas mattered most to him.

In many ways, therefore, Bayle's work is probably closer to the writings of the humanists of the sixteenth century, particularly to Michel Eyquem de Montaigne's *Essays* (1575), than to works of his own contemporaries. He certainly does not belong to that select group of authors designated as classical who enjoyed the approval of fashionable high society as well as the official protection of King Louis XIV. Furthermore, he is better known than read by the public at large, and probably more famous outside of France than in his native country. Another paradox is that his thought was submitted to serious examination and his most important works were begun to be reedited and translated only in the second half of the twentieth century.

Pierre Bayle was essentially an outsider. To be a Huguenot in Catholic France destined him to a difficult life. He was born on 18 November 1647 into a Huguenot family in the small town of Carla (now Carla-Bayle), near the Spanish border south of Toulouse. He was the second son of Jean Bayle, a Protestant pastor, and his wife Jeanne de Bruguière, who belonged to a noble family of the region. The couple had married in 1643 and had a son, Jacob, the following year. In 1656, a third son, Joseph, was born; he died in 1684.

The county of Foix had poor soil and furthermore had been subjected to successive religious wars that had torn France apart. Its economy was still essentially one of quasi-medieval bare subsistence. Roads were barely passable for carriages. Yet, small family industries, especially weaving, began to thrive, and Protestantism managed to implant itself in this poor, overpopulated region. The population still spoke Occitan, the French Medieval dialect prevalent in southern France. Only notables used French, and Bayle, who as a Huguenot had been exposed to French, at least in liturgical services, retained all his life a strong accent reminiscent of his Languedoc origins.

Bayle was strongly marked by his economically deprived native environment and even more by the increasing poverty of his family, resulting from the erosion of Protestant power throughout the seventeenth century. The situation grew even more critical in the second half of the century, with increasing pressure to force Huguenots to convert to Catholicism. Protestant churches and schools were forced to close, and dreaded dragoons were quartered in Protestant homes with untold cruelty and misery for their inhabitants. While Protestants suffered terrible oppression in France, hundreds of thousands opted for emigration from France to the Netherlands, England, and the New World.

Finally, in 1685, The Revocation of the Edict of Nantes of 1598, a decree that had been promulgated by King Henry IV and that had granted full liberty of conscience and worship to Huguenots, sealed the fate of Huguenots in France. As Protestant communities endured increasing religious and social pressure, pastors were more and more irregularly remunerated for their services. Jean Bayle, Pierre's father, found himself unable to pay for the studies of his sons Jacob and Pierre.

Pierre was therefore largely an autodidact who depended on his father's library in order to read Plutarch in the Amyot translation, Montaigne's essays, as well as the great Latin classics, some Greek authors, as well as many sixteenth-century Protestant theologians. In spite of his father's financial difficulties Pierre Bayle was able to attend the Reformed College of Puylaurens from November 1668 to February 1669. But soon expenses became too onerous for the family budget. Bayle was once more on his own and resumed his private studies and readings. He then unexpectedly on his own enrolled in the Jesuit College at Toulouse.

On 19 March 1669 Bayle converted to Catholicism. What intellectual, religious, or personal motives prompted him to convert are difficult to fathom. It is, however, quite possible to imagine what pressures were brought to bear on this young Huguenot to conform to the prevailing religious doctrine. This conversion, com-

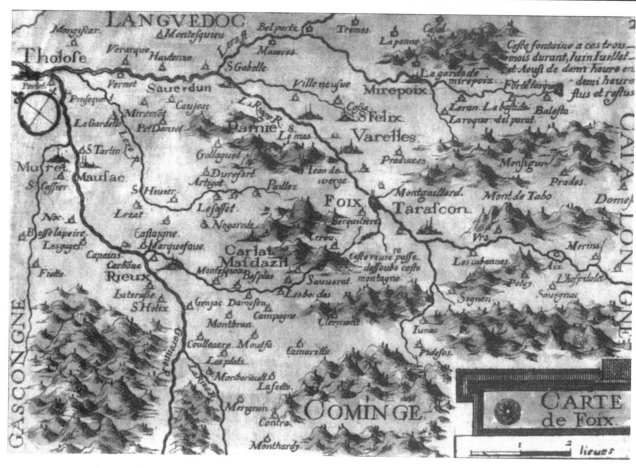

Seventeenth-century map of the area around the town of Carla, Bayle's birthplace (Tulane University Library)

ing from the son of a beleaguered Huguenot pastor, was naturally viewed by the whole Protestant community as a dreadful betrayal, and the break between Bayle and his family seemed irreparable.

On 7 August 1670 Bayle obtained his degree of bachelor of arts from the Jesuit College of Toulouse by successfully defending a thesis on the Virgin Mary. Fifteen days thereafter, and hardly eighteen months after his conversion to Catholicism, he abjured Catholicism and reverted to his Protestant faith, thereby redeeming himself with his family. This second change of religion, however, made Bayle a *relapse*, and in the France of Louis XIV that meant that he had reverted to heresy and as a consequence was liable to imprisonment or banishment.

For his own protection and in order to accomplish his full reintegration into Protestantism, Bayle was sent in 1670 to the University of Geneva, where he completed his studies of theology and philosophy, made new intellectual friendships, read avidly and widely, and also steeped himself in such new philosophers as René Descartes. No doubt Bayle's experience with both Catholicism and Protestantism broadened his

outlook and made him more receptive to different philosophies and religions. The four years in Geneva turned out to be a positive experience. Yet, he wished to return to his native country.

In 1674 Bayle secretly returned to France and embarked on a brief career as a tutor, which he felt would allow him the necessary leisure to pursue his own scholarly interests. He first went to Rouen, in Normandy, where he briefly served as a tutor, thanks to the protection and help of Jacques Basnage, an influential Protestant of that city. But after several months Bayle was irresistibly attracted to Paris, with its libraries and other rich sources of learning and ideas. Having obtained a post of preceptor, he was able to make the switch but soon had to face deep disappointment. He was treated as a domestic, and his demanding duties left him no time for reading or for frequenting libraries or bookstores, let alone literary or intellectual salons.

Thanks largely to Basnage, Bayle received an opportunity to offer his candidacy for a post as professor of philosophy at the Calvinist Academy of Sedan. Pierre Jurieu, Protestant pastor and professor of theology at Sedan, had taken Bayle under his wing and also had a great deal to do with his appointment. Bayle defeated the other candidates for the position and taught his first course beginning on 11 November 1675.

Conditions for Protestants in France quickly deteriorated, and in 1681, when the Academy of Sedan was closed by royal edict, Bayle found himself without a livelihood. For him, as for the other members of his faith, his only option was exile or emigration. After at first considering England, in October 1681 he decided to follow the example of Pierre Jurieu, his mentor and protector, and immigrated to Holland. He had been offered a post as professor of history and philosophy at the new academy in Rotterdam, the *Ecole illustre,* thereby becoming a colleague of Jurieu, who occupied the chair of theology. French was the official language at the *Ecole illustre,* a circumstance reflecting the need to welcome the growing number of French Protestants to Holland. Bayle and Jurieu thus became not only colleagues at the *Ecole illustre* but also members of the Reformed Church of Rotterdam.

Bayle's decision to immigrate to Holland is hardly surprising in light of the increasingly draconian measures taken against the Huguenots before the actual Revocation of the Edict of Nantes in 1685. The Holland of the seventeenth century was at the acme of its power. With its prosperous, teeming urban centers such as Amsterdam and Rotterdam, its political liberalism, its capitalistic entrepreneurial spirit, its religious tolerance, its freedom of the press and thriving publishing houses, its general economic prosperity largely because of its exceptionally favorable situation in the grain trade as well as its high-yield productivity in the dairy industry and its flourishing culture and arts, Holland enjoyed what has been characterized as its golden age. No wonder, therefore, that many French Huguenots such as Bayle took refuge in Holland and found there a haven from the increasingly oppressive climate in France. Of course, French Huguenots were not the only Frenchmen who lived in Holland. Already in the 1630s Descartes had settled in Amsterdam in order to pursue his grand philosophical projects without fear of repression from French religious and political authorities. But the overwhelming majority of the French community in Holland consisted of Huguenots.

Bayle's salary as a professor at the *Ecole illustre* was a modest one, but the demands on his time and energies were not heavy and enabled him to devote himself to his own research. His teaching abilities were reportedly unremarkable, and he never learned the Dutch language.

Bayle had brought along from France a manuscript on which he had already done considerable work at the Academy of Sedan; he revised and enlarged the manuscript, and the work appeared anonymously in

March of 1682, soon after his arrival in Rotterdam, under the title *Lettre à M.L.A.D.C. Docteur de Sorbonne: où il est prouvé que les comètes ne sont point le présage d'aucun malheur* (1682, translated as *Miscellaneous Reflections, Occasion'd by the Comet Which Appear'd in December 1680: Chiefly Tending to Explode Popular Superstitions,* 1708). The work was so immediately successful that it was republished in September 1683 under the new title *Pensées diverses écrites à un docteur de Sorbonne, à l'occasion de la comète qui parut au mois de décembre 1680* (Miscellaneous Thoughts by a Doctor at the Sorbonne, on the Occasion of the Comet That Appeared in December 1680).

Such natural phenomena as comets and shooting stars had profoundly disturbing effects; were occasions for general wonder, fear, and consternation; and largely fed the anxieties of the common folk. They thought that a comet or shooting star appeared as a clear signal of divine displeasure and impending doom. Comets seemed to coincide with various catastrophic occurrences such as storms and fires and reinforced a pessimistic, apocalyptic concept of human destiny.

Bayle's work on the comet is a skillful polemic that avoids invective and adopts the moderate tone of a sincere intellectual who has set out to find the truth and is above petty religious squabbles. With powerful arguments Bayle seeks to demonstrate that there is no cause and effect phenomenon with the apparition of comets. The notion that comets predict dreadful catastrophes, although widespread, was based on legend and superstition. No such belief can be borne out by scientific proof. Bayle goes on to argue, with many examples to prove his point, that even when a generally held belief is transmitted through the centuries, that is no guarantee of its truthfulness. The universal acceptance of an opinion is by no means proof of its veracity. The natural laziness of humans and their tendency to follow the path of least resistance reinforce the authority of false notions acquired by dint of tradition. Much greater effort, which most people are not ready to make, is required in order to discriminate between truthfulness and falsehood. In this respect, Bayle subscribes to the Cartesian principle that the sole dependable criterion in such matters is a rigorous critical examination.

Therefore, the popular credence that comets are supernatural manifestations and predictors of dire occurrences has no basis in fact, and by referring to the past, one can easily conclude that the apparition of comets had no influence whatsoever on the destiny of humans. Comets are natural phenomena in conformity with fixed, immutable cosmological laws, not miracles portentous of baleful human events. The superstitious dread of eclipses is similar to the fear of comets.

Bayle did not intend to attack Catholicism directly, even less to convert Catholics to Protestant-

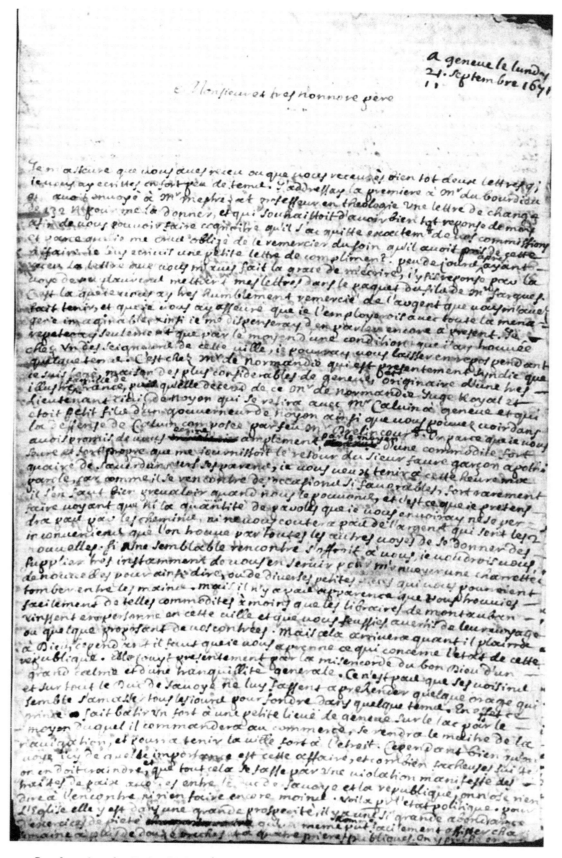

Page from a letter from Bayle to his father (Rare Book and Manuscript Library, Butler Library, Columbia University)

ism, but rather to purify religious faith and invite his readers to be better Christians by rejecting all forms of superstition. He sought, above all, to clarify dogma in order to reinforce, rather than destroy, true belief. Bayle's own experience and successive conversions had led him to the belief that salvation is possible for Christians of all denominations, providing they are sincerely convinced they are professing the true faith.

What is particularly remarkable in Bayle's work on the comets is a section titled "Atheism does not necessarily lead to the corruption of mores." In this provocative digression Bayle affirms that a lack of religious belief does not necessarily lead to immoral behavior. Indeed, atheists have been known to lead exemplary lives, as many examples from history attest. Could, therefore, a society of atheists successfully maintain itself? According to Bayle, it could if a strong system of laws governed its subjects.

How is this possible? According to Bayle's argument, human beings do not act according to their avowed principles but rather according to their primordial passions. Once more, Bayle cites many examples, from antiquity to modern times, in order to support this thesis. Christians, for instance, are expected to follow the teachings of Jesus Christ and his followers, who repeatedly recommend a courageous acceptance of human injustice and a patient resignation to God's will, even in the direst human circumstances. Yet, in actuality, Christians have been known to wage dreadfully destructive wars. Christians continue to perfect weapons of war and constantly invent more-refined and deadly machines of mass destruction. That Christians should use all their faculties and resources to such cruel and inhuman purposes is ample testimony to their ability to be deeply convinced of the truthfulness of their Christian religion and at the same time to act in a manner directly contradictory to the principles of their beliefs. In general, one's religious faith does not regulate one's moral conduct.

If, for instance, inhabitants of another planet were asked to guess what the morals of Christians were and were told that the latter believe in God and a reward in paradise for the virtuous and eternal damnation for those who do not obey God's laws, the visiting aliens would logically conclude that Christians do their best to observe the holy precepts of the gospel. This erroneous conclusion would, of course, be based on an abstract notion of human behavior, whereas if they actually lived among these Christian humans, they would after only a short fortnight be obliged to acknowledge that in this world people do not act according to the lights and dictates of their conscience. In short, historical evidence amply demonstrates that religious belief does not necessarily determine human conduct.

A positive outcome of the publication of Bayle's work on the comet was its immediate impact and publishing success. Four editions of the work appeared in Bayle's lifetime and five more by the middle of the eighteenth century. An English translation appeared in 1708. On the negative side, one of the consequences of the publication that was especially damaging to Bayle's career and reputation was that it strongly contributed to alienating Jurieu, his powerful protector and current colleague at the *Ecole Illustre,* who soon became Bayle's bitter enemy and undertook to refute Bayle's thesis that atheists could possibly be virtuous citizens by denouncing it vociferously as utterly dangerous and heretical. This break caused Bayle to relinquish his chair in 1693.

Bayle immediately followed up the initial success of his work on the comet with *Critique générale de l'histoire du calvinisme de M. Maimbourg* (A General Criticism of the History of Calvinism by Father Maimbourg), published anonymously in May 1682. He wrote the work in the short span of a fortnight. It was so well received that it was republished the same year and then officially condemned and burned after being torn to shreds by the hand of the public executioner on the Place de Grève in Paris in March 1683, a dubious honor reserved for Protestant works that had achieved notoriety through a wide dissemination.

In his *Histoire du Calvinisme* (History of Calvinism, 1682), Father Louis Maimbourg, a former Jesuit, had strongly advocated the repression of heretical beliefs by sheer force, a blatantly intolerant thesis that clearly presaged the Revocation of the Edict of Nantes, which was promulgated only three years later. While Jurieu undertook to refute Maimbourg's arguments by matching him in vehemently sectarian intolerance and polemical invective, Bayle preferred to follow a more moderate strategy already used to good effect in his work on the comet. He concentrated on pointing out Father Maimbourg's historical inaccuracies and patently tendentious interpretations and assertions. Above all, Bayle argued for mutual toleration between Catholics and Protestants, a high-minded ecumenical approach far ahead of his time. That Bayle's work turned out to be more successful than Jurieu's only served to heighten the latter's growing hostility toward his former protégé.

While the *Critique générale de l'histoire du calvinisme* was favorably received by the more open-minded and cultured Catholics as well as Protestants, it enraged Father Maimbourg, who in his efforts to have the book condemned and suppressed went so far as to appeal directly to King Louis XIV. By then, repressive persecutions against Protestants, presaging the actual Revocation of the Edict of Nantes in 1685, had increased in manifold ways, including the terrible *dragonnades* (the practice of billeting soldiers on communities or individ-

Entrance to the Reformed College of Puylaurens, which Bayle attended from 1688 to 1689

uals). No wonder, therefore, that not only was Bayle's work officially condemned but also that anyone daring to sell it in France incurred the death penalty.

In the spring of 1684 Bayle launched the first French literary periodical to be published in Holland, the *Nouvelles de la République des Lettres,* which enabled Bayle, its editor as well as its author, to establish a network with European intellectuals and to facilitate access to the latest publications not only in Holland but also in France, England, and elsewhere. As a monthly publication it offered detailed reviews of half a dozen recently published works as well as newsworthy events regarding the world of authors and books. The enterprise was highly successful, for in spite of the obstacles that the French government in particular placed in the path of the sale of the journal in bookstores, cultured readers greatly appreciated Bayle's critical perspicacity, bal-

anced judgment, and wide-ranging erudition. Thus, Bayle assumed a new role as a journalist with a special gift for disseminating and "vulgarizing" ideas and knowledge in a manner at once informative, useful, and pleasing. No wonder, therefore, that imitations soon turned up, notably the *Bibliothèques,* edited by Jean Le Clerc—*Bibliothèque universelle et historique* (1686–1693), *Bibliothèque choisie* (1703–1713), and *Bibliothèque ancienne et moderne* (1714–1727).

Bayle had a difficult year in 1685. In May he learned of the death of his father, Jean Bayle. But worse news was in the offing. Since Pierre Bayle was beyond the reach of his enemies in France, they did not hesitate, through the authority of Louvois, the powerful Minister of War of Louis XIV and a strong supporter of the Revocation of the Edict of Nantes who was largely responsible for the *dragonnades,* the brutal enforcement of that measure, to wreak their vengeance on his brother Jacob, a Huguenot pastor in Carla, by having him imprisoned in June 1685. Jacob stubbornly turned down repeated offers to buy his freedom at the cost of abjuring his Protestant faith and converting to Catholicism. Despite all of Pierre Bayle's desperate efforts, through French connections, to have his brother freed, Jacob Bayle died in his cell on 12 November 1685, doubtless as a result of the maltreatments he had incurred during his months of incarceration. That Pierre Bayle had indirectly and unwittingly contributed to his brother's tragic death doubtless caused him profound sorrow and anguish, as well as a gnawing sense of guilt that could not but enrich his inspiration as a writer and polemicist.

These experiences largely explain the intense and barely restrained bitterness and indignation that characterize Bayle's next work, *Ce que c'est que la France toute catholique sous le règne de Louis le Grand* (What Catholic France under the Reign of Louis XIV Really Is), published in March 1686. It is indeed a powerful and eloquent text denouncing Louis XIV's religious policy in the strongest possible terms. The official line that Huguenots had been treated with understanding and were being coaxed into converting to Catholicism only through gentle means of persuasion was a total sham in light of the brutal realities of the *dragonnades* and other measures of persecution, such as confiscation of personal properties, deprivation of all means of livelihood, and loss of individual freedom through forceful and inhumane incarceration.

At the end of 1686 Bayle published one of his most powerful works, *Commentaire philosophique sur ces paroles de Jésus-Chrit: Contrain-les d'entrer* (Philosophical Commentary on the Words of Jesus-Christ: "Compel Them to Come In"). Once more Bayle denounces the persecutions of Huguenots under Louis XIV but goes even further than John Locke's *Epistola de Tolerantia* (A Letter Concerning Toleration, 1689), which advocates universal toleration inclusive of all religions and sects, even Jews, Moslems, and atheists. Bayle's strikingly bold and outspoken arguments were echoed in the writings of the Encyclopedists, and more specifically, in Voltaire's 1763 work, *Traité sur la tolérance* (Treatise on Tolerance).

The title of Bayle's work refers to Jesus's parable found in Luke 14:23. It tells the story of guests who turned down an invitation to supper. The disappointed host then ordered his servant to go out, seek the recalcitrant guests, and constrain them to accept the invitation. Ever since St. Augustine, this scriptural text had frequently been invoked in order to justify the forced conversion of so-called heretics.

Bayle begins by pointing out that any literal interpretation of the Scriptures that entails the obligation to commit acts against humanity is indefensible. Such behavior is not only contrary to reason, it violates all moral principles of individual conscience. Furthermore, if one religion is allowed to resort to force, all others will follow suit. Since absolute truth is ultimately unattainable, all one can rely upon is individual conviction and sincere belief that one is not erring. God can only expect one to seek the truth as he perceives it. Therefore, tolerance is the only reasonable course of action in such matters. If a consequence of this belief is a multiplicity of religions, their existence will not result in anarchy and disorder, as Jacques-Bénigne Bossuet had asserted, but rather in a social order akin to "a beautiful concert," the pleasing harmony of which is composed of various instruments, voices, and tones, whereas a nation dominated by only two major religions will inevitably end up being torn asunder by strife and civil war, surreptitiously fomented by kings.

The publication of the *Commentaire philosophique* caused the final rupture between Bayle and Jurieu. Their relations had grown increasingly strained over the years, for as Jurieu's theological views became more sectarian and dogmatic, Bayle more and more advocated rational, liberal thought and religious tolerance. Jurieu viewed Bayle's stance as a betrayal of true Calvinism, and he did not hesitate to accuse Bayle of being a secret atheist. As happens in such cases, the dispute soon degenerated into personal accusations and recriminations. Bayle eventually lost his professorship at the *Ecole Illustre* in 1693, doubtless largely because of the vociferous campaign of vilification launched against him by Jurieu.

In early 1687 Bayle experienced something of a breakdown because of stress and overwork and had to give up the *Nouvelles de la République des Lettres,* which promptly failed when it fell into the hands of less able editors. Eventually, Bayle recovered and made tentative plans for a critical dictionary.

Having freed himself of his journalistic duties as editor of the *Nouvelles de la République des Lettres,* Bayle could now devote himself entirely to his grand project, the *Dictionaire historique et critique* (spelled *Dictionnaire* in modern editions), which appeared in 1697 in two imposing folios and which was an immediate if controversial success. These folios are the work of a single individual and clearly reflect his immense erudition and, more important, his personal beliefs and values. A second, enlarged edition was published in 1701. Thereafter, successive editions appeared in France, Holland, England, and Germany.

Bayle's dictionary was promptly attacked by Jurieu and the Consistory of the French Reformed

COMMENTAIRE
PHILOSOPHIQUE
Sur ces paroles de
JESUS-CHRIT
Contrain-les d'entrer;

Où l'on prouve par plusieurs raisons
démonstratives qu'il n'y a rien de
plus-abominable que de faire des
conversions par la contrainte, &
l'on refute tous les Sophismes des
Convertisseurs à contrainte, &
l'Apologie que S. Augustin a faite
des persécutions

*Traduit de l'Anglois du Sieur Jean
Fox de Bruggs par M. J. F.*

A CANTORBERY
Chez THOMAS LITWEL.
1686.

*Title page for Bayle's book denouncing the persecution of
the Huguenots during the reign of Louis XIV
(Bibliothèque Nationale, Paris)*

Church of Rotterdam and was also condemned in France, events that undoubtedly contributed to its notoriety. With his obsession for accuracy in historical data, Bayle had first set out to correct the errors in the *Le grand dictionnaire historique* (The Great Historical Dictionary), published in 1674 by Louis Moréri, a learned Jesuit. This reference work had gained widespread authority through several editions. Bayle was intent on pointing out Moréri's inaccuracies and theological bias, as well as his tendency to confuse history and mythology.

No doubt Bayle's dictionary provided much of the critical, strategic, and rhetorical ammunition that the philosophes used in their own struggle against religious intolerance and more generally against ideological obscurantism and dogmatism. Both Voltaire's *Dictionnaire philosophique* (Philosophical Dictionary,

1764) and Diderot's *Encyclopédie* (Encyclopedia, 1751–1772) owe a great deal to Bayle's dictionary. Diderot's encyclopedia, in particular, frequently resorted to a strategy of which Bayle had already made ample use and that consisted in fooling and confusing censors by using cross-references and also by slyly placing the most controversial and subversive statements and information in footnotes.

The format of the *Dictionaire historique et critique* made this strategy possible. The principal text of each article is presented in large print at the top of the page, and the rest, in smaller type, is devoted to famous remarks and extensive critical footnotes. Sometimes the footnotes, as is the case in the article on Desiderius Erasmus, are far more copious than the text itself. This singular mode of composition eminently suited Bayle's temperament. In his remarks and footnotes Bayle gives free rein to his scholarly virtuosity and frequently introduces a veritable disputatious dialogue with the subject of his article.

One should be wary to approach Bayle exclusively in terms of his impact on the Enlightenment movement; indeed, recent Bayle scholars, notably Elisabeth Labrousse, have suggested that too much has been made of the parallel between Bayle's dictionary and Diderot's encyclopedia. That Bayle has been viewed in widely differing ways is hardly surprising. He has been interpreted as a secret atheist, as a skeptic, as an opponent of all organized religions, as a fideist (one who relies on faith rather than reason in the pursuit of religious truth), and as a sincere man of faith and true religious believer. To the philosophes of the eighteenth century, Bayle embodied the very spirit of skepticism and was most frequently referred to as a worthy disciple of Montaigne and as the author of the article on Pyrrho, the Greek philosopher and father of skepticism, who taught that nothing can be known, for contradictory statements can be defended with equal plausibility. More recently, Bayle has been read, notably by Richard H. Popkin, as a fideist who held that to attain the truth through the imperfect human faculty of reason is impossible and who therefore must ultimately depend on a fundamental act of faith. According to this interpretation, submission to revelation is the only solution in order to avoid being mired in perpetual uncertainty and instability.

Bayle's dictionary was banned in France not only on what was deemed its antireligious bias but also on what were regarded as its licentiousness and obscenities. That Bayle probably enjoyed surreptitiously adding shocking sexual details in his articles on Greek deities as well as on such biblical figures as David, probably in order to present them as humanly fallible, created such a commotion that he felt compelled, after many discussions with the Consistory of the French Reformed Church of Rotterdam to which he belonged, to remove the objectionable parts of the article in the second edition of the dictionary.

The article "David" perhaps best exemplifies Bayle's irreverent approach to biblical figures. While the text in large print dutifully recounts the story of David in accordance with the Scripture, the remarks that were subsequently repressed tell a different, less edifying story. For instance, the main text simply states that David was the youngest of the eight sons of Jesse the Bethlehemite. In Remark A, however, Bayle comments at length on David's own admission (P. 51: 5) that he was a bastard; David declares, "Behold, I was shapen in iniquity; and in sin did my mother conceive me."

The ensuing tale stresses the resentment of Jesse, who had not been to bed with his wife for a long time and who therefore accused her of adultery. As a result, David was treated with the utmost contempt and sent off to the country where he was entrusted to shepherds. What follows is a kind of cover-up when the prophet Samuel came to seek a king in Jesse's family. Since Samuel did not find to his liking any of the sons he was shown, David had to be fetched. He was sent for most reluctantly. But when it became clear that David was the person that the prophet Samuel was looking for, the whole family, including Jesse, the cuckolded spouse, as well as the rejected sons, joined in praise and "nothing was heard but fine hymns." The ironic conclusion to Remark A is "Oh, what a fine apology! If such excuses sufficed, what a multitude of lewd people might be protected from criticism."

The lengthy article "Spinoza" is another interesting case that illustrates Bayle's own complex attitude toward religion. The main text in large print presents a biographical profile of Benedict de Spinoza as a Dutch Jew by birth who early on in his philosophical studies "became disgusted with the usual theories and was wonderfully pleased with that of Descartes." He gradually deserted Judaism, became estranged from his synagogue when he refused to conform, even outwardly, to the practices of the Jewish religion, and then after breaking off from the Jewish community, was excommunicated in 1656 and eventually espoused "atheism." Spinoza's *Tractatus Theologico-Politicus* (Theological-Political Tract), published in Amsterdam in 1670, is characterized as "a pernicious and detestable book in which he slips in all the seeds of atheism."

A far more positive message is conveyed in comments that reveal Bayle's secret admiration for Spinoza—for example, "He felt such a strong passion to search for truth that to some extent he renounced the world to be better able to carry on the search." Bayle

Title page for the first volume of Bayle's best-known work, which inspired Enlightenment philosophes such as Denis Diderot and Voltaire (from René Pomeau, L'Age Classique, volume 3, 1971)

doubtless identified to a large extent with Spinoza as the lone, independent thinker marginalized and eventually condemned by his own community. Bayle had begun working on his second edition, which appeared in 1701, as soon as the first was published in 1696, considerably adding to the text with additional articles and remarks in which he also endeavored to respond to the objections of his critics and adversaries.

For the philosophes of the Enlightenment, the *Dictionaire historique et critique* was a unique source not only of invaluable information but more importantly of elaborate stratagems of duplicity in the elaboration of arguments, in the introduction of sly innuendos, and in the use of cross-references and footnotes. That Bayle's own ideas and intentions are often obscured in this contradictory message is not surprising.

The weighty folios of the *Dictionaire historique et critique* are still a useful reference work regarding not only such great humanists of the sixteenth century as Erasmus but also many Lutheran, Anglican, and Calvinist authors, as well as Dutch, German, and English theologians and scholars who had thus far been overlooked in the exclusively Francophone culture of the period. Bayle's open-mindedness to writers other than French significantly contributed to the cosmopolitanism that characterized the Enlightenment. The main thrust of Bayle's work, however, was to highlight the discrepancy between theory and practice in the all-Catholic France of the seventeenth century and to demonstrate that religious belief has little if no bearing on moral conduct.

The dictionary, like Bayle's other works, testifies to a total lack of religious fervor, of the kind of impassioned mystical inspiration to be found, for instance, in Blaise Pascal's *Pensées* (1670). No wonder, therefore, that Jurieu so adamantly and vociferously denounced Bayle's brand of fideism as a thinly disguised brand of skepticism, if not atheism. Bayle, perhaps, even unbeknownst to himself, was a great doubter. This fact largely explains why he had such a great impact on the philosophes of the Enlightenment. Even if Bayle was a sincere Christian, modern scholars continue to debate whether his faith was merely a general and rather lukewarm adherence to the Judeo-Christian tradition, whether Manichean tendencies explain his profound pessimism, or whether his heavy emphasis on the indecencies and irrationalities in the Old Testament reveal a profound skepticism. It is therefore a nearly impossible task to attempt to ascertain whether Bayle's unquestionable influence on the Enlightenment rests on a generally faithful reading of his works, and especially of his dictionary, or whether it is a case of largely unintentional misunderstanding and misreading due to the philosophes's enthusiastic overeagerness to find like-minded thinkers in order to buttress their own weltanschauung.

Bayle's health, long undermined by overwork and pulmonary tuberculosis, grew increasingly worse after the publication of the second edition of the dictionary in 1701. He nevertheless continued to engage in polemics with Jurieu and other adversaries, whose attacks against him continued to increase in acrimony, notably in his *Continuation des Pensées diverses* (Continuation of the Miscellaneous Thoughts), which he brought out in 1705, following a fourth edition of the original work in the same year. On 28 December 1706 Pierre Bayle was still hard at work when cardiac failure finally overcame him. Bayle embodied the courageously embattled humanist and scholar who offered an exemplary model of both rigorous intellectual integrity and unswerving commitment to truth in the face of ferocious hostility and opposition on the part of both Catholics and Protestants.

Letters:

Correspondance de Pierre Bayle, 2 volumes to date, edited by Elisabeth Labrousse, Edward James, Anthony McKenna, and others (Oxford: Voltaire Foundation, 1999, 2001–   ).

Bibliographies:

Elisabeth Labrousse, *Inventaire critique de la correspondance de Pierre Bayle* (Paris: Vrin, 1961);

Labrousse, *Pierre Bayle, Hétérodoxie et rigorisme* (The Hague: M. Nijhoff, 1964).

Biographies:

Paul André, *La jeunesse de Pierre Bayle, tribun de la tolérance* (Geneva: Editions Générales, 1953);

Elisabeth Labrousse, *Pierre Bayle,* 2 volumes (The Hague: M. Nijhoff, 1963, 1964);

Labrousse, *Pierre Bayle et l'instrument critique* (Paris: Seghers, 1965); translated by Denys Potts (Oxford: Oxford University Press, 1983).

References:

Hans Bots, ed., *Critique Savoir et érudition à la veille des Lumierès. Le Dictionnaire historique et critique» de Pierre Bayle; 1647–1706* (Amsterdam & Maarsen: Apa-Holland University Press, 1998);

Léo Pierre Courtines, *Bayle's Relations with England and the English* (New York: Columbia University Press, 1938);

Elisabeth Labrousse, *Conscience et conviction: Etudes sur le XVIIe siècle* (Oxford: Voltaire Foundation, 1996);

Labrousse, *"Une foi, une loi, un roi?" Essai sur la révocation de l'édit de Nantes* (Paris: Payot, 1985);

Edmond Lacoste, *Bayle nouvelliste et critique littéraire* (Paris: Picart, 1929);

Charles Lenient, *Etude sur Bayle* (Paris: Joubert, 1855);

René Pintard, *Le libertinage érudit dans la première moitié du XVIIe siècle,* 2 volumes (Paris: Boivin, 1943);

René Pomeau, *L'Age Classique,* volume 3 (Paris: Arthaud, 1971);

Richard H. Popkin, *The History of Scepticism from Erasmus to Descartes* (Assen: Van Grocum, 1960);

John S. Spink, *French Free-Thought from Gassendi to Voltaire* (London: Athlone Press, 1960).

Catherine Bernard

(1663? – 6 September 1712)

Faith E. Beasley
Dartmouth College

BOOKS: *Frédéric de Sicile,* 3 volumes (Lyon: T. Amaulry, 1680); translated by F.S. [Ferrand Spence] as *The Female Prince; or, Frederick of Sicily* (London: Rodes, 1682);

Le Commerce galant, ou Lettres tendres et galantes, de la jeune Iris, et de Timandre, by Bernard and Bernard Le Bovier de Fontenelle (Paris: J. Ribou, 1682);

Les Malheurs de l'amour. Première Nouvelle. Eléonore d'Yvrée (Paris: M. Guérout, 1687);

Le Comte d'Amboise. Nouvelle galante, anonymous (Paris: C. Barbin, 1689); translated by P.B. [P. Bellon] as *The Count of Amboise; or, The Generous Lover* (London: Printed for R. Bentley and M. Magnes, 1689);

Brutus, tragédie (Paris: L. Gontier, 1691);

Inès de Cordoue, nouvelle espagnole (Paris: M. & G. Jouvenel, 1696)–comprises *Inès de Cordoue, Histoire de la rupture d'Abenamar et de Fatime,* "Le Prince Rosier," and "Riquet à la houppe";

Laodamie, reine d'Epire. Tragedie (Paris, 1735).

Editions: *Catherine Bernard, Œuvres,* 2 volumes, edited by Franco Pivo (Paris: Nizet, 1993)–volume 1 comprises *Frédéric de Sicile; Les Malheurs de l'amour. Première Nouvelle. Eléonore d'Yvrée; Le Comte d'Amboise; Inès de Cordoue;* volume 2 comprises *Laodamie; Brutus;* poetic works;

Le Commerce galant, ou Lettres tendres et galantes de la jeune Iris et de Timandre, edited by Piva (Paris: Nizet, 1996).

PLAY PRODUCTIONS: *Laodamie, reine d'Epire,* Paris, Hôtel Guénégaud, by the Comédiens du Roi, 11 February 1689;

Brutus, tragédie, Paris, Hôtel Guénégaud, by the Comédiens du Roi, 18 December 1690.

OTHER: *Le Mercure galant* (Paris)–includes some of Bernard's poems, between 1677 and 1700;

Recueil de plusieurs pièces d'éloquence présentées à l'Académie Françoise . . . (Paris, Coignard)–includes three prize-winning poems by Bernard, in 1691, 1692, and 1695;

"Riquet à la houppe," in Charles Perrault, *Contes,* edited by G. Rouger (Paris: G. Flammarion, 1967).

Catherine Bernard was one of the most celebrated poets of her day, winning both the prize of the Académié Française and Toulouse's Jeux Floraux prize for poetry, each three times, the most allowed. In addition to excelling in the poetic genres admired in the seventeenth century, in particular those celebrating King Louis XIV, Bernard won praise for her tragedies–a genre rarely chosen by her female contemporaries–as well as for her novels. Bernard was thus an active and recognized member of the literary establishment of the late seventeenth century. Her works reflect and respond to the tastes of her public, tastes that have often not carried over into later centuries. Changing literary tastes explain most adequately why Bernard's name and works are known by only a few literary historians specializing in the period.

Bernard's birth and literary and genealogical associations have been the subject of speculation ever since the seventeenth century. Recent research by Franco Piva points to the date of her birth as 1663. She was born in Rouen to wealthy Protestant merchants. The cultural scene in Rouen in the mid seventeenth century was lively, refined, and advanced; it centered on Protestant families such as Bernard's, so the young Catherine likely was surrounded by a literary scene not unlike that found in Paris. In the myths of literary history, Bernard is identified as a cousin of Pierre and Thomas Corneille, as well as the niece of Bernard Le Bovier de Fontenelle, but there is no concrete evidence to support such familial ties.

Bernard seems to have been particularly attracted to the novels of the period, especially the heroic novels of Madeleine de Scudéry and the shorter works founded upon history, best illustrated by Marie-Madeleine Pioche de la Vergne, comtesse de Lafayette's productions in the 1660s and 1670s. Bernard produced her first novel, *Frédéric de Sicile,* in 1680 (translated by Ferrand Spence as *The Female Prince; or, Frederick of Sicily,* 1682) when she was

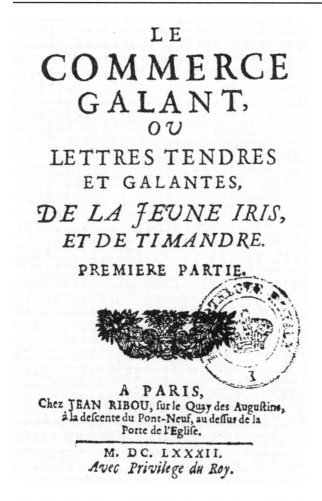

LE
COMMERCE
GALANT,
OU
LETTRES TENDRES
ET GALANTES,
DE LA JEUNE IRIS,
ET DE TIMANDRE.
PREMIERE PARTIE.

A PARIS,
Chez JEAN RIBOU, fur le Quay des Auguſtins,
à la deſcente du Pont-Neuf, au deſſus de la
Porte de l'Egliſe.

M. DC. LXXXII.
Avec Privilege du Roy.

*Facsimile of the title page for Catherine Bernard's volume of fictional
love letters (from* Le Commerce galant, *1996);
Bibliothèque Nationale, Paris)*

still in her teens and probably living in Rouen. During this period she also composed a series of gallant, fictional love letters addressed to a certain "Timandre," which were published, along with Timandre's responses, in 1682. Timandre is usually identified as Bernard Le Bovier de Fontenelle, who was serving as her literary mentor at the time. These early works reveal Bernard's intimate knowledge of the worldly literary scene and the literary productions associated with the salons. Bernard probably arrived in Paris in the early 1680s. In 1685 *Le Mercure galant* (Paris), the principal newspaper of the end of the seventeenth century, announced that she had renounced Protestantism and embraced the Catholic faith, just a few days before Louis XIV's revocation of the Edet of Nantes that had guaranteed religious choice. Bernard's decision did not meet with the approval of her family, and she remained estranged from them for the rest of her life and, more importantly, was cut off from their financial support. Bernard, who never married, thus supported herself by writing. She was acutely aware of the tastes of her pub-

lic and catered to them. She produced four more novels between 1687 and 1696: *Eléonore d'Yvrée* (Eleanor of Yvres, 1687), *Le Comte d'Amboise* (The Count of Amboise, 1689), *Inès de Cordoue, nouvelle espagnole* (Inez of Cordoba, A Spanish Novel, 1696), and *Histoire de la rupture d'Abenamar et de Fatime* (The Account of the Rift between Abenamar and Fatime), which was published in 1696 with *Inès de Cordoue*. The two fairy tales for which she is primarily known today, "Le Prince Rosier" (Prince Rosier) and "Riquet à la houppe" (Riquet with the Tuft), were inserted into her novel *Inès de Cordoue* and never published separately until the eighteenth century.

In 1688, at the height of her success as a novelist, Bernard turned to tragedy, perhaps in an effort to make more money or perhaps in order to gain favor from the more traditional literary establishment. While many women composed comedies in the seventeenth century, few ventured into tragedy, the most revered genre of the day. Bernard's two tragedies, *Laodamie, reine d'Epire* (Laodamie, Queen of Epire; performed, 1689; published, 1735) and *Brutus* (performed, 1690; published, 1691), were both presented by the "comédiens du roi" (the King's actors) in the state-sanctioned theater, where the plays received much critical and public acclaim. Bernard's correspondence reveals that she followed the productions of the plays closely in an effort to achieve as much financial gain as possible, complaining when the number of performances was limited before she felt that the success of the plays had sufficiently diminished to warrant such treatment.

Bernard abruptly abandoned the theater in 1690, most likely at the bequest of her new benefactor, Rosalie de Pontchartrain, wife of Jerome Phelypeaux, comte de Pontchartrain, minister of marines and colonies of France under Louis XIV, who probably felt, as did most of her contemporaries, that the theater was not a proper place for a woman. During this period Bernard was also protected by Françoise d'Aubigne, marquise de Maintenon, Louis XIV's second wife, and influenced by her austere and pious views. Bernard turned to composing poetry, specifically odes to glorify Louis XIV, as well as poems to commemorate friends and specific events. Most of these works were first published in *Le Mercure galant* and later included in various collections of the period. In 1691 Bernard won the prize given by the Académie Française for the best poem honoring the king. Louis XIV was so impressed that he even awarded her a pension, although it is not clear that she ever actually received it. Bernard went on to win this same prize two more times, in 1693 and 1697 (the competition took place every two years), making her one of the most successful and most recognized poets at the end of the century. In 1696 she submitted a poem to the prestigious Jeux Floraux competition in Toulouse and won first prize. Her success continued in

1697 and 1698 when she again garnered first prize. The poems she submitted for the Toulouse competition reveal her growing interest in religion and morality, inspired perhaps by her friendship with Maintenon. That one was not limited to a specific subject for the Toulouse competition attests to Bernard's personal attraction to matters of faith. Bernard's last works were in fact almost entirely dedicated to spiritual concerns. She lived the last years of her life in what had become the devout atmosphere of Louis XIV's court, dictated by Maintenon. The Academy des Ricovrati of Padoua honored Bernard with membership in 1699 and gave her the name "Calliope, the Invincible." She died on 6 September 1712, just a few years before the king she had so eloquently celebrated, her life coming to an end at the same time as the age she perfectly reflected.

Bernard's novels are clearly modeled after and inspired by those of the first generation of French female novelists, principally Scudéry; the comtesse de Lafayette; and Marie-Catherine Desjardins. While Bernard opted for the shorter genre, the *nouvelle historique* or *galante* (historical or gallant novel), practiced by Lafayette and Villedieu, among others, as opposed to Scudéry's *romans héroïques* (heroic novels), nevertheless, hints of Scudéry's influence are found throughout these later novels, in particular in Bernard's use of fate, chance, and coincidence to drive her plots. Like the novels of Lafayette and Villedieu, Bernard's are founded upon history. She fills in the gaps of official history with a plausible but fictional love story, thus conforming to the principal rule of the genre, that it be *vraisemblable,* that is, plausible, but also conforming to seventeenth-century notions of propriety. Like her predecessors, Bernard blurs the lines of history and fiction. Unlike Lafayette and Villedieu, however, Bernard places more emphasis on character development and on the psychology of her characters than on the historical component. Her primary effort is to analyze various emotions–primarily friendship, loyalty, passion, love, jealousy, and despair. In the preface to her second novel, Bernard announces her intention to produce a series of works designed to illustrate aspects of her subtitle, *Les Malheurs de l'amour* (The Misfortunes of Love). Bernard can be viewed as following in the footsteps of Villedieu and her popular *Les Désordres de l'amour* (The Disorders of Love, 1675). Bernard's choice of "malheurs" reveals what distinguishes her novels from those of her predecessors. Her view of human nature in general, but especially of love and passion, is negative. In the *Avis au lecteur* to *Eléonor d'Yvrée,* Bernard clearly explains her point of view: "Je conçois tant de dérèglement dans l'amour, même le plus raisonnable, que j'ai pensé qu'il valait mieux présenter au public un tableau des malheurs de cette passion. Je mets donc mes héros dans une situation si triste qu'on ne leur porte point d'envie" (I conceive of love, even the most reasonable, as so disturbing, that I believed

LES
MALHEURS
DE
L'AMOUR.
PREMIERE NOUVELLE.
ELEONOR D'YVRE'E.

A PARIS,
Chez MICHEL GUEROUT,
Court-neuve du Palais,
au Dauphin.

M. DC. LXXXVII.
Avec Privilege du Roy.

Facsimile of the title page for Bernard's third book, a novel about the negative side of love and passion (from Les Malheurs de l'amour, *1979)*

it would be better to present to the public a depiction of the misfortunes of this passion. I thus place my heroes in such a sad situation that no one can envy them). In Bernard's fictional lessons on love, characters have little control over their destiny and emotions, and find themselves at the mercy of fate and passion. This author takes reason out of passion and has her characters submit to emotion rather than control or dominate it. Thus, while critics and readers have frequently identified Lafayette's *La Princesse de Clèves* (The Princess of Cleves, 1678) as the model for Bernard's *Comte d'Amboise,* the latter work does not give the heroine any control over her own destiny, as Lafayette's masterpiece does. The similarities are striking– the same time period, a husband who adores his wife but whose wife does not reciprocate his love, a would-be lover, and a domineering mother. But the ending underscores the differences. The Princess of Cleves refuses to

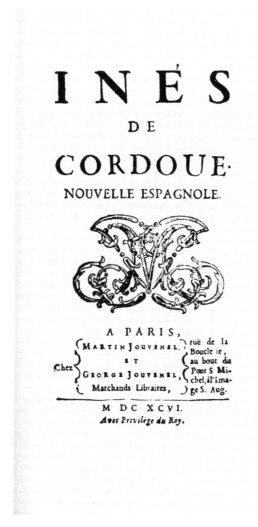

Title page for the novel Bernard set in Spain
(from Inès de Cordoue, *1979)*

marry Nemours for fear of his future infidelity, as well as for other reasons. Bernard's heroine rejects her beloved after her husband's death for the sole reason that she must remain faithful to her husband's memory. She retires to the country, like the Princess of Cleves, but only to think about the past and her emotions, "sans oser les démêler" (without daring to sort out her feelings). Her lover eventually dies. She thus remains in a state of self-denial and confusion, whereas the Princess of Cleves seems to have found peace with a decision that she herself made, not one that fate forced upon her.

All Bernard's novels end pessimistically. She seems to desire to prove that fate dictates unhappiness, and even the best of humans can do nothing to change destiny. Bernard's fictions play to her audience's taste for intricate, complicated plots, for historical novels, and for analyses of the human heart. In many respects these works can be seen as an amalgamation of Scudéry's heroic novels, with their emphasis on coincidence and fate, and a process begun by Lafayette, in which the author attempts to delve into the hearts and minds of her/his characters. But Bernard's fictions are decidedly darker and more pessimistic than almost all preceding ones. Beasts do not magically become charming princes in her fairy tales, but remain monsters with control over their wives. In "Riquet à la houppe," for example, the heroine is forced to live underground with her hideous gnome husband, in exchange for his having magically endowed her with "esprit" (wit). When the gnome discovers that her lover has secretly joined her, he transforms the lover into a gnome exactly like himself. Unable to distinguish her enemy from her lover, the heroine is forced to live out her life in despair and solitude. The bleakness of Bernard's ending, which all her novels share, is particularly evident when "Riquet à la houppe" is compared to Charles Perrault's tale of the same name. Conforming more to generic expectations, the gnome equivalent in Perrault's version becomes "l'homme du monde le plus beau, le mieux fait et le plus aimable" (the most handsome, the most perfectly created, and the nicest man) that the heroine has ever seen. The two marry and live out their lives in bliss.

Bernard's propensity to view life and love as bleak, and the human condition as one almost entirely devoid of reason as well as the ability to act, made her move to tragedy natural and explains perhaps the success she enjoyed with the genre. Following the example of Pierre Corneille, Bernard explored in her first play, *Laodamie, reine d'Epire,* a conflict between duty to the state and love. Two sisters are in love with the same man. But unlike the typical Cornelian hero, Bernard's hero, Gélon, opts for love, choosing the younger sister over a position as the husband of the reigning ruler, the older sister. As she did in her novels, Bernard analyzes love in great detail, reflecting some of the conversations that characterized seventeenth-century salon culture. Contemporaries remarked upon her ability to move her audience. She supposedly had her public in tears at the production of *Laodamie.* The play was presented twenty-six times, making it one of the most successful plays from the end of the century. Of the twenty-nine tragedies produced between 1680 and 1689, it was the sixth most financially successful. *Laodamie* was published only after Bernard's death, however, in 1735.

Bernard's second tragedy, *Brutus,* portrays the same negative opinion of love as found in her novels. It is an uncontrollable force that gives rise to the destructive passions of vengeance and despair. Bernard's heroes, with their tears and weaknesses, certainly do not conform to the seventeenth-century opinion of what constituted a perfect hero. The ending, in which Brutus agrees to execute his sons, elevates loyalty above human desires. With twenty-five performances, *Brutus* was even more successful than *Laodamie,* ranking third among the plays created between 1690 and 1700. Bernard published it almost immediately with a long preface.

She went on to write a third tragedy, "Scylla," in 1693. According to the archives of the Comédie française, the company read "Scylla" with the intention of producing it, but there is no record that the play was ever presented. This text did not survive, perhaps because Bernard had already made her decision to renounce the theater in favor of poetry, at the urging of her benefactor, Pontchartrain. Poetry had most likely been Bernard's initial calling, her first poems probably appearing anonymously in *Le Mercure galant*. As early as 1685, *Le Mercure galant* refers to her as a poetess known by polite society. But the poems Bernard composed in the last fifteen years of her life were more than the light verse cultivated and admired in the salons. She was especially drawn to honoring Louis XIV, and it was for her expertise in this domain, in which she had much competition, that she received the award of the Académie française three times. In addition to praising the monarch, Bernard used her poetic talents to moralizing and religious ends. She composed a poem, "Ode sur la foi" (Ode on Faith), for the Jeux Floraux in Toulouse and won first prize. The other two poems that received the same prize were also on religious and moral subjects, a theme that dominates her poetic production from approximately 1696. At the end of her life she turned to writing *contes en vers* (stories in verse), a genre today associated primarily with Perrault and La Fontaine. In all, forty of her poems still exist, out of what was probably a much larger corpus.

Catherine Bernard's diverse career and success in the genres most highly valued at the end of the seventeenth century make her a perfect representative and product of the literary life of her time period. Above all, as a writer inspired in particular by her female contemporaries, she reflects the prominent position of women in seventeenth-century French culture as writers, critics, and *salonnières*. Admired by her contemporaries, she is proof of what the *Le Mercure galant* said following the production of *Brutus* in 1690: "Les dames sont aujourd'hui capables de tout" (Today women are capable of doing anything).

References:

Nina Ekstein, "Appropriation and Gender: The Case of Catherine Bernard and Bernard de Fontenelle," *Eighteenth-Century Studies,* 30, no. 1 (1996): 59–80;

Ekstein, "A Woman's Tragedy: Catherine Bernard's 'Brutus,'" *Rivista di letterature moderne e comparate,* 48, no. 2 (1995): 127–139;

Perry Gethner, "Melpomene Meets Women Playwrights in the Age of Louis XIV," *Neophilologus,* no. 72 (1988): 17–33;

Gethner, ed., *Femmes dramaturges en France (1650–1750). Pièces choisies* (Paris & Seattle: Papers on French Seventeenth-Century Literature, 1993);

René Godenne, "Préface," in Catherine Bernard, *Inès de Cordoue, nouvelle espagnole* (Geneva: Slatkine, 1979);

Godenne, "Préface," in Catherine Bernard, *Les Malheurs de l'amour. Première Nouvelle. Eléonor d'Yvrée* (Geneva: Slatkine, 1979);

Henriette Goldwyn, "Catherine Bernard, ou La Voix dramatique éclatée," in *Ordre et contestation au siècle des classiques* (Paris & Seattle: Papers on French Seventeenth-Century Literature, 1992), pp. 203–211;

Marie-France Hilgar, "Les Tragédies de Catherine Bernard," in *Continental, Latin-American and Francophone Women Writers,* edited by G. Adamson and E. Myers (Lanham: University Press of America, 1990), pp. 107–114;

Marie-Thérèse Hipp, *Mythes et réalités. Enquête sur le roman et les mémoires 1660–1700* (Paris: Klincksieck, 1976);

Susan Rita Kinsey, "Catherine Bernard: A Study of Fiction and Fantasy," Ph.D. dissertation, Columbia University, 1979;

Charles Mazouer, "Le 'Brutus' de Catherine Bernard et Fontenelle. La Tradition de l'héroïsme," *Etudes normandes,* 3 (1987): 59–61;

Jacques Morel, "Catherine Bernard et Fontenelle: L'Art de la tragédie," in *Fontenelle: Actes du colloque tenu à Rouen, 1987,* edited by Alain Niderst (Paris: Presses Universitaires de France, 1989), pp. 179–190;

Niderst, *Fontenelle* (Paris: Plon, 1991);

Niderst, *Fontenelle à la recherche de lui-même (1657–1702)* (Paris: Nizet, 1972);

Catherine Plusquellec, "L'Œuvre de Catherine Bernard (Romans, Théâtre, Poésies)," Thèse pour le Doctorat du 3ème cycle en littérature et civilisation françaises, Université de Rouen, 1984;

Plusquellec, "Qui était Catherine Bernard?" *Revue d'histoire littéraire de la France,* 85 (1985): 667–669;

Monique Vincent, "Catherine Bernard," in *Nouvelles du XVIIe siècle,* edited by Raymond Picard and Jean Lafond (Paris: Gallimard, Bibliothèque de la Pléiade, 1997), pp. 1645–1648;

Heidi Wolff, *Das narrative Werk Catherine Bernards (1662–1712): Liebeskonzeption une Erzähltechniken* (New York & Paris: Peter Lang, 1990).

Nicolas Boileau-Despréaux

(1 November 1636 – 13 March 1711)

Robert Corum
Kansas State University

BOOKS: *Recueil contenant plusieurs discours libres et moraux en verset un jugement en prose sur les sciences où un honneste homme peut s'occuper* (Rouen, 1666)–includes *Satires I, VII, IV, V,* and *II,* and *Discours au Roy;*

Satires du sieur D*** [Despréaux] (Paris: C. Barbin, 1666)–includes *Satires I–VII;*

Satires du sieur D*** (Paris: L. Billaine, 1668)–includes *Satires I–IX;*

L'Arrêt burlesque, anonymous (Paris: Delphe, 1671);

Œuvres diverses (Paris: D. Thierry, 1674)–comprises *Satires I–IX; Discours au Roy; Epîtres I–IV; L'Art poétique;* Cantos I–IV of *Le Lutrin;* and *Le Traité du Sublime,* translated from the Greek by Boileau;

Œuvres diverses (Paris: D. Thierry, 1683)–comprises all titles from 1674 edition as well as *Epîtres VI–IX* (*Epître V* appeared separately in 1674) and Cantos V–VI of *Le Lutrin;*

Dialogue des Héros de roman, in *Recueil des pièces choisies et bigarrures curieuses* (Paris, 1688);

Ode . . . sur la prise de Namur (Paris: D. Thierry, 1693);

Œuvres diverses (Paris: D. Thierry, 1694)–comprises all titles from 1683 edition as well as *Réflexions critiques sur quelques vers de Longin I–IX, Satire X, Ode sur la prise de Namur,* and eight epigrams;

Epistres nouvelles du Sieur D.*** (Paris, 1698);

Œuvres diverses (Paris: D. Thierry, 1701)–comprises all titles from 1694 edition, a new *Préface, Satire XI, Ode sur les Anglais,* and miscellaneous poems;

Œuvres complètes de Boileau (Paris: Billiot, 1713)–comprises all titles from 1701 edition, *Réflexions critiques sur Longin X, XI, XII,* and miscellaneous poems and prose works;

Œuvres complètes de Boileau (Geneva: Fabri & Barrillot, 1716)–comprises all titles from 1713 edition and *Satire XII.*

Editions: *Œuvres complètes,* 7 volumes, edited by Charles Boudhors (Paris: Les Belles Lettres, 1952);

Œuvres complètes, edited by Françoise Escal, Bibliothèque de la Pléiade, 198 (Paris: Gallimard, 1966).

Au joug de la Raison asservissant la Rime;
Et, mesme en imitant, tousjours original,
J'ay sçeu dans mes Escrits, docte, enjoüé, sublime,
Rassembler en moi Perse, Horace & Juvenal.

Nicolas Boileau-Despréaux (frontispiece for Œuvres complètes de Boileau, *1713; Bibliothèque Nationale, Paris)*

OTHER: Anonymous, *Dissertation sur Joconde,* in *Contes et nouvelles de M. de la Fontaine* (Leiden: J. Sambix, 1668).

For more than three hundred years Nicolas Boileau-Despréaux has been the subject of many literary commentaries. From this mass of books, articles, pamphlets, poems, and polemical tracts, two distinct Boileaus have risen. One is the legendary *législateur du*

44

Parnasse (legislator of Parnassus), the abstract figure who coldly judged poets and writers both contemporary and past, condemning those who did not measure up to his neoclassical standards of taste and celebrating those who did. In this mythical view he emerges as the supreme authority who admitted to the Pantheon some of the most glorified writers in French literary history—Jean Racine, Molière, and Jean La Fontaine—and cast down from Mount Parnassus those writers unworthy of immortality. Generations of French schoolchildren were taught this version of an inhuman, remote, godlike Boileau who inspired only antipathy. Despite its satirical bent, his best-known work, *L'Art poétique* (The Art of Poetry, 1674), a prescriptive compendium of neoclassical poetics generally accepted by both artists and the public at the time it was composed, has been the major impetus for this reputation. His stern moralism in the latter part of his life also perpetuated this view.

A more nuanced picture of Boileau, however, compels a second view. His long career evolved markedly over various periods that reflect his personality as well as his external circumstances. Thus, historians and critics have promulgated diverse images of Boileau. In his early career (1655–1668) he was called a *jeune dogue* (young mastiff, watchdog)—a malicious, irascible, yet comical satirical poet who never hesitated to skewer those he considered bad poets and to name names. After the early *Satires* (1666, 1668) Boileau's career shifted to more-serious, even moralistic poems. In the period between 1669 and 1677 the mocking wit of the *Satires* yielded to the moral injunctions of the *Epîtres* (Epistles, 1683) and the critical imperatives of *L'Art poétique*. Satire is nonetheless present in these works and especially evident in a burlesque epic, *Le Lutrin* (The Lectern, 1674, 1683). In 1677 King Louis XIV named Boileau and the famous tragedian Racine official historians of his reign. Although eminently ill qualified for the task, Boileau continued to labor in this post for many years, although he did little work on the history after Racine's death in 1699. Boileau's literary production decreased significantly during this period, marked by traumatic trips accompanying the king's armies, ill health, and on a somewhat brighter but mitigated note, election to the French Academy in 1684. Commentators have tended to stress the last period of his life (1687–1711) as one full of bitter controversies and a poetic production of austere sermonizing on religion, morality, and literary taste. An ardent admirer of the Ancients, Boileau was embroiled in the Quarrel of the Ancients and Moderns, which pitted those who believed that the writers of antiquity could never be surpassed against those who stood for the superiority of contemporary writers. Boileau also clashed with the Jesuits and became engaged in the Jesuit/Jansenist reli-

gious controversies of the time until his death in 1711 at the age of seventy-four.

Nicolas Boileau was born 1 November 1636 in the very center of Paris, near the Sainte Chapelle on the Île de la Cité. Descended from a long line of law clerks, including his father, Gilles, and many men in his mother's family, Boileau first studied theology and was destined for a career in the church. Although tonsured, he left the religious life for the study of law. He became a lawyer in 1656 but in all likelihood never argued a case. In his first *Satire* Boileau castigates the lawyer's abuse of language and the labyrinthine system of seemingly contradictory laws; he repeats these charges in a letter to a friend written in 1704. Boileau had shown an inclination toward literature in his school days; he had written many poems in the popular style of the time and a more serious "Ode contre les Anglais" (Ode against the English) in 1656, when Oliver Cromwell was threatening France. Boileau no doubt received encouragement from his older brother Gilles, a lawyer and poet who was elected to the French Academy in 1659 at the astoundingly young age of twenty-eight. Because this older brother was so well known, Nicolas adopted the name Despréaux (of the meadows) to distinguish himself from his brother. The inheritance bequeathed on his father's death in 1657 gave the young Boileau, twenty years old, financial independence, which allowed him to write as he wished, without patronage. Following in the footsteps of his satirist brother, Boileau began to write satires in the style of the Latin satirists Horace and Juvenal and the early-seventeenth-century French poet Régnier.

Boileau's first contacts with the reading public date from 1663, when two of his poems were published in a poetic collection. Three years later a volume devoted solely to his poetry appeared, which included five of the early satires and two additional poems. Execrated by Boileau for its many errors, this was the "édition monstrueuse" (monstrous edition) that, as he said, forced him to publish later in the same year his first seven *Satires,* along with the *Discours au Roy* (Treatise to the King) in an updated, corrected edition. He added two additional *Satires* in another volume, published in 1668.

During the 1660s Boileau became well known in literary circles as an acerbic, witty, and fearless satirist. Although not a primary genre in the neoclassical value system, satire was popular among both writers and the public. It was a genre in which a bold young writer could quickly make a name. Boileau did not hesitate to mock those writers whom he considered devoid of good taste or who scoffed at his interpretation of classical principles. Chief among his victims in this period was Jean Chapelain—a poet, critic, and powerful friend

Frontispiece for Boileau's Satires du sieur D***
(1668), poems written in the style of Horace and
Juvenal (Bibliothèque Nationale, Paris)

of Jean Baptiste Colbert (first minister under Louis XIV). Although cynics charged that Boileau had chosen such a formidable foe to gain immediate attention and even through sheer malice, his contempt for Chapelain's work has stood the test of time. Chapelain is known as a classical critic, and little attention is given to his poetry today. Boileau nonetheless quickly gained a reputation as a hard-driving antagonist who more often than not prevailed over his adversaries in his witty and outspoken satires.

Although Boileau was best known as a literary satirist, many of the early satires attack what he saw as moral failings in individuals as well as all mankind. In *Satire IV* Boileau's speaker argues that all humanity is insane, that reason, paradoxically, has no sway over those who are happiest. That the search for happiness is blocked by reason itself is a frequent theme in Boileau's

Satires. The supreme example he uses is the foolish, deluded Chapelain, who, fervently believing that his poetry will make him immortal, moves in a blissful, impenetrable fog. This fact in turn makes the satirist doubt his own power to reveal to all the blind fools of the human race their true nature. This ambivalence toward the ultimate effect of satire can be seen throughout the early satires and prompts many debates within Boileau's speaker about whether to follow his instinctive love for contentious, biting satire or to abandon it in favor of poetry designed to please all its readers and perhaps to earn money and respect for its author.

Satire V abandons the uncertainty of *Satire IV* to take a principled stand against what he considers false nobles—those who, although born into an illustrious family with a long line of exemplary members, live in decadent luxury, thus betraying the glory of their ancestors. As one undeceived by surface subterfuge, Boileau's speaker vituperates against this fraudulent aristocrat in an insulting, indignant tirade, clearly distinguishing between past ephemeral honor and present manifest dishonor. The speaker is certain, however, that true nobility continues to flourish, since his admirable addressee, Dangeau, incarnates the abstract qualities of true noble greatness. The final passages of the poem are devoted to Louis XIV, who, wreathed in symbols, nonetheless demonstrates to the world through words and actions that his essence coincides with his existence. He is the model that must guide all those who pretend to glory.

In the first nine *Satires* and a short critical analysis in prose, the "Discours sur la satire" (Discourse on Satire), published in 1668, one component, *Raison* (Reason), of Boileau's speaker determines that he must leave the genre of satire in the ninth and final poem. To do otherwise would subject him to eternal calumny, to an ill-willed audience who see nothing but misanthropy, spite, and jealousy in what it considers cruel and hateful poetry. He decides on this course despite the pure pleasure another element of his psyche, *Esprit* (Spirit, Wit), enjoys whenever he ruthlessly skewers a fool. The speaker's quest for contentment and self-understanding in the early *Satires* ultimately transcends his attacks on the dullness that he perceives around him. The incessant attacks against Boileau as the *Satires* were published in the 1660s accused the satirist of insolence and of disrespect to the king, the state, and the university. Boileau was threatened with the whip and even the scaffold. His 1668 prose *Discours sur la satire* stages defensive measures, alluding to the Ancients to justify his aesthetic right to name his victims and citing the work of more-contemporary satirical poets, such as Honoré Régnier and Vincent Voiture, to vindicate his own fierce satirical thrusts. Despite this defense, Boileau never goes so far as to disavow his literary judgments and registers surprise that many readers would willingly choose to side with the "Ridicules" (ridiculous writers) rather than the "honnestes gens" (honest people). Predictably, this defiant defense did not sway his enemies. In the years after 1668, then, the character of Boileau's works changed remarkably. He still could not resist the occasional satirical jab, but he chose to exercise his talent in genres other than the satire.

The six-year silence between the 1668 *Satires* and the much longer 1674 collection titled *Œuvres diverses* (Assorted Works) reflects, as do the titles, the differences in the scope and direction of Boileau's work. After 1668 Boileau's work focuses less on vitriolic satire and more on moral questions, especially in the *Epîtres;* on literary theory and criticism in *L'Art poétique* and the *Traité du Sublime* (Treatise on the Sublime, 1674); and on the burlesque epic in *Le Lutrin*. As with the *Satires,* Boileau's choice of the epistle for his next collection of poems emulates the career of the celebrated Roman poet Horace, whom Boileau considered one of his literary forebears. Although, like the satire, a difficult genre to delimit and define, the epistle, typically addressed to a specified individual, reflects upon a moral precept or question in an entertaining, light-hearted style. Although the sardonic Boileau could hardly resist an occasional satirical jab in these poems, the *Epîtres* are generally faithful to their genre.

The first *Epître* demonstrates remarkable articulation with the ninth and last *Satire*. The poem addresses King Louis XIV, who at the close of *Satire IX* served as exemplum for the ideal reader, one who would never distort Boileau's poetic intentions and who emerged as the sole legitimate subject to whom he can in good conscience address his verse. Referred to recurrently in the *Satires* as the ultimate incarnation of good sense, taste, honor, perspicacity, constraint, and virtue that the speaker finds so rare in this world, the king is the archetypal model in the family of man. The speaker looks to the king as a means of resisting his adversaries more effectively. In rededicating himself to the king, the speaker might reconcile and eventually harmonize the heretofore incompatible forces of personal satisfaction and self-respect that war within his psyche. Although satirical barbs abound, the speaker's cheerful, but serious, counsel to the king about the blessings of peace clearly reveals the prescriptive purpose of the genre.

Composed in 1674, *Epître V* records the speaker's meditations on self-knowledge and wisdom and explicitly reconfirms the move away from trenchant literary satire. His feigned doubt as to whether to return to the "plaisantes malices" (delightful hostilities) of satire disguises his real concerns centering on moral edification. He will no longer abuse and annoy contemptible poets,

preferring to follow the road toward virtue and self-knowledge. "Je . . . me cherche cn moi même" (I am searching for myself–within myself), he says. Although he alludes to the financial advantages of abandoning the *Satires,* Boileau remains fixed on his quest for a kind of Epicurean inner tranquillity so often mentioned in the *Satires.* This goal is nonetheless ever elusive, dependent as it is upon creating "vers immortels" (immortal verse) that can "satisfaire mon cœur" (please my heart).

Boileau's growing interest in currying favor with the king and landing the royal pensions that came with it can be seen in *Epître IV,* often called *Le Passage du Rhin* (Crossing the Rhine). In this poem the speaker praises the military prowess of Louis XIV and the signal accomplishments of the French army and its illustrious noble leaders in what was actually a military operation of minor importance in the war against Holland. The boldness and bravado of some of the nobility that took part, as well as the actual presence of the king, captured the imagination of the French people. The feat became a popular subject in the genre of poetic encomium. Boileau's ostensibly serious poem mocks the harsh-sounding (to the French ear) Dutch place-names and the impossibility of finding rhymes for them, which of course also frustrates his attempts at creating harmonious verse. Nonetheless, the speaker will call on his Muse to accomplish the impossible in the realm of *vraisemblance* (that which has the semblance of truth), to make believable and imaginable an exploit about which everything is incredible. Although contemporaries criticized Boileau's apparent lack of zeal for the king and his satirical mockery in an epistle dealing with a solemn subject, the poet ingeniously adapted his own humorous and mocking style to a serious genre. The result is a poem admiring a king who had to be idolized, but without descending into fawning verbosity, as is so often the case with contemporaneous poetry in praise of Louis XIV.

In any case, the poem in all likelihood earned Boileau the opportunity to be presented formally at Louis XIV's court. The king, pleased with both Boileau and his poetry, awarded him a pension. Boileau's switch to panegyric and moralistic verse clearly alleviated the fear of poverty and royal antipathy so often expressed in the *Satires.*

Boileau's desire for a wider audience and external acceptance can also be seen in his critical works composed between 1668 and 1677. The most important of these works is *L'Art poétique,* published in 1674. As with the *Satires* and the *Epîtres,* Boileau is following the lead of his Latin predecessor Horace, who also wrote an *Ars poetica.* The last true "art of poetry" treatise had appeared in 1612 in France and was simply a compilation of the poetic principles of the Pléiade, a group of sixteenth-century Renaissance poets. In the seventeenth century, prior to Boileau, critics wrote on the aesthetic principles mainly of tragedy, but no complete treatises dealing with all of the major genres appeared. A contemporary account from a close associate of Boileau asserts that he was not content merely to have corrected his fellow poets in the *Satires,* but he wished as well to instruct them in the art of poetry. Other reasons no doubt include his desire to counter his enemies' long-standing charge that he had no positive artistic principles of his own, the wish to broaden his audience, and of course the exigencies of his career. Written in verse, the *Art poétique* offers a pleasant and rapid synthesis of contemporary literary principles. Although Boileau once again cannot resist satiric barbs aimed at various poets and poetic styles that he considered defective, there is no controversy concerning the legitimacy of the neoclassical doctrine that he propounds. Boileau does not direct his poem to an audience of intellectuals and specialists. He rather addresses an intelligent, highly literate group of cultivated readers, struggling poets in need of counsel, and future poets.

The poem is relatively short, including exactly 1,100 lines. As a comparison, Chapelain's epic poem *La Pucelle* (The Maid, 1656) included twenty-four cantos, with several thousand lines. A typical tragedy of the day included approximately 1,600–1,800 lines. The work is divided into four *Chants* (Cantos), of which the third is by far the longest. The first Canto dispenses general advice about how the aspiring poet must know and recognize his special brand of talent, submit to reason, avoid boring or confusing his reader with excessive verbosity or brevity, know how to craft a verse, and choose a trusted and wise friend as critic and censor. The second Canto defines the secondary literary genres: eclogue, elegy, ode, sonnet, epigram, rondeau, ballad, madrigal, and satire. Canto III addresses the major genres: tragedy, comedy, and epic poem. The fourth Canto offers for the most part moral advice to the poet—to reflect long and hard before sitting down to write, to love virtue above all, and to know life. Not unexpectedly, Louis XIV is hailed in the closing section of the work as a paragon of royal distinction, the ultimate subject for the poet's art.

The *Art poétique* is founded upon aesthetic assumptions that Boileau never puts into question. All of the poets of the period accepted the basic principle that literary art must have a dual purpose—to instruct and to please. Boileau never specifies what he means by the usefulness of poetic art, although most readers inferred that this quality related to moral edification. A second classical tenet addresses the necessity for the poet to combine innate genius with profound knowledge of literary art: craft and talent must go hand in hand. This dogma leads directly to the fundamental classical concept of rules governing literary art. Although convinced that "on ne va à la perfection que par les règles" (the rules alone allow us to attain perfection), Boileau nonetheless contends that reason, or as he says elsewhere, *le bon sens* (good sense), must supersede the dictates of the rules when necessary. In fact, reason must govern all elements of the artistic work. The closely allied notions of fidelity to nature and to truth accompany the primary locus of reason. Boileau's concept of truth in the *Art poétique* accords with the idea of nature. By definition, whatever exists in nature must be true; therefore, the poet must allow nature to guide him to the acquisition of truth. The imitation of nature and depiction of truth are facilitated when the poet uses the poets of antiquity as models. By imitating Horace's career and work, Boileau himself adhered faithfully to this doctrine.

Canto III focuses on the three major genres of tragedy, epic, and comedy. Boileau adds nothing original to the contemporary idea of tragedy inherited mainly from Aristotle. Tragedy should elicit from the audience the twin emotions of fear and pity—fear that the spectator may fall into the same kind of anguish felt by the major characters, but pity over their horrible misfortunes. Tragedy deals with abhorrent human behavior, but the classical dramatist must always touch the tender emotions of his public. He must make the horrible acceptable, even pleasant, to the audience: "Il n'est point de serpent, ni de monstre odieux, / Qui, par l'art imité, ne puisse plaire aux yeux" (There is no snake, nor odious monster, which, if imitated by art, cannot please the eye). Boileau goes on to emphasize the crucial importance of two allied notions—*bienséances* (roughly translated as propriety) and *vraisemblance*. The former centers for the most part on avoiding acts of violence on the stage, which in the classical view would shock the sensibilities of the audience. This rule places more importance on the value of vivid descriptions and consequently the poetic artistry of the writer. The notion of *vraisemblance* dictates that the writer must never offer to his public what is unbelievable. The reason is simple: the spectators will not be moved by what they do not believe.

The plot structure recommended by Boileau is linear, with a series of episodes linked by cause and effect, with a clear system of probability and necessity inherent in the system. The denouement of the play must be natural, well-prepared, with no farfetched, aberrant incidents that do not derive directly from the preceding action. The author should make judicious use of *peripeteia,* or well-prepared plot reversals, and *anagnorisis,* or sudden discoveries (a character's passage from ignorance to knowledge) to keep the audience engaged, in a state of anticipation, and, most importantly, entertained. The major *ressort,* or driving force, of the plot is love, but this love must not be the cloying brand proper to the lovesick shepherds in pastoral poems. Love in tragedy must be a source of weakness and shame, full of remorse, guilt, and grief. To the classical mind, this love is the surest means of touching the audience's hearts. Like Aristotle, Boileau also requires that the hero in tragedy be the victim of a tragic flaw. In this way the author will remain true to nature and truth.

Boileau's thoughts on comedy in the third canto of *L'Art poétique* follow the classicist's line of thought. The primary study of the comic poet must be human nature: "Etudiez la cour et connaissez la ville, / L'une et l'autre est toujours en modèles fertiles" (Study the court and know the city; both provide a wealth of models). A profound psychologist, the successful comic writer must be capable of depicting the abundance of human types—such as the miser, the fool, the pedant, the coquette, the spendthrift, and the snob—each in his own complexity and according to truth and nature. The object of comedy is to correct humanity's foibles, to represent to the public an image—exaggerated, to be sure—of itself. Comedy thus becomes a necessary corrective to humankind's defects: it is a source of *plaire* (entertainment) and *instruire* (moral instruction). Comedy must always remain true to its genre. It must never feature tears or sadness, nothing of the tragic. The comedy writer must beware the danger of entertaining his audience with the obscene and the vulgar. The genre must remain true to the doctrine of *bienséance.* Above all, the rule of common sense, *raison,* must be obeyed at all times. Submission to reason is the sole means of creating universal, thus ageless, works of comic art.

The fourth canto stresses morality more than technique or prescription. In this canto the speaker insists on the edifying function, as opposed to the entertainment function, of classical literary art. Contrary to the bohemian concept of the artist, which appears to equate self-indulgence with genius, the writer must adhere to the accepted moral values of his time. Boileau believed deeply in the dignity of the writer's vocation and in poetry as much more than amusement for the idle. In this vein, he disliked anyone who wrote purely for money; this goal was, in his a mind, a sure formula for dishonor. The temptation to pander to the vulgar tastes of the mob, to produce immoral poetry that made vice attractive, was too high. The classical author should be free of envy. He should rejoice when a fellow poet creates an enduring work of art and refrain from attacking it out of jealous rivalry and spite. The artist must also be an *honnête homme*—a cultured, urbane man of the world with a wide circle of cultivated friends. Boi-

Frontispiece for Boileau's first collected works, Œuvres diverses, *1674 (Bibliothèque Nationale, Paris)*

leau's classical ideal does not admit the concept of the poet as misunderstood social outcast. The great writer must know how to live within society. The knowledge derived from this interaction is one of the mainsprings of his art. The poet must strive for glory, not be content with ignoble material gain. From this thought Boileau launches into a panegyric of Louis XIV, whose divine enlightenment distinguishes the worthy artist from the unworthy and whose generosity rewards the truly exemplary poet. Thanks to his royal patronage, good poets will always have the material wherewithal that will permit them to create great poetry. The poem closes on a familiar note—the modest Boileau who begs the pardon of other, more worthy, poets, for his penchant for lowly satire. His talent lies in recognizing, applauding, and supporting the genius of others and, on a slightly more menacing note, censoring the work of the unworthy.

Despite the authority and influence of the *Art poétique,* critical opinions of the work have been generally

*Page from Boileau's 13 August 1687 letter to Jean Racine
(Bibliothèque Nationale, Paris)*

negative. As a literary historian, Boileau has earned few accolades. His comments on the ancient poets, whom he should have known better than the medieval or Renaissance poetry that he also comments upon, reveal inadequate study and false assumptions and conclusions. *Art poétique* has also been condemned for its obvious lacunae. In the second canto, in which he deals with the so-called minor genres, Boileau omits mention of basic forms, especially the epistle, a type of which he himself was particularly fond. Another criticism centers on the relative superficiality of Boileau's treatment of French poetry. On the other hand, Boileau never considered his *Art poétique* to be a profound, philosophical treatise on aesthetics. If the intent had been that serious, he would not have written it in verse. He wished to invite the reflection of his cultivated, layman reader, not to overwhelm him with a theory of literature written by and for specialists. Some of his affirmations appear contradictory. He condemns the burlesque style and yet wrote the burlesque epic *Le Lutrin;* he proclaims the noble style despite his personal taste for a lowly genre such as the satire. It is, however, ultimately unjust to castigate Boileau for faults perceived in a work that is, after all, a poem, not a formal exposition. His objectives in the *Art poétique* are much less grandiose than that. He leaves for others the task of formulating the principles of the classical doctrine and establishing the rules for carrying them out. Far from becoming the figure of the bookish pedant so savagely satirized in the *Satires* and elsewhere, Boileau wants to please and instruct the cultured public. He is, above all else, a classical poet.

Boileau's mock-heroic epic, *Le Lutrin,* the first four cantos of which were published in 1674 (the final two appeared in 1683), reveals another side of Boileau. Commentators have emphasized that the poem is a true image of his deep-seated propensity for satire, despite his "farewell" to satire in *Epître I,* published in 1670. In the poem his targets run the gamut from the church, clerics, politics, the law courts, and lawyers, to writers whose work he scorned. As always, literary satire finds a place in his work. The poem belongs to the burlesque genre, in which in most cases the principal device is to have noble, exalted characters from myth and legend speak in the language of peasants—a comical mix of the high and the low styles. Boileau reverses this technique in *Le Lutrin* to have common people speak the elevated language proper to the epic poem. *Le Lutrin* tells the "epic" tale of an inconsequential conflict among prelates in Paris's Sainte Chapelle (Boileau's own neighborhood) about the placement of a lectern. Apparently, Boileau was prompted to write the poem when friends challenged his assertion that the epic poem should never be burdened with a complicated plot and dared

him to compose an "epic" about a recent squabble at the nearby Sainte Chapelle. The work parodies Homer, Virgil, the contemporary bugaboo of Boileau, Chapelain, as well as the eminent French tragedians Racine and Pierre Corneille. Although he condemns the burlesque in *L'Art poétique* and the *Satires* as a trivial, extravagant genre contrary to the rules of right reason, his proclivity for humor and satire again prevails. In *Le Lutrin* Boileau belies his previous attempts to present himself as a more serious writer.

Boileau's interest in serious criticism can be seen in the 1674 publication of his translation of a work by the ancient Greek writer Longinus, *Le Traité du Sublime* (Treatise on the Sublime). Although a serious attempt to make known to the French public a hitherto obscure Greek theoretician (his was the first French translation of Longinus), Boileau made clear in the preface that this work was a calculated act of vulgarization; the translation was not intended merely for scholars. Above all he wanted to give his readers a version of the work that "pût être utile" (might be useful). *Le Traité du Sublime* was well received, and Boileau's translation succeeded in making Longinus known to the cultivated French audience. Even contemporaries who criticized the work on scholarly grounds recognized the same qualities as its most ardent admirers. The author who first translated the Greek work for the English public stated that "tho' not always faithful to the text, yet [Boileau's translation] has an *elegance* . . . which few will ever be able to equal, much less surpass." Boileau the poet takes precedence over Boileau the profound and erudite theoretician and critic.

The year 1677 marks another significant change in Boileau's career. He and his longtime friend, the great tragedian Racine, were chosen by Louis XIV to write a history of the reign. While financially very rewarding, this post was ill suited to Boileau's temperament, talent, and even physical constitution: he was required to accompany the king's army on its various campaigns. The mass of papers and documents produced by Boileau and Racine was destroyed in a fire in 1726. Boileau's literary production virtually ceased in the period from 1677 to 1686. Only the last two cantos of *Le Lutrin* were published, in 1683. Approaching the age of fifty, Boileau cooled his satirical ardor in the preface to the 1683 edition, in which he recognizes the talents of many of the poets he had roundly condemned and insulted in his previous work. The relative peace and calm of this period gradually began to disintegrate in the 1690s, when Boileau became the prime advocate for the poets of antiquity in the Quarrel of the Ancients and the Moderns.

The final period of Nicolas Boileau's life and career until his death on 13 March 1711 was full of acri-

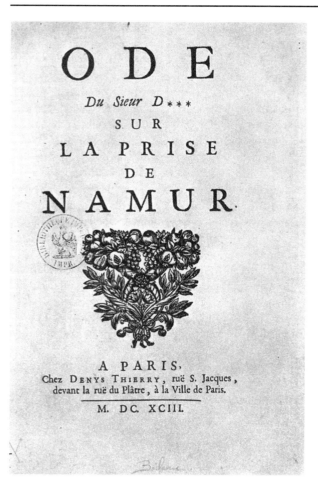

Title page for Boileau's 1693 ode on the capture of Namur by the French (Bibliothèque Nationale, Paris)

monious controversies, failing health, the loss of many lifelong friends—including the beloved Racine, in 1699—and bitter setbacks. The poetry of this period lacks the sparkle and verve of his early work, but he spent a great deal of time nonetheless on the final three *Satires* and *Epîtres, Ode . . . sur la prise de Namur* (Ode on the Capture of Namur), and nine *Réflexions critiques sur Longin* (Critical Reflections on Longinus), which derived from his earlier translation of the Greek philosopher and was his principal contribution to the Quarrel of the Ancients and the Moderns, and on a final edition of his works, published after his death. The scholarly title of the *Réflexions* belies the true nature of the work: the younger Boileau is present, full of invective and scorn for his major adversary, Charles Perrault, with an obvious desire to avoid at all cost the pedantic. Despite the cooling of his ardor in the later years, Boileau's biting wit was apparent in his moments of indignation. The best-known literary controversy of the period, the so-called Quarrel of the Ancients and the Moderns, pitted writers who proclaimed that the work of the Ancients was

clearly superior to contemporaneous work against those who thought the contemporary works were better. The former, among whom Boileau was the preeminent champion, affirmed the absolute necessity for the modern poet to be inspired by the unequaled example of the Ancients, whereas the latter declared the independence of the modern writer from what had gone before and believed in the concept of progress in literary art. Boileau's viewpoint put him in a ticklish position, inasmuch as he had ceaselessly defended and celebrated such moderns as Racine, Molière, La Fontaine, Jean de La Bruyère, and others. Boileau, in fact, was himself a modern.

Boileau became more involved in contemporary religious controversies in his later years. Although brief but vehement references can be seen in his earlier works castigating the Jesuits, his strongly Jansenist convictions took center stage in his late career. Boileau's sober and moral life matches his religious convictions. He was much more in tune with the Jansenists' strict austerity than earlier. Based less on dogma or official doctrine, Boileau's arguments with the Jesuits focused on what he considered their lax morality. Two works in particular, *Epître XII, Sur l'amour de Dieu* (On Love for God, 1697), and *Satire XII, Sur l'équivoque* (On Ambiguity, 1709), provoked the wrath of his Jesuit enemies. The latter poem is a virulent attack on the "equivocal." By equivocal Boileau means not only that which is ambiguous but also all that has prevented mankind from seeing the Truth, an error of which the Jesuits have been guilty. In 1703 the Jesuit *Journal de Trévoux* exhumed the charge of Boileau's plagiarism in its review of his 1701 *Œuvres diverses*. Never one to suffer such attacks in silence, Boileau retorted with several threatening and sarcastic epigrams. A more developed response took the form of *Satire XII,* begun perhaps as early as 1703. Boileau goes so far as to exploit images of sexual disgust to execrate his object of attack. Boileau's foremost enemy in the battle to prevent publication was *père* Le Tellier, who became confessor to Louis XIV in 1709. He and his scandalized Jesuit friends prevented the publication of *Satire XII* until several months after Boileau's death in 1711.

There is no question that Boileau was eminently successful during his lifetime. More than 125 editions of his works appeared before his death, of which more than 60 were complete works at the time of publication. The countless editions of his works through the eighteenth, nineteenth, and twentieth centuries attest to the important pedagogical function taken on by Boileau in the French schools. Unfortunately, his works had become teaching devices rather than objects of literary art. Boileau's influence in his own lifetime was not as great as many commentators have suggested, since the authors and styles he condemned kept sometimes sizable audiences despite his invective. In the eighteenth century his influence was greatest outside of France. Considered by foreigners as the quintessential model for the French spirit in art, Boileau guided other national literatures eager to exercise discipline and restraint in their own domains. In the nineteenth century, neoclassicists saw him as the great champion of the authority and symbol of tradition, reason, *bienséance,* and moderation, whereas the romantic writers viewed him as a stodgy fossil who stood in the way of artistic innovation and young talent. The long-standing legend of Boileau as the Colossus of Parnassus, whether viewed negatively or positively, has been for the most part attacked and debunked in the twentieth century. Boileau's genius lies neither with his status as legislator nor with his eminence as a critical theoretician, but with his reputation as a poet. While the legend conveniently provided unity to the classical movement and a useful function for its best-known spokesman, contemporary critics have focused on his poetry as art, not as indoctrination.

References:

Simone Ackerman, "Les *Satires* de Boileau: Un Théâtre de l'absurde avant la lettre," in *Ordre et contestation au temps des classiques,* 2 volumes, edited by Roger Duchêne and Pierre Ronzeaud (Paris, Seattle & Tübingen: Papers on French Seventeenth Century Literature, 1992), I: 255–266;

Antoine Adam, *Les Libertins au XVIIe siècle* (Paris: Buchet/Chastel, 1964);

Adam, *Les Premières Satires de Boileau (I–IX)* (Lille: Revue d'Histoire de la Philosophie, 1941; reprinted, Geneva: Slatkine, 1970);

Georges Ascoli, *Boileau, Satires I à IX* (Paris: Centre de documentation universitaire, 1967);

Bernard Beugnot and Roger Zuber, *Boileau: Visages anciens, visages nouveaux, 1665–1970* (Montreal: Les Presses de l'Université de Montréal, 1973);

E. B. O. Borgerhoff, "Boileau Satirist *animi grati,*" *Romanic Review,* 43 (1952): 241–255;

René Bray, *Boileau, l'homme et l'œuvre* (Paris: Bovin, 1942);

Bray, *La Formation de la doctrine classique* (Paris: Hachette, 1927);

Jules Brody, *Boileau and Longinus* (Geneva: Droz, 1958);

Cleanth Brooks, *The Well Wrought Urn* (New York: Harcourt, Brace, 1948);

Pierre Clarac, "Boileau," in *Les Grands Auteurs français,* edited by Daniel Mornet (Paris: Mellotte, n.d.);

Robert Corum, *Reading Boileau: An Integrative Study of the Early Satires* (Purdue, Ind.: Purdue University Press, 1998);

Nathan Edelman, "*L'Art poétique:* 'Longtemps plaire et jamais ne lasser,'" *Studies in Seventeenth-Century French Literature Presented to Morris Bishop,* edited by J.-J. Demorest (Ithaca, N.Y.: Cornell University Press, 1962), pp. 231–246;

Gustave Lanson, *Boileau* (Paris: Hachette, 1892);

Daniel Mornet, *Nicolas Boileau* (Paris: Editions C. L., 1943);

Joseph Pineau, *L'Univers satirique de Boileau. L'Ardeur, la grâce et la loi* (Geneva: Droz, 1990);

Charles Révillout, "La Légende de Boileau," in *Essais de philologie et de littérature* (Montpellier: Hamelin, 1899);

Susan Tiefenbrun, "Boileau and His Friendly Enemy: A Poetics of Satiric Criticism," *Modern Language Notes,* 91 (1976): 672–697;

H. E. White Jr., *Nicolas Boileau* (New York: Twayne, 1969);

Allen G. Wood, "Boileau and Affective Response," *Cahiers du dix-septième siècle* (Fall 1987): 61–73;

Wood, "Boileau, l'équivoque, et l'œuvre ouverte," in *Ordre et contestation au temps des classiques,* 2 volumes, edited by Duchêne and Ronzeaud (Paris, Seattle & Tübingen: Papers on French Seventeenth Century Literature, 1992), I: 275–285;

Wood, *Literary Satire and Theory: A Study of Horace, Boileau, and Pope* (New York: Garland, 1985);

Wood, "The *Régent du Parnasse* and *Vraisemblance,*" *French Forum,* 3 (1978): 251–262.

Papers:

Nicolas Boileau-Despréaux's papers are housed in the Bibliothèque Nationale, Paris, and the Bibliothèque de la Ville de Paris (Recueils de Brossette).

Jacques-Bénigne Bossuet

(27 September 1627 – 12 April 1704)

Jean-Vincent Blanchard
Swarthmore College

SELECTED BOOKS*: *Oraison funèbre de Henriette-Marie de France, reine de la Grand'Bretagne* (Paris: S. Mabre-Cramoisy, 1669);

Oraison funèbre de Henriette-Anne d'Angleterre, duchesse d'Orléans (Paris: S. Mabre-Cramoisy, 1670);

Exposition de la doctrine de l'Eglise catholique sur les matières de controverse (Paris: S. Mabre-Cramoisy, 1671); translated by W. A. Montague as *An Exposition of the Doctrine of the Catholique Church in the Points of Controversye with Those of the Pretended Reformation* (Paris: V. du Moutier, 1672);

Discours sur l'histoire universelle (Paris: S. Mabre-Cramoisy, 1681); translated as *A Discourse on the History of the Whole World* (London: Printed for M. Turner, 1686);

Conférence avec M. Claude, ministre de Charenton, sur la matière de l'Eglise (Paris: S. Mabre-Cramoisy, 1682); translated in Jean Claude, *Mr. Claude's Answer to Monsieur de Meaux's Book, Intituled, A Conference with Mr. Claude* (London: Printed for T. Dring, 1687);

Sermon presché à l'ouverture de l'Assemblée générale du Clergé de France (Paris: F. Léonard, 1682);

Oraison funèbre de Marie-Thérèse Austriche, infante d'Espagne, reine de France et de Navarre (Paris: S. Mabre-Cramoisy, 1683); translated as *A Sermon Preached at the Funeral of Mary Terese of Austria, Infanta of Spain, Queen of France & Navarre* (London: J.C. & F.C. for H.R.; sold by Samuel Crouch, 1684);

Oraison funèbre de très-haute et très puissante princesse Anne de Gonzague de Cleues, princesse Palatine (Paris: S. Mabre-Cramoisy, 1685);

Jacques-Bénigne Bossuet (portrait by Rigaud; Musée du Louvre, Paris)

Oraison funèbre de très-haut et puissant seigneur, messire Michel Le Tellier, chevalier, chancelier de France (Paris: S. Mabre-Cramoisy, 1686);

Oraison funèbre de très-haut et très puissant prince Louis de Bourbon, prince de Condé, premier prince du sang (Paris: S. Mabre-Cramoisy, 1687);

Histoire des variations des Eglises protestantes, 2 volumes (Paris: Veuve de S. Mabre-Cramoisy, 1688); translated by Levinius Brown as *The History of the Variations of the Protestant Churches*, 2 volumes (Antwerp, 1742);

*As a prominent figure of the French Catholic Church and a bishop, Jacques-Bénigne Bossuet published many books of controversy and piety, catechisms, manuals of pastoral instruction, administrative notes, sermons, and panegyrics. Only the works most often cited by religious and literary historians are listed here.

Recueil d'oraisons funèbres, edited by Bossuet (Paris: Veuve de S. Mabre-Cramoisy, 1689);

Maximes et réflexions sur la comédie (Paris: J. Anisson, 1694); translated as *Maxims and Reflections upon Plays* (London: Printed for R. Sare, 1699);

Instruction sur les estats d'oraison (Paris: J. Anisson, 1697); translated by Algar Thorold as *On Prayer: Spiritual Instructions on the Various States of Prayer According to the Doctrine of Bossuet, Bishop of Meaux* (London: Burns, Oates & Washbourne, 1931);

Relation sur le quiétisme (Paris: J. Anisson, 1698); translated as *Quakerism a-la-Mode, or A History of Quietism* (London: Printed for J. Harris & A. Bell, 1698);

Politique tirée des propres paroles de l'Ecriture sainte (Paris: P. Cot, 1709); translated as *The Political Science Drawn from the Holy Scriptures* (London: Keating & Davy, 1842);

Introduction à la philosophie, ou De la Connaissance de Dieu et de soi-même (Paris: G. Amaudry, 1722);

Elévations à Dieu sur tous les mystères de la religion chrétienne, 2 volumes (Paris: J. Mariette, 1727); translated as *Elevations to God* (London: Hamilton & Adams, 1850);

Méditations sur l'Evangile, 4 volumes (Paris: P.-J. Mariette, 1730–1731);

Traitez du libre-arbitre, et de la concupiscence (Paris: B. Alix, 1731);

Œuvres complètes, 31 volumes, edited by F. Lachat (Paris: L. Vivès, 1862–1866);

Œuvres oratoires, 7 volumes, edited by Joseph Lebarq (Lille & Paris: Desclée, de Brouwer, 1890–1897; revised and enlarged edition, 7 volumes, edited by C. Urbain and E. Levesque, Paris: Desclée, de Brouwer, 1914–1926).

Editions and Collections: *L'Eglise et le théâtre: Bossuet,* edited by C. Urbain and E. Levesque (Paris: Grasset, 1930)—comprises "Lettre de Bossuet au P. Caffaro," *Maximes et réflexions sur la comédie,* and François Caffaro's "Lettre d'un théologien illustre";

Discours sur l'histoire universelle, edited by A. Stegmann (Paris: Larousse, 1950);

Œuvres, edited by Bernard Velat & Yvonne Champailler, Bibliothèque de la Pléiade, no. 33 (Paris: Gallimard, 1961);

Oraisons funèbres, edited by J. Truchet (Paris: Garnier, 1961; revised, 1988);

Politique tirée des propres paroles de l'Ecriture sainte, edited by J. Le Brun (Geneva: Droz, 1967);

Sermons: Le Carême du Louvre (1662), edited by C. Cagnat-Debœuf (Paris: Gallimard, 2001).

Editions in English: *Biographical Sketches of Henrietta Duchess of Orleans, and Louis of Bourbon Prince of Conde: To Which are Added, Bossuet's Orations, Pro-*

nounced at their Interment, translated by Edward Jerningham (London: Printed by S. Gosnell for W. Clarke, 1799)—includes select extracts from other orations;

Select Sermons, translated by Jerningham (London: Printed by S. Gosnell for W. Clarke, 1800);

A Meditation on the Lord's Prayer, Taken from the First Volume of Bossuet's Meditations on the Gospel (Kilkenny: John Reynolds, 1824);

Selections from the Funeral Orations, edited by F. M. Warren (Boston: Heath, 1907);

Panegyrics of the Saints, edited by D. O'Mahoney (London & St. Louis: Kegan Paul, Trench, Trübner, 1924);

Letters of Spiritual Direction, translated by G. Webb & A. Walker (London: Mowbray, 1958; New York: Morehouse-Gorham, 1958);

Bossuet: A Prose Anthology, edited by J. Standring (London: Harrap, 1962);

Discourse on Universal History, translated by Elborg Forster, edited, with an introduction, by Orest Ranum (Chicago & London: University of Chicago Press, 1976);

Politics Drawn from the Very Words of Holy Scripture, edited and translated by Patrick Riley (Cambridge & New York: Cambridge University Press, 1990).

The works of Jacques-Bénigne Bossuet, bishop of Meaux, include books on matters of religious controversy, discourses on history and politics, as well as sermons and funeral orations, for which he is perhaps best remembered today. A staunch defender of the Catholic faith, he was involved in several religious polemics. His exceptional oratory talents won him the recognition of the court, and he remained close to it for most of his career. Indeed, Bossuet's sermons and funeral orations were considered to exemplify the rhetorical sublime in the age of King Louis XIV. Bossuet's eloquence was no less apparent in other genres, including less-dramatic and more-private works, in which he also displayed what the historian Henri Brémond has called lyricism.

Bossuet was born on 27 September 1627. The son of an influential family of Dijon, the capital city of Burgundy, he attended the Jesuit Collège des Godrans. His family of parliamentary magistrates favored hard work, respect for royal authority, and the piety of the Catholic Reformation. Given the civic duties of his father and the Jesuits' humanistic and religious pedagogy, Bossuet was raised in an environment in which speaking well was a prerequisite for any career. His intellectual gifts and devotion quickly made him stand out, and at fifteen he left Dijon to study in Paris until 1652. During these crucial years at the Collège de Navarre, Bossuet perfected his humanistic training while following the

Bossuet and his pupil the dauphin Louis, son of Louis XIV
(painting by Nicolas de Largillière; from Antoine Adam,
L'Age Classique, *volume 1, 1968)*

course of study in philosophy and theology to become a theologian and priest. His religious vocation was affirmed after meeting St. Vincent of Paul, a man who devoted his life to alleviating the misery of the poor and destitute. Yet, this was also the time when Bossuet was introduced to the Parisian cultural elite. Just one year after arriving in the capital, he was heard one night preaching at eleven o'clock at the Hôtel de Rambouillet. Vincent Voiture, the stalwart of this literary salon, observed that he had never heard preaching "nor so early, nor so late." The refined, if not *précieux,* taste of this milieu left little imprint on Bossuet, however. Worldly life did not appeal to him much, contrary to many other literary and religious figures of his time.

After being ordained on 16 March 1652, Bossuet left for Metz, where he rose in the hierarchy of the Church. His occupation involved preaching—including the recitation of saints' discourses of praise, called panegyrics—and political duties. Among his audience were important Protestant and Jewish communities who were required to hear his sermons. At Metz, Bossuet faced evidence of the disunity of the Church, a challenge to his pastoral duties that he took up often throughout his life.

Bossuet's career took a decisive turn when he arrived in Paris again in 1659, this time to defend the interests of his religious community. A member of the Compagnie du Saint-Sacrement, he represented the vanguard of strictly observed Catholicism. For a period of about ten years, he produced oratory works that won him a place in the canon of French literature. Bossuet preached all his life, often speaking only with the help of written outlines, improvising entire passages. His memory, according to his contemporaries, was prodigious. Thus, many of Bossuet's discourses delivered in ordinary circumstances have been lost. The prestigious quality of his works from this Parisian period earned them the largest place in the Joseph Lebarq edition.

To preach to a courtly public was a daunting task. First of all, Bossuet faced an assembly of aristocrats who, after the Fronde, a time of civil disturbances that lasted from 1648 to 1653, were more in the mood for entertainment than for spiritual edification. Among these was the young king, who displayed a taste for society and gallant company. Louis XIV went to hear Bossuet in the company of the royal mistress, Louise de La Vallière. Furthermore, what drew this courtly public to church—besides piety or the obligations of social conformity—was the artistic appeal of eloquence. This motivation shocked Bossuet, who had the highest idea of his duty to spread the word of God. To speak in church was akin to performing the sacrament of the Eucharist. Divine inspiration did not leave any space for technical understanding and artistic appreciation. Yet, Bossuet gained fame not only as an upright man of the Church but also as a superior orator. While a preacher could not seek literary glory per se, he had to face the truth that persuading earthly creatures necessitated the help of art. Today, Bossuet often stands alone as the representative of religious eloquence in the French seventeenth century. But it should be noted that his contemporaries appreciated the talent of many other orators and could give their preference to men such as Louis Bourdaloue and Esprit Fléchier.

An important part of these rhetorical productions was the sermon. Following the liturgical calendar, sermons were often organized in cycles during Lent or Advent. Such sermons lasted about an hour and could be delivered in the afternoon, not necessarily as part of mass. They were important social events. Madeleine de Sévigné, the famous epistolarian, complained about how hard it was to find places to sit at some sermons, even when lackeys had been sent three days in advance to reserve the best spots. After preaching Lenten sermons at the convents of the Minim fathers (1660) and the Carmelites nuns (1661), Bossuet was noticed by the devout queen mother, Anne of Austria, and was called

Page from the manuscript for Bossuet's 1660 sermon on demons (Bibliothèque Nationale, Paris)

*The 1669 funeral of Henriette-Marie of France, Queen of England,
for which Bossuet wrote an oration (engraving by Jean Lepautre;
Bibliothèque Nationale, Paris)*

to preach Lent before the court at the Louvre in 1662. *Le Carême du Louvre* is considered by many to be one of Bossuet's highest achievements in the field of sermons. His public included the king; the two queens; the king's brother and his wife, Henriette-Anne of England, Duchess of Orléans; and La Vallière. The cycle includes eighteen sermons, preached from Ash Wednesday to Good Friday. Bossuet had many other occasions to instill religious principles in the court. He preached Lenten sermons again at Saint-Germain-en-Laye (1666) as well as Advent at the Louvre (1665) and Saint-Germain (1669).

Bossuet also excelled in another genre—the funeral oration. His success in lamenting the loss of some of the great figures of France and in making their lives motives for religious instruction gained him immense acclaim. For contemporary readers, these pieces are among the most accessible of Bossuet's work. They dramatically evoke the Romanesque lives of fascinating and gifted characters. After mourning the death of the Queen Mother in 1667, Bossuet was called upon in 1669 to celebrate the memory of Henriette-Marie of France, Queen of England. The exiled widow of Charles I had had a life rich in dramatic political events,

and the discourse in her honor includes a celebrated description of a famous historical figure, Oliver Cromwell. For Bossuet, the hardships of Henriette-Marie—and thus the civil wars of England—represented a lesson from Providence; moreover, this lesson appeared historically necessary in light of the regained influence of Catholicism under the rule of the queen's son, Charles II. Only a year later Bossuet pronounced the funeral discourse of the daughter of the queen of England, Henriette-Anne of England (born in 1644). Henriette-Anne shone at the court of France as the wife of the king's brother, Philippe d'Orléans. Her early and sudden death stunned all. Bossuet, who had assisted her in her last moments and had been impressed with her "good death," gave a poignant speech. Again, he offered examples of the rhythmic and periodic style that came so effortlessly to him and of which Paul Valéry gave a famous description. But Bossuet's rhetorical brevity was also put to work to describe this sudden and tragic death: "Madame se meurt, Madame est morte" (Madame is dying, Madame is dead). The personality and life of the subject—charming, but rather poor in outstanding examples of piety—left ample space in the speech to expand on the worthlessness of earthly life. Such was not the case in the funeral oration of Louis II de Bourbon, better known as the Grand Condé. A military hero and a Romanesque figure of the time, he provided the inspiration for Madeleine de Scudéry's eponymous character of her famous novel, *Artamène, ou Le Grand Cyrus* (1649–1653). In Bossuet's oration, the military battle at Rocroi (1643) is recalled in vivid terms. Bossuet was actually close to Condé and pronounced this discourse a year after the death of the prince (1687) during a grandiose celebration held in the Cathedral of Notre-Dame.

The essence of Bossuet's rhetorical success lay in its never failing propriety. This sense of what was appropriate allowed him to speak of God in the widest range of tones, from the casual to the grandiloquent, while always sounding grand, yet simple, and effortlessly so. Forgotten were the curiosities and mannerisms of late Renaissance orators. His speeches include superbly crafted sentences in which every word falls into its proper place. This apparent simplicity, however, overlays a complex disposition of words, rhythmic effects, repetition, and figures of syntactic construction such as parallelism. He also used brilliant tropes. For that, the Bible was an endless source of inspiration. It might seem obvious that the Scriptures should be the most important book for a religious figure, but many men of religion of his time, while considering the Bible the founding text of their faith, often had a special taste for the writing of a particular Church Father. Yet, not even the luster of St. Augustine, whom he valued particularly, could draw Bossuet away from the words of revelation. Indeed, throughout his career, Bossuet gave all his attention to truth in its most fundamental aspects. His oratory was thus always focused on principles such as charity, the transience of earthly life, and the actions of Providence. Bossuet, while often tackling matters of morality, such as ambition or greed, was less interested in showing these flaws in realistic and psychological details. In contrast to Blaise Pascal, Bossuet's strategy did not consist in holding up an ethical mirror to his audience. Instead, Bossuet believed that preaching should show the most beautiful aspects of truth in such a light that it became irresistibly attractive.

Almost ten years after coming to Paris, Bossuet reaped the fruit of his labors. By then a famous and respected character, he was named bishop of Condom on 10 September 1669. The Académie Française welcomed him in 1670. But what proved most decisive for his work was his nomination as the preceptor of the dauphin Louis, heir to the throne. For Bossuet this nomination represented the possibility of raising an ideal monarch, and he labored hard to achieve this goal. Accounts vary on the relationship between pupil and master. For the prince, even the most sympathetic must concede that he was not the most gifted individual. The teacher appears to have lacked the qualities needed to negotiate with a child. For more than ten years, under a very strict course of study, Bossuet tried to transform the son of Louis XIV into an extraordinary human being. If all this attention did not bring the expected results, Bossuet himself learned a great deal. Writing most of the textbooks needed for the dauphin's instruction, Bossuet read a staggering quantity of books and developed his thinking on many matters. He wrote a Latin and French grammar book, a treatise on logic, and an introduction to philosophy, posthumously published under the title *Introduction à la philosophie, ou De la Connaissance de Dieu et de soi-même* (1722).

More important are his works on history and politics. In *Discours sur l'histoire universelle* (1681; translated as *A Discourse on the History of the Whole World,* 1686) Bossuet defined the Catholic interpretation of history by locating the action of divine Providence in the course of history. In this grandiose fresco spanning the age of Moses through Roman history and up to the Renaissance, every event, even the least favorable to Christianity, takes on a purpose to be interpreted in the light of God's triumph. Bossuet was not interested in simply recording events or detailing the interests of political parties and secrets of the privy chamber, but also in paying tribute to the doctrine of human freedom by highlighting, on a narrower historical scale, the role of human choices in shaping history. In *Politique tirée des propres paroles de l'Ecriture sainte* (1709, composed from

1679 and translated as *The Political Science Drawn from the Holy Scriptures,* 1842) Bossuet describes the concept of royal authority. God gives kings to people, and subjects have to conform to the kings' wills. Resistance to tyrants must be passive and is justified when individuals are required to perform acts that break the rule of religion. Bossuet never meant to justify arbitrary power, and he insisted on the necessary Christian exemplarity of the ruler. He wrote against the perceived Machiavellianism of his time and was keenly aware of political realism, having read the works of Thomas Hobbes. But having a theological mind, Bossuet logically deduced a theory of the political based on faith. As far as his own relations with the king were concerned, he was not successful. After a brief period as the king's director of conscience (1675), Bossuet was kept at a distance, and Louis remained an adulterer.

In 1681 Bossuet was named bishop of Meaux. As a good priest, he spent much of his time caring for the well-being of his diocese, down to minute details. The rest of his time consisted in dealing with important church affairs and controversies. For carrying out those duties, he kept a residence in Paris and an apartment in Versailles. In 1681 Bossuet was asked to give the opening sermon of the *Assemblée générale du Clergé de France* (1682). The purpose of the assembly was to support the king's prerogatives against the Pope in matters of religious revenues and the naming of bishops. In the speech Bossuet perilously and artfully navigated between his duty to the king, his own Gallicanism, and respect for Roman authority. His debates with the Protestants, which had begun in Metz, already included his *Exposition de la doctrine de l'Eglise catholique sur les matières de controverse* (Explanation of the Catholic Doctrine on Controversial Matters, 1671) and *Conférence avec M. Claude, ministre de Charenton, sur la matière de l'Eglise* (1682). Bossuet's apologetics culminated in the writing of *Histoire des variations des Eglises protestantes* (1688; translated as *The History of the Variations of the Protestant Churches,* 1742), in which he displayed great erudition in his defense of the Catholic Church. In 1685 Bossuet applauded the Edict of Fontainebleau, which abrogated the toleration granted by the Edict of Nantes (1598) to the Reformed religion.

For historians of literature, the smaller controversy with an obscure monk called Caffaro may be of more interest. Against Caffaro, Bossuet indignantly wrote *Maximes et réflexions sur la comédie* (1694; translated as *Maxims and Reflections upon Plays,* 1699). With a denigrating comment on Molière, Bossuet condemned theater as a device for exciting the passions. His analysis of theatrical illusion, founded on a theory of identification and self-projection, is particularly interesting for its originality.

The church at Meaux, the diocese of which Bossuet was made bishop in 1681

Unfortunately for Bossuet, the major controversy in which he participated cast an unpleasant shadow on his reputation. Known as the *Querelle du quiétisme,* or *du pur amour* (the quietist, or "pure love," dispute), this dramatic episode first involved Jeanne-Marie Bouvier de la Motte, Madame Guyon. The second central character was the dignified François de Salignac de La Mothe-Fénelon, a man of letters and faith. Guyon was spreading a mystical doctrine of prayer that concerned authorities early on, but then she found Fénelon as a protector. Bossuet took up the cause against them. Guyon's description of prayer threatened the doctrine of human freedom and responsibility. According to specialists such as Louis Cognet, there could hardly be any resolution between the dogmatic Bossuet and a woman describing her relationship with God in terms of human psychology and experience. In this long and sad affair, which also had political undertones, Bossuet harrassed Guyon and displayed acrimony toward Fénelon. The Pope resolved the issue by censuring Fénelon, all the while assuring him of his sympathy. Important texts by Bossuet on the controversy include *Instruction sur les estats d'oraison* (1697; translated as *On Prayer: Spiritual Instructions on the Various States of Prayer According to the Doctrine of Bossuet, Bishop of Meaux,* 1931) and *Relation sur le quiétisme* (1698; translated as *Quakerism a-la-Mode, or A History of Quietism,* 1698).

In his long career, Jacques-Bénigne Bossuet held the authority of the Church with unflinching determination and belief. He died on 12 April 1704 after a long illness due to kidney stones, while trying to secure a position for a relative, the abbé Bossuet, who published posthumously many of his uncle's works composed after 1695. The *Elévations à Dieu sur tous les mystères de la religion chrétienne* (1727; translated as *Elevations to God,* 1850) and *Méditations sur l'Evangile* (1730–1731) show Bossuet quietly exercising his rhetorical gift for the profit of simpler souls and his religious community.

Letters:

Correspondance, 15 volumes, edited by C. Urbain and E. Levesque (Paris: Hachette, 1909–1925).

Bibliography:

Victor Verlaque, *Bibliographie raisonnée des œuvres de Bossuet* (Paris: Picard, 1908).

Biographies:

François Ledieu, *Mémoires et journal sur la vie et les ouvrages de Bossuet,* 4 volumes, edited by Wladimir Guettée (Paris: Didier, 1856–1857); republished as *Les Dernières Années de Bossuet: Journal de Ledieu,* 2 volumes, edited by C. Urbain and E. Levesque (Bruges: Desclée, de Brouwer, 1928);

Alfred Rébelliau, *Bossuet* (Paris: Hachette, 1900);

Ernest Edwin Reynolds, *Bossuet* (Garden City, N.Y.: Doubleday, 1963).

References:

Antoine Adam, *L'Age Classique,* volume 1 (Paris: Arthaud, 1968);

Peter Bayley, "The Art of the Pointe in Bossuet," in *The Equilibrium of Wit: Essays for Odette de Mourgues,* edited by Bayley and Dorothy Gabe Coleman, French Forum Monographs, volume 36 (Lexington, Ky.: French Forum, 1982), pp. 262–279;

Bayley, "What Was Quietism Subversive Of?" in *Seventeenth- Century French Studies,* 21 (1999): 195–204;

Henri Brémond, *Bossuet,* 3 volumes (Paris: Plon, 1913);

Pierre Campion, "La Légitimation de l'éloquence sacrée dans les sermons de Bossuet," *Littératures,* 36 (1997): 33–47;

Louis Cognet, *Crépuscule des mystiques* (Paris: Desclée, 1991);

Peter France, "Bossuet: The Word and the World," in his *Rhetoric and Truth in France: Descartes to Diderot* (Oxford: Clarendon Press, 1972), pp. 116–148;

Thérèse Goyet, *Autour du Discours sur l'histoire universelle: Etudes critiques,* Langue et littérature françaises, no. 4, Annales littéraires de l'Université de Besançon, volume 3, fascicule 4 (Besançon, 1956);

Goyet, *L'Humanisme de Bossuet,* 2 volumes (Paris: Klincksieck, 1965);

Armanda Grazini, *Bossuet: Crisi di una coscienza nel contesto socio-politico dell'assolutismo* (Urbino: Argaglia, 1978);

Journées Bossuet: La Prédication au XVIIe siècle; Actes du colloque tenu à Dijon les 2, 3 et 4 décembre 1977 pour le trois cent cinquantième anniversaire de la naissance de Bossuet, edited by T. Goyet & J.-P. Collinet (Paris: Nizet, 1980);

René-Marie de La Broise, *Bossuet et la Bible* (Paris: Retaux-Bray, 1890);

Gustave Lanson, *Bossuet* (Paris: Lecène, Oudin, 1891; republished edition, New York: Arno, 1979);

Patrick D. Laude, *Approches du quiétisme: Deux Etudes suivies du Moyen court et très facile pour l'oraison de Madame Guyon (texte de l'édition de 1685)* (Paris & Seattle: Papers on French Seventeenth-Century Literature, 1991);

Jacques Le Brun, *La Spiritualité de Bossuet* (Paris: Klincksieck, 1972);

Denis Lopez, "Discours pour le prince: Bossuet et l'histoire," *Littératures classiques,* 30 (1997): 173–186;

Jean Meyer, *Bossuet* (Paris: Plon, 1993);

J.-A. Quillacq, *La langue et la syntaxe de Bossuet* (Tours: Cattier, 1903);

Sainte-Beuve, "Bossuet," in his *Causeries du lundi,* volumes 10 and 12 (Paris: Garnier, 1852–1876);

Sainte-Beuve, "Bossuet," in his *Nouveaux lundis,* volumes 2 and 12 (Paris: Calmann Lévy, 1870–1880);

Jacques Truchet, *Politique de Bossuet* (Paris: Colin, 1966);

Truchet, *La Prédication de Bossuet,* 2 volumes (Paris: Cerf, 1960);

Paul Valéry, "Sur Bossuet," in his *Variété,* volume 12 (Paris: Editions du Sagittaire, 1931), pp. 65–67;

Max Vernet, "Théâtre et usurpation du sujet: Le Monde et son image dans les Maximes et réflexions sur la comédie de Bossuet," *Etudes françaises,* 15 (1979): 149–174.

Papers:

The larger part of Jacques-Bénigne Bossuet's manuscripts is located at the Bibliothèque Nationale. This collection includes documents previously found in Henri de Rothschild's collection.

Dominique Bouhours
(15 May 1628 – 27 May 1702)

Jean-Vincent Blanchard
Swarthmore College

SELECTED BOOKS*: *La Mort de Monseigneur le Duc de Longueville* (Paris: F. Muguet, 1663);

Lettre à un Seigneur de la Cour, sur la requeste présentée au Roy par les Ecclesiastiques qui ont esté à Port-Royal (Paris: S. Mabre-Cramoisy, 1668);

Lettre à Messieurs de Port-Royal, contre celle qu'ils ont escrite à Monseigneur l'Archevesque d'Ambrun pour justifier la Lettre sur la constance et le courage qu'on doit avoir pour la vérité (Paris: S. Mabre-Cramoisy, 1668);

Les Entretiens d'Ariste et d'Eugène (Paris: S. Mabre-Cramoisy, 1671; revised, 1671);

Doutes sur la langue françoise, proposez à Messieurs de l'Académie Françoise par un Gentilhomme de Province (Paris: S. Mabre-Cramoisy, 1674);

Remarques nouvelles sur la langue françoise (Paris: S. Mabre-Cramoisy, 1675);

Histoire de Pierre d'Aubusson, Grand-Maistre de Rhodes (Paris: S. Mabre-Cramoisy, 1676); translated as *The Life of the Renowned Peter D'Aubusson, Grand Master of Rhodes: Containing Those Two Remarkable Sieges of Rhodes by Mahomet the Great and Solyman the Magnificent, Being Lately Added to Compleat the Story Adorn'd with the Choicest Occurences in the Turkish Empire at the Time* (London: Printed for George Wells and Samuel Carr, 1679);

La Vie de Saint Ignace, fondateur de la Compagnie de Jesus (Paris: S. Mabre-Cramoisy, 1679); translated as *The Life of St. Ignatius, Founder of the Society of Jesus* (London: Henry Hills, 1686);

La Vie de S. François Xavier, de la Compagnie de Jesus, Apostre des Indes et du Japon (Paris: S. Mabre-Cramoisy, 1682); translated by John Dryden as *The Life of St. Francis Xavier, of the Society of Jesus, Apostle of the*

Dominique Bouhours (portrait by Nicolas Habert; Bibliothèque Nationale, Paris)

Indies, and of Japan (London: Printed for Jacob Tonson, 1688);

Opuscules sur divers sujets (Paris: S. Mabre-Cramoisy, 1684);

La Manière de bien penser dans les ouvrages d'esprit: Dialogues (Paris: Veuve de S. Mabre-Cramoisy, 1687); translated as *The Art of Criticism; or, The Method of Making a Right Judgment upon Subjects of Wit and Learning* (London: Printed for D. Brown and A. Roper, 1705);

Suite des remarques nouvelles sur la langue françoise (Paris, 1687);

---

*Only major or representative works by Dominique Bouhours are listed here; a large number of controversial pamphlets, devotional works, and biographical essays commissioned by the Society of Jesus have been omitted. For more information on these works, see the bibliography in the *Bibliothèque de la Compagnie de Jésus,* cited at the end of this entry.

Lettres à une Dame de Province sur les Dialogues d'Eudoxe et de Philanthe, anonymous (Paris: Veuve de S. Mabre-Cramoisy, 1688).

Editions: *La Manière de bien penser dans les ouvrages d'esprit: Dialogues,* edited by Suzanne Guellouz (Toulouse: Université de Toulouse–Le Mirail, 1988);

Doutes sur la langue française, proposez à messieurs de l'Académie Française par un Gentilhomme de province, edited by Fulvia Fiorino, introduction by Giovanni Dotoli (Fasano, Italy: Schena / Paris: Didier, 1998).

TRANSLATION: *Le Nouveau Testament de Nostre Seigneur Jésus-Christ, traduit en françois selon la Vulgate,* translated by Bouhours, Pierre Besnier, and Michel Le Tellier, 2 volumes (Paris: L. Josse, 1697, 1703).

Dominique Bouhours enjoyed great respect in his time. Even the dramatist Jean Racine sought the advice of this theoretician of style on how to perfect his plays. A century later, although Bouhours's general popularity had diminished, Voltaire still held him in high regard. In the late twentieth century, after a long decline, Bouhours's importance was reappraised in view of his contribution to the definition of French classical style. While keeping its minor status in the history of French literature, the work of this Jesuit offers an excellent vantage point from which to investigate the relations among power, society, and style in the first part of King Louis XIV's reign. Despite its increasingly tight control over the arts, especially at court, the monarchy could not entirely influence another sphere of artistic creation–the salons, where women played a vital role and where classical taste was more an effect of social ethics than royal power. Most of the salon participants were courtiers themselves, but when gathered together, they could focus on their own concerns instead of those of the monarch. Bouhours's work theorizes and exemplifies the style of these *honnêtes gens* (polite men and women), whose rhetorical behavior and discourse combined individualism with the interest of the group, most notably in the practice of conversation. By underscoring also that French was an essential condition of that polite interaction and significantly contributing to linguistic standardization, Bouhours helped to define key national beliefs. His idea of French as a universal and rational instrument of communication as well as his emphasis on the value of language as an indicator of social stratification was greatly successful.

Bouhours was born on 15 May 1628. According to George Doncieux's biography, little is known about his family. That Bouhours was able to study at the Jesuit Collège de Clermont in Paris suggests that his relatives were part of the prominent bourgeoisie of the city. When sixteen years old, Bouhours entered the Jesuit novitiate for three years. After a short period of teaching, he went on to study theology. His interest in literature probably deepened while he taught rhetoric in Tours. He pronounced his final vows on 30 April 1662, in Rouen.

The Jesuits had always had a strategic and political interest in sending one of their own to tutor young aristocrats. Such was the fate of Bouhours, who was asked to oversee the education of Henri II de Longueville's two sons. The duke had been forced to retire to Normandy after having made unfortunate political choices during the Fronde (a time of civil disturbances that lasted from 1648 to 1653). The duke's death in 1663 prompted Bouhours to write his first work, *La Mort de Monseigneur le Duc de Longueville* (The Death of Monseigneur the Duke de Longueville, 1663), an account of the courage and Christian wisdom Longueville displayed during his last hours.

Bouhours was next appointed as chaplain to the garrison of Dunkirk. When, in 1666, the powerful minister of finance Jean-Baptiste Colbert noticed a report on Dunkirk written by Bouhours, he called Bouhours back to Paris to be the private tutor of his son Jean-Baptiste. This position brought the Jesuit back to the Collège de Clermont, his permanent residence for the remainder of his life. Bouhours's biography from this point forward is closely tied to the history of French literature.

Bouhours, along with René Rapin, a fellow Jesuit and author of several books on rhetoric and style, quickly became acquainted with Parisian learned circles. Each Monday, Bouhours joined Gilles Ménage and Paul Pellisson Fontanier, among others, at the residence of Guillaume I de Lamoignon, a dignitary of the Parliament. On Saturdays, Bouhours went to Madeleine de Scudéry's long-lived salon. Although she was of advancing years, the "Incomparable Sappho" was still able to gather at her salon important people such as Charles Perrault and Nicolas Boileau. Outside these circles, Bouhours frequented the salons of such illustrious women as Marie-Madeleine Pioche de La Vergne, comtesse de Lafayette; Marie de Rabutin-Chantal, marquise de Sévigné; and Madeleine de Souvré, marquise de Sablé. The influence of Scudéry's salon can be seen in the worldly nature of Bouhours's future works and in their persistent propensity toward the smoothness of gallantry, albeit a restrained and perfectly chaste gallantry. Bouhours's first claim to fame, however, was not as an arbiter of taste but as the writer of controversial tracts against the Jansenists. His success in this genre, though, was due precisely to his knowledge of the public rhetorical expectations of the salon.

The Jansenists counted such men as Antoine Arnauld and Pierre Nicole among their members. Distinguished by an austere theological orientation inspired by St. Augustine and thus opposed to the accommodating religious practice of the Jesuits, the Jansenist movement also had strong political undertones, since many Jansenists came from old parliamentary families. Their diffidence toward the religious power of the Jesuits, perceived to be an extension of the Pope's will, and toward the absolutism of the Bourbons, who had reduced the prerogatives of the parliaments, was undoubtedly politically motivated, at least in part. The Jesuits lost many battles on the terrain of style from the very beginning of their acrimonious relations with the Jansenists. In the first half of the century, a majority of the French Jesuits favored a florid rhetorical practice. Furthermore, they clumsily engaged in religious controversies, using heavy scholastic methods of explanation or attempts to inspire fear with invectives. The antagonism between Jesuits and Jansenists culminated in the mid 1650s in a storm of controversy over what is known as "L'Affaire des Provinciales," following the censure of Arnauld by the Sorbonne. By targeting an audience in the salons and at court, Blaise Pascal, in *Les Provinciales* (The Provincial Letters, 1657), successfully rallied public opinion in favor of Arnauld and the Jansenists by artfully decrying the Jesuits' lax moral practices and hunger for influence. These letters, published from 1655 to 1657, are masterpieces of discrete, elegant, and extremely effective irony. In 1668 the Jesuits were able partially to repair the damage when they asked Bouhours to vindicate the archbishop of Ambrun, who was subjected to attacks by the writers of Port-Royal, a Cistercian convent southwest of Paris. Although perhaps not comparable in stature to *Les Provinciales,* Bouhours's work shows undeniable rhetorical savvy. The controversy centered on the translation of the New Testament by the Jansenist Isaac Louis Le Maistre de Saci. Despite a condemnation by the French and Roman authorities, the book was a success. The archbishop of Ambrun had vilified it, prompting a response by Arnauld himself. The Jesuits decided to intervene and asked Bouhours to write a letter, *Lettre à un Seigneur de la Cour, sur la requeste présentée au Roy par les Ecclesiastiques qui ont esté à Port-Royal* (Letter to a Lord of the Court, on the Request Presented to the King by the Clergy Who Were at Port-Royal, 1668), condemning the Jansenists' rebellious attitude. After bitter responses by Nicole and Arnauld, Bouhours wrote a second text, *Lettre à Messieurs de Port-Royal, contre celle qu'ils ont escrite à Monseigneur l'Archevesque d'Ambrun pour justifier la Lettre sur la constance et le courage qu'on doit avoir pour la vérité* (Letter

to the Messieurs of Port-Royal, against the Letter They Wrote to Monseigneur the Archbishop of Ambrun to Justify the *Letter on the Constancy and Courage One Must Have for the Truth,* 1668). Bouhours's letters were well written and avoided the pitfalls that would have made them unreadable in a polite salon. Bouhours's strategy cleverly hinges on the idea of social unity, an idea also at the heart of *honnêtes* (polite) conversations. He systematically emphasizes the Jansenists' fierce and proud individualism in the face of the religious and temporal authorities' condemnations, depicted as representing a consensus.

These letters changed Bouhours's life: because of their success, the Society of Jesus allowed him to devote all his time to writing, and he continued to engage in polemics with the Jansenists. Significantly, Bouhours's work restored some of the Society's lost luster in the literary world. It fell again to Bouhours to further the Society's new literary fortunes with the publication of the work for which he is most often remembered, *Les Entretiens d'Ariste et d'Eugène* (The Dialogues of Ariste and Eugène, 1671).

Les Entretiens d'Ariste et d'Eugène were extremely successful. The work depicts two friends leisurely discussing matters of literary style. In the first *entretien,* the two exchange their impressions on the topic of the sea. Two other dialogues are devoted to secrets and *devises* (emblems). The theme of secrets was popular in gallant society but also in the context of political relations. A recent novel by Scudéry, *La Promenade de Versailles* (The Walk at Versailles, 1669), had used secrets as its driving motif. The latter subject, *devises,* were symbolic images, which had been extremely popular during the Renaissance. Just a year before the publication of *Les Entretiens d'Ariste et d'Eugène,* Jacques Bailly had produced a book displaying the images used on tapestries to celebrate the Sun King (*Devises pour les tapisseries du Roi,* 1670). The truly original aspects of Bouhours's work, however, are to be found in the three other dialogues, which discuss the French language, wit, and *je ne sais quoi* (literally, "I do not know what"). These concepts allow Bouhours to define his conception of French art. The Jesuit is not overly concerned with the grandiose embodiment of that art, realized, for example, in the Louvre facade that Claude Perrault remodeled from 1666 to 1670. He seeks rather to capture the elusive elegance of an informal, distinguished, and spirited conversation. According to Bouhours, this interaction is first defined by class status and must follow the example of the conversational style practiced by the most gifted men and women at court and in the salons. Taste is given a moral value, since it is based on respect for others and characterized by a lack of selfishness. Finally, taste rests on reason and common sense. Verisimilitude (defined at the time by conformity to public opinion) is a key criterion of success. In this context, artistic style is strongly grounded in ethics, and good taste nears moral worthiness.

These notions eventually came to be identified as distinctive aspects of French classicism. The concept of classicism was unknown in the seventeenth century, but Bouhours could speak of atticism, a rhetorical term inherited from antiquity, which described a simple, concise style. In *Les Entretiens d'Ariste et d'Eugène,* Bouhours claims that French atticism unites the qualities of Gaius Julius Caesar's prose, known for its clarity and simplicity, with the qualities of Cornelius Tacitus's writing, known for its capacity to strike deeply into the mind while revealing layers of wise meaning. Ideal discourse, for Bouhours, is clear and logical: the interlocutors must be able to grasp its meaning immediately. It is sober, natural, and spontaneous, because the speakers must seem to reveal themselves casually. Their words, however, should incite reflection and allow others to appropriate them. Finally, discourse must be pleasing and lively. These qualities are first and foremost the attributes of the *homme d'esprit* (man of wit), a distinction readily granted to Bouhours by his contemporaries.

In the course of this definition of French style, Bouhours runs into a difficulty when he recognizes that the very charm of esprit is impossible to describe. He first speaks of delicateness, to express that the qualities of tasteful speech are subtly intertwined and do not have an overt effect. Finally, he brings forward the *je ne sais quoi,* the part of French atticism that cannot be theorized, and dedicates an entire dialogue to something that cannot be known. In *Les Entretiens d'Ariste et d'Eugène,* as he later does in his other works of literary criticism, Bouhours proceeds to establish contrasts, to define negatively by supplying the opposite of a concept, and especially to give practical examples taken out of texts ranging from those of antiquity to those of seventeenth-century Italy and Spain. On using the *je ne sais quoi,* he risks a comparison with divine grace, whose effects are similarly indescribable but powerful. This risk proved to be reckless. Shortly after the publication of *Les Entretiens d'Ariste et d'Eugène,* Jean Barbier d'Aucour, a friend of the Jansenists, denounced in his *Sentimens de Cléanthe sur les Entretiens d'Ariste et d'Eugène* (Sentiments of Cléanthe on the Dialogues of Ariste and Eugène, 1671) the awkwardness of the comparison and more generally the worldly concerns of Bouhours. Soon after, *Les Entretiens d'Ariste et d'Eugène* reappeared in a second edition (1671), with revisions obviously motivated by Barbier's critique.

Bouhours's work also betrays the influence of the poet Vincent Voiture, the stalwart of the salon at the Hôtel de Rambouillet, which had been a temple of gal-

Frontispiece for Bouhours's Entretiens d'Ariste et d'Eugène, *dialogues between two friends discussing their views on literary style (engraving by Francois Chauveau; University of Montreal Library)*

lantry during the reign of Louis XIII. Many have considered the orientation of gallant taste to be vapid sometimes. Despite this sympathy for Voiture, *Les Entretiens d'Ariste et d'Eugène* testifies, even before Boileau's *Art Poétique* (1674), to the consolidating success of the classical style that had emerged during the reign of Louis XIV's father.

For Bouhours, the very nature of French atticism incarnates the characteristics of its national language. Not only did he set out to define what he perceived to be these French linguistic traits in a dialogue of *Les Entretiens d'Ariste et d'Eugène,* but he also steadfastly worked to improve them with erudite and prescriptive works of philology and grammar. First, in 1674 he published *Doutes sur la langue françoise, proposez à Messieurs de l'Académie Françoise par un Gentilhomme de Province* (Doubts about the French Language, Proposed to the Messieurs of the French Academy by a Gentleman of the Country), which portrays a gentleman questioning the members of the Académie Française on matters of vocabulary, grammar, and style. Bouhours pursued the same interests in *Remarques nouvelles sur la langue françoise* (New Remarks on the French Language, 1675), followed by an addition, *Suite des remarques nouvelles sur la langue françoise* (Continuation of New Remarks on the French Language, 1687). Bouhours's linguistic enterprise is founded on a remarkable knowledge of the history of French, from its Latin origins through key medieval and Renaissance texts. Bouhours also had recent examples to follow–Claude Favre de Vaugelas, author of the influential *Remarques sur la langue françoise* (1647), and Bouhours's own rival in the matter, Ménage, author of several books on language and etymology, whose *Origines de la langue françoise* (Origins of the French Language), first published in 1650, was somewhat of a landmark. Bouhours's method is again practical and consists of quoting texts to highlight their positive and negative qualities. In *Doutes sur la langue françoise,* Bouhours selects many examples of wrong and distasteful French from Jansenist authors. This fighting spirit is tempered by his also quoting his own works for the same reason. Bouhours's work represents a significant contribution to the establishment of French as a powerful instrument of national unification. In *Les Entretiens d'Ariste et d'Eugène,* the larger part of the dialogue on language is devoted to establishing differences with other European idioms, especially Italian and Spanish, deemed inferior to the French language, which is hailed as a powerful consensus builder and an integral component of the national style. Similarly, in his *Doutes sur la langue françoise,* he first examines the word "urbanité" (civility), and he emphasizes once again the differences among rival European languages. Ariste finally comes to the conclusion that "Il n'y a proprement que les Français qui parlent" (Only the French can speak), since Italian is too flowery and Spanish too hyperbolic. French, by contrast, is described as natural, balanced, and in tune with the mind's logical operations. Bouhours sees no contradiction between this naturalizing aspect and the claim that proper French must follow the linguistic practice of socially marked *honnête* conversation. Usage and reason are the main criteria for defining which words are acceptable and what is prescribed by syntax. With these principles in mind, Bouhours studies etymology, analogy, and derivation to purify vocabulary. Prepositions, agreements, and rules of order are then put to the test of logic.

Bouhours's ruthlessness in this enterprise of purification gained him the ironic title "L'Empeseur des Muses." The pun compares Bouhours's scrupulous examination of language with the starching of the Muses' dresses. To that kind of criticism, Bouhours responds in the foreword of the *Remarques nouvelles sur la*

langue françoise that although great minds often make linguistic mistakes, they are not great for that reason. His talent as a writer won him an enduring respect from the foremost authors of the time, although he quarreled with Ménage after criticizing his etymological work. Many historians believe that Bouhours provided the inspiration for the third letter of Jean-Baptiste-Henri du Trousset de Valincourt's *Lettres à Madame la Marquise *** sur le sujet de La Princesse de Clèves* (Letters to Madame the Marquise *** on the Subject of the Princess of Clèves, 1678), a famous critique of the famed novel by Lafayette published earlier that year.

After these linguistic works, Bouhours's life continued to center on literature. He participated in Lamoignon's circle, often at the country estate of Bâville. This elegant and bucolic retreat was a perfect setting for the unceremonious, yet dignified, style of rhetoric that he championed. In 1673 Bouhours met at Bâville a man who later played a significant role in his life–Roger de Bussy-Rabutin. This gentleman and military officer, a cousin of Sévigné, had been exiled from the court since 1666 for having committed several foolish and imprudent acts, including writing short stories revealing certain amorous liaisons at the court and portraying several important aristocrats in unflattering fashion in *Histoires amoureuses des Gaules* (Amorous Accounts of the Gauls, 1665). Literature was at that time Bussy's only pastime away from court, and he found in Bouhours a good interlocutor. Their two lives were hardly similar, yet they had many things in common. Like Bouhours, Bussy had studied in a Jesuit school, where he had acquired his taste for letters. There was, then, a real communion of taste in matters of style: Bussy's *Histoires amoureuses des Gaules* was written sharply, alertly, and concisely–stylistic qualities Bouhours favored.

Toward the end of his life, Bouhours–along with Pierre Besnier and Michel Le Tellier–translated the New Testament, *Le Nouveau Testament de Nostre Seigneur Jésus-Christ, traduit en françois selon la Vulgate* (1697, 1703), with what Bouhours thought was appropriate decorum; the reception was cool, however, and the Jansenists immediately decried this worldly polishing of the most sacred book. Most notably, Bouhours was ridiculed for depicting Christ speaking *à la rabutine* (in the style of Bussy-Rabutin). In their regular exchanges Bouhours and Bussy mutually corrected their writings and spoke of their projects. On 10 January 1678 Bouhours explained in a letter that he was being kept away from his favorite enterprise by a request from the Society's superiors to finish a life of Saint Ignatius Loyola (*La Vie de Saint Ignace, fondateur de la Compagnie de Jésus,* 1679;

translated as *The Life of St. Ignatius, Founder of the Society of Jesus,* 1686), this and other biographies such as a life of Saint Francis Xavier (*La Vie de S. François Xavier, de la Compagnie de Jesus, Apostre des Indes et du Japon;* translated by John Dryden as *The Life of St. Francis Xavier, Apostle of the Indies, and of Japan,* 1688), written by Bouhours likely were dues paid for the freedom to devote himself to the world of letters. The book to which he would rather have given his time was *La Manière de bien penser dans les ouvrages d'esprit* (1687; translated as *The Art of Criticism; or, The Method of Making a Right Judgment upon Subjects of Wit and Learning,* 1705). In a letter dated 17 October 1677, he explained to Bussy the design of the work. In the dialogues of *La Manière de bien penser dans les ouvrages d'esprit,* Bouhours brings his description of French atticism to completion through the conversation of two characters. The aptly named Eudoxe, who has good taste, thinks that fine examples of rhetorical style are to be found in the Roman Augustan age, especially in Virgil's epic *The Aeneid* (circa 30 B.C.); Philanthe is fond of a more florid style and is always ready to quote Torquato Tasso. Considering Bouhours's preferences and his being drawn toward the Ancients in the famous "Querelle des Anciens et des Modernes" (Quarrel of the Ancients and the Moderns), not surprisingly Philanthe ends up recognizing the superiority of Eudoxe's judgment. *La Manière de bien penser dans les ouvrages d'esprit* condemns obscure and overdone tropes, critiques the use of long sentences (preferred by the Jansenist authors), and advocates clarity and conciseness. Once again, Bouhours's work came under attack. *La Manière de bien penser dans les ouvrages d'esprit* was sharply criticized by Nicolas Andry de Boisregard in his *Sentiments de Cléarque sur les Dialogues d'Eudoxe et de Philanthe et sur les Lettres à une dame de province* (Sentiments of Cléarque on the Dialogues of Eudoxe and Philanthe and on the Letters to a Lady of the Country, 1688). Andry was much less successful than Barbier, since Bouhours had warded off the attack by writing *Lettres à une Dame de Province sur les Dialogues d'Eudoxe et de Philanthe* (Letters to a Lady of the Country on the Dialogues of Eudoxe and Philanthe), published anonymously in 1688, shortly before Andry's *Sentiments de Cléarque sur les Dialogues d'Eudoxe et de Philanthe.* In 1703 an Italian, Giovan-Gioseffo Orsi, published a vindication of his country—*Considerazioni sopra un famoso libro franzese* (Remarks on a Famous French Book)—feeling that the time had come to defend Italy's language and letters against the derisive tone used by Bouhours to describe them in *Les Entretiens d'Ariste et d'Eugène.*

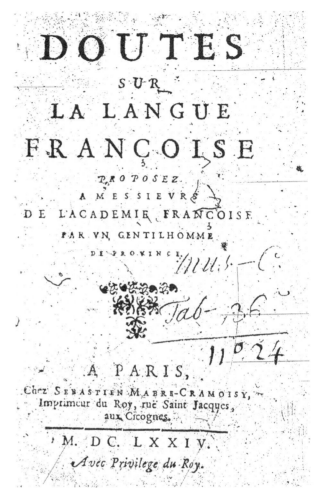

Title page for Bouhours's work in which a man from the country questions members of the Académie Française on matters of grammar and style (Sterling Memorial Library, Yale University)

Dominique Bouhours's death on 27 May 1702 was followed by many tributes, a larger part of them emphasizing the remarkable conjunction in his person of a kind soul and a dignified writer and scholar of French. He is reported to have said on his deathbed: "I have some scruples about my pleasure in dying."

Letters:

Roger de Bussy-Rabutin, *Correspondance avec le Père Bouhours,* edited by César Rouben (Paris: Nizet, 1986).

Bibliography:

"Dominique Bouhours," in *Bibliothèque de la Compagnie de Jésus,* volume 1, edited by Aloys de Backer, Augustin de Backer, and Carlos Sommervogel

(Brussels: O. Schepens / Paris: A. Picard, 1890), pp. 1886–1920.

Biography:

Georges Doncieux, *Un Jésuite homme de lettres au dix-septième siècle: Le Père Bouhours* (Paris: Hachette, 1886).

References:

Nicolas Andry de Boisregard, *Sentiments de Cléarque sur les Dialogues d'Eudoxe et de Philanthe et sur les Lettres à une dame de province* (Paris: L. d'Houry, 1688);

Anonymous, "Eloge de la vie, et de la mort de feu le Révérend Père Dominique Bouhours, Religieux de la Compagnie de Jésus," *Mémoires de Trévoux* (August 1702): 328–340;

Jean Barbier d'Aucour, *Sentiments de Cléante sur les Entretiens d'Ariste et d'Eugène* (Paris: P. Le Monnier, 1671);

Françoise Berlan, "Le Père Bouhours, ou L'Air de la cour dans la langue et le style," in *De la mort de Colbert à la révocation de l'Edit de Nantes: Un Monde nouveau?* edited by Louise Godard de Donville (Marseille: C.M.R., 1984), pp. 97–109;

Bernard Beugnot, "Prolégomènes à une édition critique des Entretiens d'Ariste et d'Eugène," in *Langue, Littérature du XVIIe et du XVIIIe siècle,* edited by Roger Lathuillère (Paris: SEDES, 1990), pp. 171–186;

Jean-Pierre Collinet, "Un Triumvirat critique: Rapin, Bouhours, Bussy," in *Critique et création littéraires en France au XVIIe siècle* (Paris: Editions du C.N.R.S., 1977), pp. 261–272;

Gilles Declercq, "Bouhours, lecteur de Balzac, ou Du Naturel," *Littératures classiques,* 33 (1998): 93–113;

Declercq, "Usage et bel usage: L'Usage de la langue dans Les Entretiens d'Ariste et d'Eugène du père Bouhours," *Littératures classiques,* 28 (1996): 113–136;

Jean-Pierre Dens, *L'Honnête homme et la critique du goût: Esthétique et société au XVIIe siècle* (Lexington, Ky.: French Forum, 1981);

Marc Fumaroli, "The Genius of the French Language," in *Realms of Memory: The Construction of the French Past,* directed by Pierre Nora, edited by Lawrence D. Kritzman, translated by Arthur Goldhammer, volume 3 (New York: Columbia University Press, 1996), pp. 555–606;

Suzanne Guellouz, "Le Père Bouhours et le je ne sais quoi," *Littératures,* 18 (1971): 3–14;

Hélène Merlin, "L'Esprit de la langue," in *L'Esprit en France au XVIIe siècle,* edited by François Lagarde (Paris & Seattle: Papers on French Seventeenth Century Literature, 1997), pp. 29–51;

Giovan-Gioseffo Orsi, *Considerazioni sopra un famoso libro franzese intitolato "La Manière de bien penser dans les ouvrages d'esprit": Cioè La maniera di ben pensare ne' componimenti, divisa in sette Dialoghi, ne' quali s'agitano alcune quistioni Rettoriche e Poetiche, e si difendono molti passi di Poeti e di Prosatori Italiani, condannati dall'autor Franzese* (Bologna: C. Pisarri, 1703);

Richard Simon, *Difficultés proposées au R. P. Bouhours sur sa traduction françoise des quatre évangélistes* (Amsterdam: A. Acher, 1697);

Jean-Baptiste-Henri du Trousset de Valincourt, *Lettres à Madame la Marquise *** sur le sujet de la Princesse de Clèves* (Paris: S. Mabre-Cramoisy, 1678);

Florence Vuillemier, "Le Père Dominique Bouhours face aux partisans de la pointe," in *Un Classicisme ou des classicismes?* edited by Georges Forestier and Jean-Pierre Néraudau (Pau: Publications de l'Université de Pau, 1995), pp. 153–216.

Jean-Pierre Camus

(3 or 4 November 1584 – 1652)

Eglal Henein
Tufts University

SELECTED BOOKS*: *Les Diversitez de Messire Jean-Pierre Camus,* 11 volumes (Paris: C. Chappelet, 1609–1614);

La Mémoire de Darie, où se voit l'idée d'une dévotieuse vie et d'une religieuse mort (Paris: C. Chappelet, 1620);

Agathonphile, ou Les Martyrs siciliens, Agathon, Philargiryppe, Triphyne, et leurs Associez: Histoire dévote où se descouvre l'Art de Bien Aimer pour antidote aux deshonnestes affections, et où par des succez admirables, la saincte Amour du Martyre triomphe du Martyre de la mauvaise Amour (Rouen: F. Vaultier, 1621);

Elise, ou L'Innocence coupable: Evénement tragique de nostre temps (Paris: C. Chappelet, 1621); translated by Jo. Jennings as *Elise, or Innocencie Guilty: A New Romance* (London: Printed by Thomas Newcomb for Humphrey Moseley, 1655);

Parthénice, ou Peinture d'une invincible chasteté: Histoire napolitaine (Paris: C. Chappelet, 1621);

L'Alexis, où sous la suitte de divers pelerinages sont déduites plusieurs histoires tant anciennes que nouvelles remplies d'enseignements de piété, 6 volumes (Paris: C. Chappelet, 1622–1623);

Eugène, histoire grenadine: Offrant un spectacle de pitié et de piété (Paris: C. Chappelet, 1623);

Spiridion, anacorète de l'Apennin (Paris: C. Chappelet, 1623);

Alcime, relation funeste, ou se descouvre la main de Dieu sur les Impies (Paris: M. Lasnier, 1625); translated as *A True Tragical History of Two Illustrious Italian Families, Couched under the Names of Alcimus and Vannoza* (London: Printed for William Jacob, 1677);

L'Iphigène de Mr de Belley: Rigueur sarmatique, 2 volumes (Lyon: A. Chard, 1625); translated by John Wright as *Nature's Paradox, or The Innocent Impostor:*

*Camus wrote more than two hundred novels, stories, essays, and homilies. The list above includes only the most significant representatives of each genre. For additional works the reader should refer to the bibliography by Jean Descrains.

Jean-Pierre Camus (from Thomas Worcester, Seventeenth-Century Cultural Discourse, *1997)*

A Pleasant Polonian History, Originally Intituled Iphigenes (London: Printed by J.G. for Edward Dod and Nathaniel Ekins, 1652);

Palombe, ou La Femme Honnorable: Histoire catalane (Paris: C. Chappelet, 1625);

Aloph, ou Le Parastre malheureux: Histoire françoise (Lyon: A. Travers, 1626);

Le Cléoreste de Monseigneur de Belley: Histoire Françoise-Espagnolle, Représentant le Tableau d'une perfaitte amitié, 2 volumes (Lyon: A. Chard, 1626);

Diotrèphe: Histoire Valentine (Lyon: A. Chard, 1626); translated by S. Du Verger as *Diotrephe, or An His-*

torie of Valentines (London: Thomas Harper, 1641);

Damaris, ou L'Implacable marastre: Histoire Allemande (Lyon: A. Travers, 1627);

Les Evénemens singuliers de Mr de Belley (Lyon: J. Caffin et F. Pleignard, 1628);

L'Amphithéâtre sanglant où sont représentées plusieurs actions tragiques de nostre temps (Paris: J. Cottereau, 1630);

Le Bouquet d'histoires agréables (Paris: G. Alliot, 1630);

Conférence académique sur le différent des belles lettres de Narcisse et de Phyllarque (Paris: J. Cottereau, 1630);

Les Spectacles d'horreur . . . (Paris: A. Soubron, 1630);

Le Voyageur inconnu, histoire curieuse, et Apologetique pour les Religieux (Paris: D. Thierry, 1630); translated by Wright as *The Loving Enemie* (London: Printed by J.G. & sold by J. Dakins, 1650);

La Tour des miroirs, ouvrage historique (Paris: R. Bertault et L. Bertault, 1631);

Les Leçons exemplaires de M. J.-P. C., E. de Belley (Paris: R. Bertault, 1632);

Les Eclaircissemens de Méliton, 2 volumes (N.p., 1635);

L'Esprit du B. François de Sales, évesque de Genève, représenté en plusieurs de ses actions et paroles remarquables, recueillies de quelques sermons, exhortations, conférences, conversations, livres et lettres de M. Jean-Pierre Camus . . . , par L.D.P., 3 volumes (Paris: G. Alliot, 1639–1641);

L'Avoisinement des protestans vers l'Eglise romaine (Paris: G. Alliot, 1640);

La Caritée, ou Le Pourtraict de la vraye Charité: Histoire dévote tirée de la vie de S. Louys (Paris: R. Bertault, 1641);

Mémoriaux historiques (Paris: J. Villery, 1643);

Les Rencontres funestes, ou Fortunes infortunées de nostre temps (Paris: J. Villery, 1644);

Les Tapisseries historiques (Paris: J. Branchu, 1644).

Editions: *L'Esprit du bien-heureux François de Sales*, 3 volumes (Paris: Gaume Frères, 1840);

Palombe, ou La Femme honorable, edited by H. Rigault (Paris: Hachette, 1853);

Agathonphile: Récit de Philargyrippe, edited by Pierre Sage, Textes Littéraires Français (Geneva: Droz, 1951; Lille: Giard, 1951);

Homélies des Etats Généraux: 1614–1615, edited by Jean Descrains, Textes Littéraires Français (Geneva: Droz, 1970; Paris: Minard, 1970);

Spectacles d'horreur, edited by René Godenne (Geneva: Slatkine, 1973; Paris: Champion, 1973);

Trente nouvelles, edited by René Favret (Paris: Vrin, 1977);

L'Amphithéâtre sanglant, edited by Stéphan Ferrari (Paris: H. Champion, 2001);

Homélies des Etats Généraux, Agathonphile, and *Palombe, ou La Femme Honnorable* are available on-line through ARTFL (American and French Research on the Treasury of the French Language): <http://humanities.uchicago.edu/ARTFL.html>.

Editions in English: *The Spirit of St Francois de Sales,* edited and translated by C. F. Kelley (New York: Harper, 1952);

A Draught of eternitie, translated by Miles Car (Menston: Scolar, 1972)–facsimile of the 1632 translation;

A Discours Hapned: Betwene an Hermite Called Nicephorus and a Yong Lover Called Tristan, Who for That His Mistresse Petronilla Entred into Religion Would Faine Become an Hermite: All Faithfullie Drawen out of the Historie of Petronilla, translated by P.S.P. (Menston: Scolar, 1973)–facsimile of the 1630 translation;

A Spiritual Combat, translated by C.P. (Ilkley & London: Scolar, 1974)–facsimile of the 1632 translation;

The Spiritual Director Disinterested (Ilkley & London: Scolar, 1974)–facsimile of the 1633 translation.

Jean-Pierre Camus, bishop of Belley, was by all accounts the most prolific French writer of the seventeenth century. The 264 titles listed by Jean Descrains in his extensive bibliography belong to three distinctive categories: essays and pamphlets published mainly at the beginning of Camus's career and around 1630; novels and short stories published between 1620 and 1640; and homilies–the only constant in Camus's literary production. The bishop's writings stem from his genuine desire to educate his flock "par la parole et par la plume" (by word and by pen). They are perfect examples of the literary goals of the Counter Reformation–*docere* (to teach) and *delectare* (to please).

Jean-Pierre Camus was born in Rouen on 3 or 4 November 1584. His family moved to Paris when he was twelve. The Camus family belonged to the "Politiques," Catholics who did not support the Ligue and who wanted the Protestant Henri of Navarre to succeed the Catholic Henri III. Camus studied law in Orléans after serving as a page at the court. His family knew and frequented the home of Roger de Saint-Lary, duc de Bellegarde, the famous sponsor of the arts who protected François de Malherbe and Honorat du Bueil, seigneur de Racan. After studying law, Camus opted instead for the priesthood. Although little is known of his early years, it is generally considered that some autobiographical details can be found in the sixth and last volume of one of his early novels, *L'Alexis, où sous la suitte de divers pelerinages sont déduites plusieurs histoires tant anciennes que nouvelles remplies d'enseignements de piété* (Alexis, in Which through a Series of Pilgrimages Many Tales, Both Old and New Are Told, Filled with Teachings of Piety, 1622–1623). The author is present under the approximate anagram of Pieriam, a young man who selects the name of Alexis when he goes on the pilgrimage described in the novel. According to Alexis's adventures, Camus seems to have loved a young woman named Saincte who became a nun; he was also apparently afraid of the dark. In 1609 François de Sales consecrated Camus, who became bishop of Belley, in Savoy. In 1629 Camus became an adjunct to the archbishop of Rouen (Normandy). In 1650 he chose to devote himself to the poor and the sick: he lived at the *Hospice des Incurables* (Hospice for the Terminally Ill), where he died in 1652. His family respected his wishes for a discrete burial. A year later a memorial was organized, and Antoine Godeau, bishop of Grasse and Vence, pronounced Camus's funeral oration.

At the age of twenty-four, Camus was already admired for his eloquence. He pronounced the funeral oration of the marquise de Rambouillet in 1610 and the panegyric of St. Ignatius Loyola the year he was canonized (1622). Camus's most prestigious homilies remained those presented in 1614 during the States General. His homily "Sur les fléaux" (On Plagues) provides a good example of his method of reasoning; each social class has its evils: the Catholic Church suffers because of Protestantism and because of the threat of the English schism; the Nobility suffer because of the spread of the deadly habit of dueling; the People suffer from taxes and from famine. For each of these evils, Camus proposes a solution: the decisions of the Council of Trent, royal edicts against dueling, and a decrease in the number of tax collectors. The bishop thus proves to be a harsh and candid critic of his society; at the same time, however, he remains an optimist and trusts the king's ability to develop new solutions to the social problems of France. The same optimism reigns in the sermons devoted to commenting on the Old or the New Testament: Camus seems to give preference to the theme of conversion, paying a great deal of attention to the story of St. Mary Magdalene and its hopeful ending. His four hundred sermons (gathered in seventeen volumes) were widely distributed to inspire other priests.

Camus's first publication was the eleven-volume collection *Les Diversitez de Messire Jean-Pierre Camus* (The Miscellanea of Messire Jean-Pierre Camus, 1609–1614), or the *Diversités,* as they are more commonly known. The work was an homage to Michel de Montaigne's *Essais* (Essays; published in 1580, 1588); "Jugement des Essais de Michel Seigneur de Montaigne" (Judgment of the Essays of Michel Seigneur de Montaigne), included in volume eight, provides a clever analysis of Camus's literary model. Large sections of the *Diversités* deal with religious

subjects: the first chapter is devoted to God; a whole volume (five) is allotted to the Beatitudes; and several other sections explore theological issues. However, readers can also appreciate Camus's thoughts on a large variety of secular topics: experience (volume one), diversity (volume two), mathematics (volume three), scepticism (volume four), eyes, exterior (volume six), and mermaids (volume seven). Volume nine focuses on passions of the soul, of which Camus distinguishes eleven. Some come from *appétit de convoitise* (lust); some from *appétit de courroux* (wrath); and the most important passion is the love of God. Camus obviously draws from Plato and Aristotle, but his favorite thinkers are Plutarch ("notre maître," our master) and Seneca ("l'admirable," the admirable), much like his friend, Honoré d'Urfé, who drew from the same sources in his *Epistres morales* (Moral Letters, 1598).

Among Camus's many essays, several dealing with a variety of topics deserve special consideration. In *Le Voyageur inconnu, histoire curieuse, et Apologetique pour les Religieux* (The Unknown Voyager, a Curious and Apologetic Story for Monks), published in 1630, he gives a detailed and invaluable account of a seventeenth-century bishop's daily life. Also published that same year, the *Conférence académique sur le différent des belles lettres de Narcisse et de Phyllarque* (Academic Conference on a Literary Dispute Between Narcisse and Phyllarque) is Camus's contribution to a famous literary controversy surrounding Guez de Balzac. A few years later, in *Les Eclaircissemens de Méliton* (The Clarifications of Méliton, 1635), Camus answers the harsh criticism made by a priest against his novels and also condemns certain religious orders. In a sort of "art poétique" (poetics), divided into four "assauts" (attacks), he vigorously defends his fiction writing. In *L'Avoisinement des protestans vers l'Eglise romaine* (The Rapprochement of the Protestants with the Catholic Church, 1640), Camus demonstrates his refusal to admit the concept of religious toleration introduced by the Edict of Nantes in 1598 and calls Protestants spiritual "lepers" who must be avoided. Camus's best-known work in the category of essays remains *L'Esprit du B. François de Sales, évesque de Genève, représenté en plusieurs de ses actions et paroles remarquables, recueillies de quelques sermons, exhortations, conférences, conversations, livres et lettres de M. Jean-Pierre Camus . . .* (The Spirit of the Blessed Francis de Sales, Bishop of Geneva, Represented in Many of His Remarkable Deeds and Words, Gathered from Some Sermons, Exhortations, Lectures, Conversations, Books, and Letters of M. Jean-Pierre Camus . . . , 1639–1641), a work that has been adapted and translated into many languages. In this six-volume biogra-

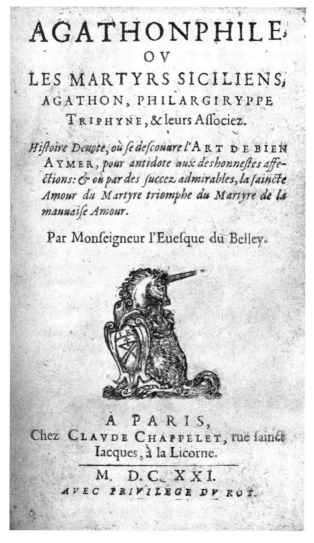

*Title page for the book in which Camus used allegory to contrast the right
and the wrong forms of love (Bibliothèques de Lyon)*

phy, Camus expresses his admiration and his gratitude for de Sales (who died in 1622), a man he considered his spiritual father.

In 1620, with the encouragement of de Sales, Camus published *La Mémoire de Darie, où se voit l'idée d'une dévotieuse vie et d'une religieuse mort* (The Memoire of Darie, Wherein Is Seen the Idea of a Devout Life and a Religious Death), the first of these moral tales that he called "ouvrages historiques," or "believable" works. Camus was following a tradition of oral and written examples given to Christians by priests in the form of entertaining stories teaching a moral lesson. One example of this tradition is Antoine d' Averoult's *Fleurs des exemples* (Flowers of Examples), published in two volumes in 1608 with the subtitle *Catéchisme historial* (Historical Catechism). In this "cat-

echism," each story illustrates a virtue or explains a commandment. Camus's *Mémoire de Darie*, by contrast, is not so systematic, and his own stories are richly imaginative. In a similar vein, he labeled his thirty novels "histoires dévotes" (devout stories). His hundreds of short stories (gathered in twenty-two volumes) are similarly "leçons exemplaires" (exemplary lessons), the title he gave in 1632 to one of these collections of stories. Camus was so convinced of the formidable power of words that he wrote a story to show how a satirical poem provoked four deaths, *Les Spectacles d'horreur* . . . (Spectacles of Horror . . . , 1630). In his *Alcime, relation funeste, ou se descouvre la main de Dieu sur les Impies* (1625; translated as *A True Tragical History of Two Illustrious Italian Families, Couched under the Names of Alcimus and Vannoza,*

1677), Camus shows a feminine Don Quixote–like character who loses her mind and kills herself because she has read too many novels.

In 1623, with *Spiridion, anacorète de l'Apennin* (Spiridion, Anchorite of the Apennins), a work made up of three independent narratives in one volume, Camus published his first collection of short stories or novellas, a genre that was becoming popular: that same year, Charles Sorel published his *Les Nouvelles françoises* (French Short Stories). In 1628 Camus abandoned long novels to devote all his energy to shorter fiction. He explained his goals and methods in the important foreword to *Les Evénemens singuliers de Mr de Belley* (The Singular Events of monseigneur de Belley, 1628). Stating that readers lack patience and do not want to pay for big books, the bishop announces that he has adapted his narratives to the public's tastes. However, in his short fictions, Camus still includes the same "agencements," or embellishments, that made his novels so long. Camus is fond of digressions and unconventional similes. His favorite addition is the introduction of verse. Well aware that his own poems are rather disappointing, he quotes hundreds of verses in Latin and French. In his opinion, "a story without verses is an egg without salt," and "a man of letters who despises poetry is like a gentleman who hates horses or dogs," as he says in volume two of *Le Cléoreste de Monseigneur de Belley: Histoire Françoise-Espagnolle, Représentant le Tableau d'une perfaitte amitié* (The Cléoreste of Monseigneur de Belley: A Franco-Spanish Tale Representing the Portrait of a Perfect Friendship, 1626).

Three collections of short stories belong to a distinctive group and are today the most often published, quoted, and studied texts of Camus. *L'Amphithéâtre sanglant où sont représentées plusieurs actions tragiques de nostre temps* (The Bloody Amphitheater Wherein Are Represented Many Tragic Actions of Our Time, 1630), *Les Spectacles d'horreur,* and *Les Rencontres funestes, ou Fortunes infortunées de nostre temps* (Disastrous Encounters, or The Unfortunate Fortunes of Our Times, 1644) are "histoires tragiques" (tragic stories) as violent as those published by François de Rosset at the beginning of the seventeenth century. The title of one story, "Morts entassées" (Piled-Up Deaths), published in *Les Spectacles d'horreur,* is a good summary of these harsh tales in which Justice often does not prevail. Camus's stories are so cruel and sometimes so brutal that Henri Coulet has called them the ancestors of horror stories that may be considered as the French equivalent of the British Gothic novels.

Writing during the first half of the century, at a time when the novel as a genre was rapidly evolving,

Camus developed an interest in narratological questions. He explains that he built one of his novels like a heroic poem, starting in medias res. He constructed another one like a play, giving it five acts. He makes clear the necessity of properly ending a narrative. He describes his aesthetic choices in prefaces and afterwords that represent important moments in the history of the novel as a genre, such as "Eloge des histoires dévotes" ("In Praise of Devout Stories," from *Agathonphile, ou Les Martyrs siciliens, Agathon, Philargiryppe, Triphyne, et leurs Associez: Histoire dévote où se descouvre l'Art de Bien Aimer pour antidote aux deshonnestes affections, et où par des succez admirables, la saincte Amour du Martyre triomphe du Martyre de la mauvaise Amour* [Agathonphile, or The Sicilian Martyrs Agathon, Philargiryppe, Triphyne, and Their Companions: A Devout Tale in Which Is Revealed the Art of Right Love as an Antidote to Unbecoming Affections, and in Which through Admirable Victories, the Holy Love of the Martyr Triumphs over the Martyr of Wrong Love, 1621]), or "Economie de cette histoire" ("Organization of This Story," from *L'Iphigène de Mr de Belley: Rigueur sarmatique* [1625; translated as *Nature's Paradox, or The Innocent Impostor: A Pleasant Polonian History, Originally Intituled Iphigenes,* 1652]). Ordinary profane novels are just "livres d'amour" (romance novels), and the bishop, in *Agathonphile,* refers to them as destructive animals: "petits livres d'amourettes qui, comme des chenilles importunes, broutent les feuilles et les fleurs" (booklets of passing fancies that eat leaves and flowers like irksome caterpillars). On the other hand, Camus composed stories in which the plot is almost a pretext, a springboard for moral observations. As a writer of fiction, he proclaims in *L'Alexis* (volume one) that he does not need to show discrimination in his choice of material: "Tout mets peut être servi en ce banquet, toute herbe venir en cette salade, toute fleur être plantée en ce champ" (Any dish can be served at this banquet, any herb can be added to this salad, any flower can be planted in this field). He does, however, use all sorts of rhetorical shields to protect his readers and explicitly refuses to include information that could induce them to sin.

To tell a story, Camus starts with many heterogeneous sources, then masterfully amplifies his tales: he attaches several anecdotes together and adds comments to consolidate and prop them up. One of his stories in *Le Bouquet d'histoires agréables* (The Bouquet of Pleasant Stories, 1630) finishes like a prayer, "Ainsi soit-il" (Amen), making the reader unable to forget that the author is a priest. Often, Camus imagines dramatic endings to expose the dangers of passions: "Le sanglant succès [en] fait une histoire qui n'est que trop véritable" (A bloody issue makes a story ring true), he notes in *Les Rencontres funestes*. The sources of his stories are sometimes religious–for instance, the hagiography of Saint Louis, Louis IX, patron of Louis XIII. Many of Camus's novels stem from myths: Ovid appears to be Camus's main source, providing an ample repertoire of stories that also inspired many other seventeenth-century novelists. Camus himself has been called the "Christian Ovid." Other authors may also be cited as sources for Camus's stories: Giovanni Boccaccio (whose writings were blacklisted by the Church) provided the inspiration for *Alcime* and "Le Cœur mangé" (The Eaten Heart; from *Les Spectacles d'horreur*), among others; d'Urfé, Camus's friend and neighbor in Savoy, inspired *L'Alexis* and several short stories included in *La Tour des miroirs, ouvrage historique* (The Tower of Mirrors: An Historical Work, 1631). Camus was extremely well read and he possessed a formidable memory. However, he rarely felt obliged to indicate his sources (with the exception of his *Diversités*) or even to remain absolutely true to the original: "Chacun au regard du récit d'une histoire pouvant abonder en son sens sans préjudice du vrai" (When it comes to telling a story, one can bend in one's direction without hurting the truth), as he says in the preamble to *Les Tapisseries historiques* (The Historical Tapestries, 1644).

Camus's major stimulation came from what he saw around him. He was inspired by what he calls his "bibliothèque animée," his animated library, the book of the world, as he says in volume one of *Les Eclaircissemens de Méliton*. He took notes in his *mémoriaux*, a sort of diary. However, he often felt the need to camouflage adventures behind the "trois rideaux des noms, des temps et des lieux déguisés" (three curtains of disguised names, times, and places), as he says in *La Tour des miroirs*. Camus traveled extensively and, as he remarks in volume two of *Le Cléoreste*, he paid more attention to "les mœurs" (the people) than to "les murs" (the architecture). This belief explains the many realistic remarks one can find in his books: information on the treatment of servants, on pilgrimages, on the celebration of St. Valentine's feast, on the relationship between Spanish and French people, on superstitions, on the daily life of students, on playing chess, and on new imported flowers (tulips, anemones, and hyacinths). Camus is fond of mixing styles and themes, as in an interesting and typical passage of *L'Alexis*, where the description of "La Fontaine des Peupliers" (The Fountain of the Poplars) combines down-to-earth details with mythical legends and religious symbols.

Modern readers of Camus may at first be surprised by his misogyny. As early as 1610, the bishop expressed his mistrust of women in his *Diversités*, when he introduced a series of quotations criticizing them under a curious heading, "Des courtisans, des avocats et des femmes" (On Courtiers, Lawyers and Women). He condemns their provocative attitudes as well as the use of cosmetics and perfumes. Although many of his novels have a woman's name in their title, few heroines in his novels deserve the reader's admiration, with the notable exception of Iphigène, who, disguised as a man, goes to war against the Turks and suffers a martyr's death. Female characters are often vicious criminals (such as Damaris) or powerless victims worthy of the reader's compassion (Parthénice, for example). Camus proclaims that women cannot live without talking, as in *Aloph, ou Le Parastre malheureux: Histoire françoise* (Aloph, or The Unhappy Stepfather: A French Tale, 1626). He also believed that to write verses like a woman meant to write badly, as he says in *L'Alexis*. In *Elise, ou L'Innocence coupable: Evénement tragique de nostre temps* (1621; translated as *Elise, or Innocencie Guilty: A New Romance*, 1655), a book dedicated to a princess expecting a child, Camus blames "ce trafic continuel qu'elles ont avec leurs miroirs" (the constant traffic women have with their mirrors) and even claims that beauty and virtue do not go together. Interestingly, in *L'Alexis*, his longest novel, Camus relegates all women to inserted stories within the main narrative. The protagonists, therefore, are all men who have often been mistreated by women. A pilgrimage, the author asserts, will cure mad lovers by separating them from women.

Modern readers will appreciate that Camus offers exceptional gems of "baroque" style. He enjoyed puns and gave many of his characters "noms signifiants" (significant names). The protagonist of *L'Iphigène* explicitly imitates Iphis and Iphigenia, and assumes other meaningful names in the novel. Another significant name is that of the eponymous hero of *Agathonphile*, lover of virtue. The hero of the last story in *Mémoriaux historiques* (Historical Memoirs, 1643) is called Final. Camus himself explains that he likes the name of *Timée* in *Diversités*, because it has "deux biais et signifiances" (two slants and significations): it means honorable in Greek and blind in Hebrew.

Camus's main stylistic characteristics are his love for long Homeric lists, his attachment to *paronomase* (juxtaposition of words that have the same sound), and his taste for the accumulation of metaphors. The following are two typical sentences–one (from *Diversités*) a vivid presentation of the seven capital sins, and the other (also from *Diversités*) a definition of eloquence:

> L'enflure de l'orgueil, le trouble de la colère, la pesanteur de la paresse, la fluxion de l'envie, l'ordure de la concupiscence, la taie de l'avarice, la réplétion de la gueule (The swelling of pride, the trouble of anger, the heaviness of sloth, the inflammation of envy, the filth of concupiscence, the blinders of avarice, the repletion of the mouth);

> La vraie éloquence qui consiste en douceur, gravité, pureté, majesté, netteté, simplicité, rondeur, bienséance, fluidité, égalité, force, polissure, jugement, abondance, pompe (True eloquence consists in sweetness, gravity, purity, majesty, neatness, simplicity, easy-going directness, smoothness, decorum, fluidity, equality, strength, polish, judgment, abundance, pomp).

The following remarks—all from *Le Voyageur inconnu*—illustrate at the same time Camus's style and his thinking on style:

> Il est aisé d'être exact en un petit ouvrage qu'on a loisir de lire, relire, polir, agencer, peigner, adoucir, limer, perfectionner (It is easy to be exact in a small book that one can leisurely read, re-read, polish, decorate, comb, soften, file, perfect);

> Je suis mon naturel, je ne marche point en dansant, je ne chemine point en cadence, je vais mon pas tout simple, sans contrefaire mon allure (I follow my nature, I do not dance while walking, there is no rhythm in my walk, I have my own simple step, I do not counterfeit my gait);

> J'avoue que le travail s'est insensiblement enflé sous la plume (et c'est le propre de la plume de s'enfler comme l'on voit aux oreillers) (I confess that my work has swelled under the quill [and it's a characteristic of the quill to swell as one sees in pillows]).

Camus himself said, in *Conférence académique sur le différent des belles lettres de Narcisse et de Phyllarque:* "Le style est le caractère le plus naïf des mouvements de l'âme" (Style is the most sincere character of the soul's movements). Camus is like his style—full of energy and full of surprises.

Considering French as a language destined to change every fifty years or so, according to *Le Voyageur inconnu,* Camus probably never paid much attention to the correction of his style; he was more interested in its effectiveness. He often presented instructive remarks on words considered new. For this reason Emile Littré, in the 1872 edition of his *Dictionnaire de la langue française,* borrows six examples from Camus: *caver* (to dig), *colombin* (pigeon-like), *dam*

(detriment), *empressement* (eagerness), *issue* (text placed at the end of a book), and *payer la gabatine* (to be duped). Camus's writings generally give the unexpected impression that their author was in a good mood. Several jokes are gathered in his "official" collection of humorous stories, *Le Bouquet d'histoires agréables,* but there are also amusing expressions in most of Camus's writings—including even the dreadful *L'Amphithéâtre sanglant,* in which one can read:

> Ce chevalier se peut bien appeler errant puisqu'il commettait tant d'erreurs ensuite l'une de l'autre (This knight can very well be called errant since he erred so often).

> Faisant deux fleuves de ses yeux, il était malaisé de juger s'il allait ou par eau ou par terre (Turning his eyes into two rivers, it was hard to judge whether he was on the water or on the ground).

Was Jean-Pierre Camus a model priest, almost a candidate for canonization? While his contemporaries admired his genuine piety, he was not considered above reproach as a Christian because he loathed mendicant orders and wrote violent attacks against monks. Was he regarded as an important writer? Godeau, Tallemant des Réaux, Théophraste Renaudot, and Charles Perrault admired his vast memory, his fiery style, his vehemence, and his extraordinary productivity. However, although Perrault included him among his "hommes illustres" (famous men), Camus's books were not analyzed or praised by the most important critics of his time. At the beginning of the seventeenth century Sorel, for instance, does not mention Camus in his parody of novels, *Le Berger Extravagant* (The Extravagant Shepherd, 1627). In his later *Bibliothèque Françoise* (French Library, 1664), he simply mentions Camus as an author who mixed fiction and moral lessons. At the end of the century, Pierre-Daniel Huet, himself a bishop, omits Camus from his famous essay "Traité de l'origine des romans" (On the Origins of Novels, 1670). Significantly also, Nicolas Boileau-Despréaux spares Camus's characters from his biting satire in the *Dialogue des Héros de roman* (Dialogue on the Heroes of Novels, 1688).

Nevertheless, Camus's novels and short stories had a definite impact: many were published more than once during the seventeenth century. *L'Iphigène,* Camus's most "romanesque" novel, the most romantic, the most fabulous and entertaining, was adapted for the English stage by John Suckling (1639) and then summarized and translated into English in 1652. Gilbert Saulnier, sieur Du Verdier, an obscure writer who plagiarized other novelists, stole some of

Camus's *Parthénice, ou Peinture d'une invincible chasteté: Histoire napolitaine* (Parthenice, or Portrait of an Invincible Chastity: A Neapolitan Story, 1621) for his *La Parténice de la cour* (Partenice of the Court, 1624). "Devout stories," however, the narrative genre that was Camus's specialty, did not flourish. Camus did not leave disciples.

With the exception of his writings against monks, all aspects of Jean-Pierre Camus's works have found modern interested scholars. Long reduced to "pre-classicism" by literary historians, the French baroque period is now recognized and valued in its own right. Moreover, the creation of SATOR (Société d'Analyse de la topique dans les œuvres romanesques avant la Révolution), an association devoted to the study of pre-Revolutionary fiction, has encouraged the examination of novels and short stories published during the seventeenth century. With his engaging personality, his astonishing imagination, and his sense of humor, Camus's work is an original and important milestone in the story of European fiction.

Bibliography:

Jean Descrains, *Bibliographie des œuvres de Jean-Pierre Camus, évêque de Belley (1584–1652)* (Paris: Société d'Etude du XVIIe Siècle, 1971).

References:

Albert Bayer, *J.-P. Camus, sein Leben und seine Romane* (Leipzig, 1906);

Peter Bayley, "Les Sermons de J.-P. Camus et l'esthétique borroméenne," in *Critique et Création littéraires au XVIIe Siècle,* edited by Marc Fumaroli and Jean Mesnard (Paris: Editions du C.N.R.S., 1977), pp. 93–101;

Henri Brémond, *Histoire littéraire du sentiment religieux en France,* volume 1 (Paris: Bloud & Gay, 1916);

Charles Chesneau (Julien Eymard d'Angers), *Du Stoïcisme chrétien à l'humanisme chrétien: Les "Diversités" de Jean-Pierre Camus (1609–1618)* (Meaux: A. Pouyé, 1952);

Henri Coulet, *Le Roman jusqu'à la Révolution,* 2 volumes (Paris: A. Colin, 1967);

Jean Descrains, *Essais sur Jean-Pierre Camus* (Paris: Klincksieck, 1992);

Descrains, *Jean-Pierre Camus (1584–1652) et ses "Diversités" (1609–1618), ou La Culture d'un évêque humaniste,* 2 volumes (Paris: Nizet, 1985);

René Godenne, *Histoire de la nouvelle française aux XVIIe et XVIIIe siècles* (Paris: Vrin, 1978);

Eglal Henein, "Le Cœur mangé . . . ruminé," in *Violence et fiction jusqu'à la Révolution: IXe Colloque de la SATOR,* edited by M. Debaisieux and G. Verdier (Tübingen: Gunter Narr, 1998), pp. 77–88;

Henein, "Les Nouvelles de Camus et les 'agencements,'" *Revue d'Histoire Littéraire de la France,* 3–4 (1977): 440–458;

Georges Molinié, "Le Projet d'édification chrétienne et les contraintes du roman baroque dans l'œuvre de Jean-Pierre Camus," in *Humanisme et foi chrétienne* (Paris: Beauchesne, 1976), pp. 203–208;

Charles Perrault, *Les Hommes illustres qui ont paru en France pendant ce siècle, avec leurs portraits au naturel* (Paris: Dezallier, 1697);

Sylvie Robic de Baecque, *Le Salut par l'excès: Jean-Pierre Camus (1584–1652), la poétique d'un évêque romancier* (Paris: H. Champion, 1999);

Charles Sorel, *De la Connaissance des bons livres* (Paris: A. Pralard, 1671);

Anne de Vaucher Gravili, "Loi et transgression dans *Les Spectacles d'horreur* de Jean-Pierre Camus, évêque de Belley," *Studi-Francesi,* 26 (January 1982): 76–81; 26 (April 1982): 20–31;

Max Vernet, *Jean-Pierre Camus: Théorie de la contre-littérature* (Paris: Nizet, 1994);

Vernet, "Péripétie et dénouement chez Jean-Pierre Camus," in *Topiques du dénouement romanesque du XIIe au XVIIIe siècle: Actes, septième Colloque international SATOR, Université Paris-Sud Orsay, 1er–3 juillet 1993,* edited by Colette Piau-Gillot (Paris: SATOR, 1993), pp. 68–74;

Thomas Worcester, *Seventeenth-Century Cultural Discourse: France and the Preaching of Bishop Camus* (Berlin & New York: De Gruyter, 1997).

Jean Chapelain
(4 December 1595 – 22 February 1674)

Jeffrey N. Peters
University of Kentucky

BOOKS: *Ode à Mgr le Cardinal Duc de Richelieu* (Paris: J. Camusat, 1633);

Paraphrase du cinquantiesme psaume, Miserere, etc. (Paris: J. Camusat, 1637);

Les Sentimens de l'Académie françoise sur la tragi-comédie du Cid, by Chapelain, Valentin Conrart, and others (Paris: J. Camusat, 1638);

Ode pour la naissance de Mgr le Comte de Dunois (Paris: Veuve de J. Camusat et P. le Petit, 1645);

Ode pour Mgr le duc d'Anguien (Paris: Veuve de J. Camusat et P. le Petit, 1646);

Ode pour Mgr le Cardinal Mazarin (Paris: Veuve de J. Camusat et P. le Petit, 1647);

La Pucelle, ou La France délivrée, poëme héroïque (Paris: A. Courbé, 1656);

Ode pour la paix et pour le mariage du Roy (Paris: A. Courbé, 1660).

Editions and Collections: *Discours pour la réception de Charles Perrault,* in *Recueil des harangues prononcées par Messieurs de l'Académie française dans leurs réceptions et en d'autres occasions depuis l'établissement de l'Académie jusqu'à présent* (Paris: Jean-Baptiste Coignard, 1689);

Liste des gens de lettres vivans en 1662, in *Mélanges de littérature tirés des lettres de M. Jean Chapelain de l'Académie française,* edited by Denis-François Camusat (Paris: Briasson, 1726);

Dialogue de la Lecture des Vieux Romans (Paris: Aubry, 1870);

Les Douze derniers chants du poème de la Pucelle, edited by H. Herluison (Orléans, 1882);

Discours de la poésie dramatique ou représentative, in *Etude sur la vie et les oeuvres de l'Abbé d'Aubignac et sur ses théories dramatiques au XVIIe siècle,* edited by Charles Arnauld (Paris: Picard, 1887);

Les Sentimens de l'Académie françoise sur la tragi-comédie du Cid, in *La Querelle du Cid: Pièces et pamphlets publiés d'après les originaux avec une introduction,* edited by Armand Gasté (Paris: H. Welter, 1898; Hildesheim & New York: Georg Olms Verlag, 1974);

Jean Chapelain (portrait by Robert Nanteuil, 1655; Biliothèque Nationale, Paris)

Discours de l'Amour, in *L'Esprit classique et la préciosité au XVIIe siècle, avec un Discours et un Dialogue inédits de Chapelain sur l'Amour et sur la Gloire,* edited by J.-E. Fidao-Justiniani (Paris: A. Picard, 1914);

Les Sentiments de l'Académie française sur Le Cid, edited by Colbert Searles (Minneapolis: University of Minnesota, 1916);

Opuscules critiques, edited by Alfred C. Hunter (Paris: E. Droz, 1936)–comprises the preface to *Le Gueux* and *Le Voleur; Lettre ou Discours de M. Chapelain à M. Favereau; Lettre sur la règle des 24 heures; Discours de la poésie dramatique ou représentative; Jugement de l'histoire des guerres Flandres du cardinal de Bentivoglio; Les Sentiments de l'Académie françoise touchant les observations faites sur la Tragi-Comédie du Cid; Projet du dic-*

tionnaire de l'Académie; Dialogue de la Lecture des Vieux Romans; Interprétation de deux passages dans la lettre de Sulpice à Cicéron sur la mort de la fille de celui-ci; the preface to *La Pucelle; Response du sieur de la Montagne au sieur du Rivage où ses observations sur le poëme de la Pucelle sont examinées; Observations sur le Clovis de Saint-Sorlin; Lettres de Monsieur Chapelain à Monsieur Colbert; Liste des gens de lettres vivans en 1662;* and excerpts from Chapelain's correspondence.

OTHER: Mateo Alemán, *Le Gueux, ou La Vie de Guzman d'Alfarache, Image de la vie humaine, en laquelle toutes les fourbes et meschancetez qui s'usent dans le monde sont plaisamment et utilement descouvertes: Version nouvelle et fidelle d'Espagnol en François, Première partie,* translated by Chapelain (Paris: P. Billaine, 1619);

Alemán, *Le Voleur, ou la Vie de Guzman, pourtraict du temps et miroir de la vie humaine: Où toutes les fourbes et meschancetez qui se font dans le monde sont utilement et plaisamment descouvertes: Pièce non encore veuë et renduë fidellement de l'original Espagnol de son premier et véritable autheur Matheo Aleman, Seconde Partie,* translated by Chapelain (Paris: T. du Bray, 1620);

Lettre ou Discours de M. Chapelain à M. Favereau, conseiller du Roy en sa cour des Aydes, portant son opinion sur le poëme d'Adonis du chevalier Marino, in Giambattista Marino, *L'Adone, Poëma del Cavalier Marino alla Maesta Christiannissima di Lodovico il decimoterzo, Rè di Francia et di Navarra, con gli Argomenti del Conte Fortuniano Sanvitale et l'Allegorie di don Lorenzo Scoto,* (Paris: O. di Varano, 1623).

Jean Chapelain was born in Paris on 4 December 1595 to bourgeois parents. His father, Sébastien Chapelain, was a respected king's notary, and Jeanne Corbière, his mother, a lover of poetry who oversaw her son's thorough education and encouraged him to pursue a literary career despite his initial interest in medicine. A devoted humanist, Chapelain learned Greek and Latin, read the Ancients, and mastered the languages and literatures of Spain and Italy. At the age of nineteen he became secretary to Sébastien le Hardy de la Trousse (who became provost-marshal of France) and later private tutor to de la Trousse's four children. During these early years, Chapelain began to write poetry and made the acquaintance of many of the most prominent literary figures of the period, including the celebrated poet François de Malherbe, whose ideas constituted the starting point of Chapelain's own thinking throughout his career. Chapelain's admiration for Malherbe as an incomparable poetic stylist who profoundly understood the nature of verse and elocution was tempered by his conviction that Malherbe's work suffered from a lack of conformity to the basic premises of Aristotelian poetics.

Through Chapelain's own writing on the formal rules of epic poetry and theater, as they could be determined from ancient treatises and their Renaissance commentaries, he was valued throughout his life for the advice on literary mechanics he provided to contemporary writers. He maintained close contact with such writers as Malherbe, Vincent Voiture, Jean Rotrou, Jean-Louis Guez de Balzac, Antoine Godeau, Jean Desmarets de Saint-Sorlin, Hippolyte-Jules Pilet de la Mesnardière, and François d'Aubignac; as Claude Favre de Vaugelas worked on his important guide to seventeenth-century usage, *Remarques sur la langue française* (Remarks on the French Language, 1647), he consulted Chapelain; Jean Racine, Jean de La Fontaine, and Nicolas Boileau-Despréaux sought Chapelain's opinion on their early work; and the epistolarian Marie de Rabutin Chantal, Madame de Sévigné considered Chapelain a mentor.

Chapelain came to the attention of the literary community in 1623. The Italian poet Giambattista Marino had recently completed *Adone* (Adonis, 1623), an epic poem that he feared might not be well received by the powerful Italian literary academies. Malherbe, whom Marino had asked to write an introduction promoting the poem, sent him to the young and unknown Chapelain after having turned down the assignment himself. Eager to demonstrate the depths of his erudition, Chapelain agreed to write a preface to Marino's poem. In the "Préface à *Adone*" (Preface to *Adonis*), Chapelain quickly concludes that *Adonis* is one of the best epic poems ever published and moves on to an elaborate discussion of *la vraisemblance,* one of the cornerstones of seventeenth-century French poetics, sometimes loosely translated as plausibility but more precisely conveyed by the technical term "verisimilitude." Drawing upon Aristotle's distinction in chapter 9 of the *Poetics* between poetry and history, Chapelain explains that poets, unlike historians, cast the world as concrete examples of universal truths. The responsibility of the poet is to construct a text that makes the events recounted seem plausible or even, to use a term Chapelain borrows from Aristotle, "probable," both within the internal logic of the poem and in relation to the reader's expectations as they have been prepared by literary tradition. Chapelain's discussion, though seminal, is only one of many versions of *la vraisemblance* that appeared over the course of the seventeenth century, and, like the others, it maintains a tension between the universality of the verisimilar event in poetry and its adherence to a set of social norms generally recognized by readers and theatergoers.

The theoretical mastery demonstrated by Chapelain in the "Préface à *Adone*" brought him the recognition he sought. Fascinated by politics and introduced by influential friends into the circle of King Louis XIII's prime minister, Armand du Plessis, Cardinal Richelieu, Chape-

First meeting of the Académie Française (1635), of which Chapelain was a founding member
(engraving by Pierre Sevin; Bibliothèque Nationale, Paris)

lain composed *Ode à Mgr le Cardinal Duc de Richelieu* (Ode to Cardinal Richelieu, 1633) in 1632. Chapelain's panegyric, considered by many at the time to be his masterpiece, raised hopes that he would become Malherbe's successor by restoring French poetry to greatness in the seventeenth century. Richelieu himself regularly consulted Chapelain on questions of literary form and even collaborated with him on the composition of *La Comédie des Tuileries* (The Comedy of the Tuileries, 1635), a play by a group named "Les Cinq Auteurs" (The Five Authors). Chapelain's literary judgments in this period thus carried real weight, and some writers feared, not without reason, that his political ambitions would result in the stifling of artistic freedom.

Chapelain's visibility in literary circles and collaborations with Richelieu led naturally to his participation in the founding of the Académie Française, which began tentatively in 1629 and gained momentum in the early 1630s. Modeled on Italy's literary academies, the Académie Française was first conceived in Chapelain's casual meetings with other poets and theorists such as Valentin Conrart, Antoine Godeau, Jean Ogier de Gombauld, and François le Metel de Boisrobert. Boisrobert met with Cardinal Richelieu to discuss the possibility of forming a literary academy in France, and Richelieu eagerly offered the financial and political support of the monarchy. Chapelain announced himself as one of the primary leaders of the movement to found the Académie Française in 1634 when he drafted his *Projet du dictionnaire*

de l'académie (Project for the Dictionary of the Academy). In this text Chapelain argued that one of the principal goals of the academy should be to oversee the composition and publication of four works: a dictionary, a grammar, a rhetoric, and a poetics. Of these four projects, only the dictionary was ever completed, but not until sixty years later in 1694 when the writer Antoine Furetière had already published his competing *Dictionnaire universel* (Universal Dictionary, 1690) and the academy had been roundly criticized for its pedantic lethargy. Most important, however, in Chapelain's 1634 dictionary essay is the initial formulation that he gives to the mandate of the Académie Française: "Le dessein de l'Académie doit être de délivrer la langue française de ses impuretés et de la rendre capable de la parfaite éloquence" (The goal of the academy must be to deliver the French language from its impurities and to render it capable of perfect eloquence).

Chapelain's statement that the primary function of the academic body should be the "purification" of the French language influenced much of the rhetoric surrounding the Académie Française during the earliest years of its existence and, indeed, throughout the seventeenth century. When the academy sent its proposal to Richelieu later in 1634 and published its official *Statuts et règlements* (Statutes and Regulations) in 1635, Chapelain's language of purification was further developed. But Chapelain's *Projet du dictionnaire de l'académie* also laid out the basic procedures to be followed by the forty members of the Académie Française. The academicians were to decide which contemporary literary works were of the highest quality and to establish a dictionary based on the vocabulary those works employed. They would then debate the meaning and use of those words before agreeing to include them in the final dictionary. Because they were also supposed to be models of pure and eloquent speech themselves, the members of the academy decided to give regular speeches before their colleagues demonstrating their chosen aesthetic criteria. In his "Discours de l'amour" (Discourse on Love), delivered before the Académie Française in 1635, Chapelain argued that love was a passion that inhibited the proper operation of human reason.

In 1637 the fledgling Académie Française turned its attention to a literary debate that became its most notorious public intervention and produced the document by Chapelain for which he is best remembered today. During the winter of 1637 the young playwright Pierre Corneille had premiered his tragicomedy Le Cid. The play was an enormous success with both audiences and critics. Richelieu professed to have loved the play, and Chapelain himself wrote in a 1637 letter to Balzac that Le Cid had given him much pleasure. Shortly after the opening of the play, however, another playwright, Georges de Scudéry, submitted a devastating critique of Le Cid to the Académie Française, demanding that its members censure the apparently irresponsible Corneille. The debate over Corneille's play, which has come to be known as the Querelle du Cid (Quarrel of Le Cid) and which pitted those who sided with Scudéry against those who supported Corneille, generated vehement responses. Members of the opposing parties wrote lengthy pamphlets against or in favor of the play, which they circulated publicly. The argument, which fundamentally debated whether theater has a social function, became so heated that Richelieu was forced to enter the discussion and submit the matter to the Académie Française. Seizing the opportunity to speak for the French crown, the Académie Française published an official decision on Le Cid and asked Chapelain, at Richelieu's request, to be its primary author.

Les Sentimens de l'Académie françoise sur la tragi-comédie du Cid (Opinions of the French Academy on the Tragicomedy of the Cid, 1638) caused Chapelain a great deal of anxiety. As he wrote in several letters, and as is evident from the text of Les Sentimens de l'Académie françoise sur la tragi-comédie du Cid, Chapelain did not wish to alienate Corneille, whom he later described in his Liste des gens de lettres vivans en 1662 (1662) (List of Writers Living in 1662) as "un prodige d'esprit et l'ornement du théâtre français" (a miracle of intellect and the ornament of the French theater). Moreover, Chapelain sincerely liked the play. But he also could not resist cultivating Richelieu's

favor by taking up the question of Le Cid. Although Les Sentimens de l'Académie françoise sur la tragi-comédie du Cid, which were revised by the academy, as well as by Richelieu himself (Chapelain's manuscript shows comments handwritten in the margins by Richelieu), concluded that Le Cid is basically flawed, Chapelain also had harsh words for Scudéry's original Observations sur le Cid (1637) and explicitly exonerated Corneille from Scudéry's charge of plagiarism. Chapelain is unyielding, however, when it comes to the issue of la vraisemblance. Repeating much of the material on verisimilitude that he had already worked out in his "Préface à Adone," Chapelain wrote that the conclusion of the play was immoral and the behavior of Chimène, its female protagonist, monstrous. Chapelain argued that although Corneille was merely following the true events of Spanish history, the French stage could not tolerate the representation of immorality that went unpunished, however true.

The conclusions drawn by Chapelain during the Querelle du Cid, together with the theoretical principles that he had begun to formulate in the "Preface à Adone," are often considered by French literary historians to have led to an emphasis on formal rules in seventeenth-century literature. Some scholars, however, have argued that Chapelain's conception of the rules of literary composition were far more subtle than historians and critics often have suggested. Occasionally pointing out that the rules needed to be flexible rather than absolute, Chapelain distinguished carefully between the technical perfection of a Malherbe and the poetic genius of a Corneille. In his letters, Chapelain wrote that the formal innovations of Malherbe were too confining and risked stifling what he called "l'agrément inexplicable" (the inexplicable pleasure), the mysterious power that could emerge in the best poetry. Chapelain, in fact, was far less concerned with rules than with notions of "régularité" (regularity). The "Préface à Adone" might be more properly described as a theory of regularity in epic poetry. According to this thinking, the subject of a poem must be fully natural, which implies conformity with forms of knowledge present in nature (lyricism is natural; magic is unnatural), proportionate to the episodes and narrative elements that convey it, and of some moral and social utility (it must instruct). Chapelain's writings on technical matters thus might also have been a way of finding access to a poetic perfection that he would never achieve through genius. Such was his beloved and, as many have written, failed epic poem, La Pucelle, ou La France délivrée (The Maiden, or France Liberated, 1656).

When Chapelain conceived of La Pucelle in the early 1630s, hopes ran high for his literary future, and he received at first an enormous amount of encouragement. Friends heard him read early versions of the poem at the Hôtel de Rambouillet, and Henri d'Orleans, duc de

Longueville, to whom it was dedicated, became so enamored of the project that he awarded Chapelain a pension. Chapelain worked for almost thirty years on *La Pucelle,* which was finally published in 1656. Reactions were politely approving, although de Longueville's wife, Geneviève de Bourbon, called the poem boring. In fact, Chapelain's poem suffered from a host of problems that guaranteed its eventual failure. As Chapelain himself knew, the epic poem had not been well represented in France. The French had no Torquato Tasso or Edmund Spenser, and epic poems by Marc-Antoine de Gérard, sieur de Saint-Amant (*Moïse Sauvé* [Moses Saved, 1653]), Saint-Sorlin (*Clovis,* 1654), and Scudéry (*Alaric,* 1654) had been unremarkable. That Chapelain chose Joan of Arc for his heroine further doomed the poem, for the medieval savior of France, a non-noble whom some considered merely the product of cultural superstition, had virtually been forgotten during the Renaissance and seventeenth century. For Chapelain, Joan represented the very soul of France. But Joan, mistreated as she had been by early modern historians, elicited little enthusiasm from among seventeenth-century readers. Moreover, many critics of the poem wanted to know how a woman could be the protagonist of an epic poem when the models for such work were the highly masculine heroes Achilles, Odysseus, and Aeneas; Aristotle himself understood women to be an error of nature. Chapelain spent several pages of his preface to *La Pucelle* defending his choice. Joan of Arc, Chapelain wrote, had been a real person, so the possibility of her heroism could not be disputed. Women, he continued, were as capable of virtuous action in the service of the fatherland as men, even if they more generally must be confined to the domestic sphere. Chapelain believed that *La Pucelle,* devoid of narrative digressions and meaningless obstacles, embodied the poetic virtues of simplicity and unity. Chapelain's readers, however, complained that the action was dull, that the story moved too slowly, that it was too full of insignificant facts and details, that it lacked imagination, and that it was sterile and rigid.

In a formal treatise, the theorist La Mesnardière, writing under the pseudonym du Rivage, systematically critiqued *La Pucelle,* claiming not only that women are not capable of heroic virtue but also that Chapelain's representation of Joan's death at the conclusion of the poem is not appropriate in an epic poem. La Mesnardière also complains that Chapelain fails to follow the principle of *bienséance,* a complex and ambiguous concept that is intended in seventeenth-century France to embody Aristotle's discussion of character, which English poetics translated as *decorum.* Although character for Aristotle involves several qualities, La Mesnardière focuses primarily on the notion of moral goodness, suggesting that King Charles VII behaves in morally unacceptable ways.

Title page for the book in which Chapelain reported the opinion of the Académie Française on the controversy inspired by Corneille's 1637 production of Le Cid *(Bibliothèque Nationale, Paris)*

La Mesnardière goes on to demonstrate that Chapelain's poem lacks the element of the supernatural that had always been present in the epic, that many of the characters are ridiculous and inconsistent, and that the poem is stylistically flawed. In a response to La Mesnardière that was never published during the seventeenth century, the *Réponse du sieur de la Montagne au sieur du Rivage où ses observations sur le poème de la Pucelle sont examinées* (Response of Mr. de la Montagne to Mr. du Rivage in Which His Observations on the Poem of the Virgin are Examined, 1936), Chapelain responds point by point to each of La Mesnardière's accusations. He tells his critic that his own response was necessitated by La Mesnardière's ignorance in matters of Aristotelian poetics. Responding to La Mesnardière, who suggests that an epic poet of great renown would be needed to undertake what Chapelain has attempted in *La Pucelle,* Chapelain writes tersely,

"Chapelain est poète épique de grand nom" (Chapelain is an epic poet of great renown).

Chapelain's conception of his own importance as a writer of epic poetry demonstrates the extent to which he believed that poetic greatness could be attained through the achievement of formal regularity. Indeed, the aesthetic qualities that made Chapelain's poem a failure as a piece of art are the same ones that summarized the theoretical principles upon which Chapelain's most significant contribution to seventeenth-century French literature was based. Chapelain's preface to *La Pucelle* includes an unironic evaluation of his own skills and demonstrates perhaps a real understanding of the nature of his literary significance: "J'avoue de n'avoir que bien peu des qualités requises en un poète héroïque. . . . J'ai apporté seulement à l'exécution de mon projet une passable connaissance de ce qui était nécessaire pour ne le pas faire irrégulier" (I admit to having few of the qualities required of the heroic poet. . . . I have brought to the execution of my project only a passable knowledge of what was necessary not to make it irregular). When Chapelain responds to La Mesnardière's critique, he does so by demonstrating how the details of his poem are consistent with the procedures of epic poetry as they had been developed in antiquity. Beyond simply suggesting that women are capable of heroic virtue as he had in the preface to *La Pucelle,* he explains that the true function of poetry, as Aristotle described it in the *Poetics,* is the representation or imitation (*mimesis*) of human action, rather than humans themselves. Joan's action in the poem is thus more important than Joan herself, while Chapelain's portrayal of her activities is justified by Aristotelian theory. With regard to La Mesnardière's assertion that Chapelain's characters do not conform to the demands of *la bienséance,* Chapelain responds that their actions are in keeping with historical record and that, more important, their behavior is consistent with their character throughout the poem. In his second *Discours de la poésie dramatique ou représentative* (Discourse on Dramatic or Representational Poetry, circa 1635), Chapelain had already defined *la bienséance* as behavior that is consistent with a character's age, sex, and social station—whether he or she is considered morally "good" or "bad." The importance of *La Pucelle,* then, according to Chapelain, derives from its representation of essential truths of human virtue that may only be derived by poets gifted with a profound understanding of the principles of ancient poetics. As he writes in an undated preface to the final books of the poem (completed in 1670), *La Pucelle* is a monument to truth, not because it demonstrates a "grande élévation d'esprit" (great elevation of intellect), but because it observes a host of formal requirements listed by Chapelain in the preface, including its adherence to the rules of imitation, the just proportion and unity of its subject, and the moral instruction it provides.

La Pucelle might quietly have been forgotten by Chapelain's contemporaries, as well as by modern scholars of seventeenth-century French literature, were it not for "l'affaire des gratifications" (the affair of the stipends). In 1662 Chapelain allied himself with his long-time friend Jean-Baptiste Colbert, Louis XIV's finance minister, who was seeking to consolidate his own influence with the king. Colbert and Chapelain chose to honor Louis XIV with a series of panegyrics written in verse and prose by the greatest writers of the century, a project that produced Chapelain's *Liste des gens de lettres vivans en 1662.* In this document Chapelain listed ninety contemporary authors, including himself, whose literary abilities made them worthy of Louis's patronage. When the writing community learned that Chapelain alone had chosen the authors who would receive stipends from the king and that Chapelain himself had received 3,000 francs for a sonnet in honor of Louis that was universally deemed absurd, scandal ensued. In particular, the writer now regarded as the central theorist of classicism in the seventeenth century, Nicolas Boileau-Despréaux, who was not included on Chapelain's list, wrote a satire (no. VII, 1663) in which he ridiculed Chapelain and his writing; he repeatedly attacked Chapelain in his later work, referring to him as a "froid, sec, dur, rude auteur" (cold, dry, hard, rude author) and a "digne objet de Satire" (worthy object of satire). As a result, a respected seventeenth-century authority on matters of literary technique became the object of much mean-spirited gossip. Chapelain became known as the author of a silly and boring epic poem and a person who had more political influence than his meager talent justified. Indeed, literary history has not been kind to Chapelain. As recently as 1954, the *Dictionnaire des lettres françaises* (Dictionary of French Letters) called the poet's work "illisible" (unreadable) and his *Pucelle* "ridicule" (ridiculous). Notable twentieth-century critics have described Chapelain's epic as being devoid of ideas and "détestable" (detestable), the ill-conceived product of a writer so concerned with pleasing—his friends, the court, the kings of France themselves—that his judgment was fatally obscured. In an irreverent assessment of Chapelain's life and work, the nineteenth-century poet Théophile Gautier wrote that reading Chapelain's verse out loud conjured wagons full of paving stones being overturned and carts bearing loads of iron bars passing in the street. Even Chapelain's generous and sympathetic biographer Georges Collas noted that *La Pucelle* lacked any bold conception, original thought, or sincere emotion.

Modern evaluations such as these are due in large part to the opinions of Jean Chapelain's contemporaries who believed that the epic poet wrongly esteemed himself the successor to Homer and Virgil

First page of the manuscript for Chapelain's Les Sentimens de l'Académie françoise
sur la tragi-comédie du Cid, *1638 (Bibliothèque Nationale, Paris)*

while wielding an unreasonable, and unwarranted, degree of political influence in the world of seventeenth-century letters. His propensity to curry political favor brought Chapelain both the scorn of those who had initially valued his insight and the opinion of history that has followed him since his death on 22 February 1674. Still considered a mediocre poet and a scheming sycophant in the service of ministers and kings, Chapelain is now recognized by modern scholars as an important theorist of the seventeenth century.

Letters:

Jean Chapelain, *Lettres,* 2 volumes, edited by P. Tamizey de Larroque (Paris: Imprimerie Nationale, 1880–1883);

Lettres inédites de Jean Chapelain à P. D. Huet, 1658–1673, edited by Léon-G. Pelissier (Nogent-le-Rotrou: Daupeley-Gouverneur, 1894);

Jean Chapelain: Soixante dix-sept lettres inédites à Nicolas Heinsius (1649–1658), edited by Bernard Bray (The Hague: M. Nijhoff, 1966).

Bibliography:

Georges Collas, "Bibliographie," in his *Jean Chapelain, 1595–1674: Etude historique et littéraire, D'après des Documents inédits* (Paris: Perrin, 1912), pp. 479–522.

Biography:

Georges Collas, *Jean Chapelain, 1595–1674: Etude historique et littéraire D'après des Documents inédits* (Paris: Perrin, 1912).

References:

Antoine Adam, *Histoire de la littérature française au XVIIe siècle, Tome III: L'Apogée du siècle* (Paris: Editions Mondiales, 1962);

E. B. O. Borgerhoff, *The Freedom of French Classicism* (Princeton: Princeton University Press, 1950);

Bernard Bray, "La Constitution du texte épistolaire: L'Exemple de Chapelain," in *Les voies de l'invention aux XVIe et XVIIe siècles: Etudes génétiques,* edited by Bernard Beugnot and Robert Melançon (Montreal: Département d'études françaises, 1993), pp. 209–223;

Bray, "Critique et forme épistolaire: le dialogue de Jean Chapelain et de Guez de Balzac," in *Critique et Création littéraires en France au XVIIe siècle* (Paris: Publications du CNRS, 1977), pp. 103–113;

René Bray, *La Formation de la doctrine classique en France* (Paris: Nizet, 1961);

Dictionnaire des lettres françaises: Le Dix-septième siècle, edited by Georges Grente (Paris: Fayard, 1954);

Joseph-Emil Fidao-Justiniani, *L'Esprit classique et la préciosité au XVIIe siècle: avec un Discours et un Dialogue inédits de Chapelain sur l'Amour et sur la Gloire* (Paris: A. Picard, 1914);

Georges Forestier, "Imitation parfaite et vraisemblance absolue. Réflexions sur un paradoxe classique," *Poétique,* 82 (1989): 187–202;

Théophile Gautier, *Les Grotesques,* edited by Cecilia Rizza (Fasano, Italy: Schena / Paris: Nizet, 1985);

Carlo Ginzburg, "Fiction as Historical Evidence: A Dialogue in Paris, 1646," in *Rediscovering History: Culture, Politics, and the Psyche,* edited by Michael S. Roth (Stanford: Stanford University Press, 1994), pp. 378–388;

Alfred C. Hunter, *Lexique de la langue de Chapelain* (Geneva: Slatikine, 1971);

John D. Lyons, *Kingdom of Disorder: The Theory of Tragedy in Classical France* (West Lafayette, Ind.: Purdue University Press, 1999);

Daniel Mornet, *Histoire de la littérature française classique* (Paris: A. Colin, 1950);

Jeffrey N. Peters, "Ideology, Culture and the Threat of Allegory in Chapelain's Theory of *La Vraisemblance,*" *Romanic Review,* 89, no. 4 (1998): 491–505;

Bradley Rubidge, "Arma Virumque: The Querelle de la Pucelle and the Gender of Epic Heroes," *Papers on French Seventeenth-Century Literature,* 19, no. 37 (1992): 457–464;

Colbert Searles, ed., *Les Sentiments de l'Académie françoise sur la tragi-comédie du Cid* (Minneapolis: Bulletin of the University of Minnesota, 1916);

Gédéon Tallemant des Réaux, *Historiettes,* 2 volumes (Paris: Gallimard, 1960);

Abby Zanger, "Classical Anxiety: Performance, Perfection and the Issue of Identity," in *L'Age du théâtre en France/The Age of Theater in France,* edited by David Trott and Nicole Boursier (Edmonton: Academic, 1988), pp. 327–339;

Roger Zuber, "Chapelain et les règles," in *Précis de littérature française du XVIIe siècle,* edited by Jean Mesnard (Paris: PUF, 1990), pp. 114–118.

Papers:

The publications, letters, and manuscripts of Jean Chapelain may be found at the Bibliothèque Nationale in Paris.

Pierre Corneille

(6 June 1606 – 1 October 1684)

John D. Lyons
University of Virginia

BOOKS: *Clitandre, ou L'Innocence délivrée* (Paris: F. Targa, 1632);

Mélite, ou Les Fausses Lettres (Paris: F. Targa, 1633);

La Vefve, ou Le Traistre trahy (Paris: F. Targa, 1634);

La Galerie du Palais, ou L'Amie rivalle (Paris: A. Courbé, 1637);

La Place Royalle, ou L'Amoureux extravagant (Paris: A. Courbé, 1637);

Le Cid (Paris: A. Courbé, 1637; Paris: F. Targa, 1637); translated by Joseph Rutter as *The Cid* (London: Printed by John Haviland for Thomas Walkly, 1637);

La Suivante (Paris: A. Courbé, 1637);

Excuse à Ariste (N.p., 1637);

Lettre apologétique du Sr Corneille, contenant sa responce aux observations faictes par le Sr Scudéry sur le Cid (N.p., 1637);

La Comédie des Tuileries, by Corneille, François Le Métel de Boisrobert, Guillaume Colletet, Claude de L'Estoile, and Jean de Rotrou (Paris: A. Courbé, 1638);

L'Aveugle de Smyrne, by Corneille, Boisrobert, Colletet, L'Estoile, and Rotrou (Paris: A. Courbé, 1638);

Médée (Paris: F. Targa, 1639);

L'Illusion comique (Paris: F. Targa, 1639); translated by John Cairncross as *The Theatrical Illusion* (Harmondsworth, U.K.: Penguin, 1975);

Horace (Paris: A. Courbé, 1641); translated by William Lower as *Horatius: A Roman Tragedy* (London: Printed for G. Bedell and T. Collins, 1656);

Cinna, ou La Clémence d'Auguste (Paris: T. Quinet, 1643);

Polyeucte martyr (Paris: A. de Sommaville et A. Courbé, 1643); translated by Lower as *Polyeuctes, or The Martyr* (London: Printed by Thomas Roycroft for G. Bedell and T. Collins, 1655);

La Mort de Pompée (Paris: A. de Sommaville et A. Courbé, 1644); translated by Katherine Philips as *Pompey* (London: Printed for John Crooke, 1663);

Le Menteur (Paris: A. de Sommaville et A. Courbé, 1644); translated as *The Mistaken Beauty, or The Lyar* (London: Printed for Simon Neale, 1685);

Pierre Corneille (engraving by Charles Le Brun, circa 1647; from the album for Corneille's Œuvres, 1862; Thomas Cooper Library, University of South Carolina)

La Suite du Menteur (Paris: A. de Sommaville et A. Courbé, 1645);

Théodore, vierge et martyre (Paris: T. Quinet, 1646);

Rodogune, princesse des Parthes (Paris: T. Quinet, 1647); translated by Stanhope Aspinwall as *Rodogune, or The Rival Brothers* (London: Printed for Stanhope

Aspinwall and sold by Dodsley [and others], 1765);

Héraclius, empereur d'Orient (Paris: T. Quinet, 1647); translated by Lodowick Carlell as *Heraclius, Emperour of the East* (London: Printed for John Starkey, 1664);

Dessein de la tragédie d'Andromède, représentée sur le théâtre royal de Bourbon, contenant l'ordre des scènes, la description des théâtres et des machines et les paroles qui se chantent en musique (Paris: A. Courbé, 1650);

Don Sanche d'Arragon (Paris: A. Courbé, 1650);

Andromède (Rouen: L. Maurry / Paris: C. de Sercy, 1651);

Nicomède (Rouen: L. Maurry / Paris: C. de Sercy, 1651); translated by John Dancer as *Nicomede* (London: Printed for Francis Kirkman, 1671);

Pertharite, roy des Lombards (Paris: G. de Luyne, 1653);

Œdipe (Paris: A. Courbé et G. de Luyne, 1659);

Théâtre de Corneille, revu et corrigé par l'autheur, 3 volumes (Paris: A. Courbé et G. de Luyne, 1660)— includes "Discours de l'utilité et des parties du poème dramatique," "Discours de la tragédie et des moyens de la traiter selon le vraisemblable ou le nécessaire," and "Discours des trois unités d'action, de jour, et de lieu";

Desseins de La Toison d'or, tragédie, représentée par la troupe royale du Marests, chez M. le marquis de Sourdéac, en son chasteau du Neufbourg, pour réjouissance publique du mariage du roy et de la paix avec l'Espagne, et ensuite sur le théâtre royal du Marests (Paris: A Courbé et G. de Luyne, 1661);

La Toison d'Or (Paris: A. Courbé et G. de Luyne, 1661);

Sertorius (Paris: A. Courbé et G. de Luyne, 1662);

Sophonisbe (Paris: G. de Luyne, 1663);

Othon (Paris: G. de Luyne, 1665);

Agésilas (Paris: T. Jolly, 1666; Paris: G. de Luyne, 1666);

Attila, roy des Huns (Paris: G. de Luyne, 1667);

Psiché, by Corneille, Molière, and Philippe Quinault (Paris: P. Le Monnier, 1671);

Tite et Bérénice (Paris: T. Jolly, 1671; Paris: G. de Luyne, 1671);

Pulchérie (Paris: G. de Luyne, 1673);

Suréna, général des Parthes (Paris: G. de Luyne, 1675).

Collections: *Œuvres,* 12 volumes, edited by Charles Marty-Laveaux (Paris: Hachette, 1862–1868);

Œuvres complètes, 3 volumes, edited by Georges Couton, Bibliothèque de la Pléiade, nos. 19, 20, 340 (Paris: Gallimard, 1980–1987).

PLAY PRODUCTIONS: *Mélite, ou Les Fausses Lettres,* Paris, Jeu de Paume Berthault, 1629–1630 season;

Clitandre, ou L'Innocence délivrée, Paris, Jeu de Paume Berthault, early 1631;

La Vefve, ou Le Traistre trahy, Paris, Jeu de Paume de la Sphère, early 1632;

La Suivante, Paris, Jeu de Paume de La Fontaine, early 1632–1634;

La Galerie du Palais, ou L'Amie rivalle, Paris, Jeu de Paume de La Fontaine, 1633;

La Place Royalle, ou L'Amoureux extravagant, Paris, Jeu de Paume de La Fontaine, 1633–1634 season;

Médée, Paris, Théâtre du Marais, early 1635;

La Comédie des Tuileries, by Corneille, François Le Métel de Boisrobert, Guillaume Colletet, Claude de L'Estoile, and Jean de Rotrou, Paris, Arsenal, 4 March 1635;

L'Illusion comique, Paris, Théâtre du Marais, 1635–1636 season;

Le Cid, Paris, Théâtre du Marais, 1636–1637 season;

L'Aveugle de Smyrne, by Corneille, Boisrobert, Colletet, L'Estoile, and Rotrou, Paris, 22 February 1637;

Horace, Paris, Théâtre du Marais, 19 May 1640;

Cinna, ou La Clémence d'Auguste, Paris, Théâtre du Marais, July or August 1642;

Polyeucte martyr, Paris, Théâtre du Marais, December 1642 or January 1643;

La Mort de Pompée, Paris, Théâtre du Marais, November or December 1643;

Le Menteur, Paris, Théâtre du Marais, 1643–1644 season;

La Suite du Menteur, Paris, Théâtre du Marais, 1644–1645 season;

Rodogune, princesse des Parthes, Paris, Théâtre du Marais, 1644–1645 season;

Théodore, vierge et martyre, Paris, Théâtre du Marais, 1645–1646;

Héraclius, empereur d'Orient, Paris, Théâtre du Marais, January 1647;

Andromède, Paris, Théâtre du Petit-Bourbon, December 1649 or January 1650;

Don Sanche d'Arragon, Paris, Hôtel de Bourgogne, 1649–1650 season;

Nicomède, Paris, Hôtel de Bourgogne, February 1651;

Pertharite, roy des Lombards, Paris, Hôtel de Bourgogne, early 1652;

Œdipe, Paris, Hôtel de Bourgogne, 25 January 1659;

La Toison d'Or, Neufbourg, 1660; Paris, Théâtre du Marais, 17 February 1661;

Sertorius, Paris, Théâtre du Marais, 25 February 1662;

Sophonisbe, Paris, Hôtel de Bourgogne, 12 January 1663;

Othon, Versailles, 3 August 1664;

Agésilas, Paris, Hôtel de Bourgogne, February 1666;

Attila, roy des Huns, Paris, 4 March 1667;

Tite et Bérénice, Paris, 28 November 1670;

Psiché, by Corneille, Molière, and Philippe Quinault, Paris, Palais des Tuileries, 17 January 1671;

Pulchérie, Paris, Théâtre du Marais, November 1672;

Suréna, général des Parthes, Paris, Hôtel de Bourgogne, December 1674.

OTHER: "P. Cornelii Rothomagensis, ad Illustrissimi Francisci, Archiepiscopi, Normaniae Primatis," in *Epinicia Musarum Eminentissimo Cardinali Duci de Richelieu,* edited by François Le Métel de Boisrobert (Paris: S. Cramoisy, 1634);

Thomas à Kempis, *L'Imitation de Jésus-Christ,* translated by Corneille (Paris: R. Ballard, 1656);

Charles de La Rue, *Poème sur les Victoires du Roy,* translated by Corneille (Paris: G. de Luyne, T. Jolly, et L. Billaine, 1667);

L'Office de la Sainte Vierge, traduit en françois tant en vers qu'en prose avec les sept pseaumes pénitentiaux, les vespres et complies du dimanche et tous les hymnes du bréviaire roman, translated by Corneille (Paris: R. Ballard, 1670).

SELECTED PERIODICAL PUBLICATIONS– UNCOLLECTED: "Sur la prise de Mastric," *Mercure Galant,* 6 (1674): 37;

"Au Roy" and "Placet au Roy," *Nouveau Mercure Galant,* 1 (1677): 46–54;

"Je suis vieux, belle Iris," *Nouveau Mercure Galant,* 3 (1677): 97–100.

The most successful playwright of the reign of Louis XIII, Pierre Corneille was the author of thirty-three plays and of the most important study of dramatic aesthetics in his century, known as "Trois discours sur le poème dramatique" (Three Discourses on the Dramatic Poem). Although his plays include comedies and tragicomedies as well, Corneille's best-known works exemplify what is now usually called French classical tragedy. He strongly influenced the work of his younger rival, Jean Racine, who eventually eclipsed Corneille in the last third of the century. Corneille favored dramatic subjects centered on individual heroism, the dialectic of love and honor, discovery or transformation of individual identity, intergenerational differences, the contrast between political ideals and realpolitik, and the stern requirements of civic or family duty. His plots and characters are often extreme and, if taken out of the carefully constructed dramatic context, appear unbelievable. In sharp contrast to Racine, Corneille almost invariably showed his protagonists as ennobled by the challenge of unusual circumstances. This optimistic view of human nature and the tendency of Corneille's tragedies to have happy endings often puzzle modern readers more accustomed to the violent denouements of Shakespearean tragedies.

An unusual characteristic of Corneille's career as a playwright is that the author himself self-consciously created public perception of that career. He generally published the texts of his plays soon after their first production, assuring for himself the *privilège* (the equivalent of copyright), profiting financially not only from the initial stage performance but also from the sale of books. Corneille thus established his independence from the companies of players and became a model for the modern concept of the freelance dramatic writer, as distinct from such earlier French playwrights as Alexandre Hardy, who were largely employees of the acting companies. Shaping contemporary and future reception of his work was one of Corneille's important concerns, and he exerted his influence over readers through his prefaces, his revised editions of his early plays, his *examens* (or retrospective critiques) of each play written prior to the 1660 collected edition, and his use of his own works as the major examples in his "Trois discours sur le poème dramatique." As a consequence of the author's using examples of his works in these essays, readers almost inevitably view each play according to the author's commentary.

Born 6 June 1606 in Rouen, Normandy, Corneille was atypical among leading literary figures of his time by remaining a provincial until late into his adult life. His father was an administrator of natural resources for the viscount of Rouen, and the young Corneille was carefully prepared for a career as a middle-class legal professional. As a student in Jesuit school in Rouen, from 1615 to 1622, he was immersed in Latin, the standard language of instruction, and he no doubt participated in the Latin plays, usually based on the lives of saints and martyrs, that were typical of the Jesuit curriculum. Debating was also a strong point of this education, and much of Corneille's drama bears the stamp of Jesuit eloquence and aspiration to heroic service.

Having received his law degree in 1624, Corneille acquired two positions in government, one in the administration of "Eaux et Forêts" (natural resources) and the other with the admiralty court of Rouen, a major port. As the second largest city in France, though with a population of no more than eighty thousand, Rouen was frequently visited by traveling theater companies, and legend has it that the young lawyer met the actor Montdory in Rouen and pressed upon him his first play, the comedy *Mélite, ou Les Fausses Lettres* (Melite, or the Forged Letters, first performed 1629–1630; first published 1633). Montdory's company gave this play its first public performance, in Paris, where the theatrical season usually ran from November to May.

Corneille's career may be divided into four stages: the early period (1629–1636), dominated by comedies, up to *L'Illusion comique;* the crucial turning point of his tragicomedy *Le Cid* and its ensuing controversy from 1637–1639; the period of his maturity from *Horace* to

Frontispiece and title page for the play that caused a literary controversy in France over the social value of theater (Bibliothèque Municipale de Caen)

Pertharite, roy des Lombards (1640–1652); the final period of slower production from *Œdipe* and the great edition of collected dramatic works until his last play, *Suréna* (1659–1674), ten years before his death. Yet, Corneille's work was so varied throughout his career that division into periods is not especially helpful.

Success came fairly early to Corneille as an author of comedies of young love, with plots based largely on misunderstandings and misinformation spread about by jealous rivals. In most of these plays the men and women characters who initially seem destined to marry are attracted to others in the course of the play, and new couples are formed in a series of shifts often described as based on a "pastoral" model of love intrigue. Of these comedies, *La Place Royalle, ou L'Amoureux extravagant* (The Place Royale, or the Extravagant Lovers, first performed in the 1633–1634 season; published 1637) and *L'Illusion comique* (The

Comic Illusion, first performed in the 1635–1636 season; published 1639) are the most original and have continued to attract the attention of critics and directors. In *La Place Royale, ou L'Amoureux extravagant* the obstacle to the hero's love for the heroine does not come from a jealous rival but from the hero himself. Alidor finds his love for Angélique too intense and limiting and therefore arranges to give her to a friend. This comedy of an internal struggle among desires for love and freedom, for self-mastery, and for glory–concepts that in the play tend to merge–is sometimes seen as prefiguring the tragic heroes and heroines of the following decades. *L'illusion comique* is an example of metatheater, or a play-within-a-play. In it a father looking for his son is aided by a magician who shows him "magical" representations of his son's adventures. Only at the end of the play does the father learn that what he has seen are his son's performances as an actor in a work that glorifies dramatic illusion. Corneille's standing as a dramatic author can be gauged by his invitation to join the group of authors working with and for the most powerful man in France, the duc de Richelieu, cardinal and prime minister. This group, known as the "Five Authors," produced the first of its negligible plays, *La Comédie des Tuileries,* in 1635.

In 1637 Corneille had his breakthrough. Although he had already written a tragicomedy, *Clitandre, ou L'Innocence délivrée* (1630–1631), and a tragedy in the manner of Seneca, *Médée* (Medea), which seems to have been a success in 1634–1635, it was his second tragicomedy, *Le Cid,* that made him well-known. Like all his other plays, *Le Cid* is written in *vers alexandrin* (twelve-syllable verse) in rhymed couplets—the established norm for drama in Corneille's day. *Le Cid* also includes two rare instances of metrical variation, called *stances,* used only in soliloquies. These stances are notable for being discourse that is divided into groups—stanzas—each of which repeats a varied metrical pattern with a relatively complex rhyme scheme. *Le Cid* was a huge popular success at its first performance at the Marais theater during the 1636–1637 season (probably in January 1637) and a success at the court (performed three times within a month of its premiere at the Louvre and twice at Richelieu's palace). That the expression "Beau comme *Le Cid* . . ." ("As beautiful as *Le Cid* . . .") remains part of the French idiom even today attests to Corneille's major theatrical achievement. Corneille's greatest moment of triumph, however, was also a critical and even political turning point for French drama in general. *Le Cid* provoked the polemic known as the "Quarrel of *Le Cid,*" prompted many broadsheets and pamphlets, and occasioned the intervention of the newly formed Académie Française at the order of the highest political authority, Cardinal Richelieu.

Le Cid, set in twelfth-century Spain, is the story of the young lovers Rodrigue and Chimène, whose apparently perfect match is disrupted by the political rivalry of their fathers. When Chimène's father publicly insults the elderly Don Diègue, the latter orders his son Rodrigue to defend the family honor by fighting a duel in his father's place. Knowing that he will offend Chimène whether he fights or not—if he fails to fight successfully he will lose his honor and thus be unworthy of his lover, but if he does succeed he will be the killer of the father of the woman he loves—Rodrigue challenges and kills the older and more experienced warrior. Upon the death of her father, Chimène immediately demands that the king execute his killer; yet, in private she admits that she not only loves Rodrigue, she "adores" him. Following the logic of *générosité* (nobility of spirit), Chimène admires Rodrigue for his decision to challenge her father. Hence, far from illustrating a direct

conflict between love and duty—as the play is sometimes said to do—*Le Cid* represents a much more complex dialectic, in which love is amplified and purified by the fulfillment of duty. In two private encounters with Rodrigue, Chimène admits that she loves him, refuses to kill him with the sword he offers her, and urges him to defeat the knight named by the king to fight a duel with Rodrigue on her behalf. Chimène's continued public calls for Rodrigue's execution are thus combined with her statements to him that she loves him precisely because he has shown himself capable of the highest feats of honor—not only did he win his duel against the greatest warrior of the kingdom but, shortly after, led a small group of Spanish fighters to victory over the Moors, earning the Arabic title of *cid,* or leader. He has thus set his reputation and that of his family over pleasure and merited her love. Chimène also argues that she must likewise pursue his death in order to prove her own honor and thus continue to be worthy of him. Chimène establishes a distinction between her private love for Rodrigue (she does not want to bring about his death but only to show that she is doing as much as she can toward that end) and the public requirement of reputation, without which she would not be worthy of him. Finally, tricked by the king into admitting her love, Chimène receives the royal command to set aside her quest for vengeance in the interest of the kingdom, since Rodrigue, *Le Cid,* is indispensable for the continuing war against the Moors.

The importance of *Le Cid* for subsequent French drama is immense, and at the core of its success is its representation of the mutual love of Rodrigue and Chimène. This depiction was considered so irresistibly touching that before the end of the century, Jacques-Bénigne Bossuet, bishop of Meaux, an outspoken enemy of all theater, denounced the play as one of the most dangerous examples of erotic love, precisely because this love appears good and noble. Racine's drama, rather than Corneille's, is usually considered to be more exclusively concerned with love. Corneille himself helped form this impression by declaring in 1660 that the dignity of the tragic genre "requires some great matter of State, or some passion that is more noble and more male than love." Yet, within *Le Cid* the hero's view that love is a crucial and noble calling, worthy of the greatest effort and fully on a par with military or political achievement, is contrasted with his father's more traditional belief that love is ephemeral and that women are basically interchangeable. No doubt influenced by the growing cultural role of women as it was manifested in such contemporary venues as the Hôtel de Rambouillet, which he frequented, Corneille celebrates the love of a couple mutually attracted by the merit and achievement of each other. Although men

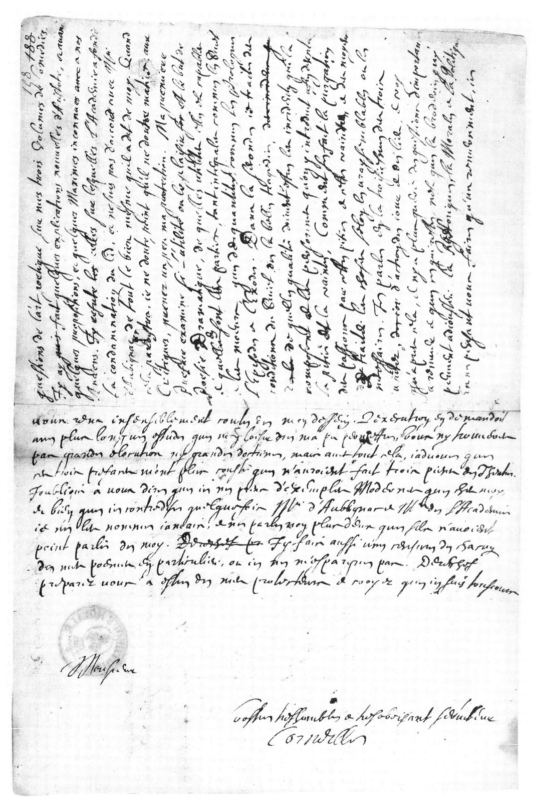

Letter from Corneille to the abbé de Pure, concerning the controversy over Le Cid *(Bibliothèque Nationale, Paris)*

and women must use different means to gain recognition–Chimène, for instance, cannot rival Rodrigue for military prowess–the central couple of the play exemplifies a certain equality of expectation and respect. Most importantly, in view of Racine's subsequent representation of love as a weakness, as independent of merit, and even as pathological, love in *Le Cid* and many other Cornelian tragedies has the logic and idealism of a pure meritocracy.

The huge success of the play not only stirred jealousy among other playwrights but also led Corneille to demand a supplementary payment from the actors, over the original fee he had charged for first-performance rights. The actors refused to pay, and Corneille published the text, obtaining a *privilège* on 21 January 1637. The angry actors mocked Corneille's cupidity, and in February Corneille circulated the *Excuse à Ariste* (Excuse to Ariste), an inflammatory defense of his poetic talents as demonstrated in *Le Cid*.

This "excuse" in French, like the earlier *Excusatio* in Latin that Corneille had addressed four years earlier to the archbishop of Rouen ("P. Cornelii Rothomagensis, ad Illustrissimi Francisci, Archiepiscopi, Normaniae Primatis," 1634), takes the form of an elaborate plea to be forgiven for not writing a certain requested work of poetry. In both cases, however, Corneille shows that his aim is less to seek pardon than to boast of his talent. To the pseudonymous and never-identified friend, "Ariste," Corneille says that he cannot write mere songs, which confine his talent and are beneath him, but that his writing for the stage soars and leaves behind his envious rivals. With astounding boldness, the playwright states that the success of his plays owes nothing to sponsors or cliques but is the result of his talent alone: "Je ne dois qu'à moi seul toute ma Renommée" (I owe my renown to myself alone). This particular boast may well have irritated the most important patron of the Parisian stage at that time, Richelieu, as well as other authors. Such an affirmation of individual merit also links Corneille's self-presentation with the hero of *Le Cid*–who repeatedly proves his worth through action, thus rising above his aristocratic peers– and with the heroes of many of his subsequent plays.

The "excuse" detonated an explosion in the milieu of playwrights. Jean de Mairet wrote a pamphlet accusing Corneille of plagiarism, claiming that he had simply translated the text of a Spanish writer, Guilhem de Castro, and Georges de Scudéry published his tract *Observations sur le Cid* in April, condemning the play in strong terms for faulty dramatic structure, implausibility, indecency, nonconformity to Aristotelian poetics, poor verse dialogue, and plagiarism. Scudéry's terms are quite violent; he even goes so far as to refer to the heroine, Chimène, as a prostitute. Corneille replied a

month later, in May, with a scornful "Lettre apologétique du Sieur Corneille," provoking Scudéry to appeal to the recently founded Académie française. The resulting document, the *Sentimens de l'Académie Française sur la tragi-comédie du "Cid"* (Sentiments of the French Academy about the Tragicomedy "Cid"), expressed in measured language a censure of Corneille, particularly in the matters of implausibility and immorality.

The judgment of the Académie Française brought to a head the complete incompatibility of academic theory and popular taste. Certainly, Corneille's plot is implausible, if plausibility is assumed to be "what usually happens." Corneille, in an effort to keep his story within the newly fashionable twenty-four-hour limit (Aristotle's "unity of a day") without giving up any of the story line, crammed an exceptional amount of activity into this period. Rodrigue not only fights and wins two duels but also conducts a successful nighttime battle within twenty-four hours. However, the difference between Corneille and the critical establishment cannot be understood as a matter of simple quantity. The compressed time within which the events occur intensifies the central ethical characteristic of the story–Chimène's continued love for Rodrigue, her two meetings with him, and her apparent final consent to marry him at the king's request. The public of 1637 as well as that in the centuries since has persistently taken Corneille's side against the Académie Française. Twenty-three years after the quarrel, Corneille formulated the theoretical basis for *Le Cid* in his "Trois Discours." *Le Cid* is often called the first great French classical tragedy–others reserve this distinction for Corneille's play *Horace* (first performed 19 May 1640; published 1641)–even though it was performed as a tragicomedy (and somewhat revised in a 1648 edition that designates the play as a tragedy); if *Le Cid* holds this position in the history of French culture, then a logical consequence is that French classical tragedy is established in opposition to the academic standards and not in conformity with them.

One aspect of the "Quarrel of *Le Cid*" that remains a mystery is Richelieu's motivation for demanding a hard line against this popular dramatic success. The resentment of less successful authors against Corneille is easier to understand, and since Richelieu apparently considered himself not only a connoisseur of the theater but also hoped to produce important and even exemplary plays through his writing team, the Five Authors, perhaps Richelieu's vanity as a would-be playwright was wounded. In a more general sense, he might have felt that Corneille's boasts of independent creativity ran counter to the government policy of organizing literary production into state-chartered or subsidized groups such as the Five Authors and the

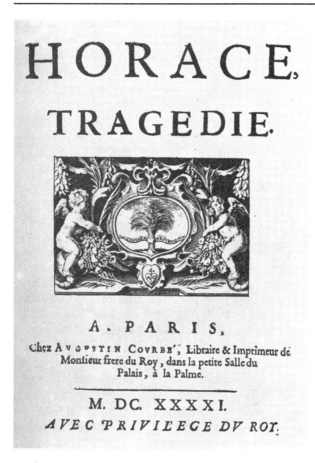

HORACE, TRAGEDIE.

A · PARIS,

Chez A v ɢ v ṣ t i n Covrbe', Libraire & Imprimeur de
Montieur frere du Roy, dans la petite Salle du
Palais, à la Palme.

M. DC. XXXXI.

AVEC PRIVILEGE DV ROY.

Title page for Corneille's play about an incident in Roman history in which patriotism motivated Horace to murder his sister and brother-in-law (Bibliothèque Nationale, Paris)

Académie Française itself. Richelieu might also have considered the content of the play politically subversive. One reason is that the aristocratic tradition of the duel as a means of settling scores appears in *Le Cid* as inseparable from true valor, and such an idea runs directly counter to Richelieu's firmly applied edict of 1634 against duels. Another reason is that the play includes many reminders that the king depends on feudal warriors such as Chimène's father and Rodrigue. The king, consequently, appears as lacking in military might and initiative of his own, even though the hero Rodrigue makes many gestures of submission to the royal will.

Humiliated by the Académie Française, Corneille did not furnish another work for the stage until 1640, when *Horace* was performed before Richelieu in February or early March and had its first public performance on 19 May. This tragedy based on an incident from Roman history was the first of a series that became staples of Corneille's production; with the exception of three subsequent tragedies drawn from Greek myth, he based all his later tragedies on

Roman, Byzantine, or early medieval history. In 1639 Corneille had already written a draft of *Horace,* which he read to various members of the Académie Française, including Jean Chapelain—main author of the Académie's censure of *Le Cid*—who criticized the ending of the play. The two-month delay between the private performance for Richelieu and the public premiere might have resulted from further criticism in high places. Yet, Corneille apparently did not bow to pressure to modify the ending and maintained the incident, found in Livy's history of Rome, of the hero Horace's murder of his sister, Camille.

If Corneille's critics found Chimène's love for her father's killer shocking, Corneille seems in *Horace* to go still farther in the direction of contradictory emotions and duties, for the hero not only kills his brother-in-law but later, arguably on patriotic grounds, also kills his own sister. The irreversible act of *Le Cid* is Rodrigue's duel, and the central event of *Horace* is also a duel. In *Horace,* the duel, rather than being an aristocratic feudal institution, appears as a humanely motivated way of avoiding the massive bloodshed that would result from pitting two whole armies against each other. In this instance, each army chooses a set of champions. Horace finds himself obliged by duty to kill his brothers-in-law, the Curiace brothers, representatives of the opposing Alban army, despite his wife's entreaties. Moreover, Horace's sister is betrothed to one of the Curiaces, and when the triumphant Horace returns from the battlefield, she greets him insultingly, cursing not only Horace's victory but Rome itself. In a fit of rage, he stabs and kills her. At this point a further similarity with *Le Cid* develops, for the Roman king must decide whether to sentence Horace to death, the usual penalty for murder, or to make an exception for a hero on whose strength and skill the very existence of the state depends.

Following *Le Cid, Horace* confirmed the pattern of most Cornelian tragedy. Promising, though not yet proven or distinguished, individuals find themselves in strange and unexpected circumstances. Although in a sense the characters simply remain faithful to their initial values and desires, the altered circumstances make everything they do seem heroic, even unbelievable. As a result, early critics used terms such as "monster" to refer to a hero similar to Horace or a heroine similar to Chimène. Horace's central value, for instance, from his first appearance in the play, is his patriotic fervor. Named as one of the combatants for Rome, he says that to die for Rome will be glorious. When his future brother-in-law, Curiace, is named as his Alban counterpart in battle, Horace simply persists in his initial commitment. His heroism, which appears to some others in the play as a lack of humanity, is based on a consistent pursuit of a certain value without regard to the change in situation. This form of heroism is echoed within the play by Horace's sister Camille's defiant fidelity to her betrothed Curiace after Horace has killed him in battle. Like her brother, Camille persists in her commitment to the overarching value of her life, her love, despite the radical shift that occurs in the world around her. Horace and Camille, as unyielding heroes, are set in contrast to more pliant or adaptive characters, such as Sabine (Horace's wife and Curiace's sister) and Curiace himself, who does battle with much less zeal than Horace.

This unswerving devotion and divergence between the hero and the surrounding world appear also, in a modified form, in Corneille's next tragedy, *Cinna, ou La Clémence d'Auguste* (Cinna, or The Mercy of Augustus, first performed in July or August 1642; published 1643). Cinna, one of the titular heroes, is a Roman noble and favorite of Augustus Caesar. Although he organizes a conspiracy to assassinate the emperor to satisfy the vengeance of his lover, Emilie, Cinna increasingly senses a contradiction between Emilie's insistent vindictiveness and his own civic and personal loyalty to the ruler. This conflict reaches its peak in Cinna's resolution to kill Auguste and then to commit suicide, thus fulfilling both of his incompatible duties, yet abandoning any hope for personal happiness or for the freedom and stability of Rome. The tragedy appears to reach an impasse at its midpoint, but at this moment Corneille shifts the dramatic movement to the other titular hero, Auguste. The emperor also has reached an impasse, for his hope to restore republican freedom to Rome by giving up imperial power is frustrated by the realization that he is surrounded by fractious conspirators, such as his counselor Cinna, who would simply renew the civil wars that brought Auguste himself to power. If Cinna and Auguste persist in their designs, one or the other—or both—will die, and Rome will be plunged into anarchy. In an unusual and radical gesture, Auguste pardons Cinna and all his coconspirators and retains imperial power. This outcome might seem at first to depart from the Cornelian hero's unswerving adherence to a set of initial values, but actually, Auguste has become heroic by choosing to rise above contingent circumstances and to take the chance that his will for peace and stability will bring them about. Through the model of Auguste, Corneille refines his conception of heroism by distinguishing it from simple stubbornness or inertia while maintaining his heroes' characteristic willingness to ignore commonsense perceptions of reality. In these unusual circumstances, the fairly ordinary Auguste rises to exceptional status by a choosing fidelity to an ideal rather than expedient violence.

Self-affirmation and even self-re-creation are central to Corneille's earlier tragedies, and *Cinna, ou la Clémence d'Auguste* brings into sharp focus an aspect of *Le Cid* and *Horace* that had been obscured at the moment of their production by criticism of such details as Chimène's proper conduct as daughter, the excessive amount of action within a twenty-four hour period, and the propriety of Horace's murder of his sister. In each case the hero (and in *Le Cid,* at least, also the heroine) attains a new identity by virtue of his own response to the altered circumstances of his life. It is a major theme, manifested also in such later works as the tragedy *Nicomède* (first performed in February 1651; published 1651) and the heroic comedy *Don Sanche d'Arragon* (first performed in the 1649–1650 season; published 1650), that birth alone does not confer nobility, even if aristocratic status creates obligations that may lead to exceptional deeds. The Auguste of *Cinna, ou la Clémence d'Auguste* was adopted by Julius Caesar. His nobility does not flow through any claim of inherited character, and indeed, only at the end of the tragedy does Auguste achieve through his own decisions a moral standing superior to that of the conspirators and participants in the civil wars. In *Le Cid,* likewise, Rodrigue and Chimène find themselves in their peculiar and touching conflict by virtue of their resolve to emulate each other in respecting the most stringent demands of the system of honor within which they were born. Their birth does not in itself distinguish them from the other nobles who surround them, but their response to the challenges of their situation gives them a nobility that can be obtained only by their own will. Almost contemporary with *Cinna, ou la Clémence d'Auguste* is the first of Corneille's two religious tragedies, *Polyeucte martyr* (The Martyr Polyeucte, first performed December 1642 or January 1643; published 1643), in which the hero Polyeucte's choice of baptism and martyrdom is explicitly presented as a transformative rebirth in defiance of social context. No one knows to what extent *Polyeucte* was appreciated by the public of its day, but this "Christian tragedy," as Corneille described it—he wrote one other, much less successful, *Théodore, vierge et martyre* (Theodore, Virgin and Martyr, performed in 1644–1645; published 1646)—has traditionally been considered one of his best. Academic critics write of the "tetralogy," the four most celebrated Cornelian tragedies, and *Polyeucte* is the fourth, after *Le Cid, Horace,* and *Cinna, ou la Clémence d'Auguste.*

The story, set in Armenia, part of the Roman empire, during the reign of Trajan (249–251 A.D.), concerns Pauline, daughter of the Roman governor; her Armenian husband, Polyeucte; and Sévère, representative and protégé of the emperor, who comes to Armenia during the wave of persecution of the Christian minority. The plot crisis arises from the simultaneous arrival of Sévère (who had once been Pauline's suitor and whom she still loves) and Polyeucte's conversion to Christianity. Zealous in his new religion, Polyeucte not only refuses to go through the usual religious rituals to mark Sévère's arrival but attacks the idols. The plot seems to offer a convenient solution for Pauline. When her father sentences Polyeucte to death for blasphemy, his death would leave Pauline a widow, free to marry the man she truly loves. But she instead chooses to remain loyal to her husband and asks Sévère to try to save him. Sévère, Pauline, and Polyeucte all in different ways exemplify the *généreux* (the noble) that is such a crucial element of Corneille's heroes and heroines, particularly from *Le Cid* to *Pertharite, roy des Lombards* (Pertharite, King of the Lombards, first performed in 1652; published 1653), and their nobility is highlighted by the contrast with the basely opportunistic quality of Pauline's father. Yet, in addition to purely human nobility, the play illustrates the power of Christian grace when, in a stunning last-minute shift after Polyeucte's martyrdom, Pauline's father becomes a Christian along with his widowed daughter.

From a modern point of view, readers may have difficulty reconciling the standard view of tragedy (as a serious play with an unhappy ending) with the "happy" ending of *Polyeucte,* in which martyrdom is a form of triumph. *Polyeucte* fits into Corneille's conception of the tragic by virtue of the author's view (accepted by his contemporaries) that a play, to be tragic, need only concern noble characters who risk death. From a Christian perspective–particularly in the militant age of Catholic missions to the Americas, Africa, and China–martyrdom and conversion are indeed happy outcomes, consonant with the poetics of admiration developed in Corneille's immediately preceding tragedies. *Polyeucte* may come the closest of all Corneille's plays to the Jesuit education that is the basis both for his eloquence and for his lifelong piety. The author is, however, careful not to represent any visible divine intervention into the world of the characters, as does Jean de Rotrou five years later in his popular *Le Véritable Saint-Genest* (The Veritable Saint Genest, 1646), in which the voice of God is heard on stage. As a consequence, *Polyeucte* remains within the ordinary plausibility of fully human drama, and one need not assume a Christian viewpoint to interpret character motivation. Pauline's father's conversion at the end could be a new, desperate example of his opportunism, the effect of remorse, or late-in-coming paternal emotion. While Pauline (often compared to the heroine of the well-known later novel by Marie-Madeleine de Lafayette, *La Princesse de Clèves,* 1678) and Sévère may be the more touching characters of the play, Polyeucte himself fits the mold of the heroes of the preceding Cornelian tragedies who undergo decisive, identity-altering transformations that reconfigure the world of the people around them.

Corneille used this concept of self-re-creation in comic plays as well as in tragedies, and it is striking that the best-known of Corneille's tragedies are framed, chronologically, by two comedies with a similar theme of disguise and transformation. These are *L'Illusion comique* (first performed the season before *Le Cid*) and *Le Menteur* (first performed in 1643–1644, the season after *Polyeucte martyr;* published 1644; translated as *The Mistaken Beauty, or The Lyar,* 1685). In both *L'Illusion comique* and *Le Menteur* the hero gains success by pretending to be someone he is not. In the first case, the pretense is that of the professional actor who assumes a variety of roles on stage. In *Le Menteur,* on the other hand, the hero positions himself within Parisian society by pretending to be a military hero when, in fact, he is only a law student. Based loosely on the Spanish play *La Verdad sospechosa* (The Suspicious Truth, first performed 1621; published 1630), which Corneille believed to be by Lope de Vega (it was in fact by Juan de Alarcon), *Le Menteur* was one of many comedies of the period based on mistaken identity. The hero, newly arrived in Paris, falls in love with one of two women he meets in a public garden. His love at first sight for one of the two becomes the source of many extreme complications because he mistakes their names, believing that the woman to whom he is attracted is Lucrèce when in fact it is Clarice. He then devotes much ingenuity to avoiding an arranged marriage to Clarice, unwittingly blocking the outcome that he ardently seeks. Another use of verbal irony occurs from the brilliant lies the hero Dorante tells about himself and his achievements, which place his verbal virtuosity next to the rather prosaic, though real, military reputation of his rivals. Tellingly, in view of the growing importance of salon and court life, Dorante's purely discursive talent makes him more attractive to the women of the play than the other suitors, whose fame rests upon military exploits.

Although it would be reductive to describe *Le Menteur* as autobiographical in inspiration, the comedy does offer a tantalizing glimpse of the conflicts between the "gown nobility" (*noblesse de robe,* the class of lawyers and judges) and the "sword nobility" (*noblesse d'épée,* the traditional upper aristocracy of warriors) in early-modern France. Corneille, from a modest background, aspired to join the former through his standing in the admiralty court. Gown nobility depended on verbal gifts rather than fighting skills, and Corneille did, indeed, achieve nobility through his eloquence. Corneille also, as a provincial from Rouen, faced the challenge of making a place for himself in a Paris that was distinguishing itself more and more as a modern capital. In August 1644,

Table that Corneille used at the Palais de justice in Rouen when he was a member of the Admiralty Court

despite the recent stage victory of *Le Menteur,* Corneille was defeated in his first bid for election to the Académie Française. It took two further attempts before, in January 1647, he was elected to that body after stating that he had arranged to reside in Paris for part of each year.

In addition to the theme of self-re-creation, the tragedies of this third part of Corneille's career are strongly marked by rivalries of sons with their fathers or their mothers, questions about the legitimacy or relevance of "birth" as a determinant of identity, and deep complexity of dramatic situation—a complexity, bordering on obscurity, that Corneille cultivated during this phase of his career. The theme of rivalry with the parent, logically connected with the motif of self-creation through acts and words, appears in variations in the tragedies *Rodogune, princesse des Parthes* (first performed 1644–1645; published 1647; translated as *Rodogune, or The Rival Brothers,* 1765), *Héraclius, empereur d'Orient* (first performed January 1647; published 1647; translated as *Heraclius, Emperour of the East,* 1664), and *Nicomède,* and in the heroic comedy *Don Sanche d'Arragon.* In the first of these works, Rodogune, a queen regent, is so determined to retain the throne that she kills one of her twin

sons and attempts to kill the other. This tragedy, proclaimed by Corneille as his favorite, is distinguished by a bizarre form of parental manipulation: the queen is the only one who knows which of the twins was born first and thus controls, by her untrustworthy and self-serving testimony, the order of inheritance. In *Héraclius*—a play so difficult to follow that Corneille with some pride admitted that a spectator would have to see it twice to understand it fully—the identity of the true heir is rendered doubtful because of a switch of babies in the cradle. The result is a situation in which there are two young men with the same set of names, one the son of the usurper and one the son of the deceased true king. In *Nicomède* there is no doubt about the hero's birth order or parentage, but Nicomède, by his nobility of action and attitude, demonstrates that he, rather than his father, is more worthy to rule—a case of the son delegitimizing the father. Finally, in *Don Sanche d'Arragon,* a military hero's humble birth (he is the son of a fisherman) is revealed and blocks his marriage with the princess he loves; but in a subsequent revelation he is reconnected with merit and birth when another story of a baby separated from parents in infancy gives reassurance that the hero is the legitimate heir of Aragon. *Don Sanche* is notable for being the first of Corneille's three "heroic comedies," designated by him as such because the hero does not risk death in the plot–a requirement, thought Corneille, for tragedy–and so the play, despite its aristocratic characters and high political stakes, remains a comedy.

The steady production of this period (thirteen plays in as many years since *Horace*) came to a halt with the massive failure of *Pertharite, roy des Lombards* in 1652. No one knows how many performances this play ran in its first production, but Voltaire claimed that it was acted only once. In any event, Corneille was sufficiently crushed by the chilly reception to cease writing for the stage for seven years. During this time he continued to work on his translation *L'Imitation de Jésus-Christ* (The Imitation of Christ), the last book of which appeared in 1656.

Œdipe (Oedipus, first performed 25 January 1659; published 1659) marks Corneille's emergence from retirement. According to Corneille's account, this venture into a mythic subject, the second of his career, resulted from his offer to write a tragedy on any subject proposed to him by the powerful Nicolas Fouquet, superintendent of finance and active patron of the arts. Corneille knew that his public was aware of Sophocles' and Seneca's plays about the Theban king, and thus his striking reworking was, according to his "To the reader," based on a recognition of modern taste with its preference for heroes not deeply tainted by crime. Although this view seems a timid retreat from the guiding principles of the theory of tragedy that, oddly, Corneille was composing at the same time, it is typical of Corneille that he solved the perceived problem by creating a second plot that is woven through the original Sophoclean one. In Corneille's account, Laius had a daughter, Dircé, as well as the son, Oedipus. In Corneille's modern tragedy, Dircé's rivalry with Oedipus and her love for Theseus, king of Athens, are presented in such a way that her brother's killing of Laius and his incestuous marriage with his mother, Jocasta, are de-emphasized. Although *Œdipe* was a success in its day, now it seems a quaint testimony to the movement to edulcorate tragedy that led to the eclipse of the genre in the eighteenth century. In comparison, Racine's tragedy of myth in the following decade is more faithful to antiquity, more violent and transgressive, and, arguably, closer to the poetics of tragedy that Corneille had been working on prior to *Œdipe* and that he spelled out in the "Trois Discours" in the year following the production of that play.

The three-volume 1660 edition of Corneille's previously written twenty-three plays is an important work because of the critical and theoretical texts that it includes. Corneille's contribution to dramatic criticism consists of his series of innovative critiques of each of his plays from *Mélite* to *Œdipe*–in other words, his entire dramatic work from 1629 to 1659. These *examens* (or examinations) are surprisingly candid accounts of what is successful and what is not in each case. While the author seizes this opportunity to shape the image that posterity will have of his oeuvre and his craft, he is more severe in some cases than the most stringent of his critics–for instance, in his enumeration of the "defects" of *Horace,* seen by many later scholars as the first great classical tragedy of France. In addition to the *examens,* printed individually in front each play, the 1660 edition includes the major theoretical work usually known as "Trois discours sur le poème dramatique." These discourses were originally printed separately as front matter to each of the three volumes of the collected plays. Instead of the collective title now used for them, the discourses had separate names: "Discours de l'utilité et des parties du poème dramatique" (Discourse on the Usefulness and on the Parts of the Dramatic Poem), "Discours de la tragédie et des moyens de la traiter selon le vraisemblable ou le nécessaire" (Discourse on Tragedy and on the Ways of Composing it in Accordance with Plausibility and Necessity), and "Discours des trois unités d'action, de jour, et de lieu" (Discourse on the Three Unities of Action, Day, and Place).

Corneille's *examens* and his "Three Discourses" are worth reading today, for they vary sharply from the idea of French "classicism" into which Corneille's work has subsequently been cast. They are also an important document of French modernism, as the seventeenth-century French moved beyond the Renaissance enthusiasm for revival of the culture of antiquity toward a more critical and self-conscious originality. Corneille's own description of his writing shows him to be overwhelmingly concerned with the audience's reception of the plays and ready to do what was necessary to maintain his reputation with critics and his box-office success with the public. Most of all, he wanted to be a popular playwright, and his theory is based on his perception of audience reaction. Yet, in order to maintain his standing with the critics, Corneille takes pains to demonstrate his extensive knowledge of Aristotle's *Poetics* (which he read in Latin and Italian translations) and of the many commentaries on that ancient work. But Corneille claims that a merely bookish knowledge of Aristotle is inferior to the insight developed as a result of the experience of applying the philosopher's precepts. Fortified by his experience, which can actually be described as a kind of experimental knowledge of Aristotelianism, Corneille does not hesitate to reject such hallowed Aristotelian concepts as catharsis and the distinction of tragedy and

Decorated title page for the Corneille tragedy in which the title character plans to kill
Caesar Augustus and then himself (Bibliothèque Nationale, Paris)

comedy based solely on the social standing of the characters. On the other hand, Corneille uses Aristotle to defend some of his own contrarian positions, including the view that pleasing the audience is the entire goal of drama.

According to Corneille, great tragedies are those that produce intense emotion in the audience through response to corresponding displays of passion and conflict on the stage. The subjects of such tragedies must always be implausible; yet, the playwright needs to persuade the audience to believe in this implausible subject—hence, Corneille develops at some length the distinction between subject and treatment. The major source of tragic stories that are believable despite their strangeness is history, since historical fact cannot be contested. Some major character of each tragedy should, in this view, engage in a significant—and implausible—transgression of ethical norms, particularly those concerning family, friendship, or love. With this view Corneille produces the theoretical foundation for *Le Cid,* written twenty-three years earlier, and he replies to the critics who censured that play and its heroine for their implausibility and lack of decorum.

The main characters of tragedy need not be virtuous as long as they are intense and exemplify their type to the fullest. Corneille sets himself apart again from his contemporary critics, who often took a moralizing approach to drama, as well as from later conceptions of drama as representation of the real. Rather than moralism or realism, Corneille presents a kind of larger-than-life intensity as the measure of heroism, claiming that drama (including comedy) requires "the brilliant and superb quality of a virtuous or criminal character." These characters can appear in both tragedy and comedy, for Corneille rejects the ancient idea that these genres should be defined simply by separating aristocratic characters (worthy of tragedy) from lower-class characters (suitable for comedy). Comedy is instead defined by its plot. Its two criteria are that the ending be happy for the main characters and that the hero not be in danger of death in the course of the play. Tragedy, on the other hand, has a plot in which the hero risks death but may survive for a happy ending. Corneille claims that an important feature of modern drama is that the audience sympathizes with a character or set of characters who are designated as the "principal characters." These characters need not be the most colorful or powerful characters in a play, but they are the ones for whom the audience cares, and this view is a major shift from ancient drama, according to the "Three Discourses."

The ideal plot for a modern tragedy, according to Corneille, is the opposite of the one preferred by Aristotle. Reviewing the latter's account of four tragic plot types based on a combination of the knowledge of kinship and the ultimate tragic act of killing a family member (for example, *Oedipus Rex*), Corneille notes that the *Poetics* describes as the best kind of tragedy the one in which a hero is about to kill a family member without recognizing him or her, then recognizes the person and refrains from the act. The worst kind of tragedy, according to Aristotle, is one in which the hero knowingly tries to kill a family member and simply fails. By promoting this last plot type, Corneille once again provides a theoretical foundation for *Le Cid* (as well as *Rodogune, Nicomède,* and others of his own tragedies). In this "tragédie à visage découvert" (tragedy without a veil), the characters move the audience to pity in situations in which a woman demands the death of her lover or a father sentences his son to death, but some superior authority or circumstance prevents the unhappy outcome.

In the last of the "Three Discourses," Corneille discusses the "three unities" that are so characteristic of seventeenth-century French drama. Although Corneille's contribution to the debates about the unities is less striking than his innovative ideas on subject, character, audience reaction, and genre, his approach to the unities is consistent with his generally audience-oriented, pragmatic stance. The expression "unities" is a term of art that can be misleading, since it was used to mean a "single instance," not a "united quality." So also the "unity of action" meant that there should be "one action" just as the "unity of day" meant that tragedy should take "one day." In discussing the one action that was allowed in each tragic plot, Corneille had the new idea of simply counting how many times the hero risked death, and he thus renamed the unity of action the "unity of peril." Once the hero had survived (or failed to survive) one mortal danger, the play should be finished. By this standard, Corneille's *Horace* fails to observe the rule, and the rule in turn is tied to the audience's emotional investment in seeing the hero risk death and escape. With regard to the "one day" allotted tragedy by Aristotle, Corneille, following a contemporary trend, felt that the perfect tragedy should have a story that took as much time to happen as to present on stage. Therefore, if a stage performance, including intermissions, takes roughly two hours, then the play should ideally represent two hours in the lives of the characters. As a practical matter, Corneille recommends being as vague as possible about time passing and allowing the audience to imagine time to suit themselves. He does say, however, that there should be a slight distortion of time in the last couple of acts of the play, since the audience will be caught up in the suspense, and the actions on the stage should be accelerated. Corneille recommends similar vagueness about the single place, usually a room in a palace, where the action of the tragedy takes place.

After the 1660 collective edition, Corneille finally moved from Rouen to Paris (in 1662) and wrote by himself nine more plays—seven tragedies and two heroic comedies—and wrote with Molière a ballet tragicomedy. Some of these plays were great successes, notably *Sertorius* (first performed 25 February 1662; published 1662), which was so popular that it was performed by all three major theater companies—the Marais Theater, Molière's company at the Palais-Royal, and the Hôtel de Bourgogne—within two years of its opening. Others were either complete or relative failures, such as the tragedies *Sophonisbe* (first performed 1663; published 1663), *Agésilas* (first performed 1666; published 1666), and *Suréna, général des Parthes* (Surena, General of the Parthians, first performed 1674; published 1675), Corneille's last play, and the heroic comedy *Tite et Bérénice* (first performed 1670; published 1671), and disappeared quickly from the repertory. In some cases, such as *Attila, roy des Huns* (Attila, King of the Huns, first performed 1667, published 1667) and the tragicomedy *Pulchérie* (first performed 1672; published 1673), the initial reception is difficult to ascertain. For the comédie héroïque ballet *Psiché* (performed for the king, 1671; published 1671), the plot was designed by Molière, and Corneille was responsible only for producing the verse dialogue. In terms of popular and commercial success, Corneille was in his declining years, while Racine, after the 1667 triumph of *Andromaque*, became the dominant playwright of France and the favorite of Louis XIV.

Yet these plays, which still appealed to a core of loyal Corneille enthusiasts (including the celebrated letter-writer Marie de Rabutin Chantal, Madame de Sévigné, who never ceased to sing Corneille's praises and to deplore the new trend toward Racine), still draw readers from among an academic public and merit attention for their continued working-through of the problems of honor, love, fidelity, history, and political change. While the plays of the last fifteen years of Corneille's career are not the most appealing in emotional terms, they include some of his most striking character creations and a brilliant ruthlessness in following the logic of heroism to the extreme. Three of them—*Sophonisbe, Othon,* and *Attila*—are worth a closer look as examples of Corneille's last work.

Corneille's house in Rouen, circa 1931

With *Sophonisbe,* Corneille challenged one of his old rivals, Jean de Mairet (an opponent during the Quarrel of *Le Cid*), whose tragedy of the same title had been an enduring success since 1634. In a deliberate gesture to call attention to his own technical virtuosity, Corneille consciously and explicitly took a subject that was known to the public primarily in Mairet's version. In the preface to his *Sophonisbe,* Corneille points out the difficulty of his task and the stimulus to plot design and dialogue creation that came from avoiding the parts of the story in which Mairet excelled. Again, as in the Quarrel of *Le Cid,* Corneille used the reference to historical authority–the Roman writer Livy's *Ab Urbe condita* (From the Founding of the City, begun in 29 B.C.), in this case–to justify the way he drew his characters, and in particular the Carthaginian queen of the title. Sophonisbe, though engaged to the Numidian king Massinisse, was married by her father to the aged Numidian king Syphax. The latter had been defeated by the Romans and their ally Massinisse. As the play opens, Sophonisbe reviews her motivations in marrying Syphax, which were purely patriotic and based on her intent to gain Syphax's military strength for Carthage and win him away from the expansionist Romans. For Sophonisbe, then, her love for Massinisse was relatively unimportant in view of her political aims, and when the victorious Massinisse asks her to marry him, she consents without hesitation, but on one condition–that she be spared the indignity of being paraded through Rome among the spoils of Syphax's defeat. When it becomes clear that the Romans, bitter enemies of Carthage, will not permit their ally Massinisse to shield their enemy by marrying her, Sophonisbe commits suicide. Throughout the play, the heroine is brutally frank in telling both Syphax and Massinisse that she views marriage with them solely in terms of her strategic aims toward Rome and of her personal glory. The distance from the structure and problematic of *Le Cid* is amazing, for in *Sophonisbe* honor and love, so inseparably intertwined in the earlier play, are starkly separate. Sophonisbe may love Massinisse or not, but this love neither energizes the heroine to greater feats of glory nor diverts her from her focused attachment to the interests of Carthage. The two main male characters are, on the other hand, in love with the heroine, and their love is only a mistake, not a quality that ennobles them. Corneille lays the foundation for the generally negative view of love that prevails in Racine's plays, but with the important difference that Sophonisbe is able to control her emotions rather than yield to them while exploiting the feelings of others.

The tragedy *Othon* (first performed at Versailles for the court in August 1664; published 1665) can be seen, in hindsight, as the beginning of the last decade of the author's career and as the first Cornelian play that overlaps the career of its author's future rival and successor, Jean Racine. The latter presented his tragic *Thébaïde, ou les frères ennemis* (The Thebes Saga, or The Enemy Brothers, first performed in 1664; published 1664), based on Sophocles' *Antigone* (circa 442–441 B.C.), in June and his second tragedy, *Alexandre,* in December of 1665 (published 1666). While at the première of *Othon,* Racine was a minor presence, after his *Andromaque* in 1667 (published 1668) he became a playwright to reckon with, and Corneille openly challenged him to a dramatic duel by staging his *Tite et Bérénice* opposite Racine's *Bérénice* (published 1671) on the same subject in 1670. The rivalry of the two dramatists, still four or five years in the future when Corneille wrote *Othon,* is worth mentioning because this somber tragedy of court intrigue and apparently unavoidable corruption might seem to be a "Racinian" play made in the mold of the younger dramatist's future works *Britannicus* (first performed 13 December 1669; published 1670) or *Bajazet* (first performed 3 January 1672; published 1672), both also set in cruel and corrupting courts. Because Corneille's *Othon,* relatively little known today, preceded the more frequently performed Racinian works that resemble it, the older playwright was clearly still capable of great originality, so great as to suggest much of the atmosphere for Racine's tragic world. The story of *Othon* is in many ways an odd subject to present to a young king in the third year of his personal reign, unless it is conceived as an admonition against devious and self-serving courtiers. Set in 69 A.D. in the court of the emperor Galba (who had overthrown Nero), *Othon* is the story of the events immediately preceding Galba's death and the start of Othon's reign as emperor (a reign destined to last only three months).

The plot is difficult to follow because of the extreme instability of the characters' alliances. Othon first begins to court Plautine, the daughter of Vinius the consul, for purely political convenience, seeking to win her father's support against other factions. However, Othon and Plautine fall in love. When Vinius makes the startling demand that Othon, in order to save Plautine's life, drop her in order to court Galba's daughter Camille—a reconfiguration required to prevent Piso from becoming emperor and killing Vinius's family— Othon finds himself in the odd situation of being motivated by his love of Plautine to court a woman he does not love. In one of those paradoxical situations that

delighted Corneille, the hero's love requires his infidelity (just as, in *Le Cid,* Chimène's love for Rodrigue is a major factor in her insistence that he be executed). The twists and turns of arranged and rearranged marriages involving Plautine, Othon, Camille, and other characters are dizzyingly hard to follow and lead to no obvious solution. In a deliberative scene that appears almost like self-parody on Corneille's part (reminiscent of Auguste's consultation of his advisors in *Cinna, ou la Clémence d'Auguste*), the emperor Galba is reduced to befuddled passivity. Only Othon's offstage success in persuading the praetorian guard to mutiny and to support him leads, in the middle of the last act, to the death of most of his rivals and of Galba.

Like the other tragedies of Corneille's last decade of writing for the stage, *Othon* is often categorized as a tragedy manifesting the "decline of the hero," the view promoted by critics Paul Bénichou and Serge Doubrovsky. Some critics have taken this judgment a step further and see the decline in the hero as a decline in Corneille's writing, as if maintaining the standards of heroism were something required of Corneille. Or in a more complex but similar statement of this view, Corneille's greatness is attributed to his ability to create political equilibrium out of the tensions of French society that are indirectly represented through tragedies set in the distant past. Thus, Doubrovsky says that after *La Mort de Pompée* (The Death of Pompey, first performed November or December 1643; published 1644; translated as *Pompey,* 1663), "The remainder of Cornelian drama is an immense effort to resolve the anguished contradiction of aristocratic ethics and politics, the conflict between existential source of power and the form of power." This effort turns out, according to Doubrovsky, to be in vain. The defect in this view, and in many traditional views of Corneille's later work, is that they take for granted a norm established by the tragedies of the late 1630s and early 1640s and then refuse to allow Corneille to adopt a different pattern with different aims. Even Doubrovsky rises above the common view of a decadence in Corneille's stagecraft to admit that *Othon* is "a neglected masterpiece" and that Corneille's writing was never better.

If *Othon* is seen as a freestanding creative work, not subject to requirements derived from the author's earlier plays, it offers much to praise. The world it describes, one that later became familiar in Racine's tragedies, is comprised of isolated individuals who cannot take for granted any friendship, love, or kinship. Using their family ties as only one of many opportunities for self-advancement or of many dangerous snares, these individuals need to recalculate their own interest and make new alliances with each scene and each new piece of information. Isolated, the characters require

Corneille's library at his house in Rouen

alliances to exist, since even the most powerful, the emperor, remains so only in the absence of a coherent alternative alignment among courtiers and army units. Not only are truth and falsehood nearly impossible for any of the characters—and, for much of the time, the audience—to distinguish, but also these concepts themselves are most often empty. Although the characters, including Othon, can be described as deceptive, most of their "deceptions" are actually reinventions of themselves—that is, they are not deceiving anyone but actually changing—in a world in which personal characteristics and emotions do not run deep. This unstable, ephemeral, decentered, networked, self-interested society is much like what is described in François La Rochefoucauld's cynical aphoristic *Maxims* (1664), which appeared the same year as the premiere of *Othon*. Rather than demonstrating Corneille's failure to repeat his previous work, the tragedies of his last decade can be considered innovative experiments with new kinds of characters and situations, some of which clearly anticipate Racine.

Attila, roy des Huns is little read today, let alone performed, though it may have been relatively successful

when it first appeared. Nonetheless, it is one of the most spectacular examples of Corneille's predilection for bizarre central characters, beings who are at the limit of the human. Corneille's tendency to focus on unusual, often psychopathic, characters is evident as early as *La Place Royalle, ou L'Amoureux extravagant* (1633–1634) in the person of the hero Alidor, an *amoureux extravagant* (literally, an "insane lover"), and these characters become increasingly extreme as the decades pass, with Horace the brother who kills his sister (1640), and with Rodogune, the queen who tries to kill both of her sons (1644–1645). Attila, the invader of the Roman empire, dominates the play that bears his name, reduces the more normal and sympathetic characters to a state of political and military paralysis, boasts sadistically of being a plague sent by God, and finally self-destructs in massive offstage hemorrhaging that is described in lurid detail as a "fountain of blood."

Despite Sophonisbe's icy patriotism, Othon's gloomy intrigue, and Attila's monstrous ferocity, Corneille's eclipse was evident in the early 1670s. He made a last attempt in 1674 with *Suréna, général des Parthes,* a tragedy in which mutual love undermines the hero's political position and leads to his death. After the failure of this play, Corneille seemed to have accepted that his career as playwright was over. He wrote only a small number of occasional verses during the last decade of his life. He died on 1 October 1684, at age seventy-eight, at his home on the rue d'Argenteuil, near the Louvre, and was buried in his parish church, Saint-Roch.

References:

Susan Read Baker, *Dissonant Harmonies: Drama and Ideology in Five Neglected Plays of Pierre Corneille,* Etudes Littéraires Françaises (Tübingen: Gunter Narr, 1990);

Paul Bénichou, *Morales du grand siècle,* Bibliothèque des Idées (Paris: Gallimard, 1948);

Claire L. Carlin, *Pierre Corneille Revisited,* Twayne's World Authors Series (New York: Twayne, 1998);

David Clarke, *Pierre Corneille: Poetics and Political Drama under Louis XIII* (Cambridge: Cambridge University Press, 1992);

Georges Couton, *Corneille et la Fronde,* Publications de la Faculté des Lettres de l'Université de Clermont (Clermont-Ferrand: G. de Bussac, 1951);

Serge Doubrovsky, *Corneille et la dialectique du héros,* Bibliothèque des Idées (Paris: Gallimard, 1963);

Georges Forestier, *Essai de génétique théâtrale: Corneille à l'oeuvre* (Paris: Klincksieck, 1996);

Marc Fumaroli, *Héros et orateurs: Rhétorique et dramaturgie cornéliennes* (Geneva: Droz, 1990);

Armand Gasté, ed., *La Querelle du Cid* (Paris, 1898; reprinted edition, Geneva: Slatkine, 1970);

Richard Goodkin, *Birth Marks: The Tragedy of Primogeniture in Pierre Corneille, Thomas Corneille, and Jean Racine* (Philadelphia: University of Pennsylvania Press, 2000);

Mitchell Greenberg, *Corneille, Classicism and the Ruses of Symmetry* (Cambridge: Cambridge University Press, 1986);

John D. Lyons, *The Tragedy of Origins: Pierre Corneille and Historical Perspective* (Stanford: Stanford University Press, 1996);

Milorad Margitić, ed., *Corneille comique: Nine Studies of Pierre Corneille's Comedy* (Paris, Seattle & Tubingen: Papers on French Seventeenth Century Literature, 1982);

Jacques Maurens, *La Tragédie sans tragique: Le Néo-stoïcisme dans l'oeuvre de Pierre Corneille* (Paris: A. Colin, 1966);

Hélène Merlin, *Public et littérature en France au XVIIe siècle* (Paris: Les Belles Lettres, 1994);

Hélène Merlin-Kajman, *L'Absolutisme dans les lettres et la théorie des deux corps: Passions et politique,* Lumière Classique, 29 (Paris: H. Champion, 2000);

Octave Nadal, *Le Sentiment de l'amour dans l'oeuvre de Pierre Corneille* (Paris: Gallimard, 1948);

Germain Poirier, *Corneille et la vertu de prudence* (Geneva: Droz, 1984);

Michel Prigent, *Le Héros et l'état dans la tragédie de Pierre Corneille* (Paris: Presses Universitaires de France, 1986);

Bradley Rubidge, "Catharsis Through Admiration: Corneille, Le Moyne, and the Social Uses of Emotion," *Modern Philology,* 95 (1998): 316–333;

Marie-Odile Sweetser, *Les Conceptions dramatiques de Corneille d'après ses écrits théoriques* (Geneva: Droz, 1962).

Savinien de Cyrano de Bergerac

(6 March 1619 – 28 July 1655)

Olivier Jouslin
Université Paris IV–Sorbonne

Translated by Claire Boulard
Université Paris III–Sorbonne

BOOKS: *Le Conseiller fidèle* (Paris: J. Brunet, 1649);
Le Gazetier des-intéressé (Paris: J. Brunet, 1649);
Lettre de consolation envoyée à Madame de Chastillon sur la mort de Monsieur de Chastillon (Paris: J. Brunet, 1649);
Lettre de consolation envoyée à Madame la duchesse de Rohan, sur la mort de feu Monsieur le duc de Rohan son fils, surnommé Tancrède (Paris: C. Huot, 1649);
Le Ministre d'Etat flambé. Rigendo dicere verum quid vetat (Paris: J. Brunet, 1649);
La Sybille moderne, ou L'Oracle du temps (Paris: J. Brunet, 1649);
Remonstrances des trois estats à la Reyne regente pour la paix (Paris: J. Brunet, 1649);
Le Pédant joué (Paris: C. de Sercy, 1654);
La Mort d'Agrippine (Paris: C. de Sercy, 1654);
Les Œuvres diverses (Paris: C. de Sercy, 1654)–comprises *Lettres, Lettres satyriques, Lettres amoureuses, Le Pédant joué; Lettres* and *Lettres satyriques*, translated as *Satyrical Characters, and Handsome Descriptions in Letters, Written to Severall Persons of Quality . . . Translated . . . by a Person of Honour* (London: Henry Herringman, 1658);
Histoire comique, par M. Cyrano de Bergerac, contenant les états et les empires de la lune (Paris: C. de Sercy, 1657); translated by Thomas St. Serfe as *Selenarchia; or, The Government of the World in the Moon* (London: Printed by J. Cottrel to be sold by Hum. Robinson, 1659);
Les Nouvelles Œuvres, 2 volumes (Paris: C. de Sercy, 1661, 1662)–comprises *Les Entretiens pointus, Les Etats et empires du soleil, Fragment de physique, Lettres; Les Etats et empires du soleil*, translated by A. Lowell as *The Comical History of the States and Empires of the Worlds of the Moon and Sun . . .* (London: Henry Rhodes, 1687).

Savinien de Cyrano de Bergerac (frontispiece to the 1709 edition of Cyrano's Oeuvres; *Bibliothèque Nationale, Paris)*

Editions and Collections: *Histoire comique des états et empires de la lune et du soleil–Fragment de physique,* edited by P. L. Jacob (Paris: Delahaye, 1858);

L'Autre Monde; ou, Les Etats et empires de la lune et du soleil, edited by Frédéric Lachèvre (Paris: Garnier, 1932);

Œuvres diverses, edited by Lachèvre (Paris: Garnier, 1933)–comprises *Lettres satiriques, Lettres amoureuses, Les Entretiens pointus, Le Pédant joué,* and *La Mort d'Agrippine;*

L'Autre Monde, edited by H. Weber (Paris: Editions Sociales, 1959);

Lettres, edited by L. Erba (Milan: All'Insegna del pesce d'oro, Collana Critica, 1965);

Voyage dans la lune, edited by M. Laugaa (Paris: Garnier-Flammarion, 1970);

L'Autre Monde, ou Les Estats et empires de la lune, edited by Madeleine Alcover (Paris: Champion, 1977);

Cyrano de Bergerac, Œuvres complètes, edited by Jacques Prévot (Paris: Belin, 1977);

La Mort d'Agrippine, edited by C. J. Gossip (Exeter: University of Exeter, 1982);

Mazarinades, edited by Marie-Madeleine Fragonard (Paris: Editions InterUniversitaires, 1989);

La Mort d'Agrippine, veuve de Germanicus: Tragédie, edited by Dominique Moncond'huy (Paris: La Table Ronde, 1995);

L'Autre Monde, ou Les Estats et empires de la lune, edited by Margaret Sankey (Paris: Minard, 1995);

L'Autre Monde, edited by Prévot in *Libertins du XVIIe siècle,* Bibliothèque de La Pléiade (Paris: Gallimard, 1998);

Lettres satiriques et amoureuses; précédées de Lettres diverses, edited by Jean-Charles Darmon and Alain Mothu (Paris: Desjonquères, 1999);

Cyrano de Bergerac, Œuvres complètes, volume 1, edited by Alcover (Paris: Champion, 2000)–comprises *L'Autre Monde, ou Les Etats et empires de la lune. Les Etats et empires du soleil. Fragment de physique;*

Cyrano de Bergerac, Œeuvres complètes, volume 2, edited by Erba and Hubert Carrier (Paris: Champion, 2001)–comprises *Lettres, Les Entretiens pointus, Mazarinades.*

Editions in English: *Satyrical Characters and Handsome Descriptions in Letters,* by *Cyrano de Bergerac,* translated, with an introduction, by Benjamin Parsons Bourland (Cambridge: Printed for the Rowfant Club of Cleveland, Ohio, 1914);

The Comical History of the States and Empires of the Worlds of the Moon and Sun, translated, with an introduction, by Geoffrey Strachan (London: Oxford University Press, 1965);

Other Worlds: The Comical History of the States and Empires of the Worlds of the Moon and Sun, translated, with an

introduction, by Strachan (London: New English Library, 1976);

Cyrano de Bergerac's Voyages to the Moon and the Sun, translated by Richard Aldington, with an introduction by John Wells (London: Folio Society, 1991).

OTHER: *Le Pédant joué,* in *Théâtre du XVIIe siècle,* volume 2, Bibliothèque de la Pléiade, edited by Jacques Schérer and Jacques Truchet (Paris: Gallimard, 1986).

A poet, novelist, and playwright, Cyrano de Bergerac was born Savinien de Cyrano in Paris on 6 March 1619 to Abel de Cyrano and his wife, Espérance de Bellanger. Abel de Cyrano was a landowner in Mauvières and Bergerac in the region of Seine et Oise, near Paris. Savinien de Cyrano lived with his parents in Paris until his father broke off with the circle of church nobility that he frequented and settled in Mauvières. There Cyrano met Henri Le Bret, one year older than he and the son of a neighboring family, who became his closest friend and later the editor of his posthumous *Histoire comique, par M. Cyrano de Bergerac, contenant les états et les empires de la lune* (1657; translated as *Selenarchia; or, The Government of the World in the Moon,* 1659). Le Bret's preface to the work was the only source of fairly accurate biographical information about Cyrano until some official records were discovered in the late nineteenth and early twentieth centuries.

Around 1631 Cyrano was sent to the College of Beauvais, a school headed by a brutal schoolmaster named Grangier, who made Cyrano's early years miserable. Cyrano later satirized Grangier in the comedy *Le Pédant joué* (The Pedant Imitated, 1654). According to Le Bret and Tallemant des Réaux, Cyrano at age seventeen was an unruly student leading a dissipated life, to such an extent that his father, who had just sold his lands at Bergerac and Mauvières, threatened to cut off his son's allowance. Cyrano was plagued with financial difficulties for the rest of his life.

At nineteen, under false pretense, he–with his friend Le Bret–joined the Gardes Nobles, a military corps composed exclusively of men from Gascony and led by Captain Carbon de Castel-Jaloux. The name of Cyrano's village, Bergerac, is common in Gascony, but Cyrano failed to reveal that he himself was not a Gascon, and that his Bergerac was located between Rambouillet and Chevreuse, near Paris. This episode marked the beginning of the lasting legend of Cyrano de Bergerac the swashbuckler. In 1639, during the Thirty Years' War, Cyrano was wounded by a bullet during the siege of Mouzon. His letter "Sur le blocus d'une ville" (About the Blockade of a Town, Letter #10 in *Les Nouvelles Œuvres,* 1661–1662), might

Cyrano's family home, Château de Mauvières, between Chevreuse and Dampierre

have been written at that time. Again, in 1640, he suffered a sword wound to the throat at the siege of
Arras. This wound, as well as the fact that promotion
within the ranks was out of his reach since the highest
ranks were reserved for the aristocracy, prompted him
to retire from the army. According to Le Bret, Cyrano
had also failed to find "un patron auprès de qui son
génie tout libre le rendait capable de s'assujettir" (a
patron whose personality would incite his free-
dom-aspiring genius to serve him).

In 1641 Cyrano returned to Paris. He lived at the
Collège de Lisieux, where he may have taught.
Although some critics question it, Cyrano might have
joined around that time a circle of *libertins* and freethinkers who listened to the lessons of the philosopher Pierre
Gassendi, recently settled in Paris. Among the members
of the group were Jean-Baptiste Poquelin (better known
as Molière) and La Mothe le Vayer the younger. Also
during this time Cyrano, who had fully recovered from

his wounds, took dueling and dancing lessons, the latter
in order to try and make his way into polite society. In
his biography *Savinien de Cyrano Bergerac, sa vie et ses
œuvres* (1893), Pierre-Antonin Brun asserts that Cyrano
traveled several times to Italy and Poland between
1643 and 1653. This information is doubtful, all the
more so since Cyrano fell ill in 1645 and was forced to
borrow 400 livres to treat his illness.

It is generally acknowledged that most of his letters were written during this period. Published only in
1654 as part of *Les Œuvres diverses* (Various Works), the
letters were known long before through manuscript circulation, a common practice at the time. Cyrano organized his letters into four different categories for
publication in one volume: sixteen *Lettres diverses* (Miscellaneous Letters), nineteen *Lettres satyriques* (Satirical
Letters), four *Lettres sur divers sujets* (Letters on Various
Subjects), and eight *Lettres amoureuses* (Amorous Letters).
Ten additional letters were included in the posthumous

edition of *Les Nouvelles Œuvres* (New Works). In 1933 Frédéric Lachèvre added two letters discovered at the Bibliothèque Nationale in Paris. In writing these letters, Cyrano was likely following fashion rather than his own taste. A favorite pastime of the Parisian salons, letter writing was also a literary genre in itself. By composing letters, Cyrano was therefore proclaiming himself a writer, following in the footsteps of admired epistolers such as Jean-Louis Guez de Balzac and Vincent Voiture, while trying to win recognition from the educated elite of the salons.

The *Lettres* represent a vast array of styles and themes. Some propose enigmas; others portray imitations of the baroque characters of *L'Astrée* (1607), the famed novel by Honoré d'Urfé. Cyrano's amatory letters adopt the contrived rhetoric of gallantry. He is also a great satirist; in his letter "Contre un gros homme" (Against a Great Man), the actor Zacharie Jacob Montfleury (not Guillaume Desgilberts Mondory, as some have supposed) is accused of plagiarizing a play. The burlesque poet and novelist Paul Scarron is also bitterly attacked. The tone of "Contre Soucidas" (Against Soucidas) shows how virulent was his quarrel with the *libertin* Charles Coypeau, Sieur d'Assouci, his erstwhile friend for whom he had previously written a preface and a poem: "Au sot lecteur et non au sage," preface to d'Assouci's *Le Jugement de Pâris* (The Judgment of Paris, 1648) and "Pour Monsieur Dassoucy sur sa métamorphose des Dieux" (For Monsieur Dassoucy on his poem "The Metamorphosis of the Gods"), a poem in d'Assouci's *Ovide en belle humeur* (Ovid in Good Humor, 1654). One should not, however, expect too much biographical information from these transient works. The *Lettre diverse XV* "Le Duelliste" (The Duelist) may include some elements on Cyrano's lodgings and on his habit of dueling, but such evidence is too sparse to be conclusive. Indeed, Cyrano himself suppressed biographical information, erasing all names prior to publication. The letters are first and foremost literary in nature and deal with fashionable, and sometimes classical, themes.

The *Lettres* were an immediate success, and an English translation appeared in 1658. They also found their detractors. In his *Bibliothèque françoise* (1664), Charles Sorel criticized Cyrano's literary trademark, the pique, which is best exemplified in his *Entretiens pointus* (Pointed Remarks, 1654). According to Sorel, the letters are "d'un stile particulier . . . qui est d'avoir la plupart de leurs pointes sur les mots par équivoque et sous une double signification; ce qui n'est fait que pour une matière de raillerie, la plupart de l'ouvrage étant d'un stile comique ou burlesque" (of a peculiar style . . . whose piques are mainly derived from double entendres and from puns, as a matter for raillery since most of this work is a comic or burlesque style). In his *Guerre des auteurs* (War of the Authors, 1671), a literary satire of ancient and modern writers, Gabriel Guéret staged a fictitious duel between Cyrano and Guez de Balzac, whose style epitomized epistolary perfection. Balzac faults Cyrano for his figurative style, his ambiguities, his impious remarks, and his vicious attacks against his opponents. Cyrano's letters are indeed extremely acerbic in tone, and some witty jibes at religion reveal that they are intentionally provocative.

These accusations and Cyrano's reputation for scandal lasted well into the twentieth century. Lachèvre and Brun still analyze the *Lettres* in moralizing terms. More recently, critics have done justice to Cyrano and focused on the literary nature of the letters, beginning with Jacques Prévot in his study *Cyrano de Bergerac, poète et dramaturge* (1978).

Prévot observes that the *Lettres diverses,* although they may appear random, are in fact thematically related—ten letters deal with Nature and rely heavily on the baroque imagery of water. The *Lettres diverses* are also grouped in contradictory pairs. A letter that propounds one view is often followed by a letter that argues the opposite. Thus, "Contre l'hiver" (Against Winter) comes before "Pour le printemps" (For the Spring), and "Pour les sorciers" (For the Witches) precedes "Contre les sorciers" (Against the Witches). The *Lettres satyriques* open and close on a criticism of cowardice with "Contre un poltron" (Against a Coward) and "Contre un faux brave" (Against a False Brave Man), which frame the serious charges against Montfleury and Scarron. Cyrano turns the procedure of an open letter into a literary genre; he does not shun personal attacks, and he turns his ideological opponent into a personal enemy. In Cyrano's system the negative seems to preexist the positive, as if the writer's task were to substitute the fragile order of art for the disorder of the world.

The *Lettres* are also the foundation of a political theory. Cyrano develops an aristocratic vision of society. The letters "Contre les frondeurs" (Against the Frondeurs) and "Contre Scarron" reveal some contempt for the common folk and portray Cyrano as a good Catholic hostile to disorder. This self-portrait may appear unusual for a *libertin,* but there was at the time no fundamental contradiction between biting satire and respect for the principles of social order. Seventeenth-century freethinkers, for all their radical views, were wary of political upheaval and extremely aware of the risks of censorship. The emblematic figure of the first generation of seventeenth-century *libertins,* the poet Théophile de Viau, had narrowly escaped a death sentence. His followers were therefore more cautious in selecting their targets. Cyrano delights in attacking

First page of the manuscript for Cyrano's novel about travel to the moon
(Bibliothèque Nationale, Paris)

some familiar figures of authority: pedantic scholars (*Lettres satyriques,* XII), doctors (XVIII), impious clergymen who feed the superstitious fears of the people (XII), and the Jesuits (*Les Nouvelles Œuvres:* "Contres un Je . . . assassin et médisant"; Against a Je . . . Assassin and Slanderer). The letter "Pour les sorciers" introduces a sorcerer; all links with reality are progressively severed, and the supernatural prevails. Only when the dream is broken does the rational order of things return. In the following letter, "Contre les sorciers" (*Lettres diverses,* XII), which encapsulates libertine thought of the period, Cyrano erects reason as the founding principle of all good and attacks superstition, saying, "La raison seule est ma reine" (reason alone is my Queen).

Cyrano's fictional world is extremely varied. The *Lettres* are often poetic and depict familiar baroque imagery, such as constant motion and the fluidity of objects, best exemplified in the seventh letter of the *Lettres diverses,* a fantastically elaborate description of the reflection of a tree on water, symbolizing a slippery and false reality. Comic effects are achieved through exaggeration, realistic descriptions, innuendoes, and crude language in a Rabelaisian vein. The letters capture a brief moment of happiness while describing its elusive and ephemeral nature.

Cyrano is also the author of two plays, a comedy (*Le Pédant joué*) and a tragedy (*La Mort d'Agrippine;* The Death of Agrippina, 1654), written between 1645 and 1647. Although *Le Pédant joué* was first published in 1654 in *Les Œuvres diverses,* an allusion in the play to the marriage of Marie de Gonzague and Ladislas VI of Poland, which took place on 6 November 1645, has caused most critics to believe the play was written some ten years earlier. The date of the first performance is unknown; critic Jacques Truchet, in fact, believes it was never staged because it was too long. Like many libertine works, it circulated in manuscript form before publication, and according to La Mothe le Vayer's pamphlet *Le Parasite Mormon* (1650), it made Cyrano famous.

The five-act plot of *Le Pédant joué* is fairly classical and draws on familiar comic patterns and characters—a peasant beating a braggart, a servant swindling his master, and an elder brother discovering his sister in amorous conversation. One of the principal characters, Granger, is an abusive father who is admired by Paquier, his pedant mirror image. Granger is obviously based on Grangier, the tyrannical headmaster of the College of Beauvais, where Cyrano spent his adolescent years. He is also a blend of comic types found in classical Latin comedy as well as in commedia dell'arte, such as the braggart soldier, the crooked servant, and the doctor. Like many comedies, *Le Pédant*

joué is also a bitter and controversial social satire that criticizes the tense and even violent relationship between parents and children, based on power or financial interest. God is absent from the play and has been replaced by superstition.

Before it was printed, the play was censored by Cyrano himself. Comparison of the version published in 1654 (republished by Prévot in *Œuvres complètes* in 1977) with the manuscript copy (edited by Truchet in *Théâtre du XVIIe siècle* in 1986) reveals that the play was expunged of its most controversial passage: Cyrano suppressed the long libertine monologue in which Granger defies death and which foreshadows the character Séjanus's stoic speech before death in *La Mort d'Agrippine.*

In its published version, *Le Pédant joué* also features some scenes openly deriding religion. Near the end of the play, the newlyweds go to bed without waiting for the sacraments. In a diatribe against apples, Granger mixes biblical and mythological references. Puns and double entendres turn references to sacred rites into sexual innuendoes: "j'avais de la peine à croire qu'un dieu peut habiter avec un homme" (I could hardly believe that a god could live with a man), says Granger to Chasteaufort (Act 1, scene 1).

Prévot has compared Cyrano to Eugène Ionesco and Samuel Beckett. According to Prévot, characters often have an alienating relation to language. Marc-Antoine de Bras de Fer, sieur de Chasteaufort, affabulates and believes in his fictions; Granger speaks Latin only to discredit Despautères (the author of a Latin grammar in use until the eighteenth century) by distorting the meaning of the examples provided by the grammarian and giving them sexual overtones. The peasant Gareau distorts language to such an extent that it sometimes loses all meaning. The servant Corbinelli may be the only character who uses language appropriately and efficiently. The play is an attempt to free language by a servant who frees himself by liberating the young people from the control of a capricious father who is himself alienated by the language of masters. The play may be the first French comedy to deserve fully the title of "language comedy."

According to Prévot, Cyrano's tragedy, *La Mort d'Agrippine,* was written around 1647 and may have been staged around 1653. The only attested performance in Cyrano's lifetime took place in Rouen in 1655. In his journal Christiaan Huygens mentions attending the performance. *La Mort d'Agrippine* is a five-act political tragedy that resembles Cornelian tragedies of the same period. Tiberius, assisted by Nerva, resists a plot fomented against him by Agrippina (Germanicus's widow and Tiberius's daughter-in-law) and Séjanus, a soldier who contemplates raising the Senate

*The Siege of Arras, at which Cyrano received a sword wound in the throat (lithograph
by Roger Viollet; from Georges Mongrédien,* Cyrano de Bergerac, *1964)*

against the emperor and using Agrippina's regency to conquer both the crown and Livilla, his mistress who had already sacrificed her husband for him. Séjanus and Livilla are sentenced to death while Agrippina's children (with the exception of Caligula) are murdered, on Tiberius's orders. In spite of the title of the play, Agrippina herself is spared by Tiberius, in order to prolong her suffering: "Je te veux voir nourrir / Un trépas éternel dans la peur de mourir" (I want you to die an eternal death in the fear of dying; Act 1, scene 7).

The play is based on a famous episode of Roman history that inspired other playwrights of the period, such as Ben Jonson (*Sejanus, His Fall,* 1603) and Jean de Magnon (*Sejanus,* 1647). From a dramatic perspective, the play conforms to the contemporary tragic model, the principal characters of which are historical figures undone by human passions. Prévot calls the play a "revenge tragedy," since vengeance is the main motivation for the characters' actions. Agrippina tries to avenge Germanicus's death by manipulating Livilla, who, suspecting an affair between Sejanus and Agrippina, demands Agrippina's death out of pure jealousy.

The play was apparently successful, largely because of its scandalous aspects. *La Mort d'Agrippine* is a tragedy without any divinity or any *fatum* (divine will of a god); it denies all forms of divine intervention within the dramatic action. The characters are responsible for their own tragic ends and never lament their

fate. In a long monologue at the end of the play, Séjanus challenges death with arguments recalling Epicurean philosophy: "Une heure après la mort nostre âme évanouie / Sera ce qu'elle estoit une heure avant la vie" (One hour after death will our fainting soul / be what it was one hour before birth). According to contemporary testimony, the line "Frappons, voilà l'hostie" (Let's strike, here is the host; Act 5, scene 5, line 1306), pronounced by Séjanus as he is about to kill Tiberius, created quite a stir.

Séjanus's character is unlike any other, and no similar fate is to be found in other plays of the period. He is a faithless conspirator of low birth, a traitor, and a perjured lover who is bold enough to manipulate Agrippina simply in order to gain power. He voices particularly subversive ideas, yet he is given a heroic death and invokes Cato in his last speech. Séjanus considers Tiberius a tyrant who must be eliminated in order to restore the republic. Because of his atheistic and egalitarian views, Séjanus is often perceived as a forerunner of the heroes of philosophical drama. His heroic character becomes more pronounced as the play progresses: "Je marche sur les pas d'Alexandre et d'Alcide / Penses-tu qu'un vain nom de traître, de voleur, / Aux hommes demi-dieux doive abattre le cœur" (I am walking in Alexander's and Alcides's steps / Thinkest thou that the vain titles of traitor and thief / From the demi-gods' hearts could abate the courage), he declares to his confidant Terence while they concoct their plot.

The violence in the play is drawn directly from the speeches rather than from the action. Except for a dagger flung by Agrippina at Tiberius's feet, no violent act is shown on stage. *La Mort d'Agrippine* is in fact a notable play in part because it observes the emerging rules of French classical tragedy—propriety and unity of action. According to Prévot, this clear, rhythmic play is the missing link between Pierre Corneille and Jean Racine.

In 1649 Cyrano inherited his father's estate, which granted him some degree of financial security. During this period, a time of civil insurrection known as La Fronde, Cyrano may have written several *Mazarinades* (political pamphlets attacking Mazarin, then prime minister). His "Lettre contre les frondeurs" (circa 1650) was, until recently, thought to be his only contribution to the rebellion, but critics now attribute seven other pamphlets, signed D.B. or B.D., to him. The "Lettre contre les frondeurs," however, seems to discredit Cyrano as the author of the *Mazarinades,* since it defends Mazarin and attacks his enemies. Several other pamphlets attributed to Cyrano, however, circulate some commonplace accusations against the cardinal. Cyrano may simply have changed his mind, or perhaps, as Prévot believes, "Lettre contre les frondeurs" may be part of the general movement of reconciliation that took place after the rebellion.

Madeleine Alcover observes that if Cyrano used the initials D.B., he never signed B.D. when writing on his own. Moreover, several other writers—such as the notorious *libertins* de Blot and des Barreaux—have the same initials. Finally, there is no contemporary testimony showing Cyrano siding with the rebels. Prévot himself recognizes that the style of the *Mazarinades* is awkward and unimaginative. For her part, Alcover concludes that the seven *Mazarinades* must be attributed to several other authors.

In the 1650s Cyrano was busy writing his novel *Les Empires et les états de la lune*. During that time he also wrote the foreword to his friend Jean Royer Le Prade's complete poetic works, published in 1650, in which Cyrano defines his own views on poetics. In 1653 Cyrano became the protégé of the duke of Arpajon. In 1654 Cyrano received a serious injury to the head in mysterious circumstances. According to Le Bret, the long brain fever that ensued caused Cyrano's disgrace and forced him to leave the duke's residence in 1655. Le Bret reports that a mysterious brotherhood of the Index, which resented Cyrano's writings, was accused of attempted murder. The Jesuits against whom he had written "Contre un Je . . . assassin et médisant" were suspected as well.

Cyrano lived for fourteen months with M. des Boisclairs, the high provost of Burgundy and Bresse

and a friend of Le Bret's. There Mother Marguerite from the convent of Charonne and Mademoiselle de Neuvillette, who was acquainted with the Jesuits, attempted to convert him. Cyrano then moved to his cousin Pierre de Cyrano's house in 1655, perhaps to escape them. There he died five days later on 28 July, having received the last rites. He was probably discreetly buried in Sannois and not, as Brun would have it, after a sumptuous ceremony at the convent of Charonne. There is no convincing evidence as to the place of his burial.

In 1657 *Histoire comique, par M. Cyrano de Bergerac, contenant les etats et les empires de la lune,* the first part of his only novel, *L'Autre Monde,* was published posthumously. The text was censored and the preface written by Le Bret. Rather than publish this bowdlerized version, which was printed by Charles de Sercy, modern editors prefer a text based on the two more complete manuscript copies now in Munich and Paris. No manuscript of *Les etats et empires du soleil,* the second part of the novel, has survived. The only existing version is that published in 1661–1662 by de Sercy in the *Nouvelles Œuvres.* Discrepancies between the first and second parts have raised some doubts as to the attribution; however, most critics believe the text is Cyrano's but that it was rewritten and even censored by the publisher, de Sercy.

The two-part novel relates a trip to the moon and another to the sun. The hero builds a machine that allows him to leave the earth, and after several episodes in different regions (Canada, Macula), he lands on the moon and later on the sun. He visits the terrestrial paradise and then the "enlightened regions." Both episodes end with the imprisonment and trial of the hero because the inhabitants of the moon (the Selenians) and those living on the sun blame him for his strangeness. The narrator narrowly escapes death, thanks to the intervention of more enlightened creatures who have visited the earth, such as Socrates' daemon (on the moon) and the magpie and the parrot (on the sun). The journey back to earth is narrated only in *Les Etats et empires de la lune; Les Etats et empires du soleil* is incomplete.

Cyrano explores and describes the universe in a traveler's tale defined by Prévot as an "epistemological novel," following in the footsteps of Sorel, who wrote an early picaresque novel, and Francis Godwin, who was inspired by the philosophy of Pierre Gassendi; Italian astronomer Gerolamo Cardano; and Tomasso Campanella, who wrote *La città del sole* (The City of the Sun, 1602) and who appears, in fact, as a character in Cyrano's novel. Cyrano relies heavily on the new cosmology of Nicolaus Copernicus, Johannes Kepler, and Galileo, whose theories were still censored by the Church. Orthodox views held the universe to be finite and harmonious, with planets in close proximity, as God had wished it. The Copernican revolution turned it into an infinite space with no center and vast distances between planets, where the earth was but a dot. Cyrano's use of language places him in the burlesque tradition; he depicts fantasy scenes in a realistic way, as in his description of paradise, where Enoch fishes and weaves robes for the eleven thousand virgins. His similes and metaphors also result in burlesque effects. God plays a game of "clique-musette" (hide and seek), and the moon becomes the "platine où Diane fait sécher les rabats d'Apollon" (the plate where Diana lets Apollo's breeches dry). Images such as the comparison between the solar system and an apple or an onion are typical of burlesque style.

Alcover and Prévot have studied the links between *L'Autre Monde* and contemporary philosophy. The novel stages the controversy between the *novatores* (the moderns) and those who side with the Aristotelian tradition, and the reader cannot decide which side Cyrano is on. In *Les Etats et empires de la lune,* the protagonist, while in Canada, is nearly jailed because he espouses principles of the new philosophy of Gassendi and Copernicus, whereas in *Les Etats et empires du soleil* the drawings that illustrate René Descartes's *Principia philosophiae* (1644) send the hero, Dyrcona (almost an anagram for Cyrano), to prison. *Les Etats et empires du soleil* also echoes the controversy fueled by the recent experiments on the void conducted by Torricelli and repeated by Blaise Pascal. Some of Gassendi's arguments can also be found, in a radical version, in the speech of the son of the Host and in the discourses of the philosophers. They develop the materialist and nominalist objections to Descartes's *Méditations* (1641), developed by Gassendi in his *Disquisitio Metaphysica* (1644). Many critics believe that Cyrano studied for a brief time with Gassendi in the early 1640s. In any case, Cyrano was well aware of recent discoveries. During his journey, Dyrcona observes the four satellites of Jupiter as well as the phases of Venus, both of which were recent astronomical observations made by Galileo, described by Gassendi and mentioned by Descartes.

Cyrano refuses to assent blindly to any one scientific system, but in antidogmatic and eclectic fashion, he sides only occasionally with a particular theory. It is therefore hard to make sense of the philosophical positions presented in the novel. Hence the debate between critics such as Alcover, who considers Cyrano a pure atheist, and Prévot, who places him in the skeptical tradition. For Alcover, Cyrano's philosophical choices are always heretical. At a time when libertinism had become more secretive, Cyrano explicitly wrote what he believed. The narrator of his novel, however,

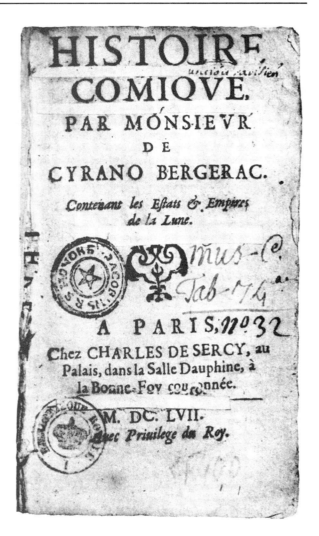

Title page for Cyrano's novel about space travel (from Mongrédien, Cyrano de Bergerac, *1964)*

reflects multiple, and sometimes conflicting, personae. He is at first a bold, enterprising character until he reaches Heaven; then he becomes gullible and fearful. This split persona is not invented in order to deflect censorship but to discredit the ideology of the time. Cyrano's freethinking is aggressive: wherever he goes, the hero quarrels with the inhabitants and questions the existing system. His life is always considered scandalous. His voyage, narrated in a falsely fideistic tone, is the adventure of nonbelief.

Prévot sees *L'Autre Monde* as teaching a lesson in skepticism: Cyrano is trying to show that man's vision of the world, the answers to his questions, and his knowledge can be reduced to verbal constructs, a belief that accounts for the many discursive layers of the novel. Cyrano assesses in a critical way the knowledge of his times and challenges an optimistic and totalitarian vision of science. Socrates's daemon takes up

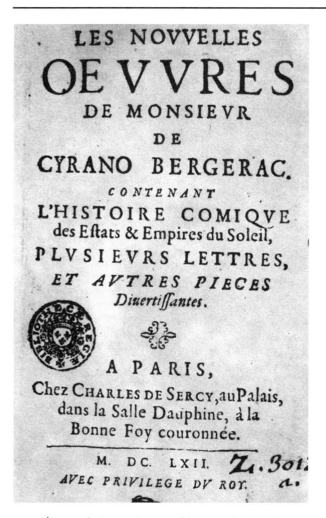

LES NOVVELLES
OEVVRES
DE MONSIEVR
DE
CYRANO BERGERAC.
CONTENANT
L'HISTOIRE COMIQVE
des Eftats & Empires du Soleil,
PLVSIEVRS LETTRES,
ET AVTRES PIECES
Diuertiffantes.

A PARIS,
Chez CHARLES DE SERCY, au Palais,
dans la Salle Dauphine, à la
Bonne Foy couronnée.

M. DC. LXII.
AVEC PRIVILEGE DV ROY.

*Title page for the second volume of Cyrano's collected works
(from Mongrédien,* Cyrano de Bergerac, *1964)*

Sorel's theory, Gonsales that of Godwin, and the moon's philosophers refer to libertine works. The jumble of new and competing theories expounded by the various characters reflects the confusion many undoubtedly felt at the time.

The *Fragment de physique* (Fragment of Physics), a work written around 1654–1655, is attributed to Cyrano, but its authorship has been questioned. In 1671 a friend of Cyrano's, the Cartesian mathematician Jacques Rohault, published *Traité de physique* (1671), which bears unmistakable resemblances to the *Fragment de physique,* as Alcover has shown. According to Claude Clersellier, who edited Rohault's *Œuvres posthumes* in 1682, Rohault wrote at a certain point a second draft of his *Traité,* or rather, a simplified version for his students. The internal order of the *Fragment de physique* is the same as Rohault's *Traité de physique.* Rohault's *Conférences* confirm that he presented his lecture in that order in 1661, and some didactic asides in the *Fragment*

de physique show that it, too, addresses the same nonspecialist audience targeted by Rohault's draft.

The *Fragment de physique* announces John Locke's and Etienne Bonnot de Condillac's sensualist theories and recalls Gassendi's conception of man rather than Rohault's, who is more Cartesian. The plan of the *Fragment de physique* is controversial: from the start, the Ancients' cosmography is rejected systematically in favor of a more open conception of science. For Alcover, Cyrano is more of an aggressive atheist than a thinker professing "a radical skepticism." The second half of the *Fragment de physique* is far less clear than the first, and Alcover believes that the text was written while Cyrano was suffering from the brain fever that ultimately caused his death. Moreover, the obscure passages cannot be attributed to Rohault and are definitely written by Cyrano, who was no mathematician. This reasoning explains why the fragment is still attributed to Cyrano even though the outline is at least partially Rohault's.

In the last hundred years, the critics have turned Cyrano de Bergerac the braggart from Gascony depicted by Edmond Rostand in his play *Cyrano de Bergerac* (1897) into a genuine Parisian writer, acquainted with *libertin* circles and receptive to new and daring philosophical ideas. What was once considered excessive language, boundless imagination, and the far too outspoken atheism of a lonely baroque writer is now acknowledged as the trademark of a major representative of Parisian worldly libertinism of the day.

Biographies:

Pierre-Antonin Brun, *Savinien de Cyrano Bergerac, sa vie et ses œuvres* (Paris: A. Colin, 1893);

Georges Mongrédien, *Cyrano de Bergerac* (Paris: Berger-Levrault, 1964);

Michel Cardoze, *Cyrano de Bergerac 1619–1655: Libertin libertaire* (Paris: J.-C. Lattès, 1994).

References:

Madeleine Alcover, *Cyrano relu et corrigé* (Geneva: Droz, 1990);

Alcover, *La Pensée philosophique et scientifique de Cyrano de Bergerac* (Paris: Minard, 1970);

Pascal Beugnot, ed., *Voyages: Récits et imaginaire, actes de Montréal (7–9 avril 1983)* (Paris: Papers on French Seventeenth Century Literature, 1984);

Olivier Bloch, "Cyrano de Bergerac et la philosophie," *XVIIe Siècle,* 149 (1985): 337–348;

Henri Busson, *La Pensée religieuse française de Charron à Pascal* (Paris: Vrin, 1933);

Mary Baine Campbell, *Wonder and Science: Imagining Worlds in Early Modern Europe* (Ithaca, N.Y.: Cornell University Press, 1999);

Jean-Charles Darmon, *Philosophie épicurienne et littérature au XVIIe siècle* (Paris: PUF, 1998);

Joan DeJean, *Libertine Strategies: Freedom and the Novel in Seventeenth-Century France* (Columbus: Ohio State University Press, 1981);

Jeanne Goldin, *Cyrano et l'art de la pointe* (Montreal: Presses de l'Université de Montréal, 1973);

Erica Harth, *Cyrano and the Polemics of Modernity* (New York: Columbia University Press, 1970);

Edward W. Lanius, *Cyrano de Bergerac and the Universe of the Imagination* (Geneva: Droz, 1967);

Maurice Laugaa, "Cyrano: Sound and language," *Yale French Studies,* 49 (1973): 199–211;

Annette Lavers, "La Croyance à l'unité de la science dans *L'Autre Monde* de Cyrano," *Cahiers du Sud,* 47 (1953): 406–416;

Christian Liger, "Les Cinq Envols de Cyrano I," *Nouvelle Revue Française,* 152 (1965): 242–256;

Liger, "Les Cinq Envols de Cyrano II," *Nouvelle Revue Française,* 153 (1965): 427–442;

Haynd Mason, *Cyrano "L'Autre Monde"* (London: Grantrand Cutler, 1984);

François Moureau, ed., *Métamorphoses du récit de voyage: Actes du Colloque de la Sorbonne et du Sénat (2 mars 1985)* (Paris & Geneva: Champion & Slatkine, 1986);

W. A. Nierenberg, "Cyrano Physicist," *Proceedings of the American Philosophical Society,* 130, no. 3 (September 1986): 354–361;

Buford Norman, "Cyrano and Pascal: A Similarity of Method," *L'Esprit créateur,* 19, no. 1 (Spring 1979): 40–49;

René Pintard, *Le Libertinage érudit dans la première moitié du XVIIe siècle* (Paris: Boivin, 1943);

Jacques Prévot, "Cyrano de Bergerac ou l'homme qui avait la tête dans les étoiles," *Littératures classiques,* 15 (1991): 145–161;

Prévot, *Cyrano de Bergerac, poète et dramaturge* (Paris: Belin, 1978);

Prévot, *Cyrano de Bergerac, romancier* (Paris: Belin, 1977);

Timothy Reiss, "Cyrano and the Experimental Discourse," in *The Discourse of Modernism* (Ithaca, N.Y.: Cornell University Press, 1982);

Cecilia Rizza, *Libertinage et littérature* (Fasano, Italy: Schena / Paris: Nizet, 1996);

Pietro Toldo, "Les Voyages merveilleux de Cyrano de Bergerac et de Swift, et leurs rapports avec l'œuvre de Rabelais," *Revue des études Rabelaisiennes,* 4 (1906): 299–334; *Revue des études Rabelaisiennes,* 5 (1907): 24–44;

Hélène Tuzet, *Le Cosmos et l'imagination* (Paris: Corti, 1965);

Jacqueline Van Baelen, "Reality and Illusion in *L'Autre Monde:* The Narrative Voyage," *Yale French Studies,* 49 (1973): 178–184.

Papers:

Savinien de Cyrano de Bergerac's manuscript of *Le Pédant joué* is located in the Bibliothèque Nationale, Paris, as are his *Lettres* (both in nouv. acq. f. fr. 4557). The manuscript of *Les Etats et empires de la lune* is also found at the Bibliothèque Nationale, Paris (nouv. acq. f. fr. 4558); another version of *Les Etats et empires de la lune* is held in Munich at the Bayerische Staatsbibliothek (Gall 419); yet another copy is held by the Fisher Library (R.B.Add.Ms.69) in Sydney, Australia.

René Descartes

(31 March 1596 – 11 February 1650)

Jeremy Sabol
Yale University

BOOKS: *Discours de la Méthode pour bien conduire sa raison, et chercher la verité dans les sciences. Plus La Dioptrique. Les Météores. Et La Géométrie. Qui sont des essais de cete Méthode* (Leiden: J. Maire, 1637);

Meditationes de prima philosophia, in qua Dei existentia et animae immortalitas demonstratur (Paris: M. Soly, 1641); enlarged as *Meditationes de prima philosophia, in quibus Dei existentia, et animae humanae à corpore distinctio, demonstrantur. His adjunctae sunt variae objectiones doctorum virorum in istas de Deo et animae demonstrationes; Cum responsionibus authoris. Secunda editio septimis objectionibus antehac non visis aucta* (Amsterdam: L. Elzevier, 1642);

Epistola Renati Des-Cartes ad celeberrimum virum D. Gisbertum Voetium. In qua examinantur duo libri, nuper pro Voetio Ultrajecti simul editi, unus de Confraternitate Marianâ, alter de Philosophiâ Cartesianâ (Amsterdam: L. Elzevier, 1643);

Principia philosophiae (Amsterdam: L. Elzevier, 1644);

Notae in programma quoddam, sub finem anni 1647, in Belgio editum, cum hoc titulo: Explicatio mentis humanae, sive animae rationalis, ubi explicatur quid sit, et quid esse possit (Amsterdam: L. Elzevier, 1648);

La Naissance de la paix: Ballet (N.p.: J. Janssonius, 1649);

Les Passions de l'âme (Amsterdam: L. Elzevier, 1649; Paris: H. Le Gras, 1649);

Musicae compendium (Utrecht: G. à Zijll et T. ab Ackersdijck, 1650); translated by William Brouncker as *Excellent Compendium of Musick* (London: Printed by Thomas Harper for Humphrey Moseley, 1653);

Lettres de Mr Descartes, 3 volumes, edited by Claude Clerselier (Paris: C. Angot, 1657–1667);

De Homine, translated into Latin by Florent Schuyl (Leiden: P. Leffen et F. Moyardum, 1662); French version published in *L'Homme de René Descartes, et Un Traité de la formation du foetus* (Paris: C. Angot, 1664; Paris: T. Girard, 1664; Paris: J. et N. Le Gras, 1664);

Le Monde de Mr Descartes, ou Le Traité de la lumière et des autres principaux objets des sens . . . (Paris: M. Bobin

René Descartes (portrait by J.-B. Weenix; Musée Central d'Utrecht)

et N. Le Gras, 1664; Paris: T. Girard, 1664; Paris: J. Le Gras, 1664);

Epistolae, partim ab auctore Latino sermone conscriptae, partim ex Gallico translatae. In quibus omnis generis quaestiones philosophicae tractantur, et explicantur plurimae difficultates quae in reliquis ejus operibus occurrunt, 2 volumes (Amsterdam: D. Elzevier, 1668);

Traité de la Méchanique, composé par Monsieur Descartes. De Plus, L'Abrégé de Musique, edited and translated by Nicolas Poisson (Paris: C. Angot, 1668);

114

Opuscula posthuma, physica et mathematica (Amsterdam: P. et J. Blaeu, 1701);

Pensées de Descartes sur la religion et la morale, edited by Jacques-André Emery (Paris: A. Le Clère, 1811);

Œuvres inédites de Descartes, 2 volumes, edited by Alexandre-Louis Foucher de Careil (Paris: A. Durand, 1859–1860).

Editions and Collections: *Œuvres de Descartes,* edited by Charles Adam and Paul Tannery (13 volumes, Paris: L. Cerf, 1897–1913; revised edition, 11 volumes, Paris: Vrin, 1974–1986);

Discours de la méthode: Texte et commentaire, edited by Etienne Gilson (Paris: Vrin, 1925);

Discours de la méthode, edited by Gilbert Gadoffre (Manchester: Manchester University Press, 1941);

Œuvres philosophiques de Descartes, 3 volumes, edited by Ferdinand Alquié (Paris: Garnier, 1963–1973);

Regulae ad directionem ingenii, edited by Giovanni Crapulli (The Hague: M. Nijhoff, 1966);

Les Passions de l'âme, edited by Geneviève Rodis-Lewis (Paris: Vrin, 1970);

Règles utiles et claires pour la direction de l'esprit en la recherche de la vérité, edited and translated by Jean-Luc Marion (The Hague: M. Nijhoff, 1977).

Edition in English: *The Philosophical Writings of Descartes,* 3 volumes, edited and translated by John Cottingham, Robert Stoothoff, Dugald Murdoch, and Anthony Kenny (Cambridge & New York: Cambridge University Press, 1984–1991).

René Descartes, considered the founder of modern philosophy, also played an important role in what is now called the scientific revolution, which inaugurated the modern conception of scientific knowledge. He elaborated a comprehensive philosophical system spanning metaphysics, physics, physiology, and ethics. Like Francis Bacon and Galileo, Descartes developed his system in conscious opposition to the dominant scholastic philosophy of the time, a Christianized Aristotelianism as interpreted by Thomas Aquinas and other late-medieval thinkers. Descartes's own philosophy was founded in what he considered to be evident truths intuited by the natural faculty of reason. His metaphysics centered on the establishment of the individual subject, a being characterized by rational thought. He considered the mind of this subject as completely distinct from all matter, including the body, although the mind and body are connected and can affect each other. This theory is the famous Cartesian "mind-body split," although the division of the soul and the body into two separate essences was a traditional distinction that preceded Descartes.

Descartes's philosophical projects often stand in sharp contrast to the conditions in which he lived and worked. Although Descartes is often called the greatest philosopher of France, little of his adult life was actually spent in France. He sought a stable foundation for philosophy in the midst of a bloody religious war that changed the face of Europe. This lack of stability extended to Descartes's personal life: he moved constantly from place to place, frequently changing his address. The thinker who dedicated his life to establishing consensus on philosophical principles was plagued with bitter controversies for most of his publishing career, and these controversies only escalated after his death—his philosophy was banned in the universities in France, and his writings were put on the *Index Librorum Prohibitorum* (Index of Forbidden Books) in Rome in 1671. Despite these difficulties, Descartes in his writings had an enormous impact on the philosophy and science of the later seventeenth century. This influence has changed but not necessarily waned; many important philosophical theories and concepts, such as rationalism and the mind-body problem, remain strongly associated with Descartes and his works.

Descartes was born on 31 March 1596 in a small village just outside Châtellerault, near Poitiers. At the time the town was called La Haye, but in 1802 its name was changed to La Haye-Descartes and then simply to Descartes. René was the third child of Joachim Descartes and Jeanne Brochard. Joachim was a councillor in the *parlement* in Rennes, and Jeanne came from a family of merchants and public administrators. A little more than a year after René's birth, his mother died, and, along with his older brother and sister, he was subsequently brought up by his maternal grandmother, Jeanne Sain, even though his father remarried in 1600.

Descartes was sent to La Flèche, a Jesuit *collège,* in 1606. The Jesuit *collèges,* like the municipal *collèges* before them, played a primary role in the formation of the French gentry class. In the early seventeenth century they were also part of the educational wing of the Catholic Reformation, forming an orthodox elite class that helped in the battle against Protestantism and heresy. La Flèche, founded in 1604, was the finest Jesuit college in France, with the possible exception of the Jesuit Collège de Clermont in Paris, the first to be established. The Jesuit curriculum was dictated by *Ratio Studiorum* (Plan of Studies, 1599), a massive and detailed document that spelled out a uniform course of study for all the *collèges.* The curriculum centered on grammar and rhetoric but also included natural philosophy and mathematics. Descartes and his fellow students were therefore fully grounded in the principal writings of Aristotle—the *Organon* (fourth century B.C.), scientific texts such as *Physics* and *On the Heavens,*

Descartes's birthplace, outside Châtellerault, near Poitiers

and *Nicomachean Ethics*—as well as relevant commentaries, from Porphyry's introduction to Aristotle's *Categories* to the influential Coimbra commentaries (works on the philosophical works of Aristotle written by the Jesuits at the University of Coimbra in Portugal) from the last part of the 1600s. These writings were supplemented with other modern texts, especially those written by Jesuits for the express purpose of being used in the educational system. These works included a range of texts from German-born Christopher Clavius's important writings on mathematics in Italy to handbooks of casuistry by authors such as the Spanish Jesuit Francis Toletus.

La Flèche was not only a place of academic learning, however; like all the Jesuit *collèges,* it was a complete environment that incorporated study, sports and other competitions, theatrical entertainment, and ceremonies. In this way, the *collèges* addressed many of the critiques leveled at the educational system during the Renaissance while reinforcing respect for the institutions of authority and the traditional corpus of knowledge.

In 1614 the eighteen-year-old Descartes left La Flèche to pursue successively two typical career choices for educated "gentlemen" of his class and generation—the law and the army. He first went to the University of Poitiers, where he graduated with a degree in civil and canon law in 1616. Then, in the summer of 1618, he volunteered as a soldier in the army of Prince Maurice of Nassau, a professional Dutch army structured according to the military organizational reforms of Maurice's mentor, the Flemish humanist Justus Lipsius.

Descartes left Maurice's army shortly to join the Catholic army of Maximilian I in Bavaria, in the beginning of 1619. In the summer of 1619 he went to Frankfurt to see the coronation of Ferdinand II. Unable to return to Bavaria in late fall of that year because of difficult weather, he stayed for the winter near Ulm, on the Danube River. While in Ulm, Descartes had a series of visions, or dreams, that significantly affected the course of his life. According to Descartes's first biographer, Adrien Baillet, the celebrated series of three dreams occurred on 10 November 1619. They were full of vivid, symbolic imagery, which Descartes allegedly began to interpret even while the last of the dreams was still occurring. The experience led Descartes to believe that the "fondamentum inventi mirabilis" (foundations of a marvelous science) had been revealed to him and that he had been entrusted by God with establishing a new philosophy that would be systematic and comprehensive. This vision convinced him to make a pilgrimage to Italy, to the shrine of the Virgin at Loretto. More important, it encouraged his intellectual ambitions and helped to determine the broad scope of his later philosophical projects.

During his military service, Descartes met Isaac Beeckman, a teacher at the Latin School in Dordrecht; Beeckman became Descartes's mentor for the next few years. He introduced Descartes to specific approaches to natural philosophy that remained with Descartes throughout his career. Both men were interested in what was called "mixed mathematics," a branch of mathematics of growing importance, in which traditional geometry was applied to physical problems. Beeckman introduced Descartes to the use of mechanistic arguments to describe physical processes. Mechanism offers explanations of the natural world based solely on the physics of invisibly small particles—atoms, which make up all matter. Although there were many atomistic, or corpuscular, natural philosophies at this time in Europe, Beeckman had an innovative approach, which Descartes learned and ultimately developed into a sophisticated system. Beeckman's corpuscularism is different from traditional atomism: he believed that the particles that make up matter are uniform, except for variation in size—therefore, speed and direction of motion determine all observable phenomena. These particles are impenetrably hard, so the laws of impact describe the only interactions that occur between them.

Under Beeckman's influence, Descartes wrote a musical treatise describing the relationship between the lengths of vibrating strings and their pitch. Beeckman and Descartes also worked on two significant physical problems, which shaped Descartes's future thinking about physics. These problems were the kinematics of freely falling bodies and the "hydrostatics paradox," in which volumes of liquid of varying volumes but identical base areas exert an identical pressure. The latter case especially provides a clear example of a mechanist explanation of an observable phenomenon. In order to analyze the pressure exerted by a volume of liquid, Descartes describes the forces, transmitted by individual particles of liquid, that act on neighboring particles.

In mid 1619 Descartes also began to work on a mathematical theory of proportional magnitudes. He had been constructing proportional compasses to solve classic unsolved geometrical problems, and his discoveries led him to believe he was on the brink of developing what he called a *mathesis universalis,* a universal mathematics, which would rely on a general theory of proportions. In such a mathematics, geometry and algebra would be simply two branches of a much more general discipline. Although Descartes did not continue to develop this *mathesis universalis,* much of his thinking during this time formed the basis for his later work in analytic geometry. This work found its final form in his essay "La Géométrie," published in 1637 with *Discours de la Méthode pour bien conduire sa raison, et chercher la verité dans les sciences* (Discourse on the Method for Guiding Reason Correctly, and Searching for Truth in the Sciences).

This attempt at finding more general approaches to branches of knowledge marked the beginning of Descartes's first important writing about method, *Regulae ad directionem ingenii* (Rules for the Direction of the Mind). As early as 1619, eighteen years before his *Discours de la Méthode,* Descartes was already considering all areas of knowledge to be, in fact, one science. He also began to think about developing a method that would consistently lead to new knowledge. No longer limiting his approach to the generalized mathematics of the *mathesis universalis,* now Descartes believed he could logically organize all of knowledge under one discipline. He begins the first rule in *Regulae ad directionem ingenii* thus: "Scientiae omnes nihil aliud [sunt] quam humana sapientia, quae semper una et eadem manet, quantumvis differentibus subjectis applicata" (All the sciences are in fact nothing else but human wisdom, which stays unique and identical to itself, regardless of the various objects to which it is applied). Although the *regulae*

share many elements in common with *Discours de la Méthode,* the early *regulae* present a method characterized by two central concerns: the method must provide a unified system of inquiry, which relates the branches of *scientia,* or knowledge; and it must emphasize certainty—only absolutely certain knowledge can be retained as *scientia* in this unified system. Certain knowledge must begin with intuition. Descartes believed that things known through intuition are directly present to the mind in their entirety. Descartes's examples and models for intuition and certainty are taken from geometry: one knows intuitively that a triangle is bound by three sides. Intuition is akin to seeing: it is like envisioning a simple object in the mind, apprehending it immediately, and knowing its essential nature for certain.

The first section of *Regulae ad directionem ingenii* presents an analysis of intuition and deduction as methods of gaining knowledge and ends with a mechanist model of how the brain interprets perceptions, both external (sensation) and internal (concepts, imagination). This model of cognition actually extends through much of the second section of the work as well, although the purpose of the second section was to present (mathematical) problems whose solutions are known and can be found by the principles presented in the first section. The third section, never begun, was to provide examples of unsolved problems, specifically problems that cannot easily be represented in the form of an equation. The goal of this section was to show how problems of this nature can be reduced to the kind treated in the second section.

Descartes most likely wrote the first eleven rules in 1620, and then apparently abandoned the project. However, he returned to it in 1626–1628, adding the rest of the extant rules and significantly altering at least one of the earlier rules before finally abandoning the project entirely. Although *Regulae ad directionem ingenii* was not published during Descartes's lifetime, manuscript copies must have been in circulation at least during the 1650s and 1660s. A substantial passage from rule 13 appears paraphrased in the second edition of *La Logique, ou L'Art de penser* (Logic, or the Art of Thinking, 1664). This text, also known as the "Port-Royal Logic," was an influential text on language written by two Jansenist thinkers, Antoine Arnauld and Pierre Nicole, and is one of the clear links between Cartesianism and the resurgence of Augustinian thinking in the seventeenth century.

Descartes had returned to France by 1622, where he sold his part of his mother's estate; the sale provided him with some yearly income. Between 1622 and 1625 Descartes appears to have been working on a treatise titled "Studium bonae mentis" (Study of the Good Mind), although no manuscript survives, nor does any-

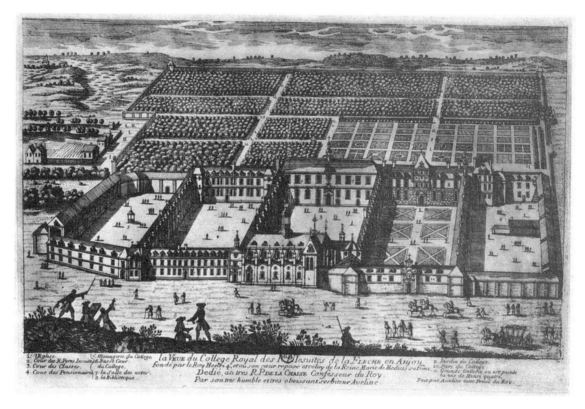

*La Flèche, the Jesuit school Descartes attended from 1606 until 1614
(engraving from Léon Brunschvicg,* René Descartes, *1937)*

one know what the treatise discussed. Descartes also continued his work in mathematics, as is evidenced from a large collection, which he put together in 1626 of the results of various mathematicians. In 1623 Descartes began a voyage to Italy with an itinerary that echoed Michel Eyquem de Montaigne's travels there almost fifty years before, which Montaigne had described in his 1581 "Journal de Voyage" (Travel Journal), although no evidence exists that this choice of route was a conscious decision on Descartes's part.

After an unsuccessful attempt at purchasing the position of lieutenant general for the region in which he was born, Descartes settled in Paris in 1625. For the next three years he lived in Paris and participated in its intellectual life, which was quite animated during the 1620s. The decade was characterized at once by a considerable growth of new thinking and a severe repression of that new thought. Giulio Vanini, an Italian philosopher and renowned atheist, had been burned at the stake in Toulouse in 1619, and the lengthy trials of the poet Théophile de Viau during the early 1620s were an alarming signal to Parisian intellectuals. These events brought the concept of libertinage (freethinking) into the forefront of public attention. Libertinage took many forms, but it was characterized by a skeptical attitude toward traditional beliefs, up to and including the

tenets of the Catholic faith. Descartes's circle included thinkers who have been called *libertins érudits* (erudite libertines). The *libertins érudits* included such men as Pierre Gassendi, François de La Mothe Le Vayer, and Gabriel Naudé. In general, they were philosophers or men of letters, often well-respected and under the protection of a powerful figure in the French court. They were receptive to new or alternative systems of thought–such as atomism and empiricism; yet, publicly, they supported the traditional political and religious institutions that maintained social order. To say what the actual beliefs of these men were is frequently difficult, as they rarely wrote or publicly acknowledged their attitudes. Their favorite genre was the dialogue, in which the author could present and contrast many perspectives without necessarily taking a stance toward any of the opinions.

Descartes was also friendly with many outspoken critics of libertinage, including Jean de Silhon, Jean-Baptiste Morin, and especially his close friend Marin Mersenne, a Minim priest who had published several books that attacked skepticism and atheism. Although Mersenne's primary concern was with Catholic apologetics, he nonetheless ardently supported the incorporation of newer philosophical methods and ideas–especially mechanist methods–in natural philosophy.

Descartes and Guez de Balzac, a critic and stylist, also became friends at this time. Descartes even wrote a public letter defending Balzac's controversial *Lettres* (1624–1626) as the ideal balance between the two reigning models of rhetoric, the Attic and Asiatic styles.

Descartes's life projects were directly influenced by his interaction with the intellectual elite during this period. The clearest example of this relationship occurred in 1628, when Descartes attended a lecture on alchemy in the private residence of the Papal Nuncio. The lecture, given by a man named Chandoux, was an exposition of a new theory of chemistry in opposition to Aristotelian chemistry. Descartes agreed with Chandoux in his criticisms of Aristotle, but he was unimpressed with the alternate system that Chandoux proposed in its stead. Apparently, Descartes stood up and offered ideas of his own. One of the other members in the audience was Cardinal Pierre de Bérulle, a religious reformer who had founded the Oratory, an order dedicated to preaching and evangelistic teaching as well as erudite research. Bérulle was impressed enough by Descartes's presentation to request a private meeting with him. The cardinal encouraged Descartes to continue his efforts to develop a systematic natural philosophy. This encouragement must not only have bolstered Descartes's resolve to undertake this project but must also have underscored the importance of a mechanist philosophy compatible with orthodox Catholicism, especially in the context of so many new systems of thought that were perceived to be heretical or dangerous to Catholic doctrine. Finding such a system certainly colored Descartes's work in the next decade, beginning the following year, when he first began to consider metaphysical and theological questions.

Descartes spent much of his time during his Paris years working on problems in optics, and in this regard he worked closely with Claude Mydorge, a wealthy man of letters who had done a great deal of work in optics. By 1628 Descartes had derived the law of refraction, which geometrically relates how light rays behave when they pass from one medium to another. This law, commonly known as Snel's law, had been developed a few years earlier by the Dutch natural philosopher and mathematician Willebrod Snel. However, Descartes is generally believed to have developed the same law independently of Snel, although Descartes's actual process of discovery is not known for certain.

In the period from 1626 to 1628 Descartes also returned to his unfinished *Regulae ad directionem ingenii*, which he had abandoned seven years before. The later rules were concerned primarily with a mechanical model of cognition. In particular, Descartes wanted to offer an explanation of how physical qualities are represented and understood by the mind. His model is based on the assumption that all perceptible qualities can be represented in two-dimensional geometric figures. These figures are imprinted on the matter of the brain in a process that functions both as perception and as memory. A memory is simply the stored imprint of a perception. These concerns led to a discussion that incorporates Descartes's work in geometrical algebra. Algebra is a generalized way to manipulate magnitudes. These magnitudes in turn can represent line lengths, which are the building blocks of the representational figures in the imagination. Algebra is therefore not only a tool for manipulating the elements of complex problems in a simple way but is also materially related to how the mind functions and perceives sensation.

Descartes left Paris at the end of 1628 or the beginning of 1629 and moved to the Netherlands, his home for the next twenty years. He had few acquaintances there and allegedly brought with him little else besides a Bible and the *Summa Theologiae* (Summary of Theology, 1265–1273; first complete printing, 1485) of Thomas Aquinas. Although Descartes's reasons for leaving France remain somewhat of a mystery, the reason that the Netherlands appealed to him is understandable: it was a vibrant center of humanistic thought, with liberal printing laws and a tolerance for new ideas, such as the Copernican model of the universe, which Descartes clearly believed to be true.

After brief stays in Amsterdam and Dordrecht, Descartes settled in the city of Franeker. In 1629 he worked on methods for grinding hyperbolic lenses, which focused all incoming light to a single point. He exchanged a great deal of detailed correspondence on this matter with his friend Jean Ferrier, an instrument maker in Paris who had worked with Descartes and Mydorge while the former was still in Paris. Their letters show Descartes's extreme attention to experimental detail and serve as one of many important correctives to the common notion that Descartes was a "pure" rationalist, with no interest in experimentation or empirical methods.

Descartes began to explore other realms of philosophy at this time; he relates in his correspondence that he planned to write a "little treatise" on metaphysics. Although nothing remains of this treatise, most critics agree that about this time Descartes began to develop the metaphysical arguments that were introduced in his *Discours de la Méthode* and more fully developed in his meditations.

Also in 1629 Descartes began his attempt at producing a general model of the physical universe. The project did not start out with such an immense scope. Initially, Descartes was concerned with explaining a meteorological phenomenon called parhelia, in which certain atmospheric conditions produce the appearance

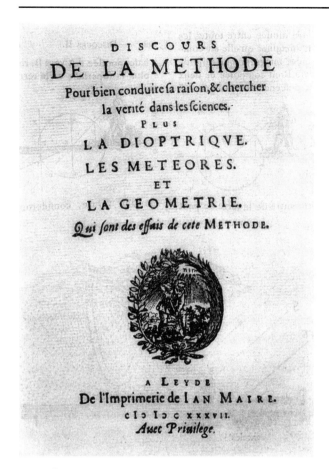

Title page for Descartes's first work, in which he attempted to define methods for scientific research (from Brunschvicg, René Descartes, 1937)

of multiple suns. This physical problem coincided neatly with Descartes's recent thinking about optics and inspired him to write a small text on meteorology, which he later published as an example of his approach to natural philosophy. Only one month later he wrote to Mersenne, explaining that the project had now grown to an explanation of the entire natural world. His work eventually led, during the next three years, to a manuscript titled "Le Traité de la lumière" (Treatise on Light).

This text, although never completed, and published only posthumously as *Le Monde de Mr Descartes, ou Le Traité de la lumière et des autres principaux objets des sens . . .* (The World of M. Descartes, or The Trait of Light and Other Principal Objects of the Senses . . . , 1664), was Descartes's first coherent description of his physics. The mechanist explanations of macroscopic phenomena clearly grew out of the work that Descartes had done with Beeckman ten years before, but they are far more ambitious and comprehensive than the piecemeal approach to particular problems that characterized their collaborative efforts. The treatise begins by asserting

that the appearances of physical phenomena are unrelated to their causes. This statement is in fact an important justification for the mechanist approach since it justifies the introduction of tiny particles that are undetectable yet completely determine the behavior of the visible world.

Descartes then details his theory of matter, reducing all phenomena to simple particles and their motion. He also argues against the existence of a void; all of space—or extension, as Descartes calls it—is synonymous with matter. The rest of the treatise is devoted to a "fable" in which Descartes imagines an unused portion of the universe, in which God creates a world, or cosmos, according to a set of laws of motion. This cosmos eventually evolves to look exactly like the present one, complete with stars and planets that revolve around a sun, thus implying that the theory of matter and the laws of motion described in the "fable" also govern the functioning of the "real" cosmos. After a compelling explanation of earthly tides, rainbows, and other atmospheric phenomena, the text breaks off and begins again with a detailed portrait of human physiology. A transitional passage, either lost or never written, would have covered the movement from the physical to the biological, perhaps addressing the origin of life and the physiology of plants and the lower animals. Just as the cosmological model of the first section was structured as a "fable," the second part of the text, *De Homine* (On Man), describes human physiology in terms of the functioning of hypothetical automata—purely physical beings that God could have created without rational minds but that share the same physiology as humans. Although Descartes's anatomical descriptions and accounts of most bodily functions are taken directly from classical and medieval sources, his mechanistic explanations of these functions are innovative—in particular, he gives a detailed model of perception, and of vision in particular, as well as an explanation for the circulation of the blood. Descartes had read the English physiologist William Harvey's *De motu cordis* (On the Motion of the Heart, 1628), and although Descartes agreed with Harvey that blood circulated through the body, he rejected Harvey's model of the heart as a pump and attempted to explain circulation by the production of heat in the heart.

In 1633 Descartes learned of the condemnation in Rome of Galileo's *Dialogo sopra i due massimi sistemi del mondo, tolemaico e copernicano* (Dialogue Concerning the Two Chief World Systems, Ptolemaic and Copernican, completed in 1630; published in 1632). Galileo's text was condemned by the Catholic Church for its affirmation of the Copernican model of the universe, in which the earth revolves around the Sun, instead of the Ptolemaic model, in which the earth was motionless at the center of the universe. Like Galileo's text, Descartes's *Le Monde* presented an explicitly Copernican planetary system; although Descartes had carefully narrated his cosmology as a fable and not as a literal account of the real universe, he judged it too dangerous to publish in the wake of the Galilean affair. In fact, this incident led Descartes temporarily to renounce the idea of publishing altogether, believing that his work should not circulate widely until after his death.

At the end of 1633 Descartes moved back to Amsterdam, where he spent two years living in the home of the headmaster of a French school and his family. During that time he became intimately involved with the serving maid for the house, Hélène, who gave birth to a daughter, Francine. Hélène's name is never mentioned in Descartes's correspondence, and Francine only once (as his "niece")–if nothing else, this behavior indicates that Descartes's relationship with Hélène did not remain intimate. Little more is known about the degree to which Descartes might have offered support for her or Francine.

Descartes did, however, form a lasting relationship in Amsterdam with Constantijn Huygens, secretary to the Prince of Orange. Constantijn and Descartes wrote to each other frequently for the rest of Descartes's life, corresponding about personal as well as philosophical matters, and Constantijn became an influential supporter of Descartes's ideas. Huygens's son, Christiaan Huygens, later became one of the most important natural philosophers of the second half of the seventeenth century. Although he made significant criticisms of Descartes's works, his own contributions to a mechanist physics were heavily influenced by Cartesian mechanism.

While in Amsterdam, Descartes continued to work on optics and some of the initial work on visual phenomena that had spurred the writing of *Le Monde*. These two areas of concern gradually became two of the three essays that he finally agreed (through Mersenne's pressuring) to publish. The third summarized much of Descartes's thinking about geometrical algebra. In late 1636 he began writing a short preface for the three essays to be published. This preface included an autobiographical narrative and gave a summary description of his suppressed texts, *Le Monde* and *De Homine*. In 1637 Descartes published his essays "La Dioptrique" (Optics), "Les Météores" (Meteorology), and "La Géométrie" (Geometry) along with the preface, which had by then become the famous *Discours de la Méthode*.

Discours de la Méthode is a complex text, serving many purposes at once. On the one hand, it is an intellectual autobiography: Descartes describes his childhood education, travels, and military service, as well as the various unpublished texts that he wrote and some of his reasons for withholding those texts. On the other hand, the *Discours de la Méthode* is an exposition of Descartes's views on moral, civic, and scientific matters–including at least two versions of a method for discovering what Descartes asserted to be certain knowledge.

In the first section of the *Discours de la Méthode*, Descartes reviews his education, both at La Flèche and during his military service. Although initially appearing to give a measured analysis of the benefits and drawbacks of the various elements of this education, the effect of the narrative is ultimately to undermine systematically the value of the humanist education and point out its inability to provide a firm basis for knowledge. Descartes's account is particularly "anti-humanist," as Henri Gouhier described it in his *L'Antihumanisme au XVII e siècle* (1987), in its portrayal of the traditional repository of wisdom–texts from antiquity. Despite centuries of study, these texts, he says, have not yet produced any absolutely certain truths. Descartes points toward the fruitlessness of the traditional scholastic exercise, the disputation: "Considérant combien il peut y avoir de diverses opinions, touchant une même matière, qui soient soutenues par des gens doctes, sans qu'il y en puisse avoir jamais plus d'une seule qui soit vraie, je réputais presque pour faux tout ce qui n'était que vraisemblable" (Considering how many diverse opinions learned men may maintain on a single question–even though it is impossible for more than one to be true–I held as well-nigh false everything that was merely probable).

Descartes's answer to this uncertainty is to renounce his education and to turn inward, to discover truth within himself. This response leads to a discussion of his method. This method has many similarities with the discussions of method in *Regulae ad directionem ingenii*, but it is more streamlined. The precepts for this method, as given in the second part of the discourse, are few and simple: "Ne recevoir jamais aucune chose pour vraie, que je ne la connusse évidemment être telle: c'est-à-dire, . . . ce qui se présenterait si clairement et si distinctement à mon esprit, que je n'eusse aucune occasion de le mettre en doute"; ". . . diviser chacune des difficultés que j'examinerais, en autant de parcelles qu'il se pourrait"; ". . . conduire par ordre mes pensées, en commençant par les objets les plus simples . . . pour monter peu à peu . . . jusques à la connaisance des plus composés"; ". . . faire partout des dénombrements si entiers, et des revues si générales, que je fusse assuré de ne rien omettre" (never to accept anything as true if I did not have evident knowledge of its truth: that is, . . . what presented itself to my mind so clearly and so distinctly that I had no occasion to doubt it; to divide each of the difficulties I examined into as many parts as pos-

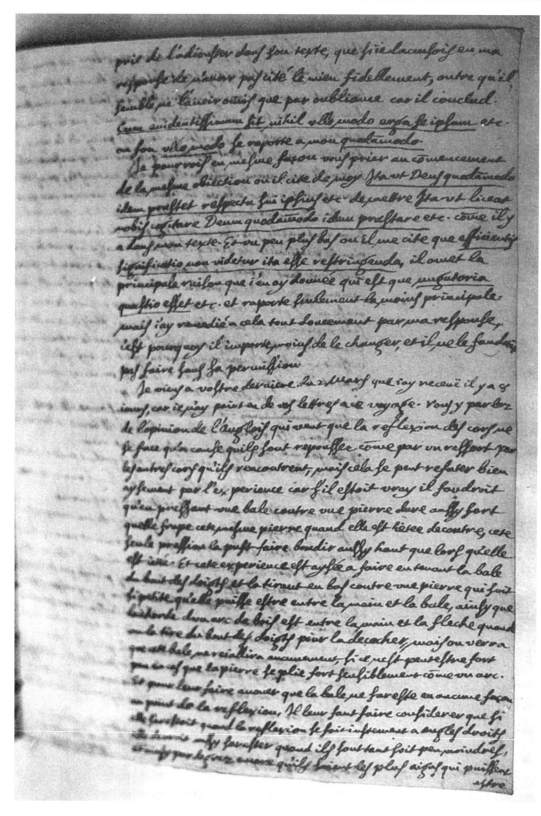

*Page from Descartes's 18 March 1641 letter to his friend Marin Mersenne, requesting changes in the text
of* Meditationes de prima philosophia *(Bibliothèque de la Sorbonne, Paris)*

sible; to direct my thoughts in an orderly manner, by beginning with the simplest . . . objects in order to ascend little by little . . . to knowledge of the most complex; to make enumerations so complete and reviews so comprehensive, that I could be sure of leaving nothing out).

This general form of the method does not give great insight into how Descartes actually applied it to his contemporary work in optics or analytic geometry. However, in the final section of the discourse, Descartes gives a more concrete account of how the third step in the method—the orderly progression of thoughts—might occur. This treatment explains how, once he has arrived at basic first principles, he deduces additional principles and so on, until arriving at purely deduced phenomena that can then be compared with those observed in the physical world. This process is in fact quite similar to Descartes's construction of the "fable" of the cosmos as it is developed in *Le Monde*.

In the third part of the discourse, Descartes gives what has been called for two reasons his "provisional ethics": first, because Descartes presents it as a temporary solution, to serve until he can develop a more coherent system; second, because it functions as a standard of behavior for situations in which one does not possess certain knowledge. In its content, this ethics is essentially a public declaration of assent to the norms dictated by legal and cultural institutions while implicitly reserving an interior freedom to investigate freely any principle or subject matter—the kind of ethics proposed by Montaigne in essays such as "De la coustume et de ne changer aisément une loy receüe" (Of Custom, and Not Easily Changing an Accepted Law, 1580) and "Des prieres" (Of Prayers) or in writings by Guez de Balzac, Descartes's friend and exact contemporary, in his 1654 "Dissertations chrestiennes et morales" (Christian and Moral Dissertations).

The fourth part of the discourse is devoted to a metaphysical foundation for knowledge. It briefly presents what is known as the *cogito* argument—I think, therefore I am—as well as three distinct arguments for the existence of God. This short discussion is the basis for the more detailed analyses of *Meditationes de prima philosophia, in qua Dei existentia et animae immortalitas demonstratur* (Meditations on First Philosophy, in Which the Existence of God and the Immortality of the Soul Are Shown), published four years later, in 1641. Descartes acknowledged afterward in a letter that this part was the weak spot in his text. He explains that in part he did not give a fuller account because he was worried that, at this stage, his discussion could lead careless thinkers toward irresponsible skepticism.

In the fifth part of the text, Descartes summarizes the analyses of his unpublished texts of the 1630s, *Le*

Monde and *De Homine*. This summary leads to a long discussion in the sixth and final part, relating Descartes's misgivings about publishing his writings. He completes this discussion with a final justification for publication—a proposal for a kind of scientific institution, which he himself would direct, in which experiments would be carried out by paid workers under his supervision. The three essays that follow the discourse are presented in this light as proof that Descartes has the expertise and methodology to justify his position at the head of such an institution.

Although the *Discours de la Méthode* was considered in later centuries to be his most important piece of writing, the immediate responses to the publication were much more focused on the three essays than on the discourse. There was a certain amount of controversy over the alleged originality of the essay on geometry, but most discussion was focused on the two physical essays on optics and meteorology, "La Dioptrique" and "Les Météores." Perhaps not until the end of the century did Descartes begin to be appreciated for his contributions to a "method" of finding knowledge.

One of the more controversial elements of the *Discours de la Méthode* was the summarized account of human physiology in the treatise *De Homine*. The discussion of automata implied that all animal behavior can be described in terms of pure mechanics, and therefore animals would have no need for a soul. Although Descartes did not make this explicit point in the text, and although he did not devote much more exposition to the question in *Meditationes de prima philosophia,* the subject was nevertheless controversial. Objections arose in part because of the further possible implication that there was no human soul either and that all human functions, including mental ones, could be explained through mechanist arguments. Descartes dealt with this subject frequently in his correspondence to worried friends or colleagues, and it was the subject of important discussions in the fifth and sixth objections and replies to *Meditationes de prima philosophia*. The controversy was heightened after Descartes's death, especially in 1664 when *De Homine* was published; it remained part of a common public perception of Cartesian philosophy. In the ninth book of Jean de La Fontaine's *Fables choisies* (Chosen Fables, 1678-1679), the "Discours à Madame de la Sablière" (Discourse to Madame de la Sablière) gives a clear portrait of this perception: "Ils disent donc que la bête est une machine; qu'en elle tout se fait sans choix et par ressorts . . . Voici de la façon que Descartes l'expose; Descartes, ce mortel dont on eût fait un Dieu" (They say, then, that the beast is a machine; that it does all without choice, with the aid of springs: no feelings, no soul, all body. . . . This is the way that Descartes describes it; Descartes, this mortal who would have been made a God). La Fontaine's text explicitly critiques Descartes's mechanist physiology. La Fontaine, as well as other important literary figures, such as Madeleine de Scudèry, were opposed to Cartesian mechanism essentially because of its implications for the human soul.

The next few years were a busy and fulfilling time for Descartes. He lived near Haarlem for most of this period and became more concerned with the welfare of his daughter, Francine. Possibly, Francine and her mother even lived with Descartes during this time; however, Francine died of fever in September 1640, in Amersfoort. Although Descartes speaks of her death only indirectly in a letter, Baillet asserts that Francine's death was the saddest moment of Descartes's life.

He spent a great deal of time responding to criticisms of the discourse and the essays, which were widely read and commented on, particularly "Les Météores." He also began to work on the text of the meditations. *Meditationes de prima philosophia,* first published in 1641, is yet another text with complex goals. As Descartes spells out in the prefatory letter to the Sorbonne, the explicit goal of the text is to prove the existence of God by the light of natural reason, as well as to prove the immortality of the soul and the nature of the distinction between mind and body. Perhaps thinking back to his meeting with Cardinal Bérulle in the 1620s, Descartes makes reference to the important 1513 Lateran council against heresy—thus aligning his text with the orthodox Catholic Reformation and against Protestantism, heresy, and libertinage. As Descartes claims in his correspondence, however, there were other goals of the text that were much more pressing concerns for him. As he indicates several times in his correspondence of the period, his primary objective was the establishment of an orthodox metaphysical grounding for his mechanist physics—something Descartes understood to be necessary after the 1633 condemnation of Galileo. By the end of the sixth and final meditation, Descartes had derived a mechanistic model for the physical world that did not rely on the natural-philosophical arguments of *Le Monde* but rather on purely metaphysical concerns, and first and foremost on God.

One of the most significant characteristics of the meditations is the role of doubt in the search for certain truth. Skepticism already played a role in the abolishment of prejudices, as well as in the establishment of certain knowledge, in the *Discours de la Méthode.* However, in *Meditationes de prima philosophia,* the role of skeptical arguments is more explicitly elaborated. The narrator of the meditations begins by suspecting his senses of deceiving him. This suspicion leads to more general doubts, such as whether any of the sensations humans perceive are trustworthy or whether they are all illusory, of the type received while one is asleep and dreaming. This question eventually leads to the more extreme doubt that there is no reality in human experiences—even in the most basic ideas about extension, shape, or geometric principles. This complete deception could be the will of an omnipotent God, or worse, it could be the result of there being no God at all—or, even more disturbingly, it could be the work of a malicious demon, who devotes all his power to maintaining humans' senses and reason in a state of total illusion. These last steps take Descartes to what is called radical, or hyperbolic, doubt—an extreme, hypothetical attitude that is consciously assumed in order to strip the mind of all prejudices, so that a solid foundation for thinking can be established. In this way, Descartes saw his strategic (and limited) use of skeptical arguments as in fact an answer to the skepticism that was prevalent in intellectual circles across Europe.

Indeed, the final product of this radical doubt is a positive, certain affirmation: if the subject has doubts, there must exist a doubting thing. This thought is the famous *cogito ergo sum* (I think, therefore, I am), in which the narrator asserts that thinking must presuppose the existence of something that can think—the thinking subject; therefore, humans can be certain of that subject. The conclusion of this argument reaffirms the initial move away from sense perception: the rational mind is and will remain more certain than knowledge of the body and the external world beyond it.

Descartes moves from this knowledge of the thinking mind to the establishment of the existence of God. As in the *Discours de la Méthode,* he presents three arguments, although they are given in *Meditationes de prima philosophia* in much fuller form. The first of these is a causal argument, and it begins with the scholastic distinction between formal and objective reality. Formal reality can be understood as actual existence, while objective reality can be understood as representational content. Descartes argues that there must be at least as much formal reality in the cause of an idea in the mind as there is objective reality in the idea itself. Since humans' idea of God is the most perfect thing they can imagine, they could not have caused it, as they do not have such a perfect degree of formal reality. The idea can only have been put into humans' heads by an agent possessing an infinite, or perfect, formal reality—and thus, God must exist.

The next argument is sometimes referred to as the cosmological argument and shares structural similarities to the causal argument. It begins by reasserting the self, a thinking thing. What created this self? One cannot have been self-created, because then one would not have the imperfections that one is aware of possessing (for example, error). One cannot claim to have

eftre diuifée entre toutes les
eut imaginer qu'elle eft com-
ement imaginer que celle de
vers B eft compofée de deux
ait defcendre de la ligne AF

UE. — DISCOURS II.   97

e bale, pouffée d'A vers B, ren-
plus la fuperficie de la terre,

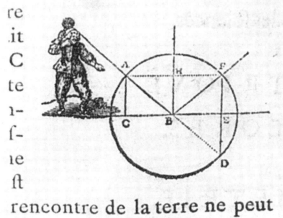

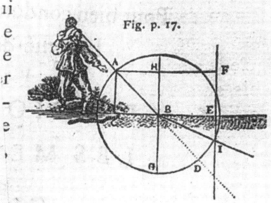

rencontre de la terre ne peut

le doit fuiure, confiderons

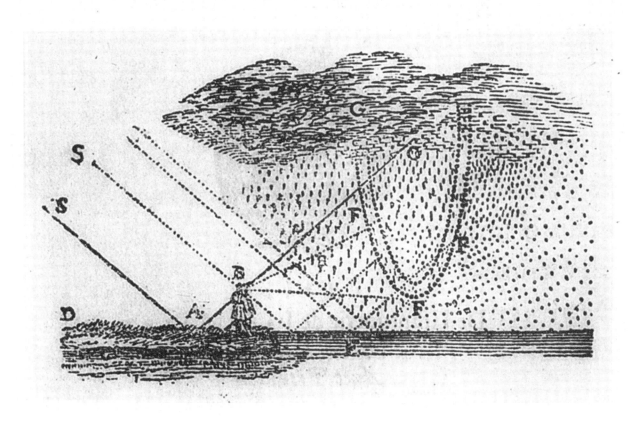

Illustrations from the essays on optics (top) and meteors (bottom) in Descartes's
Discours de la Méthode *(from Brunschvicg,* René Descartes, *1937)*

always existed and thus dispense with the need for a creator, because—in Descartes's set of assumptions—maintaining the existence of something from instant to instant is equal to the task of creating it. So if one continues to exist, something has to maintain this existence, which can be conceived as continuously creating that existence. Finally, no other imperfect creature could have created a human, because he has an idea of a perfect God within him, and this concept could not have been created by any imperfect thing. Therefore, humans must have been created by God, who must therefore exist.

The final argument for the existence of God is called the ontological argument. It presupposes the certainty of "idées claires et distinctes" (clear and distinct ideas), as asserted in all of Descartes's writings to this point. Descartes proposes that, just as it is inconceivable to think of a triangle without realizing it has three sides, it is inconceivable to think of a perfect thing whose essence is separate from its existence. Essence can be understood as the nature of a thing, regardless of whether it is real (for example, a Pegasus is a flying horse), while existence implies the actual reality of a thing. But God's essence is to be perfect, and perfection implies that essence and existence are inseparable, so God must exist.

Only after the existence of God has been firmly established does Descartes return to the question of the external world. God assures the validity of human reason, and humans can use reason to correct the sometimes uncertain knowledge provided by the senses. Humans can acquire certain knowledge about the world as long as they properly use their reason as a guide and a corrective to their perceptions.

Another important feature of *Meditationes de prima philosophia* is the form of its publication. The first published edition of the meditations was directly followed by six initial "objections" by important intellectual figures, which in turn were responded to by Descartes. A first small printing of the meditations was actually carried out in the fall of 1640, and copies were circulated, by way of Mersenne, to various important intellectual figures, including the English philosopher Thomas Hobbes, Gassendi (the principal French proponent of atomism and Epicureanism), the Jansenist theologian Arnauld, and Mersenne himself. This distribution to important figures gave the text the appearance of a public intellectual exchange and gave Descartes the opportunity to meet directly initial challenges to his arguments within the same volume.

In the following year, another edition was printed, which included a seventh set of objections by the Jesuit priest Pierre Bourdin. To Descartes's great disappointment, Bourdin's response was lengthy,

harsh, and at times bitterly sarcastic; Bourdin accused Descartes of obscurantism, as well as of an excessive and careless use of skeptical arguments that were dangerous for religious truths. Although the substance of Bourdin's criticisms was far less significant than most of those found in the other objections, Descartes's answers were extremely detailed, especially compared with his rather brusque dismissals of some of the questions posed by Hobbes and Gassendi. Descartes was greatly concerned with gaining the approval of the Jesuits, as he saw their acceptance as the principal way to get his philosophy approved and into circulation in the French schools. He appealed to a former Jesuit professor at La Flèche, Père Dinet, in a long letter, defending his case against Bourdin and appealing to Dinet to garner more support among the Jesuits after Bourdin's attack. This letter was appended to the second edition of *Meditationes de prima philosophia* and focused on the issue of the Catholic orthodoxy of Cartesian philosophy. In the letter, Descartes goes further than ever in speaking of religious matters, claiming that since truth is always identical, it is impossible for philosophically derived truth to differ from divine truth. Even further, "Omnino profiteor nihil ad religionem pertinere, quod non aeque ac etiam magis facile explicetur par mea principia, quam per ea quae vulgo recepta sunt" (I insist that there is nothing relating to religion that cannot be equally well or even better explained by means of my principles than can be done by means of those that are commonly accepted).

While Descartes's philosophy was under attack by the Jesuits, he was also involved in a vicious public debate with a Protestant professor of theology in Utrecht, Gisbertus Voetius. A polemical and somewhat caustic supporter of Cartesianism, Henri Le Roy (often known by his Latinate name, Regius), had published a series of Cartesian theses. Voetius, believing that Cartesianism was the most pernicious form of the new philosophy that was so detrimental to traditional philosophy, attacked Regius's writings and, through them, Descartes.

Although the quarrel with Voetius spanned many topics and involved many ad hominem arguments—that is, arguments speaking against the man instead of the issue—the most significant part of the debate was over Descartes's explanation of transubstantiation. In the traditional account of transubstantiation, the substance of the bread in communion becomes the body of Christ, while the form of the bread remains the same. Descartes attempted to frame his mechanist explanation within the orthodox model, but it is difficult to see how he could, since the essence of his argument was that form is entirely determined by substance. Thus, Descartes was reduced to arguing that, although the sub-

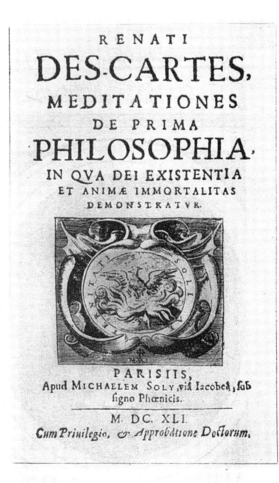

Title pages for the 1641 Latin edition and the enlarged 1647 French edition of Descartes's thoughts about God and the soul (from Brunschvicg, René Descartes, *1937)*

stance changes, the form does not *appear* differently to the senses. Therefore, the surface qualities of the host—shape and color, for example—somehow have to remain identical, even as the substance undergoes a radical transformation from bread to the body of Christ.

Significantly, although the Jesuits and Protestant scholastics such as Voetius were coming from radically incompatible positions, they essentially shared similar views on the traditional interpretation of transubstantiation, which came from the writings of Aquinas. Descartes's account undermined this interpretation and was therefore considered dangerous by Catholics and Protestants alike. These fierce polemics lasted many years—during the course of the debate, Descartes eventually separated himself from his follower Regius and published *Notae in programma quoddam* (Comments on a Certain Broadsheet, 1648), a severe criticism of Regius's version of Cartesian philosophy.

In the early 1640s Descartes made various attempts at writing a full exposition of his philosophy,

both natural and metaphysical. He considered writing his explanation in the form of an extended commentary on an existing philosophical treatise, as well as in a kind of dual format, in which his system would be compared page by page with a standard textbook on traditional scholastic philosophy. He even briefly considered writing a philosophical dialogue in French—there is an extant fragment of this dialogue, titled *La Recherche de la Vérité par la lumière naturelle* (The Search for Truth by Means of the Natural Light). Although this text is only a dozen or so pages long, it is significant because it indicates at least one of the audiences that Descartes was trying to reach: the dialogue is written in the manner of untold others of the first half of the seventeenth century—by men such as Guez de Balzac, La Mothe Le Vayer, and the Père Bouhours—and directed toward the French gentleman and the nobility. However, Descartes's primary concern was to introduce his writings into the French university curriculum. He ultimately decided on a textbook format, intended to be a kind of summa, a type of philosophical compendium used by students that covered an entire philosophical system. Descartes designed it to compete with the traditional scholastic textbooks then in use in the schools, for example, the *Summa philosophiae quadripartita: De rebus dialecticis, moralis, physicis, et metaphysicis* (Summary of Philosophy in Four Parts: On Matters of Dialectic, Ethics, Physics, and Metaphysics, 1609), by Eustache de Saint-Paul. Descartes hoped that it would replace those texts and become a staple of the French educational system, despite growing resistance from the Jesuits.

Principia philosophiae (Principles of Philosophy) was published in 1644. It was composed of four books, each devoted to a specific part of Cartesian philosophy. Although *Principia philosophiae* was originally intended to cover metaphysics, natural philosophy, medicine, and ethics, Descartes never addressed the final two subjects. The first book is foundational and addresses the same topics treated in the first five *meditationes,* except that they were now organized in a traditional scholastic format, each point logically leading to the next in a series of short articles. The second book begins with the distinction between mind and body and then moves toward a general discussion of matter as extension. Its central component, however, is the exposition of the laws of motion. Much of the content of this book and the next was first laid out in *Le Monde;* however, the material is structured in a much more traditional argument and is oriented more directly at contrasting its features with the perceived weaknesses of scholastic Aristotelian natural philosophy. The third book of *Principia philosophiae* deals with the mechanist model of the universe and the vortex theory of matter that comprised the bulk of *Le Monde.* Descartes takes great pains to downplay the Copernicanism of this model, but reactions to the text show that this ploy was not particularly successful. Finally, the fourth book deals with the particulars of the planet Earth–how it evolved and how its characteristics can be derived from mechanistic principles. Descartes originally intended to publish a fifth and a sixth book, which would discuss the physiology of living things in general, then humans, respectively–these books were never written, though the later *Les Passions de l'âme* (The Passions of the Soul, 1649) addresses some of the subject matter originally planned for them.

Although Descartes originally published many of his writings in the 1640s in Latin, he wanted his philosophy to be accessible to a wider audience in France (translated into French). At the same time, he considered it equally important that his French publications, the *Discours de la Méthode* and the essays be translated into Latin, the common tongue of all of scholarly Europe. In 1647, *Meditationes de prima philosophia* and *Principia philosophiae* were published in French transla-

tions, both of which were supervised and approved by Descartes. The meditations were translated by Charles-Louis d'Albert, duc de Luynes, and were published along with the objections and replies, which were translated by Descartes's fervent supporter Claude Clerselier as *Les Méditations métaphysiques de René Des-Cartes touchant la première philosophie . . . , et les objections faites contre ces méditations par diverses personnes très-doctes, avec les réponses de l'Auteur* (1647); the latter was responsible for the posthumous publication of three volumes of Descartes's correspondence, as well as the first publications of *Le Monde* and *De Homine.* Meanwhile, *Principia philosophiae* was translated by the Abbé Claude Picot, who began the project in 1644 when Descartes came to Paris after the Latin publication of the principles. Although the French *Méditations* follow the original Latin text quite closely, the French *Les Principes de la philosophie* (1647) differs significantly from the Latin in some places, likely indicating Descartes's own desired modifications for the French edition. The most significant addition to the French *Principia philosophiae,* however, was an entirely new preface, written as a letter to Picot as translator. In the preface, Descartes draws a now-celebrated comparison between philosophy and "Un arbre, dont les racines sont la métaphysique, le tronc et la physique, et les branches qui sortent de ce tronc, sont toutes les autres sciences, qui se réduisent à . . . la médecine, la mécanique, et la morale" (a tree, of which the roots are metaphysics, the trunk is physics, and the branches that arise from this trunk are all the other sciences . . . [which reduce to] medicine, mechanics, and ethics).

During the mid 1640s Descartes was still living in Holland, having moved from Utrecht to Endegeest to Egmond du Hoef. By 1642, after the controversy in Utrecht with Voetius, Descartes had become something of a public figure, and for people to come from The Hague or Leiden to visit him was a common occurrence. Likely one of these visitors was the twenty-four-year-old Princess Elizabeth of Bohemia, whose mother Descartes had visited in the mid 1630s. By 1643 Descartes and Elizabeth had begun writing to each other regularly. Although their correspondence began essentially as math lessons for Elizabeth, the letters grew quickly warmer and more substantial, as Elizabeth began asking excellent and difficult questions about one of the central problems raised in *Meditationes de prima philosophia*–the exact nature of the union between the mind and the body. Elizabeth's questioning led Descartes to offer a series of more and more detailed explanations about the passions and their relationship to the mind. The term "passions" had a broader sense in the seventeenth century–Descartes and Elizabeth used it to refer to any affective state that

Descartes's house at Endegeest, one of the towns in Holland where he lived during the 1640s

arose in the body but influenced the mind. In the letters that passed back and forth between Descartes and Elizabeth during 1643–1646, Descartes traced out a rough draft of what became his final published work, *Les Passions de l'âme*.

The goal of this book was to reformulate the question of the passions and their effect on the mind so that the question hinged more precisely on the nature of the relationship between body and mind. Earlier currents of thought about the passions, both in the Stoic and in the Augustinian traditions, tended to combine mental and corporeal attributes of the passions. Descartes believed this combining to be a confusion of the real issues and attempted to describe the effects of passions in a more causal framework.

The work is an attempt to explain the relation of the body to the soul in order to provide a mechanical or physiological framework for desires and emotions. Although Descartes claims, in the letters that serve as a preface to the text, that he is not writing as a moral philosopher, the work can be read as the basis for a Cartesian system of ethics. Significantly, however, Descartes consistently grounds his discussions of the passions in physiological explanations, themselves rooted in Cartesian physics. This presentation is consistent with his portrayal of philosophy as a tree, in which the higher branches, such as ethics, must be supported by the trunk, which is physics.

The text is divided into three parts, each of which is divided into many short articles. The first section provides general definitions of the concepts used in the book and introduces the framework of Descartes's theories of the passions. The second section gives a hierarchical typology of the different passions, enumerating the six "primitive passions" and explaining their functioning in the body and their interaction with the mind. The third section is dedicated to describing specific passions that are composites of the primary six discussed in the second part. These descriptions range from brief explanations of phenomena, such as derision or gratitude, to longer series of articles on important and complex passions, such as generosity.

Although Descartes focuses his explanations on the physiological basis for the passions, the text has a clearly discernible moral aspect. In Descartes's view the passions must be controlled by the rational mind. While such control is not always possible, understanding the functioning of the passions teaches ways to rein in their effects on the mind. Only through proper control of the passions may they become virtuous.

The key example of a virtuous passion for Descartes is generosity. Generosity is essentially a Stoic virtue—it is based on the knowledge that a human's only true possession is free will, and its virtue lies in using that free will to carry out what the rational mind judges to be the best course of action. Descartes's reinforcement of Stoic ethical principles is combined with a positive belief in the power of the rational mind to restrain and channel not only the emotions but also the body, and the material world in general. The goal of simultaneous control over the body and the exter-

Descartes (second from right) with Queen Christina of Sweden (center), whose court he was invited to join in 1649 (Musée de Versailles)

nal world is consonant with the final section of Descartes's first published writing, the *Discours de la Méthode,* in which he asserts confidently that the end result of rational thinking is the development of a practical philosophy that will make humans "[Les] maîtres et possesseurs de la nature. Ce qui n'est pas seulement à désirer pour . . . qu'on jouirait . . . des fruits de la terre . . . mais principalement aussi pour la conservation de la santé, laquelle est le premier bien et le fondement de tous les autres beins de cette vie" (the lords and masters of nature. This is desirable not only for . . . enjoyment of the fruits of the earth . . . but also, and most importantly, for the maintenance of health, which is undoubtedly the chief good and the foundation of all the other goods in this life).

In the spring of 1648, while Descartes was still living in Egmond, he was interviewed by a young Dutchman named Frans Burman, who came to visit

and brought a large number of questions about Descartes's philosophy. Burman took copious notes after the interview, and the notes were transcribed into Latin later by one of Burman's friends. Although not technically written by Descartes, most scholars agree that the document provides an insightful look into how the older Descartes viewed his life's work. The text especially emphasizes that Descartes saw his own contributions to physics as more central than his writings on metaphysics.

In early 1649 Descartes was invited to join the court of Queen Christina of Sweden, in Stockholm. Christina, a reader of Descartes's *Principia philosophiae* and one of his correspondents for several years, asked him to come and tutor her in philosophy. Although Descartes had misgivings about joining the court, he finally did so in September, at the age of fifty-three. He spent the fall performing various court functions, even attempting to write a pastoral com-

Constantijn Huygens, an influential supporter of Descartes, and Huygens's son Christiaan, who became an important contributor to mechanist physics during the second half of the seventeenth century (engravings from Brunschvicg, René Descartes, *1937)*

edy for the court. He finally began giving philosophy lessons at the start of the new year but was soon unable to continue as he had contracted pneumonia. René Descartes died on 11 February 1650.

The reception of Descartes's works in the second half of the century was quite mixed. Institutional reactions were almost uniformly negative. Despite Descartes's hopes of having his philosophy integrated into the French curriculum, the teaching of Cartesian principles was rarely permitted. For complex doctrinal as well as pedagogical reasons, the Jesuits devoted enormous efforts to attacking Cartesianism, from the disputations of Cartesian principles at the Clermont College in 1665, to a joint prohibition with the order of the Oratorians against teaching Descartes in 1678, to the formal condemnation in 1706. Louis XIV issued an edict against Cartesian teachings in 1671, and Descartes's writings were put on the *Index Librorum Prohibitorum* in Rome in 1663. There were diverse reasons for this seemingly uniform condemnation. Many reasons were aimed at Descartes's followers: the controversy over Jansenism in the 1650s and 1660s, for example, had an impact on the public opinion of Cartesianism. Arnauld, a polemicist as well as a

theologian, was seen as a proponent of Cartesian principles, and this connection tied Jansenism to Cartesianism in the eyes of many, including the Jansenists' fiercest opponents, the Jesuits.

Other criticisms of Cartesianism were centered on the shortcomings of Descartes's natural philosophy. The vortex theory of matter—espoused in *Le Monde* and in *Principia philosophiae*—was severely criticized in the physical writings of later important philosophers such as Benedict de Spinoza, Gottfried Wilhelm Leibniz, and Christiaan Huygens. At the same time, all of these later thinkers acknowledged their debt to Descartes and were heavily influenced by his approach to natural philosophy as well as metaphysics. Nicolas Malebranche was one of the most important French philosophers in the late seventeenth century, and his influential works were explicit extensions of Cartesian philosophy. His most important texts, *De la recherche de la vérité* (On the Search for the Truth, 1674–1675)—the title inspired by Descartes's unfinished dialogue)—and *Conversations chrétiennes* (Christian Conversations, 1677), were attempts to reconcile Cartesian philosophy more directly with orthodox Catholicism. Although the seventeenth century probably ended with more anti-Cartesians than pro-Cartesians, this fact pointed toward Descartes's central place in philosophical and scientific thinking of the century: every significant thinker in the latter part of the seventeenth century had to grapple with the issues raised by René Descartes's writings.

Letters:

Correspondance publiée avec une introduction et des notes, 8 volumes, edited by Charles Adam and Gérard Milhaud (Paris: Presses Universitaires de France, 1936–1963).

Bibliographies:

Gregor Sebba, *Bibliographia Cartesiana; A Critical Guide to the Descartes Literature, 1800–1960* (The Hague: M. Nijhoff, 1964);

A. J. Guibert, *Bibliographie des œuvres de René Descartes publiées au XVIIe siècle* (Paris: Editions du Centre National de la Recherche Scientifique, 1976);

Vere Chappell and Willis Doney, *Twenty-five Years of Descartes Scholarship, 1960–1984* (New York: Garland, 1987);

Bulletin Cartesien. Supplement to *Archives de Philosophie* (Paris, n.d.).

Biographies:

Adrien Baillet, *La Vie de Monsieur Descartes,* 2 volumes (Paris: Daniel Horthemels, 1691; fascsimile reproduction, New York: Georg Olms, 1972);

Charles Adam, *Vie et oeuvres de Descartes* (Paris: Editions du Cerf, 1910)–originally published as volume 12 of the Adam and Paul Tannery edition of the *Oeuvres de Descartes;*

Gustave Cohen, *Écrivains français dans la première moitié du XVIIᵉ siècle* (Paris: Champion, 1920);

Stephen Gaukroger, *Descartes: An Intellectual Biography* (New York: Oxford University Press, 1995);

Geneviève Rodis-Lewis, *Descartes: Biographie* (Paris: Calmann-Lévy, 1995).

References:

Ferdinand Alquié, *La découverte métaphysique de l'homme chez Descartes* (Paris: Presses Universitaires de France, 1950);

Roger Ariew, *Descartes and His Contemporaries: Meditations, Objections, and Replies* (Chicago: University of Chicago Press, 1995);

Ariew, *Descartes and the Last Scholastics* (Ithaca, N.Y.: Cornell University Press, 1999);

Jean-Marie Beyssade, *La philosophie première de Descartes: Le Temps et la cohérence de la métaphysique* (Paris: Flammarion, 1979);

Susan Bordo, *The Flight to Objectivity: Essays on Cartesianism and Culture* (Albany: State University of New York Press, 1987);

Francisque Bouillier, *Histoire de la philosophie cartésienne,* 2 volumes (Paris: Delagrave, 1868; fascimile reproduction, New York: Georg Olms, 1972);

Léon Brunschvicg, *René Descartes* (Paris: Les Editions Rieder, 1937);

Pierre-Alain Cahné, *Un autre Descartes: Le Philosophe et son langage* (Paris: Vrin, 1980);

Thomas M. Carr Jr., *Descartes and the Resilience of Rhetoric: Varieties of Cartesian Rhetorical Theory* (Carbondale: Southern Illinois University Press, 1992);

Ernst Cassirer, *Descartes, Corneille, Christine de Suède,* translated by Madeleine Francès and Paul Schrecker (Paris: Vrin, 1942);

Hiram Caton, *The Origin of Subjectivity: An Essay on Descartes* (New Haven, Conn.: Yale University Press, 1973);

Jean-Pierre Cavaillé, *Descartes; La Fable du monde* (Paris: Vrin, 1991);

John Cottingham, *Descartes* (Oxford: Blackwell, 1986);

Cottingham, ed., *The Cambridge Companion to Descartes* (New York: Cambridge University Press, 1992);

Edwin M. Curley, "Cohérence ou incohérence du 'Discours?'" in *Le Discours et sa méthode,* edited by Nicolas Grimaldi and Jean-Luc Marion (Paris: Presses Universitaires de France, 1987), pp. 41–64;

Frédéric de Buzon and Vincent Carraud, *Descartes et les "Principia" II; Corps et mouvement* (Paris: Presses Universitaires de France, 1994);

Marc Fumaroli, "Ego Scriptor: Rhétorique et philosophie dans le *Discours de la méthode,*" in *Problématique et réception du Discours de la méthode et des Essais,* edited by Henry Mechoulan (Paris: Vrin, 1988), pp. 31–46;

Gilbert Gadoffre, "La chronologie des six parties," in *Le Discours et sa méthode,* edited by Grimaldi and Marion (Paris: Presses Universitaires de France, 1987), pp. 19–40;

Gadoffre, "Réflexions sur la genèse du *Discours de la méthode,*" in *Revue de synthèse* (1948): 11–27;

Gadoffre, "Sur la chronologie du *Discours de la méthode,*" in *Revue d'histoire de la philosophie et d'histoire de la civilisation* (1943): 45–70;

Peter Galison, "Descartes's Comparisons: From the Invisible to the Visible," *Isis,* 75 (1984): 311–326;

Daniel Garber, *Descartes Embodied: Reading Cartesian Philosophy through Cartesian Science* (New York: Cambridge University Press, 2001);

Garber, *Descartes' Metaphysical Physics* (Chicago: University of Chicago Press, 1992);

Etienne Gilson, *Études sur le rôle de la pensée médiévale dans la formation du système cartésien* (Paris: Vrin, 1930);

Henri Gouhier, *L'Anti-humanisme au XVIIe siècle* (Paris: Vrin, 1987);

Gouhier, *Cartésianisme et augustinisme au XVIIe siècle* (Paris: Vrin, 1978);

Gouhier, *La pensée métaphysique de Descartes* (Paris: Vrin, 1962);

Grimaldi and Marion, eds., *Le Discours et sa méthode* (Paris: Presses Universitaires de France, 1987);

Martial Gueroult, *Descartes selon l'ordre des raisons,* 2 volumes (Paris: Editions Montaigne, 1952); translated as *Descartes' Philosophy Interpreted According to the Order of Reasons,* 2 volumes, translated by Ariew (Minneapolis: University of Minneapolis Press, 1985);

Dalia Judovitz, *Subjectivity and Representation in Descartes: The Origins of Modernity* (New York: Cambridge University Press, 1988);

Gustave Lanson, *Histoire de la littérature française* (Paris: Hachette, 1895);

Lanson, "L'influence de Descartes sur la littérature française," in *Revue de métaphysique et de morale* (July 1896);

John D. Lyons, "*Camera Obscura:* Image and Imagination in Descartes's *Méditations,*" in *Convergences: Rhetoric and Poetic in Seventeenth-Century France,* edited by Mary McKinley and David Lee Rubin (Columbus: Ohio State University Press, 1989), pp. 179–195;

Lyons, *Exemplum: The Rhetoric of Example in Early Modern France and Italy* (Princeton: Princeton University Press, 1989);

Louis Marin, *La Critique du discours* (Paris: Editions de Minuit, 1975);

Marion, *Sur la théologie blanche de Descartes; Analogie, création des vérités éternelles et fondement* (Paris: Presses Universitaires de France, 1981);

Marion, *Sur l'ontologie grise de Descartes; Science cartésienne et savoir aristotelien dans les Regulae* (Paris: Vrin, 1975);

Mechoulan, ed., *Problématique et réception du Discours de la méthode et des Essais* (Paris: Vrin, 1988);

Timothy Reiss, "Denying the Body? Memory and the Dilemmas of History in Descartes," in *Journal of the History of Ideas,* 57, no. 4 (1996): 587–607;

Reiss, *The Discourse of Modernism* (Ithaca, N.Y.: Cornell University Press, 1983);

Sylvie Romanowski, *L'illusion chez Descartes* (Paris: Klincksieck, 1974);

John A. Schuster, "Descartes and the Scientific Revolution, 1618–1634," dissertation, Princeton University, 1977;

Jean Wahl, *Du rôle de l'idée de l'instant dans la philosophie de Descartes* (Paris: Vrin, 1953);

Richard A. Watson, *The Downfall of Cartesianism* (The Hague: M. Nijhoff, 1966).

Papers:

Of René Descartes's writings, relatively few manuscripts survive. Originals or manuscript copies of fewer than half of his correspondence exist; some manuscripts of his early unpublished writings on mathematics and music are also extant. The majority of these manuscripts are located in the Bibliothèque Nationale de France, the Bibliothèque de l'Institut, and the Bibliothèque de la Sorbonne, all in Paris. The university libraries of Leiden and Amsterdam, the British Museum in London, and the Budé Collection in Geneva also hold originals or manuscript copies of many pieces of correspondence.

François de Salignac de la Mothe-Fénelon
(6 August 1651 – 7 January 1715)

Gita May
Columbia University

BOOKS: *Education des filles* (Paris: P. Aubouin, P. Emery, et C. Clousier, 1687);

De la véritable et solide piété: Entretien spirituel, anonymous (Paris: F. et P. Delaulne, 1690); enlarged as *De la véritable et solide piété: Entretien spirituel, nouvelle édition augmentée d'un traité de la prière* (Paris: F. et P. Delaulne, n.d.);

Discours prononcez dans l'Académie françoise le mardi trente-unième mars MDCLXXXXIII à la réception de M. l'abbé de Fénelon . . . (Paris: Veuve de J.-B. Coignard et J.-B. Coignard *fils,* 1693);

Explication des maximes des saints sur la vie intérieure (Paris: P. Aubouin, P. Emery, et C. Clousier, 1697);

Réponse de M. l'archevêque de Cambray à l'écrit de M. l'évêque de Meaux intitulé Relation sur le quiétisme (N.p, n.d. [1698]);

Suite du quatrième livre de l'Odyssée d'Homère, ou Les Avantures de Télémaque, fils d'Ulysse (Paris: Veuve de C. Barbin, 1699);

Seconde Partie des Avantures de Télémaque, fils d'Ulysse, 4 volumes (N.p., 1699);

Les Avantures de Télémaque, fils d'Ulysse (The Hague: A. Moetjens, 1699)—includes *Les Avantures d'Aristonoüs;*

Réflexions saintes pour tous les jours du mois (Paris: J.-B. Delespine, 1704);

Sentimens de pénitence et de piété pour tous les temps et les différents états de la vie (Paris: J.-B. Cusson, 1704);

Dialogues des morts, composez pour l'éducation d'un prince, anonymous (Paris: F. Delaulne, 1712);

Sentimens de piété, où il est traité de la nécessité de connoître et d'aimer Dieu . . . Démonstration de l'existence de Dieu, tirée de la connoissance de la nature et proportionnée à la faible intelligence des plus simples, anonymous (Paris: J. Estienne, 1713);

Entretiens spirituels sur divers sujets de piété, 2 volumes (Paris: F. Delaulne, 1714);

Prières du matin et du soir avec des réflexions saintes pour tous les jours du mois (Cambray: N. J. Douilliez, 1715);

François de Salignac de la Mothe-Fénelon
(Bibliothèque Nationale, Paris)

Réflexions sur la grammaire, la rhétorique, la poétique et l'histoire, ou Mémoire sur les travaux de l'Académie françoise (Paris: J.-B. Coignard, 1716);

Dialogues sur l'éloquence en général et sur celle de la chaire en particulier, avec une lettre écrite à l'Académie françoise (Paris: F. Delaulne, 1718);

Œuvres philosophiques, seconde partie: Démonstration de l'existence de Dieu et de ses attributs, tirée des preuves purement intellectuelles et de l'idée de l'Infini mesme (Paris: J. Estienne, 1718);

Lettres sur divers sujets concernant la religion et la métaphysique (Paris: F. Delaulne, 1718);

Œuvres spirituelles, 2 volumes (Antwerp: H. de La Meule, 1718; revised and enlarged, Rotterdam: J. Hofhout, 1738);

Dialogues des morts anciens et modernes avec quelques fables, composez pour l'éducation d'un prince, 2 volumes (Paris: F. Delaulne, 1718);

Nouveaux Dialogues des morts; Avec des contes et fables: Composés pour l'éducation d'un prince, 2 volumes (Amsterdam: Les Wetsteins, 1719);

Recueil de quelques opuscules de Messire François de Salignac de La Motte Fénelon . . . sur différentes matières importantes (N.p., 1720);

Education royale, ou Examen de conscience pour un grand prince (Amsterdam: M. Magerus, n.d. [1743]);

Œuvres de M. François de Salignac de La Mothe-Fénelon, 9 volumes, edited by abbé Gallard and Father de Querbeuf (Paris: Didot, 1787–1792);

Œuvres de Fénelon, 23 volumes (Versailles: J. A. Lebel, 1820–1830);

Œuvres complètes de Fénelon, 10 volumes, edited by Jean Gosselin (Paris: J. Leroux et Jouby, 1848–1852).

Editions and Collections: *Les Avantures de Télémaque, fils d'Ulysse* (Rotterdam: J. Hofhout, 1719);

Dialogues sur l'éloquence (Paris: Dezobry, 1846);

Lettre sur les occupations de l'Académie française, edited by Ernest Depois (Paris: Dezobry, 1846);

Les Aventures de Télémaque, 2 volumes, edited by Albert Cahen (Paris: Hachette, 1920);

De l'éducation des filles, edited by Albert Cherel (Paris: Hachette, 1920);

Ecrits et lettres politiques, edited by Charles Urbain (Paris: Bossard, 1920);

Œuvres choisies, edited by Cherel (Paris: Hatier, 1930);

Les Plus belles pages de Fénelon, edited by Henri Brémond (Paris: Flammarion, 1930);

Fénelon: Choix de textes, edited by Marcel Raymond (Paris: Egloff, 1947);

Œuvres complètes de Fénelon, 10 volumes, edited by Jean Gosselin (Paris: J. Leroux et Jouby, 1948–1952);

Œuvres spirituelles, edited by François Varillon (Paris: Aubier, 1954);

Fénelon, ce méconnu: Textes choisis, edited by Maria-Pia Chaintreuil (Paris: Fayard, 1961);

Lettre à l'Académie, edited by Ernesta Caldarini (Geneva: Droz, 1970);

Œuvres, 2 volumes, edited by Jacques Le Brun, Bibliothèque de la Pléiade, nos. 307 and 437 (Paris: Gallimard, 1983, 1997);

Traité de l'existence de Dieu, edited by Jean-Louis Dumas (Paris: Editions Universitaires, 1990);

Les Aventures de Télémaque, fils d'Ulysse, edited by Marguerite Haillant (Paris: Nizet, 1993);

Traité de l'éducation des filles, edited by Bernard Jolibert (Paris: Klincksieck, 1994).

Editions in English: *The Spiritual Letters of Archbishop Fénelon: Letters to Men,* translated by H. L. Sidney Lear (London: Rivingtons, 1877);

The Spiritual Letters of Archbishop Fénelon: Letters to Women, translated by Lear (London: Rivingtons, 1877);

Dialogues on Eloquence, translated by W. S. Howell (Princeton: Princeton University Press, 1951);

Letters and Reflections, edited, with an introduction, by Thomas S. Kepler (Cleveland: World, 1955);

Fénelon on Education: A Translation of the "Traité de l'éducation des filles," translated, with an introduction and notes, by H. C. Barnard (Cambridge: Cambridge University Press, 1966);

Fénelon's Letter to the French Academy, translated, with an introduction and commentary, by Barbara Warnick (Lanham, Md.: University Press of America, 1984);

Telemachus, Son of Ulysses, translated by Patrick Riley (Cambridge: Cambridge University Press, 1994);

The Adventures of Telemachus, the Son of Ulysses, edited by O. M. Brack Jr., translated by Tobias Smollet (Athens: University of Georgia Press, 1997);

Fénelon: Meditations on the Heart of God, translated by Robert J. Edmonson (Brewster, Mass.: Paraclete Press, 1997).

Fénelon was a great and influential Catholic churchman, theologian, pedagogical thinker, and leader of quietism, a spiritual movement eventually declared heretical, an occurrence that caused his disgrace and exile from his prestigious and influential post as bishop of Cambrai and as preceptor of the duc de Bourgogne, grandson of Louis XIV. Fénelon's 1694 eloquent letter to Louis XIV boldly criticizing the sun-king's financial and foreign policies testifies to his courageous independence of thought in an age of absolutism. He also had a lively interest in tragedy, comedy, history, and rhetoric and played a notable part in the Quarrel of the Ancients and Moderns. His 1699 pedagogical novel *Les Avantures de Télémaque, fils d'Ulysse* (The Adventures of Telemachus, Son of Ulysses), written primarily for his royal pupil, was immensely popular and testifies to a growing interest in education that culminated in Jean-Jacques Rousseau's *Emile, ou De l'éducation* (Emile, or on Education, 1762). In all his writings Fénelon was a supreme stylist who knew how to translate his ideas into a graceful, fluid prose. Eighteenth-century philosophes, in particular, felt a special kinship with the unorthodox bishop of Cambrai.

François de Salignac de la Mothe-Fénelon was born on 6 August 1651 in the ancestral château in Gascony, the thirteenth of at least fifteen children who were the offspring of his father's two marriages. His family belonged

The château near Sarlat in Gascony where Fénelon was born

to the old *noblesse d'épée* (nobility of the sword) and proudly traced its roots to the tenth century, with many of its members having served with distinction in the military, diplomacy, and the church. François first experienced life within the fortified medieval walls of the Fénelon castle, situated near the town of Sarlat, in the southwestern region of Périgord.

Like many noble families with an ancient and notable lineage, the large Fénelon clan was far from financially well off, and François's childhood was relatively austere. His early training, from 1651 to 1663, took place at home, and as he exhibited exceptional scholarly promise, he clearly appeared destined for a distinguished ecclesiastical career. When he was twelve, he was sent to the University of Cahors, where he studied rhetoric and philosophy, before he was sent to study at the famed Collège du Plessis in Paris. After he completed his theological studies at the Séminaire de Saint-Sulpice, the twenty-four-year-old Fénelon was ordained to the priesthood in 1675.

Fénelon's first preference was to do missionary work in Greece, an ambition that had a great deal to do with his strong classical background. Instead, he was assigned to the more prosaic tasks of attending to the home parish of Saint-Sulpice and preaching for common folk, duties that he performed from 1675 to 1678. No doubt Fénelon's experience as a preacher of an humble parish had a great impact not only on his rhetoric but also on his understanding of the means that could be employed to convince a recalcitrant audience.

In 1678 Fénelon was promoted to the post of superior of the Convent of Nouvelles-Catholiques (New Catholics), an institution located in the heart of Paris and dedicated to the mission of confirming Protestant girls in the Catholic faith. Thanks to his great personal charisma and exceptional powers of persuasion, Fénelon performed his duties with remarkable success from 1678 to 1688. In 1685, upon the recommendation of the powerful bishop Jacques-Bénigne Bossuet, Fénelon was entrusted by Louis XIV with the mission of evangelizing Protestants of Saintonge and Aunis, the region on the western Atlantic seaboard near the Huguenot stronghold of La Rochelle.

This mission corresponded with the 1685 Revocation of the Edict of Nantes. The 1598 Edict of Nantes had been promulgated by Henry IV in order to restore a measure of peace in France, which had been torn apart by religious wars. Its revocation marked a return to strongly repressive measures against the Huguenots.

To be sure, even before the Revocation of the Edict of Nantes, the Catholic Church did its best to persecute the so-called reformed religion. Among other measures of repression against the Huguenots, Louis XIV forbade them to build new churches, and in 1681 he sanctioned the conversion of children to Catholicism. Furthermore, the king thought he was doing his duty when, under the influence of his confessor, Père La Chaise, and his mistress Madame de Maintenon, he authorized the dragonnades, a form of persecution that involved harassing the Huguenots by housing dragoons in their homes to force them to convert to Catholicism, and disregarding the dragoons' gross misconduct, consisting in untold injuries committed against the persons and property of the Huguenots.

Fénelon fully subscribed to the mission of bringing Protestants back to the Catholic fold. He therefore did not recoil from the idea of using pressure in order to achieve this purpose. At the same time, he was loath to use sheer force and urged instead patient persuasion. His rich experience in preaching for humble folk and in evangelizing Protestants and newly converted Catholics gave him ample opportunity to reflect on the art of predication and to perfect his own rhetoric as a kindly, gentle leader of souls. Instead of reliance on force, he advocated a policy of appealing to the best in human nature.

In 1687 Fénelon published *Education des filles,* better known as *Traité de l'éducation des filles* (Treatise on the Education of Girls), the result of his experience at the Convent of Nouvelles-Catholiques. In several significant ways it foreshadowed Rousseau's *Emile,* published seventy-five years later. Fénelon's ideas on the education of young girls as expressed in his book are to make education a pleasurable experience and to teach through experience rather than book learning. In the moral domain he endeavors to make both faith and virtue attractive and amiable. Since he considers women to have a natural tendency toward coquetry, vanity, and impulsiveness, he urges them to be simple and pious and to preserve a sense of *pudeur* (modesty).

At the same time he restricts the education of young girls to their future roles as wives and mothers and strongly reacts against the preeminence accorded to women by *Préciosité* (a movement popular in the literary salons that emphasized delicacy in sentiment and taste, eventually leading to a revival of medieval courtly love). He is wary of everything that rouses the passions—notably the arts (even music), which, he believes, tend to affect the sensibilities of women and predispose them for sensuous and culpable sentiments. But he is also willing to incorporate a modest measure of culture in a young woman's education, and even in the domain of piety he recommends moderation.

Fénelon's ideal of the good woman is one entirely dedicated to her domestic duties. She is the antithesis of the fashionable bluestocking and *salonnière.* The woman in her domestic role as spouse and mother coincides with Fénelon's ideal of simplicity and conformity to nature. His primary aim is to confer to the notion of family a new status and especially to enhance the status of the mother.

Fénelon's high connections enabled him in 1689 to be named preceptor of Louis, duc de Bourgogne, grandson of Louis XIV. Fully aware of the vital importance of this task, Fénelon endeavored to shape the moral character of his pupil by refining his ideas and principles on education. He wrote *Les Avantures de Télémaque, fils d'Ulysse* (written from 1694 to 1696) primarily for the instruction of his royal pupil, and it represents Fénelon's pedagogical ideals. The first part was published in 1699 as *Suite du quatrième livre de l'Odyssée d'Homère, ou Les Avantures de Télémaque, fils d'Ulysse;* the concluding parts were published in four volumes during the same year, under the titles *Seconde* [*Troisième, Quatrième, Cinquième*] *Partie des Avantures de Télémaque, fils d'Ulysse.* Finally, the entire work was published together for the first time, also in 1699, in the Netherlands as *Les Avantures de Télémaque, fils d'Ulysse;* this latter publication included a new piece, *Les Avantures d'Aristonoüs.*

Les Avantures de Télémaque is a didactic novel that derives its inspiration from both Homer's *Odyssey* (ninth or eighth century B.C.) and Virgil's *Aeneid* (circa 30 B.C.; unfinished at his death) and features Telemachus in his endeavor to find his father, Ulysses. That Fénelon chose the novel form, a literary genre that was officially decried for its immorality yet had asserted itself impressively through its popularity, to convey his pedagogical message is both revealing and paradoxical.

The book relates the adventures of Telemachus, traveling through the Mediterranean world in search of Ulysses, his long-absent father. The youth is accompanied by the goddess Minerva, who, under the guise of mentor, guides him and teaches him to learn from his own mistakes as well as from his observations of other people. After many adventures Telemachus is eventually reunited with his father.

Since Fénelon's novel was destined for a future king of France, it also embodies essential notions on morality, politics, military strategy, and medicine. Its intent was both political and philosophical. That Fénelon was keenly aware that Louis XIV's absolutist policy was disastrous is evident throughout the novel. Fénelon's intent was that if his royal pupil were one day to be king, he would be profoundly different from the current ruler. At the same time the novel strongly appealed to the classical nostalgia for antiquity and offered a seductive picture of great heroes subtly transformed so that they conformed to the Christian mode. *Les Avantures de Télémaque* was immensely popular in France, England, and America and went through many editions and translations.

In 1694 Fénelon composed an eloquent letter to Louis XIV, which, because of its startlingly daring nature in an age of strict censorship, was offered under the protective cloak of anonymity, and its authenticity was even questioned until a manuscript in the arch-

EDUCATION
DES
FILES.
Par Monsieur L'ABBE' DE FENELON.

A PARIS,

Chez { PIERRE AUBOUIN, PIERRE EMERY ET CHARLES CLOUSIER. } { Quay des Augustins, prés l'Hôtel de Luynes à l'Ecu de France, & à la Croix d'Or. }

M. DC. LXXXVII.
Avec Privilege du Roy.

Title page of the 1687 treatise that Fénelon based on his experiences as priest at the convent of Nouvelles-Catholiques in Paris (Bibliothèque Nationale, Paris)

bishop's own handwriting was discovered in 1825. Jean Le Rond d'Alembert refers to it in his *Eloge de Fénelon,* read before the Académie Française in 1774. The text of the letter first appeared in d'Alembert's 1785 *Histoire des membres de l'Académie française* (History of the Members of the French Academy).

In this letter Fénelon began by praising the king's own innate sense of justice and equity but went on to blame Louis XIV's ministers for deliberately misleading the monarch and for the current sad state of affairs in France. The king had not been given a real opportunity to govern, and he had been misguided by his ministers, who lavished fulsome praise on him, to the extent of idolatry, which he should have rejected with indignation. Fénelon also denounced the king's foreign policy of waging wars needlessly, a policy that greatly contributed to the isolation of France. France insisted on dictating the terms of peace as a master rather than as a conciliator of moderation and equity.

Appealing to Louis XIV's sense of justice and humanity, Fénelon pointed out that his people, whom he ought to love as his children and who had been pas-

sionately committed to him, were dying of hunger. What follows is a striking picture of deserted and desolate towns and languishing trades and commerce.

The overall tone of the letter is revelatory of the intensity and even bitterness of Fénelon's feelings and goes to the core of Louis XIV's failings. The thrust of the letter is that the king had failed in his duty to seek for the unvarnished truth beyond the flattery of ministers and courtiers. Even beyond that is the probing question of whether or not there was an inherent weakness in an absolute monarchy that imposed the total suppression of criticism and opposition.

Yet, the letter ends with a moving affirmation of loyalty to the king and with a strong statement that its author had no other wish than to see the kingdom of France thrive and prosper in peace and prosperity. Was it actually delivered to Louis XIV? This question never has been fully resolved, but it is probable that because of its unusual bluntness, the king's entourage intercepted it.

Soon after the 1687 publication of *Traité de l'éducation des filles,* Fénelon had been presented to Maintenon, who had recently become Louis XIV's second spouse, but under the special provision of a morganatic marriage. Granddaughter of Agrippa d'Aubigné, the great Huguenot poet, at the age of sixteen she had married Paul Scarron, an invalid writer of satires, burlesque poems, plays, and a picaresque novel; he had died in 1660. As Scarron's widow, she became something of a celebrity in Parisian literary circles. In 1669 she was appointed governess to the offspring of the king and his mistress Françoise de Rochechouart de Mortemart, marquise de Montespan (known as Madame de Montespan). Maintenon soon managed to supplant de Montespan in the aging king's affections.

A devout Catholic, Maintenon exercised a considerable influence on the king and endeavored to lift the religious tone of the court. As the former governess of the king's illegitimate children, she had acquired firsthand experience in dealing with questions of education. Furthermore, as the founder of the school of Saint-Cyr, which was dedicated to the education of daughters of noble but poor families, she had a special interest in Fénelon's theories on the proper way of educating young girls. Fénelon's relationship with Maintenon contributed to his initial rise in Louis XIV's favor but also eventually to his downfall.

On 4 October 1688 Fénelon made the acquaintance of a Madame Guyon. Born Jeanne-Marie Bouvier de La Motte, into a family of the magistrature, she had married at the age of sixteen Jacques Guyon, who belonged to the same class. Widowed twelve years later, she became a believer in mysticism, toward which she had been inclined since her youth. At the time of her meeting with Fénelon she was forty and a passionate promoter of a new religious movement in France known as quietism. Fénelon was immediately and strongly attracted to the basic tenets of quietism, which had originated in Spain, founded by the theologian Miguel de Molinos, a Spanish priest and mystic. In his *Guida Spirituale* (Spiritual Guide, 1675) he set forth his basic quietist principle, total submission to the will of God. The essence of quietism lies in the absolute absorption of the individual soul in divine love. In 1685 he was arrested and tried by the Holy Office, and in 1687 he was condemned by Pope Innocent XI and the Inquisition for heresy. He died in prison in 1696.

Quietism had, however, somehow managed to survive this official condemnation. In France the movement began to spread under the aegis of Guyon, who, in spite of the strong opposition of the Catholic hierarchy and even in 1688 an eight-month reclusion in a convent in Paris, succeeded in acquiring powerful allies at the court of Louis XIV, mainly through women of the highest nobility and eventually even of the devout Maintenon. Quietism seemed, therefore, destined to determine the future of France, since Fénelon, the tutor of the future king, had become one of its most ardent champions.

Bossuet, bishop of Meaux, however, who had played a key role in the rise of Fénelon, was firm in his belief in the established forms of religion rather than those of personal feeling. Now the two men were pitted against each other. The great prelate who had started out by being Fénelon's promoter withdrew his support and used all his powerful oratorical skills to attack Fénelon and the quietists.

In the meantime a commission was set up that found Guyon's works upholding the quietist doctrine unacceptable. She was arrested and imprisoned in Vincennes on 27 December 1695; furthermore, the archbishop of Paris asked her to offer a retraction. At this point Fénelon entered into direct conflict with Bossuet. In spite of efforts on the part of conciliators, Fénelon refused to join in the condemnation of Guyon. He firmly believed that quietism was in the great religious tradition and fully deserved to be incorporated into the mainstream of orthodoxy.

Maintenon, for her part, became deeply concerned about the orthodoxy of quietism. Her prudent, self-restrained character had been molded by bitter personal experience. No wonder, therefore, that Fénelon lost her support as soon as quietism became controversial.

In 1699 Pope Innocent XII condemned Fénelon's writing. At this time Fénelon fell into total disgrace and was also deprived of his preceptorship of the duc de Bourgogne. Fénelon was exiled from the French court and relegated to the outpost of Cambrai, in northern France, where he devoted himself fully to his pastoral duties. Nevertheless, he and his supporters probably still held secret hopes that the end of this disgrace and exile would come with the eventual accession to the throne of his pupil, the duc de Bourgogne, for the latter would surely be guided by his mentor's spiritual principles. These hopes were dashed when the duc de Bourgogne died of smallpox in 1712.

That Fénelon would not cave in under tremendous pressure and remained loyal to quietism and Guyon, at great personal loss to his own career, is testimony to his remarkable qualities of moral fortitude and to his unswerving devotion to a cause he had so passionately endorsed. He bore his disgrace and exile with great dignity, performing his duties with exactitude and with special concern for the disadvantaged in a diocese racked with war and poverty. He also continued to write on matters close to his heart, particularly on a humane, anti-Machiavellian politics of Christian idealism and charity in which kings would be more devoted to the good of their subjects than to the aggrandizement of their realm through war. He strongly felt that one of the greatest lessons of history is that vast empires are built at the expense of a huge amount of human suffering and cause even more dreadful and fearsome ravages when they begin to crumble and eventually fall apart, as they inevitably do.

Fénelon also had a keen interest in rhetoric, poetry, tragedy, comedy, and history, and he played a significant part in the Quarrel of the Ancients and Moderns. He had been elected to the Académie Française in 1693. In the *Réflexions sur la grammaire, la rhétorique, la poétique et l'histoire, ou Mémoire sur les travaux de l'Académie françoise,* known as *Lettre à l'Académie* (Letter to the Academy, written in early 1714 but not published until 1716, one year after his death), Fénelon delineates the duties of the Académie Française as he envisions them. The Académie Française should pursue its essential project of completing the dictionary, although usage might eventually call for changes. It should also focus on a French grammar, not necessarily in order to fix the language but at least to retard its alteration as much as possible. Furthermore, every effort should be made to enrich the French language. As for rhetoric, the best mentors are the Ancients, whose ideal of simplicity should be a model in order to avoid such current tendencies toward declamation as plays on words, witticisms, and superfluous ornaments.

More important, in the *Lettre à l'Académie,* Fénelon eloquently rises to the defense of poetry. Indeed, in the Quarrel of the Ancients and Moderns, which still raged while he was writing the *Lettre à l'Académie,* he naturally tended to side with the Ancients, for he had always wholeheartedly subscribed to their ideal of simplicity and harmony. He furthermore pays generous tribute to the Ancients in having shown the way for their successors. But he expresses his own inclination in relatively moder-

Page from the manuscript for Fénelon's 1699 pedagogical novel Les Avantures de Télémaque, fils d'Ulysse, *written primarily for the young duc de Bourgogne, grandson of Louis XIV (Bibliothèque Nationale, Paris)*

ate tones. Another interesting feature of the *Lettre à l'Académie* is Fénelon's assessment of the Gothic style, to which–like most classical and neoclassical writers and critics–he remained totally impervious and which he condescendingly viewed as an example of total disproportion and immoderate ornamentation. What is also remarkable about the *Lettre à l'Académie* is its deliberately informal tone, the simplicity and directness of its rhetoric, and his lack of hesitation to express his opinions in the first person.

Fénelon was also among the few of his generation who realized that poetry was much more than a purely verbal game. The difficulty was that the French language, clear and analytical in its nature, did not lend itself to the intuitive workings of poetry. Poetry was akin to religion in that it should move the reader in simple, powerful ways. Poetry for Fénelon signified something far more profound than mere rules of prosody, versification, and rhyme. He dreamed of something akin to prose poems that would evoke the unadorned sublimity of Homer, Virgil, and the Bible. And indeed, *Les Avantures de Télémaque* contains many passages that illustrate this new poetics and that, in their musicality and descriptive virtuosity, foreshadow the prose poem and even the rhetorical techniques of *ekphrasis,* which consists in creating a strikingly vivid image of a picture through words.

François de Salignac de la Mothe-Fénelon died on 7 January 1715 at the age of sixty-three. His death preceded that of the king by only eight months, so France was still in dire economic circumstances at Fénelon's death. Fénelon was, however, a churchman above all: his main interests were of a theological, moral, pedagogical, and political nature. He just also happened to be a supreme prose artist and stylist. Even in his purely ecclesiastical works, his mystical spirituality translates into a language that rarely loses its grace and fluidity.

What may be surprising is the impact Fénelon had on eighteenth-century writers. The philosophes felt, however mistakenly, that the bishop of Cambrai was one of their own. Rousseau's didactic novel *Emile* owes a great deal to Fénelon's *Avantures de Télémaque* and his *Traité de l'éducation des filles.* In Fénelon's bold criticism of the abuses of the absolute French monarchy are clear intimations of political principles advocated in Charles de Secondat, Baron de Montesquieu's *Esprit de lois* (Spirit of Laws, 1748). Even Voltaire's philosophical tales reflect, in their more meditative and reflective passages, Fénelon's soaring rhetoric and cosmic vision of human frailty. Eighteenth-century writers, after all, grew up reading *Les Avantures de Télémaque,* and their literary imagination was nourished on Fénelon's mixture of the mythological and the didactic.

Although Fénelon no longer enjoys the same kind of popularity he had in the seventeenth and eighteenth centuries, what is now being slowly acknowledged is that he deserves to be ranked among the greatest French writers. He, moreover, affords a revealing insight into a complex chapter of French political and religious history.

Letters:
Correspondance, 13 volumes, edited by Jean Gosselin (Paris: A. Leclère, 1827–1829);
Correspondance, 18 volumes, edited by Jean Orcibal and Irénée Noye (Paris: Klincksieck, 1972–2001).

Bibliographies:
Ely Carcassone, *Etat présent des travaux sur Fénelon* (Paris: Belles-Lettres, 1939);
Nathan Edelman, *A Critical Bibliography of French Literature,* volume 3, *The Seventeenth Century* (Syracuse: Syracuse University Press, 1961), pp. 403–409.

Biographies:
Albert Cherel, *Fénelon au XVIIIe siècle: Son Prestige, son influence* (Paris: Hachette, 1917);
Jeanne-Lydie Goré, *La Notion d'indifférence chez Fénelon et ses sources* (Paris: Presses Universitaires de France, 1956);
Bernard Dupriez, *Fénelon et la Bible: Les Origines du Mysticisme fénelonien* (Paris: Bould & Gay, 1961);
Marcel Raymond, *Fénelon* (Paris: Desclée de Brouwer, 1967);
Henri Gouhier, *Fénelon philosophe* (Paris: Vrin, 1977).

References:
Jean-Robert Armogathe, *Le Quiétisme* (Paris: Presses Universitaires de France, 1973);
Roger Chartier, Dominique Julia, and Marie-Madeleine Compère, *L'Education en France du XVIe au XVIIIe siècle* (Paris: D'edition d'enseignement superieur, 1976);
Paul Hazard, *La Crise de la conscience européenne, 1680–1715,* volume 1 (Paris: Boivin, 1935);
Henk Hillenaar, ed., *Nouvel état présent des travaux sur Fénelon* (Amsterdam & Atlanta: Crin, 2000)–comprises bibliography of critical works on Fénelon published between 1940 and 2000;
Ernest Seillère, *Madame Guyon et Fénelon, précurseurs de J.-J. Rousseau* (Paris: Alcan, 1918).

Papers:
The majority of François de Salignac de la Mothe-Fénelon's manuscripts and letters are kept at the Bibliothèque Nationale, Paris, and at the Archives de Saint-Sulpice, Paris.

Bernard Le Bovier de Fontenelle

(11 February 1657 – 9 January 1757)

Gita May
Columbia University

BOOKS: *Psyché,* by Fontenelle and Thomas Corneille, adapted from the play by Molière and Pierre Corneille (Paris: R. Baudry, 1678);

Bellérophon, by Fontenelle, Nicolas Boileau-Despréaux, and Thomas Corneille (Paris: C. Ballard, 1679);

Nouveaux dialogues des morts, 2 volumes (Paris: C. Blageart, 1683); translated by John Hughes as *Fontenelle's Dialogues of the Dead* (London: Printed for Jacob Tonson, 1708);

Lettres diverses de M. le Chevalier d'Her*** (Paris: C. Blageart, 1683); enlarged as *Lettres galantes de M. le Chevalier d'Her**** (Paris: Veuve de C. Blageart, 1687);

Jugement de Pluton sur les deux parties des Nouveaux dialogues des morts (Paris: C. Blageart, 1684);

Entretiens sur la pluralité des mondes (Paris: Veuve de C. Blageart, 1686; enlarged edition, Paris: M. Guérout, 1687); translated by John Glanvill as *A Plurality of Worlds* (London: Printed for R. Bentley and S. Magnes, 1688);

Doutes sur le système physique des causes occasionnelles (Rotterdam: A. Acher, 1686);

Histoire des oracles (Paris: G. de Luyne, 1686); translated by Aphra Behn as *The History of Oracles, and the Cheats of the Pagan Priests: In Two Parts* (London, 1688);

Poésies pastorales de M.D.F., avec un Traité sur la nature de l'églogue et une Digression sur les anciens et les modernes (Paris: M. Guérout, 1688); enlarged as *Poésies pastorales, avec un Traité sur la nature de l'églogue et une Digression sur les anciens et les modernes* (Paris: M. Brunet, 1698; enlarged, 1708; enlarged, 1715);

Thétis et Pélée (Paris, 1689);

Enée et Lavinie (Paris: C. Ballard, 1690);

Œuvres diverses, 3 volumes (Paris: M. Brunet, 1724);

Elémens de la géométrie de l'infini, suite des Mémoires de l'Académie royale des sciences (Paris: Imprimerie Royale, 1727);

Endymion (Paris: J. B. C. Ballard, 1731);

Œuvres (6 volumes, Paris: B. Brunet, 1742; enlarged, 10 volumes, 1758);

Bernard Le Bovier de Fontenelle (portrait by Rigaud; Musée Fabre, Montpellier)

Eloges historiques des académiciens morts depuis le renouvellement de l'Académie royale des sciences en 1699, avec un discours préliminaire sur l'utilité des mathématiques et de la physique, 2 volumes (Paris: B. Brunet, 1742);

Théorie des tourbillons cartésiens, avec des Réflexions sur l'attraction (Paris: H.-L. Guérin, 1752);

La République des philosophes, ou Histoire des Ajaoiens (Geneva, 1768).

Editions and Collections: *Œuvres de Fontenelle,* 3 volumes, edited by Georges-Bernard Depping (Paris: A. Belin, 1818);

Choix d'éloges, edited by Paul Janet (Paris: C. Delagrave, 1888);

Histoire des oracles, edited by Louis Maigron (Paris: E. Cornély, 1908);

De l'origine des fables (1724), edited by Jean-Raoul Carré (Paris: F. Alcan, 1932);

Entretiens sur la pluralité des mondes; Digression sur les anciens et les modernes, edited by Robert Shackleton (Oxford: Clarendon Press, 1955);

Entretiens sur la pluralité des mondes, edited by Alexandre Calame (Paris: M. Didier, 1966);

Textes choisis, edited by Maurice Roelens (Paris: Editions Sociales, 1967);

Nouveaux dialogues des morts, edited by Jean Dagen (Paris: M. Didier, 1971);

Œuvres complètes, edited by Alain Niderst, 9 volumes to date (Paris: Fayard, 1989–);

Rêveries diverses: Opuscules littéraires et philosophiques, edited by Niderst (Paris: Desjonquères, 1994);

Entretiens sur la pluralité des mondes, edited by Christophe Martin (Paris: Flammarion, 1998).

Editions in English: *Letters of Gallantry,* translated by John Ozell (London: Printed for Jonas Brown and John Watts, 1715);

Week's Conversation on the Plurality of Worlds, by Monsieur de Fontenelle: To Which Is Added Mr. Addison's Defense of the Newtonian Philosophy, translated by Aphra Behn and others (Philadelphia: S. Ackerman, 1803);

Dialogues of Fontenelle, translated by Ezra Pound (London: Egoist Press, 1917);

A Plurality of Worlds: John Glanvill's translation, edited by David Garnett (London: Nonesuch Press, 1929);

Conversations on the Plurality of Worlds, translated by H. A. Hargreaves (Berkeley: University of California Press, 1990).

PLAY PRODUCTIONS: *Psyché,* libretto by Fontenelle and Thomas Corneille, music by Jean-Baptiste Lully, adapted from the play by Molière and Pierre Corneille, Paris, Académie Royale de Musique, 9 April 1678;

Bellérophon, libretto by Fontenelle, Nicolas Boileau-Despréaux, and Thomas Corneille, music by Lully, Paris, Palais Royal, Académie Royale de Musique, 31 January 1679;

Aspar, Paris, 27 December 1680;

La Comète, by Fontenelle and Jean Donneau de Visé, Paris, 29 January 1681;

Thétis et Pélée, Paris, Académie Royale de Musique, 11 January 1689;

Enée et Lavinie, Paris, Académie Royale de Musique, 7 November 1690;

Endymion, libretto by Fontenelle, music by François Collin de Blamont, Paris, Académie Royale de Musique, 17 May 1731.

Bernard Le Bovier de Fontenelle achieved the unusual feat of bridging two ages by dint of his exceptional longevity as well as by the key role he played as a highly successful, respected, and influential mediator between the classical ideal of polite and courtly elegance of expression and the new philosophical spirit of bold critical inquiry and scientific investigation. While siding with the "Moderns" in the famous *Querelle des anciens et des modernes* (Quarrel of the Ancients and Moderns), he avoided the pitfall of subscribing without qualifications to the notion of progress. His remarkable talent as a popularizer of the new science had an enormous but not sufficiently acknowledged impact on the Enlightenment philosophes.

Fontenelle was born in Rouen, the capital of Normandy, on 11 February 1657, the son of a lawyer and member of the parlement of Rouen. His mother (née Marthe Corneille) was a sister of the great dramatist, Pierre Corneille. Fontenelle bridged two centuries, not only chronologically but also because, although in many ways he was still a representative of the *bel esprit* (wit) characteristic of the elegant salons in the age of King Louis XIV, at the same time he played a key role as a precursor and contemporary of the philosophes of the Enlightenment. He managed the rare tour de force of moving with the rapidly evolving spirit of his times, despite occasional barbs from Voltaire aimed at Fontenelle's tendency to couch serious ideas in preciously gallant metaphors meant to please his modern readers.

As a direct and living link between the seventeenth and eighteenth centuries Fontenelle could casually evoke concrete details of his personal acquaintanceship with such notable figures of the Age of Louis XIV as Marie-Madeleine, comtesse de Lafayette, or Madeleine de Sévigné, and give eyewitness accounts of such events as the Revocation of the Edict of Nantes of 1685. When a mob threatened to burn down the Palais-Royal theater as an act of vengeance for the disastrous crash of John Law's financial scheme, Fontenelle, who had been housed there thanks to Philippe, duc d'Orléans, calmly refused to leave the premises. This coolness was characteristic of Fontenelle's unusually dispassionate temperament. As a result, he was a relatively old man in his youth but rejuvenated with increasing age. The main reason for this reversal of the normal order was his basically optimistic, gregarious nature. He never married, but he had a gift for social interaction and for

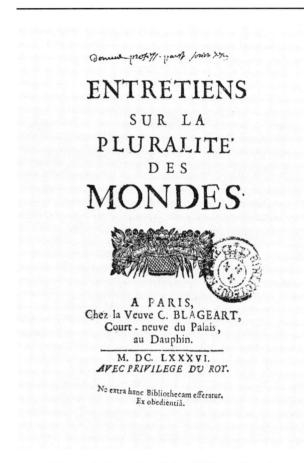

ENTRETIENS
SUR LA
PLURALITE'
DES
MONDES.

A PARIS,
Chez la Veuve C. BLAGEART,
Court - neuve du Palais,
au Dauphin.

M. DC. LXXXVI.
AVEC PRIVILEGE DU ROY.

Ne extra hanc Bibliothecam efferatur.
Ex obedientiâ.

Title page for the 1686 work in which Fontenelle sought to popularize the cosmology of astronomers such as Nicolaus Copernicus, Galileo, and Johannes Kepler (Bibliothèque Nationale, Paris)

enduring friendships, and his company was eagerly sought after because of his sunny disposition and his ability to enliven salon gatherings as a brilliant conversationalist and raconteur. Fontenelle especially enjoyed the company of women of wit and culture, and he easily became a favorite in the notable salons of such discriminating and knowledgeable hostesses as Anne-Thérèse, marquise de Lambert; Claudine-Alexandrine Guérin, marquise de Tencin; and Marie-Thérèse Rodet Geoffrin. Fontenelle outlived such major eighteenth-century figures as Charles de Secondat, baron de Montesquieu, and was still active when the younger generation of philosophes, such as Denis Diderot and Jean-Jacques Rousseau, was beginning to assert itself.

Educated at the Jesuit College of Rouen, Fontenelle lackadaisically pursued law studies, which he found dull and soon abandoned in order to devote himself entirely to belles lettres, the major passion that motivated his career. Having settled in Paris in 1677, he was from the start an active participant in the intellectual and social life of the French capital. As the nephew

of Pierre Corneille and Thomas Corneille, the dramatist's younger and less famous brother, who sponsored Fontenelle, he understandably first turned to the theater in the high hopes of attaining fame as a successful playwright. The failure of his two plays, *Aspar* (1680) and *La Comète* (The Comet, 1681), prompted him to turn to philosophy and science.

He soon assumed a leading role in the *Querelle des anciens et des modernes,* resolutely siding with the Moderns. The history of this quarrel, known in its English incarnation as the Battle of the Books, is a complicated one. It can perhaps best be summarized with the fundamental question of whether or not the Moderns could equal, or even surpass, the Ancients. This controversy, which polarized seventeenth-century intellectuals, raised for the first time the issue of whether increased knowledge meant progress.

The debate, which lasted from the classical generation (1660–1680) until well into the eighteenth century, also concerned the question of which possessed true creative genius, the Ancients or the Moderns. Critical opinion tended to side with the Ancients in the late seventeenth century, and most authors agreed with Nicolas Boileau-Despréaux–highly regarded poet, critic, polemicist, and spokesperson as well as lawgiver for the official classical doctrine–that the Ancients had provided mankind with infallible models and that they retained absolute authority, so that their examples, whether in science or the arts, continued to be ideal paradigms to be imitated and emulated. To refer to the Greek and Roman norms goes back to the Renaissance. Writers as well as artists took for granted that their works could only be created or appreciated in light of the antique model as an immutable ideal.

Classical aesthetics rested on the notion of universality. Therefore, such rationalist critics as Boileau-Despréaux were convinced that the antique ideal could be the same for every author or artist, regardless of chronology or geography. Late-seventeenth-century cultural discourse was permeated with a new sense of crisis in reviewing the hallowed notion of the supremacy of antiquity. Perhaps this feeling had something to do with fin de siècle anxiety, as Joan DeJean has suggested in *Ancients against Moderns: Culture Wars and the Making of a Fin de Siècle* (1997).

The quarrel, which so markedly split French cultural loyalties in the last two decades of the seventeenth century, with repercussions that also strongly affected eighteenth-century aesthetic discourse, has relevance today, for it marked a decisive moment when the notion of modernity emerged. The Moderns hailed a changing world, while the Ancients cautioned that the new is hardly equipped to replace the old. Champions of the Moderns were prepared to claim that contemporary literature easily rivaled that of Greece and Rome.

Charles Perrault—who gave enduring form to such fairy tales as "Sleeping Beauty," "Bluebeard," "Little Red Riding-Hood," and "Cinderella" in *Contes de ma mère l'oye* (Tales of Mother Goose, 1697)—launched the dispute in 1687 by reading his poem "Le Siècle de Louis XIV" (The Century of Louis XIV), before the Académie Française, of which he had been a member since 1671. The thrust of Perrault's poem was that, while antiquity deserved profound respect, and the Ancients were indeed great, they were also fallible as human beings. Furthermore, the authority of the Ancients had been seriously discredited in the fields of science and history, as exemplified by the many mistaken notions of Aristotle and Herodotus. Antiquity, therefore, need not be blindly venerated, and the Age of Louis XIV had fully earned the right to be ranked on a par with the Age of Augustus. In order to demonstrate that the Moderns superseded the Ancients in science, Perrault highlighted the role of the telescope and microscope in his poem. Perrault's poem, proclaiming the superiority of "The Century of Louis XIV," created a major stir in the Académie Française.

In his four-volume *Parallèle des anciens et des modernes* (Parallels between Ancients and Moderns, 1688–1696), Perrault pursued and amplified the notion of progress, especially concerning the advances made in science. The famed Dutch mathematician and astronomer Christian Huygens provided Perrault with information concerning scientific progress, while on the literary side of the dispute Perrault renewed his criticism of Homer and Virgil on the basis of the errors and implausibilities to be found in their works.

Boileau-Despréaux, on the other hand, as leader among the defenders of the Ancients and elected to the Académie Française in 1684, had staunchly upheld the Greco-Roman ideal as the absolute model in his authoritative verse treatise *L'Art poétique* (The Art of Poetry, 1674). The enmity between Perrault and Boileau-Despréaux was both ideological and personal, but the broader issues raised by the *Querelle des anciens et des modernes* are still of interest today.

Basically, the Moderns challenged the supremacy of the model of the Ancients, which had played a key role in inspiring the masterworks of the French classical generation. Defying the claims of humanist culture, the Moderns precipitated a crisis that marked the beginning of the end of the classical ideal.

Fontenelle played a key role in the quarrel. In 1683 he began to deal, rather cautiously, with the notion of progress in his *Nouveaux dialogues des morts* (1683, translated as *Fontenelle's Dialogues of the Dead*, 1708), written in the manner of Lucian, the Greek prose writer who in his own *Dialogues of the Dead* (circa second century) had vigorously satirized both ancient Olympian myths and contemporary philosophers. In Fontenelle's work, illustrious figures of both the distant and the more recent past meet on the Elysian Fields and converse on a vast range of topics, setting forth thought-provoking views that are at times unexpected and paradoxical. For instance, while Aesop reproves Homer for his use of mythology, the latter responds that unvarnished truth is unappealing to humans because of their irrepressible penchant for fiction; Michel Eyquem de Montaigne's veneration for the Ancients is modified and nuanced by Socrates, who maintains that humanity is as unreasonable, inept, and unable to use knowledge today as it was in his own day; and Paracelsus (the German-Swiss physician who established the role of chemistry in medicine) and Molière compare the insights into human nature and truths gained through science and comedy. In this exchange, Molière has the last word, for according to him, to call attention to humanity's vices and follies is to be assured of immortality.

As a skeptic as well as a generally detached and bemused observer of human affairs, Fontenelle harbored no optimistic illusions concerning a utopian concept of steady human progress. *Nouveaux dialogues des morts* exemplifies several aspects of Fontenelle's preoccupation as a writer and as a popularizer of science. His choice of the dialogue form suited his purpose of testing ideas by dialectical, polemical, and conversational argument and confrontation, as distinguished from a formal, logical demonstration. In this choice of method he exerted a singularly important influence on the Enlightenment philosophes. At the same time, he retained the stylistic elegance and, at times, the archness and preciousness of the *bel esprit* intent on pleasing and charming such formidable hostesses as Tencin, Lambert, and Geoffrin, whose salons he regularly frequented. But in his strong commitment to the dissemination of knowledge, endorsement of the new experimental method, and remarkable ability to present complex philosophical and scientific notions in a clear, understandable, and highly readable prose, he already heralded the new age. No wonder, therefore, that the Encyclopedists saw in him an essential forerunner and even went so far as to claim him as one of their own.

Fontenelle's *Histoire des oracles* (1686, translated as *The History of Oracles, and the Cheats of the Pagan Priests: In Two Parts,* 1688) embodied ideas first expressed in his *De l'origine des fables* (On the Origin of Fables, written in 1680). Its questioning of ancient oracles extends to Christian miracles and explains such beliefs in terms of the human predilection for the marvelous. In the *Histoire des oracles,* Fontenelle's main targets were credulity and superstition.

Fontenelle refused to circumscribe the *Querelle des anciens et des modernes* to a purely literary dispute and linked it directly to scientific advances. In 1688 he published *Poésies pastorales de M.D.F., avec un Traité sur la nature de l'églogue et une Digression sur les anciens et les modernes* (Pastoral Poems of M.D.F., with a Treatise on the Nature of the Eclogue and a Digression on the Ancients and the Moderns). The *Digression sur les anciens et les modernes,* a fairly brief essay of some twenty pages included in the volume, was Fontenelle's attempt to demonstrate that antiquity is not superior to modern times and to attack the notion of degeneration by way of the argument that the trees of more distant times were not taller than those growing nowadays, an argument already invoked in Montaigne's *Apologie de Raimond Sebond* (Apology for Raymond Sebond, book 2, chapter 12 of the 1580 edition of his *Essais*).

The thrust of Fontenelle's analogy is that chronology has not produced any distinct biological difference, and one may assume that present-day philosophers, orators, and poets are capable of equaling Plato, Demosthenes, and Homer, who were not made of a finer stuff. Therefore, there are no basic differences between the Greeks and the French with respect to works produced by the human imagination. But in the scientific field there is an accumulation of knowledge that gives the modern scientist a distinct edge. The supremacy of the Ancients is consequently a notion essentially based upon tradition and prejudice rather than verifiable knowledge. To be sure, the Ancients attained greatness in eloquence and poetry, but they were no match for the Moderns in the field of science. Furthermore, even in literature the Moderns have developed new genres, such as the novel.

Thus, the *Digression* constitutes a measured and nuanced defense of the cause of the Moderns, incorporates a tribute to René Descartes as a courageous role model for independent, precise, and accurate reasoning, and sounds a stern warning against an excessive veneration of the Ancients, which can only result in stifling human inventiveness and progress, as was demonstrated in the case of the uncritical devotion to Aristotle, which led to many inaccuracies and outright errors in philosophy.

Entretiens sur la pluralité des mondes (Conversations on the Plurality of Worlds), one of Fontenelle's most important and famous works, appeared in 1686. Asserting his role as a popularizer of science, Fontenelle set out to make the discoveries of Nicolaus Copernicus, Galileo, and Johannes Kepler known by a wider public by challenging the Scholastic conception

of the cosmos, which held that Earth was the center of the universe.

The work is divided into five "conversations" (a sixth was added in 1686) in the form of dialogues between Fontenelle and a marquise as they promenade at dusk in a lovely garden in the classical style under a sky brilliantly illuminated by stars. Fontenelle is the mentor who initiates his charming and eager pupil into the Copernican system. The dialogue is a lively one, and it is not without humor. The mentor resorts to various, and at times far-fetched, précieux metaphors in order to explain the new cosmology to his aristocratic student.

In *Entretiens sur la pluralité des mondes,* Fontenelle produced something new in literature as well as in science: a genre that aims at informing the lay public in the most intelligible and attractive language of the new discoveries in science, which not only were revolutionizing humanity's basic concepts about the physical world but also had far-reaching philosophical implications. In this seminal work Fontenelle had provided a model of scientific popularization in the form of dialectic and didactic discourse, which was emulated by the philosophes, notably by Voltaire in his *Eléments de la philosphie de Newton* (Elements of the Philosophy of Newton, 1736) and Diderot in *Le Rêve de d'Alembert* (D'Alembert's Dream, written in 1769, published in 1830). As a Cartesian, Fontenelle greatly prized lucidity and clarity of exposition, and the *Entretiens sur la pluralité des mondes* was thus instrumental in creating a style eminently suited for what the French call *vulgarisation,* or a highly literate form of popularization of the latest scientific knowledge.

Fontenelle's *Histoire des oracles* is a skillful adaptation of a ponderous work by a Dutch scholar, Antonius van Dale—*De Oraculis Ethnicorum Dissertationes Duae* (Two Dissertations on the Oracles of the Pagans, 1683), which embodies bold and controversial criticisms of oracles. In his preface Fontenelle acknowledges that he first thought of merely translating Van Dale's unwieldy treatise but ultimately decided to pare it down to its essentials and present it in a more comprehensible style. Fontenelle's aim is obviously to discredit any credence in supernatural phenomena, whether the predictions of Pythia, the high priestess of Apollo at Delphi in ancient Greece, or the Christian belief in miracles. The work can be viewed as a call against all forms of credulity and superstition and by the same token as an almost frontal attack against Christianity.

A rationalist, skeptic, and adept polemicist, Fontenelle undertook to demonstrate that all oracles are impostures and mystifications. As an illustration, he relates the story of the golden tooth, an anecdote that has become an anthology piece and that anticipates Voltaire in its elegant pithiness and satirical humor. In 1593 rumor had it in Silesia that a tooth of a seven-year-old child had inexplicably been replaced by a golden one. Several scholarly treatises appeared proffering complicated, contradictory, and absurd theories aiming at explaining this "miraculous" event. For instance, a Professor Horstius wrote that the golden tooth had been sent by God to the child in order to encourage the Christians in their struggle against the Muslim Turks. Other scholars, such as alchemists Martinus Rullandus and Andreas Libavius, also wrote treatises on the subject. When a goldsmith was at last summoned to look at the tooth in question, he found that it had been dexterously covered by a gold coating. Learned books had been written, and scholars had been engaged in acrimonious disputes before the idea of actually examining the tooth occurred to anyone. The message is clear: the Scholastic approach belonged to the dusty shelves of the Dark Ages. True knowledge is founded not on pedantic lucubrations but on rigorous, verifiable data and the scientific method.

Having become something of a celebrity, Fontenelle presented himself as a candidate for the Académie Française. Four attempts met with failure, thanks largely to the tenacious hostility of such staunch defenders of the Ancients as Jean Racine, Boileau-Despréaux, and Jean de La Bruyère. On his fifth try he was elected in 1691, and in view of his extraordinary longevity, his sixty-six-year membership in this august body doubtless constitutes a record among the so-called immortals. In 1697 he was elected to the recently organized *Académie des Sciences* (Academy of Sciences), soon became its secretary, and was entrusted with the task of writing its history.

Fontenelle also introduced in France the literary genre of the academic eulogy. His sixty-nine eulogies, composed from 1699 to 1740, offer a comprehensive and informative survey of the scientific achievements of his time. Particularly noteworthy are the eulogies of Gottfried Wilhelm Leibniz and Sir Isaac Newton, which stand out as models of lucid exposition, didactic discourse, and deft popularization.

De l'origine des fables delineates the major themes developed in the *Histoire des oracles*. All peoples, from the ancient Greeks to the American Indians, have conceived remarkably similar myths. The main thrust of both works is to combat all forms of irrationalism and superstition. At the same time, Fontenelle acknowledged the human tendency to ascribe uncritically to supernatural causes any event that is difficult to explain otherwise.

In the scientific field Fontenelle rejected the authoritarian system of the Scholastic but continued to

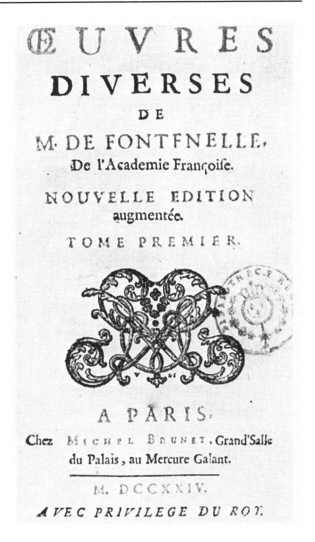

Title page for the 1724 edition of Fontenelle's works (Bibliothèque Nationale, Paris)

uphold Descartes's theory of *tourbillons* (vortexes), soon to be displaced by the Newtonian system. No wonder, therefore, that when Voltaire turned away from Descartes in favor of Newton, he enjoyed poking fun at Fontenelle's Cartesian physics.

In the field of aesthetics Fontenelle's views also reflected his adherence to the Cartesian notion of the supremacy of reason and clarity of thought and expression. He was deeply wary of enthusiasm, which as a good Cartesian he viewed as what is most untrustworthy in human behavior. At the same time, he advocated a fusion of science and poetry. Poetry should seek its inspiration in the new scientific vision of the universe.

Fontenelle can best be understood as a transitional figure who played a key role in bridging the Age of Reason and the Age of Enlightenment and exerted a powerful influence on the eighteenth-century philosophes. He awakened general interest in science and its methods and successfully goaded contemporary writers to go beyond the classical and puristic notion of belles lettres and boldly engage in the relevant and frequently controversial social, political, and religious issues of their time.

In his own lifetime and afterward, Bernard Le Bovier de Fontenelle, who died in Paris on 9 January 1757, did not receive the recognition he was due. His reputation as a *bel esprit* and liberal dispenser of bons mots (witticisms) did not enhance his status as a serious and forward-looking thinker and first-rate writer. The philosophes, notably Voltaire, who owed him much, failed to acknowledge their indebtedness to him and blithely ridiculed and caricatured the ways in which he mingled playful *badinage* (banter) with serious discourse. On the other hand, his rationalistic view of poetry had little appeal for the generation of Diderot and Rousseau, which emphasized enthusiasm, sensibility, and passion as the prime movers of poetic inspiration. Fontenelle was a pioneer who introduced the major ideological and scientific themes of the Age of Enlightenment.

Bibliographies:

George R. Havens and Donald F. Bond, *A Critical Bibliography of French Literature: The Eighteenth Century* (Syracuse, N.Y.: Syracuse University Press, 1951);

Suzanne Delorme, "Contribution à la bibliographie de Fontenelle," *Revue d'Histoire des Sciences,* 10 (1957): 289–309;

Richard A. Brooks, *A Critical Bibliography of French Literature: The Eighteenth Century; Supplement* (Syracuse, N.Y.: Syracuse University Press, 1968);

Alain Niderst, "Introduction" and "Bibliographie," in his *Fontenelle à la recherche de lui-même (1657–1702)* (Paris: Nizet, 1972), pp. 9–28, 619–660.

Biographies:

Louis Maigron, *Fontenelle: L'Homme, l'œuvre, l'influence* (Paris: Plon, 1906);

Jean-Raoul Carré, *La Philosophie de Fontenelle, ou Le Sourire de la raison* (Paris: F. Alcan, 1932);

François Grégoire, *Fontenelle: Une "Philosophie" désabusée* (Nancy: G. Thomas, 1947);

Journées Fontenelle organisé es au Centre international de synthèse . . . les 6, 7, 9 et 10 mai 1957, *Fontenelle: Sa vie et son œuvre, 1657–1757* (Paris: A. Michel, 1961);

Alain Niderst, *Fontenelle à la recherche de lui-même (1657–1702)* (Paris: Nizet, 1972);

Niderst, ed., *Fontenelle: Actes du colloque tenu à Rouen du 6 au 10 octobre 1987* (Paris: Presses Universitaires de France, 1989);

Niderst, *Fontenelle* (Paris: Plon, 1991);

Roger Marchal, *Fontenelle à l'aube des Lumières* (Paris: H. Champion, 1997).

References:

Joan DeJean, *Ancients against Moderns: Culture Wars and the Making of a Fin de Siècle* (Chicago: Chicago University Press, 1997);

George R. Havens, *The Age of Ideas* (New York: Holt, 1955);

Paul Hazard, *La Crise de la conscience européenne (1680–1715),* 3 volumes (Paris: Boivin, 1935);

L. M. Marsak, "Bernard de Fontenelle: The Idea of Science in the French Enlightenment," *Transactions of the American Philosophical Society,* 49 (1959): 1–64.

Papers:

All manuscripts of Bernard Le Bovier de Fontenelle's major works are now lost. Extant manuscripts and papers are scattered in various municipal libraries in France.

Antoine Furetière

(28 December 1619 – 14 May 1688)

Craig Moyes
King's College London

BOOKS: *L'Aenéide travestie, livre quatriesme: Contenant les amours d'Aenée et de Didon,* as A.F. (Paris: A. Courbé, 1649);

Le Voyage de Mercure: Satyre, divisé en cinq livres, anonymous (Paris: L. Chamhoudry, 1653);

Poësies diverses du sieur Furetière (Paris: G. de Luyne, 1655);

Nouvelle allégorique, ou Histoire des derniers troubles arrivez au royaume d'éloquence (Paris, 1658; Paris: P. Lamy, 1658; Paris: G. de Luyne, 1658; Amsteldam [sic]: R. Smith, 1658); translated as *The Rebellion; or, An Account of the Late Civil-Wars, in the Kingdom of Eloquence* (London, 1704);

Le Roman bourgeois, ouvrage comique, anonymous (Paris: D. Thierry, 1666; Paris: L. Billaine, 1666; Paris: T. Jolly, 1666; Paris: G. de Luyne, 1666); translated as *Scarron's City Romance, Made English* [misattributed] (London: Printed by T.N. for H. Herringman, 1671);

Fables morales et nouvelles (Paris: C. Barbin, 1671);

Les Paraboles de l'Evangile, traduites en vers, avec une explication morale et allégorique tirée des SS. Pères (Paris: P. Le Petit, 1672);

Sur la seconde conqueste de la Franche-Comté en 1674 (Paris: P. Le Petit, 1674);

Essai d'un dictionnaire universel contenant généralement tous les mots françois tant vieux que modernes et les termes de toutes les sciences et des arts . . . (N.p., 1684);

Factum pour Messire Antoine Furetière, abbé de Chalivoy, contre quelques-uns de Messieurs de l'Académie françoise (N.p., n.d. [1685]);

Second Factum pour Messire Antoine Furetière, abbé de Chalivoy, appelant tant comme juges incompétans qu'autrement, d'une prétendue sentence rendue au bureau de l'Académie françoise, le . . . janvier 1685 (N.p., n.d. [1685]);

Troisième Factum servant d'apologie aux deux precedans, pour Messire Antoine Furetière, abbé de Chalivoy, appelant d'une sentence rendue au siège de la police du Châtelet de Paris, le 24 décembre 1686 (N.p., n.d. [1687]);

Plan et dessein du poème allégorique et tragico-burlesque intitulé "Les Couches de l'Académie" (Amsterdam: P. Brunel,

Antoine Furetière, abbé de Chalivoy, at age sixty-six (engraving by Nicolas Habert, 1687; from the 1978 edition of Furetière's Le Dictionnaire universel)

1687); republished as *Les Couches de l'Académie* (Geneva, 1687); republished as *Les Couches de l'Académie, ou Poème allégorique et burlesque* (Amsterdam: H. Desbordes, 1688);

Dictionaire universel, contenant généralement tous les mots françois, tant vieux que modernes, & les termes de toutes les sciences et des arts . . . , 3 volumes (The Hague & Rotterdam: A. & R. Leers, 1690);

Nouveau Recueil des factums du procès d'entre défunt M. l'abbé Furetière, l'un des quarante de l'Académie française, et quelques-uns des autres membres de la même Académie . . . , 2 volumes (Amsterdam: H. Desbordes, 1694).

Editions: *Recueil des factums d'Antoine Furetière de l'Académie françoise contre quelques-uns de cette Académie, suivi des preuves et pièces historiques données dans l'édition de 1694,* 2 volumes, edited by Charles Asselineau (Paris: Poulet-Malassis & De Broise, 1859);

The "Poésies diverses" of Antoine Furetière: A Partial Reprint from the Edition of 1664, edited by Isabelle Bronk (Baltimore: J. H. Furst, 1908);

Le Roman bourgeois, in *Romanciers du XVIIe siècle,* edited by Antoine Adam, Bibliothèque de la Pléiade, no. 131 (Paris: Gallimard, 1958), pp. 899–1104;

Nouvelle allégorique, ou Histoire des derniers troubles arrivés au royaume d'éloquence, edited by Eva van Ginneken (Geneva: Droz, 1967);

Dictionnaire universel: Contenant généralement tous les mots françois, edited by Henri Basnage de Beauval (Hildensheim: Georg Olms, 1972);

Le Dictionnaire universel, edited by Alain Rey (Paris: SNL–Le Robert, 1978);

Le Roman bourgeois, edited by Jacques Prévot (Paris: Gallimard, 1981);

Le Dictionnaire universel, in *L'Atelier historique de la langue française: L'Histoire des mots du haut Moyen âge au XIXe siècle,* CD-ROM (Marsanne: Redon, 1999);

Dictionnaires des XVIe et XVIIe siècles, CD-ROM (Paris: Champion Electronique, 1999);

Le Roman bourgeois, edited by Marine Roy-Garibal (Paris: Flammarion, 2001).

Although a well-known literary figure in his day, Antoine Furetière is more often remembered as a lexicographer than as a writer. The burlesque poetry, satires, and occasional pieces he wrote in his youth have long since ceased to be read; his fables, published in 1671, only a few years after Jean de La Fontaine's, suffered in comparison then as they do now; and his single novel, while attracting sporadic critical interest in France since the mid nineteenth century, has not been translated into English in more than three hundred years. His dictionary, on the other hand, was instantly recognized as a major accomplishment and is still the primary reference for scholars wishing to understand the linguistic usage of the seventeenth century. In an age in which *politesse* (politeness) was the rule, in language as elsewhere in society, Furetière's *Dictionaire universel* (1690; spelled *Dictionnaire* in modern editions) was the first unilingual French dictionary to accept the "low" and archaic words still in common use but rejected by the purist lexicons of Pierre Richelet (1680) and the Académie Française (1694).

Antoine Furetière was born in Paris on 28 December 1619, the eldest of ten children. His father, a lawyer by training who was employed in the king's service, provided his son with a solid classical educa-

tion. Like his father and uncle, Furetière studied law at the Sorbonne and in 1645 graduated with a *licence,* a degree between *bachelier* and *docteur,* which allowed one to practice law. The keenly observed world and language of the legal profession as well as the social aspirations of its members later formed the background for his novel, *Le Roman bourgeois* (1666; translated as *Scarron's City Romance,* 1671).

Although Furetière was nearly thirty years old before he published his first work, he gravitated toward a literary career from an early age. While at college he met and befriended La Fontaine, and at university, Charles Perrault was his classmate. After graduating, Furetière frequented the literary salons of Madeleine de Scudéry and the Hôtel de Rambouillet, and he later joined a group of young writers to form a private literary circle. Some of these writers—such as Jean de Maucroix, Valentin Conrart, and Paul Pellisson-Fontanier—were or went on to become literary figures of some note.

Furetière probably began writing poetry and satire about this time. His first signed work of verse, *Poësies diverses* (Miscellaneous Poems, 1655), claims that most were written "in the ardor of youth and with the itch to be a writer," and from internal evidence it is possible to date the composition of several of them to the early 1640s. His first published work, appearing anonymously in 1649, was a burlesque of the first four cantos of Virgil, *L'Aenéide travestie* (The Travestied Aeneid). This publication was followed in 1653 by another unsigned work, *Le Voyage de Mercure* (The Voyage of Mercury), a biting satire of some of what Furetière believed were the major literary and social ills of his day.

If *L'Aenéide travestie* is a fairly conventional burlesque, depending for its comic effect on the contrast between the elevated subject matter of its classical reference and the low style of its vocabulary and expression, *Le Voyage de Mercure,* while also a burlesque of sorts, is less mechanical in its humor and much sharper in its social satire. The conceit of the work is familiar and was used to similar effect fifty years later by Alain René Lesage in *Le Diable boiteux* (The Hobbling Devil, 1707): a supernatural figure roams the world reporting, sub specie aeternitatis (under the aspect of eternity), on the social ills of mankind. In Mercury's report to Jupiter, little escapes the observer's ire: elevated financiers and vulgar money changers, quack doctors and unscrupulous lawyers, idle poets and poor novelists—all are brought forward to show the present state of humanity in a bad light. Though published anonymously, both works garnered Furetière a certain amount of critical notoriety.

Like almost all writers of the seventeenth century, Furetière could not hope to support himself through his literary output alone. Lacking the means of nobles such as Roger de Bussy-Rabutin or Marie-Madeleine, comtesse de Lafayette, Furetière needed some sort of regular income in order to pursue a literary career. In 1652 his legal training allowed him to move into the post of fiscal prosecutor for the *bailliage* (bailiff's court) of Saint-Germain-des-prés. Unlike many other writers, who depended on the largesse of powerful patrons to survive, Furetière could, under the cover of anonymity, strike a pose of relative social independence with regard to those in power. The dedicatory epistle of *Le Voyage de Mercure,* addressed to "No one," proclaims this position clearly.

> Moy qui sans respecter les rangs
> Satyrise petits et grands,
> Qui par tout respandant ma bile
> Sur gens de Cour et gens de Ville . . .

> (I, who throw off every yoke,
> satirize court and city folk,
> who everywhere vent my spleen
> On the great and on the mean . . .)

Despite offering relative independence, a legal career left Furetière too little time for literature. Soon afterward, through circumstances that are still unclear but that doubtless involved patronage of some sort, he managed to obtain two ecclesiastical benefices. The first position, as secular prior of the Priory of Saint-Laurent-sur-Saône, was a sinecure proper, meaning he had no charge over the care of souls (*sine cure*) and could simply receive an income. The second, at the Priory Saint-Pierre de Gigny, was what was known as a conventional benefice and required Furetière to take holy orders. As was common in the convoluted ecclesiastical world of the Ancien Régime, neither of these positions required him actually to reside in the establishments he headed, and so he could continue living the life of a worldly Parisian.

It was in the resolutely secular and increasingly fractious world of letters that Furetière was determined to make his mark. Abandoning the independent and irreverent social satire of his youth, Furetière in 1658 published *Nouvelle allégorique, ou Histoire des derniers troubles arrivez au royaume d'éloquence* (The Allegorical Novella; or, An Account of the late Civil Wars in the Kingdom of Eloquence), dedicated to Henri, prince de Bourbon. The originality of this work for Furetière's contemporaries was in its presentation of the literary rivalries of the day as an allegorical battle between two opposing military factions. On one side, the troops of Princess Rhetoric represent, under vari-

Frontispiece for Furetière's realistic novel, published anonymously in 1666 (from the 1978 edition of Furetière's Le Dictionnaire universel)

ous transparent keys, the writers and literary opinions of nascent classicism; on the other, Captain Gallimatias (literally "Captain Gibberish," although the English version of 1704 calls him "Captain Bombast") and his forces represent the pedantry and outdated aesthetic of the previous generation.

The interest for modern literary historians, however, lies as much in Furetière's original use of allegory as in what it shows of the subtle careerism of the author. A few contemporary writers are gently mocked, and their quarrels and internal divisions are alluded to, but in general, any really biting satirical attacks of the sort that characterized *Le Voyage de Mercure* are reserved for pedants and minor writers long since vanished from the literary scene. It is, moreover, no accident that the capital of the Kingdom of Eloquence is called "Academy" and that the sovereign council of Princess Rhetoric is comprised of "forty barons." By openly flattering the members of the Académie Française in this way, Furetière paved the way for his own entry into what had become, since its incorporation by the cardinal de Richelieu as a Royal Academy in 1635, the preeminent literary institution of France. *Nouvelle allégorique* was not only appreciated by the narrow band of those who saw themselves represented in its pages. As an amusing topography of the literary issues of the day, it also proved to be one of Furetière's most popular works, going through three editions in 1658 alone and regularly reprinted until 1703.

By 1662 Furetière had managed an impressive social elevation. In addition to being elected to one of the forty chairs of the Académie Française in May, in that same year he exchanged both of his ecclesiastical benefices for the stewardship of an abbey near Bourges, a change giving him the title by which he was known for the rest of his life, *L'abbé de Chalivoy*. Though now prelate and *académicien* (member of the Académie Française), he did not renounce the satirical irreverence of his youth for all that. With Molière, La Fontaine, Gilles Ménage, the young Jean Racine, and Gilles and Nicolas Boileau, Furetière met daily during the early years of the 1660s at the Croix Blanche restaurant. One of the most celebrated works to come out of these informal meetings was a cruel lampoon of Jean Chapelain, a well-known poet and critic of the preceding generation, who by that time had been appointed by Jean-Baptiste Colbert to draw up a list of "pensionable" writers likely to support the fledgling absolutist regime of Louis XIV. Parodying the insult scene in Pierre Corneille's *Le Cid* (first performed, 1637), *Chapelain décoiffé* (Chapelain Dewigged, 1663) has the old poet issuing a call to vengeance when his infamously filthy periwig is torn off by his rival Jean Puget de La Serre. Although *Chapelain décoiffé* is usually reprinted with Nicolas Boileau's works, Boileau, who soon rallied to the cultural politics of Louis XIV, disavowed all but a couple of lines, attributing the greater part of the parody to Furetière.

Furetière, despite moving in an orbit that brought him increasingly close to the center of cultural power, remained genuinely independent in his literary activity. Aside from his monumental dictionary, there is no more telling example of his originality than *Le Roman bourgeois,* published anonymously. It encountered little critical success when it was first published, although it did enjoy a brief revival at the beginning of the eighteenth century (three editions from 1704 to 1714), as well as finding some favor in England, if one counts a single English translation of 1671 that misattributed the novel to Paul Scarron and an "Imitation" by George Farquar (*The Adventures of Covent-Garden, in Imitation of Scarron's City Romance,* 1699) as favor, before being more or less forgotten until the mid nineteenth century. One can see how such a "romance" might be ill received by the literary public of the day. If the first

part is a fairly conventional burlesque romance, recounting the amorous and social misadventures of Nicodème and Javotte, two *bourgeois* (that is, upwardly mobile "townfolk," as opposed to the nobles of the Court) from the Place Maubert in Paris, the second part turns on a bizarre legalistic debate between two *chicaneurs* (squabblers), Charroselles and Collantine, who discuss the testament of a recently deceased poet, Mythophilacte. Unlike the more traditional comic novel, in which a single narrative thread is pursued, the author presents in *Le Roman bourgeois* a work with two unrelated stories sutured together by little more than the reappearance of Charroselles (an anagram of the name Charles Sorel), who has a minor role in the first part, and the anonymous voice of the publisher/bookseller, who interrupts the two stories to joke: "Pour le soin de la liaison, je le laisse à celui qui reliera [relira] le livre" (As for the task of joining them together, I leave that to the bookbinder [reader]).

Not until 1853, when Charles Asselineau "rediscovered" *Le Roman bourgeois,* was its creation recognized as an important moment in the history of the novel, if not in the history of seventeenth-century literature. Seeing it as an essentially realist work–"le premier roman d'observation qu'ait produit la litérature française" (the first novel of observation that French literature had produced), as Asselineau put it–written at a time when the novel was tending, from Scudéry to Lafayette, to a certain type of idealism, Furetière became, for the champions of narrative realism at least, a forerunner of Denis Diderot, Emile Zola, and the central tradition of the development of the novel as a modern literary genre. Those judging *Le Roman bourgeois* against other literary works of nascent classicism, on the other hand, have almost always seen it as a failed work by a minor talent–little more than a disarticulated hodgepodge of base realism, facile wit, and cheap attacks on rival writers. Commenting on a new edition of *Le Roman bourgeois,* critic Alain Niderst wrote in *Revue d'Histoire Littéraire de la France* as recently as September/December 1982: "Ce livre méchant, qui brise les grandes formes littéraires et diffame d'illustres personnalités, n'a aucune construction. Furetière l'a écrit dans la haine, l'a laissé inachevé, et a attendu une dizaine d'années avant de avant de le faire paraître. Le public de 1666 ne s'y est pas intéressé. Au XIXe sièce, on a réhabilité *Le Roman bourgeois:* Furetière devint un peu le Flaubert de la France classique; Javotte ressemblait à Mme Bovary" (Shattering the major literary forms and slandering illustrious figures, this is a nasty book with no structure. Furetière wrote it in hatred, left it unfinished, and waited ten years before publishing it. The public of 1666 was not interested. In the nineteenth century, *Le Roman bourgeois* was rehabilitated and Furetière was seen

Title page for Furetière's 1690 dictionary of the French language, the first to include "common" and archaic words still in use at that time (from the 1978 facsimile edition)

as a kind of seventeenth-century Flaubert: Javotte seemed like Madame Bovary"). Precursor of the novel or failed classic, Furetière's *Roman bourgeois* still holds this place in most textbook histories of French literature. Although more-recent readers, formed in the wake of the *nouveau roman* and deconstructive criticism, have tried to do justice to the unorthodox nature and apparent lack of structure of *Le Roman bourgeois,* its reception history has in general remained sharply divided.

Furetière only published three more purely "literary" works in his lifetime. In 1671 he returned to poetry, writing a book of fables in verse. These appeared only three years after La Fontaine's first collection and were greeted with a less than enthusiastic response from the public. Acknowledging the work of his predecessor with a backhanded compliment in the epistle dedicatory, Furetière claims that if his fables are less well written, at least the subjects are all his own invention, unlike La Fontaine's, which are largely drawn from Aesop or Phaedrus. A collection of para-

bles from the Gospels "translated" by Furetière into French verse were published the following year. These were received even less generously, with one critic going so far as to say that Furetière had put the words of Jesus into burlesque verse. Whatever their literary merit, both these works marked a change from the formal and social freedom of Furetière's youth toward a conformism more in keeping with his membership in the Académie Française and his title of abbot. Both, too, consolidated his social position by appealing to powerful patrons: the first was dedicated to the archbishop of Paris, François de Harlay, and the second to Louis XIV. A brief heroic poem addressed to the king on his conquest of Franche-Comté in 1674 continued in this direction.

Even more surprising, then, was that Furetière's final work proved responsible for his utter social undoing, destroying in four years what he had spent a lifetime building up. In 1672 the Académie Française, which had ostensibly been working on the establishment of a dictionary since its foundation in 1635, obtained an astonishing royal privilege that forbade the publication of any rival dictionary for twenty years leading up to the completion of its own, and again for a further twenty years after that. Although the early records of the Académie Française are lost, it is known that when the Académie Française decided to renew work on the dictionary under the impetus of Colbert in 1672, Furetière was an assiduous participant. Precisely when he began work on his own dictionary is unknown, although he himself later claimed to have been working on it for the better part of forty years. Clearly, however, his dictionary was largely complete by 1684 when, in circumstances that his rivals later claimed were dishonest, Furetière obtained his own privilege for a dictionary of "Arts and Sciences."

Furetière began his career in the law, and so he ended it, although as a litigant rather than as an advocate. In 1684 Furetière suddenly found himself pitted against his colleagues at the Académie Française in a dispute that became known as *La Bataille des dictionnaires* (The Battle of the Dictionaries). When he published several sample articles later in the year, in which words as ordinary as *oiseau, couleur,* and *feu* appeared, the Academy immediately saw its original privilege threatened, a threat that Furetière had foreseen but vainly tried to deflect by calling his dictionary "un Dictionnaire qui n'est pour ainsi dire que provisionnel, & le précurseur de celui qui viendra en Souverain dans une entière pureté juger tous les mots vieux et nouveau" (a dictionary that is but a provisional work and the precursor of that which will arrive free of all contamination as the sovereign judge of all words new and old). Whether these precautions were meant to be read as transparent flattery or as malicious irony, the Académie Française lost no time in defending its privilege and attacking Furetière as dishonest. In January 1685 it went to Parliament to demand that Furetière's privilege be revoked and that he remove all but the narrowly technical words from his dictionary. The chancellor Le Tellier refused to act, however, whereupon the members of the Académie Française assembled, only just quorate with twenty (including La Fontaine, Perrault, and Racine), to vote nineteen to one for the expulsion of Furetière from the Académie Française before taking their case back to the king.

From that point on, from 1685 until 1688, the year of his death, Furetière spent the greater part of his literary energies writing petitions, remonstrances, pamphlets, and most important, a series of three "factums"—quasi-legal defenses that, amidst accusations, counteraccusations, and not a little satire, presented the case for the utility and originality of his dictionary against that of the Académie Française. The first fac-

tum was released in February, just prior to his privilege being revoked in March. Despite falling gravely ill, Furetière responded with a second factum at the end of the year. Several members of the Académie Française responded in kind with (anonymous) satirical dialogues and pamphlets ridiculing Furetière at the same time as the Académie Française as a whole pursued its legal challenge. At the end of 1686 the Académie Française won an injunction, and both factums were condemned as defamatory. After several legal petitions and a third factum, darker and more acerbic than the first two, Furetière finally won his battle in the court of public opinion, even as he lost it in the court of law. With the publication of his dictionary being openly lobbied for by Pierre Bayle in his *Nouvelles de la République des Lettres,* and faced with the continuing intransigence of the Court, Furetière decided in 1687 to sell his manuscript to a publisher in the Netherlands.

Furetière never lived to see his project completed. He died in Paris on 14 May 1688 at the age of sixty-eight, two years before his dictionary, with a preface by Bayle, was published in Holland to general acclaim. When the Académie Française's dictionary finally came out in 1694, four years after the *Dictionnaire universel* (and almost sixty years after Richelieu's original mandate), it was judged by the public as a disappointment, if not a downright failure. Furetière's dictionary, on the other hand, went on in the eighteenth century to form the basis for the French Jesuit *Dictionnaire de Trévoux,* which, despite protests of plagiarism from Furetière's Dutch publisher, had seven continuously expanding French editions from 1721 to 1771. By this time the name of the obscure prelate and one-time academician who provided the lexical foundations for the monumental encyclopedia of the Jesuits was all but forgotten.

In his preface to the original edition, Bayle wrote, "la secheresse qui accompagne ordinairement les dictionnaires n'est pas à craindre dans celuy-ci. Car . . . la vaste étendüe, et la carriere immense que l'Auteur a choisie pour son dessein, fournit dans chaque page beaucoup de diversité, et ne permet pas que le lecteur fasse beaucoup de chemin sans apprendre quelque chose qui en vaut la peine" (the dryness which is normally the mark of dictionaries is not to be feared here. For . . . the great breadth and immense scope of the author's design provides diversity on every page, and does not allow the reader to go very far without learning something worthwhile). Critics of later centuries were left to measure the truth of that remark and to rescue the name of Antoine Furetière from an undeserved literary oblivion.

References:

Francis Assaf, "Furetière ou l'esthétique du contraire," *Littératures Classiques,* no. 15 (October 1991): 163–183;

Charles Asselineau, "Préface," in *Le Roman bourgeois* (Paris: Jannet, 1854), pp. 5–22;

Emmanuel Bury, "Rhétorique de Furetière: invention et lieux communs dans *Le Roman bourgeois,*" in *Prémices et floraisons de l'âge classique, Mélanges en l'honneur de Jean Jehasse* (Saint-Etienne: Presses de l'Université de Saint-Etienne, 1995), pp. 333–345;

Jean-Pierre Chauveau, "L'esprit et la lettre. Poètes débutants en face de leurs modèles: Théophile, Tristan et Furetière," *XVIIe Siècle,* no. 186 (January–March 1995): 21–38;

Joëlle Chevalier, Eugene F. Del Vecchio, and Ulrich Döring, "Fiches signalétiques des études consacrées au *Roman bourgeois* d'Antoine Furetière," *Œuvres & Critiques,* 1, no. 2 (1976): 85–91;

"Les Contes de Perrault. La Contestation et ses limites. Furetière," *Papers on French Seventeenth Century Literature, 1987,* edited by J. Alter, J. Barchilon, M. Bareau and D. Stanton (Paris: Papers on French Seventeenth Century Literature, 1987);

Jean-Charles Darmon, "Furetière et l'universel," *Stanford French Review* (Winter 1990): 15–46;

Döring, *Antoine Furetiére, Rezeption und Werk* (Frankfurt: Peter Lang, 1995);

Fabienne Gégou, *Antoine Furetière, l'abbé de Chalivoy, ou la chute d'un Immortel* (Paris: Nizet, 1962);

Calogero Giardina, *Narration, burlesque et langage dans le* Roman bourgeois *d'Antoine Furetière* (Paris: Archives des Lettres Modernes, 1992);

Pierre Hartmann, "Formalisation juridique et codification amoureuse. Une tentative d'appréhension de l'unité du *Roman bourgeois,*" *XVIIe Siècle,* no. 42 (1990): 421–431;

Maurice Laugaa, "Pour une poétique de la négation," *Revue des Sciences Humaines,* no. 164 (October–December 1976): 525–533;

Littératures Classiques, special Furetière issue, edited by Hélène Merlin (2002);

Craig Moyes, "'Il n'y a plus de Mecenas': *Le Roman bourgeois* and the crisis of literary patronage," in *Culture and Conflict in Seventeenth-Century France,* edited by Sarah Alyn Stacey (Dublin: Four Courts Press, 2002);

Jacques Prévost, "Préface," in *Le Roman bourgeois* (Paris: Gallimard, 1981), pp. 7–20;

Alain Rey, "Antoine Furetière, imagier de la culture classique," in *Le Dictionnaire universel d'Antoine Furetière* (Paris: SNL–Le Robert, 1978), pp. 7–93;

Marine Roy-Garibal, "Présentation," in *Le Roman bourgeois* (Paris: G. F. Flammarion, 2001), pp. 27–62;

Jean Serroy, "Scarron/Furetière. Inventaire de l'inventaire," *Littératures Classiques,* 11 (1989): 211–219;

J. A. G. Tans, "Un Sterne français: Antoine Furetière. La fonction du *Roman bourgeois,*" *XVIIe Siècle,* no. 128 (July–September 1980): 279–292;

Michèle Vialet, *Triomphe de l'iconoclaste: Le Roman bourgeois et les lois de la cohérence romanesque* (Paris & Seattle: Papers on French Seventeenth Century Literature, 1989);

Francis Wey, "Antoine Furetière. Sa vie, ses œuvres, ses démêlés avec l'Académie française," *Revue contemporaine,* 2 (1852): 594–618; 3 (1852): 49–78.

Marin Le Roy, sieur de Gomberville

(1600? – 14 June 1674)

Mark Bannister
Oxford Brookes University

BOOKS: *Tableau du bonheur de la vieillesse opposé au malheur de la jeunesse* (Paris: J. Laquchay, 1614);

Ode sur les heureux succez des actions du Roy (Paris: P. Chevalier, 1618);

L'Exil de Polexandre et d'Ericlée, as Orile (Paris: T. du Bray, 1619);

Discours des vertus et des vices de l'histoire, et de la maniere de la bien escrire (Paris: T. du Bray, 1620);

La Carithée de M. Le Roy, Sr de Gomberville: Contenant sous des temps, des provinces, et des noms supposez, plusieurs rares et veritables histoires de nostre temps (Paris: J. Quesnel, 1621);

Remarques sur la vie du Roy et sur celle d'Alexandre Severe, contenant la comparaison de ces deux grands princes et comme les propheties de l'heureux regne du Roy (Paris: T. du Bray, 1622);

L'Astrée de Messire Honoré d'Urfé . . . Sixiesme partie (Paris: R. Foüet, 1626);

L'Exil de Polexandre, Première partie (Paris: T. du Bray, 1629);

Polexandre, 2 volumes (Paris: T. du Bray, 1632);

Polexandre, 5 volumes (Paris: A. Courbé, 1637; revised, 1638); translated by William Browne as *The History of Polexander* (London: Printed by Thomas Harper for Thomas Walkley, 1647);

Cythérée, 2 volumes (Paris: A. Courbé, 1640; revised and enlarged, 4 volumes, 1642);

La Doctrine des mœurs, tirée de la philosophie des stoïques . . . (Paris: L. Sevestre, 1646); translated by T. M. Gibbs as *The Doctrine of Morality, or A View of Human Life According to the Stoick Philosophy . . .* (London: Printed for E. Bell, J. Darby . . . , 1721);

La Jeune Alcidiane (Paris: A. Courbé, 1651);

Les Mémoires de Monsieur le duc de Nevers, prince de Mantoue, pair de France . . . enrichis de plusieurs pièces du temps, 2 volumes (Paris: L. Billaine, 1665; Paris: T. Jolly, 1665).

Edition: *L'Astrée de Messire Honoré d'Urfé . . . Sixiesme partie,* edited by Bernard Yon (Saint-Etienne: Presses de l'Université de Saint-Etienne, 1976).

Marin Le Roy, sieur de Gomberville

OTHER: *Le Second Livre des delices de la poesie françoise, ou Nouveau Recueil des plus beaux vers de ce temps,* edited by Jean Baudoin, contributions by Gomberville (Paris: T. du Bray, 1620), pp. 267–288;

Cristóbal de Acuña, *Relation de la rivière des Amazones,* 2 volumes (Paris: C. Barbin, 1682).

Marin Le Roy, sieur de Gomberville, son of Louis Le Roy and Marie Vallençon, was born probably in 1600 or possibly in 1599. His father's profession and exact status have been the subject of debate, but he was likely an officeholder under the Crown, with all that that implied in terms of pretensions to nobility. The family estate of Gomberville was situated at Magny-les-Hameaux, near Chevreuse, to the southwest of Paris, but the family resided in the capital, and the boy was educated there at the Collège de la Marche, run by the Jesuits, who provided the soundest education available at the time. He was drawn to the literary life from an early age, having his first work, a book of verse titled *Tableau du bonheur de la vieillesse opposé au malheur de la jeunesse* (A Depiction of the Happiness of Old Age Opposed to the Unhappiness of Youth, 1614), published when he was no more than fourteen or fifteen years old. The realization that literary works could earn recognition for their author led him to produce an ode in praise of the king, *Ode sur les heureux succez des actions du Roy,* in 1618 and contributions to one of the poetic anthologies of the day, *Le Second Livre des delices de la poésie françoise, ou Nouveau Recueil des plus beaux vers de ce temps* (The Second Book of the Delights of French Poetry, or A New Collection of the Finest Verses of the Age), in 1620. His sonnets reveal the influence of Théophile de Viau, who was then inspiring the younger generation of poets with his call to follow one's own nature, both in poetry and in life.

Gomberville's education and personal preference in reading had led him to study a wide range of historical writings, an interest that marked his literary output throughout his life. The nature and function of historiography were objects of debate in the 1620s, as the chronicle-based histories of the sixteenth century gave way to the view that history was a branch of moral litterature, using the past as a repository of exempla that could be used to illuminate the human condition. Gomberville made his own contribution to the debate with his *Discours des vertus et des vices de l'histoire, et de la maniere de la bien escrire* (Discourse on the Virtues and Vices of History [or Historiography], and on Writing It Well, 1620), in which he adopted a radical approach, insisting that the historian should concern himself only with events and their causes rather than with the lives and moral disposition of individuals.

The unflattering judgments on the Italians and indiscreet remarks about Henri IV's love life in the *Discours des vertus et des vices de l'histoire* suggest that it was probably the "petit livre où il y avoit quelque chose qui n'avoit pas plû à la Reyne-mere" (little book containing something that the Queen Mother did not like) referred to by Tallemant des Réaux, which cost Gomberville the post of *secrétaire du roi* (Chancellery secretary) he had obtained in 1619. His *Remarques sur la vie du Roy et sur celle d'Alexandre Severe, contenant la comparaison de ces deux grands princes et comme les propheties de l'heureux regne du Roy* (Remarks on the Life of the King and of Alexander Severus, Containing a Comparison of These Two Great Princes, and Intended As Prophecies of the Happiness of the King's Reign, 1622), a rambling panegyric dedicated to the king but purporting to be a work of historical scholarship, was an attempt to rehabilitate himself in the eyes of the monarch.

In 1621 Gomberville married Barbe Fauveau, daughter of one of the wine merchants licensed to supply the court. They had nine children. Though his youthful writings reveal a determination to try his hand at many different genres, Gomberville's predilection for fiction emerged at an early stage. In 1619 he published *L'Exil de Polexandre et d'Ericlée* (The Exile of Polexander and Ericlée) under the anagrammatic pseudonym Orile. Most of the work is no more than some loosely connected love stories of the kind to be found in the *roman sentimental* (sentimental romance) of the day, full of disguises, mistaken identities, and escapes from abductors. Only the final chapter, in which the adventures of Polexandre and Ericlée are recounted in a book found by the other characters, points toward the concerns that increasingly preoccupied Gomberville's imaginative endeavors—the creation of a hero who surpasses other men in his noble qualities and the setting of events against a recognizable historical background, in this case the court of Henri II.

This first attempt at prose fiction seems to have had some limited success, and Gomberville embarked on what was effectively a self-imposed literary apprenticeship. His second work of fiction, *La Carithée de M. Le Roy, Sr de Gomberville: Contenant sous des temps, des provinces, et des noms supposez, plusieurs rares et veritables histoires de nostre temps* (Carithea, by M. Le Roy, sieur de Gomberville: In Which May Be Found, Hidden under Fictitious Epochs, Regions, and Names, Several Unusual and True Stories of Our Own Time, 1621), follows the prevailing fashion in claiming that the events and characters depicted are really disguised versions of "histoires de nostre temps," though there is no evidence to support the claim, despite anagrammatic references to Louis XIII and his favorite, Charles d'Albert, duc de Luynes. Its setting is "l'Isle heureuse" (The Happy Isle) on the Nile in the first century A.D., a pastoral world well known to the readers of the day in terms of the conventions on which it rested. Though Gomberville inevitably drew on Honoré d'Urfé's *L'Astrée* (1607–1625) for inspiration, he demonstrates that he is more than a mere imitator. His shepherds and shepherdesses have their own individuality: Cérinthe is no Céladon, and Philidas, the spokesman for inconstancy, is more than a replica of Hylas. Moreover, the desire to introduce a more solid historical base is apparent in the account of the life and death of Germanicus Caesar—

Decorated title page for Gomberville's first work of prose fiction, a loosely connected series of love stories published in 1619 under the pseudonym Orile (from Roméo Arbour, Un Editeur d'oeuvres littéraires au XVIIe siècle: Toussaint du Bray, *1992; Dickinson College Library)*

increasing commitment to a more heroic kind of novel. The account of the siege of Marcilly is suffused with an epic tone illuminating the value and admirable nature of human endeavor: as Bernard Yon said in the introduction to his 1976 edition of *L'Astrée,* "*L'Astrée* se transforme ainsi en une nouvelle *Iliade* qui nous éloigne certainement de ce qu'avait voulu Honoré d'Urfé" (*L'Astrée* is thus transformed into a new *Iliad,* much removed from what d'Urfé had intended).

Having learned from his work on *L'Astrée* a good deal about the art of constructing a plot, Gomberville returned to the theme of his first novel, encouraged by Nicole, duchesse de Lorraine, to devote his energies to fiction rather than to history. The result, *L'Exil de Polexandre, Première partie* (The Exile of Polexander, Part One, 1629), shows the extent to which his interest in history and his taste for exotic settings influenced the workings of his imagination. Polexandre still appears at the court of Henri II, as he had in the 1619 version, but the detail of the period is more precise: for instance, Polexandre fights against the Huguenots at the battle of Jarnac, and Catherine de Médicis's political role at court is highlighted. Polexandre and his love for Olimpe now share the center of attention with the Inca prince Zelmatide and the Mexican princess Izatide, a change that gives the author the opportunity to relate a brief history of the Incas and fill out the narration with local color. The most significant development, however, is the noticeable emphasis on the sense of brotherhood between individuals, from whatever nation, who are capable of the highest level of *générosité* (nobility of purpose) and *vertu* (moral strength).

Like its predecessor, *L'Exil de Polexandre* was unfinished, and Gomberville began work on a third version, which appeared in 1632 as *Polexandre.* Although most of the major characters reappear and many of the episodes have been modeled closely on the 1629 version, the setting has been transposed to the early eighth century. Polexandre is now Charles Martel, his name having been changed by his father to please the Franks; Zelmatide is Persian; and Izatide, Saracen. New characters are introduced and given their own subplots, linked loosely to the wanderings and exploits of Polexandre. The considerable chronological distance adopted for the 1632 version produced an effect that Gomberville presumably did not intend; it evokes an ill-defined world more reminiscent of *Amadis de Gaule* than the essentially modern, albeit exotic, settings of the two previous versions. Nevertheless, this version represents a further advance in Gomberville's vision: the existence of a universal caste of heroic warriors, committed to the highest level of *générosité,* is fundamental to all the episodes, and the female version of heroism, evolving in the character of Olimpe, requires

representing one third of the novel–and the opportunity it provides for historical detail and erudition about imperial Rome.

L'Astrée provided a more direct input into Gomberville's apprenticeship in 1625. In that year, Honoré d'Urfé died without having completed his pastoral masterpiece. Several rival parties sought to take up the master's mantle, among them Gomberville, who composed a *Sixiesme partie* (Part 6, 1626), which picked up and developed the plotlines left unresolved. The result reveals the extent to which Gomberville had immersed himself in the substance and the spirit of the original. At the same time, however, it illustrates his

the woman to demand complete submission of any suitor while herself claiming to be unmoved by love.

In 1632 Gomberville's parents transferred into his name the family estates and fiefs at Magny-les-Hameaux, four properties in some of the more fashionable quarters of Paris, and a library valued at three thousand livres. By then, as well as having financial security, he could rely on a network of influential connections, for in 1625 he had been secretary to Claude de Lorraine, duc de Chevreuse, and in 1628 was attached to the household of Henri de Lorraine, comte d'Harcourt, both of them members of a powerful family. Moreover, he was an established and respected figure in literary circles. In 1625 he had acted as mediator in the bitter quarrel between Guez de Balzac and his former teacher, Père Garasse, bringing about a reconciliation. Gomberville was one of the group of writers linked to Roger du Plessis, marquis de Liancourt, who advanced the careers of such men as Alexandre Hardy, Pierre Corneille, and Marc-Antoine Girard de Saint-Amant. Gomberville's reputation as a *bel esprit* (man of wit) and his political connections led to his being included among the original forty members of the Académie Française, founded by Richelieu in 1635.

For a man who prided himself on his dislike of order and discipline in the creative process, Gomberville showed a remarkable enthusiasm for furthering the standardizing mission of the academy, serving on the committees that established the projects for a dictionary and a grammar of the French language. That enthusiasm reveals one of the apparent contradictions in his personality, for, while admiring de Viau and writing novels that betrayed no obvious evidence of restraint or orderliness, he was also a disciple of François de Malherbe, certainly from as early as 1620, and supported Malherbe's efforts to "purify" poetic diction. Gomberville's temporary antipathy toward the conjunction *car* (for, because) was an expression of support for Malherbe's doctrine, and Gomberville tried to avoid using it in his 1629 version of *L'Exil de Polexandre,* though subsequent versions include many examples of its use. When the Académie Française became the butt of satirists in the mid 1630s for its supposed obsession with controlling the language, Gomberville was included in the satires. He appears in Charles de Marguetel de Saint-Denis de Saint-Evremond's *Comédie des Académistes* (Comedy of the Academicians), circulating in manuscript in 1637, under the name of Ladreville (Stingyville) because of his reputation for parsimony.

The fourth and final version of *Polexandre* was published in five volumes in 1637, the culmination of nearly twenty years of experiment. The essential concerns that had preoccupied Gomberville through all the changes of plot and characters now became clear. The historical element is once again revised—Polexandre, now a descendant of Charles d'Anjou, brother of Saint Louis, and of the Paleologue emperors of Byzantium, lives in the late fifteenth century—but it is subordinate to the claims of imagination. Polexandre is king of the Canary Islands, where he spends relatively little time, devoting his life to finding l'Isle Inaccessible, of which Alcidiane is queen. She for her part seems almost to be set outside the historical frame of reference. Gomberville's enthusiasm for exotic settings, however, is given free rein. The main characters are drawn from Morocco, Turkey, Peru, Mexico, Denmark, several kingdoms in Africa (Senegal, Benin, Zahara, and Thombut—that is, Timbuktu), and other real and imagined places. The action moves from one continent to another, and in each the narrator lingers over the description of an Islamic ceremony or the detail of a Mexican costume or a debate on the nature of animistic religion. The various nations and their cultures are approached with curiosity and on the whole treated tolerantly, with the exception of the Spanish who, with a hostility that must have pleased Richelieu, are invariably shown as aggressive and barbaric imperialists.

Gomberville's ambition to create a hero beyond compare is finally fulfilled. The new Polexandre is universally acknowledged to be the greatest of men. His valor is unmatched, but he is also morally superior to all other men, with a mission to help the oppressed and to further the cause of Christianity. His special status sets him morally apart from the rest of the world, as does his personal destiny—to seek out Alcidiane, even though he feels himself unworthy of her. Just as Polexandre is the epitome of male aspirations, Alcidiane is the embodiment of female perfection. She inhabits an earthly paradise lost out in the ocean and is acknowledged throughout the world as an ideal that all must respect, even if they cannot all aspire to win her. Gomberville's achievement, however, is to give Polexandre and Alcidiane characteristics that make them human as well as ideal. He makes Alcidiane an icon of the female independence that became such an important feature of feminist thinking in the 1640s and 1650s. She rejects all men, insisting on absolute freedom, and accepts Polexandre at the end of the novel only because her acceptance of him is necessary for recognizing the supremacy of heroic energy and action when combined with utter devotion. To reach that point, she had to suffer a sequence of conflicting emotions, which she records in a journal, a nice touch designed to appeal to female readers. Polexandre, too, experiences complex reactions to his quest, in particular a strong sense of his own inadequacy and a refusal to believe that he can ever attain happiness.

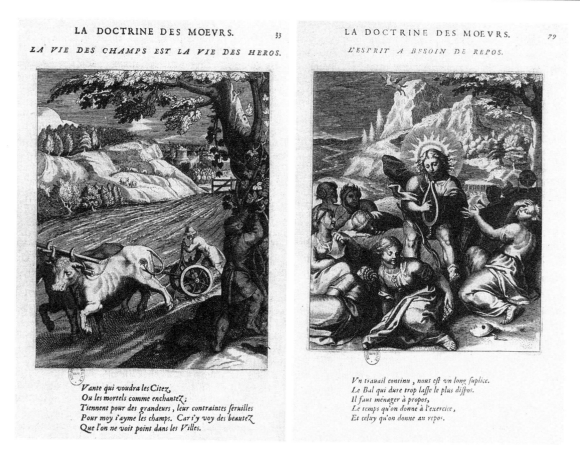

Pages from the 1646 book featuring engravings from Otto van Veen's Emblemata horatiana (1607)
accompanied by verses and commentaries by Gomberville (from Bernard Beugnot,
Le Discours de la retraite au XVIIe siècle, 1996)

If any seventeenth-century novel deserves the epithet "baroque," it is *Polexandre*. Virtually the whole of the main plot and many of the subplots are set against the background of the sea, the symbol of the vicissitudes of life so beloved by baroque art. Polexandre's base in the Canary Islands and Alcidiane's inaccessible island act as two poles exerting their forces upon the hero, pulling him from one adventure to another and frequently involving him in storms, shipwrecks, and naval battles. Islands and ships are the setting for many of the episodes. Similarly, just as baroque painters and sculptors loved to play tricks with textures and set up visual confusions, so Gomberville creates a kind of trompe l'œil around his characters. Iphidamante is second only to his brother Polexandre in terms of valor, but he is phenomenally beautiful and spends long periods as a woman. His friendship (as a man) with Bajazet is sexually ambivalent. Iphidamante's sister Cydarie, whom he closely resembles, uses his name while trying to escape from the attentions of her captor, and Iphidamante, shipwrecked in Morocco, is adored by the same

captor in her place. Zabaïm has two sons, half brothers both called Almanzor, whose careers interact through their link with Polexandre. Phélismond, who had declared that he alone was worthy of Alcidiane, finds that he is her half brother. Izatide turns out to be the daughter of the king whom Zelmatide had known, wrongly, as his father.

Polexandre represented a turning point for the seventeenth-century novel. The influences of the Greek romances, of *L'Astrée,* and of the *Amadis* cycle can be traced in it, but they have all been transcended in a new form of heroic novel. It is easy enough, too, to pick out the incoherences, the complexities, and the excesses and to complain with Antoine Adam, who says in *Histoire de la littérature française au XVIIe siècle* (1948–1956) that Gomberville "est incapable de voir le monde tel qu'il est" (is incapable of seeing the world as it is). But to pick out these flaws is to ignore the factors that appealed so much to Gomberville's generation—the breadth of vision, the imaginative power, and the shifting perspectives. Gomberville grasped the essentials of the sensibility of his day and worked them into his fiction, notably the need to believe in an idealized concept of human nature and the desire to investigate the workings of refined love based on emotional autonomy. His readers responded enthusiastically.

The success of *Polexandre* made virtually inevitable the probability that Gomberville would write another novel, and he was certainly encouraged to do so by the duchesse de Lorraine. *Cythérée* appeared in two versions. The first, published in two volumes in 1640, included an incomplete text that cannot have been other than a first draft. What appear to have been created as separate subplots in the manner of those in *Polexandre* are awkwardly brought together at the end, with the hero and heroine of each identified as Araxez and Cythérée. In the four-volume version that appeared in 1642, the first half has been considerably revised and now reveals a new tightness of construction with incidents seen from different angles in the various *tiroirs* (subsidiary narratives). The additional two volumes develop the life stories of Araxez and Cythérée and of Cythérée's parents, Arsinoé and Psyllus, parallel with the main plot, bringing them all to a happy denouement.

The plot is set in the third century B.C. in the world of the Seleucid emperor, Antiochus I, much of the action taking place in Cyprus, but Gomberville shows little concern for the historical detail and local color on which he earlier had been so keen. Indeed, the whole novel differs in conception from his earlier works in important ways. Although Araxez is intended to be another model of the ideal hero, his greatness is largely taken for granted rather than demonstrated in regular confrontations. The brotherhood of heroic virtue has been reduced in scope and involves only Araxez and Antiochus. There is even a suggestion that such heroes are likely to succumb to the same weaknesses as ordinary mortals for, despite the pagan setting, the worldview embedded in the novel is Augustinian, even though at times it is couched in Stoic terms. Mankind is beset by the sins of concupiscence; the passions are dangerous disorders of the reason; love in particular is a fever capable of leading both men and women into potentially disastrous behavior; and the sage Amasis gives frequent homilies about the inherent sinfulness of mankind.

The whole work, in fact, is a moral allegory. Cyprus, island of Venus, is being ravaged by a monstrous serpent that can only be tamed by Cythérée, ostensibly because she is descended from Aesculapius but actually because she is a quasi-divine virgin, prepared to sacrifice herself for the sake of pure—that is, spiritual—love. In *Polexandre*, the obligation to spread the truth of Christianity had been an accompaniment to the heroic mission; in *Cythérée*, set in a pre-Christian era, the fundamental doctrines of Christianity are central to the construction and elaboration of the novel. Spiritual values in this work have superseded heroic values, a development that perhaps explains the relative lack of success of *Cythérée*.

The moral tone of *Cythérée* reflects Gomberville's personal development. His long association with the Hôtel de Liancourt drew him gradually toward what, after the publication in 1640 of Jansenius's *Augustinus*, was known as Jansenist theology, and the location of his country estates only a mile or two away from the Jansenists' retreat at Port-Royal-des-Champs no doubt gave him the opportunity to meet the *solitaires* (recluses) and discuss matters of religion with them. According to Gédéon Tallemant des Réaux, by 1650, when Gomberville was churchwarden of Saint-Louis in Paris, he was so puritanical that he tried to prevent women wearing colored ribbons from attending mass.

The publication in 1646 of *La Doctrine des mœurs, tirée de la philosophie des stoïques* (translated as *The Doctrine of Morality, or A View of Human Life According to the Stoick Philosophy*, 1721), an expensively produced volume in which the 103 engravings used in Otto van Veen's *Emblemata horatiana* of 1607 have been reprinted with commentaries and verses added by Gomberville, is sometimes seen as evidence of this greater concern for strict morality. The motivation was in fact more opportunistic. Cardinal Jules Mazarin, chief minister and confidant of the regent, Anne of Austria, had recently been appointed *Surintendant de l'éducation du roi* (superintendent of the education of the king), and Gomberville hoped that dedicating to him a didactic work setting out the maxims of Stoic philosophy would attract the attention of the cardinal and establish his own credentials as a pedagogue, ideally with a post as tutor to the young king as the reward. The tide of moral thinking had, however, turned against neo-Stoicism some twenty years earlier in favor of an ethic that looked approvingly on the energy released by the passions: *Polexandre* had shown how that ethic could sustain the concept of the hero. Gomberville's choice of philosophy to impress the cardinal was therefore odd, despite his own apparent leaning toward Stoicism in *Cythérée*. In any case, as was his custom with approaches of this kind, Mazarin did not respond, an omission that may go some way toward explaining that Gomberville gained a reputation as a "grand frondeur" (great rebel) in the wave of opposition to Mazarin that broke out in 1648. Gomberville had been linked with Jean-François-Paul de Gondi, the future Cardinal de Retz and the greatest *frondeur* of them all, for some years, but he seems, perhaps surprisingly, not to have contributed by his pen to any of Gondi's campaigns of pamphlets.

The writing of novels was not generally considered compatible with Jansenist beliefs. Pressure to move away from fiction came also from other quarters. In 1646 Gomberville's friend François Maynard, in one of the sonnets in his *Œuvres,* publicly urged Gomberville to turn to more serious matters:

> Travaille utilement pour la Posterité.
> Abandonne la Fable; & prens soin de l'Histoire.
> Ton esprit plein de force, & brillant de clarté,
> Par ce beau changement augmentera sa gloire.
>
> (Work for the benefit of posterity.
> Give up fiction and concentrate on history.
> In that way, your powerful and lucid mind
> Will gain more glory.)

Nonetheless, the success of *Polexandre* had been such that Gomberville could not resist taking up the old theme again. *La Jeune Alcidiane* (The Young Alcidiane, 1651) is a sequel centered on the daughter of Alcidiane and Polexandre, but it failed to impress the readers. Its lack of popularity has usually been attributed, following Tallemant's comments ("c'est un roman de jansseniste, car les heros, à tout bout de champ, y font des sermons et des prieres chretiennes": it is a Jansenist novel, for at every turn the heroes give out sermons and Christian prayers), to the moralizing tone that undoubtedly weighs heavily on some parts. An equally valid factor is Gomberville's failure to take note of the way the reading public's taste had changed over fifteen years. Gautier de Costes de La Calprenède's *Cléopâtre* (1647–1656) and Madeleine de Scudéry's *Le Grand Cyrus* (1649–1653) were now offering a vision of heroism that placed far greater emphasis on an analysis of emotions with which the reader could identify. Though in these works the heroes are still superior to the rest of mankind, they suffer from passions that cannot be controlled by the will: the affective world they inhabit points forward to that of La Rochefoucauld and Jean Racine. In such a context, *La Jeune Alcidiane* seemed outdated, and the intended second volume was never published.

Gomberville made no further attempts to write fiction. In his later years, dogged by ill health, he finally turned his attention to serious historical scholarship. His two-volume folio edition of *Les Mémoires de Monsieur le duc de Nevers, prince de Mantoue, pair de France . . . enrichis de plusieurs pièces du temps* (The Memoirs of Monsieur le duc de Nevers, Prince of Mantua, Peer of France . . . Enriched with Several Documents of the Period, 1665) is a sound piece of work, allowing Gomberville to display his knowledge of sixteenth-century France: the book makes use of material from authentic sources and is faithful to the historiographical principles Gomberville had set out forty-five years earlier in his *Discours des vertus et des vices de l'histoire.* Other literary ventures of his last years confirm

the range of interests that he still maintained. In 1665 he was associated with Denis de Sallo in establishing the *Journal des Savants* (The Scholars' Journal); in 1671, Gomberville helped edit the *Recueil de poésies chrétiennes et diverses* (Anthology of Christian and Other Poems), which included many of his own verses; and his last work was a translation of the Spanish Jesuit Cristóbal de Acuña's account of his journey down the Amazon in 1639, published posthumously in 1682 under the title *Relation de la rivière des Amazones* (Account of the River of the Amazons). The details of the geography of the area, the customs and beliefs of the natives, their food, tools, and medicinal knowledge, are exactly the kind of cultural information that had always fascinated Gomberville. He died in Paris on 14 June 1674, and his remains were buried at Saint-Etienne-du-Mont.

Bibliography:
Philip A. Wadsworth, "Bibliography," in *The Novels of Gomberville: A Critical Study of* Polexandre *and* Cythérée (New Haven: Yale University Press, 1942), pp. 107–109.

References:
Antoine Adam, *Histoire de la littérature française au XVIIe siècle,* 5 volumes (Paris: Domat, 1948–1956), I: 408–418;

Roméo Arbour, *Un Editeur d'oeuvres littéraires au XVIIe siècle: Toussaint du Bray, 1604–1636* (Geneva: Droz, 1992; Paris: Champion, 1992);

Mark Bannister, *Privileged Mortals: The French Heroic Novel, 1630–1660* (Oxford: Oxford University Press, 1983);

Madeleine Bertaud, *L'Astrée et Polexandre: Du roman pastoral au roman héroïque* (Geneva: Droz, 1986);

Bernard Beugnot, *Le Discours de la retraite au XVIIe siècle: Loin du monde et du bruit* (Paris: Presses Universitaires de France, 1996);

Séro Kevorkian, *Le Thème de l'amour dans l'œuvre romanesque de Gomberville* (Paris: Klincksieck, 1972);

Edward B. Turk, *Baroque Fiction-Making: A Study of Gomberville's Polexandre,* North Carolina Studies in the Romance Languages and Literatures, no. 196 (Chapel Hill: University of North Carolina Department of Romance Languages, 1978);

Philip A. Wadsworth, *The Novels of Gomberville: A Critical Study of Polexandre and Cythérée* (New Haven: Yale University Press, 1942).

Papers:
A few of Marin Le Roy, sieur de Gomberville's manuscripts, letters, and poems are collected in the Bibliothèque de l'Arsenal, the Bibliothèque Nationale, and the Archives de l'Académie Française, all of which are in Paris.

Alexandre Hardy

(1572? – 1632)

Perry Gethner
Oklahoma State University

BOOKS: *Les Chastes et Loyales Amours de Théagène et Cariclée, réduites du grec de l'Histoire d'Héliodore . . .* (Paris: J. Quesnel, 1623);

Le Théâtre d'Alexandre Hardy, volume 1 (Paris: J. Quesnel, 1624)–comprises *Didon se sacrifiant; Scédase, ou L'Hospitalité violée; Panthée; Méléagre; Procris, ou La Jalousie infortunée; Alceste, ou La Fidélité; Ariadne ravie;* and *Alphée;*

Le Théâtre d'Alexandre Hardy, volume 2 (Paris: J. Quesnel, 1625)–comprises *La Mort d'Achille; Coriolan; Cornélie; Arsacome, ou L'Amitié des Scythes; Mariamne;* and *Alcée, ou L'Infidélité;*

Le Théâtre d'Alexandre Hardy, volume 3 (Paris: J. Quesnel, 1626)–comprises *Le Ravissement de Proserpine par Pluton; La Force du sang; La Gigantomachie, ou Combat des dieux avec les géants; Félismène; Dorise;* and *Corine, ou Le Silence;*

Le Théâtre d'Alexandre Hardy, volume 4 (Rouen: D. du Petit Val, 1626)–comprises *La Mort de Daire; La Mort d'Alexandre; Aristoclée, ou Le Mariage infortuné; Frégonde, ou Le Chaste Amour; Gésippe, ou Les Deux Amis; Phraarte, ou Le Triomfe des vrays amans;* and *Le Triomfe d'amour;*

Le Théâtre d'Alexandre Hardy, volume 5 (Paris: F. Targa, 1628)–comprises *Timoclée, ou La Juste Vengeance; Elmire, ou L'Heureuse Bigamie; La Belle Egyptienne; Lucrèce, ou L'Adultère puny; Alcméon, ou La Vengeance féminine;* and *L'Amour victorieux ou vengé.*

Editions: *Le Théâtre d'Alexandre Hardy*, 5 volumes, edited by Edmund Stengel (Marburg, Germany: N. G. Elwert, 1883–1884);

Théâtre du XVIIe siècle, volume 1, edited by Jacques Scherer, Bibliothèque de la Pléiade, no. 257 (Paris: Gallimard, 1975)–includes *Scédase, La Force du sang,* and *Lucrèce;*

Coriolan, edited by Terence Allott (Exeter: University of Exeter, 1978);

La Belle Egyptienne, edited by Bernadette Bearez Caravaggi (Fasano: Schena / Paris: Nizet, 1983);

Panthée, edited by Philip Ford (Exeter: University of Exeter, 1984);

La Force du sang, in *Cervantes, Hardy and "La Fuerza de la sangre,"* edited by Michael G. Paulson and Tamara Alvarez-Detrell (Potomac, Md.: Scripta Humanistica, 1984);

Mariamne, edited by Alan Howe (Exeter: University of Exeter, 1989);

Didon se sacrifiant, edited by Howe (Geneva: Droz, 1994).

Alexandre Hardy, France's first professional playwright and a pivotal figure in the transition from the Renaissance to the classical era, remains underappreciated today. Little is known with certainty about his life. Apart from a handful of statements made by Hardy himself in his published works, most of what is now known comes from archival documents, the majority of them unearthed by Sophie-Wilma Deierkauf-Holsboer.

Hardy was born in Paris. No record of his birth has been found, but scholars have proposed dates ranging from 1560 to 1577. Deierkauf-Holsboer proposes 1572, based on a statement in a dedicatory epistle written in 1622, in which Hardy claims to have been writing plays for thirty years. (She assumes, plausibly enough, that he began his career at around age twenty.) Hardy came from a respectable bourgeois family, which included many magistrates. He must have received an excellent education, since several statements by friends attest to his erudition and since he displayed great familiarity with major works of classical and modern literatures.

Around 1592 his passion for the theater impelled him to join a professional company, in which he worked as both actor and playwright. This choice of career probably alienated him from his family, who would do nothing to assist him during his many years of financial struggle. No one knows for sure which company Hardy apprenticed with, but by 1598 he had become a member of a troupe headed by Valleran Le Conte. This company, the most distinguished of its generation, was the first in

France to run an acting school—parents from respectable families apprenticed their teenaged children to Valleran—and was among the first to include actresses. Since Valleran and Hardy shared a commitment to the new dramatic genres (tragedy based on mythology or ancient history, tragicomedy, comedy, and pastoral) and since the playwright possessed extraordinary facility and fecundity, they continued to work together for more than two decades. Surviving archival records reveal that by 1598 Hardy had ceased to act and was serving the company solely in his capacity as *poète à gages* (hired playwright in residence).

When Hardy entered his theatrical career, the cultural situation in France was far from stable. The bloody civil wars resulting from the prolonged conflicts between Catholics and Protestants had disrupted cultural life for almost half a century; they also impeded the formation of professional theatrical companies. In addition, thanks to the new availability during the Renaissance of many works from Greek and Latin literature, long unknown in the West, scholars and poets aspired to re-create forms from the past. However, dissatisfaction with the dramatic genres of the Middle Ages—such as mystery and morality plays and the farce—both on aesthetic and religious grounds, was far more prevalent with the learned than with the general public. Although the playwrights of the late sixteenth century intended their works to be staged, they conceived of their plays more in rhetorical than in dramatic terms—a problem compounded by their lack of contact with professional actors. Hardy became the most important figure trying to bridge the gap between the old and new dramaturgies and between the poetic requirements of the erudite and the tastes of the spectators.

By 1594-1595 Hardy's plays had started to achieve great success. The one place where Valleran's troupe failed to win acclaim was Paris, where audiences strongly preferred older dramatic forms, especially the farce, and had little patience with the newer genres. The troupe lost so much money during its two lengthy Parisian sojourns—despite such tactics as teaming up with other troupes that specialized in farce—that Valleran frequently found himself in dire financial straits. On the other hand, the troupe consistently attracted large audiences in other parts of France, as well as in Belgium and the Netherlands. Otherwise, they would have been unable to afford a playwright in residence and, indeed, would long since have disbanded. In 1611 Hardy agreed to resume acting, apparently for no extra pay, in order to save the troupe money. No one knows how long he continued to do so.

At an unknown date, Hardy was named secretary to the prince de Condé, to whom he dedicated the early volumes of his plays. A contract from 1615 lists Hardy with this title, but the date when he formally entered the prince's service is not known, nor is whether or not he held the title without interruption for the rest of his life. The prince must have paid well, since Hardy, who had been desperately poor for much of his life, left a considerable sum of money at his death. How his acquisition of money affected his relations with the rest of the troupe is unclear.

Valleran died at an unknown date prior to October 1620, at which time the troupe was reconstituted under the leadership of Pierre Le Messier—known under the stage name of Bellerose—one of Valleran's former apprentices. The contract signed on that occasion refers to Hardy for the first time as poet ordinary of the king, and it spells out the terms of Hardy's obligations to the company: he was to furnish twelve new plays over the course of two years and to make fresh copies of several old plays that were to be revived. The contract also specifies that all plays composed thenceforth were to be the property of the troupe: Hardy could not keep any copies or drafts of his own works or try to publish them. He was to receive 75 livres tournois (£75) per play, a respectable sum for the time. He had apparently been paid only 30 livres per play at the start of his career; in the 1625 contract his fee went up to 100 livres.

When the troupe returned to Paris in 1622, it finally gained the applause it had sought for so long. A new generation of more sophisticated audiences was eager to see works from the newer dramatic genres and was able to evaluate plays according to their poetic merit. Many playwrights had begun to publish their works, thus achieving a second and more prestigious form of recognition. Hardy, who had always considered himself a serious writer and counted many poets among his friends, realized that publication was becoming essential to his literary reputation. However, he ran into a major obstacle: according to the terms of his contract with the troupe, he could not publish any plays composed for them without their permission, and Bellerose, despite his great admiration for Hardy, was reluctant to grant it. Bellerose's reason was that during that period in France a play became public domain as soon as it was printed, meaning that any company could legally perform it. Not surprisingly, the company that gave the premiere of a successful play tried to delay its publication for as long as possible. Since Hardy's plays had for years constituted the core of Bellerose's repertoire, and since the troupe was now facing stiff competition from other troupes specializing in the same types of plays, to make Hardy's works more available was clearly not in their best interest.

Finally, when pirated editions of some of Hardy's plays appeared (presumably transcribed, imperfectly, by spectators with prodigious memories, for the benefit of unscrupulous publishers) and the works of other playwrights were published under his name, the frustrated Hardy decided to take action. Starting in 1622 he sold collections of his plays to the publisher Jacques Quesnel, who paid him the sum of 15 livres per play. These volumes consisted of old plays, copies of which had been restored to him as part of the 1620 contract. His plays must have sold well, since demand caused several of the volumes to be republished a few years later. In 1625 the troupe restored five more plays to Hardy. Since he did not consider this number sufficient to fill a volume, he composed two new plays for the occasion. Moreover, since he was dissatisfied with the accuracy of the volumes published by Quesnel, he changed editors, using David du Petit Val for his next volume.

However, Hardy was still unhappy; he realized that the troupe owned literally hundreds of his plays and would not release them for publication. When Bellerose refused to return any more manuscripts, the poet issued an ultimatum: if not allowed to publish his works freely, he would sever relations and join a rival troupe. Bellerose remained firm, and Hardy made good on his threat. In November of 1626 he signed a trial contract with one of the competing companies, headed by Claude Deschamps, sieur de Villiers, giving them a single new play. The following January, since actors and playwright were satisfied with their initial collaboration, they signed a six-year contract requiring Hardy to produce six plays a year and denying him the right to publish them; moreover, instead of receiving a fixed sum per play, he would be paid a portion of the box-office receipts. Since the contract specified that he would not have to accompany the troupe while on tour, clearly he was not expected to be an actor. Moreover, the troupe chose Hardy's home in Paris as its home address, thus indicating the high esteem in which they held him. Perhaps the most revealing clause in the contract, however, is the one requiring the actors to perform the plays exactly as written; this requirement suggests that Bellerose's company had previously made substantial alterations in the texts and that Hardy had been powerless to stop them.

However, just as he seemed to have achieved the artistic recognition he craved, Hardy saw the huge success garnered by a new generation of playwrights, whose notions of dramatic style and struc-

Title page for the 1624 collection of Alexandre Hardy's plays (Bibliothèque Nationale, Paris)

ture differed radically from his own. Outraged by what he considered unjustified praise given to young and inexperienced amateurs and believing that their popularity was a threat to his own reputation, he denounced them in the preface to the fifth volume of his collected plays, published in 1628. His intemperate remarks—he called the younger playwrights, among other things, excrements of the law courts, miserable crows, and blinded dwarves—provoked the young playwrights singled out for censure, Pierre Du Ryer and Jean Auvray, to issue polemical responses, criticizing Hardy for being old-fashioned in his language, style, and dramaturgy. The older poet responded with an even more scathing pamphlet—with further comparisons of playwrights to animals—in which he lauded his own works and abilities while denying any merit at all to his younger colleagues.

Du Ryer and Auvray decided to ignore this attack, but Isaac Du Ryer (Pierre Du Ryer's father and himself a poet of note) published a poem urging Hardy to accept that the next generation had surpassed him.

Behind the personal invective, a serious aesthetic debate was going on: in his language, style, and poetic values Hardy was primarily a man of the sixteenth century, and he was unwilling to admit that times had changed. For one thing, the French language itself was undergoing rapid changes during his lifetime. Moreover, the Pléiade school of poetry (headed by Pierre de Ronsard, Hardy's idol), which had dominated French practice for more than half a century, was being abandoned in favor of a newer school headed by François de Malherbe (whom Hardy esteemed but did not take as a model). Believing that the values of the Pléiade were eternally valid and convinced that his thirty years of stage experience had made him the leading authority of the age on play writing, Hardy could not see that history was passing him by and that the young authors he so despised were really the wave of the future.

In 1631 Hardy composed his final published work—a complimentary poem to accompany the first play of Georges de Scudéry, who went on to become a major playwright of his generation and one of the few to say positive things about Hardy. Hardy probably continued furnishing plays to Villiers's troupe until the end of his life, although he must have felt frustrated that he could not publish any of them. Hardy died in 1632, a victim of the plague. The exact date of his death is unknown, but it must have been prior to 27 August, when his two paternal uncles relinquished their share in his estate in favor of his widow. This and several subsequent contracts dealing with Hardy's estate suggest that his family had reconciled with him at the end of his life, perhaps at the time he entered the service of the prince de Condé. Hardy's death inspired a handful of tributes from fellow authors, and some of his plays must have remained in the repertoire of Villiers's troupe (and probably others) for a while, but by the middle of the seventeenth century Hardy was almost forgotten.

In 1623 Hardy claimed to have written five hundred plays; in 1628 he claimed authorship of six hundred. Later writers raised that figure higher; Scudéry, for example, stated that Hardy wrote eight hundred. Although scholars consider Scudéry's figure exaggerated, they have invariably accepted Hardy's own claims as accurate; he was probably the most prolific dramatist in French history. Despite his remarkable facility and his not needing to invent his own plots—since he had read widely in both ancient and modern literatures, he had plenty of subjects to

choose from—some scholars have raised questions about the arithmetic. If contracts requiring six plays per year were the norm throughout Hardy's career as playwright in residence, he could not have reached the figure of six hundred at the end of thirty years. He might have been especially prolific at the start of his career, prior to his first formal contract, though, and the contracts he signed prior to 1620 might have called for a greater number of plays per year. Part of the answer can be derived from the 1615 contract: some of Hardy's plays (perhaps even the majority) were brief intermezzi used as fillers; he presumably considered those works unworthy of publication. However, he is unlikely to have composed large numbers of plays not intended for the troupe's use; not until Hardy became interested in publishing his compositions (around 1622) would he have had any reason to do so. In any case, only forty-one of Hardy's plays were published—thirty-four titles, since *Les Chastes et Loyales Amours de Théagène et Cariclée* (The Chaste and Loyal Love Affair of Théagène and Cariclée, 1623) is a dramatization of an ancient Greek romance consisting of eight five-act plays. About two dozen additional titles are known from contracts and other contemporary sources, but all of the plays that remained in the archives of Bellerose and of Villiers have disappeared; they may even have been destroyed deliberately at some point.

The contracts specify that Hardy had to produce works in all four of the serious dramatic forms current in his day—tragedy, tragicomedy, pastoral, and comedy. For reasons unknown, he never published any of his comedies, but he must have written some, according to the explicit language in the contracts and also because two of the unpublished plays the titles of which are known must have been comedies. Clearly, these works were full-length plays in five acts, as opposed to farces, and Hardy wrote such plays in a period when farces were popular and comedies were not. Austin Gill, who in 1957 produced a critical edition of a previously unpublished and anonymous prose comedy dating from around 1624, *Les Ramoneurs* (The Chimney Sweeps), believed that it was the work of Hardy. Although Gill presents some convincing arguments—mainly involving parallels in style, grammar, and usage between the comedy and Hardy's other works—other scholars have not accepted the attribution.

Hardy published one pastoral play with each volume of his collected works and presumably wrote far more than those five. They differ from his work in all other genres: for them he used verses of ten syllables rather than twelve. He seemed familiar with all the major pastoral novels and plays from France,

Spain, and Italy. Hardy might well have been the first French playwright to compose pastorals for a general audience, rather than the court, and he made his works far more stageworthy than those of his predecessors. He eliminated the chorus, reduced the conventional long monologues, maintained suspense and a fast pace, and showed virtually all the action on the stage. Elements of spectacle include the appearances of gods (at least one deity per play), metamorphoses, and a variety of stage sets, including temples, caves, and forests. Some of the plays feature satyrs who, whether malicious or well-meaning, are naive and ineffective; moreover, they tend to be the main source of humor. But Hardy also tended to treat the basic pastoral conventions with a gentle irony, presenting scenes that seem to mock the genre itself. For example, at the end of *Le Triomfe d'amour* (The Triumph of Love, 1626) Cupid publicly humiliates and chases away the woodland deity Pan, who has rendered a capricious verdict; in *Corine, ou Le Silence* (Corine, or Silence, 1626), instead of having a maiden judge between rival suitors with a singing contest, a shepherd indifferent to love proposes a contest of silence to the two girls who are infatuated with him; in *Alcée, ou L'Infidélité* (Alcée, or Infidelity, 1625), a shepherd refuses to take seriously the advice proffered by the echo, consequently forcing Cupidon to appear in person to deliver his message.

Hardy's tragedies, although static by modern standards, represent a crucial transitional stage between the Renaissance and classicism. Hardy reduces the role of messengers, shows all the action on the stage, no matter how violent—including rape and murder—and brings the principal antagonists face to face. He also eliminates the lyric chorus at the end of each act; according to his own statement, audiences refused to tolerate lyric choruses in performance, and only two of his plays retain them in the printed versions. He reduces the number and length of monologues, using dialogue whenever possible. He frequently employs supernatural elements—such as omens, prophetic dreams, and onstage ghosts—but avoids using the convention of the deus ex machina. Although he generally followed the tradition of using plots from mythology or classical history and dealing with gods, kings, or heroes, Hardy made occasional exceptions: the plot of *Lucrèce, ou L'Adultère puny* (Lucrèce, or Adultery Punished, 1628) is derived from a work of modern fiction, and that of *Scédase, ou L'Hospitalité violée* (Scédase, or Hospitality Violated, 1624), derived from Plutarch, deals with the misfortunes of a simple villager and his daughters. The plays retain from Seneca and his Renaissance emulators such features as the extensive use of epic similes,

mythological allusions (even in plays where they would seemingly be out of place), maxims and general comments about the human condition, and denouements that leave the audience with no sense that a moral or religious order has been restored. The weighty language and constant sense of foreboding create a solemnity and timelessness to the plays, though, making the presentation of even shocking actions bearable to the spectator.

The majority of the plays that Hardy chose to publish are tragicomedies. As Henry Carrington Lancaster has shown in *The French Tragi-Comedy* (1907), Hardy was the playwright most responsible for establishing as the standard French form of tragicomedy a play with a complicated and suspenseful plot, often based on a work of fiction and centering on the misfortunes and eventual union of noble young lovers. Dramatizations of lengthy novels sometimes expanded to multiple *journées* (full-length serial plays presented on successive days). Although the dramaturgy was largely medieval in inspiration, some critics argue that Hardy was also anticipating cinematic techniques used today—presenting to the sight of the viewer every aspect of the story he could possibly stage, fragmenting the play into a series of fairly short scenes that often followed one another abruptly, making every character clearly indicate his or her motives and aims directly to other characters or to the audience, curtailing elements not crucial to the plot (such as poetic monologues, choruses, and psychological analysis), keeping up a frenzied pace, and not worrying unduly about any unifying principle other than unity of interest. Although the celebrated three unities had not yet won acceptance in his day, Hardy's tragicomedies typically cover a much greater length of time and amount of space than his tragedies, and they sometimes consist of multiple plots that are not carefully woven together. *Elmire, ou L'Heureuse Bigamie* (Elmire, or The Fortunate Bigamy, 1628), for example, is set in three different countries on two continents, while *La Force du sang* (The Call of Blood, 1628) skips ahead seven years in the middle of an act. Hardy sometimes included comic episodes in tragicomedies, but only when the plot required them. At the same time, he could, if they were needed, feature conventions associated with tragedy, such as ghosts, omens, and scenes of lamentation. In most cases the denouement gives credit to divine providence for allowing a happy resolution after such a lengthy series of obstacles and disasters.

Hardy tended to choose for his tragicomedies plots with unusual, even shocking, situations. The surprises often involve matters of sex and marriage, as in *Elmire,* in which the Pope allows a man with two legitimate wives to keep both of them; *Gésippe, ou Les Deux Amis* (Gésippe, or The Two Friends, 1626), in which a man transfers his fiancée to his best friend; *Arsacome, ou L'Amitié des Scythes* (Arsacome, or The Friendship of the Scythians, 1625), in which the hero's friends remove the obstacles blocking his marriage to the woman he loves by murdering her wealth-obsessed father (even though he is a king) and abducting the princess; and *La Force du sang,* in which the heroine, raped in the dark by a young nobleman, is allowed to marry him seven years later, having in the meantime borne him a son. Although the main focus is on plot, Hardy can make even implausible stories more acceptable by presenting the character's internal struggles or changes of heart. A notable example is the young male protagonist of *La Force du sang,* who, in scenes added to the source (a story by Miguel de Cervantes), matures from a wild hedonist into a serious young man with a conscience and a sense of responsibility.

Hardy possibly felt some hesitation about the precise boundary between tragedy and tragicomedy, since three of the plays in the first volume of his collected works—*Alceste, ou La Fidélité* (Alcestis, or Fidelity, 1624), *Ariadne ravie* (Ariadne Abducted, 1624), and *Procris, ou La Jalousie infortunée* (Procris, or Unfortunate Jealousy, 1624)—and one play in his fourth volume, *Aristoclée, ou Le Mariage infortuné* (Aristoclée, or The Unfortunate Marriage, 1626), are sometimes designated by one label and at other times by the other. The last of these plays has a starkly tragic ending. The other three works, which are derived from mythology, feature the deaths or near deaths of the principal characters, though the endings are happy or partly so—Alceste is brought back from the underworld; Ariadne is saved from suicide by the arrival of Bacchus; and Procris dies in the arms of her beloved husband, happy and reconciled with him, but he appears likely to be consoled soon by the love of the goddess Aurore. In the case of the first volume the confusion might well have been the fault of the printer, Quesnel, rather than Hardy; Quesnel's lack of attention to textual accuracy enraged the playwright. Two other mythological plays with happy endings, *La Gigantomachie* (The Combat Against the Giants, 1626) and *Le Ravissement de Proserpine par Pluton* (Pluto's Abduction of Proserpina, 1626), bear the designation "poème dramatique," as does the eight-part serial, *Théagène et Cariclée.* The last of these works is unmistakably a tragicomedy in every respect, and the other two could logically bear the same designation. Again, whether the labels were chosen by the playwright or by the printer cannot be determined with certainty. In any case, Hardy was presumably trying to work out for himself a coherent definition for the emerging intermediate genre, to which theorists had as yet given virtually no attention.

Probably the main reason Hardy has received less attention than his historical place warrants is that his plays are not as enjoyable to read as those of the other major seventeenth-century dramatists. The main problems are his harsh style and his unusually convoluted syntax. He prided himself on imitating the complexity of Latin—using confusing inversions, placing adjectives far from the words they modified, separating relative clauses from their antecedents, often omitting subject pronouns and the "que" preceding subjunctive commands, and utilizing such devices as ablative absolutes. However, certain other aspects of his style that ancien régime readers found objectionable should no longer shock readers: directness of language and occasional vulgarity in angry exchanges, daring metaphors, and a willingness to discuss sexual matters frankly. Yet, the flaws should not distract the reader from appreciating Hardy's strengths: energy, lively pacing, often exciting dialogue, and an ability to bring to life an enormous variety of characters.

Bibliographies:

Michael G. Paulson and Tamara Alvarez-Detrell, *Alexandre Hardy: A Critical and Annotated Bibliography* (Paris, Seattle & Tübingen: Papers on French Seventeenth Century Literature, 1985);

Alan Howe, "Alexandre Hardy's Critical Bibliography: A Supplement," *Zeitschrift für französische Sprache und Literatur,* 98 (1988): 53–79.

Biography:

Sophie-Wilma Deierkauf-Holsboer, *Vie d'Alexandre Hardy, poète du roi (1572–1632)* (Paris: Nizet, 1972).

References:

Madeleine Bertaud, "Deux *Ariane* au XVIIe siècle: Alexandre Hardy et Thomas Corneille," *Seventeenth-Century French Studies,* 19 (1997): 135–148;

Carla Federici, *Réalisme et dramaturgie: Etude de quatre écrivains: Garnier, Hardy, Rotrou, Corneille* (Paris: Nizet, 1974);

Karsten Garscha, *Hardy als Barockdramatiker: Eine stilistische Untersuchung* (Frankfurt am Main: Peter Lang, 1971);

Perry Gethner, "Les Imperfections de l'Arcadie dans les pastorales de Hardy," in *Et in Arcadia ego,* edited by Antoine Soare (Paris, Seattle & Tübingen:

Papers on French Seventeenth Century Literature, 1997), pp. 277–283;

Marie-France Hilgar, "Les Pastorales d'Alexandre Hardy," in *La Pastorale française: De Rémi Belleau à Victor Hugo,* edited by Alain Niderst (Paris, Seattle & Tübingen: Papers on French Seventeenth Century Literature, 1991), pp. 37–45;

Alan Howe, "Alexandre Hardy and the French Theatre in 1615: The Evidence of Two Archival Documents," *Seventeenth-Century French Studies,* 9 (1987): 26–34;

Howe, "Alexandre Hardy, His Printers and His Patron: On an Unknown 'Privilège' for His 'Théâtre,'" *Seventeenth-Century French Studies,* 8 (1986): 132–142;

Howe, "Alexandre Hardy's *Timoclée:* A Dramatic Dinosaur," in *Ouverture et dialogue: Mélanges offerts à Wolfgang Leiner,* edited by Ulrich Döring, Antiopy Lyroudias, and Rainer Zaiser (Tübingen: Narr, 1988), pp. 219–230;

Henry Carrington Lancaster, *The French Tragi-Comedy: Its Origin and Development from 1552 to 1628* (Baltimore: J. H. Furst, 1907);

Lancaster, *A History of French Dramatic Literature in the Seventeenth Century,* 9 volumes (Baltimore: Johns Hopkins University Press, 1929–1942);

Paul Pelckmans, "Le Rêve dans le théâtre d'Alexandre Hardy," *Neophilologus,* 69 (1985): 34–45;

Timothy J. Reiss, *Toward Dramatic Illusion: Theatrical Technique and Meaning from Hardy to Horace* (New Haven: Yale University Press, 1971);

Eugène Rigal, *Alexandre Hardy et le théâtre français à la fin du XVIe siècle et au commencement du XVIIe siècle* (Paris: Hachette, 1889);

Darnell Roaten, *Structural Forms in the French Theater, 1500–1700* (Philadelphia: University of Pennsylvania Press, 1960);

Emile Roy, "Un Pamphlet d'Alexandre Hardy: La Berne des deux rimeurs de l'Hôtel de Bourgogne (1628)," *Revue d'Histoire littéraire de la France,* 22 (1915): 497–547;

Edward H. Sirich, *A Study in the Syntax of Alexandre Hardy* (Baltimore: J. H. Furst, 1915);

André Stegmann, "Unité et diversité formelles dans l'œuvre de Hardy," in *Form and Meaning: Aesthetic Coherence in Seventeenth-Century French Drama,* edited by William D. Howarth, Ian McFarlane, and Margaret McGowan (Amersham: Avebury, 1982), pp. 18–30.

Jean de La Bruyère
(17 August 1645 – 10 May 1696)

Mark A. Cohen
Bard College

BOOKS: *Les Caractères de Théophraste, traduits du grec, avec Les Caractères ou les mœurs de ce siècle* (Paris: E. Michallet, 1688; enlarged, 1689; enlarged again, 1690; 1691; 1692); enlarged and republished with *Discours prononcé dans à l'Académie* and *Préface* (1694; revised, 1696); translated as *The Characters, or, The Manners of the Age. By Monsieur de La Bruyere . . . Made English by several hands. With the Characters of Theophrastus, Translated from the Greek. And a prefatory Discourse to them, by Monsieur de La Bruyere. To which is Added, a Key to his Characters* (London: Printed for John Bullord and sold by Matt. Gilliflower, Ben. Tooke, Christopher Bateman & Richard Parker, 1699);

Discours prononcez dans l'Académie françoise à la réception de Monsieur l'abbé Bignon et de Monsieur de La Bruyère, le lundy quinze juin M.DC.LXXXXIII (Paris: Veuve de J. B. Coignard et J. B. Coignard *fils*, 1693);

Discours prononcé dans l'Académie françoise par Mr de la Bruyère, le lundy quinzième juin M.DC.XCIII, jour de sa réception (Paris: E. Michallet, 1693);

Dialogues posthumes du sieur de La Bruyère sur le quiétisme, by La Bruyère and Louis Ellies Du Pin, edited by Du Pin (Paris: C. Osmont, 1699).

Editions and Collections: *Œuvres de La Bruyère,* 6 volumes, edited by Georges Servois (Paris: Hachette, 1922);

Œuvres complètes, edited by Julien Benda, Bibliothèque de la Pléiade, no. 23 (Paris: Editions de la Nouvelle Revue Française, 1934);

Œuvres complètes, edited by Benda, Bibliothèque de la Pléiade (Paris: Gallimard, 1951);

Les Caractères de Théophraste, traduits du grec, avec Les Caractères ou les mœurs de ce siècle, edited by Robert Garapon (Paris: Garnier Frères, 1962);

Les Caractères, edited by Patrice Soler, in *Moralistes du XVIIe siècle,* edited by Jean Lafond (Paris: R. Laffont, 1993), pp. 637–1251;

Les Caractères, edited by Emmanuel Bury (Paris: Librairie Générale Française, 1995);

Jean de La Bruyère (portrait by A. Sandoz; from album for La Bruyère's Œuvres, 1922; Thomas Cooper Library, University of South Carolina)

Les Caractères de Théophraste, traduits du grec, avec Les Caractères ou les mœurs de ce siècle, edited by Marc Escola, Sources classiques, no. 17 (Paris: H. Champion, 1999).

Editions in English: *The Works of M. de La Bruyère: To Which Is Added the Characters of Theophrastus. Also, The Manner of Living with Great Men; Written after the Manner of Bruyère,* 2 volumes, translated by Nicholas Rowe (London: Printed for J. Bell & C. Etherington, 1776);

The "Characters" of Jean de La Bruyère, translated by Henri Van Laun (New York: Scribner & Welford, 1885);

Characters, translated by Jean Stewart (Harmondsworth, U.K.: Penguin, 1970).

Jean de La Bruyère is known as the author of a single masterpiece, *Les Caractères de Théophraste, traduits du grec, avec Les Caractères ou les mœurs de ce siècle* (The Characters of Theophrastus, Translated from the Greek, with the Characters or the Mores of this Century), published in ever expanding editions from 1688 to 1696, the year of the author's sudden death at the age of fifty. It is a moral-satiric work attacking the vices of contemporary French society and made up primarily of portraits and maxims but accompanied by an extraordinarily diverse set of other types of discourse treating a wide range of subject matters. The whole work was intended, as he writes in the *Préface,* to describe the *mœurs* (meaning mores, customs, and forms of behavior as well as morals) of its original readers. The mirror La Bruyère was holding up to them was not neutral. Its observational rigor was intimately connected with moral censure. The book also included La Bruyère's own translation of Theophrastus's *Characters* (circa fourth century B.C.) from the original Greek, preceded by an introduction titled *Discours sur Théophraste* (Discourse on Theophrastus), in which he underscored the moral purpose of the book: "discerner les bonnes [mœurs] d'avec les mauvaises, et à démêler dans les hommes ce qu'il y a de vain, de faible et de ridicule, d'avec ce qu'ils peuvent avoir de bon, de sain et de louable" (to separate good behavior from bad, and to untangle whatever is vain, weak, and ridiculous in men from whatever they might have that is good, healthy, and praiseworthy). Published at the height of the power and magnificence of the Sun Kingdom, *Les Caractères* showed that behind the facade the Sun Kingdom was ruled by self-interest, the worship of caste, and the destructive scramble for wealth. La Bruyère's view of France was a comprehensive one; it even included (quite exceptionally for the period) the peasantry, the most powerless and least corrupt stratum of society.

All of the major French classical writers felt sincerely that their work should instruct as well as entertain. But for the moral writer, as opposed to the storyteller or dramatist, this contradictory requirement was particularly problematic. La Bruyère discussed the predicament in the *Discours sur Théophraste.* In a society such as his, a stubborn diversity reigned, born precisely of its members' endemic egotism, because their preferences emanated from the group they belonged to rather

than the quality of the work itself. Every individual and clique therefore had different tastes: they liked different kinds of moral treatises, such as the scholastic as opposed to the Cartesian; some preferred the ancients to the moderns; others favored the contemporary. The great nobles of court scorned the city, and the writer was not able to speak honestly about the court for fear of retribution from the nobility or from royal displeasure (court and city in this context signify the whole of society). If a work attained a high level of artistic quality, this superiority did not necessarily help its moral task. A unified moral viewpoint of a general applicability could be achieved only by stringent self-criticism on the part of the reader. The reader, though, had his or her own method for resisting it. However finely the satirist wrote, even if he succeeded in depicting his targets with a beautiful or elegant barb, the reader could easily avoid censure without seeming to be evasive by pretending to judge the literary quality of the depiction as poor. To speak to the sophisticated seventeenth-century readership, whose judgment had come to dominate even learned literature, the satirist had to write well; yet, once he was judged by such criteria, the moral stakes were in danger of being forgotten. If one pandered too much to worldly tastes by lively descriptions and pictures of contemporaries, the egotistic delight in seeing one's fellows derided would override the potential for general and reflective application to oneself.

La Bruyère's solution was to mix various learned and popular, ancient and modern, forms of writing in a heterogeneous work that nevertheless converged on unmistakable moral and political positions. Worldly readers were lured into the work with comically ridiculous portraits reminiscent of the burlesque theater (*burlesque* meaning the treatment of grand figures in a denigrating manner) and portrait books. But always behind the portraits stood framing discourses of greater intellectual and moral worth. The most important was the *moraliste* tradition of Michel Eyquem de Montaigne, Blaise Pascal, and François, duc de La Rochefoucauld—a form of writing that favored discontinuous structure, disabused observations, and flashing wit that had successfully translated into worldly discourse an excoriating Augustinian view of the fallen state of human beings. La Bruyère chose to follow the example of the *moraliste* tradition and write his work in loosely organized fragments that lacked any kind of overarching doctrinal armature, carefully tabulated sets of definitions, or exhaustive divisions and subdivisions of material. The rhythm of *moraliste* writing was that of a conversation in its meandering passage from topic to topic and the presentation of multiple views of the same object. The *moraliste* made no claim to have presented a definitive treatment of his subject. His predilection for witty paradox and arresting observations was both a sign of respect for the reader's intelligence and a demand to exercise it by adding his or her own thoughts and responses to those of the writer.

The *moralistes* all shared socially and theologically conservative views, but they did not advocate them in the teeth of modern secularizing developments; on the contrary, they assumed the validity of the new science and political thought. Only thus, they believed, could they find a bedrock of sustainable belief and value that could survive any challenge. The literary forms they preferred led them to an apparent relativism and perspectivism, because each new fragment need not follow and might even contradict one that had gone before; in this way their writings were quite unlike the traditional philosophic treatise with its carefully articulated interlocking arguments. The *moralistes'* favorite topics—human ignorance, uncontrollable passions, and ineradicable inconstancy—were expressed in a disordered manner to make their readers experience the radical disorder of the human condition and the limitations of the unaided, fallen understanding, not in order to comfort their intellectual laxity. The other available moral discourses of the day were unlikely to capture the attention of the worldly reader because they were either too academic (the Aristotelian-scholastic tradition of the university), amoral (the new scientific treatises), rhetorically ostentatious (the Ciceronian), or authoritarian (the sermon).

The other important tradition to which La Bruyère turned to shape the learned part of his text was the ancient Greek Character, given its canonical form by Theophrastus in 319 B.C., with its images of the familiar and everyday. Although in England the genre had been well represented in the seventeenth century, in France until La Bruyère there were no significant examples of the genre in its own right (though it was utilized within other genres, in the works of Molière for instance). The Greek *Characters* included some thirty page-long Characters following a simple formula: an abstract title (such as Irony or Garrulousness), a one-line definition followed by a description such as "the ironical, garrulous man is one who . . . ," leading into a succession of typical actions and modes of address, as well as the embarrassments and reversals to which the Character was habitually subjected. La Bruyère was thus following the humanist example of imitation of an ancient model. The danger of using worldly literary forms for moral purposes was real. Polite conversation, for instance, was designed in part to allow its participants to avoid weightier matters. With the Character, La Bruyère was employing a Janus-faced literary form that on one side risked being taken as personal attack but on the other clearly

marked its emanation from venerable philosophic traditions—a risk exacerbated by La Bruyère's replacing of the abstract titles with Greek names, a common practice in seventeenth-century literature and one that recalled coded heroic novels and portrait books from earlier in the century. In Isaac Casaubon's magisterial late-sixteenth-century Greek-Latin edition of the *Characters,* upon which La Bruyère had relied extensively in preparing his own, the great Calvinist humanist had suggested that the Character shared many features with the biblical literature of wisdom, citing in particular the Book of Proverbs. He had judged the Character to be a highly effective form of moral instruction, midway between philosophy and rhetoric, because it represented moral philosophy in essentially dramatic actions that moved spectators, not as an externally imposed set of rules. Similarly, Theophrastus, the successor of Aristotle at the head of the Lyceum, was probably attempting in the original Greek *Characters* to provide accessible illustrations to his master's more-abstract formulations. La Bruyère's *moraliste* forebears, for their part, were equally serious. They had been deeply influenced by Augustinianism with its deep sense of irremediable sin and its doctrine of the Two Cities (one ruled by love of the world and the other by the love of God), which had for a "literary" corollary an impassioned examination of human depravity in all its puzzling and labyrinthine forms.

La Bruyère's choice of a literary model and persona underscored the same dual emphasis. The introductory *Discours* included an encomiastic biography of Theophrastus that made clear that the images of petty vice found in La Bruyère's own *Les Caractères* had been transmitted by a beloved sage; the more bizarre and disgusting the object represented, the more it reflected the sage's accuracy of vision, his charitable care in seeking to correct his fellows' faulty behavior, and his essential sanity in the face of the folly of the world. The choice of a form that combined the qualities of compositional disorder and technical simplicity was also intended to signal an act of humility before human incapacity to reach a final synthesis of knowledge without God's help and, in the same spirit, affirmed the pressing need to transmit unadorned truths that even a child could understand.

La Bruyère owes his place in the canon of European literature primarily to his brilliant renewal of the Character genre. He himself recognized its importance by placing the work as a whole under the title *Les Caractères*. The Characters were cruelly crafted images depicting the different social types populating French society. They were put on display there in a seemingly endless gallery of courtiers, financiers, nobles, churchmen, freethinkers, society ladies, parasites, hangers-on, and parvenus, and they were shown to be mostly immoral, degraded, and ridiculous figures. As they were precisely intended to be typical and exemplary of society as a whole rather than the highest ranking or well-known individuals, La Bruyère chose his targets from the middling ranks of society rather than from its leading lights, and in their everyday activities, at an indifferent moment rather than at dramatic turning points, monumental settings, or glorified historical events. They are shown in the first flush of a simple encounter, avoiding or buttonholing someone else; a reiterated, thoughtless daily occurrence such as getting up in the morning or walking down a street; or deliberating the next move in a back passage, in a doorway, behind the scenes, or in a private cabinet. In each case, La Bruyère catches them when their guard is down and their true natures cannot be hidden.

Quite unlike the modern, novelistic "character," the Greek Character is not shown developing or changing in any way, nor is any background given to explain his or her present behavior. The focus on behavior (*mœurs*) also excludes the sort of physical description prevalent in the pseudoscientific physiognomic tradition (the man with leonine features who is courageous) or the tragic character revealed when someone yields to a monstrous passion (Phèdre's criminal love for Hyppolite). Instead, the actions take place in a perpetual present in which the forward movement of the prose does not represent temporal development but a mere extension or unfolding of an ethical essence. Following the rhetorical figure is given a list of traits known as *accumulatio* or—as La Bruyère calls it—*amplificatio,* in which each successive clause or line simply adds more details in no particular order.

Few classical texts, therefore, were more "realistic" in the sense of representing traditionally underrepresented places, people, and activities; with La Bruyère's secret mania for collecting worthless observation, the way one wipes one's nose or a peasant digs the ground becomes worthy of literary and moral attention. In regard to the individual Character concerned, what the Character lacked in depth it made up for in the sheer number of striking details. With regard to the collective mass of Characters that it could ultimately display, this same lack of depth allowed the work as a whole to attain a broad social comprehensiveness. The strength of the Character's form lies in its power to imprint itself in the reader's memory and to signify immediately its moral meaning without further argument. The original meaning of the word *Character* in Greek was a stamp or distinguishing mark. Infinitely reproducible yet unmistakably demarcated, its reference to actual individuals remained tantalizingly ambiguous. A single trait might well have been observed at a certain place and time in a given person; yet, a whole portrait could equally well be a composite of many observations taken from different persons.

Just as the Character was an ancient Greek literary form perfectly suited to La Bruyère's own time, the ten-page *Discours sur Théophraste* is partly a learned humanist style of introduction to an eminent authority of the past and partly a general commentary on La Bruyère's moral project and writing. La Bruyère's translation of Theophrastus's text aims at a middle ground between accessibility for a polite seventeenth-century audience and the historical difference of the "foreign," not at word-for-word accuracy. In a further attempt to find a balance between respect and readability, he retains the apparatus of explanatory notes to illuminate certain ancient terms or customs but keeps them to a minimum. After the translation comes a three-page *Préface* more insistently focused on the contemporary audience. The preface presents La Bruyère's text simply as a portrait of the public rather than as a continuation of Theophrastus's text. La Bruyère muses on the messy expansion of his text from edition to edition, promising to stop but equally asserting that he is filling up the text with the solid "matter" of human behaviors the world has not ceased to produce. He notes the formal variety of the work as a form of "thought": "on pense les choses d'une manière différente, et on les explique par un tour aussi différent" (one considers things in a different way, and then one displays them with a different turn of phrase).

After the preface comes the French *Les Caractères,* some four hundred pages divided into what the author called "remarks"—meaning both the written form of representation and the act of noticing. These remarks are collected into thematic chapters—for example, "De La Cour" (On the Court) or "Des Femmes" (Of Women), though many could have been placed in different chapters. The chapters have no system of internal organization: a remark can be one line or many pages, and no obvious connection is used between successive remarks. More confusingly still, no space intervenes between them—as if they formed a continuous whole, with a *pied de mouche* (¶) as the only sign of demarcation of one remark from another. Furthermore, the text is heterogeneous in size and contents from year to year. La Bruyère never altered the basic sequence of the larger units—*Discours,* translation, *Préface,* the Characters—he simply added remarks to each of the sixteen chapters of the Characters. *Les Caractères* was therefore infinitely expandable, and from the first edition to the final one, the eighth, the book more than doubled in length.

Whereas the first edition had relatively few developed Characters, they made up almost a third of the

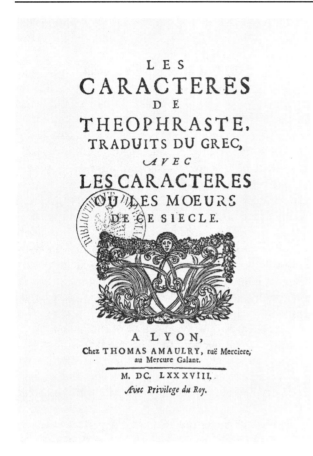

Title page for the 1688 edition of La Bruyère's best-known book, in which he translated a work by the Greek writer Theophrastus and added his own satiric sketches of seventeenth-century character types (Bibliothèque Nationale, Paris)

volume of the book in the eighth edition. In contrast, the proportion of maxims—80 percent of the first edition—steadily decreased. Finally, by the eighth edition the Theophrastan section was decidedly less important. In the first edition, the *Discours* and translation were printed in larger type than La Bruyère's Characters and took up almost half its length. By the eighth edition the expansion of the French section and its larger type caused the translation to make up less than 20 percent of the whole. To mark the emerging importance of the French section, in the fifth edition La Bruyère revealed his authorship of the book in a new remark added to "De Quelques Usages" (Of Certain Customs); until then he had remained anonymous. In his later editions La Bruyère appended two texts that presented his side of the rancorous debate that followed his controversial election to the Académie Française in 1693.

Les Caractères was contemporary with the last great exemplars of humanist encyclopedism, such as Pierre Bayle and Giambattista Vico, whose texts convey classical learning even as their "open" structures were intentionally permeable to contemporary history: they used the resources of the past to channel the assimilation of the present. Yet, *Les Caractères* has a certain conceptual progression that suggests its own specific underlying hierarchy of values. The first six chapters deal with the more personal zone of moral life—writing and literary criticism, "Des Ouvrages de l'esprit" (Of Belles Lettres); merit and reward, "Du Mérite personnel" (Of Personal Merit); women, "Des Femmes," tied to the private realm in the seventeenth century; friendship and love, "Du Cœur" (Of the Heart); personal behavior in social situations, "De La Société" (Of Society); and wealth and its despised propagators, the financiers, "Des Biens de fortune" (Of Worldly Goods). The next four chapters are larger scale, though still tied closely to the contemporary scene; they represent an ascending sociopolitical hierarchy expressed by *place* and *caste* from the town to the king—"De La Ville," "De La Cour," "Des Grands," and "Du Souverain" (Of the Town, Of the Court, Of Great Nobles, Of the Sovereign or the Republic). The next four have the widest philosophical or anthropological reference—"De L'Homme," "De Jugements," "De La Mode," "De Quelques Usages" (Of Man, Of Opinions, Of Fashion, Of Certain Customs). The final two deal directly with the most important subject of all, the Christian religion, approached by way of the language of preaching, and finally an attack on freethinkers by way of a justification of belief and a theodicy—"De La Chaire" and "Des Esprits forts" (Of the Pulpit and Of Freethinkers). A discernible parallel, counterpointed by ascension, can be seen at either pole of the work between the pagan philosopher and secular ministry of writing at the beginning and the Christian section at the end. The prescriptions suggested for good preaching are in fact close to those for good writing given in the first chapter and even indicate the virtue of the *moraliste* fragment against its Aristotelian rivals, as La Bruyère says in "De La Chaire" 29: "Il me semble qu'un prédicateur devrait faire choix dans chaque discours d'une vérité unique. . . ." (It seems to me that a preacher ought to choose a single truth for every sermon. . . .) La Bruyère's reflections on both secular and sacred speech praise self-effacing simplicity, naturalness, and the acceptance of "the already-said" as the most important "matter" for the writer to work on and to retransmit, as opposed to the showy display of intellectual prowess and the quest for novelty.

The relationship of humility to self-assertion was also central to La Bruyère's life. His adulthood was lived entirely under the personal reign of Louis XIV. It was largely uneventful; he never married nor did he ever travel beyond northern France. Born on 17 August 1645 into an undistinguished Parisian bourgeois family mainly occupied with government service and finance, he passed the bar in 1665 and bought a tax inspectorship in 1673. These paths were typical ways for someone of his class to rise slowly to attain the rank of noble. However, he probably early on preferred philosophical and literary pursuits to those for which he had qualified: no evidence exists that he ever practiced law, and he never took up residence in the *généralité* (tax district) of Caen, where he was supposed to be assessing taxes. Since the position of tax assessor was not a sinecure and earned the bearer a valuable title of nobility and a respectable income, he might have received special dispensation from the king freeing him from his duties to work on the massive edition of Latin authors being prepared for the dauphin to use in his studies. Such an occurrence would explain how La Bruyère came in contact with the tutor in charge of the prince's instruction in the "humanities," Bishop Jacques-Bénigne Bossuet, one of the leading preachers of his day but also a learned humanist, political theorist, and theologian who became the greatest defender in print of Gallican orthodoxy and later wrote a treatise justifying Louis XIV's brand of absolutism by way of biblical precepts. La Bruyère revered Bossuet for the rest of his life, but even more important, as a result of his discipleship, La Bruyère became involved with a Christian reformist group known as the Petit Concile, which had formed around Bossuet, although La Bruyère did not become part of its inner circle. From two of its leaders in particular, the Abbés Claude Fleury and François de Salignac de la Mothe-Fénelon, La Bruyère derived his most significant intellectual influences, a socially oriented Catholicism and Erasmian humanism. Together these tendencies entailed, in political terms, the concerted attempt to build a society on the principle of charity and mutual aid between the three estates—nobility, clergy, and commoners; in theological terms, they signaled a return to the primitive form of life enjoyed by the early Hebrews, Christians, and Greeks; and, in moral terms, they indicated a practical focus on moral behavior and educable human reason rather than scholastic elaborations, monastic retreat, or a dogmatic Christian rejection of pagan virtues. In effect, though the group was highly conservative in most respects and stalwart supporters of the current regime and its rigid caste system, their humanist desire to return to purer origins represented a humbling critique of the proud civilization of the Louis-Quartorzien monarchy from within its own ranks. For the members of the Petit Concile "une trop grande disposition" (too great a disproportion, as La Bruyère said in "Des Esprits forts" 49) between men threatened the traditional hierarchies and habit of obedience that were the foundation of the monarchy. It

replaced the stable society of orders governed by mutual respect and care with one governed by the destabilizing forces of money, fashion, and ambition. Only when the rulers were virtuous and the well-being of their subjects and vassals their first concern could social difference be absorbed into a transcendent ideal. The Petit Concile were also Christian humanists and sought to find the seeds of truth in the cultures of the past, both pagan and Judeo-Christian. This search served two purposes: it humiliated the present, and it reoriented moral thought to the question of practices rather than dogmas. Virtuous pagans had been in effect more Christian than many Christians, the Petit Concile thought, because they had practiced wisdom without the need of doctrine, in their daily lives. One of the first works of Christian humanist literature, Desiderius Erasmus's *The Praise of Folly* (1549), for instance, presented a panorama of a whole specifically Christian society failing to act in a Christian manner, including the priesthood. The quest to find better forms of life demanded a piecemeal approach of reconstructing and understanding other types of society and then assimilating whatever was useful into one's own. Though ancient in tone, such an approach was, paradoxically, a powerful enabling framework for legitimating reform in the present.

These emphases naturally led the group to be interested in pedagogy; indeed, they represented both the leading officially sanctioned thinkers on the subject in France and the privileged source of pedagogues for the royal family. As a result, in 1684 La Bruyère—probably through Bossuet—was recommended to be the tutor to the grandson of the prince de Condé, one of the most important, if also most controversial, men in the kingdom since Condé had been the leader of the aristocratic rebellion against royal authority that took place during Louis XIV's minority and was suspected of being a freethinker. Up until this time, La Bruyère had lived a sedentary existence in his mother's house in Paris; now he was placed in close proximity to the highest powers in the land: the Condés had rooms in Versailles, and the young Prince Louis later, in 1685, married Louis XIV's natural daughter (whom La Bruyère also tutored briefly). La Bruyère taught the young duke primarily history, geography, and genealogy with a smattering of philosophy (Cartesian) and literature (Ovid). La Bruyère's young charge was, however, neither an assiduous nor a talented student, and La Bruyère's diligent efforts did not meet with any great success. The tutorship did not last long either. When Condé died in 1686, the duke's education came to an end. La Bruyère was rewarded with a title of nobility, residence in the Condés' apartments, and a pension. In effect, he became the Condés' "man," a courtier, though one who did not have any onerous duties to perform. He seems to have had relatively little contact with either the Grand Condé or his heir and never became a particularly important member of their court.

In all probability, La Bruyère was happy to keep his distance from the Condés–haughty, dangerous, and contemptuous of common pieties as they were. The few reports about La Bruyère's character come from this period too; they are impossible to verify fully but suggest that his reluctance to be a courtier was tempered with the need to conform. La Bruyère appears to have been a figure of fun in the (notoriously cruel) Condé household because he was so gauche and ill favored, despite all his best efforts to learn to perform courtly niceties such as dancing. On the other hand, many witnesses contradict such reports. A defender of aristocratic privilege such as Louis de Rouvroy, duc de Saint-Simon, for one, praised La Bruyère's noble bearing and penetrating mind. La Bruyère says little about himself in *Les Caractères* other than to say that he is a *philosophe* and an open-hearted observer of the human race. However, what La Bruyère thought about his new condition can readily be gathered from *Les Caractères,* which is a veritable repertory of his opinions. Two chapters specifically deal with the aristocracy, court life, and the position of the virtuous in their orbit. In them he describes the court and the ambience of aristocrats as the cause of innumerable vices–especially dissimulation, pride, and servility among those people seeking their favor–and a position that is unavoidable once one is in the court. As he says in "De La Cour" 1: "Le reproche en un sens le plus honorable que l'on puisse faire à un homme, c'est de lui dire qu'il ne sait pas la Cour; il n'y a sorte de vertus qu'on ne rassemble en lui par ce seul mot" (In a way, the most honorable insult you can pay a man is to tell him that he knows nothing about the Court–by saying that one thing you attribute to him every virtue there is). La Bruyère describes aristocrats as incompetent, prideful, cruel, and disdainful of their social inferiors and intellectual betters. Yet, he does not challenge the existence of the hierarchy; indeed, he had accepted its benefits himself. He bows before its power in the manner of Pascal–that is, he recognizes its power as a physical rather than a metaphysical force that would simply overpower any resistance because of its strength. His solution to this apparent defeat of morality is to turn to a different value, which shines forth wherever one has been placed by the aleatory and capricious workings of favor–merit, the certain possession and skillful exercise of one's talents. If one has performed one's appointed tasks well, then one can take a pure and secure satisfaction that no social superior could affect in any way. La Bruyère had man-

aged to rise in social rank not by venal means but by dint of his learning. Moreover, since he did not entertain any desire to rise further in the world and was content to remain in the shadows of the Condé court, he now enjoyed a secure vantage point from which to observe the upper echelons of French society without having to compromise his own austere moral code.

Even more than through learning, La Bruyère came to incarnate merit through writing. As he says at the end of "De La Cour," the philosopher is always in danger of retreating entirely from the world out of disgust. Self-fulfillment through one's work is what saves him from misanthropy and hermeticism–neither of which agreed with La Bruyère's Christian precepts. Without a worthy function to perform in the Condé court–and perhaps disillusioned with his failure to educate a prince–La Bruyère turned to a wider field in which to demonstrate his merit and pedagogical abilities. Only at this point did La Bruyère first show his literary efforts to anyone, and his choice was Nicolas Boileau-Déspreaux, who half-mockingly dubbed La Bruyère "Maximilien" in a letter to Jean Racine, because the original edition of *Les Caractères* was so reminiscent of La Rochefoucauld's maxims in *Réflexions* (1664). Possibly, La Bruyère had been writing what would become *Les Caractères* beginning as early as 1670. They probably existed as no more than a series of notes and observations until the 1680s. His tenure with the Condés gave him a decisive impetus toward giving his work a more organized and ambitious shape. His preceptorship and social ascension had offered him access to social milieus that might otherwise have been closed to him and thus permitted him to envisage a work that would be socially encyclopedic in scope but had equally spurred him to challenge aristocratic indifference to higher human values. At some point during the 1680s he decided to insert his "remarks" into the newly devised humanist framework.

When *Les Caractères* was first published, La Bruyère was already forty-three years old and completely unknown. He originally presented his work in a rather veiled form. It was ostensibly a mere appendage to a translation of a Greek masterpiece. In the middle of the *Discours sur Théophraste,* after praising Theophrastus and the type of moral writing he had produced in the *Characters,* La Bruyère said that he had only added to the work "dans l'esprit de contenter ceux qui reçoivent froidement tout ce qui appartient aux étrangers et aux anciens" (with the intention of mollifying those who turn a cold shoulder to everything that comes from foreigners or the ancients). However, the work was an immediate success, and La Bruyère was emboldened to enlarge it almost every year until 1694. Though even at this late date his name still did not appear on the title page, he decided to tack on at the end of *Les Caractères* his controversial acceptance speech given at his induction into the Académie Française, thus making his authorship clear to all.

Les Caractères brought La Bruyère widespread public acclaim and also the respect of the learned community, which admired his graceful rendering of the work by Theophrastus. After they failed in an attempt to get him elected to the Académie Française in 1691, La Bruyère's powerful allies managed to get him elected to a vacant seat in 1693. The behind-the-scenes intrigue required to bring about his election occurred in the midst of the *Querelle des anciens et des modernes* (Quarrel of the Ancients and Moderns), which pitted those who believed that ancient literary forms no longer needed to be taken as models, the *modernes,* against those who believed the contrary, the *anciens,* of whom La Bruyère was one. His supporters were all *anciens* and included some of the greatest of the French *classiques* (classical scholars), such as Boileau, Jean La Fontaine, and Racine. Their work relied on carefully selected classical texts as models to be emulated, perhaps surpassed, but always present to guide the aspiring author. None of them, however, had coupled his work so explicitly as La Bruyère had with that of an ancient. Nor was anyone else's support for contemporary *anciens* so strident. Against the norm of simply eulogizing the dead member one was replacing when giving his acceptance speech before his fellow academicians, La Bruyère praised his *ancien* friends and ignored the *modernes*–as if to condemn them proleptically to nonclassical status. His action led to a violent quarrel fueled by the already hostile relations existing between the main parties.

Les Caractères had been attacked by some even in its original form for being a poorly constructed work that did not conform to Ciceronian standards of carefully articulated transitions from one point to another, made up as it was essentially of fragments. The now enraged *modernes* used this criticism to challenge the moral probity of the work, charging that *Les Caractères* was barely a book at all but, as the journal *Le Mercure galant* (Paris) put it in a June 1693 review, a series of personal calumnies stitched together in book form. The charge was not implausible, because La Bruyère's portraits were detailed and vivid, while the fragmentary disposition of the text made it seem to a rhetorically trained culture simply unfinished. In any case, so enamored was the tight-knit, prestige-obsessed society of the period that many *clés* (keys) sprang up in the wake of *Les Caractères* purporting to make firm identifications of a given portrait with a well-known public figure. La Bruyère tried desperately to preserve the philosophical dignity of his work by affirming that his portraits were

ARMES DE LA BRUYÈRE

La Bruyère's coat of arms

made up of traits taken from many different originals, that it was aimed at vices in general, and that this generality was the vehicle of his benevolent desire to help everyone who recognized him- or herself in the portraits, in effect becoming the one who particularized the portrait through self-reflection. To support this claim, in the fourth edition he placed as the epigraph to the text a quotation from a letter written by Erasmus in which he had defended himself from the same charges of attacking individuals in *The Praise of Folly:* "Admonere voluimus, non mordere; prodesse, non laedere; consulere moribus hominum, non officere" (We sought to admonish and not to bite, to be useful and not to wound, to improve the behavior of men and not to harm them).

In 1694 La Bruyère decided to stop adding any more material to *Les Caractères* and turned to a new project, dialogues in the style of Pascal's *Lettres Provinciales* (Provincial Letters, 1656–1657), ridiculing the mystical sect known as the quietists. In undertaking this project, La Bruyère was seconding the efforts of his mentor Bossuet in defending the established church from marginal challenges. On 10 May 1696, after reading one of them to Bossuet's brother, Jean de La Bruyère suddenly fell ill and died in the Condé apartments of Versailles, where he lived alone.

The nature of a La Bruyère Character can be illustrated with a few examples. Perhaps the best-known is Ménalque, the absent-minded man pratfalling his way through the streets and salons of Paris:

> *Ménalque* descend son escalier, ouvre sa porte pour sortir, il la referme: il s'aperçoit qu'il est en bonnet de nuit; et venant à mieux s'examiner, il se trouve rasé à moitié . . . [s]'il marche dans les places, il se sent tout d'un coup rudement frapper à l'estomac ou au visage; il ne soupçonne point ce que ce peut être, jusqu'à ce qu'ouvrant les yeux et se réveillant, il se trouve . . . derrière un long ais de menuiserie que porte un ouvrier sur ses épaules. . . .

> (Ménalque comes down the stairs, opens his door to go out, then shuts it again; he notices that he is wearing his nightcap; and when he comes to look closer, discovers that he is only half shaved . . . as he walks into the public square, he suddenly feels a sharp blow in his stomach or in his face; he can't think what it may be, until on opening his eyes and waking up, he finds himself . . . behind a long plank of wood carried on a workman's shoulder. . . .) ("De L'Homme" 7)

There is also the portrait (in "De La Mode" 2) of the tulip maniac so enamored of his prized flowers that he spends his whole day gazing at them like a lovesick fool:

> Vous le voyez planté, et qui a pris racine au milieu de ses tulipes et devant la *Solitaire;* il ouvre de grands yeux, il frotte ses mains, il se baisse, il la voit de plus près, il ne l'a jamais vue de si belle, il a le cœur épanoui de joie.

> (He seems to have been planted there, and to have taken root among his tulips, in front of the *Solitary* he opens his eyes wide, rubs his hands, bends down, examines it more closely, he has never seen it look so beautiful, his heart overflows with delight.)

Another example is the courtier, who is shown (in "De La Cour" 22) as a composite creature, at once a scheming, two-faced egotist who "se couche et . . . se lève sur l'intérêt" (sleeping and waking . . . on his self-interest); yet, he is someone who worships power to such an extent that he becomes helpless and deformed when he beholds the king ("De La Cour" 13). "De La Cour" 19 fuses the two tendencies, showing a perpetually moving but ultimately degraded human mechanism in the figures of two courtiers named Cimon and Clitander, full of "l'empressement, l'inquiétude, la curiosité, l'activité" (bustling zeal, restlessness, curiosity, activity), about whom La Bruyère comments:

> On ne les a jamais vus assis . . . on les voit courir, parler en courant, et vous interroger sans attendre de réponse. Ils ne viennent d'aucun endroit, ils ne vont nulle part. . . . Ne les retardez pas dans leur course précipitée, vous démonteriez leur machine.

> (Nobody has ever seen them sitting down . . . you see them running, talking as they run, and asking questions without waiting for an answer. They haven't come from anywhere, and they are going nowhere. . . . Don't slow them down in their mad career, you would break the machine.)

Ménalque presents the Character form at its simplest, the piling on of traits, actions, scenes, and utterances one after the other. Other forms allow the intrusion of an authorial comment, so that immediately after the passage on the tulip maniac the narrator says, "Dieu et la nature sont en tout cela ce qu'il n'aime pas" (In all this God and nature are what he is not admiring). When such a comment comes at the end of the Character, it is often shocking and sums up matters in a short phrase called a *pointe* in French rhetoric.

Occasionally, the author addresses the Character with an incredulous question or statement as part of a dramatic scene. For instance, "Des Biens de fortune" 12 presents the case of the haughty government officer who increases his power by always being unavailable; La Bruyère's persona's rush to the official's door when in need of help is accompanied by a lament because the official so persistently avoids any contact: "plût aux Dieux que je ne fusse ni votre client ni votre fâcheux!" (God preserve me from being dependent on you or having to chase you about!). Similarly, in the same remark, the persona implicitly paints his own portrait by stating what his actions would be: "le philosophe est accessible; je ne vous remettrai point à un autre jour . . . (the philosopher is accessible; I will not put you off until tomorrow . . .). He is open to others and charitable: "l'homme de lettres . . . est trivial comme une borne au coin des places; il est vu de tous, à toute heure . . . il ne peut être important, et il ne veut point être" (the man of letters . . . is easy of access like the cornerstone in any public square: he can be seen by anyone and at any time . . . he cannot be self-important and does not want to be).

However, the Characters are by no means the only constituents of the text. They form at most a third and are framed by other types of discourse that relay in piecemeal fashion a set of fundamental ideas that can only be extrapolated by making one's own connections from remark to remark, as expressed in maxims, parodies, moral tales, literary criticism, religious apology, *précieux* definitions of the passions, and political reflections. So various were the types of prose that *Les Car-*

actères displayed—and with such mastery—that the work became a veritable treasure trove for many quite dissimilar French writers to draw on in the centuries following. In a few short passages, La Bruyère reveals the absurdity of domestic customs through a naive outsider's description, a technique on which Baron Montesquieu later based his *Lettres persanes* (Persian Letters, 1721) and Voltaire his *Candide* (Candide, 1759). As in *Lettres persanes, Les Caractères* describes the French court at church as if the church were a temple devoted to idolatrous rites, since the courtiers are worshiping the king ("De La Cour" 74); looking forward to *Candide,* a fragment describes in tones of clinical detachment the increased killing power of modern weaponry as proof that human reason is progressing ("De Jugements" 119). Denis Diderot also used another of the stylistic resources of *Les Caractères* to great effect in *Le Nevue de Rameau* (Rameau's Nephew, written between 1761 and 1774; published in German, 1805) to convey the nephew's state of self-destructive adaptation to society—La Bruyère's innovative development of a nervous, jumpy prose relying on short, disjunctive clauses and reiterated words of the same grammatical category capturing a sense of the enormous energy human beings expend on pointless and ultimately repetitive actions ("il + verb, il + verb"). Some of nineteenth-century novelist Gustave Flaubert's most characteristic stylistic qualities can be traced back to La Bruyère, too: one is the use of free indirect and direct discourse as a means to condemn the stupidity of the speaker by amassing his or her clichés without the interjection of further comment on the part of the author. La Bruyère was perhaps the decisive forerunner of Flaubert's own rather peculiar artistic project—the creation of a perfect prose from the stupidity of his society's thought and speech. In the twentieth century Proust found him the most congenial of the *moralistes* and refers to him often in *A la recherche du temps perdu* (In Search of Lost Time, 1913–1927).

Each chapter of *Les Caractères,* despite all the stylistic and thematic variety of the work as a whole, traces a certain pattern reiterating the precarious place of merit and reasonable conduct in a world that does not recognize or promote them. This failure actually endangers everyone's well-being and is ultimately seen by La Bruyère as a political as much as a moral question. Every attempt to separate oneself from others by virtue of status or by greater material acquisition is shown to be self-defeating. Only the modest adhesion to one's rank and the attempt to fulfill one's talents without seeking advancement can, he implies, ultimately bring any hope of success and satisfaction. A book may be successful because of its author's reputation, but his reputation says nothing about the true quality of the

book, which must be based on hard work and critical consciousness ("Des ouvrages de l'espirit"). The fine accoutrements of a wealthy gentleman cannot hide the fact that underneath he is a fool; in a twist to the common theme of false appearances, merit is in this case to be found paradoxically on the surface: in the workmanship that went into the production of these luxuries ("Du Mérite personnel" 27). Most strikingly, La Bruyère paints prideful differentiation as an entropic mechanism. The great nobles who vie for favor at court and thus show that they are greater than their rivals end up in fact becoming as small as one another by dint of the demeaning quest for royal favor they all share ("De La Cour" 5). Once outside of Versailles presiding over their own minicourts, they become no less small in a different way. Their refusal to reward merit instead of sycophancy ends by leaving them vulnerable to the superior competence of their unscrupulous favorites, who play on the nobles' ignorance to advance themselves and finally outstrip their former masters ("Des Grands" 24). The bourgeoisie are represented as trapped within their own distinctive forms of futility. One of them spends his whole life in the struggle to acquire goods, and by the time he has succeeded is too old to enjoy them ("Des Biens de fortune" 40); another suffers a catastrophic reversal of fortune without ever having had a moment to enjoy his wealth while he had it ("Des Biens de fortune" 79). La Bruyère hammers home the lesson that the typical moneygrubbing financier or merchant who loves things rather than other human beings actually becomes a thing himself, just as those people who trade in insincere clichés and pompous language debase the language so much that they end up with something worthless even for themselves.

As these examples show, the flexible structure and insistent variation of *Les Caractères* were placed in the service of La Bruyère's socialization of his many literary and intellectual influences. La Bruyère effectively inflects the direction of *moraliste* from more-abstract metaphysical considerations on the limits of the human condition in relation to God or to the workings of self-love toward the more particularized area of social critique and possible remedies for current political problems. Some of La Bruyère's maxims, in truth, seem to have been directly taken from La Rochefoucauld's *Maximes* in all their pointed abstraction, such as "Du Cœur" 31: "L'on n'est pas plus maître de toujours aimer qu'on l'a été de ne pas aimer" (we can no more command ourselves to stay in love than we could to fall in love) or Pascal's *Pensées* (Thoughts, written 1657–1658), in which the infinite size of the universe and the intricacy of its creatures is used as a humbling proof to man of God's existence and utter superiority ("Des Esprits forts" 43 and 44). But far more often than those of his predecessors, La Bruyère's remarks have a local reference that particularizes them. They are therefore at once more banal and more susceptible of expansion into a little scene that becomes a Character or a description of social relations. A brief and unremarkable comment such as in "Des Grands" 9—"il est souvent plus utile de quitter les grands que de s'en plaindre" (it is often more advantageous to leave great nobles than to complain about them)—forms a kernel that is then fleshed out in the chapter through the many unflattering images of the ignorant noble in his relation to the meritorious servant. Likewise, whereas Pascal's Christian apologetics operated on a metaphysical and theological plane, La Bruyère no longer locates the central conceptual drama of his work in the Augustinian struggle to achieve faith but instead finds it in the struggle to stay free of the potentially overwhelming effects of the need for and pursuit of social success. For instance, in one remark, "Des Grands" 12, Pascal's metaphysical division of the world into the three orders of the flesh, the mind, and charity is re-created by La Bruyère as the difference between social classes represented by the aristocrat; the mediocre courtier, who knows how to amuse him; and the philosophe, who looks on and pities them both because they lack virtue. In the most Pascalian chapter, "Des Esprits forts," modern arguments for faith are framed by an attack on a class of people: the freethinkers. In the same vein, Christianity in *Les Caractères* is not discussed with any reference whatsoever to the particulars of the faith; instead, it is discussed as a social practice, in the conditions in which the Word of God is delivered; the thoughtlessness of the freethinkers and their different types and actions; the *faux dévots* (religious hypocrites), who pretended to be devout to please an increasingly pious king; and the divine sanction behind a "reasonable" social inequality. La Bruyère's tendency to socialize is even evident in his aesthetic comments. In one of his most innovative moves, La Bruyère opens his work with a chapter on writing itself. In this chapter he relates many of the precepts of the *anciens* party, in particular those of Boileau, but he does so in part by showing that good writing is not only a matter of following precepts or one's genius but also an eminently social role dependent on an exchange of goods that all are capable of judging correctly—"a craft, like making a clock"—while bad writing is a product of inflated reputation and uncritical egotism. In voicing such sentiments La Bruyère was perhaps the first French writer to conceive of writing as a genuine profession in the modern sense.

He certainly needed to assert the traditional lineage behind his work; yet, one of the most arresting qualities of his writing is a distinctly modern understanding of social action indicating that he was living at a time when Cartesianism was becoming more and more acceptable, even to orthodox Christians. He was favorable to René Descartes and familiar with Descartes's philosophy. Typically, he socializes Descartes. He takes Descartes's rule "qui ne veut pas qu'on décide sur les moindres vérités, avant qu'elles soient connues clairement et distinctement" (that one should not make up one's mind about the smallest truths before knowing them clearly and distinctly) as so fine that it should be applied to persons, too ("De Jugements" 42). In "Des Esprits forts" he uses Descartes's *Cogito ergo sum* (I think therefore I am) to prove a rational being's certainty about the existence of God and the impossibility of thinking at all without such a certainty. Above all, he developed a sort of protosociological dynamics to map out the almost irresistible force of social power and appearance, the equivalent in society to the laws of physics in nature. As the American critic Jules Brody has pointed out in *Du style à la pensée* (1980), La Bruyère took over Descartes's division of Being into mind and matter to portray the vast majority of human beings as soulless automatons allowing themselves to be acted on by their desires for advancement or things and thereby losing the free power of mind that they were endowed with at birth. Treating others like things, they too become thing-like in manner, a form of human existence that looked forward to an era of generalized reification in the rampant capitalism of the nineteenth century.

The connoisseur of flowers, mentioned above, is not only an eccentric figure or an allegory of transitory human pleasures but also an example of what a Marxist would call a hypertrophied attention to exchange as opposed to use value, for as "De la mode" 2 goes on to say, "il ne va pas plus loin que l'oignon de sa tulipe, qu'il ne livrerait pas pour mille écus, et qu'il donnerait pour rien quand les tulipes seront négligées et que les œillets auront prévalu" (he does not go beyond the bulb of his tulip, which he would not give up for a thousand crowns, and which he would give away for nothing when the tulips are out of fashion and carnations have won the day). Similarly, the courtiers of Versailles described in "De La Cour" are depicted in time-honored fashion familiar from at least a century of anticourtly literature, sermons, and political philosophy, which registered resistance to the elegant servility increasingly demanded by the centralizing monarchy of France; but La Bruyère's strange image of an automaton created by the convergence of the personal ambition of the courtier and an overwhelming power of the king that can grant his wishes on a whim has a peculiarly familiar resonance today. It points forward to the twinned bureaucrats in Franz Kafka's work, who appear inexpert and

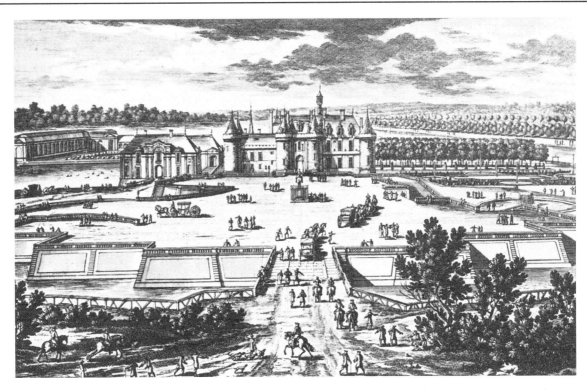

Château de Chantilly, the Condé family home where La Bruyère lived at the end of his life (Bibliothèque Nationale, Paris)

ineffective, bewildered yet ever active in the service of a mysteriously pointless authority.

Against his own intentions and driven by the energies released by his own observations in these depictions, La Bruyère often finds himself questioning the fixities of ancient faculty psychology as well as the possibility of a Christian ethics of inwardness. On many occasions the possession of character traits is no longer attached to an inner self but is the product of one's belonging to a certain social category. In "Des Biens de fortune" 83, for instance, the nature of a human being is literally demonstrated by the accumulation of traits to be a pure product of social position: Giton looks robust and acts with confidence and alertness; he blows his nose noisily and snores in company; everyone listens to him; he laughs and acts knowingly; "il est riche" (he is rich). Phedon looks sick and dreamy; he is unable to do anything well; he is furtive and ignored by others; he sneezes and spits discretely; "il est pauvre" (he is poor). The final *pointe,* had it come first, would have had the effect of a moral definition in the Theophrastan manner. But coming where it does, it delivers to the reader a sudden shock of recognition. He has been forced to try to define these Characters without a guide until the end, and when the answer is given, it is by now an inductively attained cause that explains the phenomena the reader

has encountered. Prompted by such extreme conclusions of social determinism, La Bruyère on occasion muses as to whether there is anything left of the self that could even bear something as substantial as a character, as in "De L'Homme" 6: "Un homme inégal n'est pas un seul homme, ce sont plusieurs: il se multiplie autant de fois qu'il a de nouveaux goûts et de manières différentes" (A changeable man is not one person but several: he has as many selves as he has new tastes and different manners).

La Bruyère does not dream of mounting anything like a direct attack on Louis XIV's regime itself in *Les Caractères,* but as the picture is filled in, certain inductive inferences become increasingly plausible. The placement at the center of the book of the chapter "Du Souverain" marks symbolically that the king is the center of everything in France, both juridically and spiritually. If, then, the nation was in this lamentably unspiritual state, in which neither civic spirit nor genuine religious belief was able to subsist, this suggested to the careful reader that there must indeed be something severely wrong with the political system as a whole. So virulent and effective were La Bruyère's criticisms that one reviewer, a French Protestant named Jacques Basnage, recently exiled by Louis's religious persecution, immediately hailed *Les Caractères* as a "republican" work, and later critics have judged it to be an important forerunner of the Enlightenment tradition of outspoken criticism by private individuals of all that they deemed to be of public interest. In the *Discours,* safely tucked away in the "pedantic" section of his work, La Bruyère implied that *mœurs* depended on their environing political system when he compared the democracy of ancient Athens to the monarchy of modern France in terms decidedly unfavorable to the latter. He characterizes the modern state by "the venality of offices" and the lack of "public places"; its inhabitants are said to spend their whole lives running from their own house to "shut themselves up in another's," either armed to the teeth or paying for the privilege in the case of certain houses where gambling and other types of pleasure were offered. Athens, on the other hand, was "free"–"a republic," whose "citizens were equal," with its many and well-appointed public spaces full of frugal yet highly civilized people of simple and unpretentious mores. The difference between the two polities is that in Athens "L'émulation d'une cour ne les faisait point sortir d'une vie commune" (emulating a court did not force them to abandon life in common with each other).

In the body of the text itself, when La Bruyère comes to formulate the terms of the social question at the end of *Les Caractères,* he falls back on the safer expedient of theodicy. Yet, in "Des Esprits forts" 49 the previous four hundred pages place a great deal of pressure on the word *certain,* the vague reference of which in effect makes it mean virtually the contrary of what it is supposed to mean and underlines the fragility of this type of concept: "Une certaine inégalité dans les conditions, qui entretient l'ordre et la subordination, est l'ouvrage de Dieu, ou suppose une loi divine: une trop grande disproportion, et telle qu'elle se remarque parmi les hommes, est leur ouvrage, ou la loi des plus forts" (A certain inequality in the conditions of men, which ensures order and subordination, is the work of God, and presupposes a divine law: too great a disproportion, such as is seen among men, is their own work, and the law laid down by the stronger). Occasionally in *Les Caractères* a different though related mood appears, the Bossuetian sublime, that of the Christian sage, from whose higher perspective all worldly goings-on are futile. The philosophe's desire to retire entirely from the world often causes chapters of *Les Caractères* to end on a melancholy note.

But this mood is not definitive. La Bruyère's humanism also provides him with a middle path focused on feasible human labor. He names paragons of virtue and literary excellence throughout *Les Caractères* with a reverence typical for the humanist tradition (marked by monumental capital letters for artists or identification with himself when philosophers), and his use of an ancient model is quite unlike his immedi-

ate *moraliste* predecessors' mistrust of the ancients, because as pagans they pridefully considered themselves capable of virtue without divine aid. In *Les Caractères,* humanist imitation holds out the promise that a nonegotistical form of self-assertion might be possible as one creates one's own work by paying homage to another's. Again, unlike in Pascal's work, there is little Christology in La Bruyère's, and his use of merit as a value at all is quite un-Augustinian. La Bruyère sees human misery as man-made and therefore avoidable. In an unjust system that cannot (and indeed for the conservative should not) be overthrown in rebellion, human perseverance becomes a feasible middle way of preserving a space of valid activity. In various remarks scattered throughout *Les Caractères,* social equilibrium is something the writer recognizes in the universe even if he does not experience it in the social system (the injustice of which is not ignored but is put in perspective vis-à-vis eternity and all of creation in the same chapter). Where he is able to experience social equilibrium is in personal action that has immediate and certain social benefits. In his famous remark about the peasantry ("De L'Homme" 128) the apparently brutish animals seen working on the land are first understood to be human and thus deserving of bread because they display "une opiniâtreté invincible" (an invincible tenacity) as they labor in the fields and "épargnent aux autres hommes la peine de semer" (spare other men the toil of sowing). The mindless but essential work of the peasant as well as the perfect prose and penetrating vision of the sage can present an image of a certain form of self-contemplating justice available in the everyday lives of humans through reiterated effort in any task, without the need for direct intervention on a political level.

Les Caractères is a pivotal work. It was published just as the New Science and Rationalism of Newton and Spinoza was emerging and equally at the point when the Louis-Quartorzien monarchy was entering into a period of serious decline in both its international power and its domestic affluence. *Les Caractères* delivered a penetrating analysis of French society that proved prophetic in the eighteenth century: it pinpointed the deep distortions Louis XIV's absolutism had effected in the preexistent equilibrium of social orders. Yet, it was also turned to the culture of the past in myriad ways. In good orthodox fashion it proclaimed certain forms of broader political criticism out of bounds (a fortiori action) even as certain other of its elements made those criticisms implicitly. Keeping within its own self-appointed boundaries was not an easy task in such a multifarious and expansive text obsessed with the ever proliferating matter of public vice. La Bruyère's reticence and careful avoidance of certain issues made many subsequent critics consider him nothing more than a pure observer or pure stylist, claiming that his conservatism or deference to his models revealed him to be second-rate in one way or another. But rarely in literary history does one find a text that is both a stylistic masterpiece and an historically prescient mine of insight for historians, and if La Bruyère has not had the impact of his fellow *moralistes* in terms of intellectual history, he has perhaps been more influential than any of them in the development of French prose as a register of social understanding, one of the best guides to daily life under Louis XIV, especially for discerning what were the inherent limits to its finely calibrated artifice, even as La Bruyère openly displayed that prose as a highly worked and crafted apparatus. What best defines the conceptual and textual dynamics of *Les Caractères* then is the counterpoint–played out continually in every corner of the text in one way or another–of a return to simple truths and received principles in opposition to the teeming mass of different behaviors that prevent such a return from being successful. *Les Caractères* can therefore most profitably be seen as an expression of one of the great dynamics of baroque art and thought (itself a product of the Counter Reformation), which was precisely the *containment* of what was increasingly perceived as a proliferating, infinite universe. The enormous diversity of the world could not simply be ignored or easily classified but had first to be described in all of its unpredictable, multifaceted, and often grotesque forms. One could only reach order by passing through this morass. Yet, once one did so one would still find the old trustworthy verities and traditions intact. During this time, recognizably modern science and skepticism were both gaining ground and could no longer be ignored; the centralizing monarchy was destroying the old (idealized) medieval order of strictly demarcated but mutually aiding classes. Without acknowledging disorder, then, one could not answer the pressing questions of the age; without arriving at a final or underlying order, one would be lost permanently. Jean de La Bruyère's greatest accomplishment was to have written a text that lives through this tension–between individual and type, model and imitation, multifarious behavior and simple truth, brief maxim and exfoliating Character, and acceptable and unacceptable inequality–as he grappled with the fundamental task of the moral writer, as he understood it to be, which is to convince his audience to change their behavior for the better.

Bibliography:

Marc Escola, "Bibliographie des Ecrivains français," in his *Jean de la Bruyère* (Paris & Rome: Memini & CNRS, 1996).

References:

Actes du Colloque international pour le tricentenaire de la mort de La Bruyère, *La Bruyère: Le Métier du moraliste* (Paris: Champion, 2001);

Erich Auerbach, *Mimesis: The Representation of Reality in Western Literature,* translated by Willard R. Trask (Princeton: Princeton University Press, 1953), pp. 359–367;

Roland Barthes, "La Bruyère," in his *Essais critiques,* second edition (Paris: Seuil, 1981), pp. 221–237;

Julien Benda, "A Jean de La Bruyère," *Revue de Paris,* 41 (1934): 108–124;

Paul Bénichou, *Morales du grand siècle* (Paris: Gallimard, 1948);

Elisabeth Bourguinat, Jean Dagen, and Marc Escola, *La Bruyère, le métier du Moraliste,* Papers collected from the "Colloque du Groupe d'étude des moralistes," 8–9 November 1996 (Paris: Champion, 2001);

Jules Brody, *Du style à la pensée: Trois études sur les Caractères de La Bruyère,* introduction by Jean Lafond (Lexington, Ky.: French Forum, 1980);

Emmanuel Bury, "Le Classicisme et le modèle philologique: La Fontaine, Racine et La Bruyère," *L'Information littéraire,* 3 (1990): 20–24;

Bury, *Littérature et politesse: L'Invention de l'honnête homme (1580–1750)* (Paris: Presses Universitaires de France, 1996);

Cahiers de l'Association Internationale des Etudes Françaises, special La Bruyère issue, 44 (1992);

François-Xavier Cuche, *Une Pensée sociale catholique: Fleury, La Bruyère, Fénelon* (Paris: Cerf, 1991);

Dagen, "Ce qui s'appelle penser, pour La Bruyère," *Littératures,* 23 (1990): 55–68;

Serge Doubrovsky, "Lecture de La Bruyère," *Poétique,* 2 (May 1970): 195–201;

Escola, "Ceci n'est pas un livre: Prolégomènes à une rhétorique du discontinu," *Dix-Septième Siècle,* 182 (January–March 1994): 71–82;

Roger Garapon, *Les Caractères de La Bruyère: La Bruyère au travail* (Evreux: Cercle du bibliophile, 1970);

Floyd Gray, *La Bruyère, amateur de caractères* (Paris: Nizet, 1981);

Françoise Jaouën, *De l'art de plaire en petits morceaux: Pascal, La Rochefoucauld, La Bruyère* (Saint-Denis: Presses Universitaires de Vincennes, 1996);

Doris Kirsch, *La Bruyère, ou Le Style cruel* (Montreal: Presses Universitaires de Montréal, 1977);

Michael S. Koppisch, *The Dissolution of Character: Changing Perspectives in La Bruyère's* Caractères (Lexington, Ky.: French Forum, 1981);

Maurice Lange, *La Bruyère, critique des conditions et des institutions sociales* (Paris: Hachette, 1909);

Littératures Classiques, special La Bruyère issue, supplement to 13 (January 1991);

Hamayoun Mazaheri, *La Satire démystificatrice de La Bruyère: Essais sur* Les Caractères (New York: Peter Lang, 1995);

Georges Mongrédien, *Recueil des textes et des documents contemporains relatifs à La Bruyère* (Paris: CNRS, 1979);

Octave Navarre, "Théophraste et La Bruyère," *Revue des Etudes Grecques,* 27 (1914): 23–40;

Benedetta Papàsogli and Barbara Piqué, eds., *Il Prisma dei moralisti* (Rome: Salerno, 1997);

Papers on French Seventeenth-Century Literature, special La Bruyère issue, edited by Claude Abraham, 40 (1988);

Papers on French Seventeenth-Century Literature, special La Bruyère issue, 15 (1981);

Papers on French Seventeenth-Century Literature, special La Bruyère issue, 24 (1998);

Bérengère Parmentier, *Le Siècle des moralistes* (Paris: Seuil, 2000), pp. 113–148;

Pascal Quignard, *Une Gêne technique à l'égard des fragments* (Paris: Fata Morgana, 1986);

Marine Ricord, Les Caractères *de La Bruyère, ou Les Exercices de l'esprit* (Paris: Presses universitaires de France, 2000);

Bernard Roukhomosky, *L'Esthétique de La Bruyère* (Paris, 1997);

Auguste Charles Sainte-Beuve, "La Bruyère," in *Œuvres littéraires,* volume 1, edited by Maxime Leroy (Paris: Gallimard, 1956), pp. 1000–1023;

Patrice Soler, *Jean de la Bruyère: Les Caractères* (Paris: Presses universitaires de France, 1994);

André Stegmann, *Les Caractères de La Bruyère, bible de l'honnête homme* (Paris: Larousse, 1972);

Louis Van Delft, *La Bruyère Moraliste: Quatre études sur les Caractères* (Geneva: Droz, 1971);

Van Delft, *Litterature et anthropologie: Nature humaine et caractère à l'âge classique* (Paris: Presses universitaires de France, 1993);

Van Delft, *Le Moraliste classique: Essai de définition et de typologie* (Geneva: Droz, 1982);

Van Delft, ed., *Le Tricentenaire des "Caractères"* (Paris: Papers on French Seventeenth-Century Literature, 1989);

Georges Van Den Abbeele, "Moralists and the Legacy of Cartesianism," in *A New History of French Literature,* edited by Denis Hollier (Cambridge, Mass.: Harvard University Press, 1989), pp. 327–333;

Barbara Woshinsky, *Signs of Certainty: The Linguistic Imperative in French Classical Literature* (Saratoga: Anma Libri, 1991), pp. 118–140.

Papers:

Jean de La Bruyère's manuscripts are housed in La Bibliothèque Nationale de France, La Bibliothèque de l'Arsenal, and La Bibliothèque Mazarine, all of which are in Paris. The most accessible and comprehensive scholarly collection of papers relating to La Bruyère can be found in Georges Mongrédien's *Recueil des textes et des documents contemporains relatifs à La Bruyère* (Paris: CNRS, 1979).

La Calprenède

(1609? – October 1663)

Mark Bannister
Oxford Brookes University

BOOKS: *La Mort de Mitridate* (Paris: A. de Sommaville, 1637);

Bradamante (Paris: A. de Sommaville, 1637);

Clarionte, ou Le Sacrifice sanglant (Paris: A. de Sommaville, 1637);

Jeanne, Reyne d'Angleterre (Paris: A. de Sommaville, 1638);

Le Comte d'Essex (Paris, 1639);

La Mort des enfans d'Hérodes, ou Suite de Mariane (Paris: A. Courbé, 1639);

Edouard (Paris: A. Courbé, 1640);

Phalante (Paris: A. de Sommaville, 1642);

Cassandre, 10 volumes (volumes 1–6, Paris: A. de Sommaville, 1642–1644; volumes 7–10, Paris: A. de Sommaville, A. Courbé, T. Quinet, et C. de Serey, 1645); translated by Charles Cotterell as *Cassandra, the Fam'd Romance: The Whole Work in 5 Parts* (London: Printed for Humphrey Moseley, 1652);

Herménigilde (Paris: A. de Sommaville et A. Courbé, 1643);

Cléopâtre, 12 volumes (volumes 1–5, Paris: A. de Sommaville, A. Courbé, T. Quinet, Veuve de Sercy, et C. Besongne, 1646–1648; volume 6, Paris: A. de Sommaville, A. Courbé, T. Quinet, et C. Besongne, 1649; volumes 7–8, Paris: A. de Sommaville, A. Courbé, G. de Luyne, et C. Besongne, 1653; volumes 9–10, Paris: G. de Luyne, A. de Sommaville, et A. Courbé, 1657; volumes 11–12, Paris: A. de Sommaville, G. de Luyne, et A. Courbé, 1657); translated by Robert Loveday, John Coles, James Webb, and John Davies as *Hymen's Praeludia, or Love's Masterpiece* (London: Printed for Humphrey Moseley and John Crook, 1665);

Faramond, ou L'Histoire de France, 12 volumes, by La Calprenède [volumes 1–7] and Pierre d'Ortigue de Vaumorière [volumes 8–12] (volumes 1–7, Paris: A. de Sommaville, 1661–1663; volume 8, Paris: Veuve de A. de Sommaville, 1664; volume 9, Paris: Société des Librairies du Palais, 1666;

Gautier de Costes, sieur de La Calprenède (from Sylvie Chevalley, Molière en son temps, *1973)*

volume 10, Paris: J. Ribou, 1667; volume 11, Paris: P. Trabouillet, 1668; volume 12, Paris: T. Jolly, 1670); translated by John Phillips as *Pharamond, or The History of France,* 2 volumes (London: Printed for Thomas Bassett, Thomas Dring, and William Cademan, 1677).

PLAY PRODUCTIONS: *La Mort de Mitridate,* Paris, 1635;

Bradamante, Paris, 1636;

Clarionte, ou Le Sacrifice sanglant, Paris, 1636;

Jeanne, Reyne d'Angleterre, Paris, 1637;

Le Comte d'Essex, Paris, 1637;

La Mort des enfans d'Hérodes, ou Suite de Mariane, Paris, 1638;
Edouard, Paris, 1639;
Phalante, Paris, 1640;
Herménigilde, Paris, 1641;
"Bellissaire," Paris, Hôtel de Bourgogne, July 1659.

The years 1630 to 1650 were a period of great fermentation in the development of French literature, as writers responded to the far-reaching ethical and ideological changes taking place in their world. Playwrights constructed plots around moral and affective dilemmas with which their audiences could readily identify and strove for tighter formal structures. Writers of romances—the forerunners of the modern novel—brought about a radical transformation, turning to history for their source material and making the analysis of complex emotions one of their chief concerns. Poets included those who prized, above all, order and purity of diction as well as those who upheld the claims of imagination and fantasy. La Calpranède's contributions to the theater and the romance establish him firmly as a leading figure in both genres. His determination to explore the heroic potential in human nature and the place of the individual in an increasingly regulated world struck a chord with his contemporaries and brought him success.

Gautier de Costes, sieur de La Calprenède, was born at the Château de Toulgou in the depths of the Périgord countryside, about five miles from Sarlat. The year is unknown but is likely to have been 1609 or 1610. He was the son of Pierre de Costes and Catherine du Verdier-Genouilhac. The family had deep roots in the province and, like many of the rural gentry, helped provide the network of officials on whom the royal jurisdiction depended. Pierre de Costes's father had been *lieutenant du roi* (king's lieutenant) for the local *bourg* (market town) of Salignac; his elder brother was the magistrate in Sarlat; and Pierre de Costes himself was a local judge. He was a sufficiently respected figure in the area to have founded a chapel at the convent in Salignac.

By 1635, when Pierre de Costes's wife died and he made his will (27 April), seven of their ten children were still alive. Of the three surviving sons, François, the youngest, had become a monk, and Jean, the second, who inherited the château, had entered military service, becoming Governor of Montecalvo in Piedmont, but he was killed when the fortress was besieged by the Spanish in 1639. The four daughters were given sums of money to constitute their dowries.

Gautier, the eldest child, was heir to the remainder of his father's estate and in 1639 was to gain title to the château, but having undertaken a period of study at

Toulouse, probably in law to maintain the family tradition, he had already made his way to Paris in 1632 and joined the Régiment des Gardes. The figure of the Gascon who moved to the capital to seek his fortune was a well-established stereotype: he was expected to speak with a strong accent and pepper his speech with strange expressions, to be sensitive about any perceived slight to his honor and quick to draw his sword, and to have a ready wit and an easy skill as a raconteur of outrageous stories. It seems either that La Calprenède already fitted the stereotype or that he made an effort to play up to it, for Gédéon Tallemant des Réaux commented, "Il n'y a jamais eu un homme plus gascon que cetuy-ci" (There never was a man more Gascon than he). In the *Au Lecteur* (To the Reader) to his first play, La Calprenède claimed that, when he arrived in Paris, he knew only enough French to read *Amadis de Gaule* (1540), a claim that cannot be taken seriously. Anecdotes circulated about his touchiness regarding his family honor: for instance, Cardinal Richelieu (Armand Jean du Plessis) having commented that some of the verses in one of La Calprenède's plays were "lâches" (slack, but also cowardly), La Calprenède is said to have exploded: "Comment lâches! Cadédis, il n'y a rien de lâche dans la maison de La Calprenède" (Cowardly? 'Sblood, there is nothing cowardly in the house of La Calprenède). As part of his duties as a soldier, he was assigned to the bodyguard of Queen Anne, wife of Louis XIII, and made a hit with her ladies-in-waiting by his wit and Gascon stories, thereby also coming to the queen's attention, an occurrence that stood him in good stead in his career.

Soon after his arrival in Paris, La Calprenède began to take an interest in the literary scene, attending lectures on literature and philosophy at the *bureau d'adresses* (information exchange) set up in 1631 by Théophraste Renaudot. The most dynamic branch of literature at the time, the one that offered the best chance of rapid success, was the theater. Young dramatists such as Jean Mairet, Pierre Corneille, and Jean de Rotrou were providing a new kind of theatrical experience for the more sophisticated audiences under Richelieu's ministry, and La Calprenède observed carefully the types of plays to which the public responded favorably.

His first play, *La Mort de Mitridate* (The Death of Mithradates, first performed 1635; published 1637), shows that he had learned well. The subject is drawn from Roman history and deals with the kind of psychological confrontation that can form the basis of a convincing tragedy. The scourge of Rome, Mithridate is shown in the last stage of his resistance: his son, Pharnace, has allied himself with the Romans and is besieging his father and the rest of his family in the city of

Sinope. The outcome is the suicide of all the besieged family members, but the center of interest is the conflict of principle between Mithridate and Pharnace. Mithridate is admirable for his heroic qualities and his defiance to the last, but he is stubborn, and even his warlike wife, who goes into battle alongside her husband, and his daughters urge the need for compromise; Pharnace is arguably a traitor but not a villain, for he is convinced that he has chosen the right course of action in the circumstances and that his father's obsessive hostility toward Rome has led only to the devastation of his country. The play therefore draws its strength from the tension between heroic values and political necessity that Corneille exploited so successfully in some of his major plays.

The success of *La Mort de Mitridate* established La Calprenède as one of the most promising playwrights of the new generation and brought him some financial reward. He immediately produced two more plays for the 1636 season but temporarily abandoned tragedy for tragicomedy, always in demand from play producers. *Bradamante* (first performed 1636; published 1637), a dramatized episode from Ludovico Ariosto's *Orlando furioso* (1516), and *Clarionte, ou Le Sacrifice sanglant* (Clarionte, or The Bloody Sacrifice, first performed 1636; published 1637), a run-of-the-mill tragicomedy including oracles, a monster, and a deus ex machina in the form of an army come to rescue the hero and heroine, are the kinds of plays that could be relied upon to attract an audience. From the modern point of view, they show the extent to which La Calprenède was naturally drawn toward the *romanesque* (romantic), a field in which he excelled in later years.

Over the following two years, he turned back to tragedy and revealed a particular interest in subjects drawn from sixteenth-century English history, not a source of material usually called on by French playwrights. *Jeanne, Reyne d'Angleterre* (Jane, Queen of England, first performed 1637; published 1638) deals with the trial and execution of Lady Jane Grey and is constructed around the conflict between morality and political expediency. Both Jane and Mary Tudor emerge as political innocents who believe in justice and equity: they detest the intrigues and *raison d'état* (reason of state) they are told are necessary to stay in power. Elizabeth, on the other hand, a self-confessed admirer of Herod and Tiberius, sees clemency as weakness. The worst thing Mary can wish on the counselors who have supported Elizabeth's ruthless maxims is that they should be ruled by Elizabeth after Mary's own death. No doubt the intensity of this conflict was what led La Calprenède to refer to *Jeanne, Reyne d'Angleterre* as "une tragedie que j'avois cherement aymée" (a tragedy I loved dearly), but in *Le Comte d'Essex* (The Earl of Essex,

Title page for the second volume of a later edition of La Calprenède's first novel (1642–1645), set in the time of Alexander the Great (from the 1978 facsimile edition)

first performed 1637; published 1639) he showed how the addition of a love interest to a political conflict, a formula adopted in the same year by Pierre Du Ryer for his successful *Alcionée* (1640), could create a much greater effect. The play concerns the dilemma experienced by Elizabeth when confronted with evidence that Essex, whom she loves, has been plotting against her. She puts him on trial but hopes that he will avail himself of a ring she has given him to beg for mercy. Essex is a proud man who expects others to accept him at his own estimation and scorns his judges publicly as little men who have achieved nothing. He is also unscrupulous with women and fails to consider that Lady Cecil, who had been his mistress, would feel sufficiently resentful to decide not to deliver the ring to Elizabeth. The result is another telling exploration of the tension between heroic values and political reality.

La Calprenède was now recognized as one of the major playwrights of the day. He continued to pursue his career as a soldier, however, as comments in the prefaces to his plays show. He reports that he has been in Germany, where he has suffered from starvation, and that some of his works have been printed during absences from Paris. A publisher's note in *Jeanne, Reyne d'Angleterre,* printed during one of these absences, even refers to "feu Monsieur de La Calprenède" (the late Monsieur de La Calprenède), presumably following an inaccurate report of his death. In his own mind, La Calprenède had difficulty reconciling his occupation as a dramatist with his status as a gentleman and a soldier. He comments that it is "desavantageux & fatal" (disadvantageous and disastrous) to a gentleman's reputation to be skilled at the arts: if he knows how to sing or play the lute or write verse, he will be known only for that activity, however good he is at more serious occupations.

La Mort des enfans d'Hérodes, ou Suite de Mariane (The Death of the Children of Herod, or a Sequel to Mariane, performed 1638; published 1639) was, as the subtitle indicates, an attempt to exploit the success of Tristan L'Hermite's tragedy *La Mariane,* performed and published in 1636 and greatly applauded for Montdory's representation of Herod. The tyrant as shown by La Calprenède is essentially much as he is in *La Mariane* except that he is now tormented by remorse for the death of Mariane and incapable of separating the suspicion, jealousy, and ruthlessness that have kept him in power from other emotions. The study of character and confrontation makes this play a worthy sequel to Tristan's and confirms the evolution of the concept of tragedy at the time. On the other hand, *Edouard* (Edward, performed 1639; published 1640), a tragicomedy that again draws on English history, more specifically the reign of Edward III, and *Phalante* (performed 1640; published 1642), a tragedy, reveal how permeable was the barrier between tragedy and tragicomedy. The former avoids the *romanesque* excesses of many tragicomedies and presents an emotional struggle, but it concludes happily; the latter includes a classic opposition between friendship and love of the kind regularly analyzed in novels, but it ends with the death of all three protagonists.

Herménigilde (performed 1641–1642; published 1643) is unusual in two respects and illustrates the way in which La Calprenède had learned to react to trends in the taste of the theatergoing public. It is a martyr tragedy, based on a Latin drama by Père Nicolas Caussin, confessor to King Louis XIII, and is written in prose. In the same year as La Calprenède's play was performed, or the previous year, at least five martyr plays were produced in Paris and, of those, three were in prose. La Calprenède evidently felt that this pattern would please the public, though he could not resist adding a conflict between paternal feelings and *raison d'état* to the religious theme.

Neither the fashion for martyr plays nor that for plays in prose lasted more than a year or two, but La Calprenède had in any case decided to give up the theater in favor of prose fiction. He was not alone in abandoning the theater: Georges de Scudéry, Jean Puget de La Serre, and Jean Desmarets de Saint-Sorlin wrote no plays after 1642. The death of Richelieu in December 1642 was a major factor, but the theater was already entering a difficult period with a constant search for new themes with which to please the audience. The novel (or romance), on the other hand, had found a new strength with Marin Le Roy, sieur de Gomberville's *Polexandre* (1637) and Scudéry's *Ibrahim* (1641). The former had created the archetype of a superhuman hero; the latter had established the model of the novel as a prose epic with rules and structures of its own. La Calprenède, whose creative instinct had always drawn him toward the *romanesque,* combined these characteristics in a novel that expressed better than any other the ideological essence of the 1640s.

Cassandre (translated as *Cassandra, the Fam'd Romance,* 1652) was published in five parts (ten volumes) between 1642 and 1645. Its framework is built around the history of Alexander the Great, but La Calprenède skillfully shifts the focal point so that Alexander is tangential to the main action, a force the other characters must constantly take into account but who is seldom seen. In choosing this setting, La Calprenède was responding to an increasing public interest in the heroic figures of the ancient and modern worlds, especially Alexander the Great. La Calprenède's hero, Oroondate, prince of Scythia, is Alexander's rival for the love of Statira, daughter of the defeated Persian king, Darius. The blending of history and fiction is heightened by the use of dual identities: the historical Statira becomes Cassandre for much of the novel; her brother appears under both of the names he bore in history, Artaxerxe and Arsace; and the wholly fictional Oroondate becomes Oronte. All of the factual information is intended to add plausibility to the invented episodes.

The dominant characteristic of all the heroes, and indeed of the heroines, is their moral autonomy. For the men, duties to father and country take second place to the pursuit of glory, and they feel a greater affinity with *généreux* (men of noble spirit) in the enemy camp than with many on their own side. The women maintain their moral freedom by ensuring that no one—and certainly no man—can claim to have made them do anything that might affect their heroic image adversely. In such a world, love becomes an exercise in self-assertion, a kind of emotional duel. Confrontations arise over misunderstandings; concessions have to be made with great care to ensure pride does not suffer; and honor must be satisfied.

An unusual feature of the novel is that most of the major female characters—Statira, Parisatis, Barsine, Alcione, and Hermione—are widows, which in seventeenth-century terms meant they were free from the tutelage of either a father or a husband. Tallemant's mischievous explanation is that La Calprenède was in love with a widow, "une vieille mademoiselle Hamont" (an elderly lady, Mistress Hamont), the "Caliste" to whom the work is dedicated, and that, having played the sighing lover for too long, he wrote his own novel full of widows showing cruelty to their lovers.

In a foreword to volume 5 (1644), La Calprenède announced that he was changing his style from that of the historians he had been using as sources to an epic tone, that of Homer, Virgil, and Torquato Tasso. The explanation lies in the resounding victories gained in 1643 by the duc d'Enghien, later known as le Grand Condé. Already conditioned to look for manifestations of heroism in the world around them, the French seized upon Enghien as the incarnation of the Alexander legend and loaded onto him all the attributes of the ideal hero. La Calprenède became Enghien's Virgil, and Enghien responded appreciatively, taking the latest volume of *Cassandre* with him on campaign and reading it when battle was done.

La Calprenède's second novel was written according to the same formula as *Cassandre,* mixing historical tradition with fiction. In *Cléopâtre* (1646–1657; translated as *Hymen's Praeludia, or Love's Masterpiece,* 1665), the main characters are drawn from the relatively little-known fringes of the age of Augustus: Césarion, Coriolan (Juba II), Cléopâtre (daughter of Antony and Cleopatra), Candace, and Marcel all appear in the histories but are sufficiently indistinct to allow the author to claim *vraisemblance* (verisimilitude) if not *vérité* (truth) for the adventures he has created around them. The novel is dedicated to Enghien, then approaching the peak of his heroic reputation, and La Calprenède claims him as the model for all his heroes. The reader therefore might have expected a transposition of the heroic values illustrated in *Cassandre* to the Roman world. Yet, a fundamental difference is noticeable from the start. The urge for glory and the fierce pride are still assumed but are rarely illustrated: though the heroes would still claim to be morally autonomous, they are now chiefly of interest for their submissive attitude toward the women they love. Woman has emerged as morally superior to man because she is capable of

controlling her passions, whereas his will is powerless in the face of love.

La Calprenède had sensed the change brought about by the growing current of feminism under the regency of Anne of Austria and the consequent desire for *galanterie* (gallantry) with its analysis of the metaphysics of love. Not everyone apparently was ready for the change, for at the beginning of volume 4 (1648), the author urges his readers to defer making comparisons with *Cassandre* until they have read more of the novel, which will be "plus étendu" (broader) than they may be expecting. Publication stopped temporarily after volume 6 (1649).

During this time, La Calprenède continued to devote his energies to two parallel careers. In 1649 he was a contributor to *L'Eslite des bouts rimez de ce temps* (The Best of the Rhymed-Ending Poetic Challenges of Our Time), a collection of verses remarkable only for their linguistic gymnastics, and he attended the *samedis* (Saturdays) of Madeleine de Scudéry, a literary gathering for those with *précieux* (aesthetically refined) leanings. Yet, in 1650 he was made *Gentilhomme ordinaire de la chambre du roi* (Gentleman in Ordinary of the King's Bedchamber), probably as a reward for having undertaken diplomatic missions on behalf of the Crown.

In 1648 La Calprenède confirmed his interest in widows by marrying a woman who had already buried two husbands. Magdalaine de Lyée was originally from Rouen and had married a wealthy gentleman, Jean de Vieuxpont. After his death she married Arnoul de Bracque, also an owner of estates, but he met a sudden death after only eighteen months of marriage. Common gossip had it that, while still a girl, she had been made to go through an illicit wedding ceremony with a man called La Lande, and that he had shot Bracque out of jealousy. Tallemant claimed that she married La Calprenède for his novels, which she adored, and that she inserted a clause in the marriage contract (6 December 1648) requiring him to complete his *Cléopâtre*. Since this last claim is demonstrably untrue, however, her earlier life might have been less colorful than her contemporaries liked to think. She and La Calprenède had one child—a daughter, Jeanne—who was baptized on 6 September 1653, but the couple separated in 1659.

Certainly, La Calprenède's wife was active in the literary circles of the *précieuses,* for she contributed a "Décret d'un cœur infidèle" (Decree of an Unfaithful Heart) to the *Recueil de pièces en prose* (Anthology of Prose) of 1661 and in the same year published a work of *galanterie, Les Nouvelles et divertissements de la princesse Alcidiane* (The Novels and Diversions of Princess Alcidiane). She also influenced her husband in the move toward *galanterie* in *Cléopâtre,* publication of which resumed after the Fronde (a series of conflicts during

Title page and illustration for the seventh volume (1664), the last by La Calprenède, of the historical novel about the legendary founder of the French monarchy that was completed by Pierre d'Ortigue de Vaumorière (Sterling Memorial Library, Yale University)

the minority of Louis XIV) with two volumes in 1653 and the final four in 1657. The work became thoroughly permeated by the spirit of the salons of the 1650s: groups of characters discuss the relationship between a particular hero and heroine and debate the questions of emotional principle it raises. In another respect, however, these later volumes are surprisingly out of line with the ethos of the 1650s, for they depict a tension between the authority of Augustus, absolute ruler of Rome, a man who can be cruel and use his power to perpetrate injustice, and the *généreux* princes, who represent the ideal of a morally independent aristocracy. In the aftermath of the Fronde, with the traditional code of the *noblesse d'épée* (nobility of the sword) mistrusted and an absolute royal authority recognized as the necessary guarantee of stability, such a perspective was daring in a novel.

La Calprenède's commitment to writing was such that, when *Cléopâtre* was completed, there was no question of his retiring. He took out a *privilège* (permission to publish) for a new novel, *Faramond, ou L'histoire de France* (1661–1670, translated as *Pharamond, or The History of France,* 1677), on 20 May 1658 but must have felt equally drawn to the theater, since a new tragicomedy, "Bellissaire," his first for twenty years, was performed at the Hôtel de Bourgogne in July 1659, although no evidence indicates that it was ever published. The heroic novel as La Calprenède understood it, however, posed something of a problem in the current climate, as *Cléopâtre* had shown. The ethic of moral autonomy essentially defined the kind of state for which Condé had fought during the Fronde. But Condé was now a rebel, allied with Spain, and the French had gone most of the way toward accepting the need for an absolute monarch. La Calprenède was still loyal to the legend of Condé: a letter from the great conqueror in Brussels dated 17 February 1657 indicates that La Calprenède was planning a work on him, possibly a biography, and expresses Condé's concern that the writer's position might be jeopardized. On the other hand, the first four volumes of *Faramond* did not appear until 1661, by which time Louis XIV had emerged victorious over Spain, and Condé had returned submissively to France, pardoned by his magnanimous king.

Faramond is consequently something of a hybrid. Set in the fifth-century Rhineland, it ostensibly recounts events in the life of the supposed founder of the French monarchy, Pharamond, and devotes many pages to relating the myth that had grown up around him, tracing his descent from Francus, son of Hector of Troy. The work is dedicated to the king, and the author takes every opportunity to show that his ancestor shared the characteristics attributed by eulogists to the modern ruler—a preference for peace over war, a desire to rule for the benefit of all his people, and an awareness of the need to reward merit. At the same time, the characters frequently behave like those of twenty years earlier. Indeed, the main plot bears a close similarity to that of Corneille's *Le Cid* (first performed 1637): Rosemonde is obliged to seek vengeance against Faramond for the death of her brother and promises to marry the man who kills him. Faramond offers her his life, but she insists that he must be killed in combat, while begging him to defend himself so that her love for him can retain some hope. Balamir, Viridomare, and other heroes move from one kingdom to another, like Oroondate, pursuing their own interests until the time comes for them to ascend the throne.

La Calprenède's contemporaries admired the scope of *Faramond* and approved the aim of lauding the monarchy, but de Scudéry's *Clélie* (1654–1660) had accustomed them to a novel given over totally to *galanterie,* and they found La Calprenède's approach somewhat outdated. Moreover, events cut short his career. On 31 March 1663 Jean Loret reported in *La Muse historique* that La Calprenède had had an accident. He had wanted to impress the ladies with his skill at shooting, but his gun had exploded in his face, seriously disfiguring him. Some six months later, another accident put an end to his life. The date is not known with certainty, but since Loret reported it on 20 October 1663, it is likely to have occurred during the preceding week. Other commentators indicate that La Calprenède suffered head injuries when thrown from his horse at Grand-Andely in Normandy, where he was buried. Only seven volumes of *Faramond* had appeared by then, and La Calprenède's publisher,

Antoine de Sommaville, was quick to visit La Calprenède's house to take charge of any manuscripts and notes he might have left. The work was brought to a conclusion in a further five volumes (1664–1670) by Pierre d'Ortigue, sieur de Vaumorière.

La Calprenède's death cut short his plans not only to finish *Faramond* but also to write a play for which Molière had paid him an advance of 800 livres. It also marked the end of the prose epic novel: in a letter dated 15 December 1663, critic Jean Chapelain remarked that the public was no longer reading these extended novels "qui sont tombés avec La Calprenède" (which went out with La Calprenède). Comments in the letters of Madame de Sévigné, however, indicate that, for the generation that had grown up with them, "la beauté des sentiments, la violence des passions, la grandeur des événements" (the beauty of the emotions, the strength of the passions, the scale of the events) included in them could still be a source of pleasure. La Calprenède's plays and novels are not likely, in themselves, to appeal to the modern reader. However, put back into their own context, they have much to reveal about the mindset of those who lived in mid-seventeenth-century France and, as the literature sometimes characterized as "baroque" has come to be seen as of interest in its own right rather than as merely the prelude to a greater "classical" period, La Calprenède has come into his own, recognized as a dynamic and innovative writer.

References:

Mark Bannister, *Privileged Mortals: The French Heroic Novel, 1630–1660* (Oxford: Oxford University Press, 1983);

Jean Chapelain, *Lettres de Jean Chapelain,* 2 volumes, edited by Tamizey de Larroque (Paris: Imprimerie Nationale, 1880–1883), II: 340;

Sylvie Bostarron Chevalley, *Molière en son temps, 1622–1673* (Paris & Geneva: Minkoff, 1973);

H. Carrington Lancaster, "La Calprenède, dramatist," *Modern Philology,* 18 (1920): 121–141, 345–360;

Jean Loret, *La Muze historique,* 4 volumes, edited by J. Ravenel and E. de la Pelouze (Paris: Jannet, 1857–1878), IV: 35, 114–115;

Marlies Mueller, *Les Idées politiques dans le roman héroïque de 1630 à 1670,* Harvard Studies in Romance Languages (Lexington, Ky.: French Forum, 1984);

Marie de Rabutin-Chantal de Sévigné, *Lettres,* 12 volumes, edited by Philippe A. Grouvelle (Paris: Garnéry, 1811), II: 157–158, 162, 166;

Gédéon Tallemant des Réaux, *Historiettes,* 2 volumes, edited by Antoine Adam, Bibliothèque de la Pléiade, no. 142 (Paris: Gallimard, 1960, 1961), II: 584–588.

Marie-Madeleine, comtesse de Lafayette

(1634 – 25 May 1693)

Christian Biet
Université Paris X–Nanterre, France

BOOKS: *La Princesse de Monpensier,* anonymous (Paris: T. Jolly, 1662); translated as *The Princess of Monpensier* (London, 1666);

Zayde, histoire espagnole, 2 volumes, as M. de Segrais (Paris: C. Barbin, 1670, 1671); translated by P. Porter as *Zayde, a Spanish History* (London: Printed by T. Milbourn for William Cademan, 1678);

La Princesse de Clèves, 2 volumes, anonymous (Paris: C. Barbin, 1678); translated as *The Princess of Cleves: The Most Famed Romance* (London: Printed for R. Bentley and M. Magnes, 1679);

Histoire de Mme Henriette d'Angleterre, première femme de Philippe de France, duc d'Orléans (Amsterdam: M.-C. Le Cène, 1720); translated by Ann Floyd as *Fatal Gallantry, or The Secret History of Henrietta, Princess of England, Daughter of K. Charles the I. and Wife of Phillip of France, Duke of Orleans . . .* (London: Printed for F. Clay, 1722);

Mémoires de la cour de France pour les années 1688 et 1689 (Amsterdam: J.-F. Bernard, 1731).

Editions and Collections: *Mémoires de Mme de La Fayette,* edited by Eugène Asse (Paris: Librairie des Bibliophiles, 1890);

Vie de la princesse d'Angleterre, edited by Marie-Thérèse Hipp (Geneva: Droz, 1967);

Histoire de la princesse de Montpensier sous le règne de Charles IXème, roi de France; Histoire de la comtesse de Tende, edited by Micheline Cuénin (Geneva: Droz, 1979);

La Princesse de Clèves, edited by Jean Mesnard (Paris: Imprimerie Nationale, 1980);

La Princesse de Montpensier (1662); La Princesse de Clèves (1678), edited by Christian Biet and Pierre Ronzeaud (Paris: Magnard, 1989);

Œuvres complètes, edited by Roger Duchêne (Paris: F. Bourin, 1990);

Romans et nouvelles, edited by Alain Niderst (Paris: Bordas, 1990).

Editions in English: *The Secret History of Henrietta, Princess of England, First Wife of Philippe, Duc d'Orléans; Together with Memoirs of the Court of France for the*

Marie-Madeleine Pioche de La Vergne, comtesse de Lafayette (anonymous portrait, Bibliothèque Nationale, Paris)

Years 1688–1689, translated by J. M. Shelmerdine (New York: Dutton, 1929);

The Princesse de Clèves; The Princesse de Montpensier; The Comtesse de Tende, translated by Terence Cave (Oxford & New York: Oxford University Press, 1992);

The Princess of Clèves: Contemporary Reactions, Criticism, edited by John D. Lyons (New York & London: Norton, 1994).

SELECTED PERIODICAL PUBLICATIONS–
UNCOLLECTED: "La Comtesse de Tende, Histori-
ette," anonymous, *Nouveau Mercure* (September
1718): 35–56.

Madame de Lafayette, born Marie-Madeleine
Pioche de La Vergne but known as the comtesse de
Lafayette after her marriage, came from a family of the
noblesse de robe (class who gained their nobility through
holding high office) that was well connected at court.
Her father, Marc Pioche de La Vergne, was an aristocrat and an engineer close to Cardinal Richelieu
(Armand-Jean du Plessis, duc de Richelieu), chief minister of state to Louis XIII. Her mother, the daughter of
the king's doctor, was an attendant of Marie-Madeleine
de Vignerot, marquise de Combalet, the cardinal's
niece. The family lived in the affluent Luxembourg district of Paris, the area where Lafayette lived for most of
her life. She and her parents were at the center of intellectual life; they mixed with men such as Jacques Le
Pailleur, Etienne Pascal (the father of Blaise), and the
abbé Hédelin d'Aubignac, an author and literary critic.

Marie-Madeleine's father died when she was fifteen, and in 1650 her mother married again, to René-
Renaud de Sévigné, the uncle of Marie de Rabutin
Chantal, marquise de Sévigné, later famous as a letter
writer. That same year, Marie-Madeleine became a
lady-in-waiting to Anne of Austria, the queen.
Marie-Madeleine began to study Latin, Spanish, Italian,
and history at the side of her dear friend Gilles Ménage.
Also at this time she read the fashionable novels of
Madeleine de Scudéry. This blend of classical and con-
temporary culture manifests itself in the letters Lafay-
ette wrote to Ménage throughout the years of the
Fronde, when she and the royal family were exiled in
Anjou, a difficult period for an aristocrat opposed to
Cardinal Jules Mazarin, first minister of France after
Cardinal Richelieu's death in 1642. During this time, in
1655, Marie-Madeleine married (1655) François
Motier, comte de Lafayette, a man fifteen years her
senior who had been a *maréchal* (marshal) in the king's
army. They moved to the Auvergne, and in the space
of a year she gave birth to her first son and lost her
mother, who died in 1656. In 1659 Madame de Lafayette returned to Paris to look after her husband's interests–chiefly debts. While her husband stayed in his
estates, she rejoined her friends and their literary circles. Lafayette died several years later in 1683.

She was intimately involved with the salons of
the literary life of the capital and was well known in
the *galant* circles (the social milieu of urban society that
practiced exceeding refinement of taste and speech following the *préciosité* period) of the time; she even
made an appearance, as "Féliciane," in Somaize's *Grand*
dictionnaire des précieuses (1660). She mixed with the
former *frondeurs* (rebels) who had fought against the
regent queen and Mazarin during the Fronde Revolution of 1648–1652 and also with the emerging critics
on the new literary scene. She was close to Pierre-
Daniel Huet, Jean Regnauld de Segrais, and François
La Rochefoucauld, but also to de Scudéry and
Ménage; in the company of these minds she learned to
debate matters of the heart, to discuss the perils of
"amour-propre" (self-love), and, above all, to address
such questions in a lively and contemporary style. The
first works known to be hers are two literary portraits–
a self-portrait and the "Portrait de Mme la Marquise de
Sévigné, par un inconnu" (Portrait of the Marquise de
Sévigné, by One Unknown), which was published in
an anonymous anthology of *Divers portraits,* and later,
in 1659, by Segrais, in the *Recueil des portraits et éloges en*
vers et en prose (Anthology of Portraits and Elegies in
Verse and in Prose).

Lafayette was a rather independent woman. She
was married to a man of whom she saw little, a common situation in aristocratic families, but the marriage
was unusual in that Lafayette devoted considerable
time and energy to keeping her financial liberty and
some degree of personal freedom. She even took her
battle to court and, as time went on, became skilled at
negotiating the secret rules of a patriarchal system, a
struggle pursued throughout most of her life. This
negotiation of orthodoxy can be seen in other areas of
her life as well. Lafayette appeared to follow the same
rules as other aristocratic women of the seventeenth
century: to occupy her time she read, wrote letters, and
practiced the art of conversation. But Lafayette subverted these rules in one important way, for she also
wrote historical novels. Such a rare act necessarily had
to be secretive.

As an aristocrat and a woman in seventeenth-
century France, Lafayette could not publish works of
fiction or even history in her own name. Such an action
would have been seen as socially demeaning and doubly transgressive, for the writing of novels and history
was men's work, and specifically the work of the bourgeois *gens de lettres* (writers from the educated class).
Women were limited to writing memoirs or letters,
appropriately feminine genres, as did de Sévigné, a
friend of Lafayette's. The example of de Scudéry had
shown that to publish "Grands romans," episodic
mythic or historical novels of romance or heroism, or
pastoral novels was possible. But women could not be
seen to invent anything; such an invention, especially
from a noblewoman, would have shocked the public.

La Princesse de Monpensier (translated as *The Prin-*
cess of Monpensier, 1666), Lafayette's first historical
novel, was therefore published anonymously in 1662.

Lafayette's close friend Gilles Ménage, 1666 (portrait by Bernard Vaillant; Musée Condé, Chantilly)

Lafayette uses the screen of history (specifically the period of religious wars in the second half of the sixteenth century) to disguise her vivid depictions of contemporary love, the dangers of the passions, and social comportment. But her readers were not fooled by the tactic and were desperate to uncover the true identities of the characters depicted. In the story, the female protagonist, Mlle. de Mézières, is shortly to be married to the prince de Monpensier. But she is in love with another man, the duc de Guise, and is herself loved by the desperate Chabanes, a friend of Guise. One night, when Mézières and Guise are together, Monpensier discovers that his wife has a lover. Chabanes steps in to save the day, sacrificing himself in order to save his friend. The prince's jealousy falls upon him; this poor heroic friend dies in absurd circumstances during the Saint-Barthélémy massacre. As for the lovers, the duc de Guise, true to his *galant* nature, is soon unfaithful, and the princess is so wounded by this betrayal that she dies.

Seeing the success of *La Princesse de Monpensier,* Lafayette turned to writing historical biography; her first effort was the *Histoire de Mme Henriette d'Angleterre, première femme de Philippe de France, duc d'Orléans* (written 1665–1670; published 1720; translated as *Fatal Gallantry, or The Secret History of Henrietta, Princess of England,*

Daughter of K. Charles the I. and Wife of Phillip of France, Duke of Orleans . . . , 1722); she then wrote *Zayde, histoire espagnole* (published in 1670 and 1671 under the name of de Segrais, who had indeed helped with some stylistic details; translated as *Zayde, a Spanish History,* 1678). *Histoire de Mme Henriette d'Angleterre* is the story of the daughter of Charles I of England. Born in 1644, she had married Philippe, duc de Orléans, the brother of Louis XIV. Her sudden death in 1670 at the age of twenty-six prompted Jacques-Bénigne Bossuet, bishop of Meaux, to write what is perhaps his most celebrated funeral oration. A friend of Lafayette, the princess had instructed Lafayette to write about her life. The text, however, is not hagiographic; Lafayette keeps a certain distance from her subject, constantly returning to her own concerns, such as the pleasures of gallantry, the dangers of passion, and the necessity of retreat. *Zayde* is a typical seventeenth-century novel (though shorter than those of de Scudéry); it features a linear story line that includes other, smaller stories within an overarching narrative structure, and it displays epic moments and lyrical passages. The story is set at the end of the Middle Ages, in Spain and the Orient. Consalve and Zayde, the lovers, fall for one another after a shipwreck. But before the story reaches the happy ending of their marriage, other characters—Alphonse, Belasire's jealous lover; Dom Garcie; Félime; and Alamire—intervene and present obstacles to the main couple's love. Behind these exotic and medieval characters, moreover, the atmosphere of the Fronde is suggested through thoughts on the betrayal of language and promises. Furthermore, the new analysis of the passions presages the later work of Lafayette with its simple and concise *maximes* (maxims).

In 1671 an advance *privilège* (copyright) was granted to an anonymous author for the writing of a novel called "Le Prince de Clèves." Six years later, a second such copyright was granted for *La Princesse de Clèves* (translated as *The Princess of Cleves: The Most Famed Romance,* 1679), and the novel appeared in 1678. Critics were long unable to learn the identity of the woman behind the masterpiece. Rumors circulated suggesting that Lafayette could only be a front for a real (male) writer; Huet, Segrais, La Rochefoucauld, and Ménage were all cited as possible authors of the work. Recently, many critics have ignored that seventeenth-century texts were often jointly read, debated, and reworked by a group of authors and readers. That scenario was also likely the case for Lafayette's text. But the acknowledgment of such a practice does not make Lafayette an impostor.

La Princesse de Clèves rapidly became a success, and Donneau de Visé, seeking to exploit the popularity of the new and fashionable novel, took up its promotion in his gazette, *Le Mercure Galant* (Paris). Everybody wanted to pronounce judgment on the book, and everybody wanted to read the novel and what was written about it. One of the objects of debate was the famous question of the *aveu,* the Princesse's confession to her husband of her love for Nemours, first asked in the gazette: "Did she have to confess?" At the same time, another debate was springing up about the aesthetics of the novel and the question of its author's identity. J. B. H. du Trousset de Valincour in *Lettres à Mme la marquise de * * * sur le sujet de "La Princesse de Clèves"* (Letters to Madame the Marquise of * * * on the Subject of *La Princesse de Clèves,* anonymously published in 1678) suggested that the confession (whereby a married woman confesses an adultery that has been fantasized but never committed, causing her husband to die of grief) was unlikely—that is, it went against verisimilitude, an important aesthetic category of the time. In answer to Valincour came the *Conversations sur la critique de La Princesse de Clèves* (Conversations on the Criticism of *La Princesse de Clèves,* 1679), published under the name of the Abbé de Charnes and inspired by the supporters of Lafayette. The response sought to justify this exceptional confession by naming it *grand* and *sublime,* terms used to describe Pierre Corneille's tragedies. Charnes claimed that the text was able to stimulate the passions and to move the reader to tears through a simple and straightforward style that echoed contemporary speech. The opposition of verisimilitude and exceptionality fueled aesthetic debates throughout the century, but with this novel both readers and critics seemed to be aware of a sort of birth. The work centered on the analysis of passions and feelings based upon a close observation of their physical and psychological expression. With its conjunction of understatement and hyperbole, moreover, Lafayette's style displayed a tension between the experiences of *préciosité* and the clarity of the neoclassical. Her critics found the style unharmonious, mixing everything together without ever making a choice, but most readers saw the style as the perfect medium for the description of the hesitations and contradictions of the heart.

Added to the debate was the question of how a woman could have written so impressive a work. Was such a thing possible? Was this woman the new de Scudéry, or was the author really a man who might be able to understand the passions, the realities of marriage, and the debates of theology? The anonymous authorship of the text made every answer possible, and Lafayette never officially claimed the work as her own. Her novel belongs to its time, even if it shattered previous understandings of fictional aesthetics.

The novel takes place in sixteenth-century France at the court of Henri II, just before the wars of religion that signaled the end of a world and of the Valois lineage. The novel opens with a portrait of the magnificence and gallantry of the Louvre; into this world arrives a rich young noblewoman of one of the best families in France. She comes to the court in order to be married, and since her father has recently died, her mother alone leads her through the social labyrinth. Her mother, Madame de Chartres, is a widow, severe but just in moral matters, anxious for her daughter's prospects, and above all attentive to the alliances that must be built and refused in order for her daughter to marry well. But Mlle. de Chartres and her eventual husband, M. de Clèves, are not always in line with the contemporary conventions governing marriage. Lafayette deliberately sets the action at the moment (1556) when the first important edicts place marriage under royal and paternal control, and as a result her protagonists find themselves in a sort of legal no-man's-land. This position gives them a certain liberty within an otherwise stable and hierarchical social system and allows them to subvert notions operative within the universe of the novel. Lafayette wrote at a time when a century of tension between Church and State was culminating in the affirmation of the right of the state to exercise a certain control over marriage, defined as the "seminary of the state" by secular authorities. The action of *La Princesse de Clèves* takes place at the moment when the long-existent rumblings of tension between church and state became plainly audible in the Edict of 1556 and in the discussions of canon law during the Council of Trent. Henri II, indeed, was the first king who successfully contested ecclesiastical power and encroached upon the jurisdiction of the Catholic Church.

The description of royal alliances within the novel corresponds to the emergence of marriage as a secular contract in which power was the sole consideration. The vast panorama of court affairs in the first part of the novel offers abundant testimony to the fact that court society concerned itself above all with marital alliances, which were understood as public affairs affecting the workings of the state. Ambition and gallantry were the lifeblood of the court, and they regulated the intrigues between various factions. The court was organized around marriage as a system of political alliances controlling private passions, and these passions could threaten the political system. Alliances did not negate passion; indeed, the politics of power were played out around this tension between political alliance and private passion, in which the functioning of the state itself was at stake. Even the king could not afford to break with established laws governing marriage without disrupting the delicate equilibrium between church and state.

*Interior of Lafayette's Paris apartment, where
she held her celebrated salons*

His choice of partner was ruled by politics, and he was forbidden to marry for love, a rule that applied to most of his subjects but that was even more stringently applied to the monarch. For a king, the place of love was not in marriage but in his relationship with a mistress. A marriage of passion was thought to disturb conjugal tranquility and, in the case of the king, to disrupt peace between states. The incompatibility of passion and marriage, then, was at once a declaration of principle, a prerequisite, and an observation.

Lafayette sets her novel within this world, where marriage is a contract controlled by paternal authority. By collapsing together two historical periods (the court of Henri II, where the action takes place, and the reign of Louis XIV, during which she wrote), she describes both the contemporary state of patriarchal authority and its origin in the 1560s. As if to demonstrate that, at least at court, marriage had lost its sacramental status, Lafayette insists on the importance of *galanterie* (the polite, sophisticated, and sometimes hyperbolic manners of courtly love) in a society in which love and politics are inextricably linked. Caught up in court intrigue, marriages here play a key role in the politics of power and passion; they are a game that leaves little room for noble sentiments and undermines the respect-

ability of the institution itself. At court, even those affairs that did not directly involve the king and queen could still become embroiled in politics. Lafayette seems to imply that this secular understanding of marriage is an extremely dangerous one. Draining marriage laws of their sacramental significance makes these laws an exclusively human affair and thus renders them vulnerable to manipulation. In view of this social danger, one must almost of necessity recognize the resonance of the widow Lafayette's life in the story of her princess, who chooses to retreat from the court and to refuse to remarry after her husband's death, and who thus avoids entanglement in the court politics of passion and marriage.

Against this understanding of marriage, the union of M. and Mme. de Clèves has a somewhat different character; it is subtly presented as something outside the norm. Through a series of particular circumstances, the protagonists find themselves from the beginning in an ambiguous legal situation that causes them to question, and ultimately to suffer from, the difference to which they lay claim. At first glance, nothing in the opening of the novel contradicts the rules that make marriage a contract between families and the seminary of the state. Mme. de Chartres returns to court to arrange the marriage of her daughter, "un des grands partis qu'il y eût en France" (one of the most eligible [women] in France). The court involves itself in the politics and intrigue of the match. In the interests of their house and lineage, fathers control, forbid, and debate the marriage. The proximity of these noble families to the king also turns the marriage into a bone of contention between the queen and Mme. de Valentinois. Meanwhile, the object of these dealings, Mlle. de Chartres, remains silent, refusing to voice her opinion. She will only speak up when M. de Clèves insists.

But a crack in this homogeneous system opens up when the reader learns that Mlle. de Chartres's suitors are not the first-born sons—that is, they cannot inherit the family fortunes and titles. What is more, these suitors are truly in love. Like his unhappy rival M. de Guise and his friend Sancerre, M. de Clèves is a younger son. Like them, he knows that he cannot hope for too illustrious a match. Thus, when he falls in love with an unknown woman he sees at the jeweler's, he has already broken the contract that binds him to his family line. The thought of *galanterie* does not even cross M. de Clèves's mind. What he wants is love and marriage, the classic obsession of younger sons for whom this road is usually blocked. Instead of following the model of paternal authority in marital matters, moreover, he not only wants to marry but also wishes to choose his own spouse. Inevitably, his request meets with his father's refusal. His is a double transgression since he respects neither the code of rank (the right of his father to choose for him) nor of marriage (the priority of the interests of one's house or lineage when considering marriage).

Like Guise, his rival in love, Clèves fears that people will think he is more interested in the wealth than the person of his loved one. Lafayette tells the reader the fear comes out of a lover's shyness, but with good reason in the light of prevailing customs. Both Guise and Clèves are caught in the politics of alliances and in the rivalry between factions. With little wealth and thus no room to maneuver, younger sons must renounce their desires; there is simply no way to bend the rules. Despite their passion, Guise and Clèves are bound by the theory of marriage as a contract between families. Only in relation to this particular situation will Clèves gain status as an exception. Clèves's stroke of luck—if it can be called that—is that Mlle. de Chartres is once again turned down. The prince dauphin, son of the duc de Monpensier, had appeared interested in the match, but Mme. de Valentinois steps in to thwart the plans of the Vidame and Mme. de Chartres. The traditional view of marriage as an advantageous alliance desired by both parties is henceforth shelved, like a broken dream. The situation is so grave that "personne n'osait plus penser à Mlle de Chartres, par la crainte de déplaire au roi ou par la pensée de ne pas réussir auprès d'une personne qui avait espéré un prince du sang" (no man now dared cast his thoughts in the direction of Mlle. de Chartres, whether for fear of displeasing the King or of not succeeding with a woman who had hoped for a prince of the blood royal), quite a dilemma for the marital plans of Mme. de Chartres.

This stalemate is relieved when Clèves's father, Nevers, dies, thus enabling the son (described as displaying "tant de grandeur et de bonnes qualités" and "tant de sagesse pour son âge" [courage and generosity] and [wisdom beyond his years]) to marry Mlle. de Chartres. After the death of Nevers, the lovesick Clèves is prepared to override his father's decision, even if doing so entails defying certain codes or "considerations." Clèves takes yet another step beyond societal norms and once again transgresses the customs of the court; custom forbids a younger son to go against the interests of his house, however young or in love he may be. Clèves, however, is not in the same situation as Guise, whose house rules with an iron hand. Clèves's infraction, then, is not serious, insofar as it threatens neither the House of Nevers nor the political structure of the court and state. The union proves to be without scandal, and the king, against expectations, approves it. Clèves thus ceases to be a son and becomes instead a husband and a lover. In this narrative Lafayette uses the situation of a power vacuum within a family in order to propose alternatives to the theory of marriage as family contract. Nevers dies at the right moment, and the narrator, surprisingly enough, affirms the disappearance of all political and familial ties by describing Clèves as now "dans une entière liberté de suivre son inclination" (entirely free to follow his inclination).

Clèves finds an ally in Mme. de Chartres, who had hitherto been determined to marry her daughter in accordance with the rules of court. Mme. de Chartres is now obliged to lower her expectations. Clèves declares his love to Mlle. de Chartres, seeking to gain her heart before he consults her mother; he pursues her in the name of his love for her, the principle upon which he intends to base his marriage: "Ce qui troublait sa joie, était la crainte de ne lui être pas agréable, et il eût préféré le bonheur de lui plaire à la certitude de l'épouser sans en être aimé" (The only thing that marred his joy was the fear that she might not like him enough. He would have preferred the happiness of knowing she cared for him to the certainty of marrying her without love). But the code of marital conduct—as elaborated by theologians, taught by directors of conscience, and incorporated into various catechisms—formally forbids passion between spouses; to feel passion for one's wife is to commit adultery. Clèves thus transgresses the holy laws of matrimony through his refusal of one of its terms—conjugal love as *amitié* (friendship). The interpreters of canon law see *amicitia* (the Latin word for *friendship*, here meaning something between love and friendship) as a practice that will keep passion at bay. According to this doctrine, marriage consists of *amicitia* and mutual assistance. Such a doctrine implies that the beauty, lineage, conduct, and wealth of the wife are associated with her virtue, and it connects all these attributes to the lineage, wisdom, and knowledge of the husband. Both Mme. de Chartres and her daughter share this understanding of marriage, but M. de Clèves rejects it, and he eventually falls because of his passion. This unusual husband refuses to play the usual role and instead wishes to be loved passionately.

At this point the tranquil and conformist existence of Mme. de Clèves is interrupted. The princess falls in love, becoming prey to a passion that is described as an irresistible "inclination." The object of her desire is none other than the prince of *galanterie* himself, the incomparable Nemours, whose *galanterie* is unequalled even by the Vidame. Nemours should be doubly distant from the princess; not only is he presented from the beginning of the novel as a master *galant,* but he has also been promised in marriage to the Queen of England. But he is now to enter quite another world, and in his love for Mme. de Clèves, he, too, takes on the status of exception, considering M. de Clèves as a rival for the affections of his beloved. The

Frontispiece for the second volume, published in 1671, of Lafayette's historical novel about a pair of lovers in medieval Spain (Bibliothèque Nationale, Paris)

bashful lover, Nemours takes a room in order to spy on the princess and thinks he will die of his pain. Having first toyed with the idea of an affair and having then felt jealous of the princess's husband, Nemours, like Clèves before him, is now beginning to consider the possibility of a marriage of love. Both husband and lover thus present the princess with the same model of marriage, one that brings new feelings to old roles. But the princess thinks that no man, with the exception of her husband, could remain in love with his wife, and she is even more certain that Nemours could never love in such a way. Though she had once fantasized about such a relationship with him, now the idea of enduring and reciprocal love within marriage seems impossible.

In the novel, then, only M. and Mme. de Clèves represent the theory of marriage based on love; Mme. de Clèves estimates that Nemours, despite his protests, is thoroughly incapable of such a union. And Lafayette shows her to be right in this judgment. At the end of the novel the reader learns that over the years Nemours's pain and passion have diminished. His departure from the norm was only a temporary one. Though he had experienced "la passion la plus ardente et la plus tendre qui ait jamais touché le coeur d'un homme" (the most ardent and tender passion that has ever touched a human heart), Nemours can only gaze from afar at a marriage based on love. The confusion of feelings and social roles affects the three main characters equally, but each resolves his or her confusion in a different way: Clèves never wavers from his belief in marital love and dies from it; Nemours suffers for a time but eventually returns to court life; and Mme. de Clèves almost dies from her passion but learns, as a result of this brush with death, to combat such dangerous emotion.

Mme. de Clèves may be said to have followed what Nemours reproachfully terms a "un fontôme de devoir" (phantom of duty), by literally observing her mother's words, believing that retreat (in contrast to *galanterie*) guarantees a status of exception and thus a kind of peace. But her phantom of duty is cchocd by a "phantom of *galanterie*." The princess tries in vain to resist *galanterie* but cannot. Jealousy, the husband's manipulation, and the tragic outcomes all make this tale one of a symbolically experienced *galanterie*. The exceptional status of Mme. de Clèves's avowal is undone by Clèves's disdain, a device frequently used in *galant* novels to reinforce the hero's suffering and make his death more plausible. Mme. de Clèves's marriage does not, in fact, escape from any of the established social paradigms, but neither does it fit neatly with any of them. In little more than a year, the princess learns to distinguish various marital models, and she ends by rejecting them all. At the center of debate but in a position of increas-

supposedly chivalrous Nemours initially displays all the hallmarks of the *galant*. He stoops to pettiness in order to discredit Clèves in the eyes of the princess, and he even hopes for the death of his rival. But his tactics of *galanterie*–such as manipulating the Vidame in order to gain an interview with the princess–suddenly give way, and he withdraws from the court feeling that all is hopeless. His retreat is all the more extraordinary in that he is the epitome of court life and the master of court intrigue. The most handsome, the most *galant,* the most adept at seduction–in short, the most *everything*–courtier renounces the world that has shaped him. For such a man to fall sick with love is indeed surprising, and Lafayette emphasizes the shock of his actions. A newly

ing isolation, she finds nothing in customary law that pertains to her unusual situation. She must therefore solve the problem herself, mindful of the multiple tensions of her situation and of the fact that no viable conjugal union is possible within the society of the novel. At this point the princess, exceptional in all respects like her husband and Nemours, becomes a fully developed character. At the beginning of the novel she is a creature entirely shaped by her social environment. By the end she has become an individual who subverts existing codes through her interaction with the two male protagonists who are themselves in a sort of legal limbo. This interaction brings her to withdraw from the world. Mme. de Clèves at first considers Nemours's proposal of a marriage based on love and then rejects it, fearing that his passion will diminish over time and be perverted by *galanterie*. She concludes that only her dead husband, a man whom she never loved, was able to sustain such a marriage; her conclusion underlines the illusory quality of such an ideal. The series of refusals can only lead to a rejection of the world. Her near death experience makes Mme. de Clèves realize that the sundry equivocal solutions of the secular world are all inadequate and destined for failure. To live in such a world would mean living a lie. Torn by such a possibility, she chooses instead something that previously had been hinted at but never clearly formulated—withdrawal from the world. Since nothing is possible within a universe governed by human laws and since nothing is possible outside those laws as long as one remains in the secular world, Mme. de Clèves decides both to follow and to transcend her mother's advice. Not only does she flee from the world, but she also overcomes her passion (already weakened by her illness) and directs her soul toward God. She spends her time alone, "dans une profonde retraite et dans des occupations plus saintes que celles de couvents les plus austères" (in profound retreat and in occupations more saintly than those of the most austere houses of religion).

La Princesse de Clèves is a novel about marriage and about the dangers of passion. Here, passion—*libido sentiendi*—tears people apart, leads to mistake and sin, and ruins bodies and hearts. The princess's unbending will does not prevent her from suffering. Nor does it prevent the suffering of others. Her husband's unreciprocated passion brings about his tragic end. She herself, an innocent and well-brought-up young woman, is seized by a terrible passion that threatens her world and her own salvation. Nemours, the young aristocratic hero, starts out as a conqueror and is then conquered by his own passion and the ensuing rejection. Later, his passion dissipates and he marries another. Close to La Rochefoucauld and to Jansenism, Lafayette, in her novel, reiterates their main themes: the only positive

state is retreat—the only way to escape self-love and resist passion, and the only hope of attaining virtue. A classical novel of the analysis of passions, written in a classical style (understatement, simplicity, clarity, abstraction), *La Princesse de Clèves* represents the tragic beginning of the modern novel.

After this extraordinary novel, Lafayette followed the model of her heroine. After a period at court, she retreated into retirement and solitude. She went to Savoie with Jeanne-Baptiste de Savoie-Nemours, the regent of the duchy, and like any other aristocratic woman, she wrote letters to her friends. In her illness, and greatly troubled by the death of her beloved friend La Rochefoucauld in 1680, she became closer and closer to the Jansenists. She died on 25 May 1693 in Paris, diminished by her illness and melancholy and anxious about her salvation, as her friend de Sévigné wrote later (*Lettre à la comtesse de Guitaut, 3 juin 1693*). In 1718 the *Nouveau Mercure* published a short story, "La Comtesse de Tende," attributed some six years later to Lafayette (the date of composition is unknown). Although some critics still hesitate over this attribution, this text seems like a darker and more tragic *Princesse de Monpensier*. Again set in the mid sixteenth century, it tells the tale of a woman who marries the unfaithful comte de Tende, falls in love with the chevalier de Navarre, discovers her pregnancy when her lover dies, confesses to her husband, and then dies herself, full of guilt.

If Lafayette has been, according to the French history of literature, the first modern novelist, she has become, during more recent years, a woman who lived and narrated the female experiences of the human heart. She has also become a memorialist and a major actor of the literary circles of the second half of the seventeenth century.

Letters:

Lettres de Marie-Madeleine Pioche de la Vergne, comtesse de La Fayette et de Gilles Ménage, edited by Harry Ashton (Liverpool: University Press / London: Hodder & Stoughton, 1924);
Madame de Lafayette, Correspondance, 2 volumes, edited by André Beaunier (Paris: Gallimard, 1942);
Lettres de Madame de Lafayette au chevalier de Lescheraine (Paris: Nizet, 1970).

Bibliography:

J. W. Scott, *Madame de Lafayette, a Selective Critical Bibliography* (London: Grant & Cutler, 1974).

Biographies:

André Beaunier, *La Jeunesse de Madame de La Fayette* (Paris: Flammarion, 1921);

Harry Ashton, *Madame de Lafayette, sa vie et ses œuvres* (Cambridge: Cambridge University Press, 1922);

Emile Magne, *Madame de Lafayette en ménage, d'après des documents inédits* (Paris: Emile-Paul Frères, 1926);

Marie-Jeanne Durry, *Madame de Lafayette* (Paris: Mercure de France, 1962);

Roger Duchêne, *Madame de Lafayette, la romancière aux cent bras* (Paris: Fayard, 1988).

References:

Jean-Antoine de Charnes, *Conversations sur la Critique de La Princesse de Clèves,* edited by François Weil (Tours: Université François-Rabelais de Tours, 1973);

Joan DeJean, *Tender Geographies: Women and the Origins of the Novel in France* (New York: Columbia University Press, 1991);

J.-M. Delacomptée, *Madame, la cour, la mort* (Paris: Gallimard, 1992);

Roger Duchêne and Pierre Ronzeaud, eds., "Mme de La Fayette, La princesse de Montpensier, La princesse de Clèves: journée d'étude organisée par le C.M.R. 17 (Marseille, 18 novembre 1989)," *Littératures Classiques,* supplement to no. 12 (Paris: Aux Amateurs de Livres, 1989);

R. Francillon, *L'Œuvre romanesque de Madame de Lafayette* (Paris: Corti, 1973);

Gérard Genette, "Vraisemblance et motivation," in *Figures II* (Paris: Seuil, 1969);

Elizabeth C. Goldsmith and Dena Goodman, eds., *Going Public: Women and Publishing in Early-Modern France* (Ithaca, N.Y.: Cornell University Press, 1995);

Anne Green, *Privileged Anonymity: The Writings of Madame de Lafayette* (Oxford: Legenda, 1996);

Patrick Henry, ed., *An Inimitable Example: The Case for the Princesse de Clèves* (Washington, D.C.: Catholic University of America Press, 1993);

J. A. Kreiter, *Le Problème du paraître dans l'œuvre de Madame de Lafayette* (Paris: Nizet, 1977);

Donna Kuizenga, *Narrative Strategies in La Princesse de Clèves* (Lexington, Ky.: French Forum, 1976);

Maurice Laugaa, *Lectures de Madame de Lafayette* (Paris: A. Colin, 1971);

John D. Lyons, "Narrative, Interpretation and Paradox: *La Princesse de Clèves,*" *Romanic Review,* 72, no. 4 (1981): 383–400;

Lyons, "La Présence d'esprit et l'histoire secrète: Une Lecture de La *Comtesse de Tende,*" *Dix-Septième Siècle,* 181, no. 4 (1993): 717–732;

Lyons, ed., *The Princess of Clèves: Contemporary Reactions, Criticism* (New York: Norton, 1994);

Pierre Malandain, *La Princesse de Clèves* (Paris: Presses Universitaires de France, 1985);

Alain Niderst, *La Princesse de Clèves, le roman paradoxal* (Paris: Larousse, 1973);

Bernard Pingaud, *Madame de Lafayette par elle-même* (Paris: Seuil, 1959);

Jean Rousset, *Forme et signification* (Paris: Corti, 1982);

Rousset, *Leurs Yeux se rencontrèrent* (Paris: Corti, 1981);

J. B. H. du Trousset de Valincour, *Lettres à Mme la Marquise de * * * sur le sujet de La Princesse de Clèves* (Tours: Université de Tours, 1972);

Odette Virmaux, *Les Héroïnes romanesques de Madame de La Fayette* (Paris: Klincksieck, 1981).

Jean de La Fontaine
(8 July 1621 – 13 April 1695)

Mark A. Cohen
Bard College

BOOKS: *Deuxiesme Partie des Contes et nouvelles en vers* (Paris: C. Barbin, 1646 [i.e., 1666]);

L'Eunuque (Paris: A. Courbé, 1654);

Nouvelles en vers tirée [sic] *de Bocace et de l'Arioste* (Paris: C. Barbin, 1665 [i.e., 1664]);

Contes et nouvelles en vers (Paris: C. Barbin, 1665);

Fables choisies, mises en vers, illustrated by François Chauveau (Paris: C. Barbin, 1668; revised and enlarged edition, 4 volumes, Paris: D. Thierry et C. Barbin, 1678–1679);

Les Amours de Psiché et de Cupidon (Paris: C. Barbin, 1669)–includes *Adonis, poème;*

Contes et nouvelles en vers . . . troisiesme partie (Paris: C. Barbin, D. Thierry, 1671);

Fables nouvelles et autres poësies, illustrated by Chauveau (Paris: D. Thierry, 1671)–includes 3 sections of "Le Songe de Vaux";

Poëme de la captivité de saint Malc (Paris: C. Barbin, 1673);

Nouveaux Contes (Mons: G. Migeon, 1674);

Poëme du Quinquina, et autres ouvrages en vers (Paris: D. Thierry et C. Barbin, 1682)–includes *Galatée* and *Daphné;*

A Monseigneur l'Evesque de Soissons, en luy donnant un Quintilien de la traduction d'Oratio Toscanella (Paris: A. Pralard, 1687);

L'Astrée (Paris: C. Ballard, 1691);

Fables choisies (Paris: C. Barbin, 1694 [i.e., 1693])–includes book XII;

Œuvres diverses de M. de La Fontaine . . . , 3 volumes (Paris: Didot, 1729)–volume 1 includes unpublished fragments of "Le Songe de Vaux."

Editions and Collections: *Œuvres de La Fontaine,* 6 volumes, edited by Charles Walckenaer (Paris: Lefèvre, 1827);

Fables de La Fontaine, 2 volumes, illustrated by J.-J. Grandville (Paris: H. Fournier aîné, 1838);

Œuvres de J. de La Fontaine, 12 volumes, edited by Henri Régnier (Paris: Hachette, 1883–1897);

Les Amours de Psyché; Opuscules et lettres, edited by Edmond Pilon and Fernand Dauphin (Paris: Garnier Frères, 1926 [i.e., 1927]);

Jean de La Fontaine (portrait attributed to François de Troy; Bibliothèque de Geneve)

Discours à Madame de La Sablière (sur l'âme des animaux), edited by Henri Busson and Ferdinand Gohin (Paris: Droz, 1938);

Fables, contes et nouvelles, edited by René Groos and Jacques Schiffrin, Bibliothèque de la Pléiade, no. 10 (Paris: Gallimard, 1966);

Le Songe de Vaux, edited by Eleanor Titcomb (Geneva: Droz, 1967);

Œuvres diverses, edited by Pierre Clarac, Bibliothèque de la Pléiade, no. 62 (Paris: Gallimard, 1968);

Contes de La Fontaine, avec les illustrations de Fragonard, parues dans l'édition de Didot de 1795, 2 volumes (Paris: J. de Bonnot, 1969);

Fables de La Fontaine, 2 volumes, illustrated by Gustave Doré (Paris: Lidis, 1969);

Fables de La Fontaine, avec les figures d'Oudry, parues dans l'édition Desaint et Saillant de 1755, 4 volumes (Paris: J. de Bonnot, 1969);

Les Amours de Psyché et de Cupidon, edited by Michel Jeanneret and Stefan Schœttke (Paris: Librairie Générale Française, 1991);

Œuvres complètes, 2 volumes, edited by Jean-Pierre Collinet and Clarac, Bibliothèque de la Pléiade, nos. 10 and 62 (Paris: Gallimard, 1991, 1997).

Editions in English: *Selected Works,* edited by Philip A. Wadsworth (New York: Harper, 1950);

Selected Fables of La Fontaine, translated by Marianne Moore (London: Faber & Faber, 1955);

Adonis, translated by David M. Glixon (London: Rodale Press, 1957);

The Fables, translated by Elizur Wright (London: Jupiter Books, 1975);

Selected Fables, translated by James Michie (New York: Viking, 1979);

La Fontaine Fables, and Other Poems, translated by John Cairncross (Gerrards Cross, U.K.: Smythe, 1982);

The Loves of Cupid and Psyche, translated by John Lockman (Woodbridge, Conn.: Research Publications, 1983);

Selected Fables, edited by Maya Slater, translated by Christopher Wood (Oxford & New York: Oxford University Press, 1995);

Complete Tales in Verse, translated by Guido Waldman (Manchester: Carcanet, 2000).

TRANSLATION: Augustine, *De la Cité de Dieu,* 2 volumes, translated by La Fontaine and Louis Giry (Paris: P. Le Petit, 1665, 1667).

OTHER: *Recueil de poësies chrestiennes et diverses,* 3 volumes, edited by Henri Loménie de Brienne (Paris: P. Le Petit, 1671 [i.e., 1670])–volumes 1 and 3 include works by La Fontaine;

Ouvrages de prose et de poésie des Srs de Maucroy et de La Fontaine, 2 volumes (Paris: C. Barbin, 1685)–volume 1 includes works by La Fontaine;

Mémoires de M. de Coulanges, suivis de lettres inédites de Madame de Sévigné, de son fils, de l'abbé de Coulanges, d'Arnaud d'Andilly, d'Arnauld de Pomponne, de Jean de La Fontaine, et d'autres personnages du même siècle, edited by Louis-Jean-Nicolas de Monmerqué (Paris: J.-J. Blaise, 1820)–includes letters by La Fontaine.

Jean de La Fontaine is best known for his *Fables choisies, mises en vers* (Selected Fables, Put into Verse),

published in twelve books from 1668 to 1693. Comprising more than two hundred short poems divided more or less evenly among the books, the collection employs mostly encounters between speaking animals in order to illustrate moral dilemmas. Often a *moralité* (moral) is placed at the beginning or the end summing up the lesson to be learned from the narrative. By taking an age-old genre relying on a simple and moralistic format and putting it into a more sophisticated poetic idiom, La Fontaine quickly achieved for his fables the distinction of being the most popular of all French poetry, read with pleasure by children and adults alike all over the world. From the late seventeenth century on, La Fontaine's fables became an integral part of French pedagogy. French schoolchildren learned individual fables by heart in their literature classes and the practice continues still today. Memorable lines such as "Ils sont trop verts" (They are too green), said by the fox in "Le Renard et les raisins" (The Fox and the Grapes) to cheer himself up when he sees some tasty grapes just out of reach; or "La raison du plus fort est toujours la meilleure" (The reason given by the stronger is always the best), which precedes the specious justification offered to a young lamb by a wolf before he eats it in "Le Loup et l'agneau" (The Wolf and the Lamb), are now woven into the fabric of the French language. On a higher level, adults still enjoy the bitter humor and subtle range of tones of the fables, looking for the contrapuntal ironies that sometimes play stories and morals off against one another. The fables have also inspired an important body of engravings by notable artists to illustrate luxury editions, especially in the nineteenth century. Many scenes and mottoes have taken on the emblematic status of a cherished piece of national treasure, drawing on the most primeval literary energies of mythic presence with a deft, yet cuttingly insightful, touch. If France can be said to have a single preeminent poet akin to Dante in Italy or William Shakespeare in England, then he is La Fontaine. Charles-Augustus Sainte-Beuve, in fact, called La Fontaine a French Homer, the teacher of the nation.

The impression given by a cursory reading or by the didactic use that has been made of the *Fables,* however, is that La Fontaine is a brilliant versifier who is recounting nothing more than the most banal and unoriginal moral truisms imaginable. Many of the legends that grew up around him (sometimes abetted by his own comments) tended to corroborate this idea in one way or another, portraying him as an indolent simpleton or a dreamy fantasist or a cynical, libertine arriviste–anything but an intellectually challenging artist. The reality is quite different. Partly by dint of his temperament, partly by his resolve, and partly by the way he surmounted certain personal setbacks, La Fontaine

La Fontaine's birthplace, Château-Thierry, in the Champagne region of northern France

carved out for himself a marginal yet privileged position in French literary life during the personal reign of Louis XIV (which began in 1661 when Louis XIV attained his majority and ended with his death more than fifty years later). La Fontaine was one of the oldest of the great *classiques*–more or less contemporary with Molière; Blaise Pascal; Marie de Rabutin-Chantal, marquise de Sévigné; and Jacques-Bénigne Bossuet–from the generation that followed Pierre Corneille and that was itself followed by Nicolas Boileau-Despréaux, Jean Racine, and Marie-Madeleine, comtesse de Lafayette. Over the course of his poetic career La Fontaine managed to live in relative comfort, produce a constant stream of work, garner the admiration of fellow writers, charm and entertain his patrons, join the most influential salons, and even get elected to the Académie Française (French Academy). His popularity with the general reading public was matched by savants' recognition of his deep immersion in ancient and Renaissance models. Yet, he lived outside the circuits of social intercourse normal for a poet of his stature. At the height of his career he neither attended court nor gained royal preferment. His personal life was in sham-

bles: he lived separated from his wife and child, hounded by debts and financially dependent on a series of wealthy benefactors. The difficulty of his situation, however, fortunately allowed him to preserve his independence and to escape being drawn into the propaganda machine of Versailles or indeed into any other decisive ideological commitments.

The unusual position he occupied in French letters should therefore lead readers and scholars to question the apparent simplicity of his greatest work. On closer examination his fables reveal other meanings and complexities from those first apparent on its moralistic surface–in particular, those deriving from its oblique but penetrating critique of contemporary life and its ideal counterpart, an unspoiled realm of measured pleasures away from the troubles of the world. The two realms interact in La Fontaine's work; neither wholly exists without the other, whence the ambivalent feeling that readers experience when they read his work that it is at once frivolous and somber, languid and tense. His work is therefore truly a fabulous discourse–at once airily insubstantial, overtly literary, and humbly derivative and yet often brutally true, deftly original, or sensitive to deep-rooted human needs. A full appreciation of his significance can only be properly gained if one looks at his oeuvre as a whole, of which the *Fables* makes up only a fifth. The astonishing variety and the blending of different genres, forms, and tones it comprises is unparalleled by any other French poet between Pierre de Ronsard and Victor Hugo. La Fontaine's work runs the gamut from the scabrous to the religious sublime; uses a vast range of classical, Italian, French and oriental sources; and covers a host of different genres from satire to idyll, epistle to opera. Virtually without exception, every one of his important texts openly proclaims its indebtedness to one (or more) of his sources but goes on to transform it to reflect his own favorite themes and emphases. In this respect, La Fontaine represents classicist humanism at its best with its productive combination of playfulness and respect. Poetry was La Fontaine's sole occupation and interest, but the way in which he pursued it also helped delineate his philosophy of life, loosely affiliated with the Epicurean revival of the mid seventeenth century—one that affirmed sensuality, openness to experience and change, and the value of idealized love but also the virtues of pacifism, modesty, tranquillity, and distance in carefully preserved spaces of secure happiness.

La Fontaine was born in the Champagne region of northern France at Château-Thierry on 8 July 1621. His father was a financially comfortable government official, entrusted with the upkeep of the royal domains in the region; his mother was the daughter of a family of royal doctors. As a result, La Fontaine grew up in one of the finest mansions in the town, though he spent time on the family's farm properties and in the royal forests in connection with his father's work, where perhaps he first developed an unsentimental but deeply engaged familiarity with the life of animals that he later expressed in the *Fables*. La Fontaine was well educated in the Latin classics (and possibly the Greek too) in his local school, and at age fifteen he went to Paris to complete his education. During his time at school he befriended François Maucroix—fifteen years his senior and later a poet and priest—who became his closest friend and reader. They kept up a constant correspondence (in which La Fontaine often made suggestions about translations Maucroix's friends had sent him), and in 1685 at the height of his career he generously agreed to publish a joint volume of poetry with his less well-known friend. In 1641 La Fontaine began theological studies at the Oratory in Paris, but he soon proved unsuited for the religious life and left a year later. According to later reports, he read more of Honoré d'Urfé's multivolume pastoral novel *L'Astrée* (Astrea, 1607–1627) at the Oratory than prescribed texts such as St. Augustine's works, but he also probably acquired

there his lifelong admiration for Plato and a not wholly aesthetic taste for a distinctly French vein of spirituality. Most of all, *L'Astrée* had a profound impact on La Fontaine in both ideological and formal ways. It was the founding text of a philosophical type of love in which both partners respected each other as equals, oscillating between present captivation of the senses and Neo-platonic contemplation of higher qualities. As a corollary of this *honnête* (gentlemanly, civilized) attitude, the lovers it depicts naturally renounced the ambitions and struggles of the "world," seeking instead an enchanted space where they were free to live as they wished. d'Urfé also pioneered in France an open literary form that championed an almost endlessly various mix of the genres of philosophical discussion, lyric poetry, and Greek romance. La Fontaine adopted both d'Urfé's pastoral ideal and his love of variety. Loyal always to his sources, La Fontaine wrote an opera—one of his last works—also called *L'Astrée* (1691), based on the novel by D'Urfé.

Little is known about La Fontaine's initial forays into poetry beyond the anecdotal, but almost certainly, at some point during this period, he began intensive study of François de Malherbe, the most important "pre-classical" purifier of French verse. Equally important, La Fontaine immersed himself in the works of the Latin poets Virgil, Horace, and Terence. As a result of this interest, classical mythology and styles (with a few exceptions) form the substance of his verse. Unlike the work of Jaochim du Bellay or Ronsard in the Renaissance, La Fontaine's work was by no means academic or elitist, despite its reliance on such sources. French poetry in the mid seventeenth century was a highly social phenomenon in which writers congregated in coteries to read and listen to each other's works well before they published them. In fact, they saw civilized exchange as the goal of poetry rather than the production of a body of work. This conversational ideal ensured that poetry became less academic than its Renaissance predecessor and more ready to please the audience rather than following any mystic or pedagogic imperatives. For those who still cherished the Greco-Roman classics—virtually all of the greatest writers, such as Molière and Racine, who are still read today—this preference meant that the great store of learning that had been amassed was not to be discarded, only assimilated into what first must be acceptable and entertaining as a social performance. In the chaotic political situation of the time no central authority imposed a common standard, and each literary salon freely determined its own aesthetic norms. This situation changed with the defeat of the aristocratic rebellion in the 1650s known as the Fronde and the victory of the absolutist monarchy, which attempted to install its own self-glorifying hegemony over the arts. But La Fontaine's work continued to emanate from the diverse milieus through which he passed; the circle of each new patron found in La Fontaine a ready poetic sounding board for its spirit. No one was better able to preserve the salon's combination of the playful, ironic worldliness with the savant humanist legacy under the pressures of this later period.

In 1645 La Fontaine returned to Paris to begin a study of law, the most common profession for a man of his social rank, with the intention of following in his father's footsteps to make a career in an administrative post. In Paris he became a member of a literary academy known as "La Table ronde" (Round Table), whose members called themselves paladins and whose members included Maucroix, the Hellenist Paul Pellisson, François Charpentier, Gédéon Tallemant des Réaux, and Antoine Furetière. Through these rising talents La Fontaine came into contact with the older generation of established poet-critics, including Nicolas Perrot d'Ablancourt, Jean Chapelain, Valentin Conrart, and Olivier Patru. La Fontaine's early practice of prefacing his work with a careful retailing of sources, styles, and anticipations of audience reaction reflects his acknowledgment of the critical self-awareness so characteristic of the French classicism these authors pioneered. In 1647 he married a suitable bride, Marie Héricart de la Ferté-Milon, from an equally eminent local family. A son, Charles, was born to them in 1653. Increasingly, however, he abandoned his family duties in favor of literary salons and other women. In 1652 La Fontaine bought a post similar to his father's, as inspector of the royal forests, and seemed set for a comfortable provincial existence. In 1654 he published *L'Eunuque,* an adaptation of Terence's *The Eunuch* (161 B.C.), a highly derivative piece that was not a great success. La Fontaine continued to write plays throughout his career with equally dismal results. *L'Eunuqe* did, however, give a foretaste of his typical duality of tone, taken as it was from the most urbane of the Latin dramatists; it was equally his most risqué play, centered on a rape.

Toward the end of the 1650s, La Fontaine's life became more unstable: the first fractures appeared in his marriage, and his father's death in 1658 left him saddled with his father's debts, a burden under which he labored until his own death. For the first time he was forced to look beyond his own region in search of funds. In this era, writers did not receive payment for their work and so relied for their sustenance either on their own wealth or on patronage; lacking the former, he was forced to seek the latter. In the same year, through the interposition of friends—probably Pellisson or his uncle Jannart—he met the greatest patron of the time, the minister of the treasury, Nicolas Foucquet, who combined

Marie Héricart de la Ferté-Milon, whom La Fontaine married in 1647 (from André Hallas, Jean de La Fontaine, *1922)*

wealth, taste, and the ambition to shine in equal measure. The artists he patronized are a veritable roster of the best contemporary French writers, painters, and architects—all working together to adorn his beautiful estate situated at Vaux (southeast of Paris)—who soon went on to define the officially sanctioned face of French classicism at Versailles: Molière, Charles Le Brun, André Le Nôtre, Louis Le Vau, and Charles Perrault. In *Les Fâcheux* (The Impertinents), Molière's comedy of manners (first performed at Vaux in 1661), modeled on the elegant playing with social roles of Greco-Roman New Comedy, La Fontaine was a witness to a new elegance in stage drama that assimilated the farcical to more-restrained norms of language and characterization. La Fontaine remembered this performance as a paradisiacal moment in his life, and the pleasures of a civilized community devoted to ideal love and friendship from then on colored his work. Foucquet took La Fontaine under his patronage and gracefully left him an unusual amount of liberty in fulfilling his duties. In part as a result of his new contacts and in part because of the notice his work itself began to attract, his circle of literary acquaintances grew to include Racine; Charles de Saint-Denis, sieur de Saint-Evremond; and Perrault.

In return for payment and lodging, La Fontaine agreed to a "pension poétique," a sort of poetic contract, for which he agreed to write occasional pieces every three months that dealt with events in the Foucquet household or glorified his patron in some manner. They were often preceded by fulsome prefaces praising Foucquet for his taste, grace, and dignity. Although La Fontaine was assiduous, such work to order was not really to his liking. One piece, for instance, though La Fontaine never finished it, was about the sumptuous estate Foucquet was building at Vaux. "Le Songe de Vaux" (The Song of Vaux) had to describe a château that was still in the process of being built, so La Fontaine planned to fulfill his task in two ways: by turning the ongoing construction into a dream of a finished estate and by staging an allegorical dispute, in which all the arts, allegorically represented, vied with each other to see who was the finest as they presented their specific contributions to the great project. He therefore mixed, without quite fusing, what was a venerable allegorical tradition with baroque description. To this combination in turn were added pleasurable episodes of various animals' adventures, a humorous form of what he calls *galant* (sophisticated, courtly) lyricism. He conceived of the fundamental purpose of art, both in his own work and in that of his fellow artists, as the desire to make a dream seem real. In a multitude of disparate and only loosely connected episodes, the poem constantly leaves or avoids the objects it is supposed to describe in order to imagine instead mysteries and oneiric preambles or adventures that express the magical ability of poetry always to renew its own charms.

La Fontaine also wrote at this time his first important work, *Adonis* (1669), an adaptation of a story by Ovid, rewritten by innumerable poets since classical times, including the sprawling, encyclopedic, typically baroque poem by Giambattista Marini, *Adone* (1623), to which the much shorter and more focused *Adonis* can be thought of as a classical counterpart. La Fontaine presented the work to Foucquet in 1658 in a beautifully hand-produced edition. It tells the story of a beautiful young man with whom Venus falls in love. They share a delightful period of idyllic lovemaking together, but she is forced to abandon him briefly to tend to her duties as a goddess, seeing to her cult and propagating love elsewhere. La Fontaine stresses the idyllic quality of love in its creation of a blessed zone of peace and equality, or as Venus says to Adonis, "Amour rend ses sujets tous égaux" (Love makes her subjects equal). Before leaving, she warns, "Ne chassez point aux ours, aux sangliers, aux lions / Gardez-vous d'irriter tous ces monstres félons: / Laissez les animaux qui, fiers et pleins de rage, / Ne cherchent leur salut qu'en montrant leur courage" (Do not hunt bears,

boars, and lions; / Take care not to disturb these criminal monsters: / Leave the animals alone, who, proud and full of anger / Seek their salvation in nothing but acts of courage). When she has gone, he quickly falls into despair and seeks distraction. He finds it when a nearby village calls for help against a wild boar that is ravaging the countryside. In the ensuing hunt, he manages to kill the boar heroically but is mortally wounded in the process; in order to convey this action, La Fontaine changes the genre of the poem in midstream to epic, with its breathless depiction of a hunt. The "world" is represented both by Venus attending to her "business" and Adonis's quest for glory. However necessary their respective actions might have been for the good of the community, the poem is ultimately colored by Venus's final lament over Adonis's death. La Fontaine's moral objections to heroic action are paralleled by his aesthetic preferences in his expression of distaste for the war-like but most prestigious of all the genres, epic: "Je n'ai pas entrepris de chanter dans ces vers / Rome ni ses enfants vainqueurs de l'Univers, / Ni les fameuses tours qu'Hector ne put défendre, / Ni les combats des dieux aux rives du Scamandre" (I have neither undertaken to sing in this poem / Rome nor her sons who conquered the universe / Nor the famous towers that Hector could not defend, / Nor the battles of the gods on the banks of the Scamander). The poem installs a crucial dynamic that shaped all of La Fontaine's most important future poems—the depiction of a utopian space that is abandoned but whose spirit is never lost in the more realistic second phase of the work. The choice of an animal to represent the violence that threatens civilized tranquility is in itself a surreptitious concession to human fantasy that is later exploited in all its ambiguity in the *Fables*. In its purposeful, furious rage, the destroying animal takes on human qualities but equally places the value of the warrior ethos in question by its metaphoric fusion with animality. In *Adonis* the tragic tone replaces the idyllic in a surprising turn in the middle of the poem. La Fontaine, in his greatest poetry, however, tended to choose a more homogeneously brief form as his predilection for minor genres grew more pronounced.

In the preface to the poem, La Fontaine signals admiringly Foucquet's own role in modern France, comparing it to Adonis's confrontation with the boar: "comme le héros destiné pour vaincre de la dureté de notre siècle et le mépris de tous les beaux-arts" (like the hero destined to overcome the harshness of our age and its scorn of all the fine arts). A parallel disaster awaited Foucquet, and it gave the poet a harsh lesson about the cruelty of the outside world. When Cardinal Jules Mazarin died in 1661, the young Louis XIV decided to rule without a first minister. He believed that the king

Château de Vaux (southeast of Paris), the estate of Finance Minister Nicolas Foucquet, who became La Fontaine's patron in the late 1650s (engraving by Perelle; Librairie Larousse)

should have absolute power in government and stand clearly above all others. He could not brook any competition in politics or in culture. Quite unwittingly, Foucquet roused the king's jealousy when he staged an enormous festival at Vaux to celebrate the king's accession in August 1661. Foucquet had already shown a high-handed insensitivity to the new order by his presumptuous attitude toward the king, which resulted from his assumption that the king would need in him a powerful first minister such as Armand du Plessis, cardinal de Richelieu or Mazarin to whom he could hand over the day-to-day business of government. Immediately after this event, Louis XIV, egged on by Jean-Baptiste Colbert, Mazarin's brilliant protégé, decided to arrest Mazarin on exaggerated, if not wholly false, charges of speculation and corruption. Although the king wanted Foucquet executed, mitigating circumstances and judicial independence allowed the courts to sentence him to life imprisonment instead. At great risk to himself, La Fontaine remained loyal to Foucquet and wrote two poems in his defense, which were circulated anonymously; they begged the king for clemency, a stance that alienated the new regime from La Fontaine. One of these was later known as *Elégie pour M.F. (aux Nymphes de Vaux)* (Elegy for M.F. [to the Nymphs of Vaux]). Use of a mythic scene of nymphs lamenting the misfortunes of their former cynosure in "Elégie aux Nymphes de

Vaux" might not seem realistic (in either sense of the word) against the troops, prisons, and judges of raw state power. But its mixture of the marvelous, the melancholic, and the heartfelt articulation of two great classical ideals—friendship (of La Fontaine for his master) and clemency (asked of a good king)—valorizes the fragility of the conceit: the world is harsh; the ideal is beautiful; and the pleas that emanate from the mythic realm under duress are sincere. Nevertheless, when La Fontaine published a revised version of *Adonis* in 1669—five years after Foucquet's final sentencing—he in effect bowed to the fait accompli of Foucquet's exclusion from public life and replaced the original dedication.

In 1662 La Fontaine suffered a further financial setback when he was fined for using a noble title without the right to do so. The next year he went into exile with his uncle Jannart, a close associate of the disgraced minister (whether La Fontaine was ordered to go or chose to accompany Jannart out of solidarity is not clear). Together they traveled in the Limousin region, and La Fontaine created a record of the journey in his letters home to his wife, known collectively as *Voyage de Paris en Limousin* (Voyage from Paris to Limousin, written in 1663). The first four of the letters were included in the 1729 *Œuvres diverses de M. de La Fontaine . . .* (Assorted Works of M. de La Fontaine . . .); the final two were published together with the *Mémoires de M. de*

Title page for the manuscript La Fontaine presented to Foucquet in 1658 (Collection Dutuit, Librairie Larousse)

Coulanges in 1820s. La Fontaine did not write the letters with publication in mind; yet, for all its ad hoc nature the *Voyage de Paris en Limousin* is a perfect example of French classical prose in its blend of instruction and amusement. La Fontaine stresses the constant dangers and discomfort of the trip. He makes clear that he prefers to dream at home, surrounded by the warmth of family and friends rather than to discover new things, sate his curiosity, or find glory in far-off places. As is often proved later in the *Fables,* he intimates in these letters that only in one's familiar haunts can one achieve inner peace and self-knowledge. Yet, he also makes the best of his troubles by writing the letters, imparting knowledge to his wife who, he complains, would rather read romances than learn anything new. He reveals a certain playful if problematic complicity with his wife, as he ribs her for her lack of interest and then relates picturesque details about the places he visits in the provinces, brief lessons in French history associated with them, and his flirtations with other women. Almost from the time of his return, La Fontaine and his wife started to live separate lives—the reasons for their imminent breakup can perhaps be discerned in this apparently harmless banter, though his own desire for

freedom from the mundane responsibilities also played a part in it.

On his return in 1664, La Fontaine found a new admirer in his own region, Marie-Anne Mancini, duchesse de Bouillon—a bored, lively aristocrat exiled to the country by a jealous husband who had gone off to fight the Turks. La Fontaine also found a new patron, Marguerite de Lorraine, the widow of Gaston, duc d'Orléans, who made him a *gentilhomme* of her household in Paris. La Fontaine was now sufficiently free of family and financial duties to work at his leisure, and he found in the circle of the duchesse d'Orléans, a convivial atmosphere and an avid readership for what turned out to be his first published collection of poems, the *Contes et nouvelles en vers* (Tales and Novels in Verse, 1665). In this period of the 1660s La Fontaine began his two most substantial projects, the *contes* (tales) and the *fables*. He continued to add to them both intermittently for the rest of his life. The *contes* represent La Fontaine's first important poetic success with the larger public, but they garnered him a reputation for licentiousness simply because of the subject matter of the tales—marital and amorous escapades. In the mid 1660s appeared the first signs of a reaction against the free expression of libertine sentiments after the (temporary) suppression of Molière's *Tartuffe* (first performed in 1664) for its ridicule of the religious elements of the court. The fable was traditionally a moralistic form, so La Fontaine consciously undertook fables partly to present a more acceptable face of his talent. His dedication of them to the dauphin's instruction could not have been a more orthodox gesture. They were an immediate success. But rather than focus on the *fables* and give up the *contes,* as a truly ambitious man would have done, he kept publishing new tales, often more risqué than those that had gone before. This desire for variety emerged as a fundamental attitude toward writing that is one of his most striking traits. Henceforth, he was perpetually involved in many apparently unrelated, even contradictory, projects—developing his poetic interests on several fronts at once. Despite his libertine reputation, exacerbated by his irregular family life, he even contributed to strictly Christian verse in this era, helping with a translation of St. Augustine's *City of God* (1665, 1667), contributing selections of Christian verse to *Recueil de poësies chrestiennes et diverses* (A Collection of Different Christian Poems, 1671), and writing his own deeply spiritual idyll on the life of a saint, *Poëme de la captivité de saint Malc* (Poem on the Captivity of St. Malchus, 1673), in which the sexual abstinence of its heroes is depicted with the same dream-like and transformative promise as sensuality is elsewhere in his work. At the same time his interest in adapting classical works never flagged. In 1669 he wrote his longest prose work, *Les Amours de Psiché et de*

A Limoge cinq sept 1663   275

Ce seroit une belle chose que de voyager, s'il ne se falloit point lever si matin, tant que nous estions monsieur de Chasteauneuf et moy; luy pour avoir fait tout le tour de Richelieu en grosses bottes, ce que ie crois vous avoir mandé, n'ayant pas deu obmettre une circonstance si remarquable; moy pour m'estre amusé a vous escrire au lieu de dormir; nostre promesse, et la crainte de faire attendre le voiturier, nous obligerent de sortir du lit devant que l'aurore fust éveillée. nous nous disposasmes a prendre congé de Richelieu sans le voir. il arriva malheureusement pour nous, et plus malheureusement encore pour le seneschal dont nous fusmes contraints d'interrompre le sommeil, que les portes se trouverent fermées par son ordre. le bruit courut que quelques gentilshommes de la province avoient fait complot de sauver certains prisonniers soupçonnez de l'assasinat du marquis de faure. mon impatience ordinaire me fit maudire cette rencontre, ie ne louay mesme que sobrement la prudence du seneschal. pour me contenter monsieur de Chasteauneuf luy parla, et luy dit que nous portions le paquet du Roy. aussitost il donna ordre qu'on nous ouvrist, si bien que nous eusmes du temps de reste, et arrivasmes a Chastelleraut qu'on nous croyoit encore a moitié chemin. nous y trouvasmes vostre oncle en maison d'ami. on luy avoit promis des chevaux pour achever son voyage; et il s'estoit resolu de laisser Poitiers, comme le plus long, pourveu que ie n'eusse point une curiosité trop grande de voir cette ville. ie me contentay de la relation qu'il m'en fit, et son ami le pria de ne point partir qu'il n'en fust prié par le valet de pied qui l'accompagnoit. nous accordasmes a cet ami vivieur seulement. ce n'est pas qu'il ne dependist de nous de luy en accorder davantage, monsieur de Chasteauneuf estant honneste homme, et s'acquitant de telles commissions au gré de ceux qu'il conduit aussi bien que la cour; mais nous iugeasmes qu'il valoit mieux obeir actuellement aux ordres du Roy. tout ce qui se peut imaginer de franchise, d'honnesteté, de bonne chere, de politesse, fut employé pour nous regaler. la vigne passe au pied de Chastelleraut, et en ce canton elle porte des raisins qui sont petits quand elles n'ont qu'une demi aune. on nous en servit des plus belles, avec des melons que le maistre du logis mesprisoit, et qui me semblerent excellens. enfin cette iournée se passa avec un plaisir non mediocre; car nous estions non seulement en païs de connoissance mais de parenté. ie trouvay a Chastelleraut un Pidoux dont nostre hoste avoit espousé la belle soeur. tous les Pidoux ont du nez, et abondamment. on

Page from a 5 September 1663 letter in which La Fontaine describes his trip through Limousin while in exile following Foucquet's arrest and trial for financial improprieties (Bibliothèque de l'Arsenal, Paris)

Cupidon (The Loves of Psyche and Cupid, 1669), based on Apuleius's original poem but with many similarities to "Le Songe de Vaux," and published it together with his revised version of *Adonis. Les Amours de Psiché et de Cupidon* is a highly mixed piece interspersed with verse, in which a narrator, Poliphile, shows three of his friends around the garden of Versailles (the palace of which was finished only in 1683) and then tells them his version of Psyche and Cupid. All of the many digressions, frames, and discussions in the story are marshaled to examine La Fontaine's most favored theme—the loss of a blissfully sensual state. When the long exchanges between the various participants draw to a close at the end of the poem, La Fontaine makes his strongest plea yet for the primacy of love ("Volupté") over rank (the difference of god and mortals), expressing as he does so a proto-rococo aesthetic of grace and an artificially controlled sense of natural profusion, quite obscuring the standard moral lesson warning against curiosity that is usually attached to the story.

The *contes* were adaptations primarily of tales (in French called *nouvelles* or *contes* indifferently) by Giovanni Boccaccio and Ludovico Ariosto, but also those from a native French tradition that included François Rabelais, Bonaventure des Periers, and Marguerite de Navarre, all of whom were recognized as masters of the genre but whose works were mostly considered too salacious for polite taste because of their cruel sexual reversals, deceived husbands, lecherous monks, and insatiable women. La Fontaine aimed to retain the sensuality of the tales while transmuting the rougher folk elements into something more refined, both in themes and in the use of versification. (The originals had generally been written in prose.) La Fontaine also had a simple desire to shine in carrying out such a challenge in a domain that was purposely "light" and could show off his virtuosity as pure entertainment, but he was also developing his own techniques and ideas in more interesting ways. He reflected on his own poetics as he was writing and defined his own artistic creed in one of his many asides, "Diversité, c'est ma devise" (diversity is my motto); "Pâté d'anguille" (Head of an Eel, IV, 9) in which the term *diversity* should be understood in both of its senses as *variety* and *amusement* (French *diversion*). The short form of the tale allows the poet to offer something new in each successive piece, and La Fontaine included a selection of different verse forms, subject matters, and original sources that delighted poetic connoisseurs such as Chapelain and Boileau while attracting less-cultured readers for their inoffensive, witty eroticism. Just as significant, though, was La Fontaine's skillful toning down of the violence of his originals in favor of an untroubled tolerance of human sexuality, even when it involved the infidelity or extramarital sexual experience of one's spouse—most notably, in "La Joconde" and "La Fiancée du roi du Garbe" (The Mona Lisa and The Fiancee of the king of Garbe). The sensual is not described in detail; La Fontaine is well aware of his audience's sensibilities in this regard and adds delicate veils to what had often been the more forthright language of the medieval period. His point is, nevertheless, an equalizing one, in which social rank and sexual difference pale before the peaceful embrace of love. He redefines *bienséance* (appropriateness) as what is proper for the subject chosen—in this case the venerable authors of the novella tradition, not some absolute standard or moral hierarchy. In addition, like Ariosto, he often adds to the more straightforward presentation of his stories intricate framing commentaries in which the teller offers his opinions on the themes of the story, making interpretation part of the tale in a way that makes the readers reflect on the easy immediacy of their own reactions. In his preface and many of the *contes* themselves La Fontaine foregrounded the aesthetic problems he was surmounting instead of the subject matter itself, and by often intruding himself as narrator, he established a dialectical complicity between poet and reader so that the artful and charming manner of veiling, not the erotic, was the central interest.

In the 1670s La Fontaine was at the height of his powers, publishing at the end of the decade his greatest work—the second collection of the *Fables* (1678–1679; books VII to XI), though it was not as well received as the first. In 1672 the duchesse d'Orléans died, and La Fontaine began a long and fruitful relationship with a learned and religious bourgeoise, Marguerite Hessein de La Sablière, who paid all of his expenses and saw that he was housed and fed, though not sumptuously. In joining this new milieu, La Fontaine also adopted certain of its interests and acted as a poetic conduit for its members. In La Sablière's orbit, therefore, the subject matter of his work grew broader, and he became more closely associated with the contemporary French school of Epicurean philosophy. Founded by Pierre Gassendi, who was in his day the main French opponent to René Descartes, it was ably represented in La Sablière's salon by François Bernier. La Fontaine wrote some important poems expressing his reception of their ideas, in particular the *Discours à Madame de La Sablière*, also known as "Les Deux Rats, le Renard, et l'Œuf" (The Two Rats, the Fox, and the Egg), collected in *Fables choisies* (1693), which affirmed the notion that animals possessed genuine intelligence. Scientific popularizations became an important genre in the 1670s and 1680s, and La Fontaine followed the trend. He had a genuine philosophical interest in the new scientific discoveries and above all was a supporter of an empirical attitude toward natural phenomena, including pleasure,

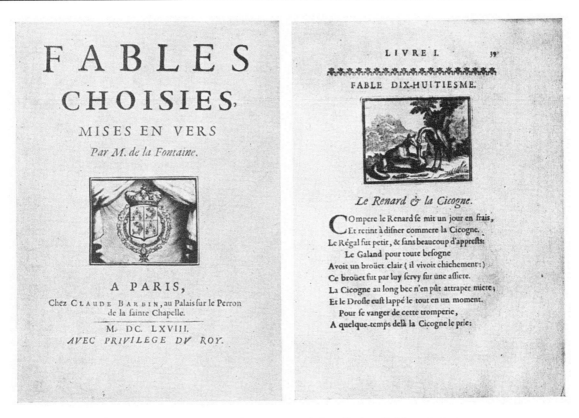

Title page and opening text page from La Fontaine's first collection of brief moral tales in verse
(from Monica Sutherland, La Fontaine, *1953)*

which for Epicureans was to be controlled by the intellect so that it could be enjoyed in constant tranquillity, not repressed. Like contemporaneous satires by Boileau and Molière, La Fontaine's "Poème du Quinquina" (1682) ridiculed those old-fashioned doctors who refused to accept new medical advances. He says of them: "Quelques-uns encore conservent / Comme un point de religion, / L'intérêt de l'Ecole et leur opinion" (Some still keep / As a point of religion, / The interest of the schools and their opinion). In his view, to the contrary, nature is bountiful in giving humans remedies: "Tout mal a son remède au sein de la nature" (every evil has its cure in the bosom of nature). As a token of respect for ancient sources, he explicitly adopts the mantle of a latter-day Lucretius, the Epicurean whose *De Rerum Natura* (Of the Nature of Things, first century B.C.) presented his philosophy in a poem whose antisuperstitious naturalized picture of the workings of the universe included a famous paean to the power of love to generate all things. Nor does he fail at the same time to modulate his modernism by praise for a more primitive simplicity in daily manners. In this matter La Fontaine can be seen as a precursor of the eighteenth-century philosophes.

After La Fontaine's defense of the disgraced Fouquet, neither Louis XIV nor Colbert was prepared to

welcome him to court or subsidize him with a royal pension. La Fontaine did not give up the quest for advancement entirely, however. Like virtually every other poet of the time, he wrote many poems in praise of the king (the praise of Versailles in the poem about Psyche, for one) and twice positioned himself as a royal pedagogue by dedicating the first and last editions of the *Fables* to the dauphin. These attempts were met with a certain success: he was officially invited to dedicate the second collection of the *Fables* to Francoise de Rochechouart de Mortemart, marquise de Montespan, then the king's mistress, in 1678. In 1674, in an attempt to ingratiate himself with the court in a different way, he wrote an opera, the most popular court entertainment. It was not a success. But in any case La Fontaine's past and the sheer breadth of his poetic production meant that he would never fit into the royal milieu. While Racine and Boileau stopped writing their own work when they became historiographers royal in 1677, La Fontaine was never prepared to make such a sacrifice for reasons of advancement.

For much of his career La Fontaine showed little interest in entering the Académie Française, then as now the pinnacle of official accomplishment in the world of French letters. But as he aged in the 1680s, he changed his mind and after an unsuccessful attempt in 1681 was finally inducted in 1684. When La Fontaine's enemy the great minister Colbert died, La Fontaine applied for Colbert's vacant seat in the Académie Française. The high esteem in which La Fontaine's peers held the *Fables* ensured that he was the preferred candidate, but the increasingly pious king and his new consort, the marquise de Maintenon, disapproved of the libertine *contes*. The king had the last word in such matters and naturally favored Boileau. He had already been appointed historiographer royal and was certain to be a more reliable propagandist for the monarchy than the unrepentant Foucquet loyalist La Fontaine. La Fontaine even went so far as to write a poem to encourage the king to decide in his favor by promising to put aside for good the more disreputable genres he had dabbled in if he were elected. The deadlock was broken when another member of the Académie Française died; that death enabled both men to be inducted together in 1684. At the induction ceremony, the abbé La Chambre began by praising the *Fables* but then, in a move that went against all previous etiquette, publicly denounced the *contes*. La Fontaine signaled his approval of the criticism at the time; yet, this retraction was probably nothing more than a politic feint. The final edition of 1674 had been banned by the authorities for the supposed licentiousness of the tales, but in the next decade La Fontaine published more *contes* and in 1693 revised a new edition for a Dutch publisher—that is, in the more freethinking environment of the most implacable enemy of France. Moreover, in his response to the abbé at the induction ceremony, La Fontaine chose to give a public reading of his Epicurean poem, the *Discours à Madame de La Sablière*. La Fontaine's position in French letters was emphasized again through his dealings with the academy when the so-called *Querelle des anciens et des modernes* (The Quarrel of the Ancients and the Moderns) blew up in 1687 between Boileau, who championed the ancients as examples, and Perrault, who saw the French moderns as equal and perhaps superiors to the ancients. La Fontaine took a moderate stance, though, leaning toward the ancients' party, recognizing the undeniable excellence of ancient models—which were, after all, those to which he had shown an exclusive predilection—without denying the many virtues of modern letters. However, he showed a way out of the impasse in his poem "Epître à Huet" (Epistle to Huet, probably begun during an earlier quarrel in the 1670s), also known as *A Monseigneur l'Evesque de Soissons, en luy donnant un Quintilien de la traduction d'Oratio Toscanella* (To Monsignor the Bishop of Soissons, on presenting him with a Quintillian translated by Oratio Toscanella, 1687), by defining his relation to the ancients as one of "imitation" as opposed to "slavishness," appropriating

them for his own ends rather than simply repeating what they had already done and in this way, too, copying the successfully creative attitude of ancients themselves in relation to their models: "Tâchant de rendre mien cet air d'antiquité" (Seeking to make my own their antique air). His independence was demonstrated yet again the following year, when he wrote a veiled appeal to the king to forgive Louis II de Bourbon, prince de Conde (known as the Great Conde), for remarks he had made about Maintenon.

There are many accounts of La Fontaine's physical and mental decline after this period. His poetic abilities also seemed to have waned, and the opera he wrote based on *L'Astrée* in 1691 is not his best work. In 1693 La Sablière died, and La Fontaine almost emigrated to the less constrained atmosphere of Restoration England at the invitation of his freethinking friend Saint-Evremond. However, he found another patron to shelter him, Anne d'Hervart, a wealthy financier and member of the Parlement. La Fontaine was by now seventy-one years old, an advanced age for the time, and soon after moving into his new home, he suffered an illness that led him to become pious and renounce his *contes* after years of robust health and creativity in which religious practice had been absent. In 1693 he published a final book of the *Fables,* which collected the fables he had published in different places over the previous decade. Those written expressly for the dauphin are somewhat stilted, but the rest are among his best. At his death on 13 April 1695, he was wearing a hair shirt, a sure sign that his apparent conversion had been sincere. Recognition of his extraordinary talent was widespread, and he was celebrated in the most glowing terms by such different writers as Perrault and François de Salignac de La Mothe-Fénelon.

The first collection of the *Fables* appeared in 1668 with six books. Dedicated to the dauphin, it was preceded by a preface that defended the genre of the verse fable, followed by a life of Aesop. The best-known fables come from these books: "La Cigale et la fourmi" (The Cicada and the Ant), "Le Corbeau et le renard" (The Crow and the Fox), and "Le Chêne et le roseau" (The Oak Tree and the Reed). The volume is carefully balanced: its reliance on the well-known ancient sources of the fable, Aesop and Phaedrus, is overt; each book has more or less the same number of fables (twenty); four have an introductory fable; and "animal" and "human" fables are divided so that in book I, for instance, fables 1–10 are about animals, while fables 11–17 are about humans (though the animal fables predominate overall). The second collection appeared in 1678 and 1679 and represents what are now numbered as books VII to XI. This collection is much more diverse, reflecting La Fontaine's connection with La

Sablière's salon. La Fontaine expanded the range of sources to include the Indian tradition of animal fable (relying heavily on Bidpai's *Fables,* translated from the seventh-century Arabic version by Gilbert Gaulmin as the *Livre des lumières* in 1644). The books vary considerably in size from one to the next, and within each book the tales are more various in tone, subject matter, and length. In many respects the second collection broke with the strictly pedagogic tradition of the Greek fable, too, by occasionally straying into "adult" areas such as philosophy, as in "L'Animal dans la lune" (The Animal in the Moon; VII, 18) and "Les Deux Rats, le Renard, et l'Œuf" (also known as *Discours à Madame de La Sablière*), which forms the unnumbered coda to book IX. The twelfth book was published in 1694, just before La Fontaine's death, and seemed to reaffirm the original modality of the earlier "pedagogic" half of the fables by being dedicated to the duke of Bourgogne, the son of the dauphin, to whom the 1668 volume had first been dedicated. But, in fact, book XII synthesizes the two manners as well as reflecting other poems La Fontaine had written entirely outside of the fable framework, the risqué *Contes,* the "heroic" style of *Adonis,* and a final reflection on the genre as a whole. Some of the books begin or end with a defense of sorts of the fabular enterprise or the author himself, addressed directly to its readers—for example, that in book II "Contre ceux qui ont le goût difficile" (Against Those Who Have a Hard-to-Satisfy Taste).

The fable came down to the seventeenth century in two rather distinct forms: as a highly valued object of erudition and as a more pragmatically oriented object of pedagogy. Authors of the Renaissance tradition in Italy took great care in translating Aesop into Latin so as to give the form dignity. To show that they had retied the broken chain of tradition from the original Greek, they equally rejected medieval versions of the fable (Ysopets and Avionnet). Instead, they considered the fable as a brilliantly "human" and therefore rhetorically effective means of transmitting wisdom. In the seventeenth century the French became assiduous scholars of the fable, taking up the Italian mantle. La Fontaine makes specific reference, too, to French versifications of fables in the sixteenth century, though they were far less distinguished than their Italian counterparts—Gilles Corrozet, Guillaume Haudent, and Philibert Hégémon. In 1596 and 1617 French scholars discovered the two lost manuscripts of Phaedrus originally written in the early Roman Empire that had lent the genre an urban civility and elegant Atticism pleasing to the austere *parliamentaire* class that formed one of the major audiences for French seventeenth-century literature. Incorporating some of these discoveries in 1610, Isaac Nicolas Nevelet published his great edition of the *Fables.* It was a huge

Marguerite de La Sablière, who became La Fontaine's patron in 1672 (portrait by Mignard; Bibliothèque Nationale, Paris)

anthology encompassing Latin translations of all the major Greek texts and many more recent humanist fables, enshrining the genre in scholarly form for the century to come. As a result, interest in the tradition of the fable remained strong in the course of the seventeenth century: two major collections of oriental fables were published in French as well as a translation of Phaedrus in 1646 in a bilingual edition by the Jansenist Le Maître de Sacy.

On the other hand, the fable was also one of the most humble genres in the humanist tradition, intimately connected with schoolboy exercises and the most basic level of moral education; its pervasiveness as a pedagogic tool made it unworthy of reflection. For instance, in 1674, when Boileau wrote what was later seen as the summa of classical poetics, *L'Art poétique,* surveying and evaluating the poetic production of the time, he completely omitted any consideration of the fable, although he was an admirer of La Fontaine and had even written fables himself. The same was true of all of the contemporary poets of the day. Whatever its venerable history, the fable was not seen as having a creative potential for those with literary ambitions; as a result, few original fables were written in France until La Fontaine's *Fables*. His exemplary success gave an impetus to the genre, with Catherine des Jardins de Villedieu, Furetière, and Pierre de Saint-Glas all publishing their own fables in the early 1670s with La Fontaine's own publisher, Claude Barbin. The success of the *Fables* launched the vogue for allegorical gardens, an idea that was realized in the Versailles gardens, whose labyrinth was decorated by thirty-nine fountains each illustrated by a different Aesopian story, etched in verse on its base. These verses, written by Isaac de Benserade, had won over those fables published by Perrault in 1677 under the title *Labyrinthe de Versailles*. Even more steeped in the ancient and humanist tradition than La Fontaine, Fénelon, preceptor of the duc de Bourgogne, grandson of Louis XIV, wrote fables for the instruction of his royal pupil, as well as translating some of La Fontaine's fables into Latin. Toward the end of La Fontaine's life, Perrault brought out his *Histoires ou Contes du temps passé, avec des moralitez* (Stories or Tales from Olden Times, with Morals, 1697), one of the first modern texts to collect fairy tales for the general adult reader, which included many animal stories as well as concluding *moralités*.

The Aesopian fable, on which the French fable is based, was a short tale most often featuring two animals (but also gods, humans, and objects) in which a moral was openly enunciated, usually at the conclusion of the tale. Stylistically, it is marked by a clear rhetorical preference for metaphorical indirection and the low comic register as opposed to the epic style of Homer, which was eminently direct and explicit, using poetic myths to tell of the great events of bygone history with all the necessary dignity and pathos of their high subject. Desiring to present himself in an Aesopian light, La Fontaine prefaced the first edition of the *Fables* with a Life of Aesop taken primarily from the ancient legends collected together by the fourteenth-century monk Planude; the preface shows how Aesop the slave was forced to use his wits in order to survive since he had no other power to help him, and the stories represent a brilliant negotiation of this situation, a peculiar blend of apparent obviousness and subtle argumentation aimed at winning in an everyday conflict. Both the Roman and the later medieval French traditions expanded the genre in various directions—using satire, picturesque epithets, and the bucolic. Their work in turn was expanded in late antiquity in the work of Avienus (or Avianus) of the fourth century, who continued the literary tendency by adding Ovidian and Virgilian vocabulary to his paraphrases of Babrius. Fables were preserved and rewritten with enthusiasm well into the Renaissance.

La Fontaine's use of his sources was a brilliant move in the triple game of simultaneously pleasing his audience, continuing the tradition, and criticizing his society. The meditative pure poet and bucolic dreamer can, from his withdrawn position, see the truth of the world more clearly, and La Fontaine was accordingly able to align himself quite unexpectedly with a thinker such as Thomas Hobbes, whose famous description in *Leviathan* (1651) of human life as nasty, brutish, and short was capped by a fable *in nuce* (in a nutshell), the motto *Homo homine lupus* (Man is a wolf for man). Presenting humans as animals was a witty way of revealing the true brutality underlying the workings of a world that prided itself on its civilization. The animal represents human life at its most basic form—just as the etymology of the word "fable" (*fari,* to speak) suggests the most basic level of human speech. Whereas La Fontaine had previously denied his desire to write in the heroic mode, in the preface to the *Fables* he affirms a new, tongue-in-cheek, panoply of heroes, more to his taste: "Je chante Les Héros dont Esope est le Père" (I sing the heros fathered by Aesop). In La Fontaine's hands the fable left the realm of venerable tradition to become a literary form of the highest subtlety.

In the preface he is keen to stress the literary quality of his *Fables:* when comparing himself with Phaedrus, he notes, "j'ai cru qu'il fallait . . . égayer l'ouvrage plus qu'il n'a fait" (I thought it necessary to make the work gayer than he did); regarding the magic of what he has accomplished, he says, "J'ai fait parler le Loup et répondre l'Agneau . . . Qui ne prendrait ceci pour un enchantement?" (I have made the Wolf speak and the lamb answer . . . Who would not think this poetry was enchanted?). This "literary" space must equally be understood as having a more than aesthetic meaning; it ensures that the moral lessons being told are anything but simplistic and the moral inferiority of pleasure not to be assumed. The first fable of book I, traditionally the first to be found in humanist school textbooks too—"La Cigale et la Fourmi"—might seem on first reading to be a simple exhortation to work hard and save for a rainy day, but its specific tonal counterpoint aims elsewhere as does the absence of any concluding *moralité,* which readers are left to adduce for themselves from the narrative. The cicada, who has been singing all summer, suddenly realizes when the winter comes that it will not survive because it has stored up no food. When the cicada explains to the ant that it has no food because it had been singing, the ant replies, "Vous chantiez? J'en suis fort aise: / Eh bien! Dansez maintenant" (You were singing? I am delighted: / Fine! Now you can dance). The poem plays off its obvious morally emblematic structure of industriousness-ant versus heedless pleasure-seeking-cicada by fleshing out their interaction and revealing through contemptuous turns of phrase the cruelty and pride that goes with the ant's merit. Moreover, if the readers perceive the ant thus, they must also begin to look differently at the cicada. It has shown a certain generosity in its actions; birdsong is, after all, a commonplace metaphor for poetry. The readers' judgment remains in tension, forced to go back and reassess the characteristics of the two protagonists.

Many of the fables in book I deal with the popular seventeenth-century theme of self-love–for example, "La Besace" (The Beggar's Bag; I, 7). But the moral is never as simple as it seems. In "La Grenouille qui veut se faire aussi grosse que le Bœuf" (The Frog Who Wants to Make Itself as Big as an Ox; I, 3) a frog tries to blow itself up to become the desired size. The animals' accompanying exchange seems quite simple: "n'y suis-je point encore? / –Nenni.–M'y voici donc?–Point du tout.–M'y voilà? / –Vous n'en approchez point" (Am I there yet? / No forsooth. Is that it then? Not at all. Did I make it? / You are nowhere near). The frog puffs itself up too much and bursts. The moral follows: "Le monde est plein de gens qui ne sont pas plus sages: / Tout bourgeois veut bâtir comme des grands seigneurs, / Tout petit prince a des ambassadeurs, / Tout marquis veut avoir des pages" (The world is full of people who are no wiser than this / Every bourgeois wants a house like great lords, / Every minor prince has ambassadors, / Every marquis wants pages). Again, as with "La Cigale et la Fourmi," a careful ear for social presentation might pick up the disdainful tone of the ox as well as the foolishness of the frog. The moral goes on a little too long, moreover, to offer any straightforward message. It starts going up the social hierarchy until it begins to question quite legitimate accoutrements for nobles, and its length suggests that it could continue all the way up to the king.

Many fables warn against trying to leave one's present condition and rise in the world because of the dangers. In "Le Loup et Le Chien" (The Wolf and the Dog; I, 5) a starving wolf is about to take up the dog's offer to join him at the court and enjoy healthy meals every day, when it notices the dog's chafed neck. The wolf discovers that in return for security, the dog has given up its freedom, a commonplace objection in moral literature to life at court. The wolf's reaction is to turn away: "maître Loup s'enfuit, et court encore" (sir Wolf runs off, and he is still running). The open ending does not tell how the wolf managed to find its next meal, intimating in the lightest of ways the pathos of animal life, in which a potentially fatal hardship is its natural condition. In the final fable of book I, "Le Chêne et le roseau," this pathos even reaches the strongest. At first the oak pities the reed for its weakness as it is tossed about by the slightest breeze, but when a terri-

POËME
DU
QUINQUINA,
ET AUTRES OUVRAGES
EN VERS
DE M. DE LA FONTAINE.

A PARIS,
Chez DENIS THIERRY, ruë
S. Jacques, devant la ruë du Plâtre
à l'enseigne de la ville de Paris.
ET
CLAUDE BARBIN, sur le second Perron
de la sainte Chapelle au Palais.

M. DC. LXXXII.
Avec Privilege du Roy.

Title page for the 1682 poem in which La Fontaine satirized physicians who refused to utilize recent medical advances (Bibliothèque Nationale, Paris)

ble storm arrives and pulls the mighty oak up by the roots, the more flexible reed survives. La Fontaine attains the sublime voice of the memento mori in reminding the king of who is the ultimate master of life when he describes the oak as "Celui de qui la tête au Ciel était voisine, / Et dont les pieds touchaient à l'Empire des Morts" (He whose head was close to the Heavens, / And whose feet were touching the Empire of the Dead).

In the first six books of the *Fables* other important themes are the tyrannical cruelty of the powerful, as in "Le Loup et L'Agneau" (The Wolf and the Lamb; I, 10) and "Les Loups et les brebis" (The Wolves and the Sheep; III, 8), and how populations can bring this cruelty on themselves, as in "Les Grenouilles qui demandent un Roi" (The Frogs Who Asked for a King; III, 3); the futility of war, as in "Le Lion et le moucheron" (The Lion

Frontispiece for the 1700 edition of La Fontaine's longest prose work, Les Amours de Psiché et de Cupidon, *originally published in 1669 (Bibliothèque Nationale, Paris)*

and the Gnat; II, 9); the difficulty of deciding on the right course of action, as in "Le Meunier, son fils et l'âne" (The Miller, His Son, and the Ass; III, 1); and the ineradicability of instinct, as in "Le Loup devenu berger" (The Wolf Who Became a Shepherd; III, 3). In a more original move La Fontaine adds poems that reflect on the fables themselves, as in "Contre Ceux qui ont le goût difficile" (II, 1). Although many fables counsel staying where one is and not seeking to improve one's situation, this conservative gesture also points to the possibility of finding pleasure and satisfaction in retreat. Ambition, the desire to accomplish great exploits or live royally, is inevitably shown to lead to tyranny, the loss of one's freedom, or death. Although to see any of these fables as direct criticism of Louis

XIV is difficult because of their archaic mise-en-scène of primal encounters to which social roles have been only metaphorically attached; yet, the criticism is penetrating because of the play of refined against more brutal language. The virulence of La Fontaine's social critique is mitigated, moreover, by his ability to vary his verse forms constantly to avoid any one obvious mode of address. Some fables have morals at the end; some at the beginning; some are integrated within the narrative. Because no pattern is ever set once and for all and because ambiguities or tonal disjunctions keep the readers pleasantly off balance from line to line, they are thereby made active participants in forging the moral.

The second half of the *Fables,* books VII to XII, is far more ambitious and wide-ranging than the first. It begins with "Les Animaux malades de la peste" (The Animals Sick of the Plague; VII, 1), a veritable anthropological study of the origins of sacrifice, in which a kingdom of animals struck by the plague, after an apparent soul-searching confession of sins led by the king, turns on its weakest and most innocent member, using his own confession against him to justify his execution so that the community can feel secure again. Ironies of power and taste continue to figure among the topics treated, but in new and more complex forms, such as the "double" fable in "Le Héron et la Fille" (The Heron and the Girl; VII, 4), scientific speculations in "Un Animal dans la Lune" (An Animal in the Moon; VII, 8), and philosophical poems in "Le Philosophe scythe" (The Scythian Philosopher; XII, 20). Further statements of the pleasures of retreat—in the orientally inspired "Le Songe d'un habitant du Mogol" (The Dream of One of the Mogul's Subjects; XI, 4) and its sociopolitical corollary, peace and justice, in "Le Paysan du Danube" (The Danubian Peasant; XI, 7)—represent an implicit rejection of Louis XIV's bellicose policies.

In one of his reflexive fables, "Le pouvoir des fables" (The Power of Fables; VIII, 4), La Fontaine gives perhaps his most pertinent definition of the fable as he understood it. An Athenian orator (probably Demosthenes) is trying to warn the people to take the threat of Philip of Macedon's invasion seriously. He tries high-handed admonition and then emotional appeal. Neither succeeds. In the end he tells them a completely unconnected story about a bird and an eel and the goddess Ceres trying to get to the other bank of a river. After relating how the first two creatures have crossed, the orator stops, and the audience begs to know "Et Cérès, que fit-elle?" (And what did Ceres do next?). In response the orator says, "Quoi! De contes d'enfant son peuple s'embarrasse! / Et du péril qui le menace / Lui seul entre les Grecs il néglige l'effet! / Que ne demandez-vous ce que Philippe fait?" (What! Ceres's people are so caught up with child's tales! /

While they are the only Greeks who do not care about the danger that is threatening them! / Why aren't you asking what Phillip is going to do next?). Only then do they come to their senses. In the original fable, Aesop attacked the frivolity of the Athenians, who let themselves get so interested in a story. But La Fontaine shows how the pleasure the fable can give is both a goad to moral reflection and something to be shared, a common pleasure that the fabulist is too human not to feel. He adds an important coda: "Au moment que je fais cette moralité, / Si *Peau d'âne* m'était conté, / J'y prendrai un plaisir extrême." (At the instant that I am stating the moral / If someone was telling me *Donkey Skin,* / I would enjoy it heartily). This space afforded to pleasure shows the fable to be something other than manipulative rhetoric. The orator's exhortation is too tyrannical, while his pathos, emanating from his own subjective feeling, is ignored.

In both cases force is being used, either force from a superior authority or the force of contamination—Horace's "si vis me flere" (if you force me to flee). But pleasure in the curious can be shared; it is a way to "adoucir les cœurs" (soften hearts). Moreover, it has a political purpose, however obliquely present, for the context of La Fontaine's poem is a sincere desire for peace: in its framing prologue he is imploring the French ambassador to be successful in his negotiations with the English.

The final fables of book XI present the most eloquent statements in all of La Fontaine's work: "Car tout parle dans l'Univers; / Il n'est rien qui n'ait son langage" (For everything in the Universe speaks; / There is nothing that does not have its own language). This book was to have been the last of the *Fables,* but when La Fontaine finally published book XII, its epilogue was about the place of poetry as opposed to such charity toward others, though in his typically balanced fashion, he does not deny the validity of charity. "Le Juge Arbitre, l'Hospitalier et le Solitaire" (The Judge, the Hospitaller, and the Solitary; XII, 27) tells of three saintly men, each of whom tries to find salvation in a different way. One becomes a judge who hopes to make the law more just by accepting no money for his services and expediting any case that comes before him. The second becomes the chief warden of a hospice to care for the sick. Neither of them finds that he is thanked by those he was trying to help: in the law courts no one ever feels the judge favored them as he should, and in the hospital the patients never feel the doctor gives them enough attention. When in despair they are forced to quit their appointed vocations, they flee to the "silence des bois" (silence of the woods) to find their third friend, the solitary, who tells them that only alone and away from the world can they ever

attain self-knowledge and satisfaction: "Troublez l'eau: Vous y voyez-vous? . . . Mes frères . . . laissez-la reposer, / Vous verrez alors votre image. / Pour vous mieux contempler demeurez au désert" (Churn up the surface of the water: Can you see yourselves? . . . My brothers . . . leave it be, / Then you will see your image. / The surer way to contemplate yourself is to stay in the desert). This fable is one that places the world and the self in stark opposition and presupposes that the former inevitably obscures the latter. La Fontaine's message is then ultimately unworldly—though not at all religious. The sheer quantity of suffering depicted in the rest of the *Fables* shows that there is nothing escapist about his vision: "Puisqu'on plaide, et qu'on meurt, et qu'on devient malade, / Il faut des médecins, il faut des avocats" (Since we go to court, we die, and we fall ill, / We need doctors, we need lawyers), but he wants to emphasize what is lost: "Cependant on s'oublie en ces communs besoins . . . Magistrats, princes et ministres, / Vous que doivent troubler mille accidents sinistres, / Que le malheur abat, que le bonheur corrompt, / Vous ne vous voyez point, vous ne voyez personne" (However, one forgets oneself in the common good . . . Magistrates, princes and ministers, / Who will find no peace from a thousand perilous disturbances, / Whom misfortune drags down and good fortune corrupts, / You do not see yourselves, you see no one). He is speaking directly to the powerful to show them that even at its best their immersion in the world does not give them the most precious thing of all: themselves. This rhetoric has sloughed off the rancor of the satirist and the idealizations of the moralist, and above all does not prescribe for others what they should do but leaves them to themselves. His poetry is a clear stream in which the self can be recuperated, not a catechism of moral precepts. Jean de La Fontaine's lesson ultimately is pure poetry.

In subsequent years the French attitude toward La Fontaine wavered between an indulgent but ultimately belittling admiration for his spontaneous fecundity (the romantic view of Sainte-Beuve) and a more elevated consideration of his deep insight into French malaise under absolutism (in Hyppolite Taine's positivistic account of the social and political critique mounted by the *Fables*) or highly conscious craftsmanship as a poet (as Paul Valéry's famous essay on the *Adonis* puts it). More recently still, in France, La Fontaine has been acclaimed by Marc Fumaroli as the last poet of the Renaissance, melding a bimillenial heritage of classical letters with a freedom of poetic treatment that translated into a highly cultured basis on which to defend one's liberty in an oppressive world.

Letters:

Lettres de La Fontaine à sa femme, ou Relation d'un voyage de Paris en Limousin, edited by Abbé Caudal (Paris: Centre de Documentation Universitaire, 1966);

Lettres à sa femme: voyage de Paris en Limousin, edited by Michel Mourlet (Paris: Trédaniel, 1995).

Bibliography:
R. de Rochambeau, *Bibliographie des œuvres de Jean de La Fontaine* (Paris, 1912).

References:
Antoine Adam, *Histoire de la Littérature française au xviie siècle,* 5 volumes (Paris: Domat, 1948–1962), IV: 7–78;

"The Art of Transition in La Fontaine," in *Leo Spitzer: Representative Essays,* translated by David Bellos (Cambridge: Cambridge University Press, 1983);

Australian Journal of French Studies, special La Fontaine issue, 16 (1979);

Jean Marc Bassetti, "A la Découverte de Jean de La Fontaine," FTPress, 2000–2001 <http://www.lafontaine.net>;

Alya Baccar, ed., *La Fontaine et l'Orient: Réception, réécriture, représentation* (Paris, Seattle & Tübingen: Papers on French Seventeenth Century Literature, 1996);

Bernard Beugnot, "La Fontaine et Montaigne: Essai de bilan," *Études Françaises,* 1 (1965): 43–65;

Jean Dominique Biard, *Le style des Fables de La Fontaine* (Paris: Nizet, 1970);

Biard, *The Style of La Fontaine's Fables* (New York: Barnes & Noble, 1966);

Michel Bideaux, ed., *Fables et fabulistes: Variations autour de La Fontaine* (Mont-de-Marsan: SPEC, 1992);

Anne Lynn Birberick, *Reading Undercover: Audience and Author in Jean de La Fontaine* (Lewisburg, Pa.: Bucknell University Press / London: Associated University Presses, 1998);

Birberick, ed., *Refiguring La Fontaine: Tercentenary Essays* (Charlottesville, Va.: Rookwood Press, 1996);

Nicolas Boileau, "Dissertation sur Jaconde," in his *Œuvres complètes,* Bibliothèque de la Pléiade, no. 188, edited by Adam and Françoise Escal (Paris: Gallimard, 1966);

Pierre Boutang, *La Fontaine politique* (Paris: A. Michel, 1981);

Elisabeth Girod Branan, *La Fontaine, au-delà des "bagatelles" des Contes et des "badineries" des Fables* (Lexington, Ky.: French Forum, 1993);

René Bray, *Les Fables de La Fontaine* (Paris: E. Malfère, 1929);

Jules Brody, *Lectures de La Fontaine* (Charlottesville, Va.: Rookwood Press, 1994);

Emmanuel Bury, *L'esthétique de La Fontaine* (Paris: SEDES, 1996);

Cahiers de l'association internationale des études françaises, special La Fontaine issue, 26 (1974);

Andrew Calder, *The Fables of La Fontaine* (Geneva: Droz, 2001);

Nicolas-Sébastien Chamfort, "Eloge de La Fontaine," in *Recueil de l'Académie des belles-lettres, sciences et arts de Marseille* (Marseille: Favet, 1774), pp. 1–48;

Pierre Clarac, *La Fontaine* (Paris: Haticr, 1959);

Jean-Pierre Collinet, *La Fontaine en amont et en aval* (Pisa: Goliardica, 1988);

Collinet, *La Fontaine et quelques autres* (Geneva: Droz, 1992);

Collinet, *Le monde littéraire de La Fontaine* (Paris: Presses Universitaires de France, 1970);

Georges Couton, *La poétique de La Fontaine* (Paris: Presses Universitaires de France, 1957);

Couton, *La politique de la Fontaine* (Paris: Les Belles Lettres, 1959);

Couton, "Le livre épicurien des *Fables:* Essai de lecture du livre VIII," in his *Mélanges Pintard* (Paris: Klincksieck, 1975), pp. 283–290;

Patrick Dandrey, *La Fabrique des Fables: Essai sur la poétique de La Fontaine* (Paris: Klincksieck, 1991);

Richard Danner, *Patterns of Irony in the Fables of La Fontaine* (Athens: Ohio University Press, 1985);

Jean-Charles Darmon, *Philosophie epicurienne et littérature aux XVIIe siècle en France* (Paris: Presses Universitaires de France, 1998);

Roger Duchêne, *La Fontaine* (Paris: Fayard, 1990);

L'Esprit Créateur, special La Fontaine issue, 21 (Winter 1981);

Europe, special La Fontaine issue, 50 (1972);

Le Fablier, Revue des Amis de Jean de La Fontaine (1988–   ) —Journal devoted to La Fontaine's *Fables;*

Marc Fumaroli, *Le Poète et le Roi: Jean de La Fontaine en son siècle* (Paris: Editions de Fallois, 1997);

Jean-Luc Gallardo, *Le spectacle de la parole: La Fontaine, Adonis, Le songe de Vaux, Les amours de Psyche et de Cupidon* (Orleans: Paradigme, 1996);

Le génie de la langue française: Autour de Marot et La Fontaine, "L'adolescence Clémentine," "Les amours de Psyché et de Cupidon," edited by Jean-Charles Monferran (Fontenay-aux-Roses, France: ENS, 1997);

Jean Giraudoux, *Les cinq tentations de La Fontaine* (Paris: Grasset, 1938);

Jürgen Grimm, *Etudes lafontainiennes,* Biblio 17, 2 volumes (Paris: Papers on French Seventeenth Century Literature, 1994, 1996);

Marcel Gutwirth, *Un merveilleux sans éclat: La Fontaine ou la poésie exilée* (Geneva: Droz, 1987);

Adnan Haddad, *Fables de La Fontaine d'origine orientale* (Paris: SEDES, 1984);

André Hallys, *Jean de La Fontaine* (Paris: Perrin, 1922);

René Jasinski, *La Fontaine et le premier receuil des Fables,* 2 volumes (Paris: Nizet, 1965, 1966);

Jean de La Fontaine, Catalogue from an exhibition held in Paris, Bibliothèque Nationale de France, 4 October 1995 – 15 January 1996, directed by Claire Lesage (Paris: Seuil, 1995);

Renée Kohn, *Le Goût de La Fontaine* (Paris: Presses Universitaires de France, 1962);

Jean Lafond, "La Beauté et la grâce: L'Esthétique 'platonicienne' des Amours de Psyché," *Revue d'Histoire littéraire de la France,* 69 (1969): 475–490;

Jean-Pierre Landry, ed., *Présence de La Fontaine,* edited by Jean-Pierre Landry (Lyon: CEDIC, Université de Lyon, 1996);

John C. Lapp, *The Esthetics of Negligence: La Fontaine's Contes* (Cambridge: Cambridge University Press, 1971);

L. Lévrault, *La Fable des origines à nos jours* (Paris: Mellottée, 1928);

Littératures classiques, special La Fontaine section, supplement to 16 (January 1992);

Louis Marin, *Des pouvoirs de l'image: Gloses* (Paris: Seuil, 1993), pp. 25–39, 64–71;

Marin, *Food for Thought,* translated by Mette Hjort (Baltimore: Johns Hopkins University Press, 1989 [1986]), pp. 44–84;

Marin, *Portrait of the King,* Theory and History of Literature, no. 57, translated by Martha M. Houle (Minneapolis: University of Minnesota Press, 1988), pp. 94–104;

Marin, *Le Récit est un piège* (Paris: Minuit, 1978);

Jean Marmier, *Horace en France, au dix-septième siècle* (Paris: Presses Universitaires de France, 1962), pp. 311–340;

Jane Merino-Morais, *Différence et répétition dans les Contes de La Fontaine* (Gainesville: University Presses of Florida, 1983);

Georges Mongrédien, *Recueil des textes et des documents du XVIIe siècle relatifs à La Fontaine* (Paris: CNRS, 1973);

P. Mornand, *L'iconographie des* Fables *de La Fontaine* (Paris: Portique, 1946);

Odette de Mourgues, *O Muse, fuyante proie: Essai sur la poésie de La Fontaine* (Paris: J. Corti, 1962);

Fanny Nepote-Desmarres, *La Fontaine, Fables* (Paris: Presses Universitaires de France, 1999);

North American Society for Seventeenth-Century French Literature, Montreal, 20–22 April 1995, *Et in Arcadia ego,* edited by Antoine Soare (Paris, Seattle & Tübingen: Papers on French Seventeenth Century Literature, 1996);

Jean Orieux, *La Fontaine: ou, La vie est un conte* (Paris: Flammarion, 1976);

Papers on French Seventeenth Century Literature, special La Fontaine issue, 4–5 (1976);

La poétique des "Fables" de La Fontaine, edited by Lane M. Heller and Ian M. Richmond (Ontario: Mestengo Press, 1994);

Revue de littérature comparée, special issue on "La Fontaine et la fable," edited by Patrick Dandrey and Pierre Brunel (1996);

David Lee Rubin, *A Pact with Silence: Art and Thought in the Fables of Jean de La Fontaine* (Columbus: Ohio State University Press, 1991);

Sainte-Beuve, "La Fontaine" in *Œuvres,* 1, Premiers Lundis and Portraits Littéraires, edited by Maxime Leroy, Bibliothèque de la Pléiade (Paris: Gallimard, 1956), pp. 696–720;

Michel Serres, "Knowledge in the Classical Age: La Fontaine & Descartes," in *Hermes: Literature, Science and Philosophy* (Baltimore: Johns Hopkins University Press, 1982 [1980]), pp. 15–28;

Serres, *The Parasite,* translated by Lawrence R. Scher (Baltimore: Johns Hopkins University Press, 1983);

Maya Slater, *The Craft of La Fontaine* (London: Athlone Press, 2000);

P. Souillé, *La Fontaine et ses devanciers* (Paris & Angers: Durand-Cosnier & Lachèse, 1861);

Leo Spitzer, "L'art de la transition chez La Fontaine," in *Etudes de style* (Paris: NRF, 1970), pp. 166–207;

Monica Sutherland, *La Fontaine* (London: Cape, 1953);

Marie Odile Sweetser, *La Fontaine* (Boston: Twayne, 1987);

Hippolyte Taine, *La Fontaine et ses Fables* (Paris: Hachette, 1861);

J. Allen Tyler, *A Concordance to the Fables and Tales of Jean de La Fontaine* (Ithaca, N.Y.: Cornell University Press, 1974);

Paul Valéry, "Au sujet d'Adonis," *Œuvres,* 2 volumes, edited by Jean Hytier (Paris: Gallimard, 1957, 1960), I: 474–495;

Michael Vincent, *Figures of the Text: Reading and Writing in La Fontaine* (Amsterdam: J. Benjamins, 1992);

Voltaire, *Le siècle de Louis XIV,* 2 volumes (Paris: Garnier-Flammarion), II: 55, 237;

Karl Voßler, *La Fontaine und sein Fabelwerk* (Heidelberg: C. Winter, 1919);

Philip A. Wadsworth, *Young La Fontaine: A Study of His Artistic Growth in His Early Poetry and First Fables* (Evanston, Ill.: Northwestern University Press, 1952);

Roger Zuber and Michele Cuénin, *Le Classicisme 1660–1680* (Paris: Arthaud, 1990), pp. 215–236.

Papers:

Jean de La Fontaine's papers are included in the Fonds Conrart at the Bibliothèque de l'Arsenal, Paris; his manuscripts are housed in the Bibliothèque Sainte-Geneviève, Paris.

François de La Mothe Le Vayer
(1 August 1588 – 9 May 1672)

David Wetsel

Arizona State University

BOOKS: *Quatre Dialogues faits à l'imitation des anciens,* as Orasius Tubero (Frankfurt: J. Sarius, 1604 [i.e., 1630]; enlarged, 1506 [i.e., 1631])–enlarged edition includes *Cinq Autres Dialogues;*

Discours de la contrariété d'humeurs qui se trouve entre certaines nations, et singulièrement entre la françoise et l'espagnole, traduit de l'italien de Fabricio Campolini, véronois (Paris: E. Richer, 1636);

Petit Discours chrestien de l'immortalité de l'âme (Paris: J. Camusat, 1637);

Considérations sur l'éloquence françoise de ce tems (Paris: S. Cramoisy, 1638);

Discours de l'histoire (Paris: J. Camusat, 1638);

De l'Instruction de Monseigneur le Dauphin (Paris: S. Cramoisy, 1640);

De la Vertu des Payens (Paris: F. Targa, 1642);

De la Liberté et de la servitude (Paris: A. de Sommaville, 1643); translated by John Evelyn as *Of Liberty and Servitude* (London: Printed for M. Meighen and G. Bedell, 1649);

Opuscules, ou Petits Traictez (Paris: A. de Sommaville, 1643);

Des Anciens et Principaux historiens grecs et latins dont il nous reste quelques ouvrages (Paris: Veuve de N. de Sercy, 1646); translated by William D'Avenant as *Notitia Historicorum Selectorum, or Animadversions upon the Antient and Famous Greek and Latin Historians* (Oxford: Printed by Leonard Lichfield for Richard Davis, 1678);

Opuscule, ou Petit Traité sceptique sur cette commune façon de parler: n'avoir pas le sens commun (Paris: A. Courbé, 1646);

Petits traitez en forme de lettres escrites à diverses personnes studieuses (Paris: A. Courbé, 1648);

La Géographie et la Morale du Prince (Paris: A. Courbé, 1651);

La Rhétorique du Prince (Paris: A. Courbé, 1651);

L'Œconomique du Prince; La Politique du Prince (Paris: A. Courbé, 1653);

François de La Mothe Le Vayer (engraving by Jac Lubin; Bibliothèque Nationale, Paris)

Œuvres, edited by François de La Mothe Le Vayer *fils,* 2 volumes (Paris: A. Courbé, 1654; revised and enlarged, 1656; revised and enlarged, 1662);

En quoy la piété des François diffère de celle des Espagnols dans une profession de mesme religion (Paris: A. Courbé, 1658);

La Logique du Prince (Paris: A. Courbé, 1658);

La Physique du Prince (Paris: A. Courbé, 1658);

Prose chagrine (Paris: A. Courbé, 1661);

La Promenade, dialogue entre Tubertus Ocella et Marcus Bibulus (Paris: T. Jolly, 1662);

La Science de l'histoire avec le jugement des principaux historiens tant anciens que modernes (Paris: L. Billaine, 1665);

Suite des Homilies académiques (Paris: L. Billaine, 1665);

Dernières Homilies académiques (Paris: L. Billaine, 1666);

Problèmes sceptiques (Paris: T. Jolly, 1666);

Doute sceptique: Si l'estude des belles-lettres est préférable à toute autre occupation (Paris: T. Jolly, 1667);

Deux Discours: Le Premier, Du peu de certitude qu'il y a dans l'histoire; Le Second, De la connoissance de soy-mesme (Paris: L. Billaine, 1668);

Observations diverses sur la composition et sur la lecture des livres (Paris: L. Billaine, 1668);

Mémorial de quelques conférences avec des personnes studieuses (Paris: T. Jolly, 1669);

Œuvres, 15 volumes (Paris: L. Billaine, 1669);

L'Hexaméron rustique, ou Les Six Journées passées à la campagne entre des personnes studieuses (Paris: T. Jolly, 1670);

Introduction chronologique à l'histoire de France pour Monsieur (Paris: T. Jolly, 1670);

Soliloques sceptiques (Paris: L. Billaine, 1670);

Cinq Dialogues faits à l'imitation des anciens, par Oratius Tubero; Quatre Autres Dialogues (Frankfurt [i.e., Trévoux]: J. Sarius, 1716).

Editions and Collections: *De la Contrariété d'humeurs qui se trouve entre certaines nations, et singulièrement entre la française et l'espagnole, ou De l'Antipathie des Français et des Espagnols,* edited by Jacques-Joseph Rouvière (Paris: de Beausseaux, 1809);

Œuvres (14 volumes, Dresde: M. Groell, 1756–1759; facsimile edition, 2 volumes, Geneva: Slatkine, 1970);

Dialogues faits à l'imitation des Anciens, edited by André Pessel (Paris: Fayard, 1988);

Lettre sur la comédie de L'Imposteur, edited by Robert McBride (Durham, N.C.: University of Durham, 1994);

Hexaméron rustique, ou Les Six Journées passées à la campagne entre des personnes studieuses, edited by Gabriel Los d'Urizen (Paris: Paris-Zanzibar, 1997).

Edition in English: *The Great Prerogative of a Private Life: By Way of Dialogue* (London: Printed by J.C. for L.C. and sold by Charles Blount, 1678).

OTHER: "Jugement de Quinte Curce," in *Quinte Curce, De la vie et des actions d'Alexandre le Grand,* translated by Claude Favre de Vaugelas (Paris: L. Billaine, 1664);

"Du moyen de dresser une bibliothèque d'une centaine de livres seulement," in *Conseils pour former une bibliothèque peu nombreuse mais choisie,* by Jean-Henri-Samuel Formey (Berlin: Haude & Spener, 1755).

SELECTED PERIODICAL PUBLICATIONS—UNCOLLECTED: "Discours sur la bataille de Lutzen," anonymous, *Mercure François,* 18 (1633);

"Discours sur la proposition de la trêve aux Pays-Bas en 1633," anonymous, *Mercure François* (1633);

"Trois Lettres de La Mothe Le Vayer," edited by Philippe Tamizey de Larroque, *Revue critique d'histoire et de littérature* (1872).

Pierre Bayle called François de La Mothe Le Vayer and Gabriel Naudé the two "savants de ce siècle qui avaient le plus de lecture et l'esprit le plus épuré des sentiments populaires" (thinkers in this century whose readings were the most extensive and whose thinking was the least contaminated by the opinions of the masses). Though the debate continues with regard to the extent La Mothe Le Vayer actually influenced the *philosophes* (philosophers) of the French Enlightenment, rarely does anyone note that his writings include the foundational texts for the beginning of historical criticism and the comparative study of religion in France. Modern scholars such as René Pintard have definitively unmasked La Mothe Le Vayer's unprecedented radical attack on revealed religion, successfully obscured by his claim that his "Christian skepticism" served only to humble the human sciences in the face of Revelation.

The son of an erudite magistrate, La Mothe Le Vayer was born in Paris on 1 August 1588; he inherited his father's position in 1625 but soon abandoned study of the law in order to devote his life to foreign travel, philosophical meditation, and frequenting the *académie savante* of the Dupuy brothers (Pierre and Jacques), where he formed close friendships with Naudé and Pierre Gassendi. Not until 1630, at the age of forty-two, did La Mothe Le Vayer publish his first work, the *Quatre Dialogues faits à l'imitation des anciens* (Four Dialogues in Imitation of the Ancients), adding *Cinq Autres Dialogues* (Five Other Dialogues) the following year. Published under the pseudonym of Orasius Tubero, these nine dialogues constitute the essence of his thought, which, though never again repeated so boldly, did not change throughout the course of his eighty-three years.

La Mothe Le Vayer's recognition of just how subversive his dialogues were is attested to not only by his use of a pseudonym but also by the false dates of publication (1604; 1506) and fake publishers and places of publication under which all the original editions appeared. A dominant theme in the work is that the true philosopher must rise above the erroneous thinking of "du vulgaire" (the masses). "De la philosophie sceptique" (On Skeptical Philosophy), the first piece in *Quatre Dialogues faits à l'imitation des anciens,* is a panegyric to the skepticism of the third-century Greek philosopher Sextus Empiricus (author of *Outlines of Pyrrhonism* and *Against the Dogmatists*). The dialogue allows La Mothe Le Vayer to enumerate paradox after paradox based upon his extensive readings about the diversity of human customs in order to elaborate a central idea—"qu'il n'y a rien de solide et d'arrêté" (that nothing is fixed and preordained)—and conclude that skepticism alone leads to the tranquility of the soul.

The second dialogue, "Le Banquet sceptique" (The Skeptical Banquet), continues in the same vein and seems to reflect La Mothe Le Vayer's many private discussions with Naudé and his circle. The third dialogue, "De la vie privée" (translated as *The Great Prerogative of a Private Life*, 1678), was inspired almost entirely by La Mothe Le Vayer's readings of the works of Roman philosopher Lucius Annaeus Seneca, who lived primarily in the first century. It pits the merits of the philosophical and retired life against the possibility of changing society. The last of the four original dialogues, "Des rares et éminentes qualitez des asnes de ce temps" (On the Rare and Eminent Qualities of the Asses of These Times), parallels the skepticism and stoicism of the ass and the philosopher—both remain impassive in the face of ill fortune and even death—and recalls in some ways Michel Eyquem de Montaigne's *De l'expérience* (On Experience, 1588).

In "De la divinité" (On Divinity), one of the five dialogues added in 1631, La Mothe Le Vayer comes closest to revealing his true opinions. The dialogue, which claims to use skepticism as a transition to Christianity, in fact represents an unprecedented scholarly attack on Revelation. La Mothe Le Vayer hardly belongs in the category of Christian skeptic. Indeed, just at the moment when the Christian apologists were beginning to discover the potential dangers of Montaigne's philosophy, La Mothe Le Vayer sought to turn skepticism loose against the very notion of revealed religion—hence the necessity of a highly ambiguous text directed to the *déniaisés* (enlightened readers) who knew how to read between the lines and understand the significance of what was left unsaid.

Whereas Montaigne had thought he could discover more resemblances than differences among the different religions of the world, La Mothe Le Vayer's aim was to document their contradictions and lack of continuity. The traditional, orthodox explanation of parallels being discovered between Christianity and the pagan religions was that the cults of the latter were but *singeries* (mimicries) created by Satan in order to cast doubt upon Christianity and its predecessor, Judaism. However, Christian fideists, including Montaigne and Pierre Charron, thought they could discern the faint light of fundamental religious truth in the religions of all the nations of the world.

La Mothe Le Vayer's itinerary could not have been more different. He boldly seeks to demonstrate the essential contradictions among as many religious

creeds as he can cite. Whereas many religions require elaborate ceremonial rituals, he observes, others direct that God must be worshiped only "en pureté d'esprit" (with a pure spirit). Many religions direct their faithful to ask God for what they need. The Greek philosopher Pythagoras, on the other hand, forbids such requests, believing that no one has true knowledge of what he really needs. Some religions require animal (and even human) sacrifices. Others have either abolished, or never had, such practices. Jews, Christians, and Muslims have chosen different days of the week as their holy day.

La Mothe Le Vayer takes care to exclude Christianity itself from his analyses. He repeatedly professes his allegiance to Christian truth. Yet, his intention of casting doubt on Christian Revelation must have been perfectly clear to the select audience of the *déniaisés* to whom the work was really addressed. When discussing the existence of God, La Mothe Le Vayer does not fail to cite traditional Christian proofs. However, he then goes into elaborate detail with regard to the arguments that nonbelievers have produced to the contrary. Drawing upon recent anthropological discoveries, he attempts to make the case that religion is hardly universal. Countries exist, he argues, that possess no vestige of religion whatsoever. The peoples of New France, he points out, worship no God whatsoever. Those of Mexico have no word in their language for God. The Mandarins who govern China believe in no other God than Nature.

Once again citing the "Athées" (Atheists), La Mothe Le Vayer directs his readers' attention to how, over the course of history, they have sought to explain the origin of human belief in Divinity. Some thinkers, La Mothe Le Vayer explains, conjecture that primitive humans first conceived the notion of Divinity in attempting to explain such frightening natural phenomena as thunder, earthquakes, and eclipses. Others, he notes, such as Epicurus, have explained the human experience of Divinity as having had its genesis in the dreams of primitive humans. The greatest among the philosophers, including Aristotle and his commentator par excellence, Averroës, recognized no other God than Nature itself, denied the Creation of the world, and rejected the notion of First Cause.

La Mothe Le Vayer's agenda with regard to revealed religion is particularly clear when he observes that even those who agree upon the existence of the Gods cannot agree upon their essential nature. His use of the plural (Gods) serves to protect him from accusations of an attack upon the Christian God, but it hardly obscures his own prejudice in the matter, including his horror at the very notion of incarnation. Some, he observes, attribute to the Gods not only the general design of the universe but also a particular interest in everything that happens in the world—hence, the notion of the reward of virtue and the punishment of vice. Others, he explains, maintain that to deny the very existence of Divinity would be better than to invest it with human passions and concerns.

La Mothe Le Vayer insists upon the total nonintervention of Divinity in human affairs. Neither modern nor ancient defenders of Divinity, he argues, seem able to agree on whether (the) God(s) require(s) the worship of humankind. Some teach that one must worship and serve the Gods, who know even our innermost thoughts and dispense punishment and reward. Others, like Epicurus, reject any kind of cult worship or adoration. La Mothe Le Vayer boldly advances the notion that the idea of an omnipotent Divinity is hardly consonant with any practical religious or moral observance. Of what use are prayers, ceremonies, or even moral behavior if everything is predestined by divine omniscience?

La Mothe Le Vayer then moves on to the question of the mortality or the immortality of the human soul. He seems delighted to be able to point out that the belief in the immortality of the soul has never been a universal tenet of all religions. Among the Jews, he explains, the Sadducees "croyaient l'âme mortelle et se mocquaient de cette prétendue resurrection" (thought the soul mortal and mocked this so-called resurrection). Among the Chinese, he goes on to observe, a religious order publicly preaches the mortality of the soul.

La Mothe Le Vayer, ever advancing toward his thesis that all religions are mired in contradiction and incoherence, first professes an essentially fideist position. "Au défaut d'avoir la foi pour aiguille aimanté qui tienne notre esprit arrêté vers le pole de la grâce divine," he claims, "il est impossible d'éviter des erreurs . . . [qui] nous porteraient enfin à un spirituel naufrage" (Lacking the compass of faith, which holds our minds fixed upon the pole of divine grace, it is impossible to avoid errors . . . [that] would ultimately carry us to spiritual shipwreck).

Among the infinity of world religions, La Mothe Le Vayer insists, every single believer thinks he alone possesses the only true religion, condemns the adherents of all other religions, and would fight until he shed the last drop of their blood. Claiming to be horrified by the carnage that religious controversy has brought upon the world, La Mothe Le Vayer takes an amazingly bold step for his time. He directs his readers' attention to those exceptional moments in history in which certain rulers have authorized liberty of conscience.

Invoking the example of the Roman emperor of the East Valens, La Mothe Le Vayer extols Solomon for having permitted his foreign wives to build temples to their own Goddesses. He lauds Manassas, King of Judah, for having installed idols and altars to a multiplicity of Gods in the Temple of Jerusalem. He likewise praises the Hebrew kings, Jehu and Joas, for having been open-minded enough to sacrifice both to the God of their Fathers and to the "golden calves."

At this point, La Mothe Le Vayer seems finally to have ceased to worry about the consequences of his words. The historical instances of religious tolerance he invokes are not only heretical by any standard but also extremely dangerous politically. La Mothe Le Vayer finally shows his underlying thought and qualifies all religions as "superstitions." Refuting the notion that atheism represents a danger to the political order, he translates word for word a passage from the *Essays* (1597–1625) of Francis Bacon:

> Atheism leaves a man to sense, to philosophy, to natural piety, to laws, to reputation: all which may be guides to an outward moral. . . . Therefore Atheism did never perturb states; for it makes men wary of themselves . . . , we see the times inclined to atheism (as in the times of Augustus Caesar) were civil times; but superstitions hath been the confusion of many states and bringeth in a new *primum mobile* that ravisheth all the spheres of government. The master of superstition is the people.

After the early 1630s La Mothe Le Vayer prudently cultivated a respectable public persona under the cover of a sincere fideism. He settled into that highly private *libertinage* (freethinking) that was the only prudent option in classical France. He took profound pleasure in contesting religious dogmas without ever believing that to go into open revolt against them was possible or even suitable. He delighted in mocking Christianity among the *déniaisés* while sharing their conviction that religion is a necessary evil for the control of the masses. He no longer openly subverted orthodox Christian doctrine and preached liberation from that orthodoxy only to a highly secret elite.

Never again, even in his most skeptical writings, did La Mothe Le Vayer return in print to the explosively dangerous theses of his dialogues. Indeed, his *Petit Discours chrestien de l'immortalité de l'âme* (Short Christian Discourse on the Immortality of the Soul, 1637) is clearly an attempt to reassure Armand du Plessis, cardinal de Richelieu, of his religious orthodoxy. The political character of the works La Mothe Le Vayer published between 1632 and 1638 equally attest to his desire to win the favor of Richelieu. "Discours sur la bataille de Lutzen" (Discourse on the Battle of Lutzen) and "Discours sur la proposition de la trève aux Pays-Bas en 1633" (Discourse on the Proposed Truce

Title page for La Mothe Le Vayer's 1638 treatise on the French language
(Bibliothèque Nationale, Paris)

in the Netherlands)–published anonymously, on Richelieu's orders, in the *Mercure François* in 1633–sought to sway public opinion in favor of the cardinal's campaign against Spain and Austria. La Mothe Le Vayer's *Discours de la contrariété d'humeurs qui se trouve entre certaines nations, et singulièrement entre la françoise et l'espagnole* (Discourse on the Contrariety of Humors to Be Found between Certain Nations, and in Particular between France and Spain, 1636), published as if a translation of observations by an Italian writer, clearly served the same end, whereas his *En quoy la piété des François diffère de celle des Espagnols dans une profession de mesme religion* (How French and Spanish Piety Differ within a Profession of the Same Religion, 1658) sought to refute possible accusations of heresy on the part of France because of its alliances with Holland and Sweden.

La Mothe Le Vayer's ambition to be named to the yet unfilled Académie Française, to which he was

elected the following year, is clear in his *Considérations sur l'éloquence françoise de ce tems* (Considerations on French Eloquence in the Present Day, 1638). His *De l'Instruction de Monseigneur le Dauphin* (On the Instruction of Monseigneur the Dauphin, 1640) likewise reveals his aspiration to be named preceptor to the young prince. *De la Vertu des Payens* (On the Virtue of Pagans), La Mothe Le Vayer's most famous work, appeared in 1642 under his own name.

Published under the personal protection of Richelieu, *De la Vertu des Payens* was ostensibly written to promote the cardinal's anti-Jansenist campaign by attacking the neo-Augustinians' extremely narrow view of salvation. The work permitted La Mothe Le Vayer to venture into a certain religious heterodoxy via a fortunate, but only partial, conjunction between his own ideas and Richelieu's intentions. In 1640 Jansenius's *Augustinus* was about to be published at Louvain. In *De la Vertu des*

Payens, La Mothe Le Vayer chose to defend the highly explosive anti-Jansenist thesis that the virtuous among the sages of antiquity had indeed attained salvation.

In *De la Vertu des Payens,* La Mothe Le Vayer argues that God never refuses his grace to those who do everything in their power to render themselves worthy of it. The virtuous pagans who followed Nature's light and submitted their free will to reason, he concludes, by all rights should be numbered among the Blessed, since they knew no other law than the natural one. To a rather extensive list of classical philosophers whom he deems worthy of salvation, La Mothe Le Vayer adds the name of Confucius. The Sage's admonition "de ne faire jamais à autrui ce que nous ne voudrions pas qui nous fût fait" (never to do unto others what we would not wish done to ourselves) strikes La Mothe Le Vayer as approaching "la morale chrétienne" (Christian morality).

La Mothe Le Vayer devotes an entire chapter to the fate of those multitudes who, though born after the Incarnation, never received the Gospel. Have they not the right to complain, as did the Japanese to Saint Francis Xavier, that God has treated them "avec tant de désavantage" (so disadvantageously)? To condemn every single one of these vast multitudes to hell "sans réserve et sans miséricorde" (without reservation and without mercy), he argues, would be illogical, inhumane, and contrary to Christian charity.

According to Antoine Arnauld, La Mothe Le Vayer's theses were not only heretical but also subversive to the point of undermining essential Christian doctrine. In his *De la nécessité de la foi en Jésus-Christ* (On the Necessity of Faith in Jesus-Christ, 1777) Arnauld mounts a broadside attack against La Mothe Le Vayer's attempt to rescue the *anciens justes* (righteous among the ancients) and the unbaptized multitudes from the fires of hell. La Mothe Le Vayer's entire enterprise, he charges, is nothing short of a revival of Pelagianism.

In *De la Vertu des Payens,* La Mothe Le Vayer appeals for mercy on behalf of a young pagan in the New World who, pious according to the lights of Nature, raises his thoughts to the Eternal Presence and prays, "Mon Dieu, qui connaissez le plus secret de mon âme, j'implore votre miséricorde, et je vous supplie de me conduire à la fin pour laquelle vous m'ávez créé" (My God, you who know the depths of my soul, I beg for your mercy, and I humbly pray that you will lead me to the purpose for which you created me). Arnauld hesitates not a moment before condemning La Mothe Le Vayer's pious pagan to that eternal fire to which he has been predestined since the beginning of time. Nor does Arnauld see any reason to exempt "ces prétendus

vertueux de paganisme" (these so-called virtuous pagans) from the fate of the damned.

Arnauld later used his influence with the queen to block La Mothe Le Vayer's aspirations to become tutor to the dauphin. "Ses discours sceptiques, sous le nom d'Oratius Tubero, ainsi que son livre de la *Vertu des Payens,*" he wrote, "font assez voir qu'il n'était pas chrétien" (His skeptical writings, published under the name of Oratius Tubero, as well as his book on the *Virtue of the Pagans . . .* make amply clear that he has not been a Christian). La Mothe Le Vayer's fortunes floundered with the death of Richelieu. Cardinal Mazarin's agenda did not include persecution of the Jansenists. It seems probable to conclude that La Mothe Le Vayer's anti-Jansenism, as well as his reputation as a freethinker, cost him the post. In 1647 La Mothe Le Vayer was named preceptor to the future duc d'Orléans, and in 1652 the Queen Mother herself chose him as preceptor of the young king. In spite of his many writings destined for the king's education–*La Géographie et la Morale du Prince* (Geography and Morality for the Prince, 1651), *La Rhétorique du Prince* (Rhetoric for the Prince, 1651), *L'Œconomique du Prince; La Politique du Prince* (Economics for the Prince; Politics for the Prince, 1653), *La Logique du Prince* (Logic for the Prince, 1658), and *La Physique du Prince* (Physics for the Prince, 1658)–the post of preceptor seems to have remained mainly honorific.

La Mothe Le Vayer's *Des Anciens et Principaux historiens grecs et latins dont il nous reste quelques ouvrages* (1646; translated as *Notitia Historicorum Selectorum, or Animadversions upon the Antient and Famous Greek and Latin Historians,* 1678), written in view of the instruction of the Prince, marks the beginning of historical criticism in France. The "Préface d'une Histoire" (Preface to a History) appended to this treatise insists that good history must be based upon authentic documents and take an impartial perspective. Avoiding plagiarisms, digressions, harangues, and invented dialogues, good history must not only relate events but also penetrate their causes. These principles are restated and subjected to a skeptical perspective in his "Du peu de certitude qu'il y a dans l'histoire" (On the Lack of Certainty in History), published in *Deux Discours* (Two Discourses, 1668).

After the death of his wife in 1665 and a bout of ill health, La Mothe Le Vayer began a slow retreat from the court to which he had once so aspired and started to send his son, the abbé Le Vayer, to replace him at his lessons with his royal pupil. La Mothe Le Vayer's retirement to a philosophical life was hastened by the death of this only son in 1664 at the age of thirty-four. Le Vayer *fils* had been an intimate friend of Molière, who addressed a celebrated sonnet to La Mothe Le Vayer upon his son's death. In 1650 the abbé Le Vayer had written a satirical comedy, *Le Parasite*

Mormon (Mormon the Hanger-on), which included a light burlesque of the style and philosophy of his father later echoed in Molière's 1664 *Le Mariage Forcé* (The Forced Marriage). Shortly after the death of his son, La Mothe Le Vayer remarried at the age of seventy-six.

François de La Mothe Le Vayer continued his philosophical meditation and writing until the year before his death at age eighty-three on 9 May 1672. *Prose chagrine* (1661), *Problèmes Sceptiques* (Skeptical Problems, 1666), and *Soliloques Sceptiques* (Skeptical Soliloquies, 1670) renew his Pyrrhonist teachings. In his last work, *L'Hexaméron rustique, ou Les Six Journées passées à la campagne entre des personnes studieuses* (The Rustic Hexameron, or Six Days Spent in the Country with Studious People, 1670)—which Bayle judged as filled with too many "impure thoughts"—La Mothe Le Vayer returns to the radical and often ribald spirit of his early dialogues.

Up until his death, La Mothe Le Vayer remained intrigued with the curiosities of life outside Christian Europe, maintaining a long correspondence with his friend François Bernier during the latter's trip to India. Indeed, at seeing Bernier, who upon his return came to visit his dying friend, La Mothe Le Vayer's last words on his deathbed were "Eh bien! Quelles nouvelles avez-vous du grand Mogol?" (Well! What news of the Great Mogul?)

References:

Antoine Adam, *Les Libertins au XVIIe siècle* (Paris: Buchet/Chastel, 1964);

Julien-Eymard d'Angers, "Stoïcisme et libertinage dans l'œuvre de François La Mothe Le Vayer," *Revue des sciences humaines,* 75 (1954): 259–284;

Joseph Beaude, "Le Dialogue d'Orasius sur le sujet de la divinité," *Recherches sur le XVIIe siècle* (1976): 50–62;

Louis Etienne, *Essai sur La Mothe Le Vayer* (Rennes: J. M. Vatar, 1849);

Peter Gay, *The Enlightenment: The Rise of Modern Paganism* (New York: Norton, 1966), pp. 290, 306–307;

Sylvia Giocanti, "De la misologie à la philosophie sceptique: Etude sur le scepticisme moderne à partir de la lecture des œuvres de Montaigne, Pascal, La Mothe Le Vayer," dissertation, Université de Rennes, 1998;

Giocanti, "La Mothe Le Vayer: Modes de diversion sceptique," *Libertinage et philosophie au XVIe siècle,* 2 (1997): 32–48;

Giocanti, "La Perte du sens commun dans l'œuvre de La Mothe Le Vayer," *Libertinage et Philosophie au XVIe siècle,* 1 (1996): 27–51;

François Ildefonse, "L'Expression du scepticisme chez La Mothe Le Vayer," *Corpus,* 10 (1989): 23–40;

René Kerviler, *François de La Mothe Le Vayer, précepteur du duc d'Anjou et de Louis XIV: Etude sur sa vie et ses écrits* (Paris: E. Rouveyre, 1879);

Gianni Paganini, "Pyrrhonisme tout pur ou circoncis? La Dynamique du scepticisme chez La Mothe Le Vayer," *Libertinage et philosophie au XVIIe siècle,* volume 2 (1997): 7–31;

René Pintard, *Le Libertinage érudit en France dans la première moitié du dix-septième siècle* (Geneva: Slatkine, 1983);

Pintard, *La Mothe Le Vayer, Gassendi, Guy Patin, Etudes et bibliographie de la critique* (Paris: Bovin, 1943);

Pintard, "Les Problèmes de l'histoire du libertinage: Notes et réflexions," *XVIIe siècle,* 127 (1980): 131–160;

Philippe-Joseph Salazar, *La Divine Sceptique: Ethique et rhétorique au 17e siècle; Autour de La Mothe Le Vayer* (Tübingen: Narr, 2000);

A. L. Sells, "Molière and La Mothe Le Vayer," *Modern Language Review,* 28 (1933): 352–367, 444–455;

J. S. Spink, *French Free-Thought from Gassendi to Voltaire* (London: Athlone Press/University of London, 1960);

Florence L. Wickelgren, *La Mothe Le Vayer: Sa vie et son œuvre* (Paris: P. André, 1934).

François, duc de La Rochefoucauld

(15 September 1613 – 16 March 1680)

Mark A. Cohen
Bard College

BOOKS: *Mémoires de M.D.L.R. sur les brigues à la mort de Louys XIII, les guerres de Paris et de Guyenne, et la prison des princes . . .* (Cologne: P. van Dyck, 1662);

Sentences et maximes de morale (The Hague: J. et D. Steucker, 1664); revised as *Réflexions ou sentences et maximes morales* (Paris: C. Barbin, 1665; revised, 1666; 1671; 1675; 1678); translated by Aphra Behn as *Reflections on Morality, or Seneca Unmasqued*, in *Miscellany: Being a Collection of Poems by Several Hands* (London: Printed for J. Hindmarsh, 1685);

Mémoires de la minorité de Louis XIV, sur ce qui s'est passé à la fin de la vie de Louis XIII et pendant la régence d'Anne d'Autriche, mère de Louis XIV (Villefranche: J. de Paul, 1688; enlarged, 2 volumes, 1689); revised and enlarged as *Mémoires de M. le duc de La Rochefoucault et de M. de La Chastre, contenant l'histoire de la minorité de Louis XIV* (Villefranche: J. de Paul, 1700);

Mémoires du duc de La Rochefoucauld, edited by Antoine-Augustin Renouard (Paris: A.-A. Renouard, 1804; revised and enlarged, 1817);

La Justification de l'amour [attributed to La Rochefoucauld], edited by J. D. Hubert (Paris: Nizet, 1971).

Editions and Collections: *Réflexions ou sentences et maximes morales de M. le duc de La Rochefoucauld*, edited by André-Charles Brotier (Paris: J.-G. Mérigot, 1789);

Réflexions, sentences et maximes morales de La Rochefoucauld, edited by Georges Duplessis, with an introduction by Charles-Augustin Sainte-Beuve (Paris: P. Jannet, 1853);

Œuvres inédites de La Rochefoucauld, publiées d'après les manuscrits conservés par la famille et précédées de l'histoire de sa vie, edited by Edouard de Barthélemy (Paris: Hachette, 1863);

Œuvres de La Rochefoucauld, 5 volumes, edited by Jean Désiré Louis Gilbert, Jules Gourdault, Adolphe Régnier, and Henri de Régnier (Paris: Hachette, 1923);

François, duc de La Rochefoucauld (engraving by de Moncornet; Bibliothèque Nationale, Paris)

Réflexions ou sentences et maximes morales; Réflexions diverses, edited by Dominique Secrétan (Geneva: Droz, 1967);

Maximes, edited by Jacques Truchet (Paris: Garnier, 1983);

Œuvres complètes, edited by Louis Martin-Chauffier and Jean Marchand, Bibliothèque de la Pléiade, no. 64 (Paris: Gallimard, 1986);

Réflexions ou sentences et maximes morales; Réflexions diverses . . . , edited by Jean Rohou (Paris: Librairie Générale Française, 1991);

Maximes, edited by André-Alain Morello, in *Moralistes du XVIIe siècle,* edited by Lafond (Paris: R. Laffont, 1992), pp. 103–226;

Mémoires; Précédés de Apologie de M. le prince de Marcillac; Et suivis des Portraits, edited by Jean-Dominique de La Rochefoucauld (Paris: La Table Ronde, 1993);

Maximes, edited by Jean Lafond (Paris: Imprimerie Nationale, 1998).

Editions in English: *Maxims of le Duc de La Rochefoucauld,* translated by John Heard Jr. (Boston & New York: Houghton Mifflin, 1917);

Maxims, translated by Leonard Tancock (Harmondsworth, U.K.: Penguin, 1959);

Maxims, translated by Stéphane Douard and Stuart D. Warner (South Bend, Ind.: St. Augustine's Press, 2001);

Seneca Unmasqued: A Bilingual Edition of Aphra Behn's Translation of La Rochefoucauld's Maximes, edited by Irwin Primer (New York: AMS Press, 2001).

OTHER: "Portrait de La Rochefoucauld fait par lui-même," in *Recueil des portraits et éloges en vers et en prose,* edited by Anne-Marie-Louise d'Orléans Montpensier (Paris: C. de Sercy et C. Barbin, 1659);

"Apologie de M. le prince de Marcillac," in *La Jeunesse de Mme de Longueville: Etudes sur les femmes illustres et la société du XVIIe siècle,* by Victor Cousin (Paris: Didier, 1868), pp. 475–490.

François, duc de La Rochefoucauld's reputation rests squarely on a single work, known as the *Maximes* (Maxims, 1664–1678), first published in 1664 as *Sentences et maximes de morale* (Thoughts and Maxims on Morality) and then as *Réflexions ou sentences et maximes morales* (Reflections or Thoughts and Moral Maxims, 1665; revised, 1666; 1671; 1675; 1678), one of the greatest masterpieces of French literature and a key document of early modern intellectual history. In a series of aphorisms, this work proclaimed with unprecedented focus the overwhelming role played by self-interest in human conduct and showed how realization of this human characteristic brought traditional conceptions of virtues and vices into question. It was a model of the understated acuity and deceptive simplicity that marked the best French classical prose and accordingly set a standard for the writing of maxims for centuries to come. This stylistic tour de force was paralleled by the landmark contribution of the *Maximes* to the secularization of moral reflection promoted by rationalist political philosophers as they increasingly theo-

rized human behavior in purely "economic," as opposed to religious or metaphysical, terms, basing their analysis on the abstract individual's desire unconstrained by any altruistic values or motives. The *Maximes,* however, was neither an exercise in style nor a straightforward exposition. As a continuation of the French *moraliste* tradition initiated by Michel Eyquem de Montaigne, it exercised moral critique indirectly by means of a discontinuous, pointedly descriptive discourse exhibiting human behavior as a paradoxical, even unfathomable, phenomenon as opposed to the more traditional types of moral treatise or religious exhortations, in which prescriptive injunction and categorical clarity were the norm. At once an entertainment and an attack on hypocrisy, the *Maximes* was at the juncture of many different and not necessarily compatible intellectual tendencies of the time and thus garnered a far broader audience than more purportedly serious works. La Rochefoucauld himself was neither a learned nor a literary man but a man of the world, a member of the *noblesse d'épée* (martial aristocracy). The *Maximes* is marked by the harsh defeats La Rochefoucauld suffered in his tempestuous life and his own soldierly temperament; yet, it is tempered by the salon milieu of civilized exchange and social observation where La Rochefoucauld found the first audience for his writing. The resulting blend of profundity and aristocratic nonchalance gives the *Maximes* its unusual quality. It sounds the depths of the human unconscious with all the sensitivity of the great religious psychologists and proffers a quasi-scientific reduction of conduct to its basic constituents in the manner of Thomas Hobbes or René Descartes without seeking to resolve the dilemmas it broaches or offer conclusions as to the ultimate truth.

François VI, duc de La Rochefoucauld, known as the prince de Marsillac until the death of his father, was born into an ancient noble family in Paris on 15 September 1613, though he was brought up mainly on his ancestral lands in the Oise valley. For the first forty years of his life he pursued the typical employments of a man of his class with unrestrained enthusiasm and blind courage—war and court intrigue, love affairs, and rebellion. His formal education was brought to an abrupt halt when he was married at age sixteen to Andrée de Vivonne (with whom he eventually had four sons and three daughters) and went off to fight his first campaign in Italy the next year. He henceforth divided his time between military service, attendance at court, and occasional exile to his estate when out of favor or as a punishment for offenses against the Crown. In La Rochefoucauld's world, family honor, political power, military prowess, and romantic attachments to noble women were the fundamental medium of individual

La Rochefoucauld's château at Verteuil, demolished by the monarchy in 1650 because of the duke's involvement
in the rebellion known as the Fronde (engraving after drawing by M. S. Barclay; from
J. D. L. Gilbert and others, eds., Œuvres de La Rochefoucauld, *1883)*

self-expression. Politically he aligned himself with the feudal aristocracy's resistance to royal dominance and anti-Catholic (meaning anti-Spanish) alliances, but to separate this position from the personal attachments he established with certain of his fellow nobles—of trust, friendship, and intimacy—is impossible. His support for the queen, Anne of Austria, for example, was intended both to counter absolutist policies at court of the first minister, Armand du Plessis, cardinal de Richelieu, and to help Marie de Rohan, duchesse de Chevreuse (La Rochefoucauld's lover) protect her mistress from Richelieu's affronts. Constantly involved in campaigns in the field and conspiracy at home, La Rochefoucauld treated political life as a game to be played to the full and personal honor as the highest of values, even when it jeopardized his own interests. When he joined the aristocratic rebellion known as the Fronde against the Regency and Richelieu's hand-picked successor, Cardinal Jules Mazarin, in the late 1640s, he did so as much out of a feeling that the queen had not rewarded him sufficiently for his services and as a loyal supporter of Louis II de Bourbon, fourth Prince de Condé (known as Le Grand Condé), the leader of the rebellion and brother of La Rochefoucauld's new lover, Anne de Bourbon, duchesse de Longueville, as to support the aristocracy's independence or to accrue political power.

The rebellion was finally defeated in 1653, and by its end La Rochefoucauld was a broken man, severely wounded in a skirmish, penniless, his estate in ruins, and facing permanent banishment. In the course of the events, he had been abandoned both by his lover, Condé's sister, and then by Condé himself, who fled to Spain. La Rochefoucauld had proved both unfailingly loyal and lacking in strategic judgment. By temperament a prey to melancholy, as he said in his self-portrait, now he had objective reasons to feel disillusioned. The development of this attitude was both compensated for and sharpened by his opting for retreat and the literary life. As he increasingly found his friends among cultivated circles, he grew less interested in promoting his family's political interests and consequently in 1671 turned over his titles to his son, François VII, who had revived the La Rochefoucaulds' name by marrying well and becoming a favorite of Louis XIV. François had sought the company of his father less and less during the 1660s, and when in the early 1670s La Rochefoucauld lost the sons he was most fond of, his wife, and his mother in rapid succession, his personal desolation after so many other setbacks could have been intense. Yet, by then he had already found another family with which to replace his own, that of some of the most gifted writers of the day.

In fact, he became a close collaborator of his relative Marie-Madeleine Pioche de La Vergne, comtesse de Lafayette, whom he had met in the salon of the comtesse du Plessis-Guénégaud, the commanding figure of which was the great Jansenist philosopher Antoine Arnauld. She had been instantly attracted by his personality and keen literary intelligence, though he had initially rebuffed her interest, perhaps because their temperaments and ages were so far apart (she was twenty years his junior, and her first reaction to the *Maximes* was horror). This stage of their relationship lasted some years until in 1667 he warmed to her, and from then on they enjoyed a deep and abiding friendship. La Rochefoucauld (and the poet Jean Regnault de Segrais) collaborated on Lafayette's novels beginning with *Zaïde* (1669) and then *La Princesse de Clèves* (finished 1672; published 1678). La Rochefoucauld also befriended Jean de La Fontaine, who praised the *Maximes* fulsomely in the *Fables* (1668–1679): "L'Homme et son image" (Man and His Image; Book I, Fable 11). He describes the *Maximes* there as a "pure stream," a mirror so beautiful that "we continue to gaze at it even when it shows us all our faults." However, the *Maximes* itself was decisively influenced by the first salon to which La Rochefoucauld belonged before he met this distinguished group, one that represented a more severe challenge to his former life while making the transition to his new existence relatively easy by virtue of its civilized, even playful, ambience, at once meeting the needs of the noble *mondain* (worldly man) bred on the chivalric romances and sharpening his taste for keener reflections than he had heretofore been accustomed to.

La Rochefoucauld was able gradually to reestablish his fortunes in the 1650s, but like many former Frondeurs he came to reassess the value of heroic action, codes of honor, and reckless adventurism. This new view did not mean that they or he rejected their own elevated social status entirely. Rather, they found a new arena for the exercise of their superiority. Forced from the political stage as they were, they turned to the more private realm of the salon and writing, aiming to cultivate the higher pleasures and so forge public taste from afar by presenting to it a model of civility to emulate or admire. Some salons were even attracted by Jansenism, a rigorist Catholic sect that espoused retreat from the world and the renewal of Augustinian thought. The Jansenists represented a nonviolent version of opposition to the government because they refused to compromise in matters of doctrine and made such a strict division between the earthly and the divine cities that they were able to look at worldly life with a steely, condemnatory precision. This view at least offered the virtues of lucidity and the sort of psychological acuity on which worldly men and women of experience, too, could pride themselves. La Rochefoucauld took this tendency to an extreme, to the point of placing the whole of his social world in question. To a large degree the *Maximes* are aimed at the demolition (as the critic Paul Bénichou has put it) of his former value system, highlighting the dubiousness of glory, the ever present possibility of betrayal, and the sheer capriciousness of fortune that ultimately renders otiose any attribution of personal credit for success. All forms of self-assertion and the pretension to great accomplishments are equally represented as having their roots in murky, suspect passions or a solipsistic ignorance. Attention was transferred from action itself, which in La Rochefoucauld's case had ended in failure, to the principles by which it operated, which he had successfully identified and deployed in the artful balance of a maxim. The daring he had once shown in battle or conspiracy was now expressed in the rapier-like thrusts of his surprising formulations.

La Rochefoucauld's chosen salon was that of Madeleine, marquise de Sablé–a learned, sickly, and pious noblewoman–who had built her house close to a Jansenist monastery but who was worldly enough to provide Epicurean meals for her guests. At her salon La Rochefoucauld began to write and circulate his maxims in letters to her and her friend, the priest Jacques Esprit, who soon became La Rochefoucauld's first readers and critics. The nineteenth-century philosopher Victor Cousin went so far as to claim that a man of La Rochefoucauld's background could not have produced such a masterpiece alone and concluded that the maxims must have been a collaborative effort. Such was not the case. La Rochefoucauld quickly realized that he had a gift for maxims, and one of de Sablé's letters mentions that La Rochefoucauld was the person who gave her the mania for writing them, not the other way around. Moreover, since both she and Esprit published their own collections of maxims in the 1670s, readers can easily see how much more conventional they are than those of La Rochefoucauld, offering orthodox Christian palliatives for sinfulness rather than tantalizing paradoxes. On the other hand, without the nurturing environment of the salon, La Rochefoucauld would not have taken the trouble to make the *Maximes* into a literary work, editing it carefully, giving it an index, and reflecting on its construction. Although he almost never took his friends' advice as to which maxims to retain or reject, that he showed the maxims to them, traded maxims for meals, or maxim for maxim, and received a constant stream of comments alerted him to the thrill of engaging and above all challenging an audience.

The *Maximes* was in consequence La Rochefoucauld's only concerted work of art, the only one for which he was willing to risk derogation by openly proclaiming his authorship (pride in the "glory" of literary fame being considered a bourgeois weakness). For although from the mid 1650s on he had produced various pieces—two hundred pages of memoirs in the 1650s, an eminently fashionable self-portrait in 1659, and a series of one- or two-page-long reflections up until the 1670s—they had been intended solely for a select group of readers. He had written them in a desultory fashion and remained wholly indifferent or even hostile to their publication. The memoirs represent his attempt to tell the truth as he saw it. They manage to balance the subjective and the objective quite admirably by relating in minute detail the events of the Fronde as La Rochefoucauld lived through them, giving a breathless sense of how he experienced the continual changes in his situation and relationships without any larger reflections or rancorous judgments clouding the narrative. Although precise information is lacking, in all probability the work was drawn up toward the end of the 1650s (and perhaps continued in the early 1660s) in two distinct drafts, one in the first person, the other in the third. A gradual if muted movement toward greater abstraction is discernible here since much of the *Mémoires* depicts an heroic La Rochefoucauld surrounded by self-interested and often pernicious aristocrats who were not living up to their code of honor. The *Réflexions diverses* represent in part an expansion of ideas voiced in many of the maxims and in part a more positive quest for a life that could be both truthful and graceful, expressed in short essays covering philosophic, worldly, scientific, and historical topics. Each of these two extremely different works can profitably be seen as sharing the incisive objectivity of the *Maximes* while offering something that reveals other facets to La Rochefoucauld's talent his masterpiece had not explored, the memoirs with a plethora of singular moments, untouched by self-pity or self-serving generalization, the reflections with a rich discursiveness and breadth of vision. La Rochefoucauld had successfully prevented publication in France of a copy of a manuscript version of the memoirs he had lent to Arnaud d'Andilly, because it stirred up old conflicts that he would rather have laid to rest. He and his friends were embarrassed by the pirated copies that began emerging in Holland (under false publishing names and locations) from 1662 until his death, yet he did not try to present an authorized edition in their stead. As a result, they were published in full and free of spurious additions only in the late nineteenth century. On the other hand, why he did not publish the reflections is not clear. They did not touch on any sensitive topics of recent history and had clearly been written with the same attention to literary effect as the *Maximes*. Nevertheless, he seems to have regarded them as in some way nothing

*Madeleine de Souvré, marquise de Sablé, at whose salon
La Rochefoucauld began to write and circulate
his maxims (portrait by Du Moustier;
Musée du Louvre, Paris)*

but a series of personal musings, and therefore he saw collecting them in a volume as unnecessary. The reflections were not published in book form until the eighteenth century, long after his death.

Although he originally affected the pretense that he had been forced into publication of even the *Maximes* because of the error-ridden pirated copy that appeared in Holland in 1664, his subsequent attitude toward the work belies his protestations. In four subsequent editions he pruned and rewrote the maxims until they were as sharp and freestanding as possible. So punctilious was he on this score that the volume actually decreased in length in successive editions, and superfluous words or religious references that were too obvious were removed. In this way he highlighted the enigmatic force of each maxim to achieve a maximum shock effect on the reader to the exclusion of all other concerns. He brought out the final, fifth edition, now considered definitive, in 1678, only two years before his death.

La Rochefoucauld's pessimism has gone down in literary history as his most distinctive feature, and the image of life the *Maximes* depicts is not a pleasant one.

His best-known maxims seek to make readers acknowledge the dominance of self-interest over human conduct and the omnipresence of the hypocrisy employed to conceal this fact. Preceding the text itself are two indicators by which La Rochefoucauld signaled his intentions. On the frontispiece he placed a literal image of the procedure that would govern what was to follow: a smiling cherub called "the Love of Truth" caught at the moment it has just removed the smiling mask from a bust of Seneca (the Stoic philosopher who had believed the attainment of virtue to be possible) to reveal a frowning, unpleasant face beneath. Even more straightforwardly, he chose as his epigraph the simple statement "Nos vertus ne sont, le plus souvent, que des vices déguisés" (Our virtues, most often, are nothing but vices disguised). In the body of the text itself, the most typical maxim takes a given virtue, such as generosity or humility, and "unmasks" it by pointing out its true source in baser motives, lending it an underlying quasi-mathematical structure of "x (a virtue) is nothing but y (a vice)" or "x is to a large extent y": "La clémence des princes n'est souvent qu'une politique pour gagner l'affection des peuples" (The clemency of princes is often nothing but a ploy to win over the people's love; M 15); "L'envie d'être plaint, ou d'être admiré, fait souvent la plus grande partie de notre confiance" (Our wish to be pitied or admired is often the main reason we confide in another; M 475). From heroism to temperance, love to good taste, the Maximes dispatches almost the whole range of the then current repertory of virtues in a similarly summary fashion. It carries out this operation so thoroughly that virtue itself starts to fade into insubstantiality and to look like a mere will-o'-the-wisp, rumored to exist but never actually seen anywhere, perhaps ultimately unrealizable: "Il est du véritable amour comme de l'apparition des esprits: tout le monde en parle, mais peu de gens en ont vu" (Trying to find an example of true love is like the appearance of spirits; everyone talks about their existence but few have ever seen one; M 76). The dual movement of constant transformation of one thing into another and the reductive direction of the change lends La Rochefoucauld's maxims a merciless yet surprising energy: readers think they know what the end will be but are kept guessing at how La Rochefoucauld will arrive at it.

At his most radical, La Rochefoucauld went much further than the commonplace suggestion that virtue was difficult and rare. He claimed to be unearthing a basic disposition present in every human being that inevitably ensured no virtue could ever be more than a false appearance, and as he did, he in effect changed the focus of moral reflection from the static binary opposition of virtue and vice to the incessant process by which virtue is always surreptitiously appropriated and exploited by vice. In his greatest and longest maxim, originally placed at the beginning of the Maximes (now known as MS 1), the source of this equivocation and the root cause of the actual if not conceptual impossibility of virtue is said to be amour-propre. This expression has been translated into English variously as "self-interest" or "self-love," and La Rochefoucauld took it from contemporary Christian discourse, which defined it in opposition to the love of God (Augustine's amor sui). La Rochefoucauld introduces it thus: "L'amour propre est l'amour de soi-même, et de toutes choses pour soi" (Self-love is the love of oneself, and of everything for oneself). He goes on to develop a "portrait" of it in memorably baroque fashion as a protean tyrant—ubiquitous, unstoppable, and endlessly inventive, almost like a person in its own right. An integral part of this description was a detailed exploration of its effects on moral behavior. The worship of oneself entailed the domination of others: "il rend les hommes idolâtres d'eux-mêmes, et les rendrait les tyrans des autres si la fortune leur en donnait les moyens" (it makes men idolize themselves, and were fortune to permit it would make them tyrants over their fellow men), and an inability really to know anything beyond the self: "il ne se repose jamais hors de soi, et ne s'arrête dans les sujets étrangers que . . . pour en tirer ce qui lui est propre" (it never rests outside of itself, and only visits foreign bodies . . . to extract from them what is its own). However, the inevitable corollary of its actions was that it ended up undermining itself. Ultimately, because it cannot exist openly in the social world, its forceful persistence in remaining in being at whatever the cost (what La Rochefoucauld's contemporary Benedict de Spinoza called conatus) means that it must therefore constantly transform itself to escape condemnation, but this necessity is what threatens to destroy it as it is forced to take increasingly bizarre and self-contradictory measures to this end: "il est souvent invisible à lui-même . . . il s'accommode des choses, et de leur privation . . . il se joint quelquefois à la plus rude austérité, et . . . entre . . . hardiment en société avec elle pour se détruire . . . "(it is often invisible to itself . . . it adapts itself to the presence of certain things or to their absence . . . sometimes it obeys the harshest discipline . . . joining forces with it to bring about its own destruction . . .). The final impression is a mystifying one: "Rien n'est si impétueux que ses désirs, rien de si caché que ses desseins. . . . On ne peut sonder la profondeur, ni percer les ténèbres des ses abîmes" (Nothing is so impetuous as its desires, nothing so secret as its plans. . . . It is impossible either to plumb its depths or to penetrate the dark fog of its abyss).

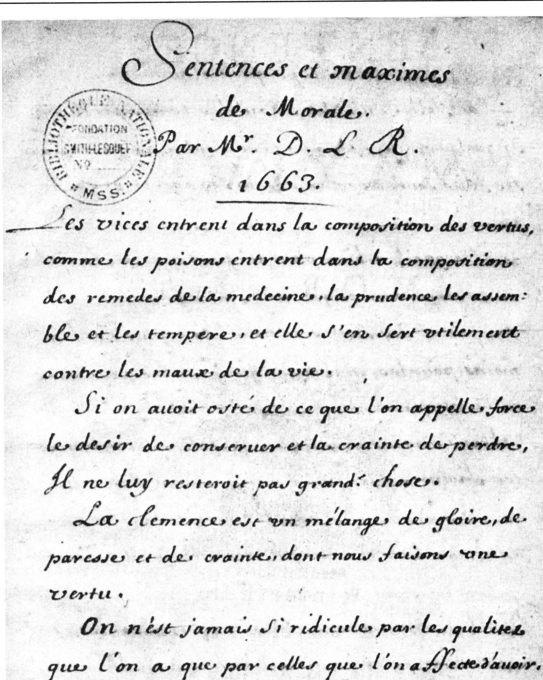

First page from the manuscript for La Rochefoucauld's collection of maxims,
published in 1664 (Bibliothèque Nationale, Paris)

La Rochefoucauld decided to remove MS 1 from all of the four subsequent editions of the *Maximes* for stylistic reasons—because of its length and because of its overly lush baroque conceits, which clashed with the less explicit, much shorter, and more antiphrastic maxims that he judged should be the predominant element of the text. But it was probably the earliest of the maxims to be written and was published as a separate piece in its own right in a collection of 1659 well before La Rochefoucauld had any idea of writing an entire book on the subject. It began life as a humorous letter to a formerly worldly lady about to enter a nunnery, a portrait of self-love written with the intention of illustrating its ability to insinuate itself where it was least expected, in the desire to give oneself to God. Portrait painting was a popular salon amusement, but MS 1 soon outgrew this context when placed at the head of his new book. Moreover, no other of his pieces defines his overall project more clearly. For rather than seeking to exhort others to avoid it or execute a systematic analysis and solution to the problems it posed, in MS 1 La Rochefoucauld limited himself to providing a description of *amour-propre* in all of its unfathomable movements. The inscrutability of self-interest was taken up in the *Maximes* itself at various points in a way that brings out the tendency toward the nonjudgmental amazement before a strange natural phenomenon already latent in MS 1. This position is clear in M 390, in which the primacy of interest is definitely trumped by a more unpredictable and less calculating quality, taste—"on renonce plus aisément à son intérêt qu'à son goût" (we tend to give up more easily on our interests than on our tastes); or in M 40, in which interest is presented as something amoral rather than immoral—"L'intérêt, qui aveugle les uns, fait la lumière des autres" (Interest, which blinds some, illuminates others). He did not seek to explain why it was as it was nor to offer a happy Christian resolution to the insuperable misery to which it consigned human beings. With few exceptions this lack of a broader philosophical framework with which to assess the relation of one sentence to another within MS 1 is true of the *Maximes* as a whole, despite the fact that the latter's prose is sparer, less imagistic, and seemingly more analytic.

In both texts, La Rochefoucauld was clearly tapping into the rich Christian language with which self-love had been condemned since the time of the church fathers and was being revived most notably by the Jansenists. Given his own quite unacademic bent and the nearly total absence of other similar classical references in the rest of his work, quite probably his attack on the proud self-sufficiency of pagan philosophers such as Seneca (who only appears in the prefatory material mentioned above) was also a reflection of the Jansenists' polemic against philosophy in general. Equally, La Rochefoucauld's constant reiteration of the primacy of passion over reason, formulaically rendered in Maxim 102 as "L'esprit est toujours la dupe du cœur" (The mind is always fooled by the heart), was a favorite Augustinian theme. In this light, reason was considered to be a purely human attribute that lacked sufficient power to save; only divine grace could do that. Many of his readers then and now have understandably assumed that La Rochefoucauld's forceful portrait of human misery, too, was intended to bring a lay reader closer to God as the only possible remedy. Yet, there is a crucial difference between La Rochefoucauld and Jansenists such as Blaise Pascal in this respect. Pascal explicitly adduces the Christian salvational framework as the obverse of fallen humanity and seeks ways to justify it in the face of modern skepticism. La Rochefoucauld, on the other hand, uses Christian references in the *Maximes* only minimally, and when he came to reedit, he removed any that remained. His text is located squarely in the world; he offers no solution, salvational or otherwise, as a way out of the miserable situation of all-enveloping self-interest that he depicts so insistently.

The removal of the Christian framework is compounded by another crucial tendency in the *Maximes* that further explored the sense conveyed by MS 1— that the apparently masterful activity of the self could easily be construed as its converse, an unconscious drive that it was powerless to control. In many maxims, passion and caprice are said to be able to overwhelm not only reason but also self-interest itself and human behavior, both good and bad, stated to be the product of predetermined factors, which thereby excluded the existence or effectiveness of free will. In M 44 moral qualities are said to derive from humoral dispositions: "La force et la faiblesse de l'esprit sont mal nommées; elles ne sont en effet que la bonne ou la mauvaise disposition des organes du corps" (Strength and weakness are misnomers; they are nothing but the result of the healthy or the unhealthy condition of our internal organs); in M 154 chance is what is said to improve us, not our own efforts: "La fortune nous corrige de plusieurs défauts que la raison ne saurait corriger" (Fortune cures us of many faults that reason could not correct). In essence, such maxims remove humans' actions from the realm of moral judgment altogether and place them in that of medicine, physics, or leave humans no way of assessing them at all, other than as the product of a chaotic, random conjunction of forces. La Rochefoucauld sometimes added further to the reader's confusion by pitting one imponderable quality against another: "Quelque grands avantages que la nature donne, ce n'est pas elle seule, mais la fortune

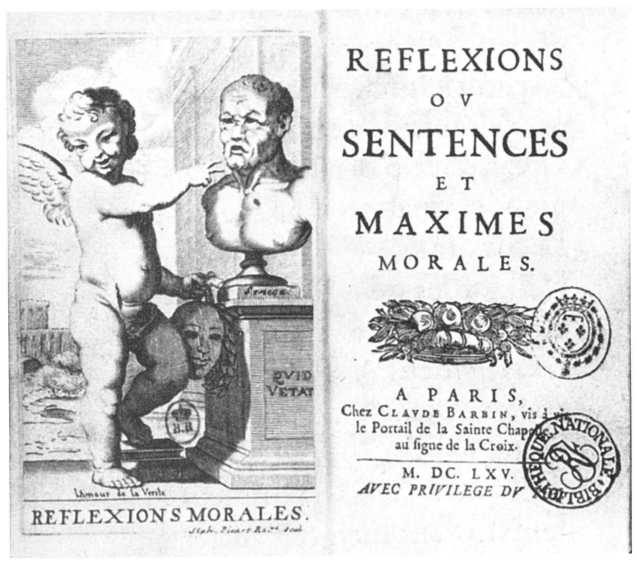

Frontispiece and title page for the first French edition of La Rochefoucauld's maxims
(Bibliothèque Nationale, Paris)

avec elle qui fait les héros" (whatever favorable attributes we are given by nature, it is not solely responsible for making us into heroes, but needs the help of good fortune; M 53). All in all, the world, from this point of view, was not a predictable or stable place, nor was it amenable to moral correction. What was being stressed was its almost infinite and prodigious diversity, forever beyond humans' grasp or control.

For all his apparent severity, then, La Rochefoucauld was not seeking to exhort his readers to change. The term "maxim," with which La Rochefoucauld liked to refer to his aphorisms (though he used others such as "reflections" or "sentences"), originally derived from the Latin expression *maxima sententia,* meaning "greatest sentence." It referred to the semantic richness that could be contained in a short phrase if it were art-

fully enough constructed. In the seventeenth century it could mean various things—a definite pronouncement that brooked no compromise or a rule of conduct (good or bad). La Rochefoucauld's maxims are closer to the former sense; they are invariably descriptive, peremptory, and shorn of argumentative support or proof. But their oracular certainty did not reside in their confirmation of common knowledge or guidance according to orthodox precepts but precisely their assertion that a paradox (from the Greek *para-doxa* meaning "against opinion")—that which goes *against* the commonly held opinion—was true. Their specific richness, rubbing against the grain of readers' expectation, was dependent on something that surprised and arrested the readers, making them think again. Not all readers might prove sufficiently liberal minded to entertain such novel ideas, while many complained that the maxims were too dense (or "obscure," as original French readers put it) to be properly understood. Following in the wake of Montaigne, with his preference for the description of human behavior in all its multifaceted and unpredictable complexity as opposed to homiletic prescription, the maxims were not presented in the voice of some authoritative persona nor organized in any systematic way but were simply numbered and indexed by theme at the end of the volume. Without subordinating rubrics or supporting argumentation, each maxim could be taken by itself or read in conjunction with others that dealt with the same theme. But La Rochefoucauld did not provide any definitive path. Readers were left the freedom (both liberating and anxiety-inducing) to roam at will through this unsettling hall of mirrors. At most, especially in the first half of the *Maximes,* one can discern thematic clusters that point to potential orderings (for example, M 5 to 12, on the passions; M 33 to 37, on pride; and M 68 to 78, on love). Some maxims that are not placed close to one another develop the same topics, encouraging the reader to compare them and ponder what each adds to the other's meaning. For instance, M 136 says, "Il y a des gens qui n'auraient jamais été amoureux s'ils n'avaient jamais entendu parler de l'amour" (There are those who would never have fallen in love if they had never heard people talking about it), which echoes M 76, repeating its emphasis on the chimeric nature of love but altering its focus to stress how doubtful its existence is in this case because it is socially produced, not because it is an attainable ideal. The final maxim is the longest and deals with finality itself, death. It sends readers back to the beginning by referring directly to the basic theme of the work—self-love, displayed in this instance in humans' refusal to accept that they will die. However, this theme cannot be compared to an overarching structural principle or the installation of an ultimate certainty. Throughout the *Maximes* it is the case that even the timeless impersonality and peremptory assertoric modality of the average maxim ("x is y") is, on closer inspection, not so absolute, because qualifying and limiting adverbs ("almost," "often," "sometimes") or their equivalents have often been unobtrusively inserted.

However tight La Rochefoucauld pulls the net to try to ensure that humans' virtues will always be shown to be vices, the next maxim is always free to salvage something from the wreckage. In the sequence devoted to unmasking the true nature of praise, for instance, one maxim (M 146) acts as a kernel by stating the inherent self-interestedness of praise. But others in the cluster complicate without simply contradicting this picture, M 149 noting the refusal of praise as something as egotistic as accepting it, M 148 the possibility of being praised by a reproach, and finally M 150 the beneficial potential of praise to encourage humans to try to conform to the ideal image of themselves they are being offered (false though it may be). Some maxims even seem to offer positive qualities that are, however, nonmoral in conventional terms, such as frankness about one's faults (M 457), strength of purpose (M 217), or reticence about one's own good qualities (M 203)—all of which praise honesty and lucidity over dissimulation and arrogance. But it is hard to show that La Rochefoucauld has thereby replaced the old values with new ones in Nietzschean fashion, as some critics have claimed; the *Maximes* are simply too various and unstructured to provide such assurances.

The prismatic quality of the *Maximes,* unframed by any "higher" discourses, religious or philosophic, makes it a fundamentally ambiguous text. It is made up of many different and not always compatible discourses, such as ancient characterology, modern medicine, Epicureanism, the refined classificatory mania of the *précieuses* (independent ladies of leisure who formed their own salons and created a refined language of poetry that drew many males' disdain), an Augustinian sense of a world bereft of ethical anchors, cynical political or court manuals such as those of Baltasar Graciàn or Niccolò Machiavelli, and above all, the nominalism of Montaigne. None are cited in a scholarly fashion but assimilated and converted to La Rochefoucauld's own uses as if they were his own. The refusal to order his text in a methodical way is paralleled by a similar refusal to center it on any philosophically consistent position. There might have been many reasons for La Rochefoucauld's attitude. One undoubtedly was his adherence to an aristocratic ethos of *sprezzatura* and refinement, the civilized sense that one should not seek to say everything or force one's interlocutor to agree by means of scholarly proofs. A man such as La Rochefoucauld simply did not need to present a conceptually unified or carefully annotated treatise. His discourse preserved the suppleness and the improvised quality of an intelligent seigneur without being shackled to the stultifying demands of the learned. Another reason, perhaps the most important because it does state a sort of higher conviction that can be fairly attributed to the author, was that life indeed was too various and unpredictable to be caught in the nets of the mind. The world had depths and surprises that could not be fathomed fully but had to be examined patiently, demanding a sort of metaphysical tact and acceptance of human limitation: "Pour bien savoir les choses, il en faut savoir le détail; et comme il est presque infini, nos connaissances sont toujours superficielles et imparfaites" (In order to understand things properly, one has to know them in detail; and since this is almost infinite, our knowledge is always superficial and imperfect; M 106). This desperate openness to further thought and striking affirmation of weakness is the ultimate message of the *Maximes*. This disabused yet empirical attitude allowed the work to play an important part in freeing moral thought from the dominant religious framework.

La Rochefoucauld's contemporaries, for the most part, did not see his work in this way. Many condemned it as the product of a disaffected misanthrope whose heart had been blackened by his own setbacks. Others admired its verbal brilliance or its clear-sightedness about human reality. When François, duc de La Rochefoucauld died on 16 March 1680, de Sévigné describes in a letter to her daughter the pain his death caused Lafayette. With such a circle to mourn him and with the constant discussion that his work aroused, La Rochefoucauld's talents did not go unrecognized in his lifetime or thereafter. The eighteenth century was different from the seventeenth in its optimism and trust of natural processes and reacted with horror to the *Maximes*. The last great maxim writer of the century, Nicolas-Sebastian Roch Chamfort, for instance, in his *Maximes et Pensées* (1796) no. 14, expressed his condemnation of La Rochefoucauld's moral extremism by lumping him in with those severe *moralistes* who were so convinced, as he put it, of the ineradicability of human turpitude that they could only see the latrines of a palace rather than the rest of it. Yet, Chamfort chose to write in maxims, too, like another prominent eighteenth-century writer who strove even more directly to oppose La Rochefoucauld's pessimism with a more positive evaluation of human passion, Luc de Clapiers, marquis de Vauvenargues, showing how influential La Rochefoucauld's literary model had been even among his intellectual foes. In more recent times La Rochefoucauld has been hailed as a precursor to Sigmund Freud and Friedrich Wilhelm Nietzsche because of his fearless exploration of the inner depths of human thought. A more accurate assessment is to see him as a lightning rod for the predicament of his own class—defeated, undaunted, and facing redundance in the machinery of the absolutist state, seeking with a newly tactful yet wickedly playful daring to see their world without illusions and find their pleasure in the mournful triumph over ignorance.

Bibliography:

Jean Marchand, *Bibliographie générale et raisonnée de La Rochefoucauld* (Paris: Giraud-Badin, 1948).

References:

Antoine Adam, *Histoire de la littérature française*, 5 volumes (Paris: Domat), I: 81–114;

Roland Barthes, "La Rochefoucauld: *Réflexions ou sentences et maximes*," in his *Le Degré zéro de l'écriture, suivi de Nouveaux Essais critiques* (Paris: Seuil, 1972), pp. 69–88;

Paul Bénichou, "La Démolition du héros," in his *Morales du Grand Siècle* (Paris: Gallimard, 1948), pp. 97–111;

Bénichou, "L'Intention des *Maximes*," in his *L'Ecrivain et ses travaux* (Paris: J. Corti, 1967), pp. 3–37;

Morris Bishop, *The Life and Adventures of La Rochefoucauld* (Ithaca, N.Y.: Cornell University Press, 1951);

Jules Brody, "Les *Maximes* de La Rochefoucauld: Essai de lecture rhétorique," in his *Lectures Classiques* (Charlottesville, Va.: Rookwood Press, 1996), pp. 260–285;

Pierre Campion, *Lectures de La Rochefoucauld* (Rennes: Presses Universitaires de Rennes, 1998);

Henry C. Clark, *La Rochefoucauld and the Language of Unmasking in Seventeenth-Century France* (Geneva: Droz, 1994);

Victor Cousin, *Madame de Sablé: Nouvelles études sur les femmes illustres et la société du XVIIe siècle* (Paris: Didier, 1882);

Peter Martin Fine, *Vauvenargues and La Rochefoucauld* (Manchester, U.K.: Manchester University Press, 1974);

Pierre Force, "Self-love, Identification, and the Origin of Political Economy," *Yale French Studies,* 92 (1997): 46–64;

Louis Hippeau, *Essai sur la morale de La Rochefoucauld* (Paris: Nizet, 1967);

Richard G. Hodgson, *Falsehood Disguised: Unmasking the Truth in La Rochefoucauld* (West Lafayette, Ind.: Purdue University Press, 1995);

Robyn Holman and Jacques Barchilon, eds., *Concordance to the "Maximes" of La Rochefoucauld* (Boulder: University Press of Colorado, 1996);

N. Ivanoff, *La Marquise de Sablé et son salon* (Paris: Colin, 1927);

Françoise Jaouën, *De l'art de plaire en petits morceaux: Pascal, La Rochefoucauld, La Bruyère* (Saint-Denis: Presses Universitaires de Vincennes, 1996), pp. 79–118;

Margot Kruse, *Die Maxime in der französischen Literatur* (Hamburg: De Gruyter, 1960);

Jean Lafond, *La Rochefoucauld: Augustinisme et Littérature* (Paris: Klincksieck, 1986);

Lafond, *La Rochefoucauld: L'Homme et son image* (Paris: H. Champion, 1998);

Lafond and Jean Mesnard, eds., *Images de La Rochefoucauld: Actes du tricentenaire, 1680–1980* (Paris: Presses Universitaires de France, 1984);

Philip Lewis, *La Rochefoucauld and the Art of Abstraction* (Ithaca, N.Y.: Cornell University Press, 1977);

Littératures Classiques, special La Rochefoucauld issue, 35 (1999);

Mesnard, "L'Esthétique de La Rochefoucauld," in his *La Culture du XVIIe siècle: Enquêtes et synthèses* (Paris: Presses Universitaires de France, 1992), pp. 236–44;

Mesnard, "La Rencontre de La Rochefoucauld avec Port-Royal," in his *La Culture du XVIIe siècle* (Paris: PUF, 1992), pp. 292–296;

W. G. Moore, *La Rochefoucauld: His Mind and Art* (Oxford: Clarendon Press, 1969);

Odette de Mourgues, *Two French Moralists: La Rochefoucauld and La Bruyère* (Cambridge: Cambridge University Press, 1978);

Bérengère Parmentier, *Le Siècle des moralistes* (Paris: Seuil, 2000), pp. 45–82;

Jacqueline Plantié, "'L'Amour-propre' au Carmel," *Revue d'Histoire littéraire de la France,* 69 (1969): 560–573;

Lucien Anatole Prévost-Paradol, *Etudes sur les moralistes français, suivies de quelques réflexions sur divers sujets* (Paris: Hachette, 1865);

Marcel Raymond, "Du jansénisme à la morale de l'intérêt," *Mercure de France* (June 1957): 238–255;

Susan Read Baker, *Collaboration et originalité chez La Rochefoucauld* (Gainesville: University Presses of Florida, 1980);

Corrado Rosso, *Procès à La Rochefoucauld et à la maxime* (Pisa: Libreria Goliardica / Paris: Nizet, 1986);

Charles Augustin Sainte-Beuve, *Portraits de femmes,* in his *Œuvres littéraires,* edited by Maxime Leroy, 2 volumes (Paris: Gallimard, 1956), II: 1241–1273;

Philippe Sellier, "La Rochefoucauld, Pascal, Saint Augustin," *Revue d'histoire littéraire de la France,* 69 (May–August 1969): 551–575;

Jean Starobinski, "La Rochefoucauld et les morales substitutives," *La Nouvelle Revue française* (1966): 16–34, 211–229;

Laurent Thirouin, "Paradoxe et contradiction dans le discours des moralistes français du XVIIe siècle," in *De la morale à l'économie politique,* edited by Force and David Morgan (Pau: University of Pau Press, 1996), pp. 19–28;

Vivien Thweatt, *La Rochefoucauld and the Seventeenth-Century Concept of the Self* (Geneva: Droz, 1980);

Tzvetan Todorov, "La Comédie humaine selon La Rochefoucauld," *Poétique,* 53 (1983): 37–47;

Louis Van Delft, *Le Moraliste classique: Essai de définition et de typologie* (Geneva: Droz, 1982), pp. 156–169;

Van Delft, *Litterature et anthropologie: Nature humaine et caractère à l'âge classique* (Paris: PUF, 1993), pp. 121–135;

Alexandre Vinet, *Moralistes des seizième et dix-septième siècles* (Paris: Les Editeurs, 1859).

Papers:

The manuscripts of François, duc de la Rochefoucauld, are housed in the Bibliothèque Nationale, Paris.

Molière
(Jean-Baptiste Poquelin)
(13? January 1622 – 17 February 1673)

Abby E. Zanger
Yale University

BOOKS: *Les Précieuses ridicules* (Paris: G. de Luyne, 1660);

Sganarelle, ou Le Cocu imaginaire (Paris: J. Ribou, 1660);

L'Escole des maris (Paris: G. de Luyne, 1661);

Les Fâcheux (Paris: G. de Luyne, 1662);

Dépit amoureux (Paris: C. Barbin et G. Quinet, 1662);

L'Estourdy, ou Les Contre-temps (Paris: G. Quinet, 1663);

L'Escole des femmes (Paris: G. de Luyne, 1663);

Remerciment au roy (Paris: G. de Luyne et G. Quinet, 1663);

La Critique de L'Escole des femmes (Paris: C. de Sercy, 1663);

Le Mariage forcé (Paris: R. Ballard, 1664);

Les Plaisirs de l'île enchantée (Paris: R. Ballard, 1664); republished with *La Princesse d'Elide* (Paris: E. Loyson, 1665);

L'Amour médecin (Paris: P. Trabouillet, 1666);

Ballet des muses (Paris: R. Ballard, 1666);

Le Misantrope (Paris: J. Ribou, 1667 [i.e., 1666]);

Le Médecin malgré luy (Paris: J. Ribou, 1667);

Le Sicilien, ou L'Amour peintre (Paris: J. Ribou, 1668 [i.e., 1667]);

Amphitryon (Paris: J. Ribou, 1668)—includes "Au roi, sur la conquête de la Franche-Comté";

George Dandin, ou Le Mary confondu (Paris: J. Ribou, 1669);

L'Avare (Paris: J. Ribou, 1669);

Le Tartuffe, ou L'Imposteur (Paris: J. Ribou, 1669);

La Gloire du Val-de-Grâce (Paris: J. Ribou, 1669);

Monsieur de Pourceaugnac (Paris: J. Ribou, 1670);

Le Bourgeois gentilhomme (Paris: P. Le Monnier, 1671);

Psiché, by Molière, Pierre Corneille, and Philippe Quinault (Paris: P. Le Monnier, 1671);

Les Fourberies de Scapin (Paris: P. Le Monnier, 1671);

Les Femmes savantes (Paris: P. Promé, 1672);

Le Malade imaginaire (Paris: Loyson, 1674);

Les Œuvres de Monsieur de Molière, 8 volumes, edited by Vinot and C. Varlet, sieur de La Grange (Paris: D. Thierry, C. Barbin, et P. Trabouillet, 1682)—vol-

Molière (engraving by J. Baptiste Nolin, 1685; Comédie-Française, Paris)

ume 7 comprises *Dom Garcie de Navarre; L'Impromptu de Versailles; Dom Juan, ou Le Festin de Pierre;* and *Mélicerte,* by Molière and Isaac de Benserade; volume 8 includes *Les Amans magnifiques* and *La Comtesse d'Escarbagnas.*

Collections: *Œuvres de M. Molière,* 2 volumes (Paris: G. de Luyne, 1663);

Les Œuvres de Monsieur Molière, 2 volumes (Paris: G. Quinet, 1666);

Les Œuvres de Monsieur de Molière, 7 volumes (Paris: C. Barbin, 1673);

Les Œuvres de Monsieur de Molière, 7 volumes (Paris: D. Thierry et C. Barbin, 1674–1675);

Œuvres de Molière, 13 volumes (Paris: Hachette, 1873–1900);

Œuvres complètes, 2 volumes, edited by Georges Couton, Bibliothèque de la Pléiade, nos. 8 and 9 (Paris: Gallimard, 1981).

Editions in English: *The Plays of Molière in French with an English Translation,* 8 volumes, translated by A. R. Waller (Edinburgh: John Grant, 1907);

Eight Plays by Molière, translated by Morris Bishop (New York: Modern Library, 1957);

The School for Wives, translated by Richard Wilbur (New York: Harcourt Brace Jovanovich, 1971);

One-Act Comedies of Molière, translated by Albert Bermel (New York: Ungar, 1975);

The Misanthrope and Other Plays by Molière, translated by Donald Frame (New York: New American Library, 1981);

The School for Husbands; and, Sganarelle, or The Imaginary Cuckold, translated by Wilbur (San Diego: Harcourt Brace, 1993);

Dom Juan and Other Plays, edited by Ian Maclean, translated by George Graveley and Maclean (Oxford & New York: Oxford University Press, 1998);

The Misanthrope and Other Plays, translated by John Wood and David Coward (London & New York: Penguin, 2000);

The Misanthrope, Tartuffe, and Other Plays, translated by Maya Slater (Oxford & New York: Oxford University Press, 2001).

PLAY PRODUCTIONS: *L'Estourdy, ou Les Contre-temps,* Lyon, summer 1655; Paris, Théâtre du Petit-Bourbon, November 1658;

Dépit amoureux, Beziers, December 1656; Paris, Théâtre du Petit-Bourbon, December 1658;

Le Médecin volant, Paris, 18 April 1659;

Les Précieuses ridicules, Paris, Théâtre du Petit-Bourbon, 18 November 1659;

Sganarelle, ou Le Cocu imaginaire, Paris, Théâtre du Petit-Bourbon, 28 May 1660;

La Jalousie du barbouillé, Paris, Théâtre du Palais-Royal, December 1660;

Dom Garcie de Navarre, ou Le Prince jaloux, Paris, Théâtre du Palais-Royal, 4 February 1661;

L'Escole des maris, Paris, Théâtre du Palais-Royal, 24 June 1661;

Les Fâcheux, Vaux-le-Vicomte, 17 August 1661; Paris, Théâtre du Palais-Royal, 4 November 1661;

L'Escole des femmes, Paris, Théâtre du Palais-Royal, 26 December 1662;

La Critique de L'Escole des femmes, Paris, Théâtre du Palais-Royal, 1 June 1663;

L'Impromptu de Versailles, Versailles, Château de Versailles, 19 October 1663; Paris, Théâtre du Palais-Royal, 14 November 1663;

Le Mariage forcé, Paris, Palais du Louvre, 29 January 1664;

Les Plaisirs de l'île enchantée, Versailles, Château de Versailles, 7–9 May 1664;

La Princesse d'Elide, Versailles, Château de Versailles, 8 May 1664; Paris, Théâtre du Palais-Royal, 9 November 1664;

Tartuffe, Versailles, Château de Versailles, 12 May 1664; revised as *Panulphe, ou L'Imposteur,* Paris, Théâtre du Palais-Royal, 5 August 1667; revised as *Le Tartuffe, ou L'Imposteur,* Paris, Théâtre du Palais-Royal, 5 February 1669;

Dom Juan, ou Le Festin de Pierre, Paris, Théâtre du Palais-Royal, 15 February 1665;

L'Amour médecin, Versailles, Château de Versailles, 15 September 1665; Paris, Théâtre du Palais-Royal, 22 September 1665;

Le Misanthrope, Paris, Théâtre du Palais-Royal, 4 June 1666;

Le Médecin malgré luy, Paris, Théâtre du Palais-Royal, 6 August 1666;

Ballet des muses, Saint-Germain-en-Laye, Château de Saint-Germain-en-Laye, 2 December 1666;

Mélicerte, by Molière and Isaac de Benserade, Saint-Germain-en-Laye, Château de Saint-Germain-en-Laye, December 1666;

La Pastorale comique, Saint-Germain-en-Laye, Château de Saint-Germain-en-Laye, 5 January 1667;

Le Sicilien, ou L'Amour peintre, Saint-Germain-en-Laye, Château de Saint-Germain-en-Laye, 14 February 1667; Paris, Théâtre du Palais-Royal, 10 June 1667;

Amphitryon, Paris, Théâtre du Palais-Royal, 13 January 1668;

George Dandin, ou Le Mary confondu, Versailles, Château de Versailles, 15 July 1668; Paris, Théâtre du Palais-Royal, 9 November 1668;

L'Avare, Paris, Théâtre du Palais-Royal, 9 September 1668;

Monsieur de Pourceaugnac, Chambord, Château de Chambord, 6 October 1669; Paris, Théâtre du Palais-Royal, 15 November 1669;

Les Amans magnifiques, Saint-Germain-en-Laye, Château de Saint-Germain-en-Laye, 4 February 1670;

Le Bourgeois gentilhomme, Chambord, Château de Chambord, 14 October 1670; Paris, Théâtre du Palais-Royal, 23 November 1670;

Psiché, by Molière, Pierre Corneille, and Philippe Quinault, Paris, Palais des Tuilleries, 17 January 1671; Paris, Théâtre du Palais-Royal, 24 July 1671;

Les Fourberies de Scapin, Paris, Théâtre du Palais-Royal, 24 May 1671;

La Comtesse d'Escarbagnas, Saint-Germain-en-Laye, Château de Saint-Germain-en-Laye, 2 December 1671; Paris, Théâtre du Palais-Royal, 8 July 1672;

Les Femmes savantes, Paris, Théâtre du Palais-Royal, 11 March 1672;

Le Malade imaginaire, Paris, Théâtre du Palais-Royal, 10 February 1673.

OTHER: "Huitaine, en l'honneur de la Confrérie de Notre-Dame de la Charité," on the engraving *La Confrérie de l'esclavage de Notre-Dame de la Charité,* Paris, 1665;

"A M. La Mothe Le Vayer, sur la mort de son fils," in *Recueil de pièces galantes en prose et en vers de Mme. la Comtesse de la Suze, d'une autre dame et de M. Pelisson, augmenté de plusieurs élégies* (Paris, 1678).

Molière's talents as both a writer and an actor were so great that at the height of his career he was often confused with the characters of his plays, whether cuckolded and browbeaten husbands, crafty servants, or, in the eyes of the antitheatricalists, the devil incarnate. As an author he was never far from the characters he invented, whether he interpreted their roles or not. In this multiple genius, Molière was rare among playwrights whose works have survived in published form. For unlike either Pierre Corneille or Jean Racine, the two other well-known dramatic writers of his epoch, Molière was not simply a writer of plays but also a practitioner of theater, intimately involved in the life of the stage as both actor and troupe director. While Molière is most commonly celebrated as the dramatist who took forms of farce and burlesque popular in early modern France to a new level of acceptance and respectability, that literary accomplishment cannot be understood separately from the challenges and skills of his professional life. As a member of the elite group of artists rising to prominence in the early years of King Louis XIV's personal rule, Molière performed on the Parisian stage, at court, and in private residences, and he wrote for all these venues and audiences. Navigating the turbulent waters of diverging and converging interests and alliances, Molière always championed the spectator's taste, whether that of the occupants of the parterre, the commoner's seats, or that of the king. He recognized that the most important goal was "to please" and that pleasing was "une étrange entreprise" (a strange enterprise). Molière reiterated this motto in prefaces to his published plays and put it into the mouths of many of his characters, in times of polemic and in periods of unchallenged success. Pleasing, however, did not mean that he was not a sharp critic.

Indeed, Molière can be ranked among the moralists of his generation, and he had a depth of knowledge of his society that was based on both observation and education. As a writer he was as much a master of poetry and prose as he was of comedic timing and gesture; he is known as a master of patois, both real and invented, and could bowdlerize Latin as only a knowledgeable linguist could do. Multitalented and professionally astute, Molière was able to ride the tides of his political service, writing for and performing in different environments (at court and in the city) and in varying genres (comedy, tragedy, ballet, court spectacle, and farce, to name a few) so that during his life, his plays and his performances enjoyed a wide reception in and around Paris, as well as in the provinces, and in such countries as England, Holland, and Sweden. While he died relatively young at age fifty-one after only thirteen years of productivity in Paris, he left a vast and varied corpus, the riches of which are still being uncovered.

The details of Molière's early life come from legal documents and from *La Vie de M. de Molière* (The Life of Molière), written by his colleague Jean-Léonor Le Gallois de Grimarest for the posthumous publication in 1682 of Molière's complete works. These facts are not always easy to verify. Indeed, the exact date of Molière's birth is not known, only that he was baptized Jean Baptiste Poquelin on 15 January 1622 at his parish church, Saint-Eustache. He was the first child of Jean Poquelin, a *tapissier,* or merchant of upholstery and other forms of tapestry for house furnishings. His father was well off, able to purchase a royal appointment as purveyor of upholstered furnishings to the king in April 1631. Jean Baptiste's mother, Marie Cressé, was from a family in the same trade. She died when he was nine years old. The inventory of her belongings upon her death indicates that she owned several books, suggesting both money for luxury items and access to literate culture. Jean Baptiste's father remarried, but the young child maintained a close relationship with his maternal grandfather, who is credited with nurturing his interest in the theater.

The Poquelins lived the life of a well-off bourgeois family, investing in and renting out property in addition to engaging in trade, and the young Poquelin was educated in the style befitting the eldest son of a successful merchant. Like many intellectuals of his generation, he studied with the Jesuits, attending the Collège de Clermont. Later, he pursued a legal education. In 1637 he received his father's royal office, his prerogative as eldest son. Whether he ever practiced either law or his family profession is not clear. In January 1643 he sold his royal appointment back to his father, abandoning a secure economic future for the uncertainty and thrill of life in the theater. He had

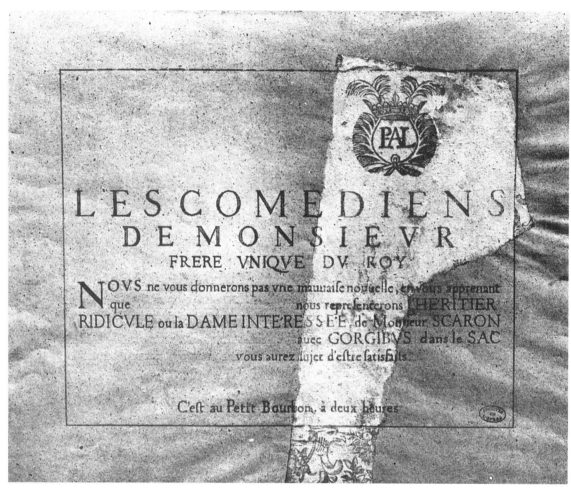

Announcement for Molière's Les Précieuses ridicules, *which premiered at the Théâtre du Petit-Bourbon on 18 November 1659 (Bibliothèque de l'Opera, Paris)*

long been drawn to the art, exposed to theater on the streets of Paris where roving performers and the sellers of medical remedies offered models of acting. He also attended plays in the permanent theaters of Paris. There he would have seen the best actors of farce, as well as those of a newly popular genre, the tragicomedy. Possibly he saw such important plays as Corneille's *Le Cid,* which premiered in 1637, causing quite a stir among Parisian intellectuals and the theatergoing classes, including many from the kind of easy bourgeois milieu to which his family belonged. The young Jean Baptiste also might have encountered drama and acting in his early education at the Collège de Clermont, where he might have been exposed to the Jesuit practice of acting plays in Latin. Only legend and little hard fact suggest why Molière turned to the theater. One legend is that he was romantically attracted to a young actress and author, Madeleine Béjart, with whom he eventually had a long romantic liaison. What is known is that about six months after renounc-

ing the trade that was his birthright, he signed a contract with the Société de l'Illustre Théâtre (Society of the Illustrious Theater). The contract established the troupe, which included Béjart and two of her siblings, as well as Jean Baptiste and several other young aspiring actors and actresses. The signature on this contract is Poquelin, but by June of that year, Jean Baptiste had taken on the stage name Molière.

Once established, the troupe rented a tennis court, a typical space for staging plays, and set about renovating it for their purposes. The Illustrious Theater opened in January 1644. It was never a great success. The troupe quickly became mired in debt. In part they were struggling because they were not located in the Marais neighborhood of Paris, where most other theaters were situated. In part they were a ragtag collection of beginners, staging out-of-fashion tragedies and more stylish tragicomedies. Molière himself was known as a terrible tragedian. In his own self-portrait, a play-about-a-play, *L'Impromptu de Versailles* (The Impromptu of Versailles, performed in 1663; first published in volume 7 of *Les Œuvres de Monsieur de Molière,* 1682), he did not subscribe to the traditional forms of tragic recitation, choosing a more natural vocalization than that to which Parisian audiences were accustomed. Even an eventual move to the Marais did not reverse the troupe's fortunes. By the summer of 1645, after just eighteen months in Paris, the troupe found itself involved in legal proceedings and one of its members, Molière, in jail for its unpaid debts. Eventually, with the help of Molière's father, the other members of the troupe were able to obtain his release. This debacle marked the beginning of a long period during which the troupe toured the provinces.

The thirteen years that the Illustrious Theater spent performing in the provinces is often referred to by scholars of Molière as a period of exile. But it was really a period of creativity and incubation, a time in which Molière found his footing as an actor of comedy, a writer, and a leader of the troupe. When he became de facto troupe leader is not certain, nor is precisely when he began providing his own material for some of the one-act plays that preceded or followed the tragicomedies and tragedies that provided the center of the programs the troupe staged. What is known is that in the provinces Molière and his fellow players joined the troupe of Bernard de Nogaret de La Valette, duc d'Epernon, and later worked under the patronage of Armand de Bourbon, prince de Conti. By the end of the 1640s France was in political turmoil, with uprisings against the royal family in the capital, Paris, and unrest in the provinces. Many of the nobility had fled Paris, accused of antiroyalist acts or sympathies, and the troupe often staged plays for these pleasure-seeking nobles in exile.

While tragedy was still considered the most noble form of theater, Molière began writing his farces during this period. In the summer of 1655 he premiered *L'Estourdy, ou Les Contre-temps* (The Bungler, published 1663)–spelled *L'Etourdi* in modern editions–and in December 1656 *Dépit amoureux* (Scorned Lovers, published 1662), two stock farces based on models from the commedia dell'arte. When the troupe returned to Paris under the patronage of the king's brother, Philippe, duc de Orléans, it chose as its central presentation a tragedy by the successful playwright Corneille. The troupe added a second, shorter play to the program–Molière's own work, *Dépit amoureux.* The king, Louis XIV, and his mother, Anne of Austria, were present at the October performance, which took place in their palace, the Louvre. The evening was a success, and the troupe soon became established on the Parisian scene, first under the patronage of the duke of Orléans and later, more significantly, under that of the young king.

One cannot overestimate the impact of such patronage on the career of Molière and on the troupe for which he wrote and acted. For the group to thrive, they needed access to an affordable space in which to perform. In their earlier incarnation in Paris as the Illustrious Theater, the troupe did not have such patronage and soon fell prey to debt. But, in their second attempt to establish themselves in Paris, the troupe had better luck. Their performance for the king so pleased him that he accorded them space to perform in the Théâtre du Petit-Bourbon, a stage already occupied by the Italian players, whose commedia dell'arte farces served as a source for Molière's own creations. The space was accorded rent-free, and the troupe was further supported by the duke. The troupe performed on the so-called off days, those when the Italians were not performing. As Molière biographer Virginia Scott has argued, this "disadvantage" was an advantage, for it allowed the troupe to perform on days when all the other Parisian theaters were closed, leaving the troupe an uncontested audience. While Molière and his colleagues continued to perform for royalty throughout their career, it was the large audience they drew in from the bourgeois of Paris that molded much of the sensibility and focus of Molière's great comedies.

When the troupe began performing at the Petit-Bourbon in November 1658, the two short farces Molière had composed in the provinces first drew in the audiences. These short plays were staged in alternation with a repertoire of well-known tragedies and tragicomedies available to any troupe for performing because they had already been published. The best and most successful troupes worked directly with playwrights to obtain new material over which they would have exclusive right of performance. Not surprisingly, by November 1659 Molière began providing his troupe such new material. To the short farces he had written in the provinces, Molière added his first fully developed play, *Les Précieuses ridicules* (The Affected Young Ladies, first performed 1659; published 1660). This play savaged the morals of contemporary Paris by parodying the pretensions and false poses of two young provincial women trying to achieve recognition in Parisian society by adopting the affected language and behavior patterns of the Parisian intelligentsia. Taking vengeance on the two girls, their spurned suitors send in their valets to court them. To the audience, the valets posing as men of society appear as pretentious as the two provincials. To the girls, ignorant of the social manners they are attempting to display, the valets seem to be the perfect society gentlemen adhering to the manners of "préciosité" (a style demonstrating delicate tastes or sentiments; in its extreme, affectation).

Molière's parody of the young women was not original. Nor was it necessarily aimed at the members of his audience who considered themselves cultivated in the style the two young women were copying. Rather, he parodied the provincials who came to Paris and tried to pass as intellectuals. His parody of the affectations of pretentious women, often characterized as scathing misogyny, is in fact not so different from the same parody of false affected women made in a passage in the most recent volume of the extremely popular novel *Le Grand Cyrus* (1649–1653), written by one of the female intellectuals of seventeenth-century France, Madeleine de Scudéry. The play, a fully developed example of the kinds of comedies of manners that Molière perfected during the course of his career, was a smash success. It also brought controversy, accusations of plagiarism, and the pirating of the play by publishers. Molière, in order to benefit from his own play, rushed it into print, even though to do so meant the troupe would lose its exclusive right to perform the comedy. In his introduction to his first published work, Molière protested the conditions of publication and underscored the difference between a work performed on the stage and one on the printed page. He also modestly protested his abilities to write seriously about drama, insisting he was not a pedant, and thus portrayed himself as a worldly Parisian gentleman. In January 1659, just two years after arriving in Paris, Molière was no longer simply an actor composing plays for performance. He was a published writer, invoking all the *topoi,* or conventional themes, of the gentlemanly reluctance to pass to print.

With his career rising along with the success of his troupe, Molière continued composing new comedies of manners. The spring of 1660 brought the premiere of *Sganarelle, ou Le Cocu imaginaire* (Sganarelle, or The Imaginary Cuckold, published 1660), a play that introduced the character Sganarelle, a bumbling bourgeois, who in this play imagines himself cuckolded. The play premiered in a quiet Paris, since the king and his court were on the banks of the Bidassoa River, the border with Spain, meeting with the court of Philip IV, king of Spain, whose daughter, María Teresa, was being married to the young Louis XIV. Once more, the bourgeois of the city became Molière's avid audience. The king and his court did not see the play until their return in late summer. But Molière was already assured of the king's approval, having received the first of many royal grants from the king in June. The actor-playwright also tried to stave off piracy of his new play, applying for official permission to publish *Sganarelle,* the earlier pieces, and a tragedy he had not yet staged but was apparently working on at this time. Drama was an extremely popular form of entertainment in the early

years of Louis XIV's reign, and published texts of popular plays being staged were a lucrative property available to a struggling print industry. Consequently, once again, and despite precautions, Molière found his play pirated. But this time, armed with his own legal protections, he pursued his right to his play in a lawsuit, although the suit was not completely successful. The details of the difficulties of Molière's attempts to control his texts in a world that did not yet recognize the rights of authors have been well documented in the work of C. E. J. Caldicott. What is most important is that by the spring of 1660, Molière was beginning to stand up for his rights as an author, using a court system he later parodied, if not for its own workings, then for the frivolous uses to which contemporary Parisians put it.

Sganarelle introduced one of Molière's stock characters. It also inaugurated one of his recurrent, successful themes, the anxiety of men about the fidelity of their wives. A stock anxiety of the Renaissance "quarrel over women," this fear of being cuckolded served Molière and his troupe well on stage. The years 1660–1663 allowed Molière to work and rework this theme in a variety of genres and professional venues. Indeed, an event beyond his control–the sudden and unannounced demolition of the Petit Bourbon theater during renovations to the Louvre–gave Molière a respite of several months from staging plays in Paris. In response to the troupe's appeals, the king awarded them a new place to perform, the theater located in the Palais-Royal. Originally built for Richelieu, the site needed extensive repairs. During this period, however, Molière returned to work on a tragicomedy that he had apparently previewed in private readings as early as 1659 and first performed in 1661. The play, *Dom Garcie de Navarre, ou Le Prince jaloux* (Dom Garcie of Navarre, or The Jealous Prince, first published 1682), was loosely based on a heroic comedy by Corneille, *Don Sanche d'Aragon* (first performed in the 1649–1650 season; published 1650). The plot concerns Dom Garcie's rivalry with Dom Alphonse, thought to be the prince of Castille, for the hand of Elvire, the princess of Léon. According to Georges Couton, each act of the play stages "a crisis of jealousy" on the part of Dom Garcie. The tension is resolved when rival Dom Alphonse is discovered to be Elvire's brother, a revelation that effectively eliminates him as a suitor and resolves any jealousy. Molière had high hopes that the play would showcase his talents in a serious genre and dispel any doubts about his status as merely a player and writer of farce. He quickly applied for permission to publish the drama. But the play was a box-office flop with a limited run and was never published during Molière's life except for verses he removed and ideas he used in other works.

Vaux-le-Vicomte, home of French finance minister Nicolas Foucquet, where Molière's Les Fâcheux
had its premiere on 17 August 1661 (Bibliothèque Nationale, Paris)

Perhaps because of the prodigious failure of his foray into tragedy, Molière's next treatment of the theme of jealousy, *L'Escole des maris* (The School for Husbands, performed and published in 1661)–spelled *L'Ecole* in modern editions–was not an immediate success. Written in three acts, *L'Ecole des maris* did, however, turn out to be Molière's first hit in the Palais-Royal venue, in which he performed for the rest of his career. In this play Sganarelle and his brother are each raising one of a pair of sisters. Opening with what became a hallmark of Molière's comedies–that is, a debate between two contrasting characters, in this case Sganarelle and his brother Ariste–the play quickly sets out two differing philosophies toward the world. Sganarelle, as his brother tells him, is too severe, too hard on the manners of their milieu, whose members find his behavior and beliefs bizarre. Ariste, on the other hand, takes a more liberal view of contemporary manners. Engaging in this disagreement, the pair anticipate another famous duo of Molière's stage, Alceste and Philante of *Le Misantrope* (The Misanthrope, performed in 1666; published 1666). Their differing views of the world also form their approach to raising the two young girls. Ariste is liberal, while Sganarelle is so mistrustful of his young charge and her desires that Lisette, one of the sister's ladies-in-waiting, wonders sarcastically in act

1 if she is not among the Turks, who believe in shutting away their women. In Molière's plays, as in many comedies, the servants and marginal characters most often speak with the greatest clairvoyance, and the younger generation rebels against the wishes of their often despotic elders. In this case Ariste ends by marrying his charge, but Sganarelle loses his tightly held prize to her young admirer, Valère, in large part because he is unable to accept modern mores. Inflexible, Sganarelle is funny, but he is also a loser in love.

Staged in June of 1661, *L'Ecole des maris* not only continued to play on the theme of jealousy and the fear of being betrayed by women, but also allowed Molière to showcase his own prodigious qualities as an actor of comedy when he took the starring role as the eccentric and inflexible Sganarelle. The play must also have further established Molière as a writer of verse. For when the finance minister of France, Nicolas Foucquet, decided to showcase his residence at Vaux-le-Vicomte with a spectacular festival, he called on all the best artists to aid in his project. Molière was among those artists. For the event, he responded to a particular challenge–that is, to conceive of a play that could meld with the ballets to be danced between its acts. While it had long been a practice to include danced interludes between the acts of plays, never before had the two forms been combined into a coherent whole. Molière's contribution to the Vaux festivities thus inaugurated a new practice and created a genre, the comedy-ballet. While his more highly developed comedies of manners are the basis on which literary scholars have canonized Molière as a playwright, his comedy-ballets were, during his life, substantially more successful and lucrative. Molière's play for performance at Vaux combined the elements for which he had become known—frustration in love and a cast of characters that provided sketches of contemporary types. Thus, the art of the piece was not in the development of character and plot but in the display or portrayal of contemporary society. In the play, *Les Fâcheux* (The Impertinents, performed in 1661; published 1662), the hero, Eraste, is plagued by encounters with bothersome individuals, *fâcheux*. In a series of descriptions and encounters on stage, Eraste bemoans all the bores of the world, many of whom are particularly irksome because they stop him from meeting his love interest. The series of delightful portraits thus allows Molière to portray through writing and acting (he played several of the roles) such contemporaries as the pompous theatergoer, who would rather display himself than watch the play (a particular irritation to Molière as actor-director); the valet, whose assiduous attentions cause Eraste's hat to fall in the dirt; the tiresome courtier, who insists Eraste listen to his latest musical composition; and the courtier, who insists on relating his tales of the hunt. This last vignette, Molière acknowledges in dedicating the published play to the king, was suggested to him by the monarch after the Vaux premiere.

Perhaps as much for the portraits it paints as for the gestures of obedience to the commands of rich patrons, *Les Fâcheux* reveals a great deal about Molière's status and strategies in these early years of his career. Summoned by Foucquet, as he tells the reader in the preface to the published play, he "conque, faite, apprise, et représentée en quinze jours" (conceived, composed, learned, and staged [the play] in two weeks). Molière was a master of accommodating to his environment, a quality necessary in the politically and socially fraught world of Louis XIV's court. When Molière refers to the production of the play as "précipitée" (precipitous), he implicitly praises himself as capable of rising to the occasion when called upon by his superiors. In describing his work as somehow lacking because of the conditions of its production, Molière also presents himself, albeit on the printed page, as a writer who is sought out and able to rise to the occasion, despite all the difficulties. He also underscores, again implicitly, the danger of his profession. For, soon after staging his festivities at Vaux, the minister Foucquet was arrested by the king and put on trial for mis-

use of funds. The political realities of that downfall may be as closely linked to a general jockeying for power immediately after the king's taking up of his personal reign upon the death of the minister Jules Mazarin, as to fiscal indiscretion and the ostentatious display of his opulent residence for which he mobilized the talents of the best artists of France. While many allies from among the intelligentsia became stained by their association with Foucquet, Molière did not suffer such a fate. Indeed, he was invited to perform *Les Fâcheux* for the king at Fountainebleau within a week of its premiere at Vaux, as if the form must be appropriated by the king from Foucquet to show the king's dominance in the world of art. Staging plays in Paris and in the various royal residences, as well as in the homes of various powerful noble patrons, was not just an aesthetic feat, it was also a political one. Indeed, in Paris in the early years of Louis XIV's reign these two realms were inextricably intertwined.

L'Escole des femmes (The School for Wives, published in 1663)—spelled *L'Ecole* in modern editions—premiered in Paris on 26 December 1662. While the gap in time between staging new material may seem large—sixteen months between August 1661 and December 1662—it was a busy period for the actor-playwright. Activities during those months included the publications of *Dépit amoureux,* the first legitimate editions of *Sganarelle* and *L'Ecole des maris,* dedicated to the king's brother, and *Les Fâcheux,* dedicated to the king; invitations to perform at the royal residences, Fountainebleau and Saint-Germain-en-Laye, the latter bringing the troupe a royal remuneration in the form of a financial award; and Molière's marriage to Armande Béjart on 20 February 1662. When Molière premiered *L'Ecole des femmes,* it was as a successful and rising actor, playwright, troupe director, and new husband. It was also as a courtier, for when the brother to whom Molière had ceded his rights to the title of *tapissier ordinaire du Roi* (tapestry purveyor to the king) had died in 1660, the title was likely returned to Molière. Biographer Virginia Scott has hypothesized that retrieving this title might have provided Molière access to rituals such as the rising and the retiring of the king (the *lever* and *coucher*) and thus added to Molière's access to the king. For this and other reasons, a spectrum of different people might have resented Molière's rising star. The success of *L'Ecole des femmes* provided both a catalyst for this animosity and an occasion for its airing.

The play itself was a witty and bitingly satiric look once again at both the foibles of the rising bourgeoisie and of the old story about men's fears of cuckoldry. It also brought to a new height Molière's mastery of the emerging genre of the comedy of manners. In five acts of verse scrupulously observing all the criteria of contemporary drama—that is, the unity of time, place, and action—the play concerns Arnolphe and his attempt to marry a young woman named Agnès, whose own love interests lie, more appropriately, with a young man, Horace. Arnolphe, whose role Molière played, is an eccentric, as his interlocutor, the moderate Chrysalde, points out in the opening dialogue. In the opening Arnolphe also informs his friend he is no longer to be called by his old name. He has purchased a property and a title, Monsieur de la Souche, or Mr. Stump, a play on the idea of rooting oneself by obtaining nobility. The pun is funny because *stump* is not an ennobling appellation. It is satiric because it is a direct reference to the way Pierre and Thomas Corneille, Molière's chief rivals as playwrights, obtained their nobility, with a title awarded to their father as "payment" for their contributions to the state as dramatists. This joke, however vicious, suggests only a fraction of the foibles Arnolphe displays. For, as the audience soon learns, he is and has long been obsessed with mocking men whose wives stray, a common event in the milieu of his day, in which women were accorded much liberty. Now Arnolphe plans to marry, despite his friend's warning that he is risking the fate for which he has so long ridiculed others; in fact he is doubly at risk—as a target of all those he has targeted *and* as a cuckold. The future groom is confident he can avoid such a fate since he has raised the bride from childhood, secreting her away in the country, and schooling her, as Barbara Johnson has argued, not in the manners of the day but in ignorance. There is, he believes, no chance she can cross him without the social graces and tools of which she has been deprived, and she is, in this state, perfectly delicious.

The intrigue and humor of the play lie in all the ways in which the ingenue Agnès is wise despite her apparent ignorance. Aided by her own feelings and by the bumbling ineptitude of Arnolphe's own house staff, she manages to meet and fall in love with Horace, son of Arnolphe's own friend. That Arnolphe has lent Horace aid in his love quest—albeit before learning the identity of the object of the young man's desires—is part of his pathos. The tension is resolved—despite much movement to and fro of the characters on the street in front of Arnolphe's house—when Agnès's father returns from abroad to reclaim his parental rights from Arnolphe, to whom he had entrusted the young girl's care many years before.

The plot and acting appealed to the audiences, and the fully developed drama was an immediate success in Paris and at court. It also provided many opportunities for Molière's enemies and jealous rivals to attack him and soon gave rise to a polemic that extended throughout 1663 and into the early months of 1664. Initially, attacks against Molière circulated orally.

Armande Béjart, whom Molière married on 20 February 1662 (Musée des Arts Décoratifs, Paris)

Not until a young and aspiring journalist, Jean Donneau de Visé, published a three-volume, nine-hundred-page compendium of poetry, short prose fiction, and literary and cultural criticism, into which he inserted a vignette recording the attacks against Molière and his play, was any criticism recorded in print.

The initial attacks—and they remained similar throughout the various performances of the polemic—were as much against Molière the person as against his play. Among the accusations were criticisms of Molière's failure as a serious tragedian, his professional opportunism, his strategies of self-promotion, and his method of appropriating ideas and characters for his theater, as well as innuendo about his morals. In many ways these attacks are interesting, because they confuse Molière the person with Molière the professional, a confusion that was maintained throughout the quarrel. At its most vicious, the polemic also consisted of attacks against the believability and propriety of the play, particularly against purported allusions to the loss of Agnès's virginity in such exchanges as her discussion of a ribbon given her paramour, and of attacks on Molière's own personal morals, namely his recent marriage to the younger sister—or more likely, daughter—of his longtime mistress, Madeleine Béjart. These three major categories of critiques—professional, aesthetic, and personal—covered the range of people who harbored animosity against the young actor-playwright. And these animosities, nurtured and mouthed at times by surrogates seeking to further their own careers, lent themselves to a dialogue that took place on the stage and in print.

Molière himself made two major interventions in the debate, both on stage. In the first, he attempted to appropriate the debate by staging his own attack against himself in a play, *La Critique de L'Escole des femmes* (Critique of The School for Wives, performed and published in 1663)—spelled *L'Ecole* in modern editions. This play moved the polemic from the protojournalism of Donneau de Visé's text and the innuendo of oral attack to the stage, where Molière could give voice and character to the attacks, framing them in such a way as to deflect, or at least ridicule, their bite. The play had probably been read aloud in Parisian salons during the months preceding its 1 June 1663 premiere. It is mentioned by Donneau de Visé in his first attack, noting, with some truth, that it would serve as clever self-advertisement on the part of Molière. Its setting is the drawing room of Uranie, a salon where the characters discuss *L'Ecole des femmes*. Not surprisingly, the most reasonable characters defend the play, while the most extravagant attack it. Many of Molière's stock characters appear—a ridiculous marquis, a pedant poet, and an extravagant, affected woman—all of whom offer the more reasonable interlocutors the opportunity to defend Molière and to expound on important problems. These issues include the nature of stage imitation, which holds a mirror up to the public while this mimesis causes chagrin in viewers who think they are targeted. Molière's portraits, however, are composites in which one should not seek out specific resemblances. Another topic is the difference between acting tragedy and acting comedy. One of Molière's mouthpieces, a gentleman named Dorante, exclaims in exasperation that comedy is much harder to perform than tragedy, in which "il suffit, pour n'être point blamé, de dire des choses qui soient de bon sens et bien écrites" (it is sufficient, in order not to be blamed, to say things that are sensible and well-written). Comedy, he underscores, "est une étrange entreprise" (is a strange enterprise) because in it one must "faire rire les honnêtes gens" (make gentlemen laugh). Warming up, he also takes a stab against pedants who cite Aristotle and Horace, but who, with all their knowledge of the "rules," have no understanding that "la grande règle de toutes les règles est de plaire" (the most important of all the rules is to please), whoever the public may be.

With these lines Molière also drew a line in the sand—namely, he gestured to the importance of his public in a manner reminiscent of and fundamentally differ-

ent from the literary polemic surrounding Corneille's *Le Cid,* which had taken place twenty-six years earlier and had also served to define the nature of the audience and its role in supporting the emergence of a new dramatic form, tragicomedy. It is reminiscent because the playwright attempts to prioritize popular reception, but it is dramatically different because Molière was supported not just by the Parisian theatergoing public but also by the king. At the same time he was fighting his polemic, Molière was receiving signs of support from the monarch. In March, Molière received a one-thousand-livre pension from the king. In August he dedicated the printed version of *La Critique de L'Ecole des femmes* to the ailing queen mother, a longtime proponent of the rival troupe of tragedians located at the Bourgogne Theater. In May he published a witty and masterful poem, *Remerciment au Roy*—spelled *Remerciement* in modern editions—in which he both thanked the king and presented himself as recognized by the monarch in public, almost as if the two are exchanging knowing winks. Finally, in October, in the midst of ongoing attacks, including a series of plays imitating *La Critique de L'Ecole des femmes* staged by rival troupes, Molière was invited to Versailles, where he staged his final answer in the polemic.

L'Impromptu de Versailles, a one-act drama, is an invaluable source of insight into the actor-playwright's ideas about his profession. It is a play-about-a-play that allows Molière to stage himself and his troupe rehearsing a play. What is most masterful about the drama is that Molière does not stage a successful enterprise, but a fitful one. The actors are late; they do not know their roles; and they are unruly. Indeed, all the actors and actresses, especially the director's newly-wed wife, rebel because they do not feel ready to perform. This resistance or breakdown in the perfect staging allows Molière to dissect what makes a successful performance, coaching each actor and overcoming all the obstacles, including a slew of bothersome interrupters who hearken back to *Les Fâcheux.* The troupe members themselves interrupt and show the collaboration behind staging plays when they offer their ideas for what the group should be doing. When they encourage Molière to answer his critics by painting their portraits, as they have recently been doing of him on stage, the actor-playwright engages in a short and virtuoso mockery of his rivals, once again distinguishing comedy from tragedy, clearly marking the former as a more challenging genre for acting. Indeed, Molière stages himself in *L'Impromptu de Versailles* less as an author and more as a director and courtier. For, in answer to the troupe's panic, he reiterates that the most important thing they can do is to obey the king. Their act of obedience will be their greatest performance and will count more than

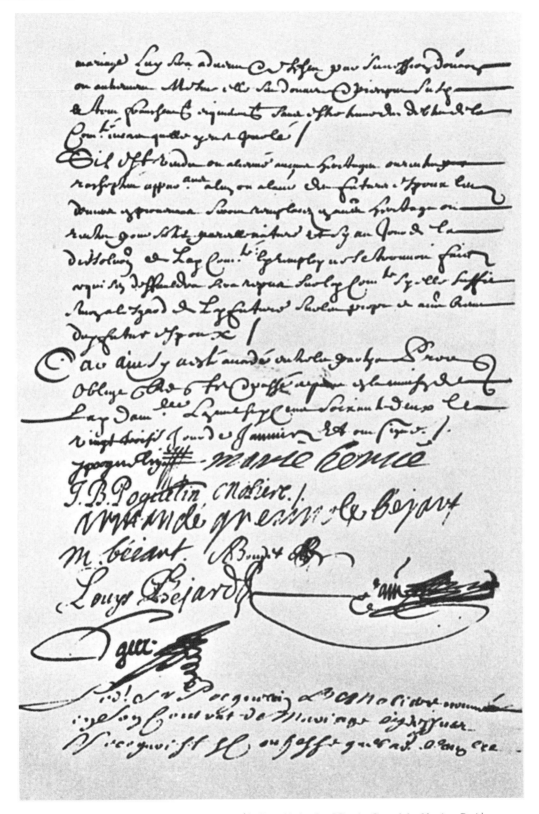

Molière's marriage license, January 1662 (Archives Nationales, Minutier Central des Notaires, Paris)

249

Sketch of a scene from a 1673 production of Molière's 1664 play Le Mariage forcé *(charcoal drawing by Claude Gillot; from Sylvie Bostarron Chevallrey,* Molière en son temps, *1973)*

the perfection of their work. Thus, when at the end of the play they are simply not ready with the work being rehearsed, the king sends the message that anything they have will be accepted. In staging this benevolence toward Molière on the part of the king at the court (and in a play with the court's name, Versailles, in its title), the actor-playwright shows that the king offers him support. When Molière tells his panicked troupe that he does not need to answer the attacks directly as they wish him to do, he is showing his relative strength, a strength he demonstrates is linked to the favor of the king, a preference that is apparently strong enough to allow him to close the chapter on what is known as "la querelle de *L'Ecole des femmes*" (Quarrel of the School for Wives), even if his detractors continued to attack him for some months to come.

While much of Molière's most remarkable writing lay ahead of him by the final months of 1663, much of the groundwork for it had already been laid. Stock characters and situations as well as the acerbic perspective on the foibles of contemporary society were already present in his first plays, while his ability to maneuver between the demands of the court and those of the city was also well established. Indeed, much of Molière's success in the coming years, when he suffered setbacks

with some of his most prized projects, depended on his ability to play off his talents of writing for the court with those of writing for an urban audience. When some of his dramas caused considerable controversy and were attacked by religious conservatives, he could always fall back on his connections at court, if not for permission to stage the banned plays, at least for more lucrative work. The year 1664 indeed establishes this pattern in Molière's career. The beginning of the year was marked by private visits sponsored by important figures at Louis XIV's court, for example, the minister of war, Michel Le Tellier, and the minister of finance, Jean-Baptiste Colbert. At the end of January, Molière premiered a new comedy-ballet for the king, *Le Mariage forcé* (The Forced Marriage, published 1664) in the queen mother's private apartments at the Louvre. In February the king served as godfather to Molière's first son, with the king's sister-in-law serving as godmother. Perhaps because of all these signs of preference, when he was invited to participate in an extended period of festivities at Versailles running throughout April and May, Molière took the risk of staging an as yet incomplete version of what eventually became *Le Tartuffe, ou L'Imposteur* (Tartuffe, or The Impostor, published 1669). In its embryonic form, the play concerned the penetration into the household of the somewhat naive and pompous Orgon by a man of the church. That the churchman, Tartuffe, is taking advantage of Orgon soon becomes apparent. The satire concerns Tartuffe's unscrupulousness; the humor, Orgon's naiveté. The traditional comic subplot concerns the marriage of Orgon's daughter, Marianne, to Tartuffe. The most prescient member of the household is the maid, Dorine, who works tirelessly to unmask Tartuffe and set things right. In 1664 the play stopped at three acts—that is, before Tartuffe's major betrayals of trying to seduce Orgon's wife, trying to take all the family's money, and having stolen potentially compromising papers from Orgon. *Tartuffe* in embryonic form was an immediate success. The king and the visiting papal legate, Cardinal Fabio Chigi, enjoyed it. It was also an immediate disaster, bringing out all of Molière's enemies, if not from among his professional rivals, at the least from among the population of pious conservatives around the queen mother, who still maintained influence at court. The fight over the play concerned issues of morality and the nature of comic satire.

If such questions had emerged around *L'Ecole des femmes,* particularly in respect to the equivocal references to sexuality seen in Agnès's giving her ribbon to Horace, and around Molière's personal mores, they did not take center stage as they did in the *Tartuffe* crisis. The other major difference in this latter debacle was that while Molière's critics did not really deter him in the polemic around *L'Ecole des femmes*—indeed the polemic actually gave him helpful publicity—in the case of *Tartuffe* they were actually able to ban performance of the play for a period of five years.

Many factors influenced this banning, but the crucial one concerned the relative strength at court of powerful nobility with ties to a severe and pious Christianity. That these groups had access to and the support of Louis XIV's mother did not help Molière, despite his support from the young and pleasure-loving king. Indeed, the festivities at Versailles in 1664 acerbated the conflict, since while they were officially dedicated to the queen, Marie-Thérèse, they were informally dedicated to the king's new mistress, Françoise Louise de La Vallière, a liaison disapproved of by the queen mother and her cohorts. That Tartuffe was portrayed as a man of the church was unbearable to this group. As Molière himself said in the preface to the play when it was finally published in 1669 and Tartuffe had metamorphosed into a mere religious hypocrite, the falsely pious were the most irate and the strongest of all those whose portraits he painted; the marquis, the affected women, the cuckolds, and the doctors all accepted their own satiric portrayals. While the play itself went through several trials and while Molière appealed twice to the king for permission to perform it, not until he made a few crucial changes, namely changing Tartuffe from a hypocritical churchman to an impostor—that is, to a man only pretending to be a cleric—and not until the queen mother died in January 1666 was Molière able to stage the play fully and freely. This victory marked not only a triumph for Molière but also one for the king, who, by 1669, the year of *Tartuffe*'s premiere at the Théâtre du Palais-Royal, was fully in authority, even over the influence of the church.

The period from May 1664, when Molière staged the first, short version of *Tartuffe* at Versailles, to February 1669, when he was finally able to stage the five-act play at the Palais-Royal in Paris, can be considered the actor-playwright's most fraught and most fertile period. During these years he wrote and staged some of his most renowned work: his treatment of the libertine in *Dom Juan, ou Le Festin de Pierre* (Don Juan, or The Stone Banquet, performed in 1665; first published in volume 7 of *Les Œuvres de Monsieur de Molière,* 1682); his portrayal of the man who rejects worldliness in *Le Misantrope;* his depiction of the miser in *L'Avare* (The Miser, performed in 1668; published 1669); the full version of *Tartuffe;* two lesser-known plays satirizing the medical profession, *L'Amour médecin* (The Love Doctor, performed in 1665; published 1666) and *Le Médecin malgré luy* (The Doctor in Spite of Himself, performed in 1666; published 1667); a stunning portrayal of cross-class marriage, *George Dandin, ou Le Mary confondu* (Georges Dandin, or The Defeated Husband, performed in 1668; published 1669)—spelled *Mari* in modern editions—and an allegorical play, *Amphitryon* (performed and published in 1668), a version of one of Jupiter's metamorphoses that can be read as a commentary on play acting as well as a condemnation of marital infidelity. At the same time, he continued to collaborate on court spectacles, composing some of his most fluent ballets for performance at the royal residences, works he also brought back to the Parisian stage with much success. Many of these works embroider, in a lighter manner, the themes of the darker comedies read and reread across ensuing centuries.

With twelve works staged between May 1664 and the end of 1669, Molière seemed to have achieved the epitome of success. Indeed, he was firmly ensconced on the list of the king's favorite dramatists and on his list of artists awarded royal pensions. In August of 1665 Molière and his troupe were singled out to become "La Troupe du Roi" (The Troupe of the King), instead of that of the king's brother, their title since coming to Paris in 1659. This change brought not only prestige and an increase in command performances but also a huge monetary payment. The troupe was also sought out by young playwrights to perform their work. These writers included the novelist Marie-Catherine Desjardins (Mme. de Villedieu) and the young dramatist Racine, whose first two plays were staged by Molière's troupe. At the same time, Molière was mired in debate over his staging of religious hypocrisy. This controversy, perhaps because of the successes elsewhere, did not deter him from taking on other forms of contemporary corruption, for, as he maintained in both the petitions he wrote appealing for his *Tartuffe* and in the preface of its published edition, comedy is at heart a serious didactic project. But, as he maintained, serious discourse is far less effective in correcting morals than is satire. As his work had shown, no one likes to be ridiculed. When he suggested that other groups did not take as great an offense as the church, perhaps he was wrong. He should have maintained other groups were not as strong as the church. For indeed, while there were little skirmishes later over his plays, there were no big defeats like the one over *Tartuffe*–or almost no big defeats.

Molière's next serious project after *Tartuffe*, his treatment of the Don Juan story, did get mired in controversy. If the controversy was not as large and incendiary as the one over *Tartuffe*, that was because Molière backed down more quickly. Indeed, the story of the libertine nobleman who seduces women for pleasure, abandoning them soon after winning their love (and most likely other treasures) must have seemed like a winning subject to Molière. Other playwrights had already adapted and staged the drama of Tirso de Molina in France without controversy. The troupe clearly expected success with the piece, investing heavily in new scenery and in mechanical apparatuses meant to add a new element to their staging, machines for the kind of baroque special effects wildly popular in the period. With the action firmly set in Spain, not France, and with the target being not the church, but the libertine activities of the main character, the drama seemed safe from controversy.

That Dom Juan seduced a young girl, Elvire, who had already taken her vows in a convent, was not the center of controversy in *Dom Juan*. Indeed, the hero of the play is a consummate gentleman in many ways that were appealing. For example, when Elvire's brothers come to avenge their sister, Dom Juan saves their lives, and they, in turn, following the codes of the noble class, spare his. Nor is he to be condemned for seducing a peasant woman in what is a performance of the nobleman's prerogative over his vassals. Rather, objections arose because of the places in the play where Dom Juan seems to take on God–or as the play says, the heavens. Indeed, with the exception of a virulent print critique of the play that attacked its principal character for being a libertine atheist, a seducer, and a hypocrite, there was,

unlike with *Tartuffe,* no overt governmental intervention to block the performance of the play.

The parts of the play deemed most offensive occur between Dom Juan and his valet, the comic sidekick Sganarelle, whose interactions with the main character allow so-called scandalous material to emerge. This material includes a scene in which Dom Juan and Sganarelle encounter a poor hermit, inciting him to blaspheme in return for money to buy food. This scene was actually cut from the play after the first performance. When the play was finally published in 1682, the scene was reintroduced, but the censors quickly removed it. Even without this scene, many exchanges between Dom Juan and Sganarelle concern issues of belief. Dom Juan, it seems, believes only in the rational, that one and one equal two. He is not afraid of statues of his victims or even the ghost who comes, in the end, to lead him to his punishment. Apparently, that Dom Juan, like Tartuffe, gets his due in the end did not matter, because he shows no fear for his fate even while his valet declares that the heavens have exercised their judgment against him for "Ciel offensé, lois violées, filles séduites, familles déshonorées, parents outragés, femmes mises à mal, maris poussés à bout" (Heaven offended, laws violated, women seduced, families dishonored, parents outraged, wives led astray, husbands pushed to their limits). "Un chacun satisfait" (All the world is content), says Sganarelle. Left alone onstage at the end of the play, he is not simply the voice of moral retribution. He is also the voice of pragmatism and perhaps even of the realities of social hierarchy. For in the original version of the play he stands watching his master led to his judgment and cries out his own fate in the simple words "Mes gages, mes gages" (My salary, my salary). Sganarelle, never happy with the behavior of his master, is nonetheless left bereft by his master's defeat because, like so many others, he gains his life by serving his master, that and nothing more. Alone onstage at the end of the play demanding his due, Sganarelle flattens the distinctions between high and low, putting into relief the issue of what one really believes in ways more profound than the antics of the libertine nobleman.

In a period of intense antitheatricality, in which Molière was labeled a libertine and the devil incarnate, the real confusion between author and character might have lain more closely between Molière and Sganarelle, and not Molière and Dom Juan. Indeed, in so many of Molière's plays, as in comedy in general, wisdom often lies less with those in power than it does with the wily subalterns, such as the valet Sganarelle in *Dom Juan* and the maid Dorine in *Tartuffe*. Molière's exquisite ability to see through social ruses ranks him among the best moralists of his generation. His ability

Posthumous portrait of Molière by Charles-Antoine Coypel,
1730 (Comédie-Française, Paris)

to stage truths places him on the line as a performer of truths, the actor in the polis whom Plato wanted to ban from his republic. What is remarkable, however, is that even in the line of greatest fire, Molière himself remained the wily subaltern, continuing to perform and profit from his performances.

If *Dom Juan* did not spawn a major quarrel, that is because Molière and his troupe voluntarily took the play off their program within weeks of its premiere, never to perform it again during Molière's life. Unlike in England, antitheatricality in France never gained a firm hold. The years that bracket the *Tartuffe* debacle and the period following *Dom Juan* were fruitful years for the actor-playwright. As "the troupe of the king," he and his players were called to court frequently. In September 1665 he wrote the first of several outright satires of medicine for a command performance at Versailles. In the preface to *L'Amour médecin* he tells the reader that the play was "proposé, fait, appris, et reprenté en cinq jours" (proposed, written, learned, and presented in five days). In the play, Sganarelle, the father, does not want to marry off his daughter because he does not want to pay the dowry. As a result, his daughter has fallen into a deep melancholy. Four doctors are called in to examine her, and each is a bigger quack than the next. The final physician is her young paramour, Clitandre, in disguise, and of course his cure is a marriage, quickly arranged, much to the disgruntled protestations of Sganarelle. The play, which actually mocked the king's own staff of physicians, was an immediate success both at court and in Paris, where it was soon performed.

At the same time as he was working at court, Molière was probably already writing one of his greatest masterpieces, *Le Misantrope,* better known by its modern spelling, *Le Misanthrope.* Like so many of the works valued today as great literature, this play was in fact not successful in its initial run in Paris. Nonetheless, it includes one of Molière's most compelling characters, Alceste. Situated among a series of opposing pairs, he is quickly contrasted to his friend Philante. While Alceste detests the social world of modern-day Paris, his friend Philante fits right into a network of social interactions that involves a bit of diplomatic hypocrisy. If Philante can smile at his peers, greeting with much fervor even those he detests, Alceste is known for telling everyone precisely what he thinks. Using the outmoded language of chivalry, he expresses a desire to distinguish himself, even if only by his contrariness. In the world of 1660s Paris, distinction was not the goal. Rather, one was supposed to fit in, to disappear behind the niceties of a courtliness in which only one person, the king, could stand out. Paradoxically, Alceste, the hater of humankind, has fallen in love. He, moreover, has not chosen the gentle and loving Eliante. Instead, he has chosen the most worldly, most coquettish of his milieu, the young widow Célimène, a choice no one understands and that causes him enormous pain. As the play unravels, so does Célimène's social status. She goes from sought-after woman to spurned woman when several suitors discover what Alceste has long suspected, that she is leading on all her lovers, declaring undying love to each of them separately.

Célimène is a talented stage director. She manipulates all the players of her world and paints pleasingly sharp portraits of those who are absent. Her downfall is that she does not rest in the oral realm but puts down her words on paper, in love letters. These documents are eventually turned on her when one goes astray and another is shared publicly. Socially shamed, she has few alternatives, it seems, at the end of the play. Yet, the play really is cyclical. It opens and closes with Alceste onstage bemoaning the ills of contemporary society. It also opens and closes with him still infatuated with the coquette Célimène: to paraphrase the Enlightenment philosopher Voltaire, himself an avid reader of Molière, "plus ça change, plus c'est la même chose" (the more things change, the more they are the same).

Perhaps because this dark comedy was not a huge hit, Molière returned to familiar ground in his next comedy, Le Médecin malgré luy (spelled lui in modern editions), which opened two months later in Paris–familiar ground not only because Molière once more satirized doctors but also because he returned to the family dynamic, more particularly the interactions between husbands and wives. In this three-act play, Martine, the wife, takes vengeance on her husband, Sganarelle, for his beatings. She portrays him as a doctor, but one who will admit as much only when he is beaten. The patient is Lucinde, whose father does not want her to marry, also a familiar theme. Sganarelle, pretending to be a doctor, must ultimately join with the young paramour Léandre to fool the father into consenting to the marriage. All turns out well in the end of a play that is, ultimately, much lighter fare than the dark moral comedy that preceded it.

During the fall of 1666 and early winter of 1667 Molière was heavily engaged with performances in which he both collaborated with other poets and dramatists and wrote pieces on his own. Of these plays, perhaps the most interesting is Le Sicilien, ou L'Amour peintre (The Sicilian, or Love's Paintings, performed in 1667; published 1667), which concerns a Greek slave named Isidore, who has been freed by her master, Dom Pèdre, a Sicilian gentleman. She is also loved by a

French gentleman, Adraste, who disguises himself as a painter and comes to paint her. In a plot twist not unlike that in L'Ecole des maris, Isidore comes to detest Dom Pèdre for his jealousy. What good is being freed if one is still imprisoned? The rest of the play involves Adraste's plot to steal the woman from the Sicilian via disguises and tricks. All ends well, despite Dom Pèdre's appeal to the law, a senator, who ignores his pleas, more interested in watching a ballet of dancing Moors.

While Le Sicilien, ou L'Amour peintre is a light comedy, it does begin to stage the elaborate plots and disguises–the theater of manipulation–that become more and more a center of the intrigues of Molière's plays in which theater and acting become the tool to get what one wants or to counter the tyranny of impossible parents. While not considered by critics as a serious piece, Amphitryon, Molière's adaption of a comedy by the Roman playwright Plautus, can be seen as pivotal in both his relations to the king and in his thinking about the conjuncture of theatrical forms in which he had been writing. The printed version of the play was prefaced by a sonnet written to celebrate Louis XIV's military triumphs in Flanders in the summer of 1667. During this period Molière also made a second, unsuccessful attempt to stage Tartuffe. In staging a play about Jupiter's transformation into a military general, Amphitryon, in order to seduce his wife, Alcmène, he is certainly making some comment about the king not only as Jupiter-like warrior but also as incorrigible warrior of love. In many ways, however, Amphitryon is most interesting as a play about acting, for Jupiter is able to seduce Amphitryon's wife because he is able to take on the form–that is, play the role–of her husband so perfectly that all around him suspend disbelief. In that sense they are living the perfect neoclassical theater experience as described by its theoreticians. Molière, as he asserts many times in prefaces to his published plays, is no theoretician but a practitioner; thus, the play is full of wonderfully comic interludes during which the illusion breaks down. These times include the encounter of Amphitryon's valet, Sosie, with his double, Mercury, playing Sosie to Jupiter's Amphitryon. While Sosie knows who he is, he is convinced he is not himself by the beating Mercury gives him.

On a more serious level, the play addresses the issue of illusion in an allegorical prologue that has the gods Mercury and Night bemoaning the roles assigned to them by the poets who have written their stories and proscribed their behavior. Proper behavior on their part–bienséance, or propriety, in the terms of theatrical theory–is seen as constraining by the actor-gods, who are, finally, underlings in the world of theater. This power struggle between practitioner actor-gods and theoretician poet-mortals that opens

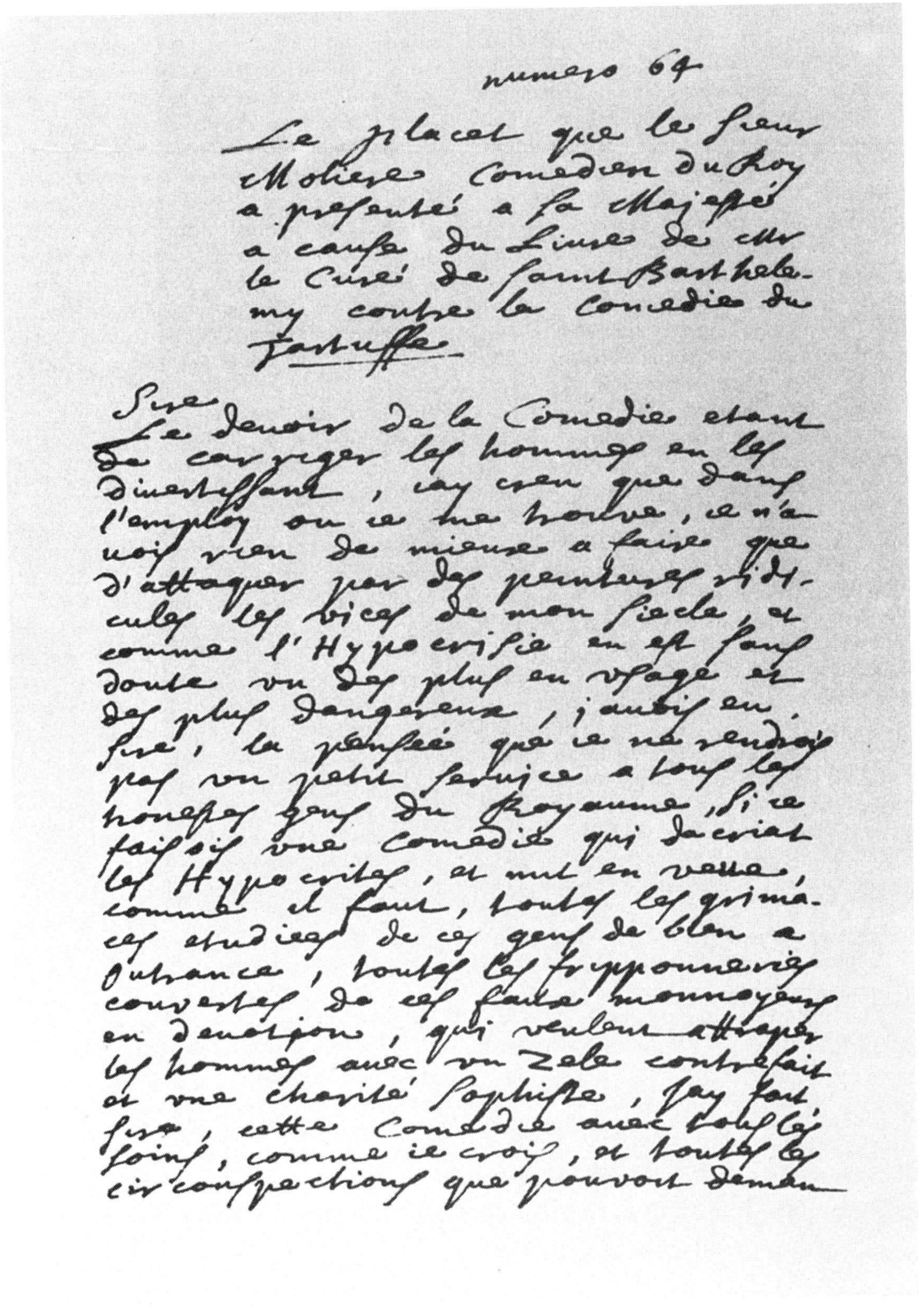

numero 64

Le placet que le sieur
Moliere Comedien du Roy
a presenté a sa Majesté
a cause du Livre de Mr
le Curé de saint Barthele-
my contre la Comedie du
Tartuffe

Sire, Le devoir de la Comedie estant
de corriger les hommes en les
divertissant, j'ay creu que dans
l'employ ou ie me trouve, il n'y
avoit rien de mieux a faire que
d'attaquer par des peintures ridicules les vices de mon siecle, et
comme l'Hypocrisie en est sans
doute un des plus en usage et
des plus dangereux, j'auois eu,
Sire, la pensée que ie ne rendois
pas un petit service a tous les
honnestes gens du Royaume, si ie
faisois une comedie qui decriat
les Hypocrites, et mit en veue,
comme il faut, toutes les grima-
ces estudiées de ces gens de bien a
outrance, toutes les frypponneries
couvertes, de ces faux monnoyeurs
en devotion, qui veulent attraper
les hommes auec un zele contrefait
et une charité sophistique, J'ay fait
faire, cette Comedie auec toutes
soins, comme ie croy, et toutes les
circonspections que pouuoit deman-

First page from the manuscript for Molière's 1664 play Tartuffe *(Bibliothèque de l'Arsenal, Paris)*

the play is turned on its head in the play proper, which pits actor-god Jupiter against mortals who are not the least poetic. That the play ends with the inimitable Sosie onstage announcing the birth of Hercules, the only god in the pantheon who is born mortal and becomes divine, suggests that one message of the play is a call to break down the barrier between poet-theoretician and actor-practitioner–that is, between divine and mortal–from Molière's perspective an artificial and unproductive distinction. More productive, he thought, were collaboration and understanding.

Indeed, during the summer of 1668 Molière was once more in intense collaboration at Versailles, working on festivities organized around the story of the Arabian nights. The event marked a recent peace treaty and served to show off the redesigned gardens of Versailles. Molière wrote words for the interludes of the festival, for which music was composed by Jean-Baptiste Lully. Within the pastoral of the spectacle, Molière also offered a comedy, *Georges Dandin, ou Le Mary confondu,* a three-act play that focuses on provincial life, and not on the social world of Paris. In this case the theme is once again dark, for it concerns a rich peasant, Georges Dandin, married to the daughter of impoverished provincial nobility, Les Sottenvilles. The family name, a combination of "sot" and "ville" (stupid and city), already suggests where the reader's sympathies should lie–that is, with the poor cuckolded husband, Dandin. He is detested and looked down on by Angélique and her parents, who are humiliated by their need for his money to enrich their bloodline. Dandin does not fully understand how low he ranks in the family and hopes to reveal to his in-laws their daughter's infidelity. By the end of the play he has accomplished his goal, but without recourse–a frustrated peasant once more with no remedy for his plight.

For a character at the end of Molière's plays to be defeated by his circumstances is a common occurrence. Indeed, neither Sganarelle in *L'Ecole des maris* nor Arnolphe in *L'Ecole des femmes* gets the young girl he has been tutoring as a future wife, while the tyrannical fathers do not get to marry off their rebellious daughters as they wish. Neither do the subalterns gain clear victory. Dandin is a different figure, however, because he is trying to put things as they should be, albeit in a world he has created that is not as it should be. *L'Avare,* the five-act comedy of manners Molière wrote and staged after the Versailles festivities, is a more traditional comedy, one that returns to portraying the urban bourgeoisie. Its main character, Harpagon, is, as the title of the play suggests, a miser. His two children suffer from his stinginess on many levels. They do not have the luxuries they wish for, and their father's mar-

riage choices for them are dictated by his economic aversions. For his daughter he has chosen an aged widower who will not demand a large dowry. He himself wishes to marry a young and fatherless woman whom his son also loves. The play is a typical comedic tangle of abusive parental authority and scheming children. Most particularly, Harpagon has buried a chest full of money, which has been discovered by his son's valet. The resolution of the play involves Harpagon's having to give up his own marriage plans, trading Marianne to his son Cléante for his coveted money chest. At the end of the play, Harpagon bemoans his treasure, which is not the lost Marianne but the chest of gold coins. He is not converted in the end, even if all the other alliances have been set aright, and he is alone on stage with existential angst prescient of Samuel Beckett's most disaffected characters.

Popular today, *L'Avare* was not an immediate success when staged in September 1668. Scholars have hypothesized that *L'Avare* had to compete with too many other hits from this extremely prolific period. Some critics have suggested one reason that *L'Avare* was not successful at first was that it was the first major comedy written entirely in prose, a fact that might have jarred the expectations of theater audiences. But perhaps, as Georges Couton has conjectured, the real reason for the tepid reception of *L'Avare* was that it lacked what *Tartuffe* had, controversial aspects. Indeed, *Tartuffe* was finally staged in its entirety in February 1669. With the staging of *Tartuffe* and following the artistic fertility of the years that bracket the controversy of the play, Molière entered the final four years of his career, years marked by more significant writing, by royal approval, by certain acceptance of his form of comedy and comedic acting in Paris and at court, and by new struggles integral to his status and that of his medium, at court and within the now established royal patronage system.

That Molière was feeling confident as an artist, courtier, and performer is clear from a small pamphlet war in which he engaged during this period, when he wrote and published a long poem about a fresco painted by his friend artist Pierre Mignard on the dome of the Val-de-Grâce Cathedral. Molière had begun reading the poem in private settings in the fall of 1668. It answered verses published by Charles Perrault in praise of the painter Charles LeBrun. LeBrun, like Perrault and Molière, was firmly ensconced in the royal patronage system. Indeed, Molière and LeBrun had collaborated on court spectacles. Mignard, on the other hand, had rejected his own appointment to the king's cadre of royal artists. Instead, he had chosen to work on a commission for Anne of Austria, a large-scale fresco on the dome of the church she had begun having built in 1638 to thank the Virgin for the long-awaited

Etching of a scene in the 1669 revised version of Tartuffe *(Bibliothèque Nationale, Paris)*

birth of her son Louis XIV. Fresco was not a popular form in mid-century Paris, and turning down invitations to work for the king, even in a less than leading role, was even less accepted. Molière's defense of Mignard and his fresco project, also the queen's project, thus seems foolhardy even while his defense of religious art commissioned by the queen on the eve of performing *Tartuffe* might seem politic. Yet, if one reads between the lines of the poem, one can also see it as a look at the king's relation to artistic projects, as a discussion of what kind of artistry is acceptable, and as a reflection of Molière's own role in producing royal entertainment. Titled "La Gloire de Val-de-Grâce" (The Glory of the Val-de-Grâce), the poem seems to comment directly on the nature of glory, whether the glory of the king, the vainglory of artists, or the apotheosis painting of the fresco, also called a "glory." All these constructs are just that, phenomena or constructs that change depending on how one views them. The same may be said of Molière's own work, which, in the final years of his career, became, if less controversial, perhaps also less straightforward in its participation in and commentary on contemporary society.

Molière continued to collaborate actively on court projects during the years 1669–1671. Invitations to court were many in this period, not only because of

Molière's popularity but also because of the king's acceleration of his own program of organizing large-scale court entertainments after his mother's death. These productions included *Monsieur de Pourceaugnac* (first performed in 1669; published 1670), a three-act comedy augmented with ballets and music concerning a provincial lawyer who comes to Paris for a marriage. The younger generation conspires against him in a wild set of capers that continue the satire of physicians from earlier plays. Performed for the king's entertainment at Chambord in October 1669, the play also fared well on the Parisian stage, to which it was brought in November. Not long after performing at Chambord, Molière was summoned in February 1670 to the residence at Saint-Germain-en-Laye to participate in another entertainment. For this occasion Molière took an idea from the king for a play not unlike the earlier *La Princesse d'Elide* (performed in 1664; published 1665). In this instance, two princes vie for the hand of a reluctant princess, Eriphile. Their weapons are not the traditional swords–at this time banned by French court society–but rather the new form of political weapon, spectacle. The play *Les Amans magnifiques*–spelled *Amants* in modern editions (The Magnificent Lovers, first performed in 1670; first published in volume 8 of *Les Œuvres de Monsieur de Molière,* 1682), is a veritable cata-

Frontispiece and title page for the 1667 publication of Molière's 1666 play about an outspoken contrarian (Bibliothèque Nationale, Paris)

logue of the kind of entertainments produced at court—ballets, pantomimes, and machine spectacles. These types are all deftly woven into a comedy in which the princess is indifferent to the performances, which mask the identities of their authors. Her mother, on the other hand, is charmed by performances concocted by other members of the court, most particularly a wily astrologer, Anaxarque, who attempts to manipulate the outcome by working on behalf of one of the princes. The foils for both princes and astrologer are Sostrate, a valiant soldier of modest birth, and Clitidas, a court wit, played by Molière. These latter two represent sincerity and genuine artistry. Taken in its entirety, the play can be read as a parable offered to the king on the dangers of performance as seduction—for those who organize, for those who perform, and for those who watch.

Les Amants magnifiques can be seen to mark a watershed moment for court performance, and thus for Molière's career. As was the practice, roles were written for the king in the ballets accompanying the comedy. It

was so routine for the king to dance in these events that initial reports of the spectacle included glowing praise of the king's performance. But these praises were soon amended because, for the first time, Louis did not participate in the court performance. Among the factors influencing this choice might have been a perceived message from Racine to the king in his recently staged *Britannicus* (1669), in which Nero's advisers warn him against too much participation in court festivities. *Les Amants magnifiques* offers another warning. When neither prince obtains the princess, losing out to an apparent commoner, they become enraged. The moral is that organizing court spectacle does not divert one's enemies but can increase their anger. Clitidas is the only performer who remains an effective producer of spectacle, although his acting and producing lead him to such unlikely acts as climbing a tree to escape dangers that well up unexpectedly in the otherwise pastoral scene. Kings can play roles and organize spectacles, but they cannot climb trees. That would not be decorous, and as the goddess Night in *Amphitryon* points out in the prologue to the play, decorum is crucial to theatrical life. If the king wants to continue to manage the stage of his court, he needs to step offstage, leaving that arena to the practitioners he employs. Symbolic power can be created by spectacle, but the boundary between what is symbolic and what is real is difficult to mediate, even for a king whose experiment in self-direction seemed well on its way to success after a mere nine years of personal rule.

Molière's next new play, also a court ballet, continued to explore this complex frontier between what is real and what is mask or performance in the staging of the extravagances of the aspiring gentleman. *Le Bourgeois gentilhomme* (The Bourgeois Gentleman, published 1671), premiered at Chambord in October 1670 and staged again at Saint-Germain-en-Laye in November, is usually considered to be one of Molière's comedies of manners. In fact, it was a comedy-ballet, a play in which the danced interludes fit seamlessly into the action but were edited out of published versions well into the twentieth century. On safer terrain than *Les Amants magnifiques*, *Le Bourgeois gentilhomme* focuses on the inability of a bourgeois to educate himself in the mores of the gentry. Despite unlimited funds that can pay for tutors of all ilks, Monsieur Jourdain does not have the innate grace of a gentleman. He cannot dance, bear arms, write poetry, or understand the music or poetry he commissions. Nor can he control the greedy tradesmen he employs. All his effort is aimed at courting a wealthy marquise. Her real lover, Dorante, is one more of the minions who are taking advantage of Jourdain. In sum, like so many of Molière's characters, the hero is ridiculous to everyone, including his daughter, wife, and servants. The plot is driven by Jourdain's daughter's desire to marry her paramour, Cléonte, who, because he is not a gentleman, is unacceptable to Jourdain. The group thus bands together to fool Jourdain, and the play ends with the realization of their goals and the further humiliation of Jourdain.

If *Les Amants magnifiques* condemns insincere performances for the sincerity of humble valor and love, *Le Bourgeois gentilhomme,* and so many other plays with similar plots of children and wives pitted against unreasonable spouses, is about how feigning or performance can set the world right again. While Jourdain cannot adequately play his desired role as gentleman, those around him capitalize on his desire for ennoblement by fabricating an elaborate fiction in which Cléonte is introduced as the son of the Grand Turc, who wishes to marry Lucille. To do so he must make her father a Mamamouchi, a made-up word that enchants the self-love of the ignorant Jourdain. Cléonte and the audience see the ruse for exactly what it is, a "mascarade."

All the actors and their costumes are ready by act 4. When Lucille happens on the Turkish ceremony of ennoblement, she asks, aptly, "Est-ce une comédie que vous jouez?" (Is this a play?) But she recognizes her lover and quickly falls in line with their acting.

Critics have long noted that Turks and all things Turkish were fashionable in the 1670s because of the presence at court of the sultan's emissary. The ballet of the Turkish ceremony certainly responded to that interest. But the emphasis on theater-within-theater must also have been popular, for it pops up again and again in the plays of this period both as a function of plot and in the language of the characters. Even the final ballet of *Le Bourgeois Gentilhomme,* which stages the scene of the spectators of a court spectacle scrambling for the booklets that include the names of the dancers, seems to respond to this taste while also staging the taste of the bourgeois for a peek at such scenes. The bourgeois, portrayed as pretentious in the play, are more prescient in the final ballet, when one bourgeois interlocutor, rattled by the struggle for recognition, begs those around him to stop him, at any price, from ever attending such an event again. While Molière's comedy-ballets were often brought back to the Palais-Royal, many bourgeois did have the opportunity to see them at court, where by the early 1670s the large entertainments were accessible to a broad array of spectators. In January of 1671, one of the most ambitious of such court productions premiered in Paris at the Palais des Tuilleries. Molière's contribution to this event was *Psiché* (published 1671),—spelled *Psyché* in modern editions—a comedy-ballet, the printed version of which bears Molière's name as author, but whose preface attests to its multiple authorship by Pierre Corneille, Philippe Quinault, and Molière. Molière wrote some verses of a play now considered a precursor of French opera. But even in the preface he is largely credited with organizing all the pieces—that is, with a kind of authorship that is less literary in the way literature as produced by a single author is thought of, and more in the way Molière's contemporaries would have understood authorship—as a form of collaboration in which real authority consisted of being the overall producer.

Many of Molière's most pleasing characters are the subalterns who organize performances. These characters include not only Clitidas in *Les Amants magnifiques* and Cléonte in *Le Bourgeois gentilhomme* but also Scapin in *Les Fourberies de Scapin* (The Trickeries of Scapin), premiered at the Palais-Royal on 24 May 1671 and published the same year. The first straight comedy by Molière in almost three years, this play is not as substantial as the five-act plays, but it does show the evolution of the valet figure as a major player, or stage director. Scapin is a "fourbe," a rascal or double-dealer.

His goal is to profit. And profit he does from the extreme disorder in the two families of Géronte and Argante. Their sons have both strayed from parental authority. Octave, Argante's son, has fallen in love with a penniless girl, Hyacinte, whom he has secretly married after the death of her mother. Léandre, Géronte's son, on the other hand, has fallen in love with Zerbinette, who is described as an Egyptian. The fathers, returning from voyages, have other plans for their children and are furious to find the valets they left in charge, Scapin and Silvestre, have not kept their sons on a straight path of obedience. The play revolves around Scapin's "fourberies" or manipulations of the fathers, first to gain money for the sons (and some for himself as well) and then to exact his own revenge in a wonderful scene in which he puts Géronte in a sack, ostensibly to hide him from an angry pursuer, the brother of Léandre's love interest. In the sack, Géronte overhears a series of virtuoso performances on the part of Scapin, who plays the roles of various people come in search of Géronte, who, in the sack, is subject to a series of beatings. Scapin enacts this comedy for his own pleasure, and perhaps for the pleasure of all the mistreated comedic valets of Molière's stage. When Géronte peers out of the bag and sees what is really happening, Scapin runs off, only to return at the end once more playing a role, that of dying man. But in the interim all the plot complications have been resolved in the usual way—"le hasard a fait ce que la prudence des pères avait déliberé" (chance having accomplished what the prudence of fathers had deliberated), since the girl each boy has fallen in love with is actually the daughter of the other man as twists of birth, kidnaping, and the like are revealed. At this point Scapin jumps up to reclaim his life, returning to his old ways as trickster.

After Molière introduced Scapin in May 1671, he did not premiere another new play for almost six months. It was a court ballet, *La Comtesse d'Escarbagnas* (The Countess of Escarbagnas, first published in volume 8 of *Les Œuvres de Monsieur de Molière*), first staged at Saint-Germain-en-Laye on 2 December 1671 but not brought back to the now more restrictive Parisian stage until July 1672. The play might be seen as a kind of female version of *Le Bourgeois gentilhomme,* although without the same cutting social commentary on class, perhaps in part because it concerned provincial and not Parisian life. The main character, the comtesse, has just returned from two months in Paris and has brought back to her native Angoulême all the airs and pretensions of a city woman. She is mean to her servants who, unfamiliar with Parisian ways, cannot help her receive visitors in the appropriate fashion. The comic interplay between the countess and her staff over misunderstood words and broken dishes is remi-

niscent of *Les Précieuses ridicules*. But the countess is also derided by her peers, a vicomte and his lover, Julie, who cannot marry because their families are feuding. The couple use visits to the countess and a feigned courtship of her by the vicomte as a pretext to meet. Meanwhile, the countess has more appropriate suitors—petty bureaucrats, a tax collector, and a low-level judicial officer. "C'est une école que votre conversation" (Your conversation is a veritable school), notes Julie, the vicomte's real lover, stifling her laughter and advertising Molière's earlier plays. The countess also does some advertising for Molière in bragging about having seen *Psiché* at court. Of course she might have, along with the six thousand other persons who would have fit easily into the Tuilleries theater.

La Comtesse d'Escarbagnas was a light play even in comparison with some of the other less developed comedy-ballets. It was also the last play involving music that Molière premiered and staged under easy circumstances. For in mid March 1672 his longtime collaborator, Jean-Baptiste Lully, gained the right to oversee and authorize any theater performed with music, a right that eventually extended to drastically reducing the number of musicians and singers allowed on Parisian stages. These prerogatives were obviously to Lully's advantage, and Molière had to have many plays in his repertoire rewritten, or at least their music, in order to function under these competitive strictures. That Molière's new work during this period of breaking with Lully was a straight comedy—one that he had, apparently, been working on for some time—is not surprising.

Les Femmes savantes (The Learned Ladies, performed and published in 1672), the first five-act nonmusical drama premiered by Molière in three and a half years, is often termed the playwright's most finished work. Indeed, it is his most literary, his work most dependent on plot and discussion as opposed to the physical comedy at the heart of many of his other dramas. The play has also long been decried as yet another example of Molière's misogyny. It concerns a family turned on its head by the lunacy of the mother, her sister, and one of her daughters. All three women are *savantes,* learned ladies, or at the least women with pretensions to learned culture. The joke is not that they think they are learned but that they are not. As in all the plays, some characters are figures of reason—in this case the somewhat henpecked husband and the apparently sane daughter, Henriette. While her sister Armande subscribes entirely to the Neoplatonism of the "précieux" movement, in which any physical relation is vastly inferior to the life of the mind, Henriette dreams of a life as a wife and mother. But she does not dream of the husband her mother has destined for her, the poet Trissotin (or thrice idiot, since *sot* is the word for idiot). While the satire of the poet and the pedant has long been associated with Molière's disdain for the intellectuals upon whom he modeled these characters—the abbé Charles Cotin and Giles Menage—the satire of learned women may be a bit more ambivalent. For when the mother, Philaminte, describes in act 3 her plan for a female academy, there is a certain poignancy about the way she claims more for her sex against the scenario men have written for it. To imagine the intent of the play as virulently antiwomen is difficult, since Molière promoted the careers of women by, for example, staging the plays of prominent female novelist Catherine Desjardins at the Palais-Royal. He was also a reader of women, utilizing comic images from the novels of another, Madeleine de Scudéry. He was playing, moreover, for a female audience, since theaters in this period in France were packed with female spectators. To imagine the play was ill received by women with aspirations, if not to learnedness in its most extreme, at least to the life of the mind, is difficult. Indeed, Marie de Rabutin-Chantal, marquise de Sévigné, known for literary letter-writing, was such a great fan of the actor-playwright that in this period she sprinkled her carefully crafted letters with references to his plays and their characters.

Les Femmes savantes was successful, but not wildly so. Yet, Molière did not again premiere a play for another year, this time a comedy-ballet, Le Malade imaginaire (The Imaginary Invalid, published in 1674). With music by Marc-Antoine Charpentier, the play did not premiere at court, where Lully held sway, but at the Palais Royal theater in February 1673. The drama was Molière's swan song. The play about a hypochondriac father, played by Molière, almost ended with a real death onstage, that of the playwright, sick for many years with what was probably tuberculosis. Considering the delicate state of his health, that Molière once more turned to doctors as a source for comic material in 1673 is not surprising. Indeed, the play brings back all the major themes of the greedy and pretentious doctors with their bowdlerized Latin discourses and bodily interventions of purging and bleeding. The main character, the invalid Argan, decides to marry off his daughter to the son of one of his physicians for its obvious advantages to him. Meanwhile, his second wife is coveting his fortune and manipulating Argan, whose delicate health pleases her. She wants him to sign over all his assets to her, thereby cutting his children out of his will. As in so many other plays, the plot involves uncovering the deceit of the family interloper and putting the right lovers together. The servant, Toinette, is central to this activity, which involves playacting, dressing as a physician, and pretending Argan has indeed died, to the

PSICHÉ
TRAGI-COMEDIE,
ET BALLET·
Danfé devant fa Majefté au mois
de Ianvier 1671.

A PARIS,
Par ROBERT BALLARD, feul Imprimeur du Roy pour la Mufique, ruë S. Iean
de Beauvais, au Mont-Parnaffe.
M. DC. LXXI.
AVEC PRIVILEGE DE SA MAIESTE.

Title page for the work by Molière and others that was first staged as part of a large court entertainment at the Tuilleries on 17 January 1671 (Comédie-Française, Paris)

delight of the wife and distress of the daughter—enlightening, if not curing, Argan.

On 17 February 1673, during the fourth night of the new play, Molière coughed up blood onstage during the performance. In this case he was not acting. Brought home, he died of a pulmonary embolism later that night. As an unrepentant actor, he was denied burial on sacred ground. Only after a direct appeal to the king were arrangements made to bury him in his parish cemetery, but at night, without any ceremony. After Molière's death, his troupe largely reconstituted itself and continued to perform its repertoire. The entirety of his theatrical corpus, including the banned Dom Juan and all the other plays not printed during his lifetime, was published posthumously in 1682, edited by one of his close aides. Prefaced by a life of Molière and heavily illustrated, this collected edition represents the first move to recognize Molière as a great writer. Indeed, his corpus influenced French and English comedy into the eighteenth and nineteenth centuries, serving as a model for the comedy of manners that evolved into the love comedies of Pierre Carlet de Chamblain

Chair in which Molière portrayed the title character of his last play, Le Malade imaginaire, *in 1673 (Comédie-Française, Paris)*

edy changed French theater performance, and his origination and development of the genre of comedy-ballet laid the foundation for what became French (as opposed to Italian) opera. Thus, Molière was not just a consummate moralist and playwright but also a participant in the evolution of the art of entertainment more generally.

Hundreds of scholarly books across the centuries have examined the work of Molière, attributing to him profound intellectual, social, and scholarly understanding, thus countering scholarship relegating comedy to the least serious of literary genres. At the same time, another portion of Molière criticism has studied him almost exclusively as a man of the theater. More recently, scholarship has tried to navigate both these facets, Molière as thinker-writer and Molière as immersed in the material culture of a performance art. This melding of perspectives has allowed the revaluation of elements of his artistic output that have long been relegated to the outer fringes of his corpus. With a growing interest in theatricality and a sense that theatrical art and its own material culture also contributed to the abstract and intellectual content of his plays, the future will likely bring a continued reassessment of Molière's role in the history of French literature and French theater that will only further emphasize the originality and depth of his writing and acting career.

Biographies:
Jean-Léonor Le Gallois de Grimarest, *La Vie de M. de Molière,* edited by Georges Mongrédien (Paris: M. Brient, 1955);

Madeleine Jurgens and Elizabeth Maxfield-Miller, *Cent Ans de recherches sur Molière, sur sa famille et sur les comédiens de sa troupe* (Paris: Imprimerie Nationale, 1963);

C. E. J. Caldicott, *La Carrière de Molière: Entre protecteurs et éditeurs* (Amsterdam & Atlanta: Rodopi, 1998);

Virginia Scott, *Molière: A Theatrical Life* (Cambridge: Cambridge University Press, 2000).

References:
Eric Auerbach, "La Cour et la Ville," in his *Scenes from the Drama of European Literature* (Minneapolis: University of Minnesota Press, 1984), pp. 133–182;

René Bray, *Molière, homme de théâtre* (Paris: Mercure de France, 1954);

Andrew Calder, *Molière: The Theory and Practice of Comedy* (London: Athlone Press, 1993);

Roger Chartier, "From Court Festivity to City Spectators," in his *Forms and Meanings: Texts, Performances, and Audiences from Codex to Computer* (Philadelphia: University of Pennsylvania Press, 1995), pp. 43–82;

de Marivaux and the biting satire of Pierre-Augustin Caron de Beaumarchais as well as for Restoration drama in England.

Molière's repertoire has remained a staple of the francophone theater scene both at the Comédie-Française and for many other smaller troupes in both France and the francophone world. It is also widely performed in translation in countries around the world. For ensuing generations, Molière became what he already was referred to by his peers, the Terence of France—that is, a writer of modern comedy. In the Quarrel of the Ancients and the Moderns, he represented the modern world, taking a lowly, degraded genre and raising it to a more serious level, even while he continued to battle the prejudices against comic theater as a genre. While later generations focused less on his importance to theater arts and more on his role as author in the romantic sense, Molière and his troupe premiered the work of the young and emerging tragedian Racine as well as that of many other playwrights, all the while developing Molière's own repertoire and staging plays by the well-known Corneille brothers and other established playwrights. His style for acting com-

Sylvie Bostarron Chevallrey, *Molière en son temps, 1622–1673* (Paris & Geneva: Minkoff, 1973);

Patrick Dandrey, *Molière, ou L'Esthétique du ridicule* (Paris: Klincksieck, 1992);

Maurice Descotes, *Molière et sa fortune littéraire* (Bordeaux: G. Ducros, 1970);

Alvin Eustis, *Molière as Ironic Contemplator* (Paris: Mouton, 1973);

Pierre Force, *Molière, ou Le Prix des choses: Morale, économie et comédie* (Paris: Nathan, 1994);

Georges Forestier, *Molière en toutes lettres* (Paris: Bordas, 1990);

James F. Gaines, *Social Structures in Molière's Theater* (Columbus: Ohio State University Press, 1984);

Jacques Guicharnaud, *Molière, une aventure théâtrale: Tartuffe, Dom Juan, Le Misanthrope* (Paris: Gallimard, 1963);

W. D. Howarth, *Molière: A Playwright and His Audience* (Cambridge & New York: Cambridge University Press, 1982);

Barbara Johnson, "Teaching Ignorance: *L'Ecole des femmes*," in her *A World of Difference* (Baltimore: Johns Hopkins University Press, 1987), pp. 68–87;

Roger Johnson Jr., Editha S. Neumann, and Guy T. Trail, eds., *Molière and the Commonwealth of Letters: Patrimony and Posterity* (Jackson: University Press of Mississippi, 1975);

Bernard Magné, "L'Ecole des femmes, ou La Conquête de la parole," *Revue des sciences humaines*, 145 (January–March 1972): 125–140;

Jean Mesnard, "Le Misanthrope, mise-en-question de l'art de plaire," *Revue d'histoire littéraire de la France*, 5–6 (November/December 1972): 863–889;

Georges Mongrédien, *Recueil des textes et des documents du XVIIe siècle relatifs à Molière*, 2 volumes (Paris: Editions du Centre Nationale de la Recherche Scientifique, 1965);

Peter H. Nurse, *Molière and the Comic Spirit* (Geneva: Droz, 1991);

Karolyn Waterson, *Molière et l'authorité: Structures sociales, structures comiques* (Lexington, Ky.: French Forum, 1976);

Abby E. Zanger, "Acting as Counteracting in Molière's *L'Impromptu de Versailles*," *Theatre Journal*, 38, no. 2 (May 1986): 180–195;

Zanger, "Classical Anxiety: Performance, Perfection, and the Issue of Identity," in *L'Age du Théâtre en France/The Age of Theatre in France*, edited by David Trott and Nicole Boursier (Edmonton: Academic Printing and Publishing, 1988), pp. 327–339;

Zanger, "On the Threshold of Print and Performance: How Prints Matter to Bodies of/at Work in Molière's Published Corpus," *Word and Image*, 17 (January–June 2001): 25–42;

Zanger, "Paralyzing Performance: Sacrificing Theater on the Altar of Publication," *Stanford French Review*, 12, nos. 2–3 (Fall/Winter 1988): 169–186;

Zanger, "The Spectacular Gift: Rewriting the Royal Scenario in Molière's *Les Amants Magnifiques*," *Romanic Review*, 81/82 (March 1990): 173–188.

Pierre Nicole

(13 October 1625 – 16 November 1695)

Erec R. Koch
Tulane University

SELECTED WORKS*: *Disquisitiones duae ad praesentes ecclesiae tumultus sedandos opportunae,* as Paulus Irenaeus (Paris, 1657);

Dissertatio de vera pulchritudine . . . , in *Epigrammatum delectus ex omnibus tum veteribus, tum recentioribus poetis accurate decerptus, &c.* (Paris: Ch. Savreux, 1659);

La Logique, ou l'Art de penser, by Nicole and Antoine Arnauld (Paris: Ch. Savreux, 1662; revised and enlarged edition, 1664, 1668; revised and enlarged edition, Lyon: Laurens, 1671; Paris: Desprez, 1683; Amsterdam: H. Wetstein, 1697); translated as *Logic, or The Art of Thinking . . .* (London: Sawbridge, 1685);

Apologie pour les religieuses de Port-Royal du Saint-Sacrement, contre les injustices et les violences du procédé dont on a usé envers ce monastère, by Nicole, Claude de Sainte-Marthe, and Arnauld (N.p., 1665);

Les imaginaires, ou Lettres sur l'hérésie imaginaire, as le sieur de Damvilliers (Liège: A. Beyers, 1667);

Les visionnaires, ou seconde partie des lettres sur l'hérésie imaginaire, contenant les huit dernières (Liège: A. Beyers, 1667);

La perpétuité de la foy de l'église catholique touchant l'Eucharistie, 4 volumes, by Nicole and Arnauld (Paris: Savreux, 1669–1713);

De l'Education d'un Prince. Divisée en trois parties, dont la derniere contient divers traittez utiles à tout le monde (Paris: Savreux, 1670);

Préjugés légitimes contre les Calvinistes (Paris: Savreux, 1671);

Preface to *Recueil de Poesies chrestiennes et diverses* (Paris: Le Petit, 1671);

Traité de l'oraison (Lyon: Rey, 1679);

Essais de Morale, 3 volumes (Paris: G. Desprez, 1693); translated as *Moral Essays,* 4 volumes (London: Manship, 1696);

Réfutation des principales erreurs des quiétistes (Paris: Elie Josset, 1695);

*The bibliography is complete except for a dozen or so minor and/or co-authored works and letters. Also, some essays from the *Essais de Morale* were published separately between and after the various iterations.

Pierre Nicole (engraving by N. Habert; Musée National des Granges de Port-Royal)

Traité de la grâce générale, 2 volumes (N.p., 1715);

Essais de Morale, 25 volumes (Paris: G. Desprez, 1733–1771).

Editions: *Traité de la comédie,* edited by Georges Couton (Paris: Les Belles Lettres, 1961);

Essais de Morale, 4 volumes; reprint of 1733–1771 edition (Geneva: Slatkine, 1971);

264

La vraie beauté et son fantôme: et autres textes d'esthétique, edited and translated from the Latin by Béatrice Guion (Paris: H. Champion, 1996);

Traité de la comédie, in *Traité de la comédie et autres pièces d'un procès du théâtre,* edited by Laurent Thirouin (Paris: Champion, 1998);

Essais de morale, selected and edited by Thirouin (Paris: PUF, 1999).

TRANSLATION: Blaise Pascal, *Litterae provinciales, de morali et politica jesuitarum disciplina,* as Willelmus Wendrockius (Colonii: Apud Nicolaum Schouten, [*i.e.,* Leyden: Elzevier], 1658).

Pierre Nicole–Jansenist theologian, philosopher, polemicist, and moralist–was born on 13 October 1625, in Chartres. From a family of the *noblesse de robe* (administrative class of the nobility), Nicole demonstrated from a young age a passion for Latin under the tutelage of his lettered father. Nicole attended the College d'Harcourt in Paris and during this time read broadly and extensively; his reading included works of heretics, both ancient and modern, and polemicists from Erasmus to Cardinal Jacques Davy Du Perron. He is also purported to have had some exposure at this point to worldly literature as well, such as the *précieux* novels (those pursuing excessively refined elegance in language and manners) of Madeleine de Scudéry. At the age of seventeen Nicole began studies for the priesthood, but he did not go beyond the stage of tonsured cleric and bachelor in theology. His studies in philosophy and theology ended with the conferral of that degree in 1649.

Like many members of the Gallican *noblesse de robe,* Nicole had strong personal ties to Jansenism and to its center of practice at the abbey of Port-Royal des Champs. Jansenism was a neo-Augustinian movement launched with the posthumous publication in 1640 of the *Augustinus* by the Belgian cleric and scholar Cornelius Jansen. That text, which analyzed at great length the Augustinian doctrine of grace, launched the eponymous movement that found adherents at Port-Royal through Jansen's friend Jean Duvergier de Hauranne, better known as Saint-Cyran, who served as confessor and spiritual director of the sisters of Port-Royal. Jansenism was a response to worldly attempts during the Counter Reformation, such as those of the Jesuits, to draw the faithful back to the Catholic Church. The claim of the Jansenists was that those efforts came at the expense of Catholic tradition and doctrine, for they devalued the nature and function of the sacraments and corrupted the doctrine of grace, both of which became focal points of controversy. Jansenists advocated a return to the teachings of the Church Fathers based on

two principles–that the fall from grace corrupted all men indelibly and that grace was a divine gift offered gratuitously to the elect. Jansenism also appealed to many in the Gallican church for political reasons–it represented defiant independence from Rome.

Nicole had begun frequenting Port-Royal at a young age because of the presence of relatives, but his ties to the abbey and its cause began to become more substantial. While working toward his bachelor's degree in theology, Nicole was exposed in 1647–1648 to the early stages of Jansenist-Jesuit controversy–in this case through two of his teachers, the Augustinian Jacques de Sainte-Beuve, with whom Nicole studied, and the renowned Jesuit Molinist Le Moine, who was excoriated in Blaise Pascal's *Lettres provinciales* (Provincial Letters, 1657). After deciding not to pursue the *licence* (a nondoctoral postbaccalaureate degree) and the *doctorat* in theology, Nicole's sympathy for the cause advocated by his teacher Sainte-Beuve helped to frame his decision to become a teacher at the *petites écoles* (small schools) of Port-Royal. Nicole began as one of five educators at Port-Royal in Paris and then moved to the famous site of des Granges, where he taught humanities and philosophy. He helped to found schools for girls in the cities of Chartres, Troyes, and Beauvais. His students included playwright Jean Racine and historian Louis-Sébastien Le Nain de Tillemont. Nicole's pedagogical responsibilities included the preparation of textbooks. He wrote many manuals on Greek and Latin grammar, but his most notable contribution was coauthoring, with Antoine Arnauld, *La Logique, ou l'Art de penser* (The Logic, or The Art of Thinking, 1662), known as "La logique de Port-Royal." This text represents an unusual convergence of faith in the power of Cartesian reason and submission to divine revelation, both of which characterize many of Nicole's writings. The work was reedited many times during the course of Nicole's life. His contributions can be traced to specific sections of books 3 and 4 of the *Logique,* texts that address moral and ethical reasoning. Chapter 10 of book 3, for example, examines logical misjudgments that are replete with the lexicon and conceptual framework of Jansenism. Nicole asserts that self-love and concupiscence are the primary sources of epistemological error. Many of these passages are extended and developed in Nicole's most mature writings, the *Essais de Morale* (Essays on Ethics, 1733–1771).

In 1654 Arnauld approached Nicole to ask his collaboration in a theological controversy in which he had become embroiled. Although reportedly timorous by nature and not inclined to polemical controversy, Nicole had knowledge of theology and elegance in writing that made him a worthy candidate for the position. He became an informal secretary and research assistant

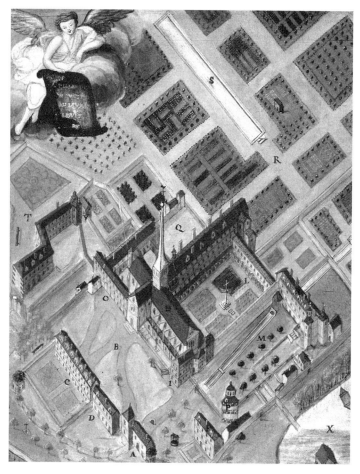

The abbey of Port-Royal des Champs in the Chevreuse Valley south of Paris, where Nicole taught philosophy and the humanities (Musée National des Granges de Port-Royal)

to Arnauld in a partnership that lasted, with occasional interruptions, for twenty years. Taking this position also launched the most consuming part of Nicole's career—advocacy and polemics dedicated to the cause of Jansenism and its controversy. Many of those contributions were made as part of a collaborative effort. At that time Arnauld was facing censure before the theological faculty of the Sorbonne. He had become embroiled in a controversy and polemical exchange that began with the confrontation of Jansenist, Augustinian interpretations of the efficacy of the sacraments when confronted with lax Jesuitical practice. This dynamic and tortuous debate culminated with the *syndic* of the Sorbonne faculty, one Nicolas Cornet, identifying five heretical theses purportedly found in Jansen's *Augustinus* and endorsed by Arnauld. Among the polemical responses launched in defense of Arnauld and Jansenism was Nicole's *Disquisitiones Pauli Irenaei* (The Discourses of Paul Irenaeus), published eventually in 1657. This treatise, forged as a general defense of Jansenism and especially of

the Jansenist notion of grace, was written largely in a dry, scholastic style, unlike the next polemical work, *Les Lettres provinciales* (1658), in which Nicole was involved, but which was written by Pascal.

Contemporary testimony that has contributed to Pascal's hagiography describes a scene dating from 1656 in which Arnauld, realizing that the specialized and arcane theology of the debate in the Sorbonne must be brought to the attention of the wider public in a more accessible way, turned at first to his secretary Nicole, who then turned the task over to the more capable hands of Pascal. Nevertheless, Nicole is believed to have contributed to the composition of *Les lettres provinciales,* one of the landmark polemical works of the seventeenth century, as something of a research assistant. Nicole might have presented Pascal with the arcane theological texts, especially those of Jesuit casuists, which provided grist for Pascal's harsh critique of the Jesuit order. Each clandestinely produced letter of *Les Lettres provinciales* was first published independently. In

1657 Nicole undertook the publication of the first edition–in one volume with a preface. A year later he published a Latin translation of *Les Lettres provinciales,* titled *Litterae provinciales, de morali et politica jesuitarum disciplina* (Provincial Letters, on the Moral and Political Science of the Jesuits) under the pseudonym Willemus Wendrockius. This translation, intended to reach a broader readership in Europe, also included Nicole's commentary on *Les lettres provinciales* and more extensive documentation than the first French version.

Nicole also contributed to the first translation of the New Testament into French, commonly known as *Le Nouveau Testament de Mons* (The New Testament of Mons, 1667), an effort undertaken by sympathizers of Port-Royal and of Jansenism. Nicole's final major collaborative effort, and one more consistent with his training as a theologian, was a text that he co-authored with Arnauld, *La perpétuité de la foy de l'église catholique touchant l'Eucharistie* (The Perpetuity of the Faith of the Catholic Church on the Eucharist, 1669–1713), an attempt to fend off two attacks on Jansenist orthodoxy. The authors defended transubstantiation against Protestant claims that its value was purely symbolic, and they forcefully dissociated themselves from Protestant beliefs in defiance of enemies who pointed to doctrinal similarities, especially those concerning grace. After his participation in the debate involving *Les Lettres provinciales* and its aftermath, Nicole engaged in writing or drafting a series of semiclandestinely circulated documents in opposition to the religious and civil authorities who opposed Port-Royal. These texts included his *Apologie pour les religieuses de Port-Royal du Saint-Sacrement, contre les injustices et les violences du procédé dont on a usé envers ce monastère* (Apology on Behalf of the Sisters of Port-Royal of the Blessed Sacrament, Against the Injustices and Violences of the Methods Used in Regard to the Monastery, 1665) and the serial *Les imaginaires, ou Lettres sur l'hérésie imaginaire* (The Imaginary, or Letters on the Imaginary Heresy), which were published in 1664 and 1666 and published together in 1667. In these ten *Imaginaires* Nicole undertakes a defense of Jansenism stylistically and rhetorically modeled on *Les lettres provinciales.* He became further embroiled in theological and religious polemics with the publication in 1667 of the *Imaginaires* and the eight letters that constitute *Les visionnaires, ou seconde partie des lettres sur l' hérésie imaginaire, contenant les huit dernières* (The Visionaries, or The Second Part of the Letters on the Imaginary Heresy, Including the Last Eight). This attack on mysticism takes as its point of departure the immensely popular contemporary comedy of Jean Desmarests de Saint-Sorlin, which also bears the title *Les visionnaires* (1637). Nicole critiques the theme of the play, mysticism in a worldly and iconoclastic mode, and condemns all playwrights as "poison-

ers of the public." Nicole's vitriolic letters prompted two sharp epistolary rebuttals from his former student at the *petites écoles* of Port-Royal, the playwright Racine. Only twenty years later were master and pupil reconciled and their friendship restored. Nicole's other sallies into religious polemics included his *Traité de l'oraison* (Treatise on Prayer, 1679) and a critique of Calvinism titled *Préjugés légitimes contre les Calvinistes* (Legitimate Prejudices against the Calvinists, 1671), which echoes many of the more detailed arguments made in the multivolume work co-authored with Arnauld, *La perpétuité de la foy.* Nicole's *Réfutation des principales erreurs des quiétistes* (Refutation of the Principal Errors of the Quietists, 1695), an attack on the mystical movement quietism, was his final salvo in polemical theological debates.

Beginning with the Peace of the Church in 1668, a brief lull for the embattled Jansenists, Nicole began to devote his efforts increasingly to his passion, Christian morality, and began to compose the texts that eventually constituted the *Essais de Morale.* The essay and other concise genres such as maxims, reflections, and portraits were the preferred discursive modes of seventeenth-century French moralists. In the tradition renewed by Michel Eyquem de Montaigne in France, the essay allowed for the nonsystematic and totalizing treatment of a moral subject, and it allowed texts to be written on common themes. At the outset Nicole's moral writings were treatises and essays not unlike the popular *réflexions* of the time. As Nicole continued work on this project over the course of more than twenty years, his writings became increasingly more fragmentary rather than fully developed. This transition might have been influenced by his editorial work on Pascal's apology, the *Pensées* (Thoughts, 1670), as well as by the continued popularity of François de La Rochefoucauld's *Maximes* (Maxims, 1665). In any case, Nicole's *Essais de Morale* are consistent with contemporary moralist writings of the time: they analyze the moral mechanisms that motivate men and describe life in society as well as prescribing a code of moral and ethical conduct. Unlike the writings of lay moralists such as La Rochefoucauld, however, Nicole's moralist writings are framed within neo-Augustinian Jansenist theology.

Nicole was able to compose the first of his essays from 1671 to 1678 while he was a resident at the *écuries* (stables) of Anne-Geneviève de Bourbon-Condé, duchesse de Longueville, that important protectress and ally of Port-Royal. During that period Nicole also frequented the Hotel de Liancourt, the residence of the moralist La Rochefoucauld's uncle. Upon the duchesse de Longueville's death in 1679 the persecutions of Port-Royal began again, and Nicole was forced to flee to Belgium. He refused to join Arnauld in his escape to Holland and made his separate peace with civil and religious authorities in France. Nicole returned first to Chartres in 1681, and then he resettled in Paris in 1683, where he led a quiet life until his death in 1695. His letter of submission to François de Harlay, the arch-bishop of Paris, upon his return to France was viewed by many of his Jansenist colleagues, however, as a betrayal of Port-Royal.

In all likelihood, many of the *Pensées* and *Instructions morales* of the posthumous fifth and sixth volumes of the *Essais de Morale* were written during the turbulent time of Nicole's departure for Belgium and return to Paris. Just as casuistry, in its proper use, examines concrete cases of moral action drawn from scriptural principles, so Nicole in the *Essais de Morale* attempts to draw the consequences of faith into the daily lives of the readers. In this way those texts may be said to resemble Loyola's spiritual exercises for the believer.

The first volume of the essays was published in 1671 and included some of the hallmark texts of the *Essais,* including "De la faiblesse de l'homme" (On Man's Powerlessness), "De la connaissance de soi-même" (On Self-Knowledge), and the "Traité de l'éducation d'un prince" (Treatise on the Education of a Prince). These works mark the convergence of moralist speculation of the time, psychology, and biblical commentary. His essays certainly resonate with the writings of moralists of the age—most notably those of La Rochefoucauld—in that they focus on man's nature as it affects his social relations. For Nicole (unlike the moralists), however, moral description and prescription are directed to the hope of drawing closer to God.

One of the more suggestive essays in this context is "De la connaissance de soi-même." In this text Nicole argues that man's self-knowledge is defined by the bifurcation of authentic and inauthentic selves, cast as two specular glances. The weight of Nicole's argument is borne by two forms of vision and their reversal—that is, seeing with the interior eye of reason and seeing with the eye of cupidity, which gazes upon projections or mirror images in the outside world. At the outset these views are associated respectively with the blindness of reason, which is deprived of sight in fallen man, and the sight of cupidity. By undoing the illusions of the eye of cupidity, Nicole argues that the two forms of vision proceed to exchange attributes in such a way that the eye of reason assumes the light of truth and the eye of cupidity assumes the obscurity of falsehood and illusion.

In this essay Nicole the moralist reminds the reader repeatedly that *amour-propre* (self-love) underlies human motivation and action and that it drives concupiscence, the principal of the three Augustinian forms of desire. Nicole generalizes and develops the specular scene of self-love that shapes the individual and cuts the self off from God. This process is again presented as a specular moment in a variety of modalities. For Nicole, self-knowledge is first an attempt to dispel the grandiose illusions of self-love. Nicole wants to bring the reader to the point in self-examination at which he sees this error and perceives the lack of being that self-love generates—a lack that can only be filled by the presence of God and the annihilation of the self and its vain phantoms. The role of reason is to perceive this state of affairs and to recognize the basis for the sense of lack, to recognize that the abysses of the self are unknowable and can only be supplemented with charity and God's grace. Self-knowledge is primarily the negative knowledge of that lack, which the illusions of self-love mask. For example, man seeks and introjects the metonyms of grandeur, such as wealth, the deference of others, and dress—those objects that draw him out of himself. Nicole's point is that man sees the self in everything, dispersed through being, but the appropriation or assumption of those objects does not lead to fulfillment because they are illusory objects of satisfaction that merely heighten the force of desire; they supply or are projected self-representations that provide no fulfillment but simply engender a further sense of lack. They are so many vain phantoms that offer the lure of satisfaction in the Augustinian dialectic of *uti/fruire* (to use/to enjoy); they underscore a lack of being of things surrounding man, because they are merely insufficient substitutes for the one source of happiness, the presence of God and self-annihilation in charity or love of the other.

Nicole's analysis dramatizes the dawn of the *moi*—that illusory wholeness of being that incites and is sustained by self-love. The implied genesis of man is that, by his fallen nature, each man is driven by *amour-propre,* whose drive in civilized society must be restricted; the natural pull of *amour-propre* must be reigned in. For Nicole, self-knowledge is recognition of the corrupt state of postlapsarian man and of the *néant* (nothingness) of worldly values that are fostered by concupiscence.

In this essay, as in others, the originary and predominant passion of fallen man is self-love, whose nefarious and corrupting effects upon him are limitless. With the repeated analysis of self-love humans also witness the development of what some scholars have seen as an early theory of the unconscious. Self-love blinds humans to its actions and its motives; it can generate illusions that deceive reason in such a way that reason will judge base actions to be virtuous and virtuous actions to be base. Those deceptive powers of self-love are most thoroughly examined in the essay titled "De la charité et de l'amour propre" (On Charity and Self-Love). In this essay, as in "De la connaissance de soi-même," Nicole contrasts the conscious surface of the mind, which is the domain of reason, with the recesses deep in the heart, which is the domain of self-love. Motives, intentions, and feelings, all serving the impulses of self-love, are more obscure than they may appear. Those ideas circulate unconsciously and are at the origin of most, if not all, conscious thought and action. The cautious introspection and self-examination advocated in "De la charité et de l'amour propre" may reveal the existence of those unconscious processes, but no human power can halt or curtail them. Again underscoring the importance of self-knowledge, Nicole emphasizes the importance of the awareness of the duplicity and ubiquitousness of self-love as the origin of most human thought and action. As it was for La Rochefoucauld, self-love for Nicole is an eye that perceives all but cannot fully turn its gaze upon itself. Nicole adds an unusual, pragmatic twist to his analysis of self-love in "De la charité et de l'amour propre": he notes that the blind and sinful, driven by self-love, may indeed perform seemingly virtuous acts from impure motives. Nicole almost seems to anticipate the positive valorization accorded to self-interest and self-love in the eighteenth century, but he tempers his paradoxical endorsement by underscoring the importance of humility to all who are devout. Pride, he argues, must never accompany a virtuous and charitable action, and in this way the power of unconscious self-love can be eroded as a motive for virtuous and charitable acts. In other words, the nefarious influence of self-love can never be eradicated as a source of human motivation, principally because it can never be fully identified as the source of human conduct, but its influence can be eroded by humility produced by acts of charity.

The anthropology that Nicole develops throughout the essays is consistent with Jansenist tradition and resonates with many elements and themes found in Pascal's *Pensées* and in other writings. Like others at Port-Royal, Nicole maintains that, with the Fall, reason was tainted and obscured while passions became excessive and surpassed the controlling scope of reason, which should have monitored the proper exercise of the will. For Nicole, as for Pascal, the corruption of the Fall is often represented in terms of the doubleness and monstrosity of postlapsarian man. Additionally, Nicole maintains that perseverance in moral and devout life is necessary but not a sufficient sign of salvation; however, in concert with traditional Augustinian doctrine, election is not possible without the gratuitous gift of the grace of God.

Nicole's most original contributions are perhaps in the domain of his social and political thought. Nicole's repeated appeals to self-knowledge and introspection must be subordinated to the interests of soci-

Title page for Nicole's 1670 treatise, collected in the first volume of his Essais de Morale *(from Jean Lesaulnier, Port-Royal insolite, 1992)*

ety and political order. Nicole was writing in a time that was profoundly affected by theories of natural law, such as Hugo Grotius's *De Jure Belli et Pacis* (About the Law of War and Peace, 1625). It is equally certain that Nicole was influenced by Thomas Hobbes's *De Cive* (Concerning Citizenship, 1642) and *Leviathan* (1660), which expound theories of sovereignty, social contract, and, paradoxically, natural law. Both of these works were written while Hobbes resided in France, and they were familiar to Port-Royal. Unlike such thinkers, Nicole attributes a disciplinary, correctional, and punitive function to the political and social order. Nicole's thesis is consistent with Jansenist anthropology in asserting that man's natural state and condition were irrevocably lost with the fall from grace. Social hierarchy is unnatural, according to Nicole, and indeed, the *libido dominandi* (desire to dominate), which underlies and sustains it, is one of the misguided desires of corrupt and fallen man. This state of affairs is necessary, however, in order to maintain rule and order in the society and political culture of concupiscent man. If social and political structures and institutions did not exist, chaos would result. Nicole's argument closely follows that of Pascal in the section of the *Pensées* titled "raison des effets" (Reasons for Effects) and in the *Discours sur la condition des grands* (Discourse on the condition of the Great, 1670). Nicole, however, goes one step further than Pascal in stating that this state of affairs is also punitive. In the essay "De l'Obéissance" (On Obedience), Nicole states that the Fall resulted from man's misuse of freedom, and while striving for redemption, man must renounce liberty and accept obedience and political submission as a form of penance for original sin. At best, life within the confines of the political and social orders can serve as a remedial exercise in assisting man to avoid temptations that led to the fall from grace.

The converse side of this argument is that the social hierarchy is entirely arbitrary and unnatural. This predicament requires the exercise of self-consciousness, by the privileged especially, as seen elsewhere in Nicole's writings. In the essay "De la grandeur" (On Grandeur), Nicole reminds humans that the establishment of a privileged nobility at the summit of the social hierarchy is the product of the Fall and not of natural order, virtue, or merit. Were it not for the Fall, Nicole contends, all men would have remained in a state of equality. Moreover, grandeur itself is doubly the product of sin, for the existence of a social hierarchy is the product of the Fall, but those who find themselves at the top of the social hierarchy were originally placed there as a result of the *libido dominandi*. Worldly power falls into the hands of those who successfully use force against their fellow men and not to those who manifest a natural superiority. Again, self-consciousness or knowledge is essential in the proper comportment of those who are privileged in society. The nobles must distinguish therefore between the outward grandeur and the inner self. In the outward manifestation they are greater than the common man, but in the inward order, the natural order, they are equal to the rest of mankind. According to Nicole, therefore, social behavior, such as displays of deference and obedience, are necessary but not just.

The essay "Des moyens de conserver la paix avec les hommes" (On the Ways of Preserving Peace among Men) shows how society is based on men's interdependence, and in "De la charité et de l'amour-propre" Nicole argues that fundamental impulses prompt humans to associate. Humans are bound together by needs that require them to live in society, and no one can do without his fellows. God

has thus forced humans to live in society as part of his design, for that is the requisite place to exercise penitential mutual love. Nicole, anticipating currents in moralism in the eighteenth century, also notes the advantages of self-interest. Self-love becomes a productive motive for exchange and a way to ensure that the needs of all are met. The social order, however, serves as a set of restraints on self-love and self-interest by providing incentives for their healthy and productive exercise and penalties for their excesses. Nicole echoes Hobbes and others in asserting the dangers of unrestrained self-love when it is not circumscribed by law and social custom. At times Nicole describes the interactions of self-love and laws as forces that act upon one another. Indeed, he resorts to the articulation of vortices in Cartesian physics to illustrate the ways in which humans are restrained in pursuing their own desires by pressure exerted by others, social institutions, and law. Ultimately, the repressive function of law and institutions assures the restriction of the tyrannical drives of self-love rather than its productive uses. Life in society, like the interior life of the individual, requires penitential submission to the will of God.

From 1671 until his death on 16 November 1695, and despite the peregrinations of 1679–1683, Pierre Nicole devoted much of his time to the serial writing and publication of his *Essais de Morale*. During his lifetime the essays were the achievement that his contemporaries admired and respected most. The essays became a model of moral reflection, savored by readers as diverse as Mme. de Sévigné, l'abbé Armand-Jean le Bouthillier de Rancé, Pierre Bayle, and even Voltaire. Nicole adopted the form of the essay because, as he explains in the preface to the first volume, Christian morality is too vast to be subsumed completely and systematically. Moreover, as a tonsured cleric, he may not have felt that he had the moral authority to write an encyclopedic Christian morality. Nicole addresses himself to the worldly *honnête homme* (gentleman), who is not to be counted among the devout but is among those who may be persuaded to believe. His efforts seem to be a response to scandalous casuistry attacked in Pascal's *Les lettres provinciales* as well as in Nicole's own writings.

The *Essais de Morale* certainly constitutes Pierre Nicole's greatest and most lasting literary achievement. Without those volumes, he would be remembered primarily as a theologian-polemicist embroiled in the recondite religious debates of his age. Significantly, his legacy is not to be found in the private devotional reading of his essays, as he may have wished, but instead in the reaction to those writings, and primarily to the moralist's analysis of self-love. Both Voltaire and Adam Smith, the founder of political economy, read Nicole, and their shared response to his writings, as well as to those of other moralists of the period, contributed to the revalorization of self-love during the Enlightenment as a positive and productive force in society. This view in turn helped to shape the nascent Modernist concepts of self, the rights of man, and capitalist democracy.

Biographies:

Abbé Goujet, *Vie de M. Nicole* (Luxembourg, 1732);

Emile Thouverez, *Pierre Nicole* (Paris: Gabalda, 1926).

References:

Jules Brody, "Pierre Nicole: Auteur de la préface du *Recueil de Poésies chrétiennes et diverses*," *XVIIe Siècle*, 64 (1964): 31–44;

Bernard Chédozeau, "Les années de Jeunesse de Pierre Nicole et son entrée à Port-Royal," *XVIIe Siècle*, 101 (1973): 51–69;

Bruce Davis, "Resisting the Pull: Pierre Nicole on the Inclination to Sin," in *Convergences: Rhetoric and Poetic in Seventeenth-Century France*, edited by David Lee Rubin and Mary B. MacKinley (Columbus: Ohio State University Press, 1989), pp. 217–233;

Béatrice Guion, "Pierre Nicole moraliste: l'humain en question," 2 volumes, dissertation, Université de Paris–Sorbonne, 1997;

Edward Donald James, "Pierre Nicole and La Logique de Port-Royal," *Seventeenth-Century French Studies*, 17 (1995): 15–24;

James, *Pierre Nicole, Jansenist and Humanist: A Study of His Thought* (The Hague: Nijhoff, 1972);

Nanerl O. Keohane, "Non-Conformist Absolutism in Louis XIV's France: Pierre Nicole and Denis Veiras," *Journal of the History of Ideas*, 35 (October–December 1974): 579–596;

Philip Knee, "Pascal, Nicole et la Morale des Lumières," *French Studies*, 52, no. 1 (January 1998): 17–27;

Jean Lafond, "Un débat d'esthétique à l'époque classique: La théorie du beau dans *L'epigrammatum delectus* de Port-Royal et sa critique par le Père Vavasseur," in *Actes du Congrès néo-latin de Tours, 1976* (Paris: Vrin, 1980), pp. 1269–1277;

Patrick Laude, "De la mort comme 'grace naturelle' chez Pierre Nicole," *Papers on French Seventeenth-Century Literature* (Paris: Papers on French Seventeenth-Century Literature, 1995), pp. 245–297;

Jean Lesaulnier, *Port-Royal insolite: Edition critique du Recueil de choses diverses* (Paris: Klinksieck, 1992);

Louis Marin, "La critique de la représentation théâtrale classique à Port-Royal: Commentaires sur le Traité de la Comédie de Nicole," in *Rethinking Classicism: Textual Explorations*, edited by David L. Rubin (New York: AMS, 1990), pp. 81–105;

Buford Norman, "Nicole's *Essais de Morale:* Logic and Persuasion," *French Literature Series*, 9 (1982): 9–17;

Jean-Marie Piemme, "Le théâtre en face de la critique religieuse: Un exemple, Pierre Nicole," *XVIIe Siècle*, 88 (1970): 49–59;

Dale Van Kley, "Pierre Nicole, Jansenism, and the Morality of Enlightened Self-Interest," in *Anticipations of the Enlightenment in England, France, and Germany*, edited by Alan Charles and Paul J. Korshin (Philadelphia; University of Pennsylvania Press, 1987), pp. 69–85;

Truls Winther, "Classicisme et cartésianisme: *Le traité de la vraie beauté* de Pierre Nicole," *Orbis Litterarum*, 33 (1978): 123–137.

Blaise Pascal

(19 June 1623 – 19 August 1662)

Erec R. Koch
Tulane University

BOOKS: *Expériences nouvelles touchant le vuide* . . . (Paris: P. Margat, 1647);

Récit de la grande expérience de l'équilibre des liqueurs . . . (Paris: C. Savreux, 1648);

Les Provinciales, ou Les Lettres escrites par Louis de Montalte à un provincial de ses amis, et aux RR. PP. Jésuites, sur le sujet de la morale et de la politique de ces peres (Cologne: P. de La Vallée, 1657); translated as *Les Provinciales, or The Mysterie of Jesuitisme: Discover'd in Certain Letters, Written upon Occasion of the Present Differences at Sorbonne, between the Jansenists and the Molinists, from January 1656 to March 1657* . . . (London: Printed by J.G. for R. Royston, 1657);

Factum, pour les curez de Paris: Contre un livre intitulé Apologie pour les casuistes contre les calomnies des jansenistes, à Paris 1657, et contre ceux qui l'ont composé, imprimé, et debité, anonymous (N.p., 1658);

Traitez de l'équilibre des liqueurs et de la pesanteur de la masse de l'air . . . (Paris: G. Desprez, 1663);

Traité du triangle arithmétique; Avec quelques autres petits traitez sur la mesme matière (Paris: G. Desprez, 1665);

Pensées de M. Pascal sur la religion et sur quelques autres sujets, qui ont esté trouvées après sa mort parmy ses papiers, edited by Etienne Périer (Paris: G. Desprez, 1669 [i.e., 1670]); translated by Jos. Walker as *Monsieur Pascall's Thoughts, Meditations, and Prayers Touching Matters Moral and Divine* (London: Printed for Jacob Tonson, 1688);

Œuvres de Blaise Pascal, 5 volumes, edited by Charles Bossut (The Hague: Detune, 1779)–volume 5 includes *Ecrits sur la grâce.*

Editions and Collections: *Œuvres de Blaise Pascal,* 14 volumes, edited by Léon Brunschvicg and Pierre Boutroux (Paris: Hachette, 1908–1923)–includes "De l'espirit géométrique et de l'art de persuader";

Pensées sur la religion et sur quelques autres sujets, 3 volumes, edited by Louis Lafuma (Paris: Editions du Luxembourg, 1951);

Blaise Pascal (engraving by d'Edelinck; Bibliothèque Nationale, Paris)

Œuvres complètes, edited by Lafuma (Paris: Editions du Seuil, 1963);

Œuvres complètes, 4 volumes to date, edited by Jean Mesnard (Paris: Desclée de Brouwer, 1964–   );

Les Provinciales, ou Les Lettres écrites par Louis de Montalte à un provincial de ses amis, et aux RR. PP. Jésuites, edited by Louis Cognet (Paris: Garnier Frères, 1965);

Pensées, edited by Philippe Sellier (Paris: Mercure de France, 1976);

Les Pensées de Pascal, edited by Francis Kaplan (Paris: Editions du Cerf, 1982);

Discours sur la religion et sur quelques autres sujets, qui ont été trouvés après sa mort parmi ses papiers, edited by Emmanuel Martineau (Paris: Fayard/A. Colin, 1992);

Œuvres complètes, edited by Michel Le Guern, Bibliothèque de La Pléiade, nos. 34 and 462 (Paris: Gallimard, 1998, 2000).

Editions in English: *The Provincial Letters,* translated by A. J. Krailsheimer (Baltimore: Penguin, 1967);

Pensées, translated by Krailsheimer (London & New York: Penguin, 1995).

OTHER: "Discours de feu M. Paschal sur la condition des grands," in *De l'éducation d'un prince, divisée en trois parties, dont la dernière contient divers traittez utiles à tout le monde,* by Pierre Nicole (Paris: Veuve de C. Savreux, 1670).

Blaise Pascal–scientist, theologian, philosopher, and rhetorician–was born in Clermont, in Auvergne, on 19 June 1623. Few writers of the seventeenth century have been as subject to hagiographic treatment. Those texts, which range from direct testimony to family lore mediated by many generations, from his sister Gilberte Périer to vicomte François-René Chateaubriand, form the core of biographical information about Pascal, but they are frequently tendentious and inaccurate.

The most challenging task presented to Pascal's biographers has been the separation of historical fact and verisimilar biographical interpretation from hagiographic fiction, not a lack of information about his life. Blaise was the only son of Etienne Pascal, a magistrate who served as president of the Cour des Aides of Montferrand, and he had two sisters, Gilberte (born 1620) and Jacqueline (born 1626). Although the family maintained titles of lower nobility–Etienne Pascal sometimes referred to himself as *chevalier* (knight), but Blaise, like his cousins, actually bore the title of *écuyer* (squire)–the Pascals more appropriately belonged among the more-privileged members of the *noblesse de robe* (rank acquired through holding a high state office), and they participated in the intellectual elite of the city of Clermont. Indeed, Etienne Pascal was a recognized and celebrated mathematician of that city. In 1631, five years after the death of his wife, Etienne Pascal began to liquidate his assets in order to engage more extensively in the intellectual milieu of the savants (men of learning, especially of science) and to devote his time to the education and guidance of his children. In the same year, the family moved to Paris.

From infancy, Blaise Pascal was sickly and suffered from the chronic illness that plagued him all of his life. He also demonstrated exceptional intellectual gifts early in childhood, as hagiographic accounts have claimed, particularly that of his sister Gilberte. She recounts that Etienne Pascal's plan for his son's education had called for him to focus first and exclusively on the study of classical languages before moving to the sciences. Gilberte said that, to satisfy his own intellectual predilections, the twelve-year-old Blaise independently worked his way to the thirty-second proposition of Euclid. In his *Historiettes* (circa 1659, published 1834), Gédéon Tallemant des Réaux offers an alternative account, in which he suggests that young Blaise had taken a copy of Euclid's *Elements* (circa third century B.C.) secretly to circumvent his father's prohibition. Gilberte also says that her younger brother wrote a treatise on sound at the age of eleven.

At this time, Etienne Pascal continued to establish his reputation as a mathematician and scientist. He was one of the original members of the informal scientific *académie* founded by Marin Mersenne, which drew together such distinguished mathematicians as Gérard Desargues, Gilles de Roberval, and Jacques Le Pailleur, who also had the distinction of being a recognized poet. In 1634 Armand de Plessis, cardinal de Richelieu, named Etienne Pascal as one of five commissioners charged with assessing the discoveries of Jean-Baptiste Morin on the calculation of longitude. This episode also suggests the developing ties and involvement of Etienne Pascal with the royal court, which were enhanced by the favor shown to his daughter Jacqueline by the queen and one of Richelieu's nieces. By 1638 Blaise Pascal had had exposure to court life and to the intellectual societies of bourgeois literary salons and scientific academies. At approximately this time he also wrote his first mathematical work, "Traité des coniques" (Treatise on Conics), no copies of which are extant.

In that same year Etienne Pascal seems to have participated in the protests by a group of rentiers who objected to the low rate of return on their investments, and he was forced to flee Paris and go into hiding in his native Auvergne. In 1639 Richelieu pardoned him, according to hagiography, because the cardinal was moved by the dramatic performance of Jacqueline and her pleas for her father. Richelieu sent Etienne Pascal to Rouen, where he was assigned to serve under the intendant of Normandy as *commissaire deputé par Sa Majesté pour l'impôt et la levée des tailles* (commissioner in charge of tax collection) in the wake of several episodes of popular rebellion in that province.

While Blaise Pascal continued to suffer from the chronic illness that afflicted him throughout his life, the years spent in Normandy from 1639 to 1647 were extremely productive in his mathematical and scientific research. During the winter of 1639–1640 he wrote his

Pascal's birthplace, the Hôtel de Langeac in Clermont-Ferrand, photographed circa 1900

Essai pour les coniques (Essay on Conics), which, heavily influenced by the work of Desargues, was applauded by the members of the *académie* Mersenne and was published in Paris in late 1640. In 1642 Pascal began work on a calculating machine, the first machine capable of "thought," which he designed to assist his father in the calculation of tax revenue. In 1645 Pascal offered the prototype to the *chancelier* Pierre Séguier and dedicated the invention to him. The text of this dedication, in its confident assertion of modernist ideals and the promise of progress, displays the pride of the inventor as well as his talents in rhetoric.

In the course of 1646 Pierre Petit, the intendant of fortifications, informed the Pascals of a series of experiments conducted by the Italian engineer and student of Galileo, Evangelista Torricelli. The experiments assayed the effects of placing an inverted tube filled with mercury into a vat of mercury, which caused the level of that liquid to descend in the tube. Torricelli speculated that the cause of the apparent suspension of the mercury was the counterbalancing force of the weight of air. Mersenne and others had been unable to repeat the experiment in Paris, but Petit proposed that Etienne and Blaise Pascal do so in Rouen, a major European center for the manufacture of glass. The Pascals succeeded in repeating and extending those experiments in October 1646, but

Blaise Pascal's attention was drawn by another phenomenon—the apparent "void," or vacuum, left in the tube as the mercury descended. Contrary to Aristotelian physics, which posited that nature abhorred vacuums and did not tolerate them, Pascal speculated that there were limits to this "abhorrence" and that the limit was a column of water measuring thirty-two feet. Pascal began to summarize his ideas in a series of accounts of the experiments that he had conducted.

While in Normandy, Pascal underwent a religious experience that has come, perhaps hyperbolically, to be known as the first conversion. More important, this experience marks Pascal's first sustained, although mediated, contact with Jansenism (defense of the theology of St. Augustine promoted by followers of Cornelius Jansen). After an accident in January 1646, Etienne Pascal was tended to by two devout and charitable men, Deslandes and de la Bouteillerie, who were members of the sect of "rouvillistes"—that is, followers of curé de Rouville, friend of Antoine Arnauld, who received spiritual direction from Jean Duvergier de Hauranne, abbé de Saint-Cyran. Saint-Cyran had been an associate of Jansen and shared his adherence to the austere doctrine of St. Augustine. The Pascal family was moved by the spirit of Jansenism; Blaise and his sister Jacqueline were particularly affected by the message of the two itinerant missionaries, and they experienced a renewed enthusiasm for piety. This experience inspired what Blaise Pascal later described as the sense of the presence of God and of his grace. His sister Jacqueline was seized by particularly fervent devotion after a life of relative religious laxity.

Blaise Pascal's renewed zeal also explains his first involvement in a matter of religious controversy. An itinerant former Capuchin monk, Jacques Forton, sieur de Saint-Ange, was traveling through Normandy at that time preaching unusual theological beliefs. Those theses were recorded in his three-volume work *La Conduite du jugement naturel* (The Direction of Natural Judgement, 1637–1641). Most significantly, Saint-Ange attempted to reconcile, in an awkward way, reason and faith, and consequently he reduced the importance of revelation and divine grace. Although the local episcopate refrained from taking any action against the former monk, Pascal and two of his devout friends, the mathematician Adrien Auzoult and Raoul Hallé, hounded Saint-Ange and demanded a retraction of his heretical views. Eventually, the zealous pursuit by Pascal and his friends resulted in Saint-Ange's public renunciation of his beliefs.

In 1647 Pascal, for reasons of health, returned to Paris, accompanied by his sister Jacqueline. While Jacqueline continued to pursue her lay pious vocation, Pascal resumed contacts with the *académie* Mersenne, where he earned Mersenne's admiration for his work on conic sections. The unpublished "Generatio conisectionum" (Generation of Conic Sections), written at this time, was rediscovered and made public by Gottfried Wilhelm Leibniz in 1677. Pascal also presented to the academy his repetition and extension of Torricelli's experiments. Discussion continued to center on whether the space at the top of the tube was really a vacuum, as Pascal speculated, or contained some form of "subtle matter." Debate also persisted on the question raised by Torricelli himself, namely on the causes of this phenomenon. The academy was divided between two explanations: either atmospheric pressure caused the descent of the mercury in the tube, or some form of inherent attraction, consistent with Aristotelian physics, drew the mercury downward. On 23 September 1647 Pascal met with René Descartes, who proposed the experiments that Pascal had his brother-in-law, Florin Périer, carry out at Puy-de-Dôme one year later. Pascal had Périer re-create the Rouen experiments at various levels of elevation to determine whether the variations in the descent of mercury in the tube confirmed his hypothesis that atmospheric pressure caused that phenomenon. Pascal published the account and results of these experiments in the *Récit de la grande expérience de l'équilibre des liqueurs . . .* (Account of the Grand Experiment on the Equilibrium of Liquids) in 1648.

While awaiting the opportunity to conduct this decisive experiment, Pascal began to write and have published his results to date. He published his *Expériences nouvelles touchant le vuide . . .* (New Experiments Concerning the Void . . .) in October 1647. This text summarized his experiments; it also proposed that nature did not abhor a vacuum, while cautiously advancing the claim that the space in the tube *appeared* to be empty of all substance. Pascal also seems to have begun drafting a treatise on the "void," of which only the preface is extant. This text is highly representative of the time in its expression of confidence in the modernist spirit, the ability of science to unlock the secrets of nature, and man to dominate and productively exploit his world. It opens with the important distinction between disciplines subject to authority, such as history and theology, and disciplines subject to reason. Pascal's forceful advocacy of scientific progress echoes the texts of Francis Bacon closely. More significant, this text is an early example of the mature style of Pascal's writings—reasoned discourse that assumes natural and appropriate stylistic ornaments in the form of figures and tropes, which heighten the aesthetic qualities of his thought. The strong rhetorical and stylistic flourishes already were becoming the hallmark of Pascal's craft.

Pascal as an adolescent (portrait by Jean Domat; Musée National des Granges de Port-Royal)

The publication of *Expériences nouvelles touchant le vuide* launched a stinging debate between Pascal and one of the champions of Aristotelian physics and the nonexistence of the vacuum in nature, the Jesuit Etienne Noël. The exchange of two letters and responses—Pascal's second was addressed more publicly to Le Pailleur—are examples of Pascal's nascent talent as rhetor, and his contributions to the exchange anticipate the lively, engaging, mock, and provocative style of *Les Provinciales, ou Les Lettres escrites par Louis de Montalte à un provincial de ses amis, et aux RR. PP. Jésuites, sur le sujet de la morale et de la politique de ces peres* (1657; translated as *Les Provinciales, or The Mysterie of Jesuitisme: Discover'd in Certain Letters, Written upon Occasion of the Present Differences at Sorbonne, between the Jansenists and the Molinists, from January 1656 to March 1657 . . . ,* 1657). Significantly, much of the debate has to do with epistemological language and the encroachment of the rhetoric of tropes in a domain in which it does not belong. Pascal and his father, in a supplementary letter, challenge the use of such terms as the "abhorrence" of nature for the "void" as metaphors that undermine the epistemological value of language. Pascal's argument anticipates what he later wrote in "Réflexions sur la géométrie en général: De l'esprit géométrique et de l'art de persuader" (Reflections on Geometry in General: On Geometric Thought and the Art of Persuasion). Like that text, Pascal's two letters in response to Noël assert the differences between nominal and real definitions, and acknowledge the primacy and undefinability of primitive terms such as *space, time,* and *motion.* While noting the epistemological risks involved in conflating real and nominal definitions, Pascal also asserts, and states even more clearly in "De l'esprit géométrique et de l'art de persuader," that those primary terms, which found epistemological discourse, themselves function as tropes. As always, Pascal acknowledges the centrality of epistemology, of questions of truth and falsehood, and the place of rhetorical language in this configuration. In other words, the letters to Noël, just as many other of Pascal's writings, are not simply texts that employ and deploy rhetoric through stylistic mastery. Rhetoric may be said to constitute the crux of the argument that he makes here and elsewhere. If the originality of Pascal's experiments and his interpretation of the results may be deemed unoriginal and even uninteresting by many scholars, the questions that Pascal raises about the articulation of epistemology and rhetoric should be cause to reconsider what the stakes of the debate may truly be.

In September 1647 Pascal and his sister Jacqueline began regularly to attend sermons of Antoine Singlin, supérieur de Port-Royal, the confessor of the nuns at Jansenist Port-Royal. By early 1648 Jacqueline had placed herself under his spiritual direction. Pascal himself was not unaffected by his sister's deepening devotion (at this time, by some accounts, Pascal began to form the intention of writing an apology of the Christian religion), and he supported his sister before their father in her desire to enter the convent of Port-Royal. Indeed, already at this time, Pascal's letters reveal an increasing piety and acceptance of the Jansenist position preached by Singlin. Up to his death in 1651 Etienne Pascal, however, resisted allowing his daughter to pursue this vocation. After that event there seemed to be no obstacle to Jacqueline's acceptance of vows, but Blaise Pascal, perhaps fearing a second loss in his immediate family, now displayed reluctance to allow her to enter Port-Royal. The most contentious point for him was allowing her to bring a large dowry to Port-Royal, but this obstacle was finally overcome when Jacqueline was allowed to enter with none. Jacqueline began her novitiate year in 1652 and eventually took vows.

Alone for the first time, Pascal entered a period of his life described by his sister Gilberte, in her hagiobiography of her brother, as "le temps de sa vie le plus mal employé" (the most wastefully used period of his life). This characterization is perhaps excessive, for the "worldly" period of Pascal's life was certainly not one of debauchery and dissipation. Pascal's piety was unquestioned and certainly consistent with devotion typical of the period, but his energies were not exclusively devoted to religious pursuits. In this period,

which really extends from his return to Paris in 1647 until 1654, Pascal did, however, reenter society with renewed vigor. Pascal's activities during those years are archivally undocumented, but the reader can assess a general picture from his sister's biography and from contemporary testimony in letters. The period was not extremely productive in scientific research. Pascal did continue to participate in the academy that was successor to Mersenne's. He also began writing in late 1651 his *Traitez de l'équilibre des liqueurs et de la pesanteur de la masse de l'air . . .* (Treatise on the Equilibrium of Liquids and the Weight of Air . . .), which summarized the experiments that Florin Périer performed for him at Puy-de-Dôme. This work remained unpublished until 1663, after Pascal's death.

After the death of his father, Pascal seems to have decided to aspire to the magistrature and to marriage. He ventured more frequently into society and the social world. He developed a lasting friendship with the worldly Artus Gouffier, duc de Roannez, a peer of France who shared Pascal's passion for mathematics. Pascal also began to associate with known libertines—such as Antoine Gombaud, chevalier de Méré; Damien Mitton; and Melchisédech Thévenot—associations that exposed him to religious laxity and moral humanism. This group, valuing elegance and grace in social life, made an important counterpoint to Pascal's academic and savant milieu and left a profound impression on him, as witnessed by sections of the *Pensées de M. Pascal sur la religion et sur quelques autres sujets, qui ont esté trouvées après sa mort parmy ses papiers* (Thoughts of M. Pascal about Religion and about Some Other Subjects, Which Were Found after his Death among His Papers, 1669), which draw on his familiarity with *mondain* (worldly) society.

Pascal's worldly period was interrupted by the events of the night of 24 November 1654 and the memorial that records his experience. This brief text, which Pascal, in accordance with the custom of his time, had sewn into the lining of his jacket, is a powerful personal declaration of faith, of acceptance of the truth of the Christian religion, of his embrace by divine love, and of the rapture experienced during the course of his religious meditation. The second, or major, conversion was not wholly unexpected. Pascal had been a believer and was moderately devout. Contemporary accounts say that his temperament began to change at about this time and that he developed a more cautious and suspicious view of society and life in society. Several days after the second conversion, Pascal attended another sermon by Singlin and placed himself under Singlin's spiritual guidance. Pascal apparently decided to devote his life to relative material simplicity and charity. On Singlin's recommendation, he went on a retreat with Charles d'Albert, duc de Luynes, in January 1655. Pascal was placed under the guidance of Lemaistre de Saci, and he asked for and received a cell among the Solitaires of Port-Royal, although urgent affairs forced him to return to Paris.

Pascal was now a friend of Port-Royal but did not belong to Port-Royal, as he explains through the narrator of *Les Provinciales*. He did not move exclusively within that milieu, nor did he have much contact with his later collaborators, Arnauld and Pierre Nicole. Indeed, at this point Pascal continued to have contact with worldly and savant circles. He pursued amicable contact with the libertines Méré and Mitton. At this time, he might also have continued to frequent or at least have contact with Parisian society, most notably with the *salonnière* Magdeleine, marquise de Sablé.

Pascal also continued to participate in savant circles after the second conversion. He attended the Saturday meetings of a circle of mathematicians that included Pierre Gassendi, Roberval, Desargues, and Pierre de Carcavi, with whom Pascal corresponded until nearly 1660. In 1656 Pascal began important work on probability and game theory, which his worldly and libertine friends had encouraged him to undertake. That group of savants, known as the "très célèbre académie parisienne" (famous Parisian academy), was the one through which Pascal issued his challenge of solving the problem of the roulette in 1658–that is, determining geometrically the center of the cycloid. After solving the problem himself as a distraction from a toothache, according to Gilberte Périer, Pascal challenged members of the mathematical community in Europe to do the same with the promise of a generous reward. In December 1660 Pascal received a visit from Christian Huygens at the residence of his friend the duc de Roannez. Pascal also showed interest in applied science during this period. He contributed in 1660 to a technical improvement to the transport carriages known as *haquets;* he displayed interest in an improvement in clock making that substituted a spring mechanism for the cumbersome pendulum. Finally, he played an important role in the design of the first system of public transportation, the *carrosses à cinq sous* (coaches at five sous). As a result of Pascal's planning, the duc de Roannez signed an agreement with Louis François du Bouchet, marquis de Sourches, to create such a line of public transportation; it was inaugurated on 18 March 1662.

These worldly activities were counterbalanced at first by Pascal's dedication to Port-Royal. He participated in religious lectures and discussions that took place at Vaumurier, at the residence of the duc de Luynes, a fervent supporter of Port-Royal. From the point of the second conversion on, however, Pascal

Pascal's older sister, Gilberte Pascal Périer, who wrote a biography of her brother (portrait by M. Ojardieas; Musée d'Histoire Locale, Clermont-Ferrand)

became a consistent partisan of the causes of Port-Royal, bringing his talents as rhetor to the service of Jansenism. The first major example of this loyalty was his composition of the text that has come to be known as *Les Provinciales*. This text is the product of a long-term theological debate launched with the publication of Jansen's *Augustinus* in 1640 (two years after his death), the text that constituted the credo of that eponymous neo-Augustinian movement. In *Augustinus,* Jansen argued against the new laxity of the Catholic Church that followed in the wake of the Counter Reformation and advocated a return to the doctrine of the patristic fathers of the church–most notably, of course, that of St. Augustine. The extensive discussion of grace in that text proved to be the greatest source of theological controversy. In the name of orthodoxy, the *Augustinus* maintained that grace was an absolutely gratuitous gift that God bestowed upon the elect.

In 1643 Arnauld began this debate by publishing *De la fréquente communion.* Two worldly penitents, one under the direction of the Jansenist Saint-Cyran and the other under the direction of the Jesuit confessor Pierre de Sesmaisons, compare the instructions of their respective confessors on the efficacy of the sacraments regardless of the penitent's acts before and after communion.

Arnauld criticizes Sesmaisons's apparent endorsement of the lack of contrition by the penitent and the general moral laxity endorsed by the Jesuit order. This text resulted in popularizing an arcane theological debate and began the drawing of battle lines in the public and within the ranks of the religious establishment. At issue in Arnauld's work, as later in *Les Provinciales,* was the way to integrate religious life and life in society.

Although sixteen French bishops and twenty doctors of the Sorbonne endorsed Arnauld's position in *De la fréquente communion,* the backlash against Arnauld, especially among Jesuits, was severe. The debate was eventually carried to the confines of the Sorbonne, where the syndic of the Faculté de Théologie de Paris, Nicolas Cornet, drew up a list of five propositions on grace that he claimed to have drawn from Jansen's text and that he asked his colleagues to condemn. The propositions were transmitted to Rome, where Pope Innocent X condemned them as heretical in the bull *Cum occasione* (With Occasion) of 31 March 1653. The matter seemed to have been resolved until early in 1655, when the vicar of Saint-Sulpice refused absolution to Roger Du Plessis, duc de Liancourt, on the grounds of the duke's association with Port-Royal. Arnauld responded in February 1655 with his *Lettre à une personne de condition* (Letter about a Person of Rank), in which he condemned the five heretical theses and declared himself to have adopted the doctrine of St. Augustine on grace. King Louis XIV's confessor, François Annat, accused Arnauld of embracing Calvinism instead. Arnauld responded in July 1655 with his *Seconde lettre à un duc et pair* (Second Letter to a Duke and a Peer) addressed to the duc de Luynes, a supporter of Port-Royal. A commission of the Faculté de Théologie discerned two errors in Arnauld's text. On 14 January 1656 the Faculté de Théologie condemned Arnauld on the first point and threatened to do the same on the second.

At this important juncture Pascal entered the debate. The Port-Royalist supporters wanted to bring the debate before the broader public, but Arnauld and his collaborator up to that point, Nicole, were ill equipped for this vulgarizing rhetorical mission. One contemporary account relates a meeting of Arnauld, Nicole, and Pascal in which Arnauld urged Nicole to take up the defense of the Jansenist cause. Nicole then turned to Pascal as the one most capable of defending Arnauld's position. Thus, according to hagiography, was launched the first of the *Lettres écrites par Louis de Montalte à un provincial de ses amis,* a compelling combination of satirical narrative and vulgarized theological polemics. The division of labor in the writing of these texts, as portrayed in contemporary accounts, is also revealing. The rigorous theology and references to recondite texts and arguments were to have Nicole as

their source and Pascal as rhetorical craftsman. This account is compelling, since it provides a convenient and informative bifurcation in the process of the production of the text, one that again displays the singular talents of Pascal to make accessible and aesthetically pleasing the highly specialized debate in an ideal fusion of *l'agréable* (the pleasant) and *l'utile* (the useful).

The eighteen letters appeared serially and anonymously in 1656 and 1657 and were interspersed with counterattacks launched by the Jesuits. The first collective edition was published in 1657 under the pseudonymous title *Les Provinciales.* The first letter was published in January 1656, and it bore no publishing *privilege* (copyright). At the core of the letter, addressed to an interested *honnête homme* (honorable man), is the candid narrator's fictional account of a discussion between Molinists and Thomists, adherents of the theological systems developed by the Spanish Jesuit Luis de Molina and St. Thomas Aquinas respectively, which, narratively played out as a *showing,* understates the absurdity of the debate on grace involving the doctrine of *pouvoir prochain* (proximate power). What becomes painfully obvious to the reader is that the agreement on the words themselves has nothing to do with the radically different meanings ascribed by the two groups and that their concurrence is motivated by political expediency. Moreover, the Molinists' understanding has nothing to do with the common meanings of the words *pouvoir* or *prochain.*

The eight-page pamphlet met with such resounding success that Pascal, drawing on the theological expertise of Arnauld and Nicole, turned immediately to the composition of the second letter, which targeted the theory of *grace suffisante* (sufficient grace). The narrator's naive candor again underscores the absurdity of Jesuits' understanding of the term as well as its divergence from the orthodox understanding of grace. Despite the official reaction against the letter and the pursuit of its author and publisher by the police, Pascal wrote the third letter in the series over a period of ten days. In this letter, Pascal, continuing his examination of the notion of grace, initiates a direct defense of Arnauld on the fall of St. Peter. Pascal demonstrates unequivocally, and again in a way that was readily accessible to the public, how Arnauld's position was extremely consistent with orthodoxy, and how his condemnation was implicitly a condemnation of the fathers of the Church.

The fourth letter begins a series of conversations between the narrator and a risible Jesuit who represents the fragmented and heterogeneous writings and practices of that order. In this letter the attention focuses on the nexus of grace and free will. Pierre Le Moyne had articulated the Molinist position that, in order to commit a sin, the agent had to be fully cogni-

Pascal's calculating machine, which he developed in 1642–1645 to assist his father in his work as commissioner of tax collection in Rouen (from Jean Anglade, Pascal, l'insoumis, 1988)

zant of the good action to do and the evil to avoid. Barring the existence of those conditions, there could be no commission of sin. In other words, only those choices made clearly and lucidly would carry any moral weight. To forestall the obvious objection, Le Moyne suggested that God always bestows sufficient grace on man to enable him to make such lucid and clear choices. This position, which Arnauld had lengthily criticized in his *Apologie des Saints Pères* (Apology of the Holy Fathers) of 1651, became an irresistible target for Pascal's trenchant satire. Pascal exposed the absurdity of this position by arguing compellingly that some men do not have a sentiment of committing sins by their actions, and indeed, some never have the sentiment of the presence of God. To suppose, as Le Moyne and other Jesuit authors did, that all men are inclined naturally to do good and are supremely capable of doing so would be ridiculous.

Nearly one month separated the publication of the fourth and fifth letters in *Les Provinciales,* and during that time Pascal, under the tutelage of Arnauld and Nicole, discovered the Jesuit casuists (those authors on Christian morality who turn general rules and principles drawn from the Scriptures to specific, earthly, and unusual circumstances, and develop guidelines for the mediation between theory and praxis) and especially Antonio Escobar y Mendoza. Continuing the narrator's conversations with the risible representative of the Jesuit order, Pascal turned his arguments to the sphere of morality. This turn in the fifth letter marks an important development in Pascal's strategy: instead of restricting the debate to the theological points that provoked Arnauld's censure, Pascal instead began to challenge the moral authority of those who attacked the legitimacy and orthodoxy of Port-Royal. Pascal exploits this strategy masterfully in letters 5–8. The host of casuists quoted and paraphrased in these letters are shown to endorse simony, lying, usury, murder, and adultery—to name only a few topics—through their tendentious interpretation of the Scriptures and the decisions of councils and popes. Pascal's rhetorical mastery and his ability to dramatize and illustrate Jesuitical excess make the critique far more effective than one carried out in the tone and diction of traditional theological debate. At every juncture, the rhetorical devices, as well as the explicit statements themselves, underscore the distance of Jesuits and their allies from the revealed truths and, conversely, the proximity and consistency of the Jansenists to the truths and traditions of the church. The Jesuit casuists' advocacy of religious subjectivism suggests that the church itself, its hierarchy, and its sacraments are, at best, optional on the road to salvation. In those letters, Pascal also underscores on several occasions the disjunction between the excessive practices advocated by the Jesuits and the restraint demanded by civil law and authority. Pascal's critique of the moral authority of the Jesuits is doubly effective in setting them against both religious and civil authority.

Although Pascal writes in a note in the eighth letter that "après ma 8e, je croyais avoir assez répondu" (after my eighth, I believe that I had sufficiently responded), the attack against the Jesuit order continues in a somewhat similar vein by taking on the recommendations for Jesuit devotional practice and spiritual direction. Drawing largely from Paul de Barry's *Le Paradis ouvert à Philagie par cent dévotions à la mère de Dieu* (Paradise Opened to Philagie through One Hundred Acts of Devotion to the Mother of God), the letter, like Arnauld's previous polemical efforts, exposes the mechanical nature of devotion recommended and practiced by the Jesuits. Pascal illustrates the absurdity of such recommendations in a religion whose core, for Jansenists, was love of God and of other, or *caritas* (charity). Pascal turns to this love—or charity—in letter 10. The letter largely targets the work of Antoine Sirmond on charity. In addition to the degradation of the sacred, Pascal takes exception to a doctrine such as Sirmond's, which advocates the exercise of pagan virtue as a substitute for the practice of charity, the moral center of the Christian religion.

This series of letters provoked a sharp response from the Catholic Church and from secular authorities. Pascal's literary efforts resulted in a series of condemnations of casuistry by the Gallican episcopate. Those events and the mordant satire of the letters themselves provoked the Jesuits to write responses, such as Jacques Nouet's *Réponse aux lettres que les jansénistes publient contre les Jésuites* (Response to the Letters the Jansenists Publish against the Jesuits), in defense of their doctrines and practices. Those writings in turn prompted Pascal's letters 11–15, which he wrote from August to November 1656. In those letters, Pascal drops the literary guise of his candid narrator to address his Jesuit detractors directly. The diction of the letters shifts from satire to what Jean Mesnard has described as "une éloquence indignée" (an eloquence of indignation). Pascal largely repeats, clarifies, and further documents the arguments that he had presented earlier in literary guise. In most cases, the letters, which approach more-traditional forms of theological debate, turn the Jesuits' defensive countercharges against them—namely, that the Jesuits had deformed and misinterpreted the texts that they cited, and that they often miscited. Letters 11–15 also, and more explicitly than their predecessors, broach questions of language and the language of truth by claiming that the Jesuits speak only the seductive language of pleasure.

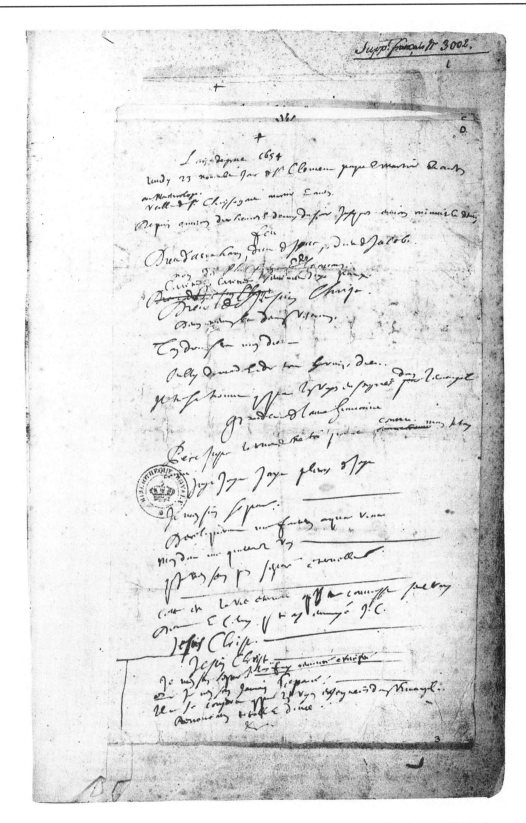

Page from the manuscript for the memorial Pascal wrote to commemorate the night of 24 November 1654, when he experienced a profound, mystical recommitment to his religious faith (Bibliothèque Nationale, Paris)

The Jesuits supplemented this open and public debate with efforts to silence the author of *Les Provinciales* through more forceful means. The Jesuits' attempts to exploit their influence with the young king, the chancelier Séguier, and the majority of French bishops prompted the hurried composition of letter 16, which is usually acknowledged as the least effective of the series. The Jesuits' efforts might also have influenced the polemical stance that Pascal assumed in letter 17, which, appearing in early 1657, stresses the turn of the debate from the theological domain to the political domain. In letter 17 Pascal suggests that the Jesuits had fabricated the Jansenist heresy in order to undermine the only opposition in France to their political hegemony. Pascal also attempts in this letter to return the debate to its original point of contention by forcefully developing the distinction between *droit* (right) and *fait* (fact), and by compiling convincing support for his claim that the Jansenists had condemned the five propositions as heretical while also demonstrating that they were not to be found in the writings of Jansen.

This return to the inaugural issue in the controversy suggests that the energy of Pascal and his collaborators was just about spent. Political developments helped to bring the debate to closure. Pope Alexander VII's bull of 16 October 1656 was presented to the king on 10 March 1657. This document denounced the five propositions and acknowledged their presence in Jansen's *Augustinus*. On 28 March 1657 the Assemblée du clergé issued an edict that all French clergymen sign a statement accepting both aspects of the papal denunciation. In this atmosphere Pascal wrote the final published letter of *Les Provinciales*. This letter, written in close collaboration with Arnauld and Nicole, is a last desperate attempt to settle the questions of *droit* and *fait* in the Jansenists' favor.

This last Jesuit attempt did not succeed in silencing Pascal, however, as the nonpublication of the drafted letter 19 would suggest. Instead, it simply forced Pascal to find another venue. The opportunity arose with the publication in 1657 of the Jesuit Père Pirot's *Apologie pour les casuistes* (Apology for the Casuists). At the synod of the *curés de Paris* of 7 January 1658, those ecclesiastics decided to pursue the condemnation of that publication, and their protest was recorded in the *Factum pour les curés de Paris* (Factum for the Curates of Paris), which was largely, if not entirely, written by Pascal. The *Deuxième écrit des curés de Paris* (The Second Letter from the Curates of Paris), which appeared in April of 1657, is also believed to have been written largely by Pascal, as was the *Cinquième écrit des curés de Paris* (Fifth Letter from the Curates of Paris) of 11 June 1658.

For many critics *Les Provinciales* represents the dawn of a new form of rhetoric and rhetorical persuasion. The

work marks a significant shift in style, a departure from and vulgarization of lofty Ciceronian and Quintilian rhetorics. The effects of *Les Provinciales* are consistent with the dawning classical aesthetic of *l'agréable* and *l'utile:* they affect the passions and provoke pleasure while simultaneously addressing the mind and reason. The publication of this text also coincides with the moment in the evolution of rhetoric when this art becomes restricted to the literary use of figures and tropes, ornaments of discourse. Rhetoric was increasingly reduced to this function rather than embracing, as it had since Aristotle, an art of discursive reasoning that included *inventio, dispositio, elocutio, memoria,* and *pronuntiatio* (invention, disposition, elocution, memory, and delivery).

The literary qualities of *Les Provinciales* again underscore Pascal's mastery of rhetoric in this new and restricted sense. The first ten letters advance the case of the deviance and departure of the Jesuits from orthodoxy through images of metonymic concatenation and fragmentation. For example, the letters include a ponderous list of Jesuit casuists who substitute their mutually contradictory texts for the sole source of truth, the Scriptures. As Louis MacKenzie has noted, Jesuit casuists invest numbers and plurality in spiritual doctrine, where there should be the metaphoric unity and totality of tradition. The same observation holds for the Jesuits' forced linkage of images of concupiscence and charity. For example, in letter 11, a gallant poem from Le Moyne's *Peintures morales* (Moral Portrait, 1640) draws together the blush of passion of a *belle dame* (beautiful lady) and the incommensurate angelic fire of charity. The letters oppose such metonymic concatenation to another figural structure around which the many themes of the letters can be organized, namely metaphoric totalization. Metaphoric wholeness characterizes images and descriptions of the unity of the Catholic Church in its doctrine, its hierarchy, and its history. One figure developed later in letter 14 illustrates this point decisively. It idealizes the image of the analogical correspondence of God, church, and man. Through mimesis, the three form a metaphoric whole. The critique of the Jesuits is founded on rhetorical structures that contrast metonymic and arbitrary contiguity with the metaphoric totality of tradition.

Les Provinciales may be read as an example and an illustration of Pascal's rhetorical mastery in an age when rhetoric was increasingly moving toward the restriction to *elocutio,* to figures and tropes, stylistic ornaments of discourse. The popular reception of the work is an attestation to this movement, and it is memorialized in the provincial correspondent's reply to the second letter, which cites the praise of two readers for the author's extraordinary mastery of style. *Les Provinciales* does, however, also address the question of another form of rhetoric. Beginning in letter 11, Pascal broaches rhetoric not only as the ornamental system of figures and tropes but also as a modality of discourse, and he argues cogently that Jesuitical seductions are a function of this more extended definition of rhetoric. Pascal makes this point most forcefully in letter 11, the first in which the narrator openly addresses his Jesuit detractors. In this letter Pascal opposes truth and force and the discourses that these two govern. The language of force posits or imposes truth; it is a performative function of language that opposes the constative and referential language of truth. This rich analysis does not simply dwell on political strategies and counterattacks in the ongoing struggle between truth and force, it also assesses the language of the two. Pascal asserts that Jesuitical language of seduction is positional and performative; it posits truths that please. The language of orthodoxy, however, is the referential language of truth. The question for readers of *Les Provinciales* must thus become whether Pascal's text, as discourse of truth, can itself maintain the distinction made in its own rigorous analysis. In other words, one must ask, in echo of Pascal's Jesuit detractors, whether *Les Provinciales* is caught up in the problem that it attempts to analyze and master.

This analysis of rhetoric is entirely consistent with an unpublished text by Pascal written at about the same time, in either 1657 or 1658, "De l'esprit géométrique et de l'art de persuader." Pascal had originally intended this work to be a text used for the instruction of students at the *petites écoles* (little schools) of Port-Royal. A long proof on the existence of the two infinities, which resembles fragment 199 of the *Pensées* (Lafuma edition), "Disproportion de l'homme" (Disproportion of Man), helps to situate this fragment at about the time when Pascal was beginning to compose his apology for the Christian religion. The "Réflexions," too, distinguishes two modes of human discourse. The first is the discourse of truth by reasoning *more geometrico*—that is, of starting with primary terms, principles, and axioms, and proceeding deductively from these. This form of discourse is the only epistemologically sound one. It is also one that bears its own pitfalls, not simply because it is, as Pascal regretfully notes, underutilized in human affairs, but also because it is as flawed and limited as humans themselves are. The text cites, for example, the importance of the distinction between real and nominal definitions. The latter are names arbitrarily given to things and not definitions of their natures or essences. Real definitions alone list the properties of entities as they are in their own being, but they are, in fact, nothing more than propositions to be proven. According to Pascal, the conflation of those two is the source of many epistemological errors. A more important epistemological problem is presented

by primitive terms, such as *space, time,* and *motion.* All real and nominal definitions depend on primitive terms, which are not susceptible to definition because such definitions would necessarily be real definitions—that is, nothing more than propositions to be proven. Pascal describes them merely as directional motions, vectors toward the things in themselves, which, as Paul de Man has argued in his article "Pascal's Allegory of Persuasion," is identical to Pascal's definition of figures or tropes in the *Pensées.* Reasoning *more geometrico* is in itself impossible not only because, as Pascal notes, it would require an infinite regression to define all terms used, but also because the foundational primitive terms at which this regression is halted themselves function as tropes, as figures rather than as proper meanings. This belief suggests that reasoning *more geometrico* is itself founded necessarily on metaphors that undo all proper and referential meaning in the discourse of truth.

The second half of the text goes on to examine the other mode of discourse, persuasion, which Pascal allies with seduction and pleasure. Pascal states that, unlike with geometric discourse, codifying the persuasive discourse of seduction exceeds his abilities because of the infinite variability of pleasure among men and the instability of its apparent principles. Pascal contends that because of man's fallen nature, mankind hopes that truth and pleasure can be allied and articulated in the art of discourse, but he goes on to express his uncertainty about the possibility of doing so. One important reason for such doubts is broached in *Les Provinciales*—namely, that the seductive discourse of pleasure has nothing properly to do with truth or falsehood because it is a performative and nonreferential mode of language. The "Réflexions sur la géométrie en général" also poses the question of divine persuasion, which is the most efficacious form of persuasion but one that is incomprehensible to mankind. This mode of persuasion is the sole source of divine truths and revelation, and one for which the rhetoric of seduction may serve as the corrupt image. Pascal's hesitant analysis of divine persuasion exposes the importance of charity to its efficacy. In reasoning *more geometrico,* one finds that the value of truth leads to love of the truth, but in divine persuasion, love (charity) precedes any act of understanding. This important theme is adumbrated in *Les Provinciales* and receives more extensive treatment in the *Pensées.*

The controversy that fueled the publication of *Les Provinciales* slowly diminished up to early 1661. Until 1660 civil and religious authorities in France had not shown a great deal of zeal in requiring the signature of the formulary denouncing the five theses attributed to Jansen, but in December of that year the king intervened personally. The Assemblée du clergé required all clerics

Les Granges, the residence of the Jansenist "Solitaires" at the abbey of Port-Royal des Champs, where Pascal went to live in January 1655

in France to sign that document, and the Conseil d'Etat ratified this measure, recommending severe penalties for those who did not comply. Two positions predominated at Port-Royal. To condemn Jansen was, in the eyes of some at Port-Royal, also to condemn St. Augustine and the orthodox notions of grace. Arnauld led the moderate camp, which endorsed signing the denunciation, but with explanation—namely, that the signators agreed that the propositions were heretical but that they were not to be found in works of St. Augustine—and therefore implicitly not in works of Jansen either—although that polemical battle had already been fought and lost. The other camp at Port-Royal, led in spirit by Martin de Barcos, argued that any condemnation of Jansen, however it might have been implicitly or explicitly attenuated, would also encompass an unsanctionable condemnation of St. Augustine, St. Paul, and the grace of Christ himself. Pascal became embroiled in this affair and forcefully advocated the latter position in his *Ecrit sur la signature du formulaire* (On the Signing of the Formulary). Also, at about this time he composed the *Ecrits sur la grâce* (Writings on Grace). This text is both a further vulgarization of theological doctrine on grace and an eloquent expression of the strictest Jansenist position on that matter. Few

sided with Pascal on the subject of the formulary; most shared Arnauld's concerns about the terrible political consequences for Port-Royal if its supporters did not sign the denunciation.

Perhaps as the result of this rift with his colleagues at Port-Royal, but certainly as a result of his failing health, Pascal began to lead a life of increasing solitude. During this period he wrote the "Prière pour demander à Dieu le bon usage des maladies" (Prayer for Asking from God the Good Use of Maladies)—first published in *Divers traitez de piété* (Various Treatises on Piety, 1666)—and an important text, "Discours sur la condition des grands" (Discourse on the Status of Nobles), which appeared in Nicole's *De l'éducation d'un prince* (On the Education of a Prince, 1670). Pascal's discourse, which consists of three essays, was composed for the formation of the young Charles de Lorraine, duc de Chevreuse, the son of the Jansenist duc de Luynes. Pascal's pedagogical aim in the text is to undo the presuppositions of the nobleman on the nature and origin of his grandeur. In the first discourse Pascal argues that the wealth and status bestowed on noblemen are the result of chance, not of natural necessity or worth. The second discourse distinguishes between natural and institutional social grandeur. Although the latter requires a show of respect, only the former is worthy of admiration. A life devoted to the practice of Christian virtue is the loftiest example of natural grandeur. Building on this important distinction, Pascal, in the final discourse, goes on to analyze three stages of royalty and royal rule: force, concupiscence, and charity. A nobleman, while living by the social conventions of worldly concupiscence, must recognize them as mere conventions for maintaining social order. At the same time the nobleman must strive to imitate the king of charity, Jesus Christ.

The years 1656 to 1658 were extremely productive literarily for Pascal. At the end of this period he devoted much of his time to collecting many of the materials for his unfinished apology for the Christian religion, his masterpiece which has come to be known as the *Pensées*. As his health permitted, Pascal continued to work on this text until his death on 19 August 1662. Scholars believe that Pascal began to formulate the project of an apology for the Christian religion in 1656 or 1657. The miraculous healing of his niece by the touch of a thorn from the crown of Christ prompted Pascal's reflections on miracles, which constitute some of the earliest fragments of the *Pensées*. The debate with the Jesuits and his contact with libertines such as Méré and Mitton further fueled his interest to work on this project. Pascal had originally planned an apology that would ground the truth of the Christian religion in miracles, but, as the project unfolded, he turned to argumentation based on the Bible and its interpretation. The overall plan and main lines of argumentation for this project were presented in a conference that Pascal gave at Port-Royal in 1658. Nicolas Filleau de la Chaise's notes taken at this conference, and published in 1672 as the *Discours sur les Pensées* (Discourse on the *Pensées*), form the basis of the only written record of this presentation.

The status of the text, composed entirely of fragments, presents a formidable challenge to scholarly commentary on the *Pensées*. The unfinished apology is made up of a series of notes that Pascal recorded on large sheets of paper. He separated the beginning and end of each fragment by a line and then cut these large sheets and regrouped the fragments into *liasses* (bundles) bound together by string. At his death Pascal's manuscript consisted of twenty-eight bundles bearing titles, the *papiers classés* (classified bundles), and thirty-one bundles that, for the most part, did not bear titles, the *papiers non classés* (unclassified bundles). Upon his death Pascal's colleagues at Port-Royal made two copies of the manuscript and then proceeded to undo and reorder the fragments and bundles. These efforts led to the first edition of the *Pensées* in 1670, known as the

Port-Royal edition and titled *Pensées de M. Pascal sur la religion et sur quelques autres sujets, qui ont esté trouvées après sa mort parmy ses papiers,* which not only reordered the fragments but also suppressed many and presented rewritten versions of others. Pascal's first editors launched two traditions that subsequent editors have followed—either founding editions on the two copies or projecting a finished version modeled on Pascal's apparent intentions. The first strategy presupposes acceptance of the manuscript as a work in progress that would necessarily remain unfinished; the second strategy presupposes the possibility of constructing a version of the text that is consistent with Pascal's intentions based on evidence internal to the manuscript, contemporary testimony, and, most important, the judgment of the editor. The latter strategy has been the guiding principle for most editions of the *Pensées* during the seventeenth, eighteenth, nineteenth, and early twentieth centuries, including those of Charles, abbé Bossut (1779), Prosper Faugère (1844), and Léon Brunschvicg (1904). This tendency has continued late in the twentieth century with the editions of Francis Kaplan (1982) and Emmanuel Martineau (1992). In comparing those editions, the reader is struck by the radical differences among those texts, differences that are the product of varied ordering and emphases. One of Pascal's fragments describing the writing of his apology is also applicable to the predicament of his editors. Defending the originality of his work, Pascal states in fragment 696 of the Lafuma edition, "Qu'on ne me dise que je n'ai rien dit de nouveau, la disposition des matières est nouvelle, . . . J'aimerais autant qu'on me dise que je me suis servi de mots anciens. Et comme les mêmes pensées ne formaient pas un autre corps de discours par une disposition différente, aussi bien que les mêmes mots forment d'autres pensées par leur différente disposition" (Let no one say that I have said nothing new, the order of the materials is new . . . I would just as well have someone say that I used ancient words. And the same thoughts constitute a different discourse by their order, just as the same words form different thoughts by their altered order). Kaplan is perhaps the most straightforward about the significance of these differences, arguing in his preface that *any* edition of the *Pensées* must also necessarily be a tendentious interpretation.

The second editorial tradition was launched by Louis Lafuma with his 1951 edition of the *Pensées* based on the first copy. More recently, Phillipe Sellier published an edition in 1976 based on the second copy. The content of the bundles is essentially the same in the two copies, but their order is slightly different. Sellier argues that the second copy is more authentic because the notebooks that constitute the first copy were erroneously reshuffled when that copy was made. Jean

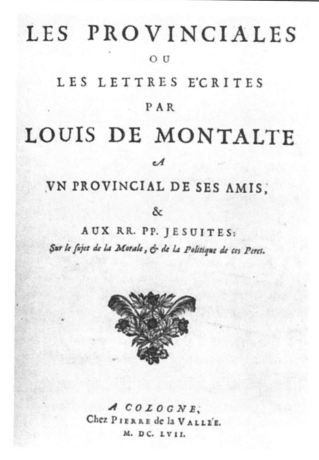

LES PROVINCIALES
ou
LES LETTRES ECRITES
PAR
LOUIS DE MONTALTE

VN PROVINCIAL DE SES AMIS,
&
AUX RR. PP. JESUITES:
Sur le sujet de la Morale, & de la Politique de ces Peres.

A COLOGNE,
Chez PIERRE de la VALLÉE.
M. DC. LVII.

Title page for the 1657 collection of eighteen letters that
Pascal wrote supporting the Jansenists' position in their
debate with the Jesuits (Edmonds Collection,
Boston University Libraries)

Mesnard's uncompleted edition of the *Pensées* promises to be a combination of the two copies. Both copies more accurately represent the status of the *Pensées* upon Pascal's death. They may both be divided into four principal sections. The first is made up of the twenty-eight classified bundles, which represent the most developed sequence of arguments for the apology. The second consists of the thirty-one unclassified bundles. Lafuma had thought that these were notes waiting to be integrated within the classified section of bundles, but scholars today believe that the classification in section 2 is as authentic as the classification in section 1. The third section groups fragments on miracles, and the final section groups fragments found in many different sources, including the original manuscript itself. These difficult editorial issues are compounded by the question of the mode of discourse that would have been adopted in the final version of the apology. The fragments themselves are predominantly discursive, but they also include examples of letters and dialogues.

One primary division in Pascal's argument is that obtaining between an anthropological prelude, an exam-

ination of the human condition, and the theological portion of the *Pensées*. Pascal's strategy seems to have involved the examination of the human condition and an assessment of its incomprehensibility in view of preparing the reader to accept the truth of the Christian religion, which alone can account for the human condition. This strategy seems appropriate for Pascal's projected readers, the worldly nonbelievers, many of whom he had encountered during the period preceding and following his second conversion. This first, anthropological movement of the *Pensées* analyzes the human condition through a critical assessment of philosophy, social conventions, existential schemes, and morality. Many of these fragments, which are to be found primarily in the first fourteen bundles of section 1 and in the earlier bundles of section 2, resonate with the contemporary writings of *moralistes* and account for the place that Pascal occupies in their ranks despite the religious tenor of his text. Those sets of fragments, moreover, defy any linear thematic development. Instead, they may be said to group and regroup the examination of the human condition into a series of binary oppositions that undermine each other's discursive authority. Perhaps the most clearly developed example of this problem is the philosophical opposition of dogmatism and Pyrrhonism in the examination of the human condition. At first glance, Pascal's fragments may be mistakenly interpreted as in the tradition of Michel Eyquem de Montaigne's skepticism, but this point is far from the final one in the development of Pascal's argument. Instead, the fragments that address dogmatism and Pyrrhonism can be grouped in such a way as to subvert the authority of both traditions. In Pascal's argument the confrontation of dogmatist confidence in progress and knowledge with Pyrrhonian skepticism launches an interminable debate in which the strengths of each camp consistently undermine the weaknesses of the other in such a way that no final conclusion can be reached. This argument is replicated in "L'Entretien avec M. de Saci" (The Conversation with M. de Saci), the summary of Pascal's conversation with his confessor in 1655 or 1656, which delineates the strategy that he planned to adopt in his apology.

The other themes developed throughout the anthropological portion of the *Pensées* proceed in a similar manner. Those fragments unfold a series of binary oppositions that advance by dialectical reversal of priorities. The themes include natural/positive law, nature/custom, ennui/desire, imagination/reason, and justice/force, to name only a few. The discursive development is difficult to trace for obvious reasons, but related fragments within the fabric of the *Pensées* progress by a constant reversal in the priority and privileged position accorded to the opposing terms. The reader is compelled to conclude that there is no other conclusion than the acceptance of a series of paradoxes. The argument may well be exemplified by bundle 7 of the first section, "Contrariétés," in which man's dignity and grandeur, represented by one of the two terms, is constantly undermined by his misery in such a way that the final image of man is one of a "monstre incompréhensible" (incomprehensible monster [Lafuma, fragment 130]). The argument unfolds, as Pascal himself says, by the "renversement continuel du pour au contre" (continuous reversal from pro to con [fragment 93]), in which there can be no final, decisive outcome, at least none in anthropology or the discourse of man on man. The human condition is a contradictory and incomprehensible condition that cannot be resolved, reconciled, or accounted for in philosophical or any other discourse.

At this point in the argument, there would be a transition to the theological part of the *Pensées*. After the anthropological prelude, Pascal argues that the only reconciliation of those contrarieties can be found in Christian revelation. Many of the fragments of the *Pensées* seem to dramatize this transition by moving the reader from a sense of absence and lack to the only solution to his predicament, through faith and seeking God. The most notable fragment of this kind is the famous fragment on the "pari," the wager on the existence of God (fragment 418). This fragment, written for the libertine gamesman, perhaps best exemplifies Pascal's attempts to move and convince the worldly reader. This fragment, which is drawn from Pascal's own research on probability theory, presents an argument for the infinite gain that the reader could make if he made the move to belief in the existence of God. This wager, in keeping with Augustinian doctrine, is one that offers no assurance of success. God in Jansenist doctrine is the *Deus absconditus,* the hidden God, who must be sought through faith but who showers his grace only upon the elect. The practice of faith is sustained by the principal law of Christianity in the Jansenist milieu, namely charity or love of the other. Fragment 372 summarizes this ethos. Drawing from contemporary models of political and religious authority, it describes Christendom as a body, an organic whole, in which each part, each individual, may maintain the illusion of autonomy but is really dependent on the totality. Charity is simply defined as this love of the other, of the totality of which one is a part.

Recently, scholars have identified a specific apologetic strategy within the disparate and digressive theological musings in the *Pensées*. Pierre Force's seminal study of the *Pensées, Le problème herméneutique chez Pascal* (The Hermeneutical Problem in Pascal), has determined the importance of the Bible and biblical hermeneutics within the second, theological part of the *Pensées*. Force has argued that the large number of fragments that include citations of and commentaries on the Bible reveal a conscious and consistent strategy of biblical interpretation—namely, reconciling contrarieties within the Scriptures, especially those that obtain between the Old and the New Testaments. Following in the wake of Augustinian hermeneutics, Pascal demonstrates the unity of the carnal and spiritual moments of the Bible through figural interpretation. Ultimately, the tension of those oppositions is summarized and condensed within the figure of Christ, who unites these opposites within himself, the man-God, and also reconciles the contrarieties of grandeur and misery developed in the anthropological part of the *Pensées*. This strategy heightens the persuasiveness of Pascal's text by mobilizing divine persuasion in the apologetical enterprise.

Much recent commentary on the *Pensées* has stressed the paradoxical nature of the text. The first study to exploit such an approach was Lucien Goldmann's *Le Dieu caché: Etude sur la vision tragique dans les Pensées de Pascal et dans le théâtre de Racine* (The Hidden God: A Study of Tragic Vision in the *Pensées* of Pascal and in the Plays of Racine). Goldmann underscores the irreconcilable nature of contradictions and contrarieties in the anthropological fragments of the *Pensées* and argues for the impossibility of their synthesis or reconciliation. An outstanding example of this point can be found in fragment 199, "Disproportion de l'homme," one of the most celebrated of the *Pensées*. This text represents the vertiginous place of man caught between two infinities and the incomprehensibility of a universe that flees, like the two infinities themselves, his efforts at understanding. Goldmann's work is also seminal in signaling the dialectical nature of tensions and contrarieties within the text. For Goldmann the theological resolution of the anthropological part of the *Pensées* is no resolution at all. The *Pensées* is merely the expression of the negative theology of the *Deus absconditus,* who may subtend and reconcile contrarieties within some form of totalization that is ultimately inaccessible to man.

Recent critical efforts take their starting point from, and often do not move far beyond, Goldmann's analysis of dialectical paradox in the thought of Pascal. Many of these recent efforts, however, turn from cognition and acts of understanding in Pascal's thought to the language of the text itself—that is, the language that would mediate an understanding, although a negative one. At this point, the focus of study again becomes rhetoric in Pascal's work. For example, Sara Melzer, in her *Discourses of the Fall,* gauges in Pascal's *Pensées* the incapacity of language to speak the truth. The *Pensées,* therefore, is always in the realm of the rhetorical rather than in the realm of truth. Louis Marin's study of the *Pensées* and Arnauld and Nicole's *Logique de Port-Royal,* titled *La Critique du discours* (The Critique of Discourse), examines in a more rig-

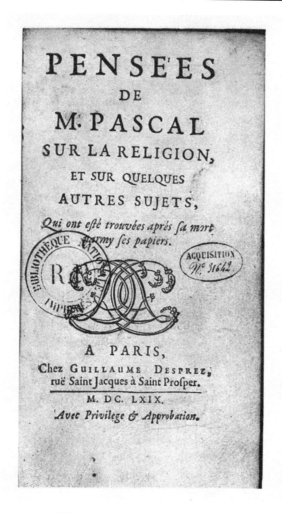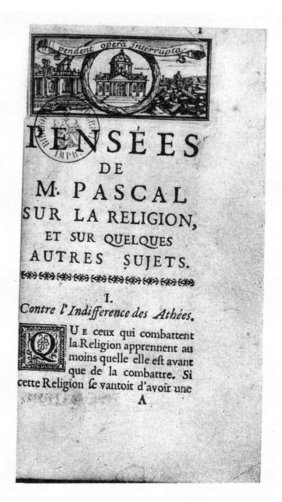

Title page and first text page from the posthumously published 1669 collection of writings Pascal had intended to shape into a defense of the Christian religion (Bibliothèque Nationale, Paris)

orous way the same problem through the theories of the sign and of discourse developed in those texts. Marin examines the many ways in which rhetoric in the *Pensées* undoes the theory of linguistic representation and its transparency. In neither case does the analysis of the *Pensées* move far from the negative lessons and negative theology of Lucien Goldmann: the transcendent truth is now not simply inaccessible to man but, through the play of rhetoric, is unrepresentable in language.

To analyze rhetoric in the *Pensées* in a slightly different way is more revealing. Rather than looking at the text as a series of explicit statements about rhetoric, as Marin and Melzer have done, the reader will profit from taking a closer look at the rhetoric of the fragments themselves. Two forms of rhetoric arise in Pascal's writings: the rhetoric of tropes and the performative rhetoric of persuasion. Upon closer exami-

nation, the *Pensées* may be read as the dramatization of the play of these two forms of rhetoric—a play that undermines the status of the text as unproblematic transmission of a message in any form, whether positive or negative. For example, Pascal does not account for tropological motions in the *Pensées*. Closer scrutiny of fragment 199 reveals that it includes not only a lesson on the two infinities but also a lesson on the rhetoric of tropes. This fragment states that the language of cognition, which is exemplified by scientific discourse, is always based on rhetoric, on tropological exchanges between mind and matter, beginning with the first proper concepts. Such substitutions, of which Pascal's own text could not be exempt, render unstable *any* determination of meaning, whether positive or negative.

The dramatization of this predicament in the *Pensées* does not stop with this problem. It can be argued that if language does not embrace the cognitive function, then it must be purely conventional and performative. The *Pensées* undoes this assumption as well. The bundle titled "Raisons des effets" is precisely about such conventions, which are thematic within such human institutions as law. The fragments build to a crescendo in the dialectical opposition of force and justice, which oppose performative language and cognitive language, as Paul de Man has ably demonstrated. The problem is that the performative language of force, ultimately determined to be at the origin of the cognitive language of justice, cannot dispense with the cognitive and referential functions, most evidently in stating that such is the nature of language. This analysis places an entirely different emphasis on the question of rhetoric in Pascal's work. Rhetoric would not simply be a linguistic tool mastered by Pascal. Instead, rhetoric becomes a problem that is presented, in exemplary fashion, by Pascal's texts, and one, arguably, to be confronted in any text and in any attempt to understand and interpret his texts. This lesson, perhaps, is the final and most lasting one of and about rhetoric in Pascal's work.

Since their consecration in the eighteenth century by Voltaire, Pascal's major writings, *Les Provinciales* and the *Pensées,* remain canonical texts of the French classical age. Pascal, more than any other writer of that period, has prompted response and reaction from a wide range of disciplines. He has engaged philosophers as divergent as Adam Smith, Friedrich Nietzsche, Jean-Paul Sartre, and Stanley Cavell. Blaise Pascal continues to be an important point of reference for theologians as well as mathematicians, and he still provokes debate among specialists of literature and literary theory.

Bibliographies:

Albert Maire, *Bibliographie générale des œuvres de Blaise Pascal,* 5 volumes (Paris: Giraud-Badin, 1925–1927);

Lane M. Heller and Thérèse Goyet, *Bibliographie Blaise Pascal: 1960–1969* (Clermont-Ferrand: Adosa, 1989).

Biographies:

Jean Mesnard, *Blaise Pascal: L'Homme et l'œuvre* (Paris: Boivin, 1951);

Francis X. J. Coleman, *Neither Angel nor Beast: The Life and Work of Blaise Pascal* (New York: Routledge & Kegan Paul, 1986);

Jean Anglade, *Pascal, l'insoumis* (Paris: Perrin, 1988);

John R. Cole, *Pascal: The Man and His Two Loves* (New York: New York University Press, 1995);

Jacques Attali, *Blaise Pascal, ou Le Génie français* (Paris: Fayard, 2000);

André Le Gall, *Pascal* (Paris: Flammarion, 2000).

References:

Hugh M. Davidson, *Pascal and the Arts of the Mind* (Cambridge: Cambridge University Press, 1993);

Paul De Man, "Pascal's Allegory of Persuasion," in *Allegory and Representation,* edited by Stephen J. Greenblatt (Baltimore: Johns Hopkins University Press, 1981);

Gérard Ferreyrolles, *Blaise Pascal, Les Provinciales* (Paris: Presses universitaires de France, 1984);

Pierre Force, *Le Problème herméneutique chez Pascal* (Paris: J. Vrin, 1989);

Lucien Goldmann, *Le Dieu caché: Etude sur la vision tragique dans les Pensées de Pascal et dans le théâtre de Racine* (Paris: Gallimard, 1959);

Henri Gouhier, *Blaise Pascal, commentaires* (Paris: J. Vrin, 1966);

Françoise Jaouën, *De l'art de plaire en petits morceaux: Pascal, La Rochefoucauld, La Bruyère* (Saint-Denis: Presses Universitaires de Vincennes, 1996);

Erec R. Koch, *Pascal and Rhetoric* (Charlottesville, Va.: Rookwood Press, 1997);

Louis A. MacKenzie, *Pascal's Lettres provinciales: The Motif and Practice of Fragmentation* (Birmingham, Ala.: Summa, 1988);

Louis Marin, *La Critique du discours: Sur la Logique de Port-Royal et les Pensées de Pascal* (Paris: Editions de Minuit, 1975);

Antony McKenna, *Entre Descartes et Gassendi: La Première Edition des Pensées de Pascal* (Paris: Universitas / Oxford: Voltaire Foundation, 1993);

Sara Melzer, *Discourses of the Fall: A Study of Pascal's Pensées* (Berkeley: University of California Press, 1987);

Jean Mesnard, *Les Pensées de Pascal* (Paris: Société d'édition d'enseignement supérieur, 1976);

Robert J. Nelson, *Pascal, Adversary and Advocate* (Cambridge, Mass.: Harvard University Press, 1981);

Richard Parish, *Pascal's Provincial Letters: A Study in Polemics* (Oxford: Oxford University Press, 1989);

Walter E. Rex, *Pascal's Provincial Letters: An Introduction* (London: Hodder & Stoughton, 1977);

Philippe Sellier, *Pascal et Saint Augustin* (Paris: A. Colin, 1970).

Papers:

Blaise Pascal's manuscripts are located at the Bibliothèque Nationale, Paris.

Charles Perrault

(12 January 1628 – 15 May 1703)

Jeanne Morgan Zarucchi

University of Missouri–St. Louis

BOOKS: *Les Murs de Troye ou l'origine du burlesque,* by Charles and Claude Perrault (Paris: L. Chamhoudry, 1654);

Dialogue de l'Amour et de l'Amitié (Paris: E. Loyson, 1660);

Ode sur la paix des Pyrénées (Paris: C. de Sercy, 1660);

Ode sur le mariage du Roy (Paris: C. de Sercy, 1660);

Le Miroir, ou La métamorphose d'Orante (Paris: C. de Sercy et C. Barbin, 1661);

La Peinture (Paris: F. Léonard, 1668);

Courses de testes et de bague faites par le Roy et par les princes et seigneurs de sa cour, en l'année 1662 (Paris: Imprimerie Royale, 1670);

Critique de l'Opéra, ou Examen de la tragédie intitulée Alceste, ou Le Triomphe d'Alcide (Paris: C. Barbin, 1674);

Recueil de divers ouvrages en prose et en vers (Paris: J.-B. Coignard, 1675);

Banquet des dieux pour la naissance de Monseigneur le duc de Bourgogne (Paris: J.-B. Coignard, 1682);

Saint Paulin, évêque de Nôle, avec une épître chrétienne sur la pénitence et une ode aux Nouveaux convertis (Paris: J.-B. Coignard, 1686);

Le Siècle de Louis le Grand (Paris: J.-B. Coignard, 1687);

Parallèle des anciens et des modernes, en ce qui regarde les arts et les sciences, 4 volumes (Paris: J.-B. Coignard, 1688–1697);

Le Cabinet des Beaux-Arts (Paris: G. Edelinck, 1690);

La Chasse (Paris: J.-B. Coignard, 1692);

L'Apologie des femmes (Paris: J.-B. Coignard, 1694);

Griselidis, nouvelle, avec le conte de Peau d'Ane et celui des Souhaits ridicules (Paris: J.-B. Coignard, 1694);

Le Triomphe de Sainte Geneviève (Paris: J.-B. Coignard, 1694);

Les Hommes illustres qui ont paru en France pendant ce siècle, avec leurs portraits au naturel, 2 volumes (Paris: A. Dezallier, 1696, 1700);

Adam, ou la création de l'homme, sa chute et sa réparation (Paris: J.-B. Coignard, 1697);

Histoires, ou Contes du temps passé, avec des moralitez (Paris: C. Barbin, 1697); translated by Robert Samber as *Histories or Tales of Past Times* (London: J. Pote, 1729); revised as *Fairy Tales or Histories of Past*

Charles Perrault (portrait by Philippe Lallemand; Musée de Versailles)

Times, with Morals (Haverhill, Mass.: P. Edes, 1794);

Mémoires de ma vie (circa 1700), edited by Paul Bonnefon (Paris: Renouard, 1909; reprinted, with an introduction by Antoine Picon, Paris: Macula, 1993); translated and edited by Jeanne Morgan Zarucchi as *Charles Perrault: Memoirs of My Life* (Columbia: University of Missouri Press, 1989);

Pensées chrétiennes de Charles Perrault (1694–1702), edited by Jacques Barchilon and Catherine Velay-Vallantin, Biblio 17, no. 34 (Paris, Seattle & Tübingen: Papers on French Seventeenth Century Literature, 1987);

Devises pour les tapisseries du Roi (circa 1665), edited by Marc Fumaroli and Marianne Grivel (Paris: Herscher, 1988).

Editions and Collections: *Perrault's Tales of Mother Goose: The Dedication Manuscript of 1695 Reproduced in Collotype Facsimile,* 2 volumes, edited by Jacques Barchilon (New York: Pierpont Morgan Library, 1956);

Parallèle des anciens et des modernes en ce qui regarde les arts et les sciences, edited by Hans Robert Jauss and Max Imdahl (Munich: Eidos, 1964);

Contes, edited by Gilbert Rouger (Paris: Garnier, 1967);

Contes de Perrault: Fac-similé de l'édition originale de 1695–1697, introduction by Barchilon (Geneva: Slatkine, 1980);

Contes, suivi du Miroir ou La métamorphose d'Orante, de La peinture, poème, et du Labyrinthe de Versailles, edited by Jean-Pierre Collinet (Paris: Gallimard, 1981);

Contes, edited by Roger Zuber (Paris: Imprimerie Nationale, 1987);

Contes, edited by Marc Soriano (Paris: Flammarion, 1989);

"Critique de l'Opéra, ou Examen de la tragedie intitulée Alceste, ou Le Triomphe d'Alcide," in *Alceste, suivi de La Querelle d'Alceste, anciens et modernes avant 1680* (1674), by Philippe Quinault and others, edited by William Brooks, Buford Norman, and Jeanne Morgan Zarucchi (Geneva: Droz, 1994).

OTHER: "Le Portrait d'Iris" and "Portrait de la voix d'Iris," in *Divers portraits,* by Anne-Marie-Louise-Henriette d'Orléans, duchesse de Montpensier, edited by Jean Regnauld de Segrais (Caen: P. Huet, 1659);

Gabriele Faerno, *Traduction des Fables de Faërne,* translated by Perrault (Paris: J.-B. Coignard, 1699);

"Le Corbeau guéri par la Cigogne" (1674), in *Remarques critiques sur le dictionnaire de Bayle,* by Philippe-Louis Joly, volume 2 (Paris: H. Guérin, 1748), p. 632–633;

"'Discours sur l'Art des Devises': An Edition of a Previously Unidentified and Unpublished Text by Charles Perrault," edited by Laurence Grove, *Emblematica,* 7 (1993): 99–144.

Charles Perrault was the author of a fairy-tale collection that has become better known than virtually any other work of Western literature. His *Histoires, ou Contes du temps passé, avec des moralitez* (1697; translated as *Histories or Tales of Past Times,* 1729) includes "La Belle au bois dormant" (Sleeping Beauty in the Woods), "Cendrillon ou La Petite pantoufle de verre" (Cinder-

ella, or the Little Glass Slipper), "Le Maître chat ou le chat botté" (The Master Cat, or Puss in Boots), and "Le Petit chaperon rouge" (Little Red Riding Hood), tales that, in many translations and adaptations, have been part of European folk culture for more than three hundred years.

Perrault was also an influential figure at the court of King Louis XIV, playing a key role in politics as the closest adviser to Louis's finance minister, Jean-Baptiste Colbert. Perrault became a major figure in the Quarrel of the Ancients and Moderns, the cultural debate over whether classical or contemporary works should serve as literary models. His life exemplifies the interrelation of art and politics in seventeenth-century France.

Charles Perrault was born on 12 January 1628, the seventh child of Pierre Perrault, a member of the Paris Parlement, and Pâquette Leclerc Perrault. Following in the footsteps of his father and eldest brother, Jean, Charles received training as a lawyer, but he found a more attractive pursuit in the writing of poetry. In 1654 he moved in with another brother, Pierre, who had purchased a post as the principal tax collector of the city of Paris. Pierre was also a personal friend of Colbert, who in 1661 became the unofficial prime minister of Louis XIV.

Colbert and Louis XIV undertook the construction of a royal image that included patronage of the arts in order to secure political authority by controlling the representation of the king in a wide variety of media. In 1663 Colbert selected a "Little Academy" of artistic advisers, later formally recognized as the Academy of Inscriptions and Medals, which was charged with inventing the mottoes that were to celebrate Louis on public buildings, statues, and commemorative medals.

As one of the four founding members of the newly formed "Little Academy," Colbert appointed Perrault, who by that time had worked as a clerk for his brother Pierre for ten years. Perrault had also published several poems, including *Ode sur le mariage du Roy* (Ode on the King's Marriage, 1660) and *Ode sur la paix des Pyrénées* (Ode on the Treaty of the Pyrenees, 1660), which served as the justification for his appointment alongside three much more distinguished writers: Jean Chapelain and Amable de Bourzéis, both founding members of the Académie Française, and Jacques Cassagnes, the king's librarian. Perrault's appointment to the Little Academy at the age of thirty-five set the stage for the rest of his career. Based on his status as a loyal insider, he achieved positions of influence in the arts but then found that his legitimate accomplishments were undermined by critics who denounced him as a political shill.

Perrault also assumed a professional role as Colbert's administrative aide and played an influential part

*Frontispiece from the 1675 collection of Perrault's
prose and verse (Musée Condé, Chantilly)*

in the design of a new eastern facade for the Louvre. Perrault succeeded in promoting the work of another of his brothers, Claude, a medical doctor and amateur architect. In 1665 Claude's design was ultimately chosen over rival plans drawn by leading architects such as Gian Lorenzo Bernini and François Mansart. Factors leading to this choice included the fear of astronomical costs, for which other architects were infamous, and personal antagonism between Louis XIV and Bernini. In bestowing the commission upon Claude Perrault, Colbert favored a conservative design that cvokcd the glory of the Roman Empire, and he also kept control of the project by hiring a member of a family whose loyalty to him was unquestioned. Although Perrault's Colonnade of the Louvre received worldwide admiration as the architectural epitome of seventeenth-century French classicism and inspired many imitations, the episode increased resentment against the Perrault clan.

While continuing to serve as Colbert's administrative deputy, Charles Perrault published a quantity of circumstantial poetry, such as *La Peinture* (Painting, 1668), honoring the king's first painter, Charles Le Brun, and *Courses de testes et de bague* (Head and Ring Races, 1670), written to commemorate the 1662 celebrations staged by Louis for his mistress, Louise-Françoise de La Baume le Blanc, duchesse de La Vallière. In 1671, with Colbert's endorsement, Perrault was elected to the Académie Française, but only after several unsuccessful attempts at being nominated to fill vacancies. The following year he married nineteen-year-old Marie Guichon. The couple had three sons: Charles-Samuel, born in 1675; Charles, born in 1676; and Pierre, born in 1678. Marie died in October of that year, only months after Pierre's baptism.

Perrault soon cultivated an alliance with his fellow academician and poet Philippe Quinault, a longtime friend of the Perrault family, who was gaining a reputation as a librettist for the new musical genre known as opera, collaborating with composer Jean-Baptiste Lully on several works. After Quinault and Lully's opera *Alceste* (1674) was denounced by traditionalists, who rejected it for deviating from classical theater, Perrault wrote *Critique de l'Opéra* (1674), in which he praised the merits of *Alceste* over the tragedy of the same name by Euripides. Perrault's treatise was one of the first documents of the literary debate that was later to become known as the Quarrel of the Ancients and Moderns.

In 1682 Perrault suffered a grave setback in his professional life. Colbert wanted to promote the fortunes of one of his own sons, Jules-Armand, marquis d'Ormoy, and gave him many of the duties that Perrault had performed, thus forcing Perrault into retirement at the age of fifty-six. Colbert's death the following year deprived Perrault of the protection of his former mentor. He was immediately removed from the Little Academy by Colbert's jealous successor, François-Michel Le Tellier, marquis de Louvois. All that remained for Perrault was his membership in the Académie Française, which was a life appointment that could not be revoked.

After this date Perrault sought to affirm his poetic talent and deflect his critics by writing poetry incorporating exemplary moral values and expressing his genuine devotion to Christianity. In 1686 he published *Saint Paulin, évêque de Nôle* (St. Paulinus, Bishop of Nola), an epic poem based on the life of an early Christian martyr. The combination of epic poetry, at that time the most admired but most difficult literary genre, and a religious subject was not a success. Like *La Pucelle, ou la France délivrée* (1656), the epic poem about Joan of Arc, for which his friend Jean Chapelain had been much derided, *Saint Paulin* became a target of mockery by Perrault's enemies in the Académie Française, including the celebrated satirist Nicolas Boileau-Despréaux.

The pivotal event of Perrault's literary career occurred in 1687, when the Académie Française convened a session to recite works written in celebration of Louis XIV's recovery from a life-threatening operation.

Perrault's contribution was *Le Siècle de Louis le Grand* (The Age of Louis the Great), a poem that was consistent with his many previous works praising the king. In this case, however, Perrault introduced a new twist: he argued that because of Louis's enlightened rule, the present age was superior in every respect to ancient times. Perrault claimed that even modern French literature was superior to the works of antiquity, and that, after all, even Homer nods.

The Académie Française erupted in shouts of protest, led by Boileau, accusing Perrault of literary heresy. Although *Le Siècle de Louis le Grand* had been intended as an encomium of the king, it was received as an insult to the classical models that formed the basis of a humanist education and were thought to define the notion of the sublime. Perrault was charged with making an ill-considered jest that merely revealed his own ignorance.

In reaction to this outpouring of criticism, Perrault declared his poem to be a true reflection of his sentiments, and he embarked on the writing of a treatise to defend the cause of the "Moderns" against the partisans of the "Ancients." The first volume of *Parallèle des anciens et des modernes* (Parallel of the Ancients and Moderns) was written quickly and published in 1688; subsequent volumes were published in 1690, 1692, and 1697, and the complete work totaled more than twelve hundred pages. In it Perrault admires the progress of civilization since classical times, not only in the arts but also in areas such as geographic exploration, scientific discovery, and advances in medicine. Even moral values are superior in the modern age, he argues, because of the spiritual enlightenment of Christianity.

The format of *Parallèle des anciens et des modernes* is also a model of the art of persuasion. It is constructed as a series of conversations among three parties: a "President," a self-important bureaucrat and narrow-minded traditionalist who defends the Ancients (a lampoon of Perrault's opponents in the Académie Française); a "Chevalier" representing a well-born but ignorant follower of fashion; and an "Abbot," the voice of pragmatic reason, who offers relentless arguments in favor of the moderns.

Parallèle des anciens et des modernes represents a turning point in European intellectual history, shifting emphasis away from the long-standing equation of the sublime with classical antiquity and moving culture toward a new value system giving primacy to modernity and the "progress" of civilization. This debate, occurring in Europe's most influential royal court and among the academicians who effectively set the standards of judgment in their day, had a profound influence upon eighteenth-century philosophical and political views. The very notion of "enlightenment," which served the radical cause in both the American and

French Revolutions, is a direct outgrowth of the modernist position ardently defended by Perrault.

Around 1690 a vogue arose within aristocratic salons for imaginative tales that incorporated "the marvelous." The verse fables of Jean de La Fontaine, modeled upon the tales of Aesop, had enjoyed great success since their publication in 1668, and Perrault himself had commemorated statues depicting scenes from the fables in *Le Labyrinthe de Versailles* (The Labyrinth of Versailles), first published in his *Recueil de divers ouvrages en prose et en vers* (Collection of Various Works in Prose and Verse, 1675). The current novelty, however, was for tales created from the contemporary imagination, not those based upon existing classical models. Such tales eventually became known as *contes de fée* (fairy tales).

Perrault embraced the new genre of the fairy tale, which allowed him to combine his natural talent for light verse—which he claimed in his memoirs to be his greatest gift—with "modern" subjects that could reflect the progress of civilization since antiquity. His first effort in the genre was a poem originally titled "La Marquise de Salusses, ou la Patience de Griselidis" (The Marquise of Salusses, or the Patience of Griselidis) but later retitled "Griselidis," based on a tale by the fourteenth-century Italian writer Giovanni Boccaccio. It was read aloud to the Académie Française, not by Perrault but by his friend the Abbé de Lavau, on 25 August 1691 and published in a collection of poems presented to the academy that year. "Griselidis" was well received, according to the literary journal *Le Mercure Galant*. Perrault followed with two more verse tales in 1693: "Les Souhaits ridicules" (The Ridiculous Wishes), based on a classical tale but substituting modern French peasants for the foolish protagonists, and "Peau d'Ane" (Donkey-Skin). All three tales were collected in 1694 as *Griselidis, nouvelle, avec le conte de Peau d'Ane et celui des Souhaits ridicules.*

Perrault's verse tales incorporate elements of magic, including a fairy godmother, but their key story elements are didactic, demonstrating the importance of wisdom, virtue, and obedience. In a preface to the third edition of the 1694 collection, published in 1695, Perrault referred to the conflict between partisans of the Ancients and Moderns, criticizing the fables of the Ancients because "la plupart [des Fables] qui nous restent des Anciens n'ont été faites que pour plaire sans égard aux bonnes moeurs qu'ils négligeaient beaucoup" (most of [the Fables] left to us by the Ancients were created only to please, without regard for sound morals, which the Ancients greatly neglected); in contrast, Perrault writes that his modern forebears "ont toujours eu un très grand soin que leurs contes renfermassent une moralité louable et

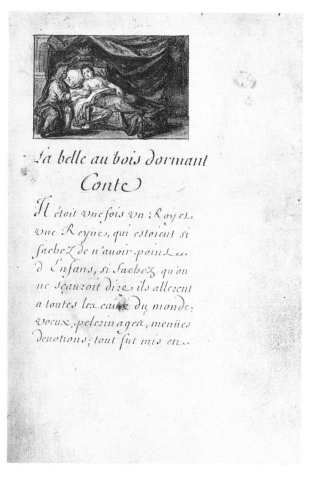

Opening page of "Sleeping Beauty," a story in "Contes de Ma Mère l'Oye," the manuscript Perrault presented to Elisabeth-Charlotte d'Orléans in 1695 (Pierpont Morgan Library, New York)

instructive" (always took great care that their tales should include a praiseworthy and instructive moral).

The public response to "Les Souhaits ridicules" and "Peau d'Ane" was much less favorable than that accorded to "Griselidis," and critics such as Boileau derided Perrault's treatment of such base subject matter, even though La Fontaine had used similar material with great success. In 1693 Boileau published an epigram that included the lines "Si du parfait ennuyeux / Tu veux trouver le modèle / Ne cherche point . . . / Un poëte comparable / A l'auteur inimitable / De Peau d'Ane mis en vers" (if you wish to find the model of perfect boredom, do not seek . . . a poet comparable to the inimitable author of Donkey-Skin put into verse). Perrault's response to these attacks was entirely in character. In order to prove that he was serious and to establish the legitimacy of the new genre, he wrote more tales, changing the format to prose text accompanied by a verse moral.

Five of Perrault's new prose tales were compiled as "Contes de Ma Mère l'Oye" (Tales of Mother Goose), a manuscript presented by the author to Louis XIV's niece Elisabeth-Charlotte d'Orléans in 1695. The designation of this distinguished recipient, who was then nineteen years old, reflects the seriousness with which Perrault viewed this work and his desire to assure its protection by obtaining a royal patron. It was officially signed by "P. Darmancour," purportedly a pseudonym for Perrault's seventeen-year-old third son, Pierre, but the work was nevertheless recognized as Perrault's own by his contemporaries.

The five tales in Perrault's presentation manuscript were "La Belle au bois dormant," "Le Petit chaperon rouge," "Le Maître chat ou le chat botté," "La Barbe bleue" (Bluebeard), and "Les Fées" (The Fairies), a version of which is better known in English as "Diamonds and Toads." "La Belle au bois dormant" was first published in 1696 in *Le Mercure Galant*. In 1697 a compilation of eight of Perrault's prose tales, *Histoires, ou Contes du temps passé, avec des moralitez,* was published, including the five from the 1695 presentation manuscript as well as three new ones: "Cendrillon ou La Petite pantoufle de verre," "Le Petit Poucet" (Little Thumbkin), and "Riquet à la houppe" (Ricky with the Tuft). The last of these is the only one that has not become well known in English. Although some of the stories share common elements with other documented folktales, the actual versions composed by Perrault are generally considered to be his original creations.

The full title of the 1697 volume reflects how Perrault distinguished his tales from the fables of antiquity: by the incorporation of moral observations. In the dedication "To Mademoiselle" (Elisabeth-Charlotte, then twenty-one years old) he states that the tales "Renferment tous une Morale très sensée, et qui se découvre plus au moins, selon le degré de pénétration de ceux qui les lisent" (all contain a very sensible Moral, which is more or less apparent according to the level of understanding of those who read them).

All eight tales are structured in a similar manner, with a story in prose followed by one or two morals in verse. The morals do not always follow directly from the story, as in "La Belle au bois dormant," in which the moral ignores the elements of the plot and instead chides contemporary young women for their impatience to be married. In the eighteenth and nineteenth centuries literary scholars used this apparent conflict of style and content to attribute authorship of the prose texts to someone other than Perrault, including his son Pierre. Critics after 1980, however, have argued that the morals are not intended to be obvious lessons derived from the tale but are sophisticated moral observations of contemporary society. Marc

Fumaroli has argued that the presumably naive quality of the prose is characteristic of a rhetorical "simple style." The format of juxtaposing a prose text and verse moral had also been used by Perrault two decades earlier, in *Le Labyrinthe de Versailles.*

The reception of Perrault's prose tales was muted in literary circles, but the collection gained immense popularity in the public sphere. Over the next century individual tales were reprinted in broadsides, translated into many languages, and retold orally, to the extent that when Jacob and Wilhelm Grimm compiled stories for their landmark *Kinder- und Hausmärchen* (1812–1815; translated as *German Popular Stories,* 1823–1826), versions of Perrault's tales were included as part of that German folk heritage.

The rise of children's literature as a distinct genre in the nineteenth century influenced a redefinition of Perrault's tales as intended for an audience of children. That was true of many edited versions, but the original identity of the collection was largely ignored, as was its history of having been addressed to a woman of the royal court and the members of the Académie Française. Even in France, most present-day readers of the "contes de Perrault" are unfamiliar with the original text, from which the verse morals and certain brutal elements of the stories are usually removed as too "adult." Only in the last two decades of the twentieth century did scholars begin to reassess Perrault's original work in the context of seventeenth-century moralist literature and cultural history.

Perrault's last significant prose work was *Les Hommes illustres qui ont paru en France pendant ce siècle* (Illustrious Men Who Have Appeared in France During This Century, 1696, 1700). This two-volume collection of brief biographical portraits unites political and military figures, theologians, writers, and artists, furthering Perrault's argument that the greatest century in the history of mankind had produced men of awe-inspiring achievement. Since all of the subjects were deceased, Perrault included his own brother Claude and left out his rival Boileau.

In the last years of his life Perrault worked on two manuscripts that were left incomplete at his death: "Mémoires de ma vie" (Memoirs of My Life), first published in 1909, and "Pensées chrétiennes" (Christian Thoughts), published in 1987. Both of these works reflect his lifelong struggle to be taken seriously as an intellectual, and the memoirs in particular are not so much a record of his life as they are a justification of his family's accomplishments. He defends the moral integrity of his brother Nicolas, a theologian allied with the Jansenist religious philosopher Blaise Pascal; he defends the honesty of his brother Pierre, who was stripped of his financial post by Colbert in the same

Opening page of "Puss in Boots," a story in Perrault's Histoires, ou Contes du temps passé, avec des moralitez *(1697), which includes the five stories in the 1695 manuscript he gave to Elisabeth-Charlotte d'Orléans (Bibliothèque Nationale, Paris)*

manner that Perrault lost his own position of favor; he defends the architectural genius of his brother Claude; and he defends his own talent as a poet and loyalty as a public servant. Perrault virtually ignores details of his personal life in the memoirs, and the reader is barely aware of the existence of his wife and children. Instead, the memoirs document the highs and lows of an extraordinary career, in which political patronage shaped and eventually overshadowed Perrault's artistic achievements.

Perrault's advocacy of the modernist cause did not prevail among his contemporary opponents, but it was a clear precursor of eighteenth-century philosophical views. Without the Quarrel of the Ancients and

Moderns, fueled by Perrault's arguments in defense of absolute monarchy, the fate of Europe in succeeding centuries would have been vastly altered.

Charles Perrault's greatest literary legacy, however, is unquestionably the fairy tales, which have entered so thoroughly into the fabric of Western culture that most people who know them by heart are unaware that they had an original author. Although they may not have proved the superiority of modern culture over the mores of classical antiquity, the overwhelming success of the fairy tales as literature, and the universality of their appeal to generations of readers, are reason enough to ensure Perrault a place among the world's most influential authors.

Bibliography:

Claire-Lise Malarte, *Perrault à travers la Critique depuis 1960: Bibliographie annotée,* Biblio 17, no. 47 (Paris, Seattle & Tübingen: Papers on French Seventeenth Century Literature, 1989).

Biographies:

André Hallays, *Les Perrault* (Paris: Perrin, 1926);

Marc Soriano, *Le Dossier Perrault* (Paris: Hachette, 1972).

References:

Jacques Barchilon, *Le Conte merveilleux français de 1690 à 1790: Cent ans de féerie et de poésie ignorées de l'histoire littéraire* (Paris: H. Champion, 1975);

Barchilon and Peter Flinders, *Charles Perrault* (Boston: Twayne, 1981);

Paul Bonnefon, "Charles Perrault, commis de Colbert, et l'administration des arts sous Louis XIV," Parts 1–3. *Gazette des Beaux-Arts* (September 1908): 198–214; (October 1908): 340–352; (November 1908): 426–433;

Bonnefon, "Charles Perrault: Essai sur sa vie et ses ouvrages," *Revue d'histoire littéraire de la France,* II (1904): 365–420;

Bonnefon, "Charles Perrault, littérateur et académicien," *Revue d'histoire littéraire de la France,* 12 (1905): 549–610;

Bonnefon, "Les dernières années de Charles Perrault," *Revue d'histoire littéraire de la France,* 13 (1906): 606–657;

Peter Burke, *The Fabrication of Louis XIV* (New Haven: Yale University Press, 1992);

Marc Fumaroli, "Les enchantements de l'éloquence: *Les Fées* de Perrault ou De la littérature," in *Le Statut de la littérature: Mélanges offerts à Paul Bénichou,* edited by Fumaroli (Geneva: Droz, 1982), pp. 153–186;

Jeanne Morgan, *Perrault's Morals for Moderns* (New York: Peter Lang, 1985);

Marc Soriano, *Les Contes de Perrault: Culture savante et traditions populaires* (Paris: Gallimard, 1968);

Mary Elizabeth Storer, *La Mode des contes de fées, 1685–1700* (Paris: H. Champion, 1928).

Papers:

The principal collection of manuscripts and first editions of the works of Charles Perrault is in the Bibliothèque Nationale, Paris.

Philippe Quinault

(June 1635 – 26 November 1688)

Buford Norman
University of South Carolina

BOOKS: *Les rivales* (Paris: G. de Luyne, 1655);

Les coups de l'Amour et de la Fortune (Paris: G. de Luyne, 1655);

La généreuse ingratitude (Paris: T. Quinet, 1656); translated by Sir William Lower as *The Noble Ingratitude* (The Hague: J. Ramzey, 1659);

L'amant indiscret, ou le Maître étourdi (Paris: T. Quinet, 1656); translated by Alexandra Kaminska as *Philippe Quinault's Comedy The Indiscreet Lover; or, The Master Blunderer* (Hicksville, N.Y.: Exposition Press, 1976);

Le fantôme amoureux (Paris: C. Barbin, 1657); translated by Lower as *The Amourous Fantasme* (The Hague: J. Ramzey, 1660);

La comédie sans comédie (Paris: G. de Luyne, 1657);

Amalasonte (Printed in Rouen and sold in Paris by A. Courbé, 1658);

Le feint Alcibiade (Paris: G. de Luyne, 1658);

Le mariage de Cambyse (Paris: A. Courbé et G. de Luyne, 1659);

La mort de Cyrus (Paris: A. Courbé et G. de Luyne, 1659);

Stratonice (Printed in Rouen and sold in Paris by G. de Luyne, 1660);

Agrippa, roy d'Albe, ou le faux Tibérinus (Paris: G. de Luyne, 1663); translated by John Dancer as *Agrippa, King of Alba, or The False Tiberinus* (London: N. Cox, 1675);

Astrate, roi de Tyr (Paris: G. de Luyne, 1665); translated by Lacy Lockert as *Astrate* in *More Plays by Rivals of Corneille and Racine*, edited by Lockert (Nashville: Vanderbilt University Press, 1968);

La mère coquette, ou les amants brouillés (Paris: T. Quinet, 1666);

La grotte de Versailles (Paris: R. Ballard, 1668);

Pausanias (Paris: G. de Luyne, 1669);

Bellérophon (Paris: G. de Luyne, 1671);

Psyché, by Quinault, Molière, and Pierre Corneille (Paris: R. Ballard, 1671);

Les fêtes de l'Amour et de Bacchus (Paris: F. Muguet, 1672);

Philippe Quinault (Musée Condé, Chantilly)

Cadmus et Hermione (Paris: C. Ballard, 1673);

Alceste (Paris: R. Baudry, 1674); translated by N. Hartmann in *Alceste*, music by Jean-Baptiste Lully, CBS Records, 79301, 1975;

Thésée (Paris: C. Ballard, 1675);

Discours au Roy, par M. Quinault, sous le nom de l'Académie (Lyon: J. Certe, 1675);

Atys (Paris: C. Ballard, 1676); translated by Derek Weld in *Atys*, music by Lully, Harmonia Mundi, 401257.59, 1987;

Isis (Paris: C. Ballard, 1677);

Proserpine (Paris: C. Ballard, 1680);

Le triomphe de l'Amour (Paris: C. Ballard, 1681);

Persée (Paris: C. Ballard, 1682);

Phaéton (Paris: C. Ballard, 1683); translated in *Phaéton*, music by Lully, Musifrance, 4509-91737-2, 1994;

Amadis (Paris: C. Ballard, 1684);

Roland (Paris: C. Ballard, 1685);

Le temple de la paix (Paris: C. Ballard, 1685);

Armide (Paris: C. Ballard, 1686); translated in *Armide*, music by Lully, Erato, STU 715302, 1984;

Œuvres choisies de Quinault, 2 volumes (Paris: P. et F. Didot, 1811, 1817)—comprises *La mère coquette, Alceste, Thésée, Atys, Proserpine, Persée, Amadis, Roland, Armide,* and "Sceaux, poème en deux chants";

Sceaux, poème par Philippe Quinault (Paris, 1813);

Cinq questions d'amour, proposées par Mme de Brégy, avec la réponse en vers par M. Quinault, par l'ordre du Roy (N.p., n.d.).

Editions and Collections: *Le Théâtre de Mr Quinault, contenant ses tragédies, comédies et opéra,* 5 volumes (Paris: P. Ribou, 1715); revised as *Le Théâtre de Monsieur Quinault, contenant ses tragédies, comédies et opéra,* 5 volumes (Paris: Compagnie des Libraires, 1739); revised as *Théâtre de Quinault, contenant ses tragédies, comédies et Opéra,* 5 volumes (Paris: Veuve Duchêne/Libraires Associés, 1778; reprinted, Geneva: Slatkine, 1970);

Chefs-d'œuvre lyriques de Quinault, 3 volumes (Paris: Au Bureau général des Chefs-d'œuvre dramatiques, 1791)—comprises *Isis, Proserpine, Le triomphe de l'Amour, Persée, Phaéton, Amadis, Roland, Le temple de la paix,* and *Armide;*

Œuvres choisies de Quinault, 2 volumes (Paris: Crapelet, 1824)—comprises *Astrate, La mère coquette, Alceste, Thésée, Atys, Isis, Proserpine, Persée, Phaéton, Amadis, Roland, Armide,* and "Sceaux";

Théâtre choisi, edited by Victor Fournel (Paris: Laplace, Sanchez, 1882)—comprises *Les rivales, La comédie sans comédie, Astrate, La mère coquette, Cadmus et Hermione, Alceste, Atys, Amadis, Roland,* and *Armide;*

La mère coquette, edited by Etienne Gros (Paris: H. Champion, 1926);

La comédie sans comédie, edited by Jean Dominique Biard (Exeter, U.K.: University of Exeter, 1974);

Astrate, edited by Edmund J. Campion (Exeter, U.K.: University of Exeter, 1980);

Amalasonte and *Astrate,* in *Théâtre du dix-septième siècle,* volume 2, edited by Jacques Scherer and Jacques Truchet, Bibliothèque de la Pléiade, no. 330 (Paris: Gallimard, 1986), pp. 967–1100;

Stratonice, edited by Elfrieda Teresa Dubois (Exeter, U.K.: University of Exeter, 1987);

Bellérophon, edited by William Brooks and Campion (Geneva: Droz, 1990);

Atys, edited by Stéphane Bassinet (Geneva: Droz, 1992);

Atys and *Armide,* in *Théâtre du dix-septième siècle,* volume 3, edited by Truchet and André Blanc, Bibliothèque de la Pléiade, no. 391 (Paris: Gallimard, 1992), pp. 3–94;

Alceste, suivi de la querelle d'Alceste: Anciens et Modernes avant 1680, edited by Brooks, Buford Norman, and Jeanne Morgan Zarucchi (Geneva: Droz, 1994);

Livrets d'opéra, 2 volumes, edited by Norman (Toulouse: Société de littératures classiques, 1999).

PLAY PRODUCTIONS: *Les rivales,* Paris, Hôtel de Bourgogne, 1653;

La généreuse ingratitude, Paris, Hôtel de Bourgogne, 1654;

L'amant indiscret, ou le Maître étourdi, Paris, Hôtel de Bourgogne, 1654;

La comédie sans comédie, Paris, Théâtre du Marais, April 1655;

Les coups de l'Amour et de la Fortune, Paris, Hôtel de Bourgogne, late August or early September 1655;

Le fantôme amoureux, Paris, Hôtel de Bourgogne, no later than early July 1656;

Amalasonte, Paris, Hôtel de Bourgogne, first half of November 1657;

Le feint Alcibiade, Paris, Hôtel de Bourgogne, no later than 1 March 1658;

Le mariage de Cambyse, Paris, Hôtel de Bourgogne, summer 1658;

La mort de Cyrus, Paris, Hôtel de Bourgogne, late December 1658 or early January 1659;

Stratonice, Paris, Hôtel de Bourgogne, 2 January 1660;

Lysis et Hespérie, Paris, Hôtel de Bourgogne, 26 November 1660;

Agrippa, roy d'Albe, ou le faux Tibérinus, Paris, Hôtel de Bourgogne, October or November 1662;

Astrate, roi de Tyr, Paris, Hôtel de Bourgogne, late December 1664 or early January 1665;

La mère coquette, ou les amants brouillés, Paris, Hôtel de Bourgogne, mid October 1665;

La grotte de Versailles, Versailles, château, April 1668; revised as *L'Eglogue de Versailles,* Versailles, gardens, 11 July 1674;

Pausanias, Paris, Hôtel de Bourgogne, 16 November 1668;

Bellérophon, Paris, Hôtel de Bourgogne, mid January 1671;

Psyché, by Quinault, Molière, and Pierre Corneille, tragedy-ballet, Paris, Palais des Tuileries, 17 January 1671;

Les fêtes de l'Amour et de Bacchus, Paris, jeu de paume de Bel-Air, 11 November 1672;

Cadmus et Hermione, opera, Paris, jeu de paume de Bel-Air, no later than 27 April 1673;

Alceste, opera, Paris, Palais-Royal, 11? January 1674;

Thésée, opera, Saint-Germain-en-Laye, château, 11 or 15 January 1675;

Atys, opera, Saint-Germain-en-Laye, château, 10 January 1676;

Isis, opera, Saint-Germain-en-Laye, château, 5 January 1677;

Proserpine, opera, Saint-Germain-en-Laye, château, 3 February 1680;

Le triomphe de l'Amour, ballet, Saint-Germain-en-Laye, château, 21 January 1681;

Persée, opera, Paris, Palais-Royal, 17 or 18 April 1682;

Phaéton, opera, Versailles, Riding School, 6 or 8 January 1683;

Amadis, opera, Paris, Palais-Royal, 16? January 1684;

Roland, opera, Versailles, Riding School, 8 January 1685;

Le temple de la paix, ballet, Fontainebleau, château, 20 October 1685;

Armide, opera, Paris, Palais-Royal, 15 February 1686.

OTHER: Tristan L'Hermite, *Osman,* dedication by Quinault (Paris: G. de Luyne, 1656);

Recueil des plus beaux vers, suite de la seconde partie (Paris: R. Ballard, 1668)—includes twenty airs by Quinault;

Nouveau recueil des plus beaux airs de cour (Paris: R. Ballard, 1669)—includes sixteen airs by Quinault;

"Grand Roy, vos ennemis ne trouvent point d'asiles," in *A la gloire de Louis le Grand, conquérant de la Hollande, par MM. Corneille, Montauban, Quinault et autres,* by Quinault, Pierre Corneille, and others (Paris: O. de Varennes et P. Bienfaict, 1672), p. 7;

"Relation nouvelle du Parnasse, à M. Perrault," in *Deux poèmes à la loüange du Roy avec la traduction en vers latins,* by Quinault and Charles Perrault (Paris: J. Chardon, 1674), pp. 6–21;

"Tableau de la Chute de l'Hérésie," in *Bibliographie des recueils collectifs de poésies publiés de 1597 à 1700,* edited by Frédéric Lachèvre, volume 3 (Paris: H. Leclerc, 1904; reprinted, Geneva: Slatkine, 1967), pp. 490–494;

Protée (Paris: Collège de Pataphysique, 1958)—comprises excerpts from *Phaéton.*

Philippe Quinault was one of the most versatile and most successful writers in seventeenth-century France. By the time he was thirty-six, in 1671, he had had eighteen of his plays performed and was about to begin a "second career" as librettist for Jean-Baptiste Lully's operas, a position that brought him the reputation throughout the ancien régime as one of France's greatest lyric poets. Quinault was also well known for his contributions to ballets and other court spectacles; for songs, witty light verse, and elegant occasional verse; and for his talents as an orator.

Title page for the 1662 edition of Quinault's 1655 play, which includes plays-within-plays illustrating the dramatic genres of pastoral, comedy, tragedy, and tragicomedy (British Library, London)

Indeed, Quinault was probably the most frequently performed and the best remunerated playwright of the seventeenth century. *Astrate, roi de Tyr* (Astrate, King of Tyre, 1665) was staged at least 40 times in 1664–1665, a record rarely matched even by Jean Racine, and *Thésée* (Theseus, 1675) could have had as many as 150 performances since it ran for a year in 1675–1676. Quinault received 3,000 livres from Lully for each libretto and a royal pension of 3,000 or 4,000 livres per year, which rose to 12,000 per year by the end of his life. In comparison, Racine generally had a pension of 1,500–2,000 livres and rarely received more than 1,500 livres for the publication of a play. Quinault's reputation slipped considerably near the end of the eighteenth century, but the success of revivals of several Lully-Quinault operas since 1986 has renewed interest in his works and career and led to the rediscovery of a great deal of information.

Philippe Quinault was baptized in Paris on 5 June 1635, probably no more than two or three days after his birth. His father, Thomas, was a master baker, but some of his relatives, such as young Philippe's godparents, held important administrative posts. The family of his mother, Prime Riquier, was from the province of La Marche (now the department of the Creuse).

The details of Quinault's early years are unclear. Contemporary sources agree that he entered the service of the poet and playwright Tristan L'Hermite (who also had roots in the Marche region) as a valet around 1643; Quinault, however, referred to himself only as the student (*élève*) of Tristan. Whatever their exact relationship might have been, it was clearly a close one, and Quinault benefited from Tristan's experience and connections. When Tristan's play *Osman* (written in 1647) was published posthumously in 1656, Quinault wrote the dedication for it.

Later in his life Quinault's enemies accused him of having had no other education than what he picked up while in the service of Tristan, but a document discovered by Jérôme de La Gorce certifies that from 1646 to 1651 Quinault was a boarder with Philippe Mareschal, a *maître écrivain* (master writer) who ran a school in Paris. During this time Quinault learned enough Latin to be qualified to enter the Collège du Cardinal Lemoyne. (This document was drawn up at Quinault's request in 1671, but his presence at the baptism of Mareschal's son in 1656 confirms their earlier relationship.) It seems most likely, then, that he was in the service of Tristan from about 1643 to 1646 and that he continued his relationship with his mentor while he received a more formal education.

In the early 1650s Quinault began to learn two professions, that of attorney and that of poet and playwright. According to Charles Perrault in his *Les Hommes illustres qui ont paru en France pendant ce siècle* (Illustrious Men Who Have Appeared in France During This Century, 1696, 1700), Quinault began working with an *avocat au conseil* (attorney) when he was fifteen years old, by which time he was already writing some "very agreeable" comedies. His first play to be performed (1653) and published (1655), the comedy *Les rivales* (The Rivals), met with great success. According to an anecdote in Claude and François Parfaict's *Histoire du théâtre françois* (1734–1749), *Les rivales* was the first play for which the author was paid a percentage of the box-office revenues rather than a fixed fee. According to this

charming but unauthenticated story, the actors of the Hôtel de Bourgogne were willing to buy the new play when Tristan presented it as his own but balked when they found out that it was the work of a newcomer. As a compromise, they agreed to pay Quinault a ninth of ticket revenues during the first run.

Two more of Quinault's plays were performed the following year, 1654, and published in 1656: *La généreuse ingratitude* (translated as *The Noble Ingratitude*, 1659), a pastoral tragicomedy, and another comedy, *L'amant indiscret, ou le Maître étourdi* (translated as *The Indiscreet Lover; or, The Master Blunderer*, 1976). By this time he was not only popular with the Parisian public but also a successful attorney. In *Les Hommes illustres* Perrault tells how Quinault surprised a client while they were waiting for an appointment with a *rapporteur* (judge) by taking him to the theater, where the audience was as receptive to *L'amant indiscret* as the judge was to Quinault's presentation of his client's case a few hours later.

Quinault wrote seven more plays for the Parisian stage during the next four years, beginning with the remarkable *Comédie sans comédie*, first performed in 1655 and published in 1657. After an opening act that, in the original production, featured well-known actors playing under their own names, four plays-within-plays illustrate popular dramatic genres: pastoral, comedy, tragedy, and tragicomedy. The last, which took advantage of the Marais theater's popular machines in the original production, presents an episode from Torquato Tasso's *Gerusalemme liberata* (1581; translated as *Jerusalem Delivered*, 1600) featuring Renaud and Armide, who were to be the hero and heroine of Quinault's last libretto, *Armide* (1686).

Quinault's next five plays were tragicomedies, an extremely popular genre that featured romantic intrigues, sometimes involving historical characters, that ended happily after considerable complications and unexpected twists of plot. Quinault frequented fashionable and précieux salons, such as those of Madeleine de Scudéry; Gilles Ménage; Henriette de Coligny, comtesse de la Suze; and Antoinette Du Ligier de La Garde, Madame Deshoulières. Barely into his twenties, Quinault enjoyed a considerable reputation for well-crafted plays and for the elegant expression of tender sentiments, the *tendresse* that became his trademark.

The ambitious young Quinault was not content with his success in the world of the arts. A *gentilhomme* (gentleman) in the service of the powerful duc de Guise since 1656, he was also courting other powerful patrons. He attracted the attention of Cardinal Mazarin, to whom he dedicated *Amalasonte* (produced, 1657; published, 1658), and of Queen Christina of Sweden. Louis XIV was so pleased with *Amalasonte* that he gave its author a generous gift, an incident detailed in Jean Loret's gazette *La Muse historique* (17 November 1657). In 1658 the powerful minister and patron Nicolas Fouquet expressed his approval of *Le feint Alcibiade* (The False Alcibiades), and Quinault dedicated the published version to him later that year.

Perhaps because of his desire to be more than a successful playwright, the rate of Quinault's production began to decline after 1658; he wrote only six more spoken plays in the next twelve years, whereas he had written ten in the first six years of his career. He also began to move away from tragicomedy toward tragedy, a move that paralleled the taste of his public. Quinault's first tragedy, *La mort de Cyrus* (The Death of Cyrus, produced, 1658; published, 1659), was not a success, and he returned—quite successfully—to tragicomedy with *Stratonice* (1660) and *Agrippa, roy d'Albe, ou le faux Tibérinus* (Agrippa, King of Alba, or The False Tiberinus, produced, 1662; published, 1663). These plays, however, had historical subjects and were considerably more serious than the lighthearted tragicomedies of Quinault's first years, such as *Les coups de l'Amour et de la Fortune* (The Blows of Love and Fortune, 1655). But more had changed by 1662 than the subject of his plays; by then he was married with children, had new titles, was on familiar terms with Louis XIV, and, most important for his later career, had begun to participate in the creation of spectacles for the court.

On 29 April 1660 Quinault married Louise Goujon, a rich young widow. According to Boscheron in his manuscript biography, Quinault described his courtship in a novella, "L'amour sans faiblesse," which has since disappeared. He continued to improve his social status. Described as an attorney ("avocat en la cour de Parlement") in the marriage contract, by the baptism of his first daughter, Marie-Louise, on 23 March 1661 Quinault claimed a position at court: "escuyer, valet de chambre du Roy" (esquire, servant of the king).

Several early biographers wrote that Quinault abandoned the theater after his marriage, but they were working with incorrect dates for his later plays and thought his wedding took place in 1668. One of the first things he did after his marriage was to write, at the request of Mazarin and in collaboration with the minister Hugues de Lionne, an allegorical pastoral, "Lysis et Hespérie," to celebrate the Spanish alliance and the marriage of Louis XIV to Marie-Thérèse of Austria. The work was performed at the Hôtel de Bourgogne on 26 November 1660 and at the Louvre on 9 December of that year, but it was never printed, and the manuscript disappeared in the eighteenth century.

Certainly, "Lysis et Hespérie," which employed stage machinery and perhaps musical interludes, if not sung passages, was what Quinault was referring to

BELLEROPHON

TRAGÆDIE:

A PARIS,

Chez GUILLAUME DE LUYNE, Libraire Juré, au Palais en la Salle des Merciers, sous la montée de la Cour des Aydes, à la Justice.

M. DC. LXXI.

Avec Privilege du Roy.

Title page for Quinault's last work for the spoken theater (from the 1990 facsimile edition)

when he wrote to the king in 1684 that he had been working for twenty-four years "pour les Divertissements de Votre Majesté" (for Your Majesty's *Divertissements*). From 1660 until 1672, the beginning of his regular collaboration with Lully as librettist, Quinault divided his time between writing spoken plays and a variety of texts to be set to music as songs or as part of court spectacles. His next play and his last tragicomedy, *Agrippa, roy d'Albe, ou le faux Tibérinus,* confirmed his success with the theatergoing public and with the court. One of his greatest successes and the most frequently revived—along with *Astrate, roi de Tyr* and *La mère coquette, ou les amants brouillés* (The Flirtatious Mother, or the Quarreling Lovers, produced, 1665; published, 1666)— of his spoken plays, *Agrippa, roy d'Albe, ou le faux Tibérinus* had a longer run than another play of 1662, Claude Boyer's *Oropaste ou le faux Tonaxare* (Oropaste, or the False Tonaxare), which had a similar but more historically accurate subject. A sure sign of Quinault's success at court is the dedication to Louis XIV in the 1663 published version of *Agrippa, ou le faux Tibérinus,* in which Quinault mentions not only that the king was fond of the play but also that he had helped Quinault with the plot. The playwright's success in literary society was no less great. Around 1662 the king asked Quinault to respond to the "questions d'amour" posed by Charlotte Saumaise de Chazan, comtesse de Brégy, which required cleverly worded poetic answers to questions such as whether the presence of one's beloved causes more joy than signs of his or her indifference cause pain. It was a parlor game, but one that involved situations that Quinault also depicted on the stage.

Quinault's next two plays were the greatest successes of this first stage of his career, before he devoted himself exclusively to the musical theater. *Astrate, roi de Tyr* opened in late 1664 or early 1665 and ran for at least three months, about forty performances, an extremely long run for a new play at that time. It presents the story of a young man who is about to marry a queen when he discovers that he is the son of the legitimate ruler she had had put to death when she came to power. Featuring tender love scenes and debates about whether one should follow nature or love, *Astrate, roi de Tyr* brought in so many spectators that the Hôtel de Bourgogne doubled ticket prices.

Quinault had had jealous enemies since his early successes in 1654, but in the mid 1660s he became the butt of satires by a writer who managed to impose his own view of seventeenth-century French literature on most of nineteenth- and twentieth-century literary history, Nicolas Boileau-Despréaux. Until the modern revival of interest in Quinault following the success of performances of Lully-Quinault operas, he was known to most readers only as the writer whose name offered itself as the perfect rhyme in opposition to "sans défaut" (without fault) in Boileau's second *Satire* (written, 1663 or 1664; published, 1666) and as a favorite author of the ridiculous country gentleman who, in the third *Satire* (written, December 1665; published, 1666), dared prefer *Astrate, roi de Tyr* to Racine's *Alexandre le Grand* (1666). In this manner the seventeenth-century aesthetic known as *galante* (light, refined, in tune with the taste of the time), which recent research has shown to be the dominant aesthetic of the 1660s and 1670s, came into conflict with what is traditionally called the classical aesthetic, represented chiefly by Boileau and Racine. No one can doubt the genius of these latter two, but theirs was a minority view that was never adopted by the larger public, who, like the dramatists Edme Boursault and Jacques Pradon, appreciated Quinault's *tendresse* as they did the lyricism of "le tendre Racine."

The increasingly popular Quinault was sometimes at odds with other writers. In 1665 his comedy *La mère coquette, ou les amants brouillés* ran at the Hôtel de Bourgogne while Molière's troupe was playing Jean Donneau de Visé's comedy of the same name. Charles Robinet's gazette describes a "war between two authors" and suggests that Donneau de Visé's accusations that Quinault "stole" his topic are justified. Nonetheless, Quinault's play enjoyed great success up through the nineteenth century. This was not the first time Quinault had been accused of using the ideas of others; for his first play, *Les rivales,* he borrowed heavily from Jean Rotrou's *Les deux pucelles* (The Two Virgins, 1636). François Le Métel de Boisrobert accused Quinault of having taken the subject of *Les coups de l'Amour et de la Fortune* from his play of a similar name, although both were based on a play by Pedro Calderón.

At the same time that Quinault was writing his most successful spoken plays, he was becoming more involved with the ballets and other spectacles involving poetry, music, and dance that were so popular with Louis XIV's court. In groundbreaking research Frédéric Lachèvre and, more recently, Anne-Madeleine Goulet attribute approximately sixty airs to Quinault in various collections published between 1660 and 1674. (These attributions do not include songs Quinault included in *La généreuse ingratitude* and *La comédie sans comédie.*) Many of these were *airs de cour* and not associated with a particular stage work—it is difficult to determine Quinault's role in many of the ballets performed during the 1660s—but he definitely played a role in the elaboration of the various versions of *Ballet des Muses* in 1666 and 1667. Robinet writes of two "comedies" by Quinault that were part of the excerpts from the ballet performed at the Hôtel de Bourgogne in June 1667, by which he may mean entrées (sections) of the ballet, perhaps "Les Poètes" and the Greek and Roman orators, or adaptations of them. Quinault also contributed text for other parts of the ballet, and it is possible that "Les Madrigaux," which is listed among Quinault's works in Boscheron's 1715 biography, was part of this ballet.

In 1668 Quinault was involved in spoken theater as well as court festivities. He contributed two airs to the masquerade *Le carnaval* in January 1668, but his role in the overall elaboration of the work was probably small. (He was more involved in the 1675 revision, but, again, it is not clear to what extent.) Quinault wrote the libretto for *La grotte de Versailles,* which was performed at Versailles in April 1668 and was revived in 1674 as *L'Eglogue de Versailles* and again in 1685, with Racine's *Idylle sur la paix.* The music for all these works was by Lully.

Quinault's tragedy *Pausanias* (published, 1669) opened in November 1668 and had a fairly short run,

Illustration from the 1708 edition of Quinault and Jean-Baptiste Lully's 1674 opera Alceste
(Bibliothèque Nationale, Paris)

though he had certainly been hoping to emulate the success of Racine's *Andromaque,* which had premiered in November of the previous year. Quinault had more success with his next work, *Bellérophon* (1671), a play with a subject similar to that of Racine's *Phèdre* (1677). It was Quinault's last work for the spoken theater, marking the end of a remarkably successful stage in a career that had brought him election to the Académie Française a few months earlier in 1670. He was praised during the reception ceremony for his ability to touch hearts and evoke passion, a skill he used from then on for words set to Lully's music.

Collaboration between Lully and Quinault was not new, and Lully certainly would not have chosen Quinault as his principal librettist if the latter had not had considerable experience. Their work together is documented as early as the 1666 version of *Ballet des Muses* but certainly goes back farther, and Quinault stated in 1681, in a letter reproduced by Emile Campardon in 1884, that he had known Lully well for twenty years. There is no indication in contemporary sources that the choice of Quinault by Lully and Molière to contribute the sung verses for the 1671 *Psyché* (except for the Italian lament) was in any way surprising. (Lully

wrote another opera of the same title in 1678, with a libretto by Thomas Corneille.) Furthermore, when in 1672 Lully purchased his privilege to operate the Académie Royale de Musique and set out to create the first French opera, it is inconceivable that he would have decided to devote almost all of his considerable talent and energy to a yet unproven form if he had not been sure of the collaboration of a competent librettist. From a seventeenth-century point of view, there was no doubt that the *livret* (libretto) was the key element in the success of an opera, and Lully must have consulted Quinault frequently before launching this complex and costly new venture. Quinault was now in an even higher position at court, having obtained the important—and expensive—rank of auditor in the Chambre des Comptes on 18 September 1671, despite the resistance of some members of the group, who did not like the idea of having a playwright of humble origins in their august company.

From a somewhat simplistic teleological perspective, French opera, first called *tragédie en musique* and now better known as *tragédie lyrique,* is the culmination of efforts—including court ballet, pastoral, machine plays, and comedy-ballet—to create a type of theater that was to include music and dance as well as dialogue. The first production of the new Académie Royale de Musique was *Les fêtes de l'Amour et de Bacchus* (The Festivals of Cupid and Bacchus, 1672), patched together by Quinault from earlier works by Lully and Molière, such as *Le bourgeois gentilhomme* (1670; translated as *The Would-Be Gentleman*, 1926), *Les amants magnifiques* (The Magnificent Lovers, 1670), *George Dandin* (1669), and *La pastorale comique* (1667), to the last of which Quinault himself had perhaps contributed. When it came to creating his first true opera with Lully the following year, *Cadmus et Hermione* (1673), Quinault came up with something quite different, a tragedy (with a happy ending, as was often the case at the time) conceived to be sung from beginning to end and to incorporate dance, spectacle, and the supernatural. After an allegorical prologue in praise of the king, the five-act drama presented a mythological hero who must overcome considerable obstacles, human and divine, to win his beloved. The text was in rhyming lines of various lengths, sung mostly to recitative, a type of vocal music that closely followed the rhythms and intonations of French as it was spoken and, in particular, declaimed at the time. There were more-lyrical passages for moments of intense emotion, including monologues, and each act included a *divertissement,* featuring choruses and catchy dance tunes.

Cadmus et Hermione was met with considerable acclaim and by a *cabale* that included not only those who did not like the new art form or were jealous of Quinault and Lully's success but also the many writers, composers, and performers who were excluded by Lully's near monopoly on theatrical performances involving music. An important literary quarrel, in many ways the beginning of the Quarrel of the Ancients and Moderns, followed the next Lully-Quinault opera, *Alceste* (1674), based loosely on Euripides' tragedy *Alcestis* (438 B.C.) and seen as a direct rival to spoken tragedy. Perrault defended the libretto in his *Critique de l'Opéra, ou Examen de la tragédie intitulée Alceste* (Critique of the Opera, or Examination of the Tragedy Titled *Alceste,* 1674), while Racine took up the cause of the Ancients in the preface to his *Iphigénie* (produced, 1674; published, 1675).

Alceste was a success, running from January 1674 until a revival of *Cadmus et Hermione* in October, but it was not clear in the beginning that the *cabale* would not prevail, and Quinault's lucrative position as Lully's librettist was temporarily in jeopardy. His rivals included not only little-known authors such as Henry Guichard, who had collaborated with Pierre Perrin in establishing the first Académie de Musique (1669), but also Jean de La Fontaine, Racine, and Boileau. La Fontaine wrote a libretto, "Daphné," in mid 1674, but Lully rejected it.

Although some critics place Racine and Boileau's collaboration on *La Chute de Phaéton,* which they never completed, near the end of Quinault's temporary disgrace in 1677–1679, there is also considerable evidence that it took place in 1674.

Quinault prevailed, however, and his next libretto, *Thésée,* was so successful that it ran for almost a year in 1675–1676. He took some of the earlier criticism to heart, especially that directed at the comic secondary characters, but he did not change the basic format of the new *tragédie en musique. Atys* (1676), however, marks at the same time a culmination and a new direction. It is both literally and figuratively more human: the goddess Cybèle behaves much like a mortal, and Atys is more of a confused young lover than a heroic demigod. *Atys* is the most Racinian of Quinault's librettos, as if he had reached the goal of emulating spoken tragedy, but he tried a new direction with *Isis* in 1677, moving away from tightly knit tragic plots and unity of action.

Isis was not received well at court, and Lully made some changes before it opened at the Académie Royale in August 1677. The timing was unfortunate for Quinault because Françoise-Athénaïs de Rochechouart, marquise de Montespan, who had made a triumphant return to favor in mid 1676 after Louis XIV's infatuation with Marie-Elisabeth de Ludres, discovered in June 1677 that her rival had regained the king's favor. She wreaked terrible vengeance on Ludres, and courtiers immediately interpreted the persecution of Io by the excessively jealous Juno in *Isis* as an unflattering portrait of the royal mistress, who had Quinault removed as librettist for the next two years. His replacement, Thomas Corneille, found his task difficult and even had to call on Quinault for help with his *Bellérophon* in 1679. Corneille was not eager to continue, and by later that year Quinault was officially working on a new opera, *Proserpine* (1680).

Proserpine was fairly dark, featuring rivalry among the gods and the refusal of the patriarchy to acknowledge the desires and rights of women. The next year, 1681, was the only year during Quinault's collaboration with Lully in which the composer did not write a new *tragédie en musique.* Instead, he and Quinault helped to celebrate the arrival of the new dauphine at court with a lavish ballet, *Le triomphe de l'Amour* (The Triumph of Love), in many ways the last in a series of court ballets going back to 1581. It was a huge success, and the Paris public was eager to see it, so Lully brought it to the Académie Royale, using, for the first time, professional danseuses to take the parts danced by young nobles in court performances. The rivalry and ungallant behavior found in *Proserpine* return, however, in the next two operas, *Persée* (Perseus, 1682) and *Phaéton* (1683), as if Quinault had already sensed that the glory years of the reign of Louis XIV were coming to an end.

Quinault's next libretto, *Amadis* (1684), is indeed an indication of change, both in its subject matter and in the reaction to it. As in Quinault's next—and last—two librettos, the subject came from chivalric romance rather than from classical mythology. *Amadis* is similar to earlier librettos in that it features a hero who must overcome supernatural obstacles to win his beloved; yet, this type of plot must have struck audiences as more and more nostalgic. In the January 1684 *Mercure galant* Deshoulières published a ballade, to which several writers responded, complaining of the brutal lovers of her day, both in real life and in Racine's tragedies. The exchange highlights conflicts among coexisting traditions, conflicts that often involved the increasing role of women in society and the arts.

Quinault's last two librettos, *Roland* (1685) and *Armide* (1686), feature another conflict, that between love and duty. In both works love causes the hero temporarily to abandon his duty, but he returns to it at the end. One senses a reflection of the changing mood at court, as the sobering influence of Françoise d'Aubigné, marquise de Maintenon, was felt on the aging king in a time of increasing economic and political problems, and this changing mood is perhaps reflected in the fact that *Armide,* unlike most of the earlier Lully-Quinault operas, did not have its premiere at court. Nonetheless, it is generally considered Lully's masterpiece and, along with *Atys,* one of Quinault's best librettos. The magician Armide is magnificently drawn, full of pride as well as of love, a victim of her passions and worthy of the spectator's pity. The plot is carefully constructed and moves quickly toward the dénouement, although the fourth act interrupts the action to present new characters whose adventures parallel those of the hero, Renaud.

Armide had been running for less than two months when the court learned in early April 1686 that Quinault had received permission from the king to step down from his post as librettist. The official reason was concern for his soul, given the church's opposition to the theater in general and to opera in particular. His health was declining, as he stated in two letters written in 1686, but he did write a fairly long poem about the destruction of the Protestant heresy, "Le poème de l'hérésie détruite" (published in 1904 as "Tableau de la Chute de l'hérésie"). (The Edict of Nantes had been revoked in November 1685, leaving Quinault just enough time to add a reference to Louis's victory over the "monster" of Protestantism in the prologue to *Armide.*)

Little is known of the last year and a half of Quinault's life. He continued to fulfill his duties as a

Engraving of the palace of Armide from the first edition of Quinault and Lully's 1686 opera Armide *(Bibliothèque de l'Opera, Paris)*

member of the Académie Française, the Académie des Inscriptions et Belles-Lettres (of which he had been a member since 1674), and the Chambre des Comptes. He was wealthy and respected and had even reconciled with Boileau in 1683. Quinault became seriously ill in June 1688 and died on 26 November that same year.

Quinault had a long and successful career; certainly, no other writers could say that they had been chosen as Molière's successor or that they had succeeded in a domain where La Fontaine, Boileau, and Racine had failed. Quinault's first fourteen plays had been translated into at least one other European language by 1711 and most into several languages. The Lully-Quinault operas were performed, and the librettos published, all over Europe. Three editions of Quinault's selected works were published in the nineteenth century, but twentieth-century readers knew him almost solely as the object of Boileau's ridicule—unless, that is, they saw one of the eight Lully-Quinault operas that have been performed to considerable critical and popular success since the 1986–1987 production of *Atys.* Philippe Quinault truly deserves the label that Jean de La Bruyère gave him: "le phénix de la poésie chantante" (the phoenix of musical poetry).

Bibliographies:

William S. Brooks, *Bibliographie critique du théâtre de Quinault*, Biblio 17, no. 38 (Paris, Seattle & Tübingen: Papers on French Seventeenth Century Literature, 1988);

Carl B. Schmidt, *The Livrets of Jean-Baptiste Lully's Tragédies Lyriques: A Catalogue Raisonné* (New York: Performers' Editions, 1995).

Biographies:

Boscheron, *La vie de Philippe Quinault de l'Académie Françoise*, in Quinault, *Le théâtre de Mr Quinault, contenant ses tragédies, comédies et opéra*, volume 1 (Paris: P. Ribou, 1715), pp. 5–64;

Boscheron, "Vie de M. Quinault de l'Académie Françoise avec l'origine des opera en France," (1722), ms. 24329, Paris, Bibliothèque Nationale, fonds français;

Etienne Gros, *Philippe Quinault: Sa vie et son œuvre* (Paris: E. Champion, 1926; reprinted, Geneva: Slatkine, 1970);

Johannes B. A. Buijtendorp, *Philippe Quinault: Sa vie, ses tragédies et ses tragi-comédies* (Amsterdam: H. J. Paris, 1928).

References:

Nicolas Boileau-Despréaux, *Œuvres complètes*, edited by Françoise Escal, Bibliothèque de la Pléiade, no. 188 (Paris: Gallimard, 1966);

William S. Brooks, "Boffrand, Boscheron, and Biographies of Quinault," *Nottingham French Studies*, 16 (1977): 19–28;

Brooks, "Theatrical Success and the Chronology of Productions at the Hôtel de Bourgogne: New Evidence from Racine and Quinault," *Theatre Survey*, 30 (1989): 35–44;

Emile Campardon, *L'Académie royale de musique au XVIIIe siècle; documents inédits découverts aux Archives nationales par Emile Campardon*, 2 volumes (Paris: Berger-Levrault et Cie, 1884; reprinted, New York: Da Capo Press, 1971);

Manuel Couvreur, "La Collaboration de Quinault et Lully avant la *Psyché* de 1671," *Recherches sur la Musique Française Classique*, 27 (1991): 9–34;

Antoinette du Ligier de La Garde, Madame de Deshoulières, *Poësies de Madame Deshoulières* (Paris: Veuve de S. Mabre-Cramoisy, 1693);

Anne-Madeleine Goulet, "Musique de ruelle: les livres d'airs de différents auteurs publiés chez Ballard de 1658 à 1694," dissertation, Université de Paris X, 2002;

Jean de La Bruyère, *Les caractères de Théophraste*, edited by Robert Garapon (Paris: Garnier, 1962);

Jérôme de La Gorce, *Jean-Baptiste Lully* (Paris: Fayard, 2002);

La Gorce, "Un proche collaborateur de Lully, Philippe Quinault," *Dix-septième Siècle*, 161 (1988): 365–370;

Frédéric Lachèvre, *Bibliographie des recueils collectifs de poésies publiés de 1597 à 1700*, 4 volumes (Paris: H. Leclerc, 1901–1905; reprinted, Geneva: Slatkine, 1967);

Jean Loret, *La Muze historique, ou recueil des lettres en vers contenant les nouvelles du temps, écrites à son Altesse Mademoiselle de Longueville, depuis duchesse de Nemours (1650–1665)*, volume 2, edited by Charles-Louis Livet (Paris: P. Daffis, 1877);

Buford Norman, *Touched by the Graces: The Libretti of Philippe Quinault in the Context of French Classicism* (Birmingham, Ala.: Summa, 2001);

Claude and François Parfaict, *Histoire du théâtre françois depuis son origine jusqu'à présent*, 15 volumes (Paris: A. Morin et P. G. Le Mercier, 1734–1749; reprinted, New York: B. Franklin, 1968);

Charles Perrault, *Critique de l'Opéra, ou Examen de la tragédie intitulée Alceste, ou Le Triomphe d'Alcide* (Paris: C. Barbin, 1674); reprinted in Quinault, *Alceste, suivi de la querelle d'Alceste: Anciens et modernes avant 1680*, edited by Brooks, Norman, and Jeanne Morgan Zarucchi (Geneva: Droz, 1994), pp. 79–102;

Perrault, *Les Hommes illustres qui ont paru en France pendant ce siècle, avec leurs portraits au naturel*, 2 volumes (Paris: A. Dezallier, 1690, 1700; reprinted, Geneva: Slatkine, 1970);

John S. Powell, *Music and Theatre in France, 1600–1680* (Oxford: Oxford University Press, 2000);

Charles Robinet, *Lettres en vers à Madame*, in *Les continuateurs de Loret: Lettres en vers de la Gravette de Mayolas, Robinet, Boursault, Perdou de Subligny, Laurent et autres (1665–1689)*, edited by James de Rothschild and Emile Picot, volume 1 (Paris: D. Morgand et C. Fatout, 1881).

Jean Racine

(December 1639 – 21 April 1699)

Georges May
Yale University

BOOKS: *La Nymphe de la Seine à la Reyne, ode,* anonymous (Paris: A. Courbé, 1660);

Ode sur la convalescence du Roy (Paris: P. Le Petit, 1663);

La Renommée aux Muses, ode (N.p., n.d. [1663]);

La Thébayde, ou Les Frères ennemis (Paris: C. Barbin, 1664);

Alexandre le Grand (Paris: T. Girard, 1666);

Lettre à l'auteur des Hérésies imaginaires et des deux Visionnaires (N.p., n.d. [1666]);

Andromaque (Paris: C. Barbin, 1668);

Les Plaideurs (Paris: C. Barbin, 1669);

Britannicus (Paris: C. Barbin, 1670);

Bérénice (Paris: C. Barbin, 1671);

Bajazet (Paris: P. Le Monnier, 1672);

Mithridate (Paris: C. Barbin, 1673);

Iphigénie (Paris: C. Barbin, 1675);

Œuvres de Racine, 2 volumes (Paris: C. Barbin, 1675, 1676; revised and enlarged edition, Paris: D. Thierry, 1687; revised and enlarged edition, Paris: P. Trabouillet, 1697)–1697 edition includes volume 1, *La Thébaïde, Alexandre le Grand, Andromaque, Britannicus, Bérénice, Les Plaideurs, Harangue de l'Académie,* and *Idylle sur la paix;* volume 2, *Bajazet, Mithridate, Iphigénie, Phèdre, Esther, Athalie,* and *Cantiques;*

Phèdre et Hippolyte (Paris: C. Barbin, 1677);

Idylle sur la paix, pour estre chanté dans l'Orangerie de Sceaux (N.p., n.d. [1685]); revised and enlarged as *Idylle sur la paix, avec L'Eglogue de Versailles . . .* (Paris: C. Ballard, 1685);

Esther (Paris: D. Thierry, 1689);

Athalie (Paris: D. Thierry, 1691);

Relation de ce qui s'est passé au siège de Namur . . . [authorship uncertain] (Paris: D. Thierry, 1692);

Cantiques spirituels (Paris: D. Thierry, 1694);

Campagne de Louis XIV, par M. Pelisson [misattributed] (Paris: Mesnier, 1730); republished as *Eloge historique du Roi Louis XIV, sur ses conquêtes depuis l'année 1672 jusqu'en 1678,* by Racine and Nicolas Boileau-Despréaux (Amsterdam & Paris: Bleuet, 1784);

Jean Racine (portrait by Auguste Sandoz; from the album for Racine's Œuvres, 1885; Thomas Cooper Library, University of South Carolina)

Abrégé de l'histoire de Port-Royal (Cologne, 1742; enlarged edition, Paris: Lottin le Jeune, 1767);

Œuvres de Jean Racine, 7 volumes, edited by Julien-Louis Geoffroy (Paris: Le Normant, 1808)–volume 5 includes "Le Paysage, ou Promenade de Port-Royal des Champs."

307

Editions: *Œuvres de J. Racine,* 8 volumes, edited by Paul Mesnard (Paris: Hachette, 1865–1873);

Œuvres complètes, 2 volumes, edited by Raymond Picard, Bibliothèque de la Pléiade, nos. 5 and 90 (Paris: Gallimard, 1951, 1952);

Œuvres complètes, edited by Georges Forestier, Bibliothèque de la Pléiade, no. 5 (Paris: Gallimard, 1999).

PLAY PRODUCTIONS: *Les Frères ennemis,* Paris, Théâtre du Palais-Royal, 20 June 1664;

Alexandre le Grand, Paris, Théâtre du Palais-Royal, 4 December 1665;

Andromaque, Paris, Palais du Louvre, 17 November 1667; Paris, Hôtel de Bourgogne, a few days later;

Les Plaideurs, Paris, Hôtel de Bourgogne, November 1668;

Britannicus, Paris, Hôtel de Bourgogne, 13 December 1669;

Bérénice, Paris, Hôtel de Bourgogne, 21 November 1670;

Bajazet, Paris, Hôtel de Bourgogne, early January 1672;

Mithridate, Paris, Hôtel de Bourgogne, December 1672 or January 1673;

Iphigénie, Versailles, Château de Versailles, 18 August 1674; Paris, Hôtel de Bourgogne, December 1674 or January 1675;

Phèdre et Hippolyte, Paris, Hôtel de Bourgogne, 1 January 1677;

Idylle sur la paix, music by Jean-Baptiste Lully, Sceaux, Château de Sceaux, 16 July 1685;

Esther, music by Jean-Baptiste Moreau, Maison de Saint-Cyr, 26 January 1689;

Athalie, music by Moreau, Maison de Saint-Cyr, 5 January 1691.

OTHER: *Le Bréviaire romain en latin et en français . . . ,* edited by Nicolas Le Tourneux (Paris: D. Thierry, 1688 [i.e., 1687])–includes hymns translated into verse by Racine;

"Urbis et ruris differentia," in *Recueil de pièces d'histoire et de littérature,* 4 volumes, edited by François Granet and Pierre Nicolas Desmolets (Paris: Chaubert, 1731–1738);

Plato, *Le Banquet,* translated by Racine and Marie-Madeleine-Gabrielle de Rochechouart de Mortemart (Paris: P. Gandouin, 1732);

"Discours prononcé à l'Académie Française à la réception de M. l'abbé Colbert le 30 octobre 1678," "Plan du premier acte d'Iphigénie en Tauride," "Extrait du traité de Lucien intitulé: Comment il faut écrire l'histoire," "Fragments historiques," "Réflexions sur l'Ecriture sainte," "Hymnes du Bréviaire romain," "Discours prononcé à la tête du clergé par M. l'abbé Colbert," and "Relation de ce qui s'est passé au siège de Namur," in *Mémoires sur la vie de Jean Racine,* edited by Louis Racine (Lausanne & Geneva: M. M. Bousquet, 1747);

"Epigrammes de J. Racine," in *Œuvres de M. L. Racine . . . revue et augmentée par l'auteur,* volume 1 (Paris: M. M. Rey, 1750).

SELECTED PERIODICAL PUBLICATION–UNCOLLECTED: "Stances à Parthénice" [authorship uncertain], *Journal général de France,* 2 October 1788.

Jean Racine has long been held as one of the foremost writers in the whole of French literature, though his fame rests essentially on but ten plays. His literary output beyond these plays is, moreover, surprisingly small when compared to that of writers of equal stature. He may be the French writer whose rank is most exclusively based on the quality of his work. Most of his plays are still regularly performed, some of them even in translation, in spite of their being exceptionally difficult to translate because of the particular quality of his poetry. They continue to be republished as well, especially in editions designed for use in French schools, where they have long occupied a privileged place.

Baptized on 22 December 1639, Racine was presumably born a few days before this date in the small town of La Ferté-Milon in the province of Champagne, some fifty miles northeast of Paris, to a lower-middle-class family. His father, also named Jean, occupied a modest and poorly paid position in the tax-collecting bureaucracy. In January 1641 Racine's mother, Jeanne Sconin Racine, died while giving birth to her second child, Marie. In February 1643 the children's father, who had remarried three months earlier, also died, leaving Racine and his sister destitute. Their paternal grandparents took charge of the boy, the maternal grandparents of the girl. In October 1649 the young Racine was enrolled as a nonpaying student at the "Petites Ecoles" (Little Schools) in Cheureuse.

The Petites Ecoles were run by the abbey of Port-Royal, a convent of Cistercian nuns. At the time the abbey had two locations, one south of Paris in the Chevreuse valley, known as Port-Royal des Champs, and the other in Paris proper, known as Port-Royal de Paris, located on what is now the Boulevard de Port-Royal. The admission of the penniless and orphaned Racine to the prestigious Petites Ecoles resulted from the close connections that had long existed between the abbey and Racine's family. In 1625 Suzanne Desmoulins, the sister of Racine's paternal

TITE
ET
BERENICE.
COMEDIE HEROIQUE.

Par P. CORNEILLE.

A PARIS,
Chez Loüis BILLAINE, au Palais, au second
pillier de la grand'Salle, à la Palme,
& au grand Cesar.

M. DC. LXXI.
AVEC PRIVILEGE DU ROY.

BERENICE
TRAGEDIE.
PAR M. RACINE.

A PARIS,
Chez CLAUDE BARBIN, au Palais,
sur le Second Perron de la Sainte Chapelle.

M. DC. LXXI.
AVEC PRIVILEGE DV ROY.

Title pages for the 1671 editions of Pierre Corneille's and Racine's plays on the accession of the Roman emperor Titus, which had their premieres a week apart in November 1670 (Bibliothèque Nationale, Paris)

grandmother, had been admitted to the convent. In 1642 Agnès Racine, Racine's father's sister, also entered the convent, later becoming its superior as Mère Agnès de Sainte-Thècle. And in 1638–1639 another of Racine's aunts, Claude Racine Vitart, had offered shelter in La Ferté-Milon to three of the austere gentlemen who had chosen Port-Royal as a retreat and who were known as the "Messieurs de Port-Royal" or the "Solitaires" (Solitaries). They had been forced to leave their retreat when the abbey was suspected of showing too much sympathy for the doctrine known by its opponents as Jansenism (named for Cornelius Jansen, a proponent of St. Augustine); disapproved of both by the church and by the king, Jansenism was eventually condemned as heretical. In 1649, after the death of her husband, Racine's grandmother and godmother, Marie Desmoulins Racine, also moved to Port-Royal, where she was employed as a housekeeper.

Racine studied at the Petites Ecoles of Port-Royal from October 1649 to September 1653. The school provided him with a superior education, which, contrary to the then prevailing fashion, was conducted not in Latin but in French and emphasized a close study of the vernacular. It included a sustained study of Latin and Greek—in which Racine soon became remarkably fluent—as well as the modern languages of Spanish and Italian.

After his four years at Port-Royal, Racine entered the Collège de Beauvais in Paris, an institution sympathetic to the abbey, where he studied for two years, returning to Port-Royal in the fall of 1655. He spent three more years as a student there before entering the Collège d'Harcourt in Paris, where he studied for a final year (1658–1659), completing an education of virtually unparalleled scope and quality, one far superior to what a destitute and provincial orphan could have hoped for.

During this period Racine composed a few poems, both in French and in Latin, including seven odes published posthumously under the title "Le Paysage, ou Promenade de Port-Royal des Champs" (The Countryside, or A Walk through Port-Royal des Champs; included in volume 5 of the *Œuvres de Jean Racine* [Works of Jean Racine], 1808). At least some of his translations of several Latin hymns into French verse, later used by Nicolas Le Tourneux in his 1687 *Bréviaire romain en latin et en français* . . . (Roman Breviary in Latin and in French . . .), were probably also composed at this time.

Having benefited from an education out of proportion with his expectations, yet devoid of family fortune and in need of making a living, the nearly twenty-year-old Racine faced the difficult choice of an occupation. Rather than going back to La Ferté-Milon and becoming a humble and obscure office worker like his father and grandfather before him, Racine accepted the hospitality offered to him by his cousin Nicolas Vitart (a nephew of his maternal grandmother), who managed the estates of the wealthy and influential Charles d'Albert, duc de Luynes, and who sheltered his cousin in the vast townhouse of the de Luynes family in Paris. In the Paris house and later in the duc de Luynes's country estate of Chevreuse, Racine made his first attempts at writing for a living.

The poems he had written during his adolescent years at Port-Royal were all rather conventional, of a kind not uncommon for a young man with a primarily literary education. But once out of school, Racine tried to seize upon current events to compose poems intended for important personages in the hope of receiving monetary rewards from them. In 1659 he wrote a sonnet, now lost, on the occasion of the peace treaty between France and Spain. In 1660 he composed a 240-line ode for the new queen of France, Marie-Thérèse, whose marriage to Louis XIV had just been celebrated on 9 June of that year. This poem, *La Nymphe de la Seine à la Reyne* (The Nymph of the Seine to the Queen, 1660), is the first of his works to have been printed, albeit anonymously. Neither it nor the lost sonnet seems to have had the expected results. Racine then turned his attention to another possible source of income from literature, writing two plays. Both are lost and little about them is known, but the second appears to have featured the Roman poet Ovid as its hero. The plays were turned down successively in 1660 and 1661 by two different Parisian theaters. This rejection did not, however, prevent Racine's aunt Agnès and others at Port-Royal from chiding him for these excessively worldly literary efforts.

Still in need of a means of support and having already had to borrow money to survive, Racine agreed to a plan conceived by his family in La Ferté-Milon to obtain for him a church benefice. He left Paris in October 1661 for the small Provençal town of Uzès, where his uncle Antoine Sconin (his mother's brother) occupied an influential ecclesiastical position. The plan eventually failed, and Racine had to go back to Paris empty-handed, sometime between August 1662 and June 1663. During his stay in Uzès he read many of the classics, as well as some works of theology. Several volumes from his library have been preserved, notably those by Greek poets, with handwritten annotations dating back to this period. He also wrote some poetry, including, if it is indeed by him, the short poem known as "Stances à Parthénice" (Stanzas to Parthenice, 1788).

Once back in Paris, Racine resumed his poetic efforts and eventually succeeded in obtaining a financial recompense for poems intended to celebrate the reign of Louis XIV. After the death of the powerful Cardinal Jules Mazarin on 9 March 1661, the newly married Louis XIV decided to take control of the government himself and turned to his principal aide, Jean-Baptiste Colbert, to set up institutions intended to glorify his reign through the commissioning of works of art and literature. With the assistance of Jean Chapelain, a celebrated poet of his day, Colbert put in place in 1662–1663 a system of royal pensions that emulated in part the model of the Roman emperor Augustus and his supporter, the banker Maecenas. Eager to benefit from this innovation, Racine wrote and published in July and November 1663 two odes, one on the occasion of Louis XIV's recovery from the measles—*Ode sur la convalescence du Roy* (Ode upon the King's Recovery)—and another to thank the king for having responded favorably to the first—*La Renommée aux Muses* (Fame to the Muses). The reward for the two works, approved in 1663 and granted in August 1664, was an annual pension of six hundred livres—a substantial sum at the time—which placed Racine on the list of officially recognized French writers, albeit at the bottom. The top pension on the list, awarded to Chapelain, amounted to two thousand livres. During this period Racine was introduced to the court by an influential aristocrat, François de Beauvilliers, duc de Saint-Aignan, to whom he soon dedicated his first performed tragedy.

Prior to the establishment of this elaborate system of pensions and rewards, aspiring writers and poets had to depend on the sponsorship of influential benefactors. By far the most important of these had been the wealthy minister of finance, Nicolas Foucquet, who held court at his sumptuous Château de Vaux-le-Vicomte (thirty miles east of Paris) and who counted among his beneficiaries such luminaries as Pierre Corneille, Jean de La Fontaine, and Molière. Foucquet's arrest in 1661, followed by a lengthy trial and his incarceration in 1664, cleared the way for Louis XIV to become the chief patron of artists and writers under his

Acte 1.er Scene 1.   95.

Iphigenie vient auec vne captiue Grecque, qui s'estonne
de sa tristesse. Elle demande si c'est qu'elle est affligée
de ce que la feste de Diane se passera sans qu'on luy
immole aucun estranger. Tu peus croire dit Iphigenie
si c'est la vn sentiment digne de la fille d'Agamemnon
Tu scais auec quelle repugnance j'ay preparé les
miserables que l'on a sacrifiez depuis que je preside
a ces cruelles ceremonies. Je me faisois vne joye de
ce que la Fortune n'auoit amené aucun Grec pour
cette journeé, et je triomphois seule de la douleur
commune qui est respandüe dans cette Isle, ou l'on
conte pour vn presage funeste de ce que nous manquions
de victimes pour cette feste. Mais je ne puis resister
a la secrette tristesse dont je suis occupeé depuis le
songe que j'ay fait cette nuit. J'ay crû que j'estois
a Mycene dans la Maison de mon Pere, il m'a
semblé que mon Pere et ma More nageoient dans
le sang, et que moy mesme je tenois vn poignard
a la main pour en esgorger mon frere Oreste.
Helas mon cher Oreste! Mais Madame vous
estes trop esloignez l'vn de l'autre pour craindre

First page from the manuscript for Racine's 1674 tragedy, Iphigénie *(from Roselyne de Ayala
and Jean-Pierre Guéno,* Belles Lettres, *2001)*

reign. One of the effects of the royal institutionalization of the arts and letters was a partial lifting of the stigma attached by the church to the theater, and this change in attitude perhaps explains why Racine chose to renew his efforts as a playwright.

His first tragedy, *Les Frères ennemis* (The Enemy Brothers, published in 1664 as *La Thébayde* [*Thébaïde* in most editions], *ou Les Frères ennemis*), premiered in June of 1664. It is the story of the violent death of Oedipus's three children, a subject that had inspired all three of the great Greek tragic poets and that had already been treated by several French playwrights; in the 1675 preface to the play–published in volume one of the *Œuvres de Racine*–Racine refers to the myth as "le sujet le plus tragique de l'antiquité" (the most tragic subject in antiquity). Racine's version was performed on the stage of the Théâtre du Palais-Royal by Molière's company, which at the time was relatively new to the Parisian theater world. The play met with modest success. As was often the practice, the Hôtel de Bourgogne, home of the Comédiens du Roi and rival theater to the Palais-Royal, staged a competing play on the same subject, a tragedy by abbé Claude Boyer titled *La Thébaïde,* which had failed in 1647 and did not fare much better with its reprise in 1664. Three more of Racine's tragedies were also to be *doublées* (doubled, or presented at the same time as a rival play on the same subject), as the practice was known. Racine's *Thébaïde* illustrates another common practice of the time, in that it was a "remake" of a well-known earlier play, in this case Jean Rotrou's *Antigone* (1637), as Racine acknowledges in his 1675 preface.

Although less than he had hoped for, the reception of his tragedy was favorable enough to encourage Racine to persist in this new endeavor. The year 1664 marks the starting point of a period of just more than twelve years during which Racine produced the ten plays that eventually earned him a reputation as the most worthy successor of his illustrious predecessor and rival, Corneille. Surprisingly little is known of Racine's life during this period. Of his correspondence, practically nothing has survived between the letters he had written while in Uzès and those he wrote much later to his elder son and to Nicolas Boileau-Despréaux.

On 4 December 1665 Racine's second play, *Alexandre le Grand* (Alexander the Great, published 1666), was performed on the same stage, again by Molière's company, and the work met with greater success than his first. Based on Alexander the Great's conflict with King Porus during his campaign in India, the play presents Alexander as a young, brilliant, and magnanimous monarch, equally irresistible in his conquest of kingdoms and of women–in brief, a transparent image of the rising Louis le Grand (Louis XIV). On 18 December, the day of the sixth performance of *Alexan-*

dre le Grand at the Palais-Royal, the same play was unexpectedly staged by Molière's rival company at the Hôtel de Bourgogne. What led Racine to this unethical move is not entirely clear. His decision to shift alliances might have resulted from the fact that the Comédiens du Roi were a more prestigious venue for an aspiring author and enjoyed a higher reputation in the field of tragedy than Molière's company; it might also have been influenced by the serious opposition Molière had encountered ever since his efforts in 1664 to obtain permission to perform his *Tartuffe* (published 1669). Molière's sense of outrage at Racine's betrayal was aggravated a few months later when the actress who had performed the leading role of Axiane in his production of *Alexandre le Grand* left to join the Comédiens du Roi, on whose stage Racine's next eight plays were performed. The actress, Marquise Duparc, was well known at the time for her talent, as well as for the number and social standing of her several lovers, including Racine himself.

Born circa 1633 as Marquise-Thérèse de Gorla (her father was Italian), at the time of *Alexandre le Grand* she was married to another member of Molière's company, René Berthelot–known by the stage name Duparc–who died in 1664. In 1668 she gave birth to a daughter, who was baptized on 12 May. The girl's godmother was Marie-Anne Duparc, Marquise Duparc's elder daughter, and her godfather was Racine; indeed, for a time she was widely believed to be his own daughter, though the rumor was most likely false. Marquise Duparc's death on 11 December that year gave rise to further unsubstantiated rumors–that she was pregnant at the time, that she died of a failed abortion, or that she was poisoned. Racine's goddaughter died in 1676.

When *Alexandre le Grand* was published in January 1666, it was dedicated to Louis XIV, an indication that the king had granted the author the flattering favor of accepting the dedication. Shortly thereafter, Racine's pension was raised to eight hundred livres. Around the same time, Racine became embroiled in a bitter dispute with Port-Royal. Beginning in 1664, one of the most respected "Messieurs" of the abbey, the philosopher and theologian Pierre Nicole, had written a series of letters defending Jansenism and formally condemning the theater as an unchristian and pernicious activity. Racine responded with a vigorous and aggressive defense, his *Lettre à l'auteur des Hérésies imaginaires et des deux Visionnaires* (Letter to the Author of the Imaginary Heresies and the Two Visionaries, 1666). He composed a sequel as well, but his cousin Nicolas Vitart seems to have dissuaded him from publishing it. The dispute, which lasted until the spring of 1667, marked the height of Racine's estrangement from Port-Royal.

Meanwhile, perhaps as a belated result of the efforts of his uncle in Uzès, Racine, although a layman, received his first ecclesial appointment, as prior of Sainte-Pétronille de l'Epinay. The sinecure added to both his status and his income. Four years later he traded in this benefice for another, the priorship of Saint-Jacques de la Ferté, which was more profitable and also closer to his family roots. The revenue from such appointments, which depended largely on personal favor, was indispensable for writers such as Racine, devoid of personal fortune. Royalties from Racine's plays were never high enough to constitute a major source of income. According to the practice of the time, as soon as a play was published, it became public property and could be performed without compensation to the author.

Racine's first real success was *Andromaque* (Andromache, published 1668), performed first before the court on 17 November 1667 and then, no more than a week later, before the public at the Hôtel de Bourgogne. Marquise Duparc played the title role, Hector's widow, who after the Trojan defeat was held captive together with her son, Astyanax, at the court of Pyrrhus, the son of Achilles. When the play was published in January 1668, it was dedicated to the king's sister-in-law, Henriette, daughter of King Charles I of England, known as Henriette d'Angleterre; perhaps the most influential lady at the French court, she was much admired by Louis XIV and highly respected for her good taste and judgment in literary matters.

The success of *Andromaque* was the occasion of bitter attacks on the part of Racine's rivals. One such attack, *La Folle querelle, ou La Critique d'Andromaque* (The Foolish Quarrel, or The Critique of Andromaque, 1668), a satirical comedy by Adrien de Perdou de Subligny, was performed in the spring of 1668 by Molière's company, perhaps in retaliation for Racine's slight of Molière during the production of *Alexandre le Grand*. But Racine's fame was growing, as was his royal pension, which reached 1,200 livres in 1668. Two years later it was raised again, to 1,500 livres.

In 1668 Racine also premiered his only comedy, *Les Plaideurs* (The Litigants, published 1669). It opened in November on the stage of the Hôtel de Bourgogne, as a sign of the unwillingness on the part of the Comédiens du Roi to abandon comedy altogether to Molière's company. Based in part on Aristophanes' *The Wasps* (422 B.C.), this farcical and satirical comedy in three acts pokes fun at the passion for litigation as well as the trappings of the legal system. Its reception was not especially favorable, except at the court, though it has fared better since, becoming one of Racine's most frequently performed plays.

A year later, on 13 December 1669, Racine's fourth play, *Britannicus* (published 1670), premiered at the Hôtel de Bourgogne. Based on Roman history, the

IPHIGENIE

Frontispiece for the 1676 edition of Racine's 1674 tragedy (engraving by François Chauveau; Bibliothèque Nationale, Paris)

play is a tragedy centered around Nero's first crime, the murder of his half brother. Corneille, the then recognized master of Roman drama, was in attendance, as well as several of his admirers. The play was harshly criticized by Corneille's partisans, who viewed it as an attempt to rival Corneille's *Cinna* (1642), one of his early and most successful tragedies based on Roman history. Though *Britannicus* was eventually recognized as one of Racine's best tragedies, its premiere was a partial failure. Disappointed and obviously angered, Racine, when he published the play early the following year, added a preface in which he systematically and sarcastically attacked Corneille. The published play was also preceded by a flattering dedication to the "duc de Chevreuse," which was one of the titles of the duc de Luynes, the employer of Racine's cousin Vitart.

On 21 November 1670 his next tragedy, also based on Roman history, premiered. *Bérénice* (published 1671)–the tale of Titus's accession as Roman emperor and of his resulting forced separation from Bérénice, regardless of their shared love–was performed by the Comédiens du Roi; just one week later Molière's company premiered Corneille's new play on the same subject, *Tite et Bérénice*. Although the concurrent production of rival plays on a similar theme was by no means unheard-of at the time, the opening of this particular pair of plays, composed as they were by the two best-known tragic playwrights of their day, has been the topic of much speculation and many scholarly disquisitions. Was the competition instigated by Henriette d'Angleterre, Louis XIV's sister-in-law? Was the plot, featuring a Roman emperor's sacrifice of love for duty, an allusion to Louis XIV's own unfulfilled youthful love for Marie Mancini, the late Cardinal Mazarin's niece? The consensus among scholars today is that these rumors are unfounded, and that they were probably spread long after the event. In any case, Racine's play generated a greater and more lasting success than Corneille's, although the latter was in no way a failure at the time. The dual premieres also marked the height of the younger poet's rivalry with the elderly Corneille.

The title role of Bérénice, designated in the play as queen of Palestine, was performed by an actress known as La Champmeslé, the late Marquise Duparc's successor both on stage and in Racine's affection. Née Marie Desmares in 1643, she was married to Charles Chevillet, from whose stage name of Champmeslé she derived her own name. La Champmeslé became famous both for her talent and, as had been the case with Marquise Duparc, for the number and distinction of her lovers. Although her liaison with Racine was by no means short-lived–she played leading roles in his next five tragedies–their relationship appears to have been somewhat casual, rather than based on a passion comparable to that featured in Racine's plays.

When Racine's next tragedy, *Bajazet* (published 1672), had its first run at the Hôtel de Bourgogne in January 1672, La Champmeslé seems to have played the part of Princess Atalide in some of the performances, and that of the other female lead, Sultana Roxane, in others, thus demonstrating the versatility of her talent. Based on recent events at the Ottoman court in Constantinople, this play is one of Racine's bloodiest after *La Thébaïde* and perhaps the one featuring the most unbridled and passionate love. It met at first with some denigration on the part of Corneille's admirers but soon surmounted their opposition. Nevertheless, when Racine published it in February of the same year,

he still felt the need to compose for it a polemical preface, though one milder in tone than that which he had composed for *Britannicus*.

Enjoying the personal support of Louis XIV and the all-powerful Colbert–to whom he had dedicated the published *Bérénice*–Racine was elected to the Académie Française in December 1672. His formal reception took place on 12 January 1673, around the time of the premiere of his next tragedy, *Mithridate* (Mithridates, published the same year). This new play, which might have opened as early as December 1672, was based on a well-known episode of the Roman colonial wars and was written from the perspective of the defeated kingdoms of the eastern Mediterranean. The role of Monime, played by La Champmeslé, appears to have been one of the most unforgettable depictions of young and heroic womanhood of its day. *Mithridate* was an instant success and was said to be Louis XIV's favorite play by Racine. On 17 February 1673, between the premiere of *Mithridate* and its publication in March, Molière died. His death was followed by the slow decline of his company and its eventual fusion with that of the Comédiens du Roi.

Racine's reputation was further enhanced by his next tragedy, *Iphigénie* (Iphigenia, published 1675), perhaps Racine's greatest success up to that time. The play premiered on 18 August 1674, with La Champmeslé in the title role. Marking Racine's return to Greek legend, its plot was based on the planned sacrifice of Agamemnon's daughter Iphigenia in order to placate the gods and allow the Greek invasion fleet, marooned in the harbor of Aulis, to sail forth toward Troy. As he explains in the preface he wrote for the edition of 1675, the play was modeled after Euripides' *Iphigenia at Aulis* (circa 405 B.C.). Among several pieces later appended by Racine's son Louis to his 1747 *Mémoires sur la vie de Jean Racine* (Memoirs of the Life of Jean Racine) is a fragment labeled "Plan du premier acte d'Iphigénie en Tauride" (Plan for the First Act of Iphigenia in Tauris). This document, an outline in prose of an unwritten tragedy Racine had planned to base on another play by Euripides, offers valuable clues to his methods of composition.

Despite Racine's established reputation, his adversaries had not given up their denigrating efforts, and *Iphigénie* was one more of his plays to be "doubled." On 24 May 1675 a play by the same title, authored by Michel Le Clerc and Jacques Coras, premiered on the stage of the Guénégaud theater. The Palais-Royal stage, which had been associated with Molière's career, had been turned over after his death to the newly founded Parisian Opéra. What was left of Molière's company had settled in the playhouse of the Rue Guénégaud, where they remained until their fusion with the Comé-

Cantique Spirituel
à la louange de la Charité
tiré de S.t Paul. 1. Corinth. ch. 13.

Les Meschans m'ont vanté leurs mensonges frivoles.
Mais je n'aime que les paroles
De l'éternelle Vérité.
Plein du feu divin qui m'inspire
Je consacre aujourdhuy ma Lyre
A la céleste Charité.

En vain je parlerois le langage des Anges.
En vain, mon Dieu, de tes loüanges
Je remplirois tout l'univers.
Sans Amour, ma gloire n'égale
Que la gloire de la cymbale
Qui d'un vain bruit frappe les airs.

Que sert a mon esprit de percer les abimes
Des mysteres les plus sublimes,
Et de lire dans l'avenir?
Sans Amour, ma science est vaine
Comme le songe, dont a peine
Il reste un leger souuenir

Manuscript for one of the four religious poems collected in 1694 as Cantiques spirituels
(Bibliothèque Nationale, Paris)

Drawing of Racine by Charles Le Brun
(Collection Chauffard)

diens du Roi in 1680. The play, overtly intended to compete with Racine's, was performed only five times and caused it no real harm. Another sign of the survival of opposition to Racine around this time was the publication in July 1675 of a bitterly satirical work by Jean Barbier d'Aucour titled *Apollon vendeur de Mithridate, ou Apollon charlatan* (Apollo, Peddler of Mithridate, or Apollo the Charlatan).

In the fall of 1674 Racine received the honorific appointment of *Trésorier de France,* a lucrative sinecure normally purchased by the beneficiary but in this case a gift from the king. Its annual income was higher than the royal pension he was already receiving and therefore represented a sign of unusual favor on the part of the king. Racine's prominence was further secured with the publication of the first collected edition of his works. The *Œuvres de Racine* (1675, 1676) was printed in two volumes illustrated with engravings by François Chauveau. In preparation for it Racine had minutely reviewed and carefully corrected and amended his original texts.

Racine's next play, *Phèdre et Hippolyte* (Phaedra and Hippolytus, published 1677)–later known simply as *Phèdre*–premiered on 1 January 1677 at the Hôtel de Bourgogne, with La Champmeslé once again in the lead role. This fourth and last of Racine's Greek tragedies was based on a mythological episode already treated by several French playwrights, centering on the overwhelming and eventually murderous love of Phèdre for her stepson Hippolyte. Though it is today per-

haps Racine's best-known and most admired tragedy, at the time the play gave rise to a particularly acrimonious and extended dispute. Two days after the premiere of Racine's *Phèdre et Hippolyte,* a play by Nicolas Pradon opened under the same title at the Guénégaud theater. For a while the two plays met with equal success, and it took several weeks for the superiority of Racine's play to become obvious. The quarrel lasted, however, longer than on previous similar occasions and did not conclude until March or April. It involved in particular the spreading of several scurrilous sonnets, threats of violence, and the intervention of such highly placed personages as Philippe Mancini, duc de Nevers, on Pradon's side and Louis II de Bourbon, prince de Condé, on Racine's. It was also an occasion for Boileau to defend Racine, in contrast to his former support of Molière at the transferral of *Alexandre le Grand* from his theater more than ten years earlier.

An intimate and lasting friendship between Racine and Boileau soon ensued, sealed in the fall of 1677 by the joint appointment of the two writers as the official historiographers of Louis XIV's reign. They each received from the king on this occasion a princely gift of six thousand livres in addition to their regular pensions, plus a further six thousand for the procurement of provisions necessary for escorting the king during wars. This highly honorific appointment marked a surprising choice on the part of the king and generated considerable jealousy, both among other hopeful writers and among aristocrats, who were shocked to see mere commoners entrusted with the honor of writing the history of the king's reign.

After having written what is now considered his masterpiece, *Phèdre,* Racine for a long time abandoned writing for the stage. His old plays continued to be performed frequently, though, not only in France but in several other countries as well. And Racine did not stop writing altogether; aside from his work as an historiographer, he produced several commissioned works, including occasional verse and librettos for operas and ballets. Still, his relatively abrupt turn from theater has long puzzled scholars, who have offered several more or less tenable explanations. His return to a more religious life–some call it a conversion–has been posited as one reason for his dissociating himself from the theater. The enduring petty hostility against him, exemplified in particular by the temporary but grating success of Pradon's play, might also have contributed to the shift in his career. But the most likely explanation lies in the fact that Racine's new appointment as historiographer to the king was no mere sinecure; rather, it demanded on the part of both Racine and Boileau an exclusive devotion to their new mission, including not only considerable research but attendance at the court and at all military actions led by the king personally.

On 1 June 1677 Racine had married the twenty-four- or twenty-five-year-old Catherine de Romanet, a member of a notable bourgeois family from La Ferté-Milon that was related by marriage to the Vitart branch of Racine's family and that had been granted noble status in return for services to the Crown. She was a pious woman who was said to be indifferent to her husband's literary career and never to have read any of his works. Her fortune at the time was roughly on par with Racine's, who had by then become a moderately wealthy man. After his appointment as royal historiographer, Racine became a regular courtier and was able to live on a much higher scale. Various monetary gifts from Louis XIV are estimated to have totaled no less than forty-three thousand livres during the decade 1678–1688. Racine was able to use this income to support his new family, which in the first fourteen years of his marriage came to include seven children: Jean-Baptiste in November 1678, Marie-Catherine (known as Cathau) in May 1680, Anne (Nanette) in July 1682, Elisabeth (Babet) in August 1684, Jeanne-Françoise (Fanchon) in November 1686, Madeleine (Madelon) in March 1688, and Louis (Lionval) in November 1692. Of the five daughters, three eventually entered monastic life, which required a dowry, as did the marriage of Marie-Catherine toward the end of Racine's life. As for his sons, they were given costly educations, especially the elder, Jean-Baptiste, for whom a diplomatic career was planned.

All indications are that Racine, who until then had not always led an exemplary life, turned out to be a good husband and father, in spite of his new duties, which often kept him away from his family. In addition to spending much of his time at the court, from 1678 to 1687 he regularly followed the king on military campaigns, first together with Boileau and then, after 1681 (the date of the taking of Strasbourg), alone because of Boileau's ill health.

Taking his mission to heart, Racine had prepared himself by studying the historians of classical antiquity. He visited the sites of important events of the recent past and interviewed highly placed witnesses of significant occurences of the reign. The results of his and Boileau's efforts are now almost entirely lost, their manuscripts having been destroyed in a fire in 1726. Of the few surviving fragments it is often impossible to identify with certainty which are from Racine's own hand. Several times Louis XIV had sections of the work-in-progress read to him, and in 1688 he granted Racine and Boileau a new award of ten thousand livres each.

With Racine's newly recovered religious faith, a rapprochement with Port-Royal also began in 1677, the first positive contact since the quarrel of 1666. During this period he had begun to occupy an increasingly influential position at the court, enjoying the good graces of the king's favorites: first the powerful Françoise-Athénaïs de Rochechouart, marquise de Montespan, followed by the even more powerful Françoise d'Aubigné, marquise de Maintenon, whom Louis XIV is said to have secretly married in 1683, a few months after the death of Queen Marie-Thérèse. Racine was also well acquainted with the Colbert family and the Condés, both of which wielded considerable influence. These connections enabled him to intervene discreetly on more than one occasion on behalf of Port-Royal, which was then being viewed with increasing suspicion and disfavor by Louis XIV and his entourage. Racine's aunt became Port-Royal's mother superior in 1690, and he visited her there on several occasions. Their meetings were not without danger: Racine's enemies eventually denounced him to the king as a Jansenist, which could have opened him to disgrace. As another sign of his attachment to the cause of the abbey, he composed in secrecy, during the last few years of his life, his *Abrégé de l'histoire de Port-Royal* (Concise History of Port-Royal), which was not published in its entirety until 1767, more than sixty years after his death.

Racine had already found himself in a dangerous situation in 1679, during the infamous *Affaire des Poisins* (Affair of the Poisons), when an official inquiry was launched into widespread allegations of poisoning among commoners and nobles alike. Catherine Deshayes, Madame Monvoisin (known simply as La Voisin), in the course of being tried for witchcraft and poisoning, accused Racine of having himself poisoned Marquise Duparc eleven years earlier. Although a warrant for his arrest was requested and issued, it was never served, and Racine seems to have survived the affair unscathed. Indeed, in 1679 his annual pension reached two thousand livres.

In 1683 Racine received a ten-thousand-livre grant from the king for a libretto, co-authored with Boileau, of a ballet for the carnival preceding Lent. The same year, he and Boileau were chosen as two of the nine members of the newly created Académie des Inscriptions (or "Petite Académie"), which was responsible for devising inscriptions for public monuments, medals, and engravings. In compensation for all these signs of royal favor, Racine and Boileau composed in 1684, as an aside to their work as historiographers, an *Eloge historique du Roi Louis XIV, sur ses conquêtes depuis l'année 1672 jusqu'en 1678* (Historical Eulogy of King Louis XIV, on His Conquests from the Year 1672 to

Racine's gravestone at Port-Royal des Champs, south of Versailles

1678). Originally published in 1730 under the title *Campagne de Louis XIV,* the work was at the time misattributed to Paul Pellisson. Only in 1784 was it republished under the correct names of Racine and Boileau.

In January 1685 Thomas Corneille was received into the Académie Française, taking the seat of Pierre Corneille, his elder brother, who had died three months earlier. On the occasion of his reception Racine delivered a stirring eulogy of the elder Corneille, his former rival; his speech was also filled with lavish praise for the king, especially in his role as patron of the arts and protector of the theater. Later the same year, on the occasion of the reception of Louis XIV and Colbert at the newly built and magnificient Château de Sceaux, Racine composed his *Idylle sur la paix* (Idyll on Peace), which was set to a musical score by Jean-Baptiste Lully. First published in 1685, the piece was included two years later in the first volume of a newly revised and

enlarged edition of the *Œuvres de Racine.* The same volume also included Racine's "Discours prononcé à l'Académie française à la réception de MM. de Corneille et de Bergeret" (Discourse Delivered to the French Academy at the Reception of MM. de Corneille and de Bergeret).

The most important literary event in Racine's life during this period was an invitation from the powerful marquise de Maintenon to write a play to be performed by the students of Saint-Cyr, an educational institution near Versailles created by her in 1686 for impoverished girls of noble birth. At its height it housed as many as 250 students, some of whom resided and studied there for up to twelve years. Among their extracurricular activities, one of the more significant was the staging of plays suitable for their age and their sex. Because of her religious devotion and her conservative convictions, the marquise de Maintenon had prescribed that these plays should be morally edifying and, most importantly, that they should include no love interest. An invitation of this kind, coming from her, was tantamount to a royal order, and Racine promptly went to work on what was to be his first play since *Phèdre* a dozen years earlier. He chose as his subject the book of Esther, which had already been adapted by other French playwrights. The biblical story recounts the way Queen Esther saved the Jewish people from being massacred by the Persians. Departing from Racine's previous tragedies, the play had not five acts but three, and it included choral interludes to be sung to a musical score composed by Jean-Baptiste Moreau, the successor of Lully, who had died in 1687. These interludes were doubtless inspired by classical Greek tragedy, but they also catered to the fashion of the newly imported genre of the opera.

Esther (published 1689) premiered at Saint-Cyr on 26 January 1689 in front of a select audience including Louis XIV. Attendance was limited to 250 people and was by invitation only. All of the roles were performed by students of the school, and all of the ensuing performances were likewise held at Saint-Cyr; indeed, the first truly public performance of the play did not take place until 1721, more than twenty years after Racine's death. Led by Louis XIV, who went to several of the performances, the audience was enthusiastic, and the marquise de Maintenon soon approached Racine with a request for another play.

Scholars have speculated that *Esther* might have included allusions to events of Racine's day: the salvation of the Jews from persecution might have been a metaphor for the plight either of the Protestants, still reeling from the Revocation of the Edict of Nantes in 1685, or of the Jansenists, who were being subjected to an increasing hostility from the church and the Crown; likewise, the coronation of Esther in place of the destitute former queen, Vasthi, might have been an allusion to the marquise de Maintenon's succession of the marquise de Montespan in the king's affection. No evidence exists either to support or to dismiss such interpretations.

Racine's dutiful compliance with the marquise de Maintenon's wishes enhanced the favor in which he was held at the court. He was more than once invited by Louis XIV to join the few similarly privileged at his new residence of Marly, a few miles north of Versailles. Built from 1679 to 1686, Marly had become Louis XIV's favorite retreat from the overcrowded court of Versailles. Racine's presence at this more intimate court—where all the guests were present by invitation only and were personally known to the king—was a sign of exceptional favor; the king's high regard for Racine was further confirmed in 1689, shortly after the

success of *Esther,* when Louis XIV granted him personal lodgings at Marly.

Asked by the marquise de Maintenon as early as 1689 to supply Saint-Cyr with another play, Racine once again chose a biblical episode. The final play of his career, *Athalie* (Athaliah, performed 1691; published the same year) follows the story of the restoration to the throne of Judah of the last descendant of David, and of the defeat and death of the usurper Athaliah, the villainous daughter of Ahab and Jezebel. This second biblical drama was a more ambitious undertaking than *Esther,* not only because it was a five-act tragedy, complete with important choral sections following the model of the great Greek tragedies, but also because of its grander setting, the temple of Jerusalem. The performance featured music by Moreau and a spectacular set in line with those used in the increasingly popular opera.

Racine completed the choral parts first, and their rehearsals began shortly thereafter; rehearsals of the entire play began in July 1690. In January and February 1691 it was rehearsed in front of Louis XIV and other distinguished guests, in particular the dauphin and the exiled queen of England, Mary of Modena, to whom, along with her husband, the recently dethroned James II, Louis XIV had in 1689 offered the hospitality of the Château de Saint-Germain-en-Laye. *Athalie* was never fully staged at the time, however, not even in private as was *Esther,* in part because of a lingering hostility in the church toward theater in all its forms. Consequently, all of the performances at Saint-Cyr were called *répétitions* (rehearsals). Even in the case of a biblical play, some viewed it as scandalous that young girls should participate in a spectacle on the stage. Whereas the performances of *Esther* had included elaborate oriental costumes, the schoolgirls participating in the rehearsals of *Athalie* wore instead their austere school uniforms.

Despite the fact that *Athalie* was never performed publicly in its day, like *Esther,* the play has been subjected to interpretations referring to current events: either to the persecutions being endured by Port-Royal and its friends, or to the hope of the restoration to the English throne of the Stuart royal family, then exiled in France. No scholarly consensus exists, however, on any of these readings.

During the period of these biblical productions Racine's status continued to rise, though more as a courtier than as a writer. In 1690 he was authorized to purchase from the widow of the previous incumbent the position of *Gentilhomme de la chambre du Roi.* It was not an especially profitable position—Racine had to pay the widow fifty-three thousand livres for it, and its annual revenue was a mere two hundred livres—but it conferred nobility upon its new owner. In 1693 the title of *Gentilhomme* was made hereditary by the king, thus guaranteeing the future of Racine's elder son, Jean-Baptiste, then fifteen years old, a matter of the utmost importance for his ambitious father. In 1696, as a final mark of the noble status newly conferred upon the family, its coat of arms was formally registered. Originally bearing the figures of a rat and a swan (in French *rat* and *cygne,* forming the patronym *Racine*), it was changed to represent just a swan, eliminating the unsavory figure of the rat: "d'azur au cygne d'argent becqué et membré de sable."

At the suggestion of the marquise de Maintenon, and as a sign of his religious devotion, Racine composed four poems published together under the title *Cantiques spirituels* (Spiritual Canticles, 1694). The first three were set to music by Moreau and the fourth by Michel Delalande, and they were sung at the court in the king's presence. The following year Louis XIV gave Racine the high privilege of housing in the Versailles palace. During the king's illness in 1696, this arrangement allowed him to have Racine, known for the exceptional quality of his voice and his diction, share his apartment and read to him at night when he could not sleep. One of the texts then chosen was Plutarch's *Life of Alexander* (circa A.D. 100).

In 1696 Racine was also allowed to purchase another position, this one bearing the exalted title of *Conseiller secrétaire du Roi,* though it in fact had no real responsibilities attached. The availability of such honorific titles resulted in part from the financial and economic crisis France was undergoing at the time, a consequence of the long succession of wars in which the country had been embroiled, as well as of the king's profligate ways; selling meaningless offices had long been an expedient resorted to by the Crown to aid its treasury. They were often in no way profitable investments for their status-seeking purchasers: Racine had to borrow money in order to pay the 55,000 livres for this one, which brought in an annual income of only 2,200 livres. A few years earlier, in 1692, already because of the financial crisis, Racine's annual stipend as an historiographer had been reduced to 2,000 livres. Nonetheless, his growing family–his seventh and last child, Louis, was born in 1692–managed quite well. In 1697 a third edition of Racine's collected works appeared, the final to be published in his lifetime: two handsome volumes resulting from his assiduous work of correcting and revising.

The year 1698 was a difficult one for Racine. Accused of Jansenism by some of his enemies and feeling obliged to defend himself, he composed a long letter addressed to the marquise de Maintenon, but he seems to have kept it in his personal papers without sending it. In May of the same year, La Champmeslé died; no

record of Racine's reaction exists. In October he suffered the initial symptoms of what has since been diagnosed as liver cancer. On 10 October he substituted for the will he had written five years earlier a new one in which he expressed the wish to be buried at Port-Royal des Champs, next to the grave of his former teacher at the Petites Ecoles, Jean Hamon. In spite of his health, Racine managed to attend the ceremony in Melun in which his daughter Anne entered the order of the Ursulines on 6 November. In January 1699, although increasingly ill, he attended the wedding of his daughter Marie-Catherine, the only one of his daughters to marry, to a lawyer, Colin de Moramber de Riberpré.

Racine died on 21 April 1699. Louis XIV authorized his burial at Port-Royal, in spite of his growing antagonism toward all that it stood for. The king's final favor to Racine was to grant a pension to his widow and to his elder son, Jean-Baptiste. In 1710 Louis XIV ordered the demolition of Port-Royal; the following year, Racine's remains were exhumed and transferred to the church of Saint-Etienne du Mont in Paris, where Blaise Pascal had been buried in 1662.

Racine's death marked the virtual demise of the literary genre he had so ably illustrated. In the century that followed, many tragedies were written in emulation of Racine's, but none succeeded in matching his, and almost none have survived, in spite of the talent of some of their authors, Voltaire in particular. Not until the early nineteenth century was it finally realized that, with Racine, French tragedy had reached both its zenith and the beginning of its decline.

Bibliographies:

Edwin E. Williams, *Racine depuis 1885: Bibliographie raisonnée des livres, articles, comptes-rendus critiques relatifs à la vie et l'œuvre de Jean Racine, 1885–1939* (Baltimore: Johns Hopkins University Press, 1940);

Albert-Jean Guibert, *Bibliographie des œuvres de Jean Racine publiées au XVIIe siècle et œuvres posthumes* (Paris: Editions du Centre National de la Recherche Scientifique, 1968);

Raymond Picard, *Nouveau Corpus Racinianum: Recueil-inventaire des textes et documents du XVIIe siècle concernant Jean Racine* (Paris: Editions du Centre National de la Recherche Scientifique, 1976).

Biographies:

Louis Racine, *Mémoires sur la vie de Jean Racine* (Lausanne & Geneva: M. M. Bousquet, 1747);

Geoffrey Brereton, *Jean Racine: A Critical Biography* (London: Cassell, 1951);

Raymond Picard, *La Carrière de Jean Racine* (Paris: Gallimard, 1961);

Alain Viala, *Racine: La Stratégie du caméléon* (Paris: Seghers, 1990);

Jean Rohou, *Jean Racine: Entre sa carrière, son œuvre et son Dieu* (Paris: Fayard, 1992);

Georges Forestier, "Chronologie," in *Œuvres complètes,* edited by Forestier, Bibliothèque de la Pléiade, no. 5 (Paris: Gallimard, 1999), pp. lxix–xc;

Jean-Michel Delacomptée, *Racine en majesté* (Paris: Flammarion, 1999).

References:

Claude K. Abraham, *Jean Racine,* Twayne's World Authors Series, no. 458 (Boston: Twayne, 1977);

Roselyne de Ayala and Jean-Pierre Guéno, *Belles Lettres: Manuscripts by the Masters of French Literature,* translated by John Goodman (New York: Abrams, 2001);

Roland Barthes, *Sur Racine* (Paris: Seuil, 1963);

Charles Bernet, *Le Vocabulaire des tragédies de Jean Racine: Analyse statistique* (Geneva: Slatkine / Paris: Champion, 1983);

Philip Butler, *Racine: A Study* (London: Heinemann, 1974);

Peter France, *Racine's Rhetoric* (Oxford: Clarendon Press, 1965);

Bryant C. Freeman and Alan Batson, *Concordance du théâtre et des poésies de Racine,* 2 volumes (Ithaca, N.Y.: Cornell University Press, 1968);

Lucien Goldmann, *Le Dieu caché: Etude sur la vision tragique dans les "Pensées" de Pascal et dan le théâtre de Racine* (Paris: Gallimard, 1956);

Judd D. Hubert, *Essai d'exégèse racinienne, les secrets témoins* (Paris: Nizet, 1956);

Roy C. Knight, *Racine et la Grèce* (Paris: Boivin, 1950);

John C. Lapp, *Aspects of Racinian Tragedy* (Toronto: University of Toronto Press, 1955);

Charles Mauron, *L'Inconscient dans l'œuvre et la vie de Racine* (Paris: Ophrys, 1957);

Georges May, *Tragédie cornélienne, tragédie racinienne: Etude sur les sources de l'intérêt dramatique* (Urbana: University of Illinois Press, 1948);

Odette de Mourgues, *Autonomie de Racine* (Paris: Corti, 1967);

Alain Niderst, *Les Tragédies de Racine: Diversité et unité* (Paris: Nizet, 1975);

Henry Phillips, *Racine: Language and Theatre* (Durham, U.K.: University of Durham, 1994);

Jean Pommier, *Aspects de Racine* (Paris: Nizet, 1954);

Jean Rohou, *Evolution du tragique racinien* (Paris: SEDES, 1991);

Jacques Scherer, *La Dramaturgie classique en France* (Paris: Nizet, 1950);

Jean Starobinski, *L'Œil vivant, essai: Corneille, Racine, Rousseau, Stendhal* (Paris: Gallimard, 1961);

Ronald W. Tobin, *Jean Racine Revisited,* Twayne's World Authors Series, no. 878 (New York: Twayne, 1999);

Martin Turnell, *Jean Racine–Dramatist* (London: Hamilton, 1972);

Eugène Vinaver, *Racine et la poésie tragique: Essai* (Paris: Nizet, 1951);

Bernard Weinberg, *The Art of Jean Racine* (Chicago: University of Chicago Press, 1963);

Philip John Yarrow, *Racine* (Oxford: Blackwell, 1977).

Papers:

No autograph manuscripts of Jean Racine's plays are extant. Racine's younger son, Louis, donated many of his father's writings to the Crown; these manuscripts are now kept at the Bibliothèque Nationale, Paris, which also houses most of his correspondence, as well as some books in which Racine made handwritten annotations.

Jean-François-Paul de Gondi, cardinal de Retz

(15 September 1613 – 24 August 1679)

Malina Stefanovska
University of California, Los Angeles

SELECTED BOOKS*: *Très-humble et très importante Remonstrance au Roy, sur la remise des Places maritimes de Flandres entre les mains des Anglois,* anonymous (Paris, 1658); translated as *France No Friend to England; or, The Resentments of the French upon the Success of the English, as It Is Expressed in a Most Humble and Important Remonstrance to the King of France upon the Surrendring of the Maritime Ports of Flanders into the Hands of the English, Wherein Much of the Private Transactions between Cardinal Mazarin and the Late Protector Oliver Are Discovered* (London, 1659);

La Conjuration du comte Jean-Louis de Fiesque, anonymous (Paris: C. Barbin, 1665);

Mémoires de Monsieur le Cardinal de Retz, 4 volumes (Amsterdam: F. Bernard / Nancy: J.-B. Cusson, 1717); revised as *Mémoires du cardinal de Retz, publiés pour la première fois sur le manuscrit autographe,* edited by Jacques Joseph Champollion and Aimé Louis Champollion (Paris: E. Proux, 1837); *Mémoires de Monsieur le Cardinal de Retz* translated by Peter Davall as *Memoirs of the Cardinal de Retz: Containing the Particulars of His Own Life, with the Most Secret Transactions at the French Court During the Administration of Cardinal Mazarin, and the Civil Wars Occasioned by It, to Which Are Added Some Other Pieces Written by the Cardinal De Retz, or Explanatory to These Memoirs,* 4 volumes (London: J. Tonson, 1723).

Editions and Collections: *Œuvres du cardinal de Retz,* 12 volumes, edited by Alphonse Feillet, Jules Gourdauld, and Régis Chantelauze (Paris: Hachette, 1870–1929);

La Conjuration de Fiesque: Edition critique publiée d'après le texte de 1665, avec des variantes provenant de manuscripts inedits, edited by Derek A. Watts (Oxford: Clarendon Press, 1967);

*Only major or book-length works of cardinal de Retz are listed above. Short pamphlets and works of uncertain attribution have been omitted.

*Jean-François-Paul de Gondi, cardinal de Retz
(Musée des Beaux-Arts, Blois)*

Œuvres, edited by Marie-Thérèse Hipp and Michel Pernot, Bibliothèque de la Pléiade, no. 53 (Paris: Gallimard, 1984);

Mémoires, 2 volumes, edited by Simone Bertière (Paris: Garnier, 1987).

SELECTED BROADSIDES: *Défense de l'ancienne et légitime Fronde* (Paris, 1651);

Le Solitaire aux deux désintéressés (Paris, 1651);

Les Contretemps de sieur de Chavigny (Paris, 1652);

Les Intérêts du temps (Paris, 1652);

Manifeste de Monseigneur le duc de Beaufort, général des armées de Son Altesse Royale (Paris, 1652);

Le Vrai et la Faux de Monsieur le Prince et de Monsieur le cardinal de Retz (Paris, 1652);

Le vraisemblable sur la conduite de Monseigneur le cardinal de Retz (Paris, 1652).

A High Church figure and leader of a political faction, an admired preacher as well as a pamphleteer, the controversial cardinal de Retz remains best known in French literary history for his posthumously published *Mémoires de Monsieur le Cardinal de Retz* (1717). The public was immediately attracted to Retz's account of his life during the Fronde for its historical interest as well as its literary value. The memoirs went through two editions in 1717, five in 1718, and one in 1719; they have since remained among the best known in French literature, have been compared with Saint-Simon's and Chateaubriand's memoirs, and are thought to have influenced Stendhal and Marcel Proust.

Jean-François-Paul de Gondi, coadjutor to the archbishop of Paris and later cardinal de Retz (or Rais, as he chose to spell it), was born on 15 September 1613 into an old Florentine merchant family, naturalized in France since the sixteenth century and ennobled by Catherine de Médicis, who bestowed on the family considerable favors, including the duchy of Retz. The youngest of three sons in a family that traditionally boasted of important positions in the Church, Retz was groomed for an ecclesiastical career, one for which, according to him, he had no inclination whatsoever. Expected to succeed his uncle, the archbishop of Paris, the young Retz—who dreamed of exceptional deeds but was unwilling to lead a life of strict moral standards—decided instead to throw himself into politics. While his critics' accusations that he aimed as high as the prime minister's office might have been exaggerated, it is clear from his own account that his ambition was to become a cardinal and wield a decisive influence in state affairs.

The period was a propitious one for the politically ambitious: the conflict between nobility and the monarchy, brewing throughout the reign of Louis XIII, had escalated upon his death in 1643. Regencies in France were traditionally fraught with political tensions, and that of Anne of Austria was complicated by the unpopularity of the cardinal de Mazarin, her prime minister and suspected lover. An Italian of merchant extraction and newly naturalized in France, Mazarin was generally despised by the French nobility and became the focus of popular discontent provoked by the crown's attempt to raise taxes in order to finance foreign wars.

In 1648 a revolt erupted, first among the Parlement of Paris, and soon spread to the Parisian populace. It was the beginning of the Fronde, which was to engulf the nobility, most crown princes, and several

provinces and was to shake the kingdom until 1652. As coadjutor to the archbishop of Paris, Retz was particularly visible in the capital and influential among the clergy. In his memoirs he recounts how, after he was mocked by the court for his attempts to negotiate an agreement between the queen regent and the insurgents, he joined the Frondeurs. Louis XIV, then a child, never forgave Retz his role as a faction leader and an adviser to the duke of Orléans when that prince became involved in the revolt. In 1652 the Pope named Retz a cardinal, but Louis never formally recognized the appointment. Instead, in the middle of what is known as the ecclesiastical Fronde, Retz was arrested and incarcerated in the prison of Vincennes. Eighteen months later he escaped and spent eight years roaming throughout Europe as an exile. Retz was finally pardoned in exchange for relinquishing the archbishopric of Paris, inherited after his uncle's death. The king's pardon, however, was half-hearted, and although Retz faithfully served Louis's interests at the papal conclaves, he never received much recognition for it. The end of Retz's life was marked by long stays at his estate at Commercy, where he wrote his memoirs between 1675 and 1677, and by a religious conversion in which he unsuccessfully sought to resign his cardinalship. He died on 24 August 1679 at the Abbey of Saint-Denis in Paris, where he spent the last year of his life. By Louis's order, Retz's tomb was left unmarked.

An admiration for glory acquired through extraordinary deeds—which no doubt also informed a life of Julius Caesar, composed early on in Retz's life and now lost—is the striking feature of *La Conjuration du comte Jean-Louis de Fiesque* (The Conspiracy of Count Gian Luigi Fieschi), published anonymously in 1665. Retz claimed that he wrote the work when he was eighteen, but Derek A. Watts has proved that it was most likely composed in 1639, when Retz was twenty-six. *La Conjuration du comte Jean-Louis de Fiesque* is the narrative of a failed sixteenth-century conspiracy in Genoa led by Gian Luigi Fieschi, written after Agostino Mascardi's historical account, published in Italy in 1629. Retz's text was meant as an exemplum, composed in high rhetorical style with long debates on topics such as the legitimacy of conspiring. Though admittedly not a masterpiece, it is interesting for several reasons. In opposition to Mascardi's defense of the historical victors, Retz sides entirely with the unfortunate Fieschi who, in the middle of carrying out his insurgency, perished by drowning in the muddy Genoan harbor. In Retz's mind, France under Cardinal Richelieu bore a striking resemblance to the Ligurian city dominated by the tyrant Andrea Doria. Richelieu himself, having read a copy of Retz's book that was inadvertently allowed to circulate, had no doubts about its message, since he

LA
CONIVRATION
DV COMTE
IEAN-LOVIS
DE FIESQVE.

A PARIS,
Chez CLAVDE BARBIN, fur
le grand Perron de la Sainte
Chapelle.

M. DC. LXV.
AVEC PRIVILEGE DV ROY.

Title page for Retz's narrative about a failed conspiracy in sixteenth-century Genoa (Bibliothèque Nationale, Paris)

exclaimed, "Voilà un dangereux esprit" (Here is a dangerous mind).

La Conjuration du comte Jean-Louis de Fiesque encapsulates most of the views that give Retz's memoirs their unique physiognomy. His admiration for heroism led him to describe Fieschi as "l'un des plus beaux et des plus élevés esprits du monde, ambitieux, hardi et entreprenant" (among the most beautiful and elevated minds in the world, ambitious, bold and enterprising) and prompted him to assert that "C'est cette amour de la belle gloire, et cette hauteur d'âme qui fait les hommes véritablement grands et qui les élève au-dessus du reste du monde; c'est la seule qui peut vous rendre parfaitement heureux" (This love of high glory, and this elevation of soul makes men truly great and places them above the rest of humanity; it, alone, can make you perfectly happy). *La Conjuration du comte Jean-Louis de Fiesque* reveals Retz's belief that historical

outcome was less important than the beauty and heroism involved in an action, his idealization of factional politics developed against the backdrop of Niccolò Machiavelli's political realism, his passionate involvement in history writing, and the irony lying in the questionable choice of a failed hero who uncannily foregrounded Retz's own political destiny. René Pintard has aptly called this work "l'héroïsation du factieux" (the heroization of a faction leader).

As much as this early historical narrative, Retz's other works, too, testify to his conviction that writing was subordinate to action. This is not to say that the former did not command his attention: his involvement in literary circles and scholarly academies and his friendships with such well-known figures as Jean Chapelain, Gédéon Tallemant des Réaux, and Paul Scarron show a man of impressive culture and good taste. But more often Retz's talent was placed in the service of politics: his admired sermons, his letters, and his political pamphlets were all rooted in particular historical circumstances and bear their mark. More than that, in them Retz strove to have an effect on history. Christian Jouhaud's analysis of Retz's political pamphlets as part of the well-known "Mazarinades" (publications attacking the cardinal) shows how the cardinal's rhetorical strategies contributed to what Jouhaud calls "la Fronde des mots" (the Fronde of words).

Retz's main work and by far the most important, however, is his *Mémoires*. His was a time of renewed interest in history: the publication of sixteenth-century memoirs and of historical novellas such as Marie-Madeleine, comtesse Lafayette's *La Princesse de Clèves* (1678), which came out a year after Retz wrote his account but probably circulated in salons earlier, accompanied a decline in popularity of the baroque adventure novel. Retz was not unaware of his antecedents, since he saw himself in a tradition embodied by the widely read memoirs of the sixteenth-century magistrate Jacques-Auguste de Thou and by Caesar's life. Indeed, Retz's own *Mémoires* stand out among the literature of his century, much as Saint-Simon's do in the eighteenth.

Retz's original title, *La vie du cardinal de Rais* (The Life of the Cardinal de Rais), shows that his memoirs are as much an autobiography as an historical account. The narrative, which comprises 926 pages in the 1984 Pléiade edition, begins with Retz's birth in 1613 and, after a few selected episodes from his youth (part 1), covers his involvement in the Fronde, his arrest and escape from prison (part 2, by far the longest), and his arrival at the papal conclave in Rome in 1655 (part 3), where the narrative abruptly stops. The book is an account of the circumstances and reasons that attracted Retz to become a faction leader, of his acts and

Page from the manuscript for Retz's memoir, published posthumously in 1717 (Bibliothèque Nationale, Paris)

thoughts, and of the personal consequences of his decision to join the Frondeurs. Yet, while following a strict chronological order and recapitulating the main events in which Retz participated, the memoirs are not an eyewitness account proper but rather a rememoration, the lucid, introspective glance of a mature author at the man he once was. André Bertière has established that Retz wrote the work between 1675 and 1677, more than twenty years after the events narrated.

In his memoirs Retz states, "l'on ne se connaît jamais assez bien pour se peindre raisonnablement soi-même" (one never knows oneself well enough to paint oneself accurately). Understandably, he does not provide a self-portrait as such. All throughout the narrative, however, he discloses his passions and interests, his (sometimes concurrent) love affairs, his capacity to persuade and manipulate others, and his keen psychological observations of others. He presents a detailed picture, confirmed by contemporaries, of an agile mind and an exceptionally active man. A frantic lobbyist, an impenitent Don Juan, and a dandy before his time, Retz infused his memoirs with a distinct personality rarely found in the literature of the classical age. His subjectivity is also detectable in the personal perspective provided on popular uprisings, human passions, and political greatness. For Retz as an historian, the Fronde was caused by the gradual deterioration of the traditional, unspoken, social pact between the monarchy and its subjects. As a protagonist in the movement, he also notes its immediate causes: Mazarin's tyranny and ignorance of French institutions, the queen regent's acrimony and lack of intuition, and the Parlement's formalistic spirit. This same analytical vein pervades Retz's examination of the insurgents: he draws an unforgettable gallery of their portraits, delineating the various characters and passions revealed in minute gestures, hidden glances, and inflections of the voice. No less pointed is his self-examination: he reports embracing the Fronde after a long night of thinking in which his passion for glory came together with his childhood dream of leading a faction. Retz was probably drawn to political opposition because of its inherent fragility and its dependence on public opinion. He deemed leading a political faction more difficult than governing the world and felt that succeeding in such extraordinary circumstances would have given him eternal glory and that failing, as he did, made his choice no less heroic. This perspective, more than his political destiny, paints Retz as an historical actor and gives depth to his thought.

Retz's writing was thus, above all, a quest. Marie-Thérèse Hipp notes that the memoirs are constructed around an existential interrogation. Simone Bertière describes them as "ni apologie ni règlement de comptes, mais quête de soi et revendication d'identité" (neither an apology nor a settling of accounts, but a quest for the self and an affirmation of identity). His quest, however, did not take the shape of an aesthetic or a philosophical one. Although true happiness for Retz might have lain in writing rather than in life, as was the case with Jean-Jacques Rousseau, Stendhal, and Proust, he was unaware of it. Like most men of his time and stature, Retz considered himself a public figure and a man of action. The pursuit of glory in the realm of politics was the sole prism through which he saw his destiny, and even his love affairs were integrated into the dynamics of the Fronde. One should not assume, therefore, that he describes his personal sentiments in the same vein as his literary heirs. As a true seventeenth-century aristocrat, Retz claims that his narrative has been written negligently, without any artfulness, and that his sole interest lies in establishing the historical truth. Echoing other memoirists from the nobility, he favors writers who have personally witnessed and created history over royal historiographers, most of low birth, whom he disdainfully relegates to the "poultry yard" and to whom he denies any true understanding of events.

While ideologically motivated, this passionate involvement in history is what gives Retz's writing its distinctive form: the aphorisms and maxims woven into his narrative, the gallery of portraits, and his thoughts on human motivation and group dynamics are all testimony to his will to understand the lessons of history. Yet, in spite of this desire to see history as an exemplum, he represents historical action in human terms, with all its contingencies and limitations. In spite of his professed distaste for Machiavelli, such a perspective makes them akin, as does Retz's belief that history belongs to those who can recognize the right moment: "Il n'y a rien dans le monde qui n'ait son moment décisif, et le chef-d'œuvre de la bonne conduite est de connaître et de prendre ce moment" (Everything in the world has its decisive moment, and the consumate art in good conduct is to know and seize that moment). Yet, while not believing in providential order, Retz avoids entirely subordinating history to man's machinations, as did Tacitus. Retz insists on the unreconcilable contradictions of history and often admits his ignorance, letting the reader decide between conflicting interpretations. His ultimate pessimism as an historian is paralleled by his destiny as the protagonist of his narrative. Retz's eloquent speeches to the duc d'Orléans, the prince de Condé, and the queen, quoted at length; his descriptions of the "comédie humaine" unfolding before his eyes; his pointed and sometimes contradictory political maxims; and his many reflections on political action, all lead to the same conclusion: that his failure as a faction leader was inevitable, in spite of all his capacities and efforts. This conclusion seems to be the point at which Retz suddenly stops writing.

Yet, Retz's acknowledged failure as a political actor and perhaps even as an historian was ultimately his literary redemption. As is the case with many great writers, his life turned out to be far less significant than its rewriting. What gives him stature is thus neither the historical truth he claimed nor his destiny but his reflections on the past. Hence, while much early scholarship on Retz was dedicated to determining whether his memoirs accurately reflected his role in the Fronde, that question is seen as less important today. Instead, critics have turned to his quest for personal truth. In her study *Le cardinal de Retz, historien et moraliste du possible* (Le Cardinal de Retz, an Historian and Moralist of Possibilities, 1966), Janet T. Letts aptly describes Retz's attempts to make sense of his acts in concrete, historical circumstances. Analyzing every event both as a case study and as a possible exemplum, Retz takes the stance of the historian as well as of a moralist author. His interest lies in individuals rather than "man," in "circumstances" rather than "history." As he considers the motivations of every protagonist, including himself, both strands of his writing–history and moral introspection–come together. They give his memoirs a distinctive speculative style and a subtle analytical vein that anticipate Proust.

Retz's memoirs are dedicated to a woman whose identity remains unknown, though scholars have suggested Marie de Rabutin Chantal, Madame de Sévigné, a long-time friend of Retz, or her daughter, Madame de Grignan. Addressing her simply as "Madame," he opens his autobiography by stating the peculiar "pact" that governs it: in spite of his reluctance to unveil a life filled with sins and mistakes, he promises to open up the most hidden recesses of his heart on her request. To this relationship of trust and intimacy, carefully cultivated by the narrator, the memoirs owe their particular tone and charm. Retz's complicity with his interlocutor and first reader, perceptible at every juncture of the narrative, gives it the appearance of a leisurely, heart-to-heart conversation, a confession in which sincerity does not preclude seduction. Expressions such as "I told you before" or "you will agree with me" regularly punctuate the text, as does Retz's surprise at the unexpected pleasure of revealing his hidden self to her. Her figure, gradually woven into the text through such passing remarks, is that of a sympathetic listener who guarantees the authenticity of the narrative, shares the author's pleasure, and makes his writing into a gesture of giving. The resulting exchange is more introspective than a letter, yet more dynamic than a confession: a dialogue with the self as much as with the other, an earnest

Cardinal de Retz (engraving after a portrait by Audran; Bibliothèque Nationale, Paris)

account in which the lucidity and disenchantment of the mature author do not hide the enthusiasm and frantic quest for glory of the young prelate.

Through such qualities Retz introduced the genre of the memoir into the great French tradition of psychological prose, from Madame de Lafayette to Proust, and proved himself able to transform, long after the fact, a failed life into a literary triumph. Banished from action in his lifetime, disputed as an impartial historian, he triumphed in writing. Through his writing, his life acquired its unity.

Biographies:
Régis Chantelauze, *Le Cardinal de Retz et l'affaire du chapeau,* 2 volumes (Paris: Didier & Cie, 1878);
Louis Batiffol, *Biographie du cardinal de Retz* (Paris: Hachette, 1929);

François Albert-Buisson, *Le cardinal de Retz: Portrait* (Paris: Plon, 1954);

Pierre-Georges Lorris, *Un agitateur au XVIIe siècle: le cardinal de Retz* (Paris: A. Michel, 1956);

Richard M. Golden, *The Godly Rebellion: Parisian Curés and the Religious Fronde, 1652–1662* (Chapel Hill: University of North Carolina Press, 1981);

Simone Bertière, *La vie du cardinal de Retz* (Paris: Editions de Fallois, 1990).

References:

André Bertière, *Le Cardinal de Retz, mémorialiste* (Paris: Klincksieck, 1977);

Hubert Carrier, "Un désaveu suspect de Retz: l'*Avis désintéressé sur la conduite de Monseigneur le Coadjuteur,*" *XVIIe siècle,* no. 124 (1979): 253–263;

Carrier, "Sincérité et création littéraire dans les *Mémoires* du cardinal de Retz," *XVIIe siècle,* nos. 94–95 (1971): 39–74;

Jacques Delon, *Le cardinal de Retz, orateur* (Paris: Aux amateurs de livres, 1989);

Marc Fumaroli, "Retz: des *Mémoires* en forme de conversation galante," in his *La diplomatie de l'esprit: De Montaigne à La Fontaine* (Paris: Hermann, 1994), pp. 247–281;

Donald Furber, "Humor and the Ridiculous in Retz' *Mémoires,*" *French Review,* 36 (1962–1963): 352–358;

Marie-Thérèse Hipp, "La 'Galerie des portraits' dans les *Mémoires* du cardinal de Retz," *Littératures,* 17 (1987): 49–67;

Hipp, *Mythes et réalités: Enquête sur le roman et les Mémoires, 1660–1700* (Paris: Klincksieck, 1976);

Christian Jouhaud, *Mazarinades: La Fronde des mots* (Paris: Aubier, 1985);

A. J. Krailsheimer, *Studies in Self-Interest from Descartes to La Bruyère* (Oxford: Clarendon Press, 1962);

Janet T. Letts, *Le cardinal de Retz, historien et moraliste du possible* (Paris: Nizet, 1966);

Louis Marin, "Bagatelles pour meurtres," in his *Le récit est un piège* (Paris: Minuit, 1978), pp. 35–66;

Jean-Pierre Morelou, "Le cardinal de Retz moraliste politique," *Contrepoint,* 24 (June 1977): 81–98;

Chantal Morlet, "Jean-Louis de Fiesque, héros de roman," in *XVIIe siècle,* no. 109 (1975): 33–50;

René Pintard, "*La conjuration de Fiesque* ou l'Héroïsation d'un factieux," in *Héroïsme et création littéraire sous les règnes d'Henri IV et de Louis XIII,* edited by Noémi Hepp and Georges Livet, Actes et colloques, no. 16 (Paris: Klincksieck, 1974), pp. 225–232;

J. H. M. Salmon, *Cardinal de Retz: The Anatomy of a Conspirator* (London: Weidenfeld & Nicolson, 1969);

Derek A. Watts, *Cardinal de Retz: The Ambiguities of a Seventeenth-Century Mind* (Oxford: Oxford University Press, 1980);

Watts, "The Enigma of Retz," *French Studies,* 12 (1958): 203–221;

Watts, "Quelques réflexions sur *La Conjuration de Fiesque,*" *Revue des sciences humaines,* no. 126 (1967): 289–302;

Watts, "Retz and Tacitus," in *The Classical Tradition in French Literature. Studies presented to Professor R. C. Knight by Colleagues, Pupils and Friends,* edited by H. T. Barnwell and others (London: Grant & Cutler, 1977), pp. 135–144;

Watts, "Le sens des métaphores théâtrales chez le cardinal de Retz et quelques écrivains contemporains," *Travaux de linguistique et de littérature,* 13, no. 2 (1975): 385–399.

Papers:

Of Jean-François-Paul de Gondi, cardinal de Retz's papers, four manuscripts of *La Conjuration du comte Jean-Louis de Fiesque* exist, none of them autographs and all copied considerably earlier than the publication year of 1665: copy A (Bibliothèque Nationale de France, manuscrits fr., 24.717), copy B (Bibliothèque Mazarine, manuscrits, 1924), copy C (Bibliothèque Nationale de France, nouv. acq. fr., manuscrits, 1517), and copy D (Bibliothèque Nationale de France, manuscrits fr., 6050). Each shows variations in style, but overall, the text of copies C and D has been revised and modernized and is written in the same hand. One autograph manuscript of *Mémoires de Monsieur le Cardinal de Retz* is at the Bibliothèque Nationale de France (three volumes in quarto, manuscript nos. 10325, 10326, and 10327), as well as several copies. The original manuscript is missing several parts, of which the first and most extensive is about seventy pages long.

Jean Rotrou

(August 1609 – June 1650)

Perry Gethner
Oklahoma State University

BOOKS: *L'Hypocondriaque, ou Le Mort amoureux,* published with *Autres Œuvres poétiques du Sr Rotrou* (Paris: T. Du Bray, 1631);

Cléagénor et Doristée (Paris: A. de Sommaville, 1634); republished as *La Doristée* (Paris: T. Quinet, 1635);

La Bague de l'oubli (Paris: F. Targa, 1635);

La Diane, published with *Autres oeuvres du même auteur* (Paris: F. Targa, 1635);

Les Occasions perdues (Paris: A. de Sommaville & T. Quinet, 1635);

La Célimène (Paris: A. de Sommaville, 1636);

Hercule mourant (Paris: A. de Sommaville & T. Quinet, 1636);

L'Heureuse constance (Paris: A. de Sommaville & T. Quinet, 1636);

Les Ménechmes (Paris: A. de Sommaville & T. Quinet, 1636);

Agésilan de Colchos (Paris: A. de Sommaville, 1637);

La Céliane (Paris: T. Quinet, 1637); republished as *La Belle Céliane* (Paris: T. Quinet, 1642);

Clorinde (Paris: A. de Sommaville, 1637);

Le Filandre (Paris: A. de Sommaville, 1637);

L'Heureux naufrage, also published as *Cléandre, ou L'Heureux naufrage* (Paris: A. de Sommaville, 1637);

L'Innocente infidélité (Paris: A. de Sommaville, 1637);

La Pélerine amoureuse, also published as *Angélique, ou La Pélerine amoureuse* (Paris: A. de Sommaville, 1637);

Amélie (Paris: A. de Sommaville, 1638);

L'Aveugle de Smyrne, by Rotrou, Pierre Corneille, François Le Métel de Boisrobert, Guillaume Colletet, and Claude de l'Estoile (Paris: A. Courbé, 1638);

La Comédie des Tuileries, by Rotrou, Corneille, Boisrobert, Colletet, and l'Estoile (Paris: A. Courbé, 1638);

Les Sosies (Paris: A. de Sommaville, 1638); republished as *La Naissance d'Hercule, ou L'Amphytrion* (Paris: A. de Sommaville, 1650);

Antigone (Paris: A. de Sommaville & T. Quinet, 1639);

Jean Rotrou (engraving from Oeuvres de Jean Rotrou, *1967)*

La Belle Alphrède (Paris: A. de Sommaville & T. Quinet, 1639);

Les Deux Pucelles (Paris: A. de Sommaville & T. Quinet, 1639);

Laure persécutée (Paris: A. de Sommaville & T. Quinet, 1639);

Les Captifs, ou Les Esclaves (Paris: A. de Sommaville, 1640);

Crisante (Paris: A. de Sommaville & T. Quinet, 1640);

Iphygénie (Paris: A. de Sommaville, 1641); republished as *Le Sacrifice d'Iphigénie* (Paris: T. Quinet, 1642);

Clarice, ou L'Amour constant (Paris: A. de Sommaville, T. Quinet & A. Courbé, 1643);

Le Bélissaire (Paris: A. de Sommaville & A. Courbé, 1644);

Célie, ou Le Vice-roy de Naples (Paris: A. de Sommaville, T. Quinet & A. Courbé, 1646);

La Soeur (Paris: A. de Sommaville, T. Quinet & A. Courbé, 1647);

Le Véritable Saint Genest (Paris: T. Quinet, 1647; Paris: G. de Luynes, 1666); translated by Lacy Lockert as *Saint Genest* in *More Plays by Rivals of Corneille and Racine* (Nashville: Vanderbilt University Press, 1968);

Dom Bernard de Cabrère (Paris: A. de Sommaville & T. Quinet, 1648);

Venceslas (Paris: A. de Sommaville, 1648); revised by Jean-François Marmontel (Paris: S. Jorry, 1759); revised by Charles-Pierre Colardeau (Paris: Veuve Duchesne, 1774);

Cosroès (Paris: A. de Sommaville / Leyden: B. & A. Elzevier, 1649); revised by Bernin de Valentiné, sieur d'Ussé (Paris: P. Ribou, 1705); translated as *Cosroes* by Lockert in *The Chief Rivals of Corneille and Racine* (Nashville: Vanderbilt University Press, 1956);

Dom Lope de Cardone (Paris: A. de Sommaville, 1652);

La Florimonde (Paris: A. de Sommaville, 1655).

Editions and Collections: *Œuvres,* 5 volumes, edited by E. L. N. Viollet Le Duc (Paris: T. Desoer, 1820)—comprises all extant plays plus the tragedy *L'Illustre Amazone,* not accepted by later scholars as Rotrou's work;

Théâtre choisi, 2 volumes, edited by D.J., with an introduction by Louis de Ronchaud (Paris: Librairie des bibliophiles, 1882)—comprises *Hercule mourant, Antigone, Le Véritable Saint Genest, Dom Bernard de Cabrère, Venceslas,* and *Cosroès;*

Théâtre choisi, edited by Félix Hémon (Paris: Laplace, Souchez & Cie, 1883)—comprises *Les Sosies, Laure persécutée, La Soeur, Saint Genest, Dom Bernard de Cabrère, Venceslas,* and *Cosroès;*

Venceslas, edited by Wolfgang Leiner (Saarbrücken, Germany: West-Ost, 1956);

La Soeur, edited by André Tissier (Paris: Larousse, 1970);

Hercule mourant, edited by Derek A. Watts (Exeter, U.K.: University of Exeter, 1971);

Le Véritable Saint Genest, edited by Elfrieda Dubois (Geneva: Droz, 1972);

Théâtre du XVIIe siècle, volume 1, edited by Jacques Scherer, Bibliothèque de la Pléiade, no. 257 (Paris: Gallimard, 1975)—comprises *La Bague de l'oubli, La Belle Alphrède, Laure persécutée, Le Véritable Saint Genest, Venceslas,* and *Cosroès;*

Les Sosies, edited by Damien Charron (Geneva: Droz, 1980);

Cosroès, edited by Watts (Exeter, U.K.: University of Exeter, 1983);

L'innocente infidélité, edited by Perry Gethner (Exeter, U.K.: University of Exeter, 1985);

Laure persécutée, edited by Jacques Morel (Mont-de-Marsan: J. Feijóo, 1991);

Théâtre complet, edited by Georges Forestier and others (Paris: Société des textes français modernes, 1998–);

L'Hypocondriaque ou Le mort amoureux, edited by Jean-Claude Vuillemin (Geneva: Droz, 1999).

Having emerged from a long period of relative obscurity, Jean Rotrou is now generally recognized as the greatest French playwright of the seventeenth century after the great trio of Pierre Corneille, Jean Racine, and Molière. Much remains sketchy in Rotrou's biography, including such key dates as the precise years he moved from one city to another. Likewise, the exact number of his plays and the dates of their premieres are largely a matter of speculation. Jean Rotrou was born in the city of Dreux in Normandy, the oldest of four children, and was baptized on 21 August 1609. His father, also named Jean, was a respectable merchant; his mother, Elisabeth Facheu, likewise came from a commercial family. Little is known of Rotrou's childhood.

Rotrou received his schooling in Paris and stayed there to pursue legal studies, although there is no evidence that he ever practiced law. In any case, his grounding in the classics of Latin literature, as well as his knowledge of Italian and Spanish, were to serve him well during his career as a dramatist. Since his first play was staged in 1628, it is assumed that Rotrou remained in the capital after completing his studies, having already decided on a literary vocation. Given his extreme financial difficulties during the following decade, it would seem that his family did not approve of his choice of career and refused to help him. Legend has it that Rotrou was a debauched young man who gambled to excess and spent much of his time in taverns, but there is no solid evidence to support this characterization, other than an ostensibly autobiographical poem, published in 1631, in which he repents the follies (left vague) of his misspent youth.

Rotrou accepted a position with the Comédiens du Roi troupe based at the Hôtel de Bourgogne theater. The manager and lead actor, Pierre Le Messier (better known by his stage name, Bellerose), eager to replace his previous *poète à gages* (hired playwright in residence), Alexandre Hardy, signed the promising young man in 1629. Although the earliest contracts do not survive, it appears that Rotrou was required to supply six new

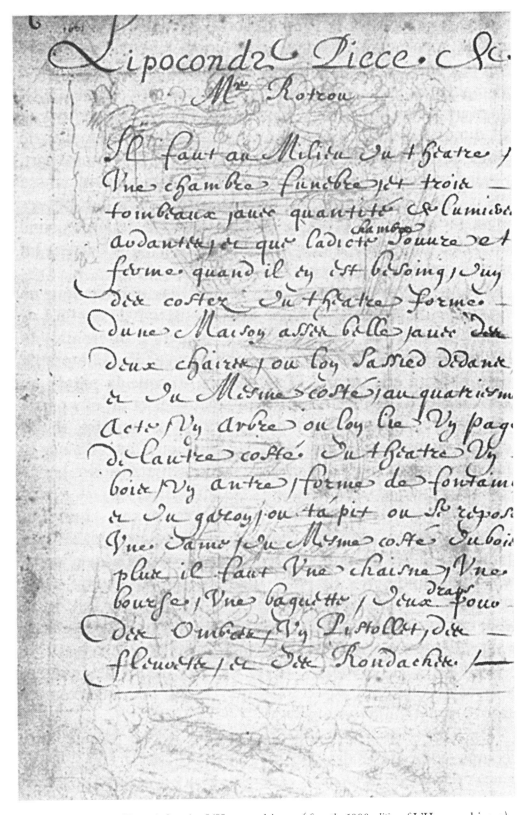

Page from the manuscript of Rotrou's first play, L'Hypocondriaque *(from the 1999 edition of* L'Hypocondriaque*)*

plays a year and received a sum, probably quite modest, for each. Because a play at that time entered public domain as soon as it was published, theatrical companies tried to prevent authors from publishing their works until the work had at least exhausted its initial run. In the case of a hired playwright-in-residence, the contract typically forbade publication altogether, requiring the author to turn over all manuscript copies to the troupe.

Meanwhile, Rotrou was quickly making a name for himself, acquiring several noble patrons, including the comte de Belin, who provided both encouragement and financial support for some of the leading playwrights of the era. Rotrou's second play, *La Bague de l'oubli* (The Ring of Forgetfulness, 1635), won the approval of King Louis XIII, who accepted its dedication, and another, *Les Occasions perdues* (Missed Chances, 1635), brought Rotrou to the attention of the all-powerful minister, Armand du Plessis, cardinal de Richelieu, who had become an eminent patron of the drama. In 1633 the cardinal recruited Rotrou to join a team of five authors, each of whom was assigned to compose one act of a play devised by Richelieu. It was presumably through his work for the cardinal that Rotrou first came to know Corneille, another of the five chosen dramatists, who went on to be recognized as the preeminent playwright of the age. The team wrote at least three plays that were staged in the cardinal's palace; two of them, the comedy *La Comédie des Tuileries* and the tragicomedy *L'Aveugle de Smyrne* (The Blind Person from Smyrna), were published in 1638. The part of each collaborator in these collective efforts has not been determined with absolute certainty. Richelieu was so pleased with Rotrou's talent and zeal that he conferred upon him a title of nobility; the date is uncertain, but it must have happened by 1639, because in that year Rotrou, signing his name on a baptismal certificate, referred to himself as "gentilhomme ordinaire" to Richelieu. Although Rotrou was acquainted with many of the original members of the Académie Française, which the cardinal founded in 1634, and was highly esteemed by Jean Chapelain, the most influential poet in the academy, he was never to win a seat in that august body. The most likely reason is that he was viewed as too young; in the following decade, moreover, Rotrou ran afoul of the rule, then strictly enforced, that academy members had to reside within commuting distance of Paris.

Having quickly achieved both popular success and critical acclaim and finding himself increasingly in the company of fellow authors and influential patrons, Rotrou came to realize that securing the right to publish his plays was vital. But his highly restrictive contract with Bellerose prevented him from publishing any of his works except his first play, *L'Hypocondriaque, ou Le Mort amoureux* (The Melancholy Madman, 1631), composed before he became an employee of the Hôtel de Bourgogne. Bellerose, having fought bitterly with Rotrou's predecessor, Hardy, over that same issue, was determined not to yield. In 1634 the young playwright took the bold step of keeping a copy of a new play, *Cléagénor et Doristée,* and selling it to one of the leading publishers of the day, Antoine de Sommaville, who published it that year. To save face, Rotrou claimed that the manuscript had been stolen and published without his permission. Apparently, a standoff ensued, but Bellerose finally compromised and agreed to turn over to Rotrou some of his earliest plays in the troupe's archives for publication. If Rotrou's claim that *Cléagénor et Doristée* was the youngest of thirty sisters is taken literally, then approximately fifteen of his early plays were never restored to him and are now lost. In 1637 Bellerose, who was facing increasingly stiff competition from the rival Marais theatrical troupe and its leading playwright, Corneille, finally decided to sign a new and far less restrictive contract with Rotrou. Henceforth, the poet could compose at his own pace, with no fixed number of new plays to be written each year, and he would be allowed to publish every subsequent play after it had been in the troupe's possession for eighteen months. (These contracts were rediscovered and published by the nineteenth-century historian Auguste Jal.)

In 1637 one of the most acrimonious literary quarrels of the century took place. Corneille's tragicomedy *Le Cid* generated an unprecedented amount of popular and critical acclaim. But when Corneille imprudently published a brief autobiographical poem in which he declared that he had definitively surpassed all his rivals, his boast provoked furious responses from two of the other leading playwrights of the day, Georges de Scudéry and Jean Mairet. Since Rotrou was on good terms with all of these writers, and since Mairet was a fellow protégé of the comte de Belin, who was himself involved with the anti-Corneille faction, he found himself in a difficult position. A little pamphlet titled *L'Inconnu et véritable ami de Messieurs de Scudéry et Corneille* (The Unknown and True Friend of Scudéry and Corneille, 1637), signed D.R. and generally attributed to Rotrou since the eighteenth century, was one of the few attempts to reconcile the opposing factions and assure the warring playwrights that they were all deserving of high praise. The pamphlet had no effect, but Rotrou seems to have continued to get along with all the participants in the dispute, including Corneille, on whom he was later to bestow a glowing tribute.

In 1639 Rotrou moved back to his native city, where he acquired an important magisterial position. Although his new duties as "lieutenant-particulier au bailliage de Dreux" (special lieutenant of the bailiwick of Dreux) were demanding, he still managed to find some time for writing, producing an average of one play a year. These included his greatest masterpieces in both comedy and tragedy. On 9 July 1640 he married Marguerite Camus, and the couple went on to have six children, only three of whom survived infancy. (Since the son became a priest, one daughter became a nun, and the other daughter never married, Rotrou had no direct descendants.) Rotrou died during an outbreak of the plague and was buried on 28 June 1650. Although urged by family and friends to leave Dreux and take shelter in a safer area, he refused, insisting that he would not desert his post. According to an early biographer, Rotrou wrote to his brother during his final days that the church bells were sounding at that moment for the twenty-second person to die that day, and that the bells could sound for him whenever it pleased God. This anecdote, though rejected by some modern scholars, accords with what is known of the playwright's character: modest, conscientious, loyal, and honest.

That Rotrou's plays were popular in his own day is confirmed by Bellerose's desire to retain his services even after their quarrel, as well as by indications that some of the plays were revived during Rotrou's lifetime and for at least a decade after his death by troupes in both Paris and the provinces. Molière's troupe frequently performed *Venceslas* (1648) and on one occasion revived *La Soeur* (The Sister, 1647), which gave Molière some ideas for his comic masterpiece, *Le Bourgeois gentilhomme* (The Bourgeois Gentleman, 1670). But by the time the Comédie-Française was founded in 1680 as the sole national troupe, the only Rotrou play remaining in the standard repertory was *Venceslas,* and subsequent revivals presented it in an increasingly rewritten and edulcorated form. Apart from an isolated revival of *Cosroès* (1649) early in the eighteenth century, the Comédie-Française did not stage any other of Rotrou's works until the final decades of the twentieth century. This neglect corresponded to a consensus among scholars that Rotrou was nothing more than a minor playwright of modest ability whose role in ushering in the classical era of the French stage was secondary.

Rotrou was in fact one of the key participants in the transition toward classical dramaturgy, with its complex set of rules and unities, but he also epitomized the spirit of an earlier era that scholars since the mid twentieth century have labeled baroque. Among the specifically baroque characteristics of his work are a fascination with human mutability, role-playing, disguise, metamorphosis, and surprise, and a search for a divine providence that often seems to be absent. Rotrou gave especially memorable treatment to such baroque devices as a play within the play, transsexual disguise,

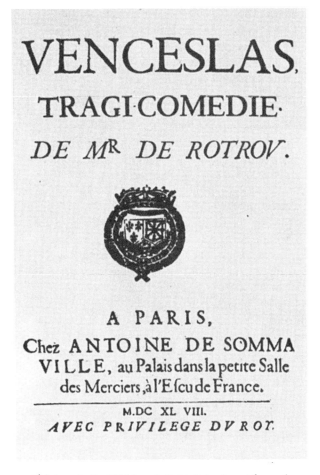

Title page for the 1648 tragedy that is Rotrou's most frequently performed play (Comedie-Français, Paris)

and the alteration of characters' feelings and personalities by means of magic. His style, though at times uneven, is often powerful or gracefully lyrical. He was a master of complex and exciting plots, filled with unexpected twists and turns and often featuring startling endings. Although some of Rotrou's early plays include an unwieldy amount of material, his best work displays a mastery of structure. He adopted the unities of time and place as they came to be promulgated during the course of his career, and he showed an increasing concern for dramatic decorum and verisimilitude, though later generations, having adopted more-stringent standards in these areas, viewed some of his situations as unacceptably risqué or contrived.

The most glaring imperfections in Rotrou's plays arose because he composed quickly and never supervised the publication of his plays. Of course, in his early days he had to write hastily in order to satisfy his onerous contract with the Hôtel de Bourgogne, but early biographers state that writing came easily to him throughout his career. Stylistic flaws include occasional violation of the poetic rule mandating alternation between masculine and feminine rhymes. Dramaturgical problems include inadequate motivation for characters' actions or change of heart and failure to explain the fate of some characters at the end. Especially troubling is the mislabeling of the genre of a play in the original edition. For example, *Venceslas* is labeled a tragicomedy in the original Paris edition but a tragedy in the Leyden edition that was published later in the same year; on the title pages of the original editions of *Le Bélissaire* (1644) and *Iphygénie* (1641) the plays are called tragedies, but the running heads throughout the volumes read "tragi-comédie." The case of *Crisante* (1640), the first edition of which consists of two radically different versions (apparently, a large section of the text was temporarily mislaid by printers and some unknown person composed a bridge passage to cover the missing segment), is the clearest proof of Rotrou's indifference to the fate of his plays once they had premiered. The haste with which he had to compose for much of his career may also explain his heavy reliance on source plays, which he tended to adapt closely, at times making a near literal translation. It should be added that most other playwrights of the period, not always bound by such time constraints, did just the same, and that modern ideas about the value of originality had not yet emerged.

Rotrou's corpus of thirty-five extant plays covers not only all four dramatic genres known to his generation (tragedy, tragicomedy, comedy, and pastoral) but also features a variety of possibilities within each.

Comedy, as opposed to farce, was unpopular in France during the first three decades of the seventeenth century, and only a handful of works in that genre survive. Rotrou and Corneille deserve the bulk of the credit for restoring the five-act comedy to public favor, and in fact they composed between them more than half the total number of comedies produced in Paris during the 1630s. Both playwrights believed that the genre needed to appeal to and mirror a new generation of more-sophisticated theatergoers who insisted on poetic excellence, cleverly constructed plots, and moral decency. Rotrou and Corneille preferred to set their comedies not among the ranks of ordinary citizens but rather among the elegant and wealthy members of the upper-middle class or lower aristocracy. They gave greater prominence to the feelings of young lovers, subordinated the role of stock comic types (such as the clever valet and the braggart soldier), and emphasized internal obstacles in the young lovers (for instance, jealousy or the desire to manipulate others) more than the traditional external obstacles, such as tyrannical fathers. Though laughter and farcical episodes are rare in most of these comedies, they typically feature characters who

provide ironic commentary on the action. Although the tone is lighthearted for the most part, the plays feature moments of genuine pathos. One of the key differences between the two playwrights' approaches is that Corneille was moving in the direction of what was subsequently to be called comedy of character and comedy of manners, whereas Rotrou preferred pure comedy of intrigue, in which characters receive only sketchy development and little or no reference is made to contemporary mores.

Rotrou published a total of twelve plays designated as comedies, and they constitute an extremely heterogeneous corpus. One, *La Belle Alphrède* (1639), is a stock romantic tragicomedy virtually devoid of comic elements and was presumably mislabeled by the printer; five are pastoral comedies that belong in a category of their own; three are adaptations of Latin comedies by Plautus, and two are adaptations of recent Italian plays. Rotrou's first comedy, *La Bague de l'oubli*, published in 1635 but first performed in 1629, is a transitional work midway between comedy and tragicomedy in tone and plot. It is also the first French play to be adapted from a Spanish *comedia*. (There had been previous French dramatizations of Spanish novels and short stories.) Rotrou, who presumably read Spanish fluently, would frequently draw on *comedias* for his material in all genres.

La Bague de l'oubli qualifies as a genuine comedy because of the prominent role given to the jester Fabrice and because of the drastic personality changes experienced by King Alfonse, the central character, which happen every time he puts on or takes off a magic ring. The tone of the play, however, is also extremely somber, especially at the start of act 5, where the heroine's father is about to be wrongfully executed and the audience sees the erected scaffold and the executioner. This comedy displays several of the themes that recur throughout most of Rotrou's plays: metamorphosis, disorientation, and redemption. Thanks to the ring, the king is allowed to exhibit two radically contrasting identities. Normally, he is aggressive, lustful, and immoral; transformed by the ring, he is weak, confused, and easy to manipulate but also concerned with virtue, justice, and basic existential questions. The comic aspect of the transformations is reinforced by the fact that the ring also causes amnesia, making the wearer unable to recall his identity or to recognize other people. Disorientation spreads throughout the cast as Alfonse's beloved and various courtiers, baffled by the contradictory treatment they receive from him, struggle to rethink what they thought they knew about the king's identity or their own. Thus, Fabrice, deprived of a promised sum of money every time the king puts on the ring, logically but mistakenly attributes his master's refusals to pay up to avarice and ingratitude. At the conclusion of the play, Alfonse, shocked by the havoc he has caused, reforms and turns into a model ruler, combining the best features of his two identities. He rewards the most virtuous of his senior courtiers, converts his feelings of lust for Liliane into pure love and agrees at last to marry her, and even forgives a group of conspirators, whose crimes, as they pointedly remind him, were caused by love.

Rotrou's adaptation of his Spanish source for *La Bague de l'oubli* provides a good illustration of his adroitness in combining imitation and originality. Aside from the obvious general alterations required by French taste (the use of five acts rather than three and the consistent use of alexandrine verse in rhyming couplets), he eliminated several superfluous characters, improved the pace, expanded on or condensed scenes, and gave additional prominence to his favorite themes, such as role-playing and metamorphosis. He also altered the predominantly tragicomic tone of his source play, making the denouement a completely happy one, converting the court musician into a jester with a sharp wit, and adding various types of verbal and gestural humor.

The three comedies adapted from works by Plautus, *Les Ménechmes* (The Menaechmi Twins, 1636), *Les Sosies* (The Two Sosias, 1638), and *Les Captifs* (The Captives, 1640), likewise display Rotrou's knack for adapting source plays to fit the Parisian taste of his day. They are also the funniest of Rotrou's comedies, in large measure because he retained so much of the visual and verbal humor already found in the Latin plays. He probably made some of his most striking modifications in order to conform to the increasingly strict demands of dramatic decorum and to satisfy popular demand for love scenes in urbane style. In *Les Ménechmes,* for example, he transformed Plautus's courtesan into a virtuous widow; changed Sosicle, the newly arrived twin brother, from an amoral opportunist into an honorable man and gallant lover; gave the married twin brother a sense of shame over his conduct; and made the wife a more sympathetic character. For *Les Captifs* Rotrou added four new characters, allowing him to include both a serious love plot with a strong element of pathos and a contrasting comic love plot involving a jailer who fancies himself a poet. For *Les Sosies,* considered the finest of the set, Rotrou added several new scenes that make the reactions of the gods to Jupiter's philandering a more integral part of the play. In particular, he added a prologue for the goddess Junon (inspired not by Plautus's original play but by Seneca's tragedy *Hercules furens*) and a comic monologue in which Mercure relates the merrymaking on Olympus to celebrate the impending birth of Hercule. Rotrou expanded the episodes in which characters agonize over the loss of their identities, attempt to battle forces beyond their control, and doubt whether they are really themselves. Their existential anguish climaxes in

the opening scenes of act 5, which are totally of Rotrou's invention.

In his last two comedies, *Clarice, ou L'Amour constant* (1643) and *La Soeur,* both derived from Italian sources, Rotrou gave unusual prominence to standard comic types. The former play gives major roles to a pedantic doctor and a braggart captain, while much of the intrigue in the latter is handled by a wily valet. *La Soeur,* generally acknowledged to be Rotrou's best comedy, is an example of comic imbroglio managed with supreme ease. The convoluted plot, with its constant reversals and surprises, always remains clear to the audience, even as it keeps both them and the characters in suspense. Examples of humor and wit range from the pseudo-Turkish gibberish that the valet, Ergaste, speaks to a young man who knows Turkish but no French, to eavesdropping, exchanges of overt sarcasm, prolonged misunderstandings between characters, and the marriage that the two servants arrange between themselves in six rapid-fire verses at the end of the play. Role-playing involving rapid improvisation, as well as elaborate lying, occurs with great frequency. In some instances the manipulators lose control of the situation, especially in a scene in which Constance, the newly returned mother, promises to assist with her son's deception and pretends to recognize Aurélie as her long-lost daughter; it turns out that the recognition is genuine and that Aurélie really is her daughter. In the final act, after all the secrets have been revealed, the parents and heroines play a gratuitous trick on the young men, pretending to compel them to marry against their wishes and not revealing the truth until after enjoying this "plaisir plein d'appas" (pleasure full of charms). The darker side of *La Soeur* includes, most notably, the danger of incest when Constance reveals that the woman her son has secretly married and passed off as his sister is indeed his sister. Only the last-minute revelation of a substitution of infants many years before allows the play to end happily.

Rotrou never used the designation of pastoral, probably because this dramatic genre was starting to lose popularity by 1630. Nevertheless, five of the plays labeled as comedies—*La Diane* (1635), *La Célimène* (1636), *Le Filandre* (1637), *La Florimonde* (1655), and *Clorinde* (1637)—and two labeled as tragicomedies (*La Céliane,* 1637, and *Amélie,* 1638) are fully or largely pastoral in character, owing to their rustic settings, their use of chains of frustrated lovers (in the most extreme case, A loves B, who loves C, who loves D), and the frequency with which one of the young lovers tries to manipulate the emotions of other members of the group. The manipulation, sometimes playful but sometimes malicious, typically involves attempts to break up or reunite a couple. The schemes do not always work as planned, but the plots inevitably end happily. Rotrou derived the plots for *La Célimène* and *La Florimonde* from the most popular of French pastoral novels, Honoré d'Urfé's

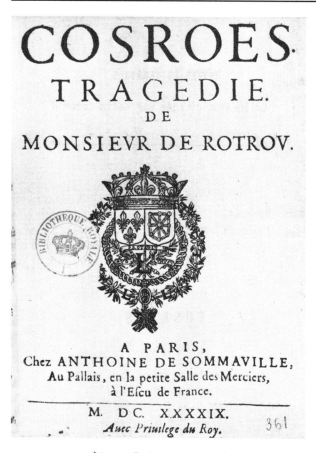

COSROES.
TRAGEDIE.
DE
MONSIEVR DE ROTROV.

A PARIS,
Chez ANTHOINE DE SOMMAVILLE,
Au Pallais, en la petite Salle des Merciers,
à l'Escu de France.

M. DC. XXXXIX.
Auec Priuilege du Roy.

*Title page for Rotrou's last tragedy
(Bibliothèque Nationale, Paris)*

L'Astrée (1607–1627). Revealingly, Rotrou originally designed *La Célimène* as a pastoral play, something that became known only when, after his death, some of his friends discovered a manuscript sketch of the first version, which they asked the respected poet and playwright François Tristan L'Hermite to complete and rework for the stage. (The result, with the new title *Amaryllis,* was staged in 1652.)

In the version published by Rotrou, *La Célimène* is one of the most pleasing of his pastoral comedies. The play focuses on the power of disguise to transform personalities and hearts, empowering the characters and providing both pleasure and astonishment. The plot evolves from a conversation between Florante and the lover who has jilted her, Filandre. The young man admits to being dazzled by the narcissistic Célimène, who spurns all her suitors, but he agrees to go back to Florante if she, disguised as a man, can successfully woo Célimène and open her heart to love. The heroine, under the name of Floridan, impersonates a male swain so flamboyantly that Célimène immediately falls under her spell. Floridan also, however, makes an unwanted conquest in Félicie, who had previously reciprocated the love of Lysis. Floridan's successes lead Lysis and Célimène's other suitor, Alidor,

to join forces in attacking their rival. Floridan cleverly calms them down by promising to aid them in regaining their ladies, which she does by arranging a midnight tryst in the woods at which everyone shows up and all is revealed. In order to convince the ladies whom she has tricked that she is really a woman, she shows them her breasts. Filandre, delighted at the spectacle he has been privileged to watch throughout the play, willingly returns to Florante, while the humiliated Félicie and Célimène accept their original suitors. As in Rotrou's other pastoral plays, the obstacles are more internal than external and require the characters to sort out their true feelings. At the end, true love and fidelity triumph: the inconstant characters return to their original suitors, while those who considered themselves indifferent to love finally acknowledge its power.

During the second quarter of the seventeenth century, tragicomedy reached the zenith of its popularity among French audiences, and Rotrou was among the most prolific suppliers of such plays. By the time he began to write, the dominant model of the tragicomedy involved a complicated and suspenseful plot, often based on a novel, with several implausible plot twists, two-dimensional characters, little or no comedy, and a happy ending ascribed by the characters to divine providence. Rotrou helped to refine this model by deepening the pathos, providing eloquent expression of intense feelings (including a special fondness for *stances,* lyrical monologues in strophic form), and often propelling the action at breakneck speed. He relished "nightmare" episodes in which characters agonize over a tragic situation that proves to be either temporary or altogether illusory. He employed with great skill and also great frequency such baroque devices as a play within the play, cross-dressing that fools onlookers, and false death announcements.

Jacques Morel's division of Rotrou's tragicomedies into "road" plays and "palace" plays, although it risks obscuring the many thematic links between the two categories, is nonetheless useful. The characters in the road plays, drawn from the upper bourgeoisie or lower aristocracy and occasionally from royalty, are well educated, strong willed, and impatient of any attempts to restrain their passions. Facing obstacles to their love lives, they must leave home, either in flight from parents or rivals, or in pursuit of the beloved. In the course of their travels they meet with hair-raising adventures, such as encounters with robbers, would-be rapists, and pirates; shipwrecks; and unexpected rescues.

Rotrou's first play, *L'Hypocondriaque,* features a whole arsenal of baroque devices, such as mad scenes, onstage violence, magic, cross-dressing, and a ceremony held in a funeral chamber. Chance and fate rule in a seemingly chaotic universe, although in retrospect all is shown to have been for the best. The voyage that sets the plot in motion is that of Cloridan, ordered by his father to travel to Corinth and leave behind his beloved, Perside. Along the way he saves a young woman, Cléonice, from rape and kills her two attackers. To his dismay she falls passionately in love with him and persuades him to spend a few days with her family. When a page arrives bearing a letter to Cloridan from Perside, Cléonice alters a single word to make it appear that Perside is dead and bribes the page to keep the secret when he delivers the revised letter. But once again actions have unintended consequences: Cloridan goes mad and believes that he himself is dead, even insisting on lying in a coffin. Perside, disguised as a man, and her cousin Aliaste, who happens to be in love with Cléonice, consult a magician, who delivers an enigmatic oracle: Perside will wed a dead man, while Cléonice will prefer a dead man to Aliaste. The cousins thereupon decide to seek Cloridan in Corinth, and on the way they find the page, who has been attacked by robbers and tied to a tree. After he reveals his deception, they track down Cloridan but have difficulty persuading him that he is really alive. Finally, when a fellow "dead" man rises from his coffin and fires a blank at him, Cloridan sees that his terror of being killed proves that he is not dead, after all. He is reunited with Perside, while Cléonice agrees to marry Aliaste. From the standpoint of later generations the play is loosely structured and includes material that is not strictly necessary, such as Cloridan's mad scenes (in fact, the striking lyricism of these scenes is a highlight of the play) and a humorous episode in which Aliaste, exchanging clothes with his cousin, tries to pass as Perside in order to distract her parents while she steals out of the house. The speed with which the characters can change their identities or affections fits well with the baroque fascination with instability and mutability, both human and cosmic.

The "palace" tragicomedies have royalty as main characters, eliminate the traveling and surprise encounters, and feature political considerations among the obstacles faced by the young lovers. While in his early years Rotrou used both models interchangeably, by around 1637 he abandoned the "road" model altogether. One reason was the need to observe the dramatic unities of time and place, which had gradually won acceptance. As a result, Rotrou tightened the structure of his plays and reduced the number of plot complications, though to the end he reveled in unexpected plot twists and flouted the principle of verisimilitude.

Arguably the finest of the palace tragicomedies is *Laure persécutée* (The Persecuted Laura, 1639). An irritable and overbearing king tries to block the union of his son, Prince Orantée, with Laure, a girl of unknown birth. He uses force, arresting the prince and threatening Laure's execution, and trickery, staging a charade in which Laure's maid, dressed in her mistress's clothes, has a late-night meeting with her own suitor, with the prince watching from the shadows. Laure, who is resourceful as well as virtuous, dons disguises (first as a page, then as a wronged woman who requests the king's aid) and manages to win the king's esteem with the first disguise and his heart with the second. Since, however, all of these deceptions are soon revealed, they provide suspense and excitement without moving the plot toward resolution. It takes a well-worn convention, the last-minute revelation of identity, to provide the desired denouement. The arrival of the Polish princess to whom the prince was betrothed, and who, incidentally, takes the side of the lovers against the king, allows Laure's foster father to produce a long-concealed letter proving that she is in fact the princess's sister. Laure can now marry the man she loves, while the king agrees to marry the princess himself. As is often the case in Rotrou's tragicomedies, the most effective scenes are the "nightmare" episodes in which characters feel devastated by a loss that turns out to be illusory—in this case, Orantée's outpouring of grief and anger when he is led to believe that Laure has betrayed him.

The highly complex plots of the tragicomedies reinforce two of Rotrou's favorite themes: the powerlessness and mutability of the characters, especially in their attempts to master their feelings and control the people around them, and the benign role of divine providence, which somehow arranges everything for the best. The final act of *Les Occasions perdues,* in which six characters who have set up late-night assignations mistake one another in the dark but ultimately end up with the partners most suitable to their rank, shows with special clarity how this conception of providence bolsters dynastic and social stability. Monarchs who love an inappropriate person suddenly find that their original passion vanishes as soon as the mate destined for them appears. In *L'Innocente infidélité* (The Innocent Infidelity, 1637) the instantaneous shift from one genuine passion to the next is effected by means of black magic, but the same result occurs without magic in such plays as *L'Heureuse constance* (The Fortunate Constancy, 1636) and *L'Heureux naufrage* (The Fortunate Shipwreck, 1637). Of the many deceptions and disguises, those undertaken for self-preservation or altruistic reasons always succeed, whereas those engaged in for selfish or sinister reasons invariably fail. Both patterns may occur within the same play, as in *L'Innocente infidélité,* in which the king's discarded mistress, Hermante, uses a magic ring to regain his love and take him away from his new bride, while the king's faithful minister resorts to ruses in order to save the innocent queen's life and to restore the royal marriage. Deceptions intended as harmless pastimes, although not evil, also backfire. In *L'Heureux naufrage* the heroine Floronde, already in an awkward situation (disguised as a boy, she has been forced to announce her own death in order to rejoin her lover), asks her beloved to pretend to respond to the advances of the queen's sister, who has fallen in love with him. Disaster ensues when the sister's suitor hires assassins to murder the hero, who manages to defend himself and then kills his rival, for which he is condemned to death and is rescued only at the last minute. In this and other road plays, killings may occur on the stage, with the good characters always prevailing against murderers, thieves, and rapists.

Rotrou's tragedies, like his work in other genres, form a heterogeneous corpus, indicative of his constant willingness to experiment with new possibilities. His first tragedy, *Hercule mourant* (The Death of Hercules, 1636), is among the earliest French plays to follow the newly proclaimed three dramatic unities. Although closely based on Seneca's play on the same subject, Rotrou's version adds a love plot, features greater suspense (including a last-minute change of heart in which the dying hero spares his rival's life), and makes the main characters more complex and more noble. Although the title character's transformation from tyrannical ruler and unfaithful husband into an heroic figure worthy of being received among the gods is not handled as convincingly as it might be, the final apotheosis is moving and shows the playwright's fascination with the themes of martyrdom and spiritual redemption.

Rotrou's second tragedy, *Crisante,* probably first performed in 1635 but not published until 1640, is less classical in that it does not observe the unities of time and place and features much violence on the stage (three murders and three suicides). On the other hand, the Roman lieutenant Cassie is a complex character whose conflict between his sense of duty and honor and his uncontrollable passion for a captured queen leads him to the crime of rape and then to expression of remorse through public confession and suicide. Crisante, the unfortunate captive queen, has an extremely austere sense of honor but finds herself persecuted and misunderstood by the men around her. When, following the rape, she returns to her husband, the exiled king Antioche; he disbelieves her story and refuses to take her back. When she proves herself guiltless by coming back with the severed head of her attacker and then stabbing herself in front of her husband, Antioche, finally remorseful, commits suicide in hope of expiating his misconduct and of rejoining his wife in the hereafter. Although the gods never manifest their presence in the play, the three principal characters all see their deaths as redemptive.

Rotrou's next two tragedies, both based on classical mythology, feature effective scenes of political discussion, heroic self-affirmation, pathos, and lamentation. *Antigone* (1639), although it includes an excessive amount of action in an attempt to show the downfall of the whole household of Oedipus and Jocasta, adds some revealing features to the Greek and Latin source plays. Rotrou develops the love interest between Antigone and Hémon, with the lat-

ter behaving like a chivalrous knight; gives Créon both a good and a bad adviser who spell out the pros and cons of his fateful edict; and creates an important role for Argie, the wife of Antigone's brother Polynice. Rotrou skillfully evokes pathos with such moving scenes as one in which the sister and wife meet for the first time as they search for the body of the slain Polynice. *Iphygénie* also develops the love interest, although, significantly, the heroine does not seem to requite the ardor of Achille. Among Rotrou's innovations in the play is an attempt to justify the wrath of the goddess Diane against the Greeks: Clytemnestre belatedly remembers that many years before she had pledged her daughter Iphygénie to the service of Diane. In the final act, instead of using messengers to report the sacrifice of Iphygénie, Rotrou shows the sacrificial scene on the stage, including the descent of Diane to declare that, now that she has taken the maiden to be her priestess, the vow is fulfilled and the Greeks may set sail. The initially timid Iphygénie quickly evolves into a genuinely heroic figure. She is the only character to exhibit greatness of soul, unlike her weak and ineffective father, Agamemnon, and the other Greek leaders, who are overly calculating and ruthless.

If Rotrou's next tragedy, *Le Bélissaire,* based on the death of the Roman general Belisarius, shows the hero as somewhat akin to a Christian martyr—he providentially escapes a series of assassination attempts, converts evil characters to goodness, and, when wrongfully punished, dies with an aura of sanctity—*Le Véritable Saint Genest* (The True St. Ginesius, 1647) is a full-fledged religious drama. Written at a time when Cardinal Richelieu was encouraging the composition of tragedies on Christian subjects and in response to the overwhelming success of Corneille's *Polyeucte martyr* (1643), the play depicts an actor who becomes converted to Christianity during the course of rehearsing and performing a play about the recent death of a martyr. Genest, known as the most brilliant actor of his era, has a special talent for putting himself totally into the characters he plays, so that when he starts to improvise during the performance the audience is slow to grasp that he has stopped acting and is literally following in his character's footsteps.

The play within the play, dealing with the conversion and martyrdom of Adrian, a former official of Emperor Maximin who enthusiastically carried out persecutions of Christians but has become impressed by the indomitable faith and fortitude of the martyrs, features striking parallels with Genest's own life. In one key area, however, Rotrou deliberately leaves the symmetry imperfect. Adrian still feels affection for his wife, Natalie, and regrets the misery his death will cause for her, only to discover that she is already a Christian herself and has long prayed for his conversion; she provides moral support during his final hours (and denounces him when she mistakenly thinks that he has abandoned his new faith). But when Genest receives a visit in prison from his colleague Marcelle, who played Natalie in the internal play, she remains firm in her pagan belief and pleads with him to recant for the sake of the troupe, which could not survive his loss. (There is no suggestion of an amorous relationship between them.) When the emperors, Dioclétien and Maximin, finally realize that Genest is proclaiming his own conversion, not his character's, they condemn him to death, which is precisely the fate he desires. From this point on the play is filled with allusions to roles and role-playing, with the Christian and non-Christian characters disagreeing on the nature of Genest's real-life drama. He now views earthly life as an illusion and his transformation as part of a cosmic drama created by God in which he has been honored with a glorious role. The others see him as a madman who has bungled his role as a distinguished actor and court favorite.

The frame plot of *Le Véritable Saint Genest,* taking up the first act and portions of the remaining acts, serves primarily to glorify the theater, though it also mirrors elements in the religious drama. Valérie, daughter of Dioclétien, has had a prophetic dream announcing that she will wed a shepherd. The prophecy immediately comes true when her father betroths her to his coemperor, the victorious general Maximin, who had begun life as a shepherd; the young people fall in love at first sight. To celebrate their nuptials, Genest and his troupe are summoned to perform, and Maximin, who, like Dioclétien, is a dedicated and sophisticated patron of the arts, is delighted to view an episode from his own life on the stage. The emperors are so fascinated by an actor's ability to impersonate a figure quite different from himself that they feel no discomfort at the prospect of witnessing a play in which the religion they abhor receives a sympathetic portrayal. During their interview with Genest they discuss the value of theater and praise its power to charm and excite. Genest, who expresses a preference for the great playwrights of earlier times, also lavishes high praise on an unnamed contemporary author, obviously a reference to Rotrou's eminent colleague, Corneille. It may seem surprising that fanatical persecutors of Christians are shown in such a favorable light, especially in an overtly religious play. Probable reasons include advocacy for the doctrine of the divine right of kings as eternally valid; the fact that the shepherd who becomes a great leader parallels the career of Christ, but on an earthly scale; the belief that divine providence extends to the entire human race, including non-Christians; and Rotrou's desire to glorify royal patrons of the drama (alluding indirectly to Richelieu and his successor, Jules, Cardinal Mazarin).

Rotrou's last two tragedies come closest to the classical ideal represented by Corneille; these works, together with *Le Véritable Saint Genest,* are generally agreed to be his

*Marble bust of Rotrou by J.-J. Caffiere, 1783
(Comedie-Française, Paris)*

masterpieces. *Venceslas,* the most frequently performed of his plays, features powerful dramatic scenes, memorable characters, a well-crafted plot filled with suspense, and a fascinating combination of political and psychological conflicts. The title character is a seasoned, majestic, and just king whose advanced years make him overly dependent on young generals. He has a deep affection for his sons, especially his older son, Ladislas, despite the fact that the latter is violent, aggressive, and impatient with all forms of authority. Because of his obsessive love for the duchess Cassandre, who rejects him, Ladislas cannot abide her other suitor, the valiant Duke Fédéric, who has led the army to a glorious victory, and he loathes his own brother, Alexandre, for being a close friend and supporter of the duke. Neither Ladislas nor the audience discovers until much later that Fédéric really loves Théodore, the princes' sister; the duke has pretended to court Cassandre in order to conceal her secret romance with Alexandre. When Ladislas discovers that the lovers are planning to wed secretly at night, he surprises them, duels in the dark with the man he believes to be Fédéric, and kills him. In one of the most gripping scenes in all of Rotrou's works, Ladislas openly boasts to the court of his murderous exploit, only to see Fédéric enter the room; a moment later Cassandre appears to reveal that the prince has in fact slain his own brother. Venceslas, despite his love for his older son, and despite Ladislas's genuine shock and remorse, condemns him to death. When faced, however, with a popular uprising in favor of the prince, the king decides, after an agonizing inner struggle, to adopt the only viable alternative. He abdicates in favor of Ladislas, whose criminal past will be automatically expunged once he succeeds to the throne. In the final moments of the play the new king, apparently touched by a kind of divine grace, shows signs of becoming a worthy monarch, retaining Fédéric's services and granting him the hand of Théodore, formally apologizing to Cassandre, and demonstrating a newfound ability to control his wild passions. Venceslas urges Cassandre to consider marrying Ladislas at a future date, and that possibility is left open.

Cosroès likewise features a conflict between a weak king and his two sons, but the vision is darker since power and virtue are shown to be incompatible. The Persian king Cosroès gained the throne by murdering his own father, and his guilty conscience manifests itself in periodic outbreaks of madness; in fact, his first appearance in the play is in a mad scene. His haughty and ambitious second wife, Syra, pressures him to disinherit his elder son (from a previous marriage), Syroès, in order to crown her own son, Mardesane, as successor. When Cosroès abdicates in favor of Mardesane, the partisans of the valiant and virtuous but overly timid and respectful Syroès stage a successful countercoup. Syroès feels no compunction in ordering Syra to kill herself with the poison she had prepared for him. He tries to spare Mardesane's life, but the latter proudly refuses: having been proclaimed king, he prefers to die rather than relinquish that title. Syroès, however, being too dutiful a son to punish his father, returns power to Cosroès and, despite the personal risk, even accedes to his father's demand that he pardon Syra and Mardesane. But when the order comes too late and Cosroès kills himself in despair over the deaths of his wife and younger son, Syroès holds himself responsible. The denouement is left ambiguous: if the new king goes mad like his father, the cycle of political and personal chaos will be perpetuated; if he manages to overcome his guilt feelings and become a competent and just ruler, the outcome is both happy and providential. Uncharacteristically, the love interest plays only a secondary role. Syroès is in love with Narsée, the beautiful and virtuous daughter of Syra, who returns his love but urges him to spare her mother. It is later revealed that she is not Syra's daughter after all, having been switched in infancy. Although some critics consider Narsée's presence in the play unnecessary, she serves to emphasize the tender and conflicted nature of Syroès and to remind the audience of the limits on both self-knowledge and human control over events.

Little need be said of Rotrou's nondramatic compositions, which consist of two short collections of verse published with two early plays, about a dozen occasional poems (most of which are compliments to other writers

used as prefatory material to their work), and two pamphlets sometimes attributed to him. The verse collections are of greater biographical than literary interest, mentioning personal feelings and problems that might or might not have been autobiographical, indicating who Rotrou's friends were, showing his gratitude to his noble patrons, and demonstrating that he was a member of the most influential Parisian salon of his day, that of Catherine de Vivonne, marquise de Rambouillet. There is no conclusive evidence that Rotrou wrote *L'Inconnu et véritable ami de Messieurs de Scudéry et Corneille,* the conciliatory pamphlet published during the 1637 quarrel over Corneille's *Le Cid.* It is also unlikely that Rotrou was the author of *Dessein du poème de la grande pièce des machines de la Naissance d'Hercule,* the libretto published in 1649 on the occasion of a revival of his comedy *Les Sosies* by the rival Marais troupe with elaborate theatrical machinery. In all probability the libretto, giving a plot synopsis with a detailed description of the sets and special effects, was composed by members of the Marais company.

Rotrou's accomplishment is among the most remarkable of the seventeenth century, both in quantity and quality. His plays have considerable historical importance in that they display both the flowering of baroque tendencies and the gradual move toward classic regularity. Aesthetically, they remain both enjoyable to read and eminently worthy of being staged. Although it is not clear that Rotrou possessed a well-defined philosophical outlook, his passionate exploration of existential and religious questions and his willingness to explore a wide range of human conduct, from saintliness to monstrous criminality, make him a worthy object of study.

Biography:

Henri Chardon, *La Vie de Rotrou mieux connue: Documents inédits sur la société polie de son temps et la Querelle du Cid* (Paris: A. Picard, 1884).

References:

Imbrie Buffum, "A Baroque Tragedy: Saint Genest," in his *Studies in the Baroque from Montaigne to Rotrou* (New Haven: Yale University Press, 1957), pp. 212–247;

David Clarke, "'User des droits d'un souverain pouvoir': Sexual Violence on the Tragic Stage (1635–1640)," *Seventeenth-Century French Studies,* 18 (1996): 103–120;

Sophie-Wilma Deierkauf-Holsboer, *Le Théâtre de l'Hôtel de Bourgogne,* 2 volumes (Paris: A.-G. Nizet, 1968–1970);

Georges Forestier, *Esthétique de l'identité dans le théâtre français, 1550–1680: Le déguisement et ses avatars* (Geneva: Droz, 1988);

Forestier, "Ironie et déguisement chez Rotrou: une richesse de moyens exemplaire," *Papers on French Seventeenth Century Literature,* 17 (1982): 553–570;

Forestier, *Le Théâtre dans le théâtre sur la scène française du XVIIe siècle* (Geneva: Droz, 1981);

Robert Garapon, "Rotrou et Corneille," *Revue d'Histoire littéraire de la France,* 50 (1950): 385–394;

Perry Gethner, "La chronologie du théâtre de Rotrou: Mise au point," *Revue d'Histoire du théâtre,* 43 (1991): 242–257;

Hubert Gillot, "Le Théâtre d'imagination au XVIIe siècle: Jean de Rotrou," *Revue des Cours et Conférences,* 15–16 (1933): 577–590, 673–687;

John Golder, "*L'Hypocondriaque* de Rotrou: Un essai de reconstitution d'une des premières mises en scène à l'Hôtel de Bourgogne," *Revue d'Histoire du théâtre,* 31 (1979): 247–270;

William O. Goode, "Nature and Fortune: A Tragic Dislocation of Values in Rotrou's *Cosroès,*" *Papers on French Seventeenth Century Literature,* 25 (1986): 93–112;

Alan Howe, "A Lost Play by Rotrou," *Papers on French Seventeenth Century Literature,* 12 (1980): 245–262;

Judd D. Hubert, "Le réel et l'illusoire dans le théâtre de Corneille et de Rotrou," *Revue des sciences humaines,* 91 (1958): 333–350;

Jules Jarry, *Essai sur les oeuvres dramatiques de Jean Rotrou* (Lille: L. Quarré, 1868);

Gillian Jondorf, "'What Is a King?': The Figure of the King in Rotrou," *Seventeenth-Century French Studies,* 10 (1988): 40–52;

Barry Kite, "The Poet Figure in the Plays of Jean Rotrou," *Seventeenth-Century French Studies,* 8 (1986): 143–151;

Kite, "Rotrou and Italian Comedy, 1641–1645," *Seventeenth-Century French Studies,* 12 (1990): 53–64;

R. C. Knight, "*Cosroès* and *Nicomède,*" in *The French Mind: Studies in Honour of Gustave Rudler,* edited by Will Moore, Rhoda Sutherland, and Enid Starkie (Oxford: Clarendon Press, 1952), pp. 53–69;

Harold C. Knutson, *The Ironic Game: A Study of Rotrou's Comic Theater* (Berkeley: University of California Press, 1966);

Henry Carrington Lancaster, *A History of French Dramatic Literature in the Seventeenth Century,* 9 volumes (Baltimore: Johns Hopkins Press, 1929–1942);

Raymond Lebègue, "Le Baroque," in his *Etudes sur le théâtre français,* volume 1 (Paris: A.-G. Nizet, 1977), pp. 299–395;

Wolfgang Leiner, "Deux aspects de l'amour dans le théâtre de Jean Rotrou: Le romanesque et le réalisme," *Revue d'Histoire du théâtre,* 11 (1959): 179–204;

Jean Lelièvre, "Documents inédits," *Revue d'histoire du théâtre,* 3 (1950): 287–290;

John D. Lyons, *A Theatre of Disguise: Studies of French Baroque Drama, 1630-1660* (Columbia, S.C.: French Literature Publications, 1978);

Jacques Morel, "Les Criminels de Rotrou en face de leurs actes," in *Le Théâtre tragique,* second edition, edited by Jean Jacquot (Paris: Editions du Centre national de la recherche scientifique, 1965), pp. 225–237;

Morel, *Jean Rotrou, dramaturge de l'ambiguïté* (Paris: A. Colin, 1968);

Joseph Morello, *Jean Rotrou* (Boston: Twayne, 1980);

Robert J. Nelson, *Immanence and Transcendence: The Theater of Jean Rotrou 1609-1650* (Columbus: Ohio State University Press, 1969);

Francesco Orlando, *Rotrou: Dalla Tragicommedia alla Tragedia* (Turin: Bottega d'Erasmo, 1963);

Paul Pelckmans, "Le Rêve apprivoisé: Notes sur le thème onirique dans le théâtre de Rotrou," *Studia Neophilologica,* 54, no. 1 (1982): 129–140;

Heljé Porré, "Sur les pas de cet illustre père du comique: Rotrou's Adaptations of Plautus," *Romance Notes,* 20 (1979): 94–102;

Jean-Paul Raffinot, "Une Innocence de la dualité: Les femmes travesties dans les pastorales de Rotrou," in *Et in Arcadia ego: Actes du XXVIIe Congrès annuel de la North American Society for Seventeenth-Century French Literature, Université de Montréal, Université McGill (20–22 avril 1995),* edited by Antoine Soare, Biblio 17, no. 100 (Paris, Seattle & Tübingen: Papers on French Seventeenth Century Literature, 1997), pp. 233–240;

Alain Riffaud, "Le Réseau des images chez Rotrou: L'exemple d'*Iphigénie,*" *Papers on French Seventeenth Century Literature,* 53 (2000): 509–525;

Jean Rousset, *La Littérature de l'âge baroque en France: Circé et le paon* (Paris: J. Corti, 1954);

Micheline Sakharoff, *Le Héros: Sa liberté et son efficacité, de Garnier à Rotrou* (Paris: A.-G. Nizet, 1967);

Colette Scherer, *Comédie et société sous Louis XIII: Corneille, Rotrou et les autres* (Paris: Nizet, 1983);

Jacqueline Van Baelen, *Rotrou: Le Héros tragique et la révolte* (Paris: A.-G. Nizet, 1965);

Jean-Claude Vuillemin, *Baroquisme et théâtralité: Le théâtre de Jean Rotrou,* Biblio 17, no. 81 (Paris, Seattle & Tübingen: Papers on French Seventeenth Century Literature, 1994);

Derek A. Watts, "*Cosroès:* A 'Providential' Tragedy?" *Papers on French Seventeenth Century Literature,* 19 (1983): 499–515.

Madeleine de Scudéry

(15 November 1607 – 2 June 1701)

Elizabeth C. Goldsmith
Boston University

BOOKS: *Ibrahim ou L'Illustre Bassa,* as Georges de Scudéry, 4 volumes (Paris: A. de Sommaville, 1641); translated by Henry Cogan as *Ibrahim or the Illustrious Bassa, an Excellent New Romance* (London: Printed for Humphrey Moseley, William Bentley & Thomas Heath, 1652);

Les Femmes illustres ou Les Harangues héroïques, as Georges de Scudéry, by Madeleine de Scudéry and Georges de Scudéry, part 1 (Paris: A. de Sommaville et A. Courbé, 1642); part 2 (Paris: Quinet et de Sercy, 1642); translated by James Innes as *Les Femmes Illustres, or The Heroick Harrangues of the Illustrious Women* (Edinburgh: Printed by Thomas Brown, James Glen & John Weir, 1681);

Artamène ou Le Grand Cyrus, as Georges de Scudéry, 10 volumes (Paris: A. Courbé, 1649–1653); translated by Francis Gifford as *Artamenes, or The Grand Cyrus, an Excellent New Romance,* 5 volumes (London: H. Moseley & T. Dring, 1653–1655);

Clélie, histoire romaine, as Georges de Scudéry, 10 volumes (Paris: A. Courbé, 1654–1660); translated by J. Davies and G. Havers as *Clélia, An Excellent New Romance,* 5 volumes (London: H. Moseley & T. Dring, 1655–1661);

Célinte, nouvelle première, anonymous (Paris: A. Courbé, 1661);

Mathilde d'Aguilar, anonymous (Paris: E. Martin & F. Eschart, 1667);

La Promenade de Versailles, anonymous (Paris: C. Barbin, 1669);

Discours sur la gloire (Paris: Le Petit, 1671); translated as *An Essay upon Glory* (London: J. Morphew, 1708);

Conversations sur divers sujets, 2 volumes (Paris: C. Barbin, 1680); translated by F. Spence as *Conversations upon Several Subjects,* 2 volumes (London: H. Rhodes, 1683);

Conversations nouvelles sur divers sujets, 2 volumes (Paris: C. Barbin, 1684);

Conversations morales, 2 volumes (Paris: Sur le Quai des Augustins, 1686);

Madeleine de Scudéry (from Alain Niderst, Madeleine de Scudéry, 1976)

Nouvelles conversations de morale, 2 volumes (Paris: S. Mabre-Cramoisy, 1688);

Entretiens de morale, 2 volumes (Paris: J. Anisson, 1692);

Mademoiselle de Scudéry, sa vie et sa correspondance avec un choix de ses poésies, edited by E. J. B. Rathéry and A. Boutron (Paris: L. Techener, 1873).

Editions and Collections: *Choix de conversations de Mademoiselle de Scudéry,* edited by Phillip J. Wolfe (Ravenna: Longo, 1977);

Célinte: Nouvelle première, edited by Alain Niderst (Paris: A.-G. Nizet, 1979);

"De l'air galant" et autres Conversations: Pour une étude de l'archive galante, edited by Delphine Denis, Sources classiques, no. 5 (Paris: H. Champion, 1998);

Mathilde, edited by Nathalie Grande, Sources classiques, no. 38 (Paris: H. Champion, 1998).

Novelist, philosopher, moralist, and feminist, Madeleine de Scudéry was a figure of enormous influence in the development of French literature in the seventeenth century. Her writings immortalized the style of speech cultivated in the salons. She accompanied her analyses of the delicacy of human relations with creative and visionary speculations on the nature of social institutions and practices: marriage, friendship, conversation.

Born on 15 November 1607 in the busy trade city of Le Havre on the Atlantic coast of France, Madeleine de Scudéry was one of five children born to Georges de Scudéry and Madeleine de Martel de Goutimesnil, both from provincial aristocratic families of relatively modest means. In 1613 both parents died, leaving their two surviving children to the care of an uncle in Rouen, the provincial capital where Madeleine was to spend most of her youth. Here she was educated according to standards somewhat higher than those for most girls of her social background and time; she was encouraged to read widely and was taught Italian, Spanish, writing, dancing, and painting. Her brother, Georges, after a successful career in the military, moved to Paris to pursue his literary ambitions. In 1637 Madeleine joined him there, in time to share in his newly acquired prestige as a playwright. With her brother she began to frequent the literary coteries that met in the salons of the Marais district of Paris, where she and Georges had established a household.

The next several years were a time of fruitful cooperation between brother and sister, a period in which both published works of fiction that enjoyed immediate popularity. In 1641 Madeleine de Scudéry published her first novel, *Ibrahim ou L'Illustre Bassa* (Ibrahim or the Illustrious Bassa), under her brother's name. She continued to use this pseudonym for most of her prolific career as a writer, despite the fact that her own authorship was both recognized and discussed by her readers in the gazettes, memoirs, and letters of the time. She herself did not attempt to disguise her authorship, openly discussing her writing in correspondence with friends, but in print she persisted in hiding behind her brother's name. Her writings themselves offer the most reliable explanation of her reasons for making such a choice. In several conversations her characters discuss the risks for women of assuming the public identity of a writer or indeed of any deviation from prescribed social roles for women. The decision to publish under Georges's name might also have had more immediate practical motivations. Since he was already an established writer, books attributed to him were bound to

sell, but the finances of the Scudéry household were never on solid ground. Georges clearly collaborated to some extent with his sister in the writing of her novels. According to their friends, he was responsible for the many detailed battle scenes in *Ibrahim ou L'Illustre Bassa,* and he wrote the prefaces to several of her books.

Ibrahim ou L'Illustre Bassa is based loosely on travelers' accounts and historical sources, recounting the tale of a former Greek slave (transformed into a prince in Scudéry's version) and his rise and fall at the court of a Turkish sultan. Drawing liberally from published descriptions of Constantinople to evoke a plausible backdrop for her exotic story, Scudéry devised a series of romantic plots and subplots linking sentimental adventure with political tensions between different social groups–Christians, Muslims, Romans, Persians, and Turks. The narrative is punctuated with digressions in which the characters tell each other stories and converse on the moral and philosophical implications of their situation. The preface, written by Georges, theorizes about rules for a new narrative genre, the heroic novel, over which Scudéry was to exert so much influence.

In 1642 Georges de Scudéry was appointed governor of Notre-Dame-de-la-Garde, a fortress overlooking the port of Marseille, and his sister accompanied him on his move. Though the post was considered prestigious, Madeleine's letters make clear that she considered her years there a form of exile from Paris and the literary milieu in which she had come to occupy an important place. In the same year that they left Paris, Georges and Madeleine collaborated on the publication of a series of fictional letters by legendary women, titled *Les Femmes illustres ou Les Harangues héroïques.* Formally modeled after a collection of discourses that Georges had just translated, *Les Femmes illustres* also gives voice to several arguments for women's equality that Madeleine was to develop in her later works. In a letter Sapho admonishes her young admirer, Erinne, to transform herself from a muse into a writer, and in so doing to create her own immortality rather than wait for others to do it for her.

When Scudéry returned to Paris with her brother in 1647, she found that she was a candidate for the position of governess to Cardinal Mazarin's nieces, a clear mark of recognition for her education and culture. She was not appointed to the post, but she resumed her writing and published a second novel, *Artamène ou Le Grand Cyrus* (Artamène or The Great Cyrus), in ten volumes, from 1649 to 1653. This novel was enormously successful both in France and abroad and was translated into English, German, Italian, and Arabic.

Like *Ibrahim ou L'Illustre Bassa,* the setting of *Artamène ou Le Grand Cyrus* is the Orient, during a

Madeleine de Scudéry's brother, writer Georges de Scudéry, whose name she used as a pseudonym for most of her career (portrait by Nanteuil; Bibliothèque Nationale, Paris)

remote historical period at the court of the legendary conqueror Cyrus. While drawn from some historical sources, however, the characters and setting of the novel are more obviously comparable to Scudéry's own social world and the French court. From the beginning *Artamène ou Le Grand Cyrus* was viewed as a roman à clef, in which most of the major characters could be identified with corresponding real people among Scudéry's contemporaries. Keys to the identities of the characters were circulated in manuscript form as an appendix to an edition of the novel and published in 1657. The lengthy character portraits in the novel were analyzed apart from the many exotic and improbable adventures that the characters embark upon, and their behavior and speech were studied as examples of gallantry and civility to be emulated by readers. Among these character sketches was a self-portrait in which Scudéry describes herself as the poet Sapho, whose most pronounced quality is her intellect and who expounds with her friends on the virtues of platonic love and the life of the mind.

In 1653, as the final volume of *Artamène ou Le Grand Cyrus* was published, Scudéry established her own salon, known as the *samedi* (Saturday), as it was on Saturdays that she received her guests. In the wake of the turbulent period known as the Fronde, both

Madeleine and Georges struggled to retain their favor at court while also participating openly in the disputes between conflicting political interests. Both sympathized with the families of the old nobility against the efforts of Anne of Austria and her minister, Mazarin, to weaken their traditional power. In 1654 Georges fled Paris under threat of arrest for his support of the rebellious princes, and in the same year he married, events that marked the end of his shared household with his sister. Madeleine had managed to escape disgrace despite her political allegiances. Her *samedi* endured for five years as the most prestigious literary coterie in Paris, regularly receiving notable figures such as Marie de Rabutin Chantal, Madame de Sévigné; Marie-Madeleine, comtesse de Lafayette; Valentin Conrart; Claude Perrault; Jean Chapelain; and François, duc de La Rochefoucauld. Hosting her gatherings with her was Paul Pellisson, a writer and academician who was to become her lifelong companion.

The final volumes of *Artamène ou Le Grand Cyrus* were published just as the civil wars of the Fronde were coming to a close. Scudéry had dedicated the novel to the duchesse de Longueville, who had played a prominent role in the uprisings against the throne, and the hero of the novel, Cyrus, was thought by readers to be the fictional representation of the duc de Condé, brother of the duchesse de Longueville. But in the final volume of her novel Scudéry turned away from a narrative dominated by military exploits and epic voyages to return to another heroic figure that she had taken as her own eponymous model, Sapho. In the long story of Sapho that occupies much of volume 10 of *Artamène ou Le Grand Cyrus,* Scudéry develops several personal themes that also appear in her subsequent writings. Sapho's retreat to the land of the Amazons occasions a description of a kind of female utopia, where women govern according to carefully elaborated codes of love and gallantry and where intellectual pursuits and writing are the highest vocations a woman can pursue.

As Scudéry became more interested in writing fiction that incorporated the philosophical discussions of salon society, she moved away from epic romance as a narrative model. The publication in 1654 of the first volumes of her third novel, *Clélie,* came as the meetings of the *samedi* were gaining prestige and recognition. Her printer and bookseller, Augustin Courbé, pressed her to produce more volumes to satisfy an ever growing demand for her works, but even Scudéry's impressive capacity for writing could not keep up with the demand, and Courbé had to content himself with reprinting the first volumes of *Clélie* while waiting for the sequels. In the end the novel was published in ten volumes between 1654 and 1660. In *Clélie,* Scudéry pursued her transformation of novelistic action into social interaction, to the point that most of the novel consists of conversations and character portraits. The plot is drawn from Roman historical sources and reflects Scudéry's careful reading of Livy and Plutarch, but the story focuses on the psychological portrayal of the characters as expressed by stories they tell about each other. In the most famous moment of the novel, a group of speakers gathers around an allegorical map of the human heart, called the "Carte du pays de Tendre" (Map of the land of Tenderness). Examining the different features of this topographical landscape, they discourse on the ways in which voyagers might make their way from the town of "Nouvelle Amitié" (New Friendship), past the villages of "Générosité" (Generosity) and "Exactitude" (Exactitude), avoiding a detour to the village of "Oubli" (Forgetfulness) or the "Lac de l'Indifférence" (Lake of Indifference), to arrive at the safe destination of "Tendre sur Estime" (Tenderness on Esteem). The conversations in the novel that are generated by this map are part of a lengthy elaboration of a theory of love that places reason over passion, discourages marriage, and promotes the cultivation of specific emotions for the promotion of happiness and durable relationships.

In *Clélie,* Scudéry continues her practice of elaborating, through fiction, the code of *galanterie* (gallantry) and refining the concepts of *honnêteté* (noble behavior) and harmony in social relations, particularly between the sexes. While clearly drawing on the tradition of courtly love, she proposes a vision of amorous relationships based on behavior that people can cultivate and control. Passion is neither fatal nor inevitable. Platonic love is not only superior to physical passion, but it is also learnable. Scudéry's characters promote the ideal of "spirituel" (spiritual), or intellectual, marriage, a mutual commitment built on an intimacy between two people that must be continually nourished by verbal reflection and the shared pursuit of erudition and study of philosophy. Scudéry's readers entered enthusiastically into her project and found in her novels an original, serious engagement with important social questions. Her characters' speculations about marriage were perceived by some as subversive—a challenge to existing norms of behavior for women and a menace to conjugal harmony. Nicolas Boileau-Despréaux published a lengthy satire of novels in which he singled out *Clélie* and the "Carte du pays de Tendre" as encouraging dangerous thinking that would ultimately lead to female adultery and the decline of marriage as a social institution.

After *Clélie,* Scudéry ceased to write long novels and turned to the shorter fictional form called the *nouvelle* (novella). She published three, all anonymously: *Célinte* (1661), *Mathilde d'Aguilar* (1667), and *La Promenade de Versailles* (1669). Unlike her novels, these works had contemporary settings that would have been familiar to her readers. In the opening pages of *Célinte* readers would have recognized a description of the property of the minister of finance, Nicolas Fouquet; in *Mathilde d'Aguilar* a group of friends leaves Paris by carriage for a house in the country on the banks of the Seine; and the first hundred pages of *La Promenade de Versailles* present a detailed description of the new Versailles gardens. In *Célinte* and *La Promenade de Versailles,* Scudéry points to the realism and veracity of her own story, assuring the reader that the narrative is a true account, in contrast to what she describes as the ordinary practice of novels. While turning her attention to the development of new, shorter narrative forms, Scudéry continued to portray characters who themselves are captivated by epic novels and their heroic plots. In the first part of *Mathilde d'Aguilar* the company retreats to the country in order to cut themselves off from the rest of society, where they select pseudonymous identities taken from *Clélie* and *Artamène ou Le Grand Cyrus.* In *La Promenade de Versailles* the friends tell each other stories in which the conduct of the heroes is explicitly contrasted with the manner in which characters from an

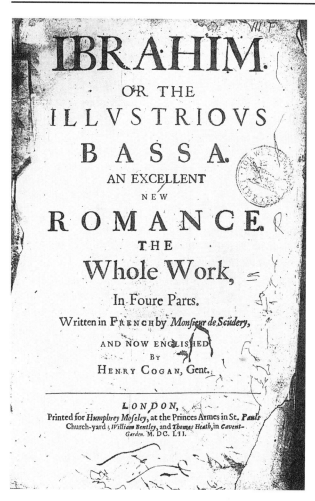

*Title page for the 1652 English translation of Scudéry's
first novel,* Ibrahim ou L'Illustre Bassa
(Bodleian Library, Oxford)

to the post of royal historiographer. In 1671 Scudéry was the first recipient of a prize awarded to authors by the Académie Française, for a somewhat uncharacteristic rhetorical harangue she published that year titled *Discours sur la gloire.* For the next nine years she published no more writings until the appearance of a two-volume work excerpting conversations from her novels, *Conversations sur divers sujets* (1680), which was printed with a dedication to Marie-Anne-Christine-Victoire of Bavaria, the young bride of the dauphin, Louis de France. In 1683 Louis XIV awarded Scudéry a royal pension, and that same year she was honored with election to the illustrious Academei dei Ricovrati of Padua.

Toward the end of her career as a writer, from 1683 to 1692, Scudéry published ten more volumes of "conversations." These were regarded at the time as representing the best of her writing, even though as a genre the conversation collections were quite different from the long novels that had established her literary reputation. But while the novels had been widely read, even her leisured, aristocratic audience had complained of the excessive length of her fiction. Sévigné wrote that Scudéry's best writing was "drowned" in her novels, and it was common for readers, who would typically read Scudéry's books aloud to each other, to break them into fragments in order to excerpt the best parts. The conversations in the novels were the parts that readers often judged to be the best.

In fact, one of the reasons that Scudéry's novels are so long is that the action regularly pauses, sometimes for hundreds of pages, while the characters form a group and retreat to an idyllic setting to converse on an agreed-upon topic. These long segments reflect the collective efforts of Scudéry's milieu to cultivate the art of talk and develop new notions of conversation based on aesthetic as much as practical motivations. Of course, as a social practice, conversation was not new, but as an activity that was itself an object of definition and reflection, conversation had, in a sense, been invented in the late Renaissance. Beginning with Baldassare Castiglione's *Book of the Courtier* (1528), a new literature of social behavior had developed, describing conversation as a kind of project or skill essential for amusement and maintenance of one's social status. In seventeenth-century France the growth of a new leisure class that had spare time and was persuaded of the importance of sociable interaction led to the refinement of conversation as an art and a mark of exclusivity. In salon gatherings such as Scudéry's *samedis,* conversation became the most valued forum for literary debate, arbitration, and discussion of aesthetic questions, matters of taste, and more-political issues, such as the social value of marriage and the legal rights of women.

epic novel would have behaved. Thus, even as she moved away from the genre of the heroic novel, Scudéry pointed to the pervasive influence that her earlier works of fiction had on the collective imagination of her readers.

The 1660s were the first decade of the reign of Louis XIV, a period during which the king consolidated his control over developments in the arts and when members of literary coteries such as Scudéry's struggled to retain their influence and favor at court. The regular meetings of the *samedi* had stopped in 1659, and in 1661 the political disgrace of Scudéry's friend and patron Fouquet resulted in exile and imprisonment for him and several of his closest associates. Pellisson and Scudéry were among the small number of authors who dared to write appeals to the king on Fouquet's behalf during his trial. Pellisson himself was imprisoned in 1661 and was not released for five years. Unlike Fouquet, though, who spent the rest of his life in a dungeon, Pellisson was rehabilitated and eventually named

In choosing to republish excerpts from her novels in the form of "conversations," Scudéry was clearly placing them in the tradition of "conduct" literature. By 1680 the reading public was familiar with several French works in this genre, the most popular being courtesy manuals by Nicholas Faret and Antoine de Courtin and a collection of original conversations by Antoine Gombaud, chevalier de Méré. Works such as these were fostered in the social milieu of the salon, an historical space that, like Scudéry's writing, lent itself to descriptive metaphors contrasting large and small, grand and insignificant. The ideal of a radically restricted, enclosed space was crucial to the earliest manifestations of salon culture. Salons were an important locus of French elite culture from the first decades of the seventeenth century, when courtiers were increasingly interested in learning the techniques of verbal etiquette in the Italian tradition, while at the same time the social credentials of the royal entourage were no longer uniformly aristocratic. Salon life was thought to be sheltered from the distractions of courtly politics and strongly committed to cultivating ideal courtly behavior.

Scudéry's *samedis* followed the model established in the 1630s by Catherine de Vivonne, marquise de Rambouillet, in her famous *chambre bleue* (blue room), a prototypical salon that is often referred to as a kind of birthplace of French sociability. Salon habitués cultivated the notion that they constituted an ideal elite that could always close ranks and create a separate reality even when surrounded by a heterogeneous crowd of courtiers. By the time that Scudéry began publishing her conversations, maintaining one's elite status meant frequenting the court of Louis XIV. Salon society, self-consciously set apart from the royal court, came to define itself not so much by a concrete space as by its habitués' principal activity, conversation.

As the principal expression of salon culture, ideal conversation was understood to be possible only if all participants were confident of their equal standing within the group as well as their collective superiority to all who were outside it. The coterie of speakers had to be sure of the boundaries separating them from the rest of society; at the same time, they had to be able to contemplate that society comfortably. Ideal conversation had to seek this balance of closure and openness, of internal equilibrium and external orientation. In Scudéry's written conversations, her speakers usually initiate the encounter by moving slightly away from the rest of a social group to a spot such as an outdoor pavilion on the grounds of a château. That this encounter is in no way contrived, though, seems important to its success—the conversation begins when "chance" brings the right people together at the right place and time.

Although Scudéry published all of her novels either anonymously or under her brother's name, she allowed the conversation collections to be published with her own name on the title pages. In other respects, too, she was more attentive than with her novels to the preparation of these texts for publication and circulation. The books were published in small format, designed to be easily carried in a pocket. They feature tables of contents for easy reference, and the conversations have titles reminiscent of those of the essays of Michel de Montaigne: "On Pleasures," "On Politeness," "On Experience," "On Conversation." Contemporary readers remarked on the instructiveness of Scudéry's conversations. She received a pension from Louis XIV after the publication of the first two volumes in 1680, and for a time her books of conversation were actually used as textbooks for the instruction of young aristocratic women at St.-Cyr, a school founded by Françoise d'Aubigné, marquise de Maintenon, the king's mistress.

Scudéry's decision to reframe her novelistic conversations and create original conversations written for the collections represents an effort to transform the idyllic and vast landscapes of her novels into a more movable space for inventing ideal social interaction. It was important to her that these spaces be understood as transferable and imitable, if only by readers who were worthy of the task and could approach it with the requisite leisure. Readers are invited to observe how her speakers create the conditions necessary for perfect conversation by cutting themselves off—even if temporarily and artificially. In the conversations it is often unclear exactly where the speakers are, but certain features of their location are noted, features that stress the fact that the group is cut off from their usual milieu yet not far away from it. Members of the coterie had to be sure of the boundaries separating them from the rest of society and at the same time be able to comfortably contemplate and discuss that society.

A Scudéry conversation typically progresses in three stages. First, the separateness of the group is established, either by a description of the particular qualities of each member of the company, or by their installation in a protected, enclosed space, or both. There follows a kind of inventory of the subject at hand; each speaker contributes examples for all to discuss. Finally, after the increasingly centripetal movement of the discussion has led the company to a state of total self-absorption, the frame of reference again shifts to a broader perspective of the world outside the circle, but from the vantage point of an exclusive group that has freshly examined the qualities that make it superior to that world.

Almost invariably in these conversations, a speaker remarks on how successfully the group has managed to conduct an ideal interaction. Read collectively, they thus offer a catalogue of the ingredients nec-

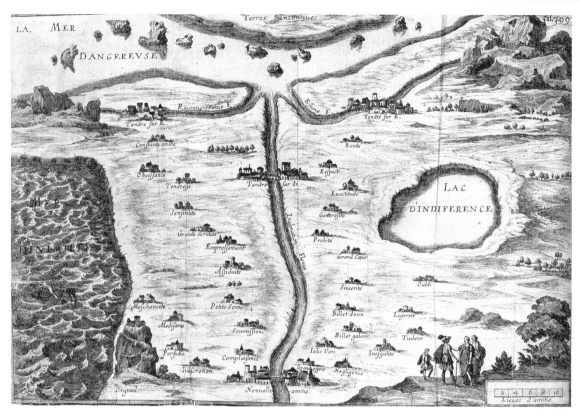

Foldout frontispiece from the first volume of Scudéry's novel Clélie *(1654–1660), an allegorical map of the human heart*
(Bibliothèque Nationale, Paris)

essary for a successful conversational "happening." A conversation always has more than two people but never more than six or seven. It must be a mixed company of men and women. One person always acts as a kind of host. The topics under discussion must never be either explicitly personal or strongly political. As in actual salon conversations, the speakers often refer to each other by pseudonyms (like Scudéry's "Sapho"), a practice that helps to locate conversation somewhere between the private and the public.

Scudéry's pedagogical project of publishing these conversations as models for others to emulate brought her more official praise than her other writings had, but it also failed dramatically in the one instance in which the books were actually introduced as schoolbooks. Maintenon was not pleased with the effect they had on young readers, and she had them removed from St.-Cyr when she realized they were not serving the practical purpose she had intended– teaching young girls how to speak well–but rather were having the effect of encouraging daydreams and fantasy. Even in their own time Scudéry's conversations did not work as didactic tools; they are diffuse and leisurely and do not encourage the reader to remember what was said so much as the atmosphere

and the sense of pleasure the speakers seem to take in their activity. Maintenon replaced Scudéry's books with her own compositions, shorter dialogues on more-practical and narrow moral topics that the girls could memorize.

The early career of Scudéry's conversation books reflects an important historical shift in standards of sociability that occurred in the last decades of the seventeenth century. When she decided to publish a collection of conversations removed from the context of her novels, she made them more accessible to a broader audience, including readers who might not care for her lengthy heroic narratives but were interested in learning "how to live" leisured social lives. Her anthologies also responded to the new taste for shorter texts that could easily be adapted from written to spoken form, that could be freely borrowed and imitated in the verbal marketplace of court and salon. How-to texts teaching ambitious readers the art of polite interaction were much in demand. Maintenon's use of Scudéry's volumes indicates the extent to which they were considered plausible pedagogical tools. With her subsequent rejection of the books and of the verbal excess that they encouraged, Maintenon was attempting to promote a new, more domestic image of proper interaction in society, stressing economy, restraint, and a systematic suspicion of sociability.

The Scudéry conversations did adapt well, though, to the dissemination of coterie literature via written correspondence, as their style came to seem more suited to letter writing than to speech. There is never a sense in a Scudéry dialogue that an urgent reply is needed, and there is rarely even a sense that the topic under discussion is closed when the reader comes to the end of the text. Equanimity, balance, and carefully cultivated democracy within the membership are more crucial to Scudéry's ideal conversation than having one person win a debate. Blunt, even honest, talk is not always held up as a virtue. Some of her conversations, such as "De la Politesse" (On Politeness), from *Conversations nouvelles sur divers sujets* (1684), and "De la Dissimulation et de la sincérité" (On Dissimulation and Sincerity), from *Conversations sur divers sujets*, engage directly with contemporary debates about the ethics of courtliness and reflect a new concern with forms of communication that cannot be categorized according to a primarily aesthetic code. In "On Sincerity," Scudéry's speakers examine the risks as well as the rewards of sincere speech, treating it as a new and slightly dangerous practice that, if imposed too aggressively, could threaten the equanimity so crucial to their notion of ideal conversation. As they try to define sincerity and mull over its useful functions, they also work to defuse whatever threat it might pose to the balanced verbal economy they are trying to maintain. Sincerity is clearly distinguished from "natural" talk, the latter term describing an unconstrained style of expression free of self-conscious pedantry. *Le naturel* was to remain the key term describing the aesthetic imperative of conversation in the French tradition, a term both vague and compelling enough to inspire generations of writers to work at its definition and description for centuries to come.

Scudéry's conversations were translated almost immediately into English. Her reputation as both a novelist and a *salonnière* extended beyond the boundaries of France within her own lifetime, and she promoted the dissemination of her published works. The translations of her books formed part of a body of literature describing new, "French" styles of living that were imitated by elite circles in England, Germany, Italy, and Spain. The new prestige accorded the "conversational" style in both writing and speech also meant that women, who were not educated in the rhetorical arts as men were, could participate more fully in intellectual life. Women were thought to have a natural propensity for conversation and to be better at it than men. As aspiring writers and courtiers began recommending the company of women as a way of learning the new styles of speech and writing, salon culture, managed by women, came to occupy a central position in the world of letters. Salons took power away from the academic sphere and helped to create the modern idea of an enlightened public capable of reasoning about important issues of the day or pronouncing on the value of a work of art.

Madeleine de Scudéry continued to write until her death at the age of ninety-three on 2 June 1701. In her last years, as deafness and infirmity made it difficult for her to leave her home in the Marais district, she devoted an increasing amount of time to epistolary correspondence. Letter writing, about which she had theorized in her novels and conversations, became for her an aesthetic practice as well as a way of assuring her continued presence in a social world in which one's speech and rhetorical skills were all-important. Scudéry's extraordinary longevity meant that the letters she wrote in her last years came to constitute a series of eulogies of friends and illustrious figures who preceded her in death. She died knowing herself to be not only the most acclaimed French novelist of her time but also an author whose profound influence on later generations of novelists was already well recognized, both in France and abroad.

Bibliography:

Georges Mongrédien, "Bibliographie des oeuvres de Georges et Madeleine de Scudéry," *Revue d'Histoire littéraire de la France,* 40 (1933): 225–236, 413–425, 538–565.

Biographies:

Claude Aragonnès, *Madeleine de Scudéry, reine du Tendre* (Paris: Colin, 1934);

Dorothy McDougall, *Madeleine de Scudéry: Her Romantic Life and Death* (London: Methuen, 1938).

References:

Nicole Aronson, *Mademoiselle de Scudéry,* translated by Stuart R. Aronson (Boston: Twayne, 1978);

Aronson, *Mademoiselle de Scudéry, ou, Le voyage au pays de Tendre* (Paris: Fayard, 1986);

Daniella Dalla Valle, "Le Merveilleux et la vraisemblance dans la description des romans baroques: *La Promenade de Versailles* de Madeleine de Scudéry," *Dix-Septième Siècle,* 152 (July–September 1986): 223–230;

Joanne Davis, *Mademoiselle de Scudéry and the Looking-Glass Self* (New York: Peter Lang, 1993);

Joan DeJean, "The Politics of Tenderness: Madeleine de Scudéry and the Generation of 1640–1660," in her *Tender Geographies: Women and the Origins of the*

Novel in France (New York: Columbia University Press, 1991), pp. 71–93;

Delphine Denis, *La Muse galante: Poétique de la conversation dans l'oeuvre de Madeleine de Scudéry* (Paris: H. Champion, 1997);

René Godenne, *Les Romans de Mademoiselle de Scudéry* (Geneva: Droz, 1983);

Elizabeth C. Goldsmith, "Excess and Euphoria in Madeleine de Scudéry's 'Conversations,'" in her *Exclusive Conversations: The Art of Interaction in Seventeenth-Century France* (Philadelphia: University of Pennsylvania Press, 1988), pp. 41–75;

Nathalie Grande, *Stratégies de romancières: De Clélie à La Princesse de Clèves, 1654–1678* (Paris: H. Champion, 1999);

Caren Greenberg, "The World of Prose and Female Self-Inscription: Scudéry's *Les Femmes Illustres*," *Esprit Créateur*, 23 (Summer 1983): 37–43;

Katherine Jensen, "Madeleine de Scudéry," in *French Women Writers: A Bio-Bibliographical Sourcebook*, edited by Eva Martin Sartori and Dorothy Wynne Zimmerman (New York: Greenwood Press, 1991), pp. 430–439;

Barbara Krajewska, *Du Coeur à l'esprit: Mademoiselle de Scudéry et ses samedis* (Paris: Kimé, 1993);

Renate Kroll, *Femme poète: Madeleine de Scudéry und die "poésie précieuse"* (Tübingen: Niemeyer, 1996);

Donna Kuizenga, "*Des choses heureusement inventées:* Verisimilitude in *Clélie*," *Cahiers du Dix-Septième Siècle*, 3 (Spring 1989): 77–87;

Marie-Gabrielle Lallemand, *La Lettre dans le récit: Etude de l'oeuvre de Mlle de Scudéry* (Tübingen: G. Narr, 2000);

Maurice Magendie, "Les Romans de Mlle de Scudéry," in his *La Politesse mondaine et les théories de l'honnêteté en France au XVIIe siècle, de 1600 à 1660* (Paris: F. Alcan, 1925), pp. 629–692;

Chantal Morlet-Chantalat, *La Clélie de Mademoiselle de Scudéry: De l'épopée à la gazette, un discours féminin de la gloire,* Lumière classique, no. 1 (Paris: H. Champion, 1994);

James S. Munro, *Mademoiselle de Scudéry and the Carte de Tendre* (Durham, U.K.: University of Durham, 1986);

Alain Niderst, *Madeleine de Scudéry, Paul Pelisson et leur monde* (Paris: Presses Universitaires de France, 1976);

Rita Santa Celoria, *Le grand Cyrus, Clélie, hystoire romaine: Episodes choisis avec le résumé des deux romans* (Torino, Italy: Giappichelli, 1973);

Domna Stanton, "The Fiction of *Préciosité* and the Fear of Women," *Yale French Studies*, 62 (1981): 107–134;

Linda Timmermans, *L'Accès des femmes à la culture (1598–1715): Un débat d'idées de Saint François de Sales à la Marquise de Lambert,* Bibliothèque littéraire de la Renaissance, series 3, no. 26 (Paris: H. Champion, 1993).

Maric de Rabutin Chantal, Madame de Sévigné

(5 February 1626 – 17 April 1696)

Elizabeth C. Goldsmith
Boston University

BOOKS: *Lettres de Madame Rabutin-Chantal, Marquise de Sévigné, à Madame la Comtesse de Grignan sa fille,* 2 volumes (The Hague: P. Gosse & J. Neaulme, 1726); translated as *Letters of Madame de Rabutin Chantal, marchioness de Sévigné, to the Comtess of Grignan Her Daughter,* 2 volumes (London: N. Blandford, 1727);

Lettres inédites de Madame de Sévigné, edited by Charles-Hubert Millevoye and Claude-Xavier Girault (Paris: J. Klostermann, 1814);

Lettres de Madame de Sévigné, de sa famille et de ses amis, edited by L. J. N. Monmerqué, 10 volumes (Paris: J. Blaise, 1818); revised and enlarged as *Lettres de Madame de Sévigné, de sa famille et de ses amis: Edition orné de 25 portraits dessinés par Devéria, augmenté de plusieurs lettres inédites, des 105 lettres publiées en 1804 par Klostermann,* 12 volumes (Paris: Dalibon, 1823); revised and enlarged as *Lettres de Madame de Sévigné, de sa famille et de ses amis,* 14 volumes (Paris: Hachette, 1862–1868);

Lettres, edited by Emile Gérard-Gailly, 3 volumes, Bibliothèque de la Pléiade, nos. 97, 112, 124 (Paris: Gallimard, 1953–1963);

Correspondance, edited by Roger Duchêne, 3 volumes, Bibliothèque de la Pléiade, nos. 97, 112, 124 (Paris: Gallimard, 1972–1978).

Collections: *Letters from Madame la marquise de Sévigné,* selected, translated, and introduced by Violet Hammersley, with a preface by W. Somerset Maugham (New York: Harcourt, Brace, 1956);

Lettres, selected and edited, with an introduction, by Bernard Raffalli (Paris: Garnier-Flammarion, 1976);

Selected Letters, translated, with an introduction, by Leonard Tancock (Harmondsworth, U.K. & New York: Penguin, 1982).

Marie de Rabutin Chantal, Madame de Sévigné, 1645 (from Jean Cordelier, Madame de Sévigné par elle-même, *1967)*

The correspondence of Madame de Sévigné, covering almost fifty years of a rich and turbulent period in French history and culture (1648–1696), has been the favorite reading of great writers from Voltaire to Virginia Woolf. From the time of their first publication in 1726, Sévigné's letters have provided a standard against which other important letter collections can be measured. Writing in an era when epistolary style was cultivated as an art, Sévigné's correspondence grew out of

351

this tradition, but she transcended it with her original, personal, and creative approach to letter writing.

Marie de Rabutin Chantal was born in Paris on 5 February 1626, the only child of Marie de Coulanges and Celse-Bénigne de Rabutin, baron de Chantal. On her mother's side she descended from a wealthy bourgeois family, while her father was a titled nobleman from an ancient Burgundian line. Both parents had died by the time their daughter was seven, and Marie was left to the care of the large and affectionate Coulanges family headed by her maternal grandparents, in whose house she had lived since birth. Her education under their guardianship was based on a wide range of readings in French and Italian. Her tutoring in religion encouraged piety and rejected the sort of fanaticism exemplified in the life of her famous paternal grandmother, Jeanne de Chantal, who had abandoned a young son to follow her mystical calling.

At the age of eighteen Marie was married to Henri de Sévigné, a young nobleman from Brittany, and they had two children: Françoise-Marguerite, born in 1646, and Charles, born in 1648. The marriage was troubled and short-lived, ending with Henri de Sévigné's death in a duel fought over a mistress on the day after his wife's twenty-fifth birthday. Madame de Sévigné was not an inconsolable young widow. Within months she and her children moved back to Paris from her husband's Breton estate, where the family had been living. With the help of an uncle, the abbé de Coulanges, she managed to restore order to the family finances, much damaged by her late husband's spending habits.

Thus reestablished in her beloved Marais, the district of Paris where she had spent her youth, Sévigné was quickly assimilated into the elite social circles of court and city. As a widow of some means who enjoyed the support of her extended family, she had considerable freedom in the conduct of her life, a fact that may explain why she never remarried. She frequented the salon of Madeleine de Scudéry, whose novel *Clélie* (1654–1661) included a description of Sévigné. The young widow was also closely associated with Louise d'Orléans, duchesse de Montpensier (known as "la Grande Mademoiselle"), cousin of Louis XIV, and she renewed her girlhood intimacy with Marie-Madeleine, comtesse de Lafayette, who was to become the most renowned French novelist of the seventeenth century. Lifelong friendships with other well-known intellectual figures from these circles, including François, duc de La Rochefoucauld, and Jean-François-Paul de Gondi, cardinal de Retz, were to have an enduring influence on her own writing. Until the end of her life Sévigné maintained her principal residence in the Marais, in a building now known as the Musée Carnavalet, which has preserved one wing as a monument to her life and achievement.

As a writer, Sévigné occupies a special position in the history of French literature. She wrote nothing but letters, thousands of them, letters that constitute a treasure of information for historians and that have been admired as masterpieces of style. Sévigné's body of work, though, has not been stable—it has changed its shape at least once every few decades since the end of the seventeenth century. Since the letters were first written, they have been edited, corrected, copied, recopied, and even willfully destroyed by a long line of readers with a variety of motives. During Sévigné's lifetime the letters were published only once, when her cousin Roger de Bussy-Rabutin included a few of them in a volume of his memoirs, which he presented to Louis XIV. After her death on 17 April 1696, a larger number of letters was included in the published correspondence of Bussy-Rabutin, generating enough public interest to persuade Sévigné's granddaughter Pauline de Simiane to undertake the task of preparing her grandmother's letters for publication. This project resulted in the intermittent release of selected letters at intervals over the next hundred years and spawned enough family quarreling and tension between the copyists and de Simiane's descendants that in 1784 her son-in-law burned all of the several hundred letters she had left in his possession.

When the literary scholar L. J. N. Monmerqué undertook the first critical edition of Sévigné's letters in 1818, there were already few original autographs left. He had to verify his material by comparing the many published editions of selected letters and the copies of letters that had been compiled by editors and never published. Since the first "complete" edition of the letters was published from 1862 to 1868 (Monmerqué having spent more than thirty years on the project), there has been one major discovery of a 1720 manuscript copy of some of the letters and two new critical editions, the definitive one being Roger Duchêne's edition of the correspondence published in three volumes from 1972 to 1978. Duchêne's edition includes more than 1,500 letters by Sévigné and more than 1,000 letters addressed to her, and it draws on all of the available copies of the letters as well as the relatively few autographs that remain in museums and archives across France.

Most readers of Sévigné, however, encounter her writing in the many published selections of her letters. Already thoroughly abridged by historical circumstances, her legacy has thus been restructured and rearranged for the public by editors and readers who find in the fragmented form of correspondence a structure easily permitting selective reading. Interpretations of Sévigné's letters, and of her character, have changed more radically over the centuries than is usually the

The Château Les Rochers, Sévigné's country estate near Vitré in Brittany

case for an author as well known as she. These changes are reflected in the different choice of letters that is presented to each new generation of her readers. There is the Sévigné of court and salon, a master of gossipy anecdotes written in a style that perfectly renders the excitement of conversation. The most famous of her letters is probably one of these, a letter of 15 December 1670 written to Bussy-Rabutin and announcing the surprising news of a marriage in the royal family (here and following, quotations are from the Duchêne edition; translations are by Charles G. S. Williams unless otherwise indicated):

> Je m'en vais vous mander la chose la plus étonnante, la plus surprenante, la plus merveilleuse, la plus miraculeuse, la plus triomphante, la plus étourdissante, la plus inouïe, la plus singulière, la plus extraordinaire, la plus incroyable, la plus imprévue, la plus grande, la plus petite, la plus rare, la plus commune, la plus éclatante, la plus secrète jusqu'aujourd'hui, la plus brillante, la plus digne d'envie; enfin une chose dont on ne trouve qu'un exemple dans les siècles passés, encore cet exemple n'est-il pas juste; une chose que nous ne saurions croire à Paris (comment la pourrait-on croise à Lyon?); une chose qui fait crier miséricorde à tout le monde; une chose qui comble de joie Mme De Rohan et Mme De Hauterive; une chose enfin qui se fera dimanche où ceux qui la verront croiront avoir la berlue; une chose qui se fera dimanche, et qui ne sera peut-être pas paite lundi. Je ne puis me résoudre à la dire.

Devinez-la; je vous le donne en trois. Jetez-vous votre langue aux chiens? Eh bien! Il faut donc vous la dire. . . .

(I am going to tell you a thing that is the most astonishing, the most surprising, the most marvelous, the most miraculous, the most supreme, the most dizzying, the most unheard, the most singular, the most extraordinary, the most incredible, the most unforeseen, the greatest and the smallest, the rarest and most common, the most public and until today the most secret, the most brilliant, the most envied—in short a thing known only once in past centuries—and that not really the same—a thing that we cannot believe in Paris (how could it be believed in Lyon?)—a thing which makes everyone cry mercy—a thing that is the crowning joy of Mme de Rohan and Mme de Hauterive—a thing finally that will be done Sunday and that those who see will not believe—a thing that will be done Sunday and perhaps will not be finished Monday. I cannot make myself tell you what. Guess. I'll give you three guesses. Give up? Very well, then, I must tell you. . . .)

There is a cagier, political Sévigné, reporting on important events or orchestrating the social advancement and marriage of her daughter, Françoise-Marguerite. There is the Sévigné engaged in family disputes or negotiating between quarreling correspondents, determined to keep the web of her epistolary community intact. And there is Sévigné the mother, inconsolable over her separation from her daughter. In one of her first letters to Françoise-Marguerite, dated 2 February 1671, she writes:

Ma douleur serait bien médiocre si je pouvais vous la dépeindre; je ne l'entreprendrai pas aussi. J'ai beau chercher ma chère fille, je ne la trouve plus, et tous les pas qu'elle fait l'éloignent de moi. Je m'en allai donc à Sainte-Marie, toujours pleurant et toujours mourant. Il me semblait qu'on m'arracchait le coeur et l'âme, et en effet, quelle rude séparation! Je demandai la liberté d'être seule. On me mena dans la chambre de Mme Du Housset, on me fit du feu. Agnès me regardait sans me parler; c'était notre marché. J'y passai jusqu'â cinq heures sans cesser de sangloter; toutes mes pensées me faisaient mourir. J'écrivis à M De Grignan; vous pouvez penser sur quel ton. J'allai ensuite chez Mme De La Fayette, qui redoubla mes douleurs par la part qu'elle y prit. Elle était seule, et malade, et triste de la mort d'une soeur religieuse; elle était comme je la pouvais désirer. M De La Rochefoudauld y vint. On ne parla que de vous, de la raison que j'avais d'être touchée, . . . Je revins enfin à huit heures de chez Mme De La Fayette. Mais en entrant ici, bon dieu! Comprenez-vous bien ce que je sentis en montant ce degré? Cette chambre où j'entrais toujours, hélas! J'en trouvail les portes ouvertes, mais je vis tout démeublé, tout dérangé, et votre pauvre petite fille qui me représentait la mienne. Comprenez-vous bien tout ce que je souffris?

(My affliction would be mediocre indeed if I could describe it, so I shall not try. I search everywhere for my dear child, I do not find her, and her every step takes her farther from me. In this state I went to Sainte-Marie, always weeping and always dying. It seemed my heart and soul had been torn from my body. How cruel separation is! I asked to be alone and was led to Mme du Housset's room and given a fire. Agnès stayed with me, without speaking, as agreed. I spent five hours sobbing. Every thought brought death. I wrote to M. de Grignan, in a tone you can imagine. I went to see Mme de Lafayette, who renewed my sorrow by her sympathy. She was alone, ill, afflicted by the death of a friend, in the right state for me. M. de La Rochefoucauld came. They spoke of you, of how right I was to be concerned. . . . About eight I came home, and entering, good Lord, do you know how I felt going up the stairs? That room I always entered was open, but empty and in disorder. Your poor little girl there made me see mine. Do you really know how I suffered?)

Underlying all of these facets of Sévigné's rich and complex character is a writer's skill, honed in the daily practice of conversation as well as epistolary communication and nurtured in a cultural milieu that placed a high value on the art of writing letters.

In seventeenth-century France, epistolary style and practice was commonly discussed in social conversation and published manuals. In this period familiar letters were first collected and printed for their intrinsic interest rather than for the information they conveyed about a high court official or an author already known for works in another genre. Whether or not a private correspondence had been printed, its readers often included many people not originally envisaged by the writer. Reputations were made for skill in the letter-writing genre, and exemplary texts were widely distributed to be copied and imitated.

There were many reasons for the rapid growth of interest in the familiar letter that occurred in France at this time. The most obvious of these was an increasingly sophisticated culture associated with court society. This society cultivated conversation as an art, and theoreticians of the letter proposed conversation as a formal model for "natural" epistolary writing. Early in the seventeenth century the introduction of a central postal system, established by royal authority, provided a situation that fostered new interest in letter writing. By 1627 regular courier routes had been set in place across the country, and after the rebellions of the Fronde, Anne of Austria and her prime minister, Cardinal Mazarin, established a special postal service within Paris in order to facilitate quick letter communication between neighborhoods.

The increasing concentration of political and economic power in the person of the monarch also made it more expedient, in the last three decades of the seventeenth century, for members of the nobility to maintain constant contact with events at court. Whether traveling in the provinces or exiled indefinitely from Paris, anyone who hoped to gain favor with the king had to be informed of the most recent news from the capital. Printed pamphlets such as the *Gazette de Hollande* and the *Muse historique* were also published during this period, but they were distributed no faster than private letters, and a reliable correspondent could provide at least as much information to aristocrats absent from court as a printed newsletter.

These conditions encouraged interest in the art of letter writing and facilitated its practice. Many epistolary manuals were published throughout the seventeenth century, addressed to an increasingly broad readership eager to cultivate the letter writer's art. Though Sévigné's letters were not published during her lifetime (apart from the small number included in Bussy-Rabutin's memoirs), they were read and admired by many readers beyond their immediate addressees. Her letters do not, however, seem to follow the sorts of rules that writers of letter manuals were fond of establishing, nor can they be easily fit into the specific categories of letters that the epistolary theorists laid out. Sévigné's style can best be characterized as conversational. Her long letters typically cover a wide variety of topics; they are suggestive of speech and invite reading aloud. Her most admiring readers through the centuries have commented on their capacity to evoke an entire world of speakers sharing a common culture.

One of the most famous portions of Sévigné's correspondence is the series of letters to her friend Simon de Pomponne in 1664, during the trial for treason of Nicolas Foucquet, minister of finance to the young Louis XIV. The Foucquet affair is now regarded as a pivotal moment in the history of Louis XIV's relations with the nobility. At the time of Foucquet's arrest and trial, his friends and protégés could only speculate on the far-reaching political implications of the events as they unfolded. Foucquet's disgrace threatened both Sévigné and Pomponne personally. Pomponne was exiled early in the trial under suspicion of having conspired to draw Foucquet closer to Jansenist circles. Sévigné had sought favors from Foucquet in the past, had written him letters that were confiscated when he was arrested, and had cultivated close ties with his family in the hope that her own children would benefit from the patronage of the wealthy and powerful minister.

Foucquet's trial polarized Parisian high society; his guilt was hotly debated, and it was not easy to tell from the outset what side even his friends would take. To Sévigné, Foucquet's behavior was nothing short of heroic. Her reports to Pomponne supported this view by including conversations with several people who shared her and Pomponne's sympathies and who offered their interpretation of daily events down to the smallest detail. Sévigné rarely transcribed what Foucquet actually said in his own defense (this information would have been accessible to her correspondents from other sources) but instead focused on the manner in which he spoke and the gestures that punctuated his testimony—a refusal to be seated, a polite salutation, whether or not he removed his hat. Her descriptions of the defendant and of those who watched him are carefully framed for dramatic effect. Her accounts of the behavior of the judges and even the king highlight the gallantry of Foucquet and his sympathizers and the brutality of those hostile to him. What emerges from these descriptions is a clear interpretation of the trial, even though, in the risky context of a letter exchange, Sévigné never expresses her outrage directly.

As time went on, Sévigné was to see other close friends suffer disgrace or exile. An important purpose of her correspondence was to keep social groups connected at a distance and to sustain the impression of ongoing conversations among people. As in her letters to Pomponne, Sévigné's other letters invite her far-flung correspondents to participate in the talk of the group and remain, at least through writing, on the "inside." In her letters to her cousin Bussy-Rabutin, who spent most

Sévigné's daughter, Françoise-Marguerite de Sévigné, comtesse de Grignan, who carried on a voluminous correspondence with her mother (portrait by Pierre Mignard; from Roselyne de Ayala and Jean-Pierre Guéno, Belles Lettres, 2001)

of his adult life trying in vain to regain favor at court, she regularly reported how his letters were read aloud, absorbed into conversations, and given real power in a social world where gossip and political action were never very far apart. In her letters to other friends unwillingly absent from court, she assumed a consolatory, retrospective tone. In these letters Sévigné sought both to sustain old contacts and to create new connections in compensation for other, broken ones. As in her descriptions of Foucquet, the exiles become heroes and are placed in the company of grand figures from history or legend.

The separation that had the most profound effect on Sévigné was the departure of her daughter, Françoise-Marguerite, who married the comte de Grignan in 1669 and left Paris two years later with her husband, who had been given the post of governor of Provence. In Sévigné's letters to her daughter, the awareness of Françoise-Marguerite's social alienation is compounded by the shock of personal separation. Although it was an honor to be named the personal representative of the king, Grignan's departure for Provence entailed absence from the court and a heavy financial burden on the family. Sympathetically sharing

Page from Sévigné's 13 September 1679 letter to her daughter (from Antoine Adam, L'Age Classique, *volume 2, 1969)*

her daughter's new position, Sévigné strove to construct in their correspondence a new, compensatory experience of intimacy. Dialogue in letters, for her as for many of her contemporaries, helped to transform the experience of political exclusion into a more gratifying image of deliberate escape. The letters to her daughter also record a passionate attachment and an obsession with finding the words to describe that attachment in writing.

Of the published letters that were written after 1671, more than three-fourths are from mother to daughter, and they reveal an intense, often contradictory relationship that is today the subject of most studies done on Sévigné and her writing. Grignan's move to Provence precipitated a profound loneliness and sense of isolation in her mother, feelings that were new to a woman who was known by all of her friends as a paragon of sociability. In the letters to her daughter Sévigné writes with an urgency not seen in her correspondence with others, and in the process she discovers her vocation as a writer. She was acutely aware of the elements of her letters that would assure their value in the eyes of Françoise-Marguerite and her family, and she worked hard to provide them with news that would enable Grignan to continue to participate in the social world from which he and his wife had been separated. Even without having access to the letters written by the daughter in response, modern readers can perceive the fact that Françoise-Marguerite was overwhelmed by her mother's continual expressions of affection. Sévigné understood that the worth of her letters in her daughter's eyes had to be assured by the communication of useful information. To her own descriptions of events she adds a popular gazette to "nourish" her daughter in public conversations. And she vaunts her own superiority as a source of news, reminding Françoise-Marguerite that other informants have been less accurate than she. When Sévigné herself was away from Paris, she apologized for the reduced interest her letters would inevitably have for her daughter.

At the same time, Sévigné discovered in this new epistolary relationship with her daughter an interest that she had not anticipated and an opportunity for self-expression that she could not repress. Thus, in the letters written from her country estate of Les Rochers, in Brittany, she indulges herself and seems to relish the separation from society experienced there. Traveling to Les Rochers was a voyage into a territory imbued with memories she could share with her correspondent, where distractions were pared down to a few encounters with people and places familiar to her daughter from her youth. At Les Rochers it was easier to summon a mental image of Françoise-Marguerite, even

Courtyard of the Hôtel Carnavalet in the Marais district of Paris, where Sévigné lived from 1677 until her death in 1696

though it was more difficult to muster information that would be of interest to her. The correspondence between Les Rochers and Provence drew upon a narrower world for sustenance, but it invited both writers to nourish their exchanges with other references, from shared memories of places and people or from readings. Picking up on her daughter's comment that she wished she could be "a shepherdess" with her in the fields surrounding their country home, Sévigné compares herself to a character from a popular pastoral romance of the day. She fills her descriptions of the woods with literary allusions, reminds her daughter of some of the games they had played there as they read together, and reports that the verses they had carved on two trees in the garden are still there, suggesting the permanence of their affection. Intrusions on her solitary promenades were unwelcome, unless the visitor offered to read with her from Torquato Tasso or Ludovico Ariosto.

While Sévigné's letters from Paris offer chronicles of behind-the-scenes events in an extremely volatile social milieu, with each return to Brittany she rediscovered the same stable "company" of her favorite landscapes and books. Letters from Les Rochers written in

Late portrait of Sévigné by Pierre Mignard
(Collection Giraudon)

1671, 1675, 1684, and 1689 show the writer embracing a return to the same imaginative world, reassuringly unchanged, and the same favorite authors, who became her points of reference even in some incongruous situations. Immersing herself in a new history of the Crusades on her 1675 visit, Sévigné reports that the book makes her want to reread Tasso's epic poem *Jerusalem Delivered* (1575). Her daughter's aggressive confidence in the arrangement of a business affair makes her think of the courage of Rinaldo, the hero of Tasso's epic, in traversing the illusory perils of an enchanted wood. Walks in the woods bring to mind the woodland scenes of Ariosto's epic *Orlando Furioso* (1532). Even Françoise-Marguerite's letters, at their best, are compared to Ariosto's epic. The Italian language itself becomes a way for Sévigné to make a connection with her daughter or with other friends from whom she has been separated. Italian phrases and references to works in Italian are frequent in the letters immediately following her separations from her daughter.

Sévigné read widely, but her love of the Italian epic romances continued throughout her life, eventually out of resistance to the disparagement of the genre by classical French academicians. Many of her favorite characters and episodes were precisely those that were most vigorously discredited—the female warriors Clorinda, from *Jerusalem Delivered,* and Bradamante, from *Orlando Furioso,* fascinated her, while such figures were criticized by the classical theoreticians. Ariosto and

Tasso's use of the fantastic in their epics was also disparaged, but Sévigné's repeated allusions to their enchanted forests, mythical creatures, and palaces of illusion suggest that for her, as for many of her generation, the neoclassical aesthetics were not compelling. As her correspondence evolved, Sévigné revealed a growing awareness that her literary culture was part of a nostalgic attachment. This nostalgia became more pronounced as the Sévigné and Grignan financial problems worsened and as it became more obvious that Grignan and her husband would not be recalled to Paris. In a remarkable series of letters written in May 1680 Sévigné reports to her daughter that her son cut down the trees from one of their beloved woods in order to pay his debts. For her the experience signified the destruction of a magic forest, an imaginary landscape rich with shared associations for the correspondents, whose defacement was a kind of death and marked the loss of her own inspiration.

As Sévigné's letters are read chronologically, they inevitably seem more preoccupied with time, change, and death. Sévigné lived a long life by the standards of her day, and she outlived many of her friends. But her obsessive love for her daughter appears not to have diminished in the long span of time during which they corresponded, and the mother's overwhelming commitment to this relationship is all the more impressive when one considers that they were in fact apart for only nine of the twenty-three years following the Grignans' move to Provence.

Mother and daughter visited each other for lengthy periods, and Sévigné also lived with Françoise-Marguerite for the last years of her life. The repeated experience of separation and reunion perpetually renewed Sévigné's commitment to finding a way of expressing her passion. The theme of the inadequacy of language for the expression of love recurs throughout her correspondence, but this sense of inadequacy seemed to energize rather than discourage her efforts to describe her emotions. To put her maternal feeling into words, she drew on a multitude of discourses from her culture—the language of religion, erotic love, and myth—and in so doing created a particular model of a mother's passion that has become an important point of reference for both historical and contemporary discussions of the mother-daughter bond.

Though little is known of the nature of the relationship between Sévigné and her daughter outside of their epistolary record of it, they apparently quarreled often when they were together. Particularly in the correspondence with her daughter, Sévigné found in the practice of writing letters a kind of pleasure that she could not experience in actual conversation. As her family's links to court society weakened, she became more focused on the routines organizing her epistolary world, at the center of which was her correspondence with her daughter. Writing to Françoise-Marguerite was a means of escaping everything else. Françoise-Marguerite's letters enabled Sévigné to put herself in her daughter's place and imagine herself totally in that distant world. This intimacy meant that many of the conventional rules of conversation, at which Sévigné was so adept, did not apply, and in fact such rules interfered with the kind of mutual absorption she tried to cultivate with Françoise-Marguerite. Sévigné instructed her daughter in this new kind of writing, telling her to write only of herself, and as unself-consciously as possible, with no thought of responding to the "old news" from previous letters. In her love letters to her daughter, Sévigné experienced the unfamiliar feeling of being at a loss for words. This discovery ultimately led her to invent new styles of expression that had not been cultivated in the intensely sociable world that had shaped them both.

Françoise-Marguerite suffered a lengthy illness during the winter and spring of 1696, and her mother exhausted herself in attending to her. In April, Sévigné fell ill and died two weeks later. In a letter to a friend written in the first days after the loss of her mother, Madame de Grignan seems to echo her mother's expressions, written twenty-five years earlier, of the agony of their separation: "Il est vrai, Monsieur, il faut une force plus qu'humaine pour soutenir une si cruelle séparation et tant de privation. . . . Je ne puis encore tourner mes regards autour de moi, et je n'y vois plus cette personne qui m'a comblée de biens . . . " (It is true, sir, one needs a strength that is more than human to bear such a cruel separation and so much deprivation. . . . I can still only look around me, and I no longer see that person who gave me so much . . .) (28 April 1696; translation by Elizabeth C. Goldsmith).

Biographies:

Roger Duchêne, *Madame de Sévigné; ou, La chance d'être femme* (Paris: Fayard, 1982);

Frances Mossiker, *Madame de Sévigné: A Life and Letters* (New York: Knopf, 1983);

Jeanne A. and William T. Ojala, *Madame de Sévigné: A Seventeenth-Century Life* (New York: Berg, 1990);

Anne Bernet, *Madame de Sévigné: Mère Passion* (Paris: Perrin, 1996).

References:

Antoine Adam, *L'Age Classique*, volume 2 (Paris: Arthaud, 1969);

Harriet Ray Allentuch, *Madame de Sévigné: A Portrait in Letters* (Baltimore: Johns Hopkins Press, 1963);

Roselyne de Ayala and Jean-Pierre Guéno, *Belles Lettres: Manuscripts by the Masters of French Literature*, translated by John Goodman (New York: Abrams, 2001);

H. T. Barnwell, "'Il faut que je vous conte . . .': Fact into Fiction in the Letters of Madame de Sévigné," *Seventeenth-Century French Studies*, 19 (1997): 109–124;

Bernard Beugnot, "Madame de Sévigné telle qu'en elle-même enfin?" *French Forum*, 5 (1980): 201–217;

Bernard Bray, "Quelques aspects du système épistolaire de Madame de Sévigné," *Revue d'Histoire littéraire de la France*, 69 (1969): 491–505;

Bray, "Le Style épistolaire: La Leçon de Madame de Sévigné," *Littératures classiques*, 28 (1996): 197–209;

Jean Cordelier, *Madame de Sévigné par elle-même* (Paris: Editions du Seuil, 1967);

Roger Duchêne, *Réalité vécue et art épistolaire: Madame de Sévigné et la lettre d'amour* (Paris: Bordas, 1970);

Duchêne and Pierre Ronzeaud, eds., *Autour de Madame de Sévigné: Deux colloques pour un tricentenaire* (Paris: Papers on French Seventeenth-Century Literature, 1997);

Michèle Longino Farrell, *Performing Motherhood: The Sévigné Correspondence* (Hanover, N.H.: University Press of New England, 1991);

Elizabeth C. Goldsmith, "Sociability and Intimacy in the Letters of Madame de Sévigné," in her *Exclusive Conversations: The Art of Interaction in Seventeenth-Century France* (Philadelphia: University of Pennsylvania Press, 1988), pp. 111–141;

Michael Hawcroft, "Historical Evidence and Literature: Madame de Sévigné's Letters on the Trial of Foucquet," *Seventeenth Century*, 9 (1994): 57–75;

Louise K. Horowitz, "Madame de Sévigné," in her *Love and Language: A Study of the Classical French Moralist Writers* (Columbus: Ohio State University Press, 1977);

Catherine Montfort Howard, *Les Fortunes de Madame de Sévigné au XVIIème et au XVIIIème siècles* (Tübingen, Germany: G. Narr / Paris: Editions J.-M. Place, 1982);

Dagmar Weiser, "Proust et Madame de Sévigné," in *Marcel Proust*, Revue d'Histoire Littéraire de la France, no. 100 (Paris: Presses universitaires de France, 2000), pp. 91–106;

Charles G. S. Williams, *Madame de Sévigné* (Boston: Twayne, 1981);

Virginia Woolf, "Madame de Sévigné," in her *The Death of the Moth, and Other Essays* (New York: Harcourt, Brace, 1942), pp. 51–57.

Charles Sorel
(circa 1600 – 7 March 1674)

Jean-Pierre van Elslande
University of Neuchâtel, Switzerland

SELECTED BOOKS: *Epithalame sur l'heureux mariage du très-chrétien roy de France, Louis XIII de ce nom . . .* (Paris: E. Richer, 1616);

L'Histoire amoureuse de Cléagénor et de Doristée, 4 volumes (Paris: T. du Bray, 1621);

Le Palais d'Angélie, as sieur de Marzilly (Paris: T. du Bray, 1622);

Les Nouvelles françoises, où se trouvent les divers effects de l'amour et de la fortune . . . (Paris: P. Billaine, 1623); revised and enlarged as *Les Nouvelles choisies, où se trouvent divers incidens d'amour et de fortune,* 2 volumes (Paris: P. David, 1645);

L'Histoire comique de Francion, anonymous (Paris: P. Billaine, 1623; revised and enlarged, 1626); revised and enlarged as *La Vraye Histoire comique de Francion,* as Nicolas Moulinet, sieur du Parc (Paris: P. Billaine, 1633); translated as *The Comical History of Francion* (London: F. Leach, 1655);

Le Berger extravagant, où, parmy des fantaisies amoureuses, on void les impertinences des romans et de la poésie, 2 volumes (Paris: T. du Bray, 1627; enlarged, 1628); revised and enlarged as *L'Anti-Roman, ou L'Histoire du berger Lysis,* as Jean de la Lande, 4 volumes (Paris: T. du Bray, 1633); translated by J. Davies as *The Extravagant Shepherd: The Anti-Romance; or, The History of the Shepherd Lysis* (London: T. Heath, 1653);

Avertissement sur l'Histoire de la Monarchie française (Paris: C. Morlot, 1628); revised and enlarged as *Histoire de la Monarchie française, où sont décrits les faits mémorables et les vertus héroïques de nos anciens rois* (Paris: C. Morlot, 1629; enlarged, Paris: L. Boulanger & J. Camusat, 1633); republished as *Histoire de France, contenant les faits mémorables et les vertus héroïques de nos rois* (Paris: L. Boulanger, 1647);

La Science des choses corporelles, première partie de la Science humaine, où l'on connoist la Vérité de toutes les choses du Monde par les forces de la Raison, et l'on trouve la réfutation des Erreurs de la Philosophie vulgaire (Paris: P. Billaine, 1634);

Charles Sorel (Bibliothèque Nationale, Paris)

Première partie de la Science universelle, contenant la science des choses corporelles, qui est la vraie physique (Paris: P. Billaine, 1637)—includes *La Science des choses spirituelles;*

De l'Usage et de la perfection de toutes les choses du monde, troisiesme volume de la Science universelle de Sorel (Paris: T. Quinet, 1641);

La Science universelle, 3 volumes (Paris: T. Quinet, 1641)—comprises *La Science des choses corporelles, La Science des choses spirituelles,* and *De l'Usage et de la perfection de toutes les choses du monde;* revised and enlarged as

*La Science Universelle, où la vraye philosophie plus esten-
düe que la vulgaire, et reduite en un ordre naturel, avec la
refutation de plusieurs erreurs,* 4 volumes (Paris: T.
Quinet, 1644, 1647)—comprises *La Science des choses corporelles, La Science des choses spirituelles, De
l'Usage et de la perfection de toutes les choses du monde,*
and *La Perfection de l'âme* (1644); revised and
enlarged as *La Science Universelle, dernière édition augmentée,* 4 volumes (Paris: N. Le Gras, 1668);
La Maison des jeux, 2 volumes (Paris: N. de Sercy, 1642);
*Discours sur l'Académie Françoise establie pour la correction et
l'embellissement du Langage, pour sçavoir si elle est de
quelque utilité aux Particuliers et au public et où l'on void
les Raisons de part et d'autre sans desguisement* (Paris:
G. de Luyne, 1654);
La Bibliothèque françoise (Paris: Compagnie des Libraires
du Palais, 1664; revised and enlarged, 1667);
*De la connaissance des bons livres, ou Examen de plusieurs
autheurs* (Paris: A. Pralard, 1671).

Editions: *Histoire comique de Francion,* 4 volumes, edited
by Emile Roy (Paris: Hachette, 1924–1931);
Histoire comique de Francion, in *Romanciers du XVIIe siècle:
Sorel, Scarron, Furetière, Madame de La Fayette,* edited
by Antoine Adam, Bibliothèque de la Pléiade, no.
131 (Paris: Gallimard, 1958);
La Bibliothèque françoise (Geneva: Slatkine, 1970);
Le Berger extravagant (Geneva: Slatkine, 1972);
*Les Nouvelles françaises, où se trouvent divers effets de l'amour
et de la fortune* (Geneva: Slatkine, 1972);
*De la connoissance des bons livres, ou Examen des plusieurs
auteurs,* edited by Lucia Moretti Cenerini (Rome:
Bulzoni, 1975);
La Maison des jeux (Geneva: Slatkine, 1977);
Histoire comique de Francion, edited by Yves Giraud (Paris:
Garnier-Flammarion, 1979);
Histoire comique de Francion, edited by Fausta Garavini
(Paris: Gallimard, 1996).

Charles Sorel is regarded by critics today as one
of the most interesting pioneers of the modern novel.
He was also one of the most prolific authors of his era,
having tried his hand at a dizzying variety of genres. In
addition to writing novels, he left behind verse, historical and ethical works, bibliographies, pedagogical documents, and scientific articles, as well as collections of
cultural games, news articles, and pamphlets. Such a
diverse oeuvre made Sorel an extraordinary polymath,
pursuing on varied fronts a single coherent enterprise.
From novels to scientific treatises to moral lessons, his
aim was to unmask—often satirically—social pretense,
intellectual imposters, and aesthetic artifice. Lucidity
was Sorel's guiding principle; that is, to erase prejudice
in all its forms. In this regard, and because he trusted in
reason to gain access to a more authentic form of

knowledge, his ideas are close to those of René Descartes. Intent on moving beyond accepted ideas and
attacking defenders of tradition, Sorel belonged to the
freethinking current of the time, exemplified by philosophers such as François de La Mothe Le Vayer and
Gabriel Naudé and writers such as Savinien de Cyrano
de Bergerac and Théophile de Viau.

In order to achieve this vast enterprise of demystification, Sorel did not hesitate to take recourse to fiction
and its most subtle ruses. Contradictory though it may
seem, Sorel in fact expected his readers not to be duped
by the fictional worlds evoked in his novels. Rather
than allowing themselves to be naively transported by
the story, they had to be fully aware of the playful
dimension of the work, and Sorel never failed to
remind his readers of this dimension, frustrating their
expectations. This forced complicity between author
and public, which undermines the power of illusion in
fiction, may be considered one of Sorel's trademarks.

Charles Sorel was born in Paris, around 1600, to
a bourgeois family whose roots lay in Picardy, in northern France. His grandfather was the magistrate of
Picardy, but his father had recently moved to Paris in
order to pursue a career as *procurateur* (attorney). There
he married the sister of Charles Bernard, the first historiographer of France. The couple had two children:
Charles and his sister, Françoise. Although bourgeois,
the Sorels had aristocratic pretensions and claimed to
be descended from an important Picardy family, the
Sorels of Ugny, who themselves were descendants of
English kings and who counted among their relatives
Agnès Sorel, the celebrated favorite of King Charles
VII of France. Charles Sorel liked to refer to this prestigious, though undoubtedly false, genealogy.

Between 1621 and 1626 Sorel followed the court
throughout France. He was secretary for Adrien de
Monluc, comte de Cramail, then for the comte de Marcilly and François de Baradat. Afterward Sorel spent the
rest of his life in Paris, living a bourgeois existence in a
house on the rue Saint-Germain l'Auxerrois, which he
shared with his sister and brother-in-law and their children. Sorel lived off the money he had earned as historiographer of France, a post formerly held by his uncle,
from whom he had purchased it.

Sorel began his literary career with two popular
novels. In 1621 *L'Histoire amoureuse de Cléagénor et de
Doristée* (The Love Story of Cléagénor and Doristée)
was published in Paris by Toussaint du Bray. The following year *Le Palais d'Angélie* (Angélie's Palace) was
published under the pseudonym de Marzilly by the
same publisher. These two books, each exceeding several hundred pages, were well suited to the educated
public's taste for adventure and were extremely successful. There is little original about these works: as in

other novels of the period, they include people in disguise, kidnappings followed by happy reunions, and several cases of mistaken identity. Sorel returned to some of these themes and structural elements in later novels, notably with episodes involving disguise and the insertion, within the primary narrative, of secondary narratives recounted by the characters themselves.

In 1623 Sorel published *Les Nouvelles françoises,* a collection of novellas ostensibly more realistic than his previous works. As the title indicates, the action takes place in France rather than in a distant, mythical setting. The characters are given contemporary names rather than names borrowed from Greek mythology. As for the stories, their originality lies in their depiction of amorous relations between members of different social classes. Sorel aimed to depict situations, people, and emotions relevant to daily life.

At the same time, however, Sorel was composing verse *ballets de Cour* (court ballets), which mixed dance, singing, and recitation to create a spectacular performance full of mythological references. Sorel worked with other poets such as Théophile, François de Malherbe, and Honorat de Bueil, seigneur de Racan, since the verses recited at these dances were generally composed by several poets rather than just one. Sorel's talents were particularly at the service of Henri I de Savoie, duc de Nemours, who was quite fond of such festivities. During this time Sorel frequented the aristocratic salons of Paris, where he was introduced as the secretary of Cramail. In these salons he participated in conversations dominated by questions of gallantry and scientific discovery, undertaken in a spirit of enlightened inquiry.

Sorel's most famous novel, *L'Histoire comique de Francion* (translated as *The Comical History of Francion,* 1655), was also published in 1623. The book appeared without the author's name, and several subsequent editions were also published anonymously. *L'Histoire comique de Francion* became one of the most successful novels of the period. The title itself designates the novel a "comic story," thus placing it in a particular narrative tradition that included such writers as Théophile and, later, Cyrano, Tristan L'Hermite, Paul Scarron, and Antoine Furetière.

At the beginning of the seventeenth century the comic story was in the process of establishing itself as a separate genre. In contrast to its contemporary rival, the heroic or gallant novel, the comic story portrayed characters and their actions more naturally—even, in fact, with a certain rawness. Just as comic theater was distinguished from tragedy in portraying not mythical or heroic figures but ordinary people and action, the comic story replaced chevaliers, nymphs, and shepherds with people from all social conditions and recounted their ordinary daily existence. The geograph-

LES
NOVVELLES
Françoifes.

Où fe trouuent les diuers effects de
l'Amour & de la Fortune,
& defquels voicy
les tiltres.

Le Pauure Genereux.
Les mal-Marie〉.
La Sœur Ialoufe.
Les trois Amants.
La recognoiffance d'vn Fils.

A PARIS,
Chez PIERRE BILLAINE , ruë
S. Iacques , à la Bonne Foy.
1623.
Auec Priuilege du Roy.

Title page for the collection of novellas Sorel revised and enlarged in 1645 (from the 1972 facsimile edition)

ical and historical circumstances of the comic story also differed from those of the traditional novel: exotic locations and distant epochs gave way to contemporary France and its realistic portrayal. This realism, however, was not the objective realism of nineteenth-century writers such as Honoré de Balzac or Emile Zola. Rather, it was a realism defined in its opposition to the idealism of the contemporary novel, while at the same time providing the satirical and caricatural elements the public expected of such works.

Thus, the comic-story genre presented a style quite different from that of the heroic novel. Instead of the précieux metaphors and ornamental mythology characteristic of the works of Antoine de Nervèze, Nicolas Des Escuteaux, and François Du Souhait, writers in the comic-story genre adopted a direct tone and did not resort to affected expression, except in parody. In general, repetitions, ornate descriptions, and allegorical portraits are either absent from the comic story or convey derision of such narrative devices. Moreover, the comic story readily admits popular idiom, vulgar words, and picaresque expressions.

This reevaluation of the traditional forms of the contemporary novel led, finally, to a critique of established values, which explains why authors of the comic story were sometimes linked with libertine and free-thinking movements and became the target of official censure. The satirical approach of the genre spared no tradition and found expression in subversive episodes that upset moral, social, and political norms.

Indeed, *L'Histoire comique de Francion* is in many ways a baffling work. Its deliberately composite character precludes any assignation to a particular convention or type. The adventures of Francion are related both in the first and third person, generating narrative instability and an ambiguous perspective. Francion is thus perceived from the interior and exterior at once. One scene may be governed by an omniscient perspective, thus making readers privy to Francion's personal motivations, while another may be told from an external but limited point of view, thus keeping his motivations unknowable.

L'Histoire comique de Francion does not develop through a logical cause-and-effect sequence of episodes. Rather, it conforms to a mode of reading that is more episodic than linear. One scene may be radically different from the last, giving the reader an impression of rupture, but the various episodes continue to echo throughout the entirety of the novel, giving it cohesiveness. Similarities and differences between various parts of the story are not really visible until a second reading. At first the reader is struck, rather, by the many digressions, the fragmented episodes, and the lack of apparent narrative continuity.

Each scene of *L'Histoire comique de Francion* constitutes an autonomous narrative fragment that can be related to one or several other narrative fragments, creating a network of meaning. From this perspective, Sorel's novel is a modular work that baffles the readers and plays with their expectations. The deliberately incomplete information about the characters and their situations engages the reader in the pursuit of additional information, which is interspersed throughout the rest of the work.

The conclusion of *L'Histoire comique de Francion* is constantly delayed, particularly in the first edition of 1623, which openly suggested to the reader an incomplete story begging for an ending. Thus, the structure of Sorel's novel necessitated the continuation of the story. The appearance of a second edition in 1626 and a third in 1633 confirms this point. By adding episodes to the preceding version, each subsequent edition brought about corrections, additions, and omissions that redistributed the narrative elements, redirected the reader's

attention, and delayed as much as possible the conclusion of the work.

The characters' construction is consistent with this formal analysis of the structure of the novel. Multifaceted and sometimes contradictory, their complexity is striking. It seems impossible to assign them a stable identity or to define them once and for all. *L'Histoire comique de Francion* represents a complex universe in the middle of which beings and events avoid easy definitions; diversity and contradiction reign. Francion himself exhibits a dizzying array of divergent traits and finds himself engaged in multiple and extravagant adventures. A noble by birth, he is an adventurous character with a love for travel, and this mobility is emblematic of his whole personality. He makes friends, becomes attached, leaves, finds his companions again, and knows both honor and disgrace. He interacts with diverse social worlds—the court, the bourgeoisie, the lower classes— and he loves many women. He disguises himself frequently as a pilgrim or shepherd, which often permits him to trick others. He shares these characteristics with others in the novel, however, to the point that these other characters seem almost to be Francion's doubles. In fact, Sorel so efficiently blurs the identity of his characters that the bemusing episodes of mistaken identity mimic the confusing effects the story produces for the reader.

This taste for disguise and incessant movement corresponds with the philosophy Francion proclaims on several occasions, which evokes the ideals of the *libertins* and freethinkers, particularly those associated with Théophile. Francion wants to combat ignorance and stupidity, break taboos, castigate narrow minds, and live according to nature, however it may shock common opinion. The exercise of freedom interests him above all. Pleasure is legitimate, and Francion seeks to rehabilitate it against constraining value systems.

At the same time, certain narrative elements in Francion's successive adventures seem to advocate a course leading from the immediate satisfaction of the senses to the search for idealized love. In the 1623 edition the novel begins in medias res with Francion's attempt to seduce Laurette, turns to a retrospective narrative of his tumultuous youth, and then returns to the present to depict an orgy at which the participants declare themselves in favor of free love and the search for pleasure. In the course of these adventures, however, Francion falls in love with the beautiful Nays after having seen her portrait and vows to find her in order to marry her. He thus turns his back on Laurette and the pleasures of the senses in order to devote himself to a quest for beauty. Some critics have called attention to this progression. Hervé D. Béchade evokes Francion's "itinéraire moral" (moral itinerary), while Jean Serroy insists on the "évolution psychologique du héros" (psychological evolution of the hero), and Félix R. Freudmann speaks of the "mouvement ascendant du profane vers l'idéal" (ascending movement of the profane towards the ideal), all of which are characteristic of narrative development and hero psychology.

Sorel's rewriting of each subsequent edition of *L'Histoire comique de Francion* seems to conform to such an interpretation. In both the 1626 and 1633 editions the text is reworked so that the most audacious elements are omitted, as if Sorel wanted to purify his text at the same time that he was leading his hero to a less carnal form of love. The incomplete fifth and last book of the first edition shows Francion preparing to leave for Italy in search of Nays. The hero's new adventures in the 1626 edition are organized around this perspective and are finally capped by his marriage with Nays in the 1633 version of the novel.

Certain critics, however, reject the hypothesis that *L'Histoire comique de Francion* is a linear and progressive novel. Martine Debaisieux proposes to question "les concepts d'évolution, de 'profondeur,' attribués à Francion, et de faire ressortir au contraire l'aspect dispersé, partiel et contradictoire de sa représentation" (the concepts of evolution, of "profundity," attributed to Francion, and to emphasize instead the dispersed, partial and contradictory aspects of his representation). Given the unstable nature of Francion, the succession of masks, and the playful effect of his doubling in other characters, it is problematic to speak of psychological and moral development. Similarly, Fausta Garavini notes that "le parcours qui conduit à Nays est sinueux et soumis à de fréquentes déviations" (the path that leads to Nays is sinuous and subject to frequent deviations) and that the pursuit of ideal love is ironic in that Francion's professions of his love for Nays resemble those that are openly ridiculed elsewhere in the novel.

The 1626 and 1633 editions of *L'Histoire comique de Francion,* even with their important revisions leading apparently to a greater sense of morality, include even more thinly veiled allusions to a philosophy of pleasure freed from restrictions. Between a reading that insists on the progression and unity of the novel and one that insists, on the contrary, on an aesthetic of discontinuity and paradox, it is undoubtedly necessary to abstain from choosing one over the other. It is precisely these ambiguities that furnish all the richness of Sorel's novel.

In *Le Berger extravagant* (1627; revised and enlarged as *L'Anti-Roman, ou L'Histoire de berger Lysis,* translated as *The Extravagant Shepherd: The Anti-Romance; or, The History of the Shepherd Lysis,* 1653) Sorel parodies sentimental novels, particularly Honoré d'Urfé's *L'Astrée* (1607–1627), a pastoral novel that had been passionately devoured by the public. *L'Astrée* depicts a society of

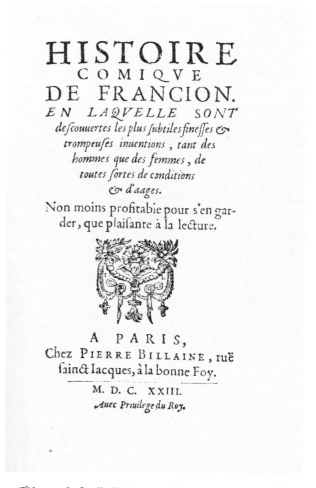

Title page for Sorel's third novel, published anonymously in 1623 (from the 1982 reprint edition)

aristocrats who have chosen to live far from the cities and the court in order to escape the ill effects of ambition. All dressed as shepherds, they devote their lives to idealized love, which they discuss, sometimes at great length, in a highly stylized fashion.

In order better to denounce the artificiality of d'Urfé's novel, Sorel creates the character of a shepherd, Lysis, who is in love with the beautiful Charite. Lysis is in reality named Louis and is a Parisian bourgeois, the son of a silk merchant, and his passion for pastoral literature has driven him mad. Much like Don Quixote, who identifies himself entirely with heroic characters of chivalry, Louis/Lysis completely identifies with the shepherds of pastoral literature. He thus leaves Paris for the countryside of Saint-Cloud, disguises himself as a shepherd, adopts the gallant language of d'Urfé's characters, and no longer considers any reality other than that filtered through his reading. As for the beautiful Charite, she is really named Catherine and is the servant of a rich Parisian woman vacationing in Saint-Cloud.

A series of adventures follows, in the course of which Lysis is ridiculed and derisively treated. Anselme, a noble Parisian he encounters by chance, takes him under his protection and proposes to cure him of his madness. In truth, the cure to which he submits Lysis, with the help of a group of friends, permits Anselme to amuse himself at Lysis's expense. Everyone is in on the game, convincing Lysis that he is actually in Forez, the region where d'Urfé's shepherds lived. One character presents himself as a musician and persuades Lysis that he has transformed him into a girl, echoing a famous episode in *L'Astrée* in which the shepherd Céladon dresses as a woman. Another character hides in order to repeat Lysis's words and make him believe that he is hearing an echo. At one point Lysis wishes for a faithful portrait of Charite, and Anselme fabricates one according to Lysis's description of his beloved. Because the description, inspired by the mannered verbal portraits characteristic of pastoral literature, uses several metaphors to describe the young woman's physical traits, the resulting portrait is monstrous: the eyes have become suns, the eyebrows are real arches, the cheeks veritable flowers, and the lips pieces of coral. Having been well amused, Anselme and his friends reveal to Lysis that they have tricked him. The young man, sorry to see his bucolic dream dissolve, comes to his senses and ends up marrying Catherine/Charite. Everything returns to order: reason triumphs over absurdity.

In *Le Berger extravagant* Sorel mocks the public's passion for the pastoral and the lack of believability of such novels. In his madness Lysis is a caricature of the public. But the parodic dimension of the book also allows Sorel to reflect on the art of the novel and, more generally, on the conventions that underlie the genre. In the preface to the 1627 edition he affirms his wish to write "un livre qui se moquât des autres et qui fût comme le tombeau des Romans et des absurdités de la Poésie (a book that would mock others and would be the tomb of the novel and of poetic absurdities). Likewise, in the second edition, which was published in 1633 and was significantly titled *L'Anti-Roman, ou l'Histoire du berger Lysis* (The Antiromance, or the History of the Shepherd Lysis), Sorel specifies that the adventures of his hero are "arrangées comme celles des Romans" (arranged like those in novels), but that "cela n'est fait que pour en montrer les impertinences" (that is only done in order to show their extravagance).

This effort toward demystification not only finds expression in Lysis's adventures but also in several remarks in the appendices (in the first as well as in subsequent editions) Sorel inserted at the end of each of the fourteen books of the novel. These remarks offer commentary and analysis on scenes from the narrative. From this point of view *Le Berger extravagant* is a novel

about the art of writing and reading novels. Sorel unveils the structure of his novel and thus invites the public not simply to follow the adventures of the characters passively but to reflect actively on the choices of the author who presides over the story and on the subtle tricks that underlie the story. Periodically interrupted, the narrative no longer allows readers to abandon themselves to the fictional world; instead, it becomes subject to the possibility of refashioning.

In order to denounce the artifice of the novel genre, Sorel wrote one nevertheless. *Le Berger extravagant* recounts a coherent story, even if it is one of disillusionment. The character of Lysis is much more complex than first appears. At times he seems aware of the artificial nature of his bucolic existence. For example, before throwing himself into the water, as Céladon does at the beginning of *L'Astrée*, Lysis attaches to his arms two buoys that will save him from drowning. Thus, he is not entirely duped by the character he plays. One day, after having allowed himself to be convinced by Anselme and his friends that he has turned into a tree, he attests that he never really believed it. He simply pretended to believe them in order to trick them in turn and amuse himself at their expense. In passages such as these, the satiric intent of the novel becomes much more complex, since, in order to appreciate it, the reader must also be familiar with the novels Sorel is deriding. Here, as in *L'Histoire comique de Francion*, the interest of the work lies in such paradox and ambiguity.

In 1628 Sorel published a work titled *Avertissement sur l'Histoire de la Monarchie française* (Foreword to the History of the French Monarchy) in which he continued the effort at demystification begun in *L'Histoire comique de Francion* and *Le Berger extravagant*. In this case he was no longer aiming his criticism at novelists but at historians concerned with the origins of France. In *Avertissement sur l'Histoire de France* Sorel blames such historians for relying on legendary accounts rather than basing their research on viable sources. He particularly condemns the consistent practice of modeling the history of France on those of ancient Greece and Rome. Rather than imitate the style and methods of ancient historians, projecting their model onto a reality that has become quite different, Sorel argues, it would be better to examine what France has really been. In his view the history of France includes enough remarkable examples on its own to merit historians' interest. The tradition of mixing French history with stories from classical antiquity that have nothing to do with truth but convey something of a national legend must be cast aside. King Arthur and the Round Table, Charlemagne at Roncevaux, and the miraculous liquefaction of the holy oil at the king's crowning ceremony are deceptive stories, unworthy of being included in serious historical work.

Finally, Sorel asserts, it is necessary to adopt a clear style, avoid general philosophical reflection, and eschew rhetorical tricks.

Not surprisingly, *Avertissement sur l'Histoire de France* was immediately censured. Sorel revealed that the sources for the fantastical genealogies and celebrated stories that the monarchy relied on for its prestige were nothing but fables. In 1629 he published a second edition of the work, rewritten and amended to render it more orthodox. The same prudence guided the alterations to subsequent editions in 1633 and 1647.

Between 1634 and 1644 Sorel extended his enterprise of demystification to the terrain of knowledge. Several of his works were published during this period, all of which were dedicated to the project of constructing a universal science. The first lines of *La Science des choses corporelles* (The Science of Corporeal Things, 1634) define a complete program: the quest for knowledge must begin with a systematic reexamination of ancient physics, followed by a critical examination of metaphysical tradition and of all branches of knowledge inherited from the past. Sorel targets in particular the false scholars who blindly follow the Aristotelian tradition and abuse their authority in all aspects of knowledge, perpetuating errors and superstitions and encouraging men's ignorance and credulity. It is thus necessary to reexamine, in turn, medicine, alchemy, astrology, magic, the art of divining, arithmetic, geometry, music, optics, mathematics, grammar, rhetoric, history, poetry, morals, economics, and politics. In this quest, experience should always count for more than the abstract categories cherished by Aristotle's followers, such as matter, form, emptiness, time, place, infinity, cause, and consequence.

Thus, beginning in 1634, Sorel was engaged in the creation of a veritable critical encyclopedia of human knowledge. Such a project revealed an extraordinary confidence in the capacities of reason to distinguish truth from falsehood and lead men to wisdom and happiness. Sorel was seeking, after all, a total liberation of thought, following a plan that led from the corporeal to the spiritual. In 1637 a revised edition of *La Science des choses corporelles* was published, including *La Science des choses spirituelles* (The Science of Spiritual Things). In 1641 a third volume, *De l'Usage et de la perfection de toutes les choses du monde* (On the Use and Perfection of All Things in the World), was published, and the three works were collected that year as *La Science Universelle* (The Universal Science). From one publication to the next, Sorel reassessed, condensed, and reworked his material, creating a scientific summa of sorts. In 1644 a fourth volume, more particularly consecrated to the art of language and titled *La Perfection de l'âme* (The Perfection of the Soul), was added. Sorel had

Frontispiece for the 1628 enlarged edition of Sorel's Le Berger extravagant, *first published in 1627 (Bibliothèque Nationale, Paris)*

thus attained his goal, but he was again to feel the need to retouch his encyclopedia. In 1647 the third edition of *La Science Universelle,* in four volumes, appeared, harmonizing the collection of treatises published thus far. The last edition reviewed by Sorel was published in 1668.

In 1642 Sorel published *La Maison des jeux* (The House of Games), the story of a group of gentlemen and ladies gathered at a country house in autumn. To enjoy themselves they adopt fictitious identities, borrow Hellenistic names, and engage in spirited games. Throughout the course of these games, several themes are treated, such as the usefulness of the novel and the artificial nature of life, love, admiration, and surprise, as well as many other aspects of morality. One of the characters defends an opinion while another champions the opposing point of view in a well-ordered dialectic. The art of conversation takes on a resolutely playful dimen-

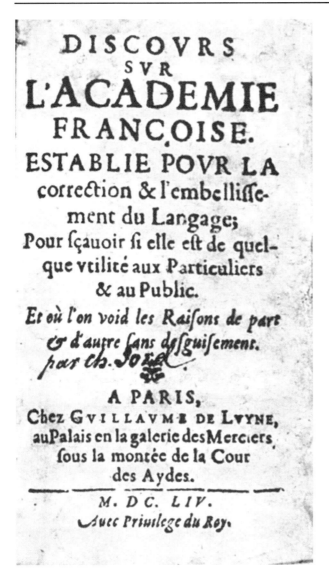

Title page for Sorel's critique of the Academie Française
(Archives de l'Académie Française)

sion in a game of identity willingly played by the members of the little circle.

Hermogène, the master of ceremonies, speaks in defense of these games that, according to him, preside over all aspects of life in society. The world is a scene in which all play a character, sometimes without even realizing it. To live means to acknowledge the playful aspect of existence, and to speak means to play with all the possibilities offered by language. The protagonists support their points of view by recounting stories that become the object of their commentaries, which themselves give rise to subsequent stories. Stories within stories multiply; voices crisscross in the game, which involves the collective composition of a book. In this game a participant begins a fictional story and then interrupts himself in the middle to allow someone else

to take over. Each character draws on his reading and improvises from memory. In this way all of the narrative recipes and types of composition–including the most extravagant–are instantly placed in the work and commented upon.

Thus, in *La Maison des jeux,* Sorel pursues his reflections on the novel by parodying the fashions that prevailed in the salons of the time. The artificial character of worldly society and the works it has produced is made plain, but the novel also demonstrates a legitimate style of life and a coherent aesthetic, notably as portrayed by Hermogène.

In 1664 Sorel, this time writing as a literary historian, published *La Bibliothèque françoise* (The French Library). In it he examines different literary genres and their rules and then analyzes French literary works that best represent these genres. He includes studies of the dramatic genre, lyric poetry, and epistolary works and also examines the problem of translating foreign works into French. Judicial, political, and religious eloquence are also discussed, as well as certain aspects of language. Sorel generally commends works that avoid artificiality. He praises Pierre Corneille for having given his dramatic characters a realistic tone. Sorel expresses his reservations, however, regarding the rules governing the composition of tragedy, which he finds confining and contrary to common sense. In addition, he defends actors whose performance is not overblown and whose elocution is as natural as possible.

In 1671 Sorel published *De la connaissance des bons livres* (On the Knowledge of Good Books). The treatise is a sort of complement to *La Bibliothèque françoise* and consists of a catalogue of what Sorel deems the most remarkable works composed by his favorite authors. Like *La Bibliothèque françoise, De la connaissance des bons livres* returns to the importance of *naturel* in writing. Sorel declares war on all artificiality, especially if it is legitimated by tradition. In these two bibliographical works he explains, summarizes, and uses examples borrowed from the works of those authors he had defended in *L'Histoire comique de Francion* and in *Le Berger extravagant.*

When he died on 7 March 1674, Charles Sorel left an exceptionally varied and abundant body of work. Throughout his life he remained convinced that *La Science Universelle* was his greatest work and the one that would ensure his posterity. Today, however, he is best remembered as the author of *L'Histoire comique de Francion* and *Le Berger extravagant,* two novels that unmask prejudice and demystify the world while paradoxically taking recourse in a fiction that voluntarily undermines the illusion it creates and cloaks its philosophical project under a playful guise for the reader's pleasure.

Bibliographies:

Wolfgang Leiner, "Fiches signalétiques des études traitant de l'*Histoire comique de Francion* de Charles Sorel," *Œuvres et critiques,* new series 1 (1976): 63–110;

Volker Schröder, "Fiches signalétiques des études traitant de l'*Histoire comique de Francion* de Charles Sorel," *Œuvres et critiques,* second series 14, no. 2 (1989): 7–63;

Patrick Dandrey, *Charles Sorel, Histoire comique de Francion: Anthologie critique, assortie d'un relevé de variantes (éditions de 1623, 1626 et 1633), et d'une bibliographie analytique* (Paris: Klincksieck, 2000).

Biography:

Emile Roy, *La Vie et les œuvres de Charles Sorel, sieur de Souvigny, 1602–1674* (Paris: Hachette, 1891; reprinted, Geneva: Slatkine, 1970).

References:

Jean Alter, "La Bande à Francion ou les pièges de l'histoire," *Esprit Créateur,* 19 (1980): 3–13;

Alter, "C'est moi qui parlons: Le Jeu des narrateurs dans *Francion,*" *French Forum,* 5 (1980): 99–105;

Roméo Arbour, "Langage et société dans les *Nouvelles françaises* de Charles Sorel," *Revue de l'Université d'Ottawa,* 41 (1971): 169–191;

Hervé D. Béchade, *Les Romans comiques de Charles Sorel* (Geneva: Droz, 1981);

Daniel Chouinard, "*L'Anti-roman* de Charles Sorel: Poétique d'une lecture, lecture d'une poétique," dissertation, University of Montreal, 1983;

Chouinard, "Sorel (anti)romancier et le brouillage du discours," *Etudes Françaises,* new series 14 (1978): 65–91;

Martine Debaisieux, "*Francion,* ou la libre pensée travestie," *Neophilologus,* 72 (1988): 191–199;

Debaisieux, "L'Histoire comique, genre travesti," *Poétique,* 74 (April 1988): 169–181;

Debaisieux, *Le Procès du roman: Ecriture et contrefaçon chez Charles Sorel,* Stanford French and Italian Studies, no. 63 (Saratoga, Cal.: Anma Libri, 1989);

Joan DeJean, *Libertine Strategies: Freedom and the Novel in Seventeenth-Century France* (Columbus: Ohio State University Press, 1981);

Wim De Vos, *Le Singe au miroir: Emprunt textuel et écriture savante dans les romans comiques de Charles Sorel* (Leuven, Belgium: Universitaire Pers / Tübingen, Germany: G. Narr, 1994);

Anna Lia Franchetti, *Il Berger extravagant di Charles Sorel* (Florence: L. S. Olschki, 1977);

Félix R. Freudmann, "La recherche passionnée du *Francion,*" *Symposium,* second series 21 (1976): 101–117;

Fausta Garavini, "L'Itinéraire de Sorel: Du *Francion* à la *Science universelle,*" *Revue d'histoire littéraire de la France,* 77 (1977): 432–439;

Garavini, *La Maison des jeux: Science du roman et roman de la science au XVIIe siècle* (Paris: H. Champion, 1998);

Richard Hodgson, "L'Activité ludique dans l'œuvre de Charles Sorel," *Papers on French Seventeenth Century Literature,* second series 15 (1981): 351–358;

Hodgson, "Poétique et pratique du roman dans l'œuvre de Charles Sorel," dissertation, University of Toronto, 1977;

Robin Howells, *Carnival to Classicism: The Comic Novels of Charles Sorel,* Biblio 17, no. 48 (Paris & Seattle: Papers on French Seventeenth Century Literature, 1989);

Hubert Judd, "Les Nouvelles françaises de Sorel et de Segrais," *Cahiers de l'Association internationale des études françaises,* 18 (1966): 31–40;

Jean Lafond, "Le Songe de Francion revisité," *Saggi e ricerche di letteratura francese,* 29 (1990): 45–76;

Wolfgang Leiner, "Le Rêve de Francion: Considérations sur la cohésion intérieure de *L'Histoire comique de Francion,*" in *La Cohérence intérieure: Etudes sur la littérature française du XVIIe siècle présentées en hommage à Judd D. Hubert,* edited by Jacqueline van Baelen and David L. Rubin (Paris: J. M. Place, 1977), pp. 157–175;

Jean-Pierre Leroy, "La *Bibliothèque française* de Charles Sorel," *Revue Française de l'histoire du livre,* 24 (1979): 709–734;

Leroy, "Réflexions critiques de Sorel sur son œuvre romanesque," *XVIIe Siècle,* 105 (1974): 29–47;

Beverly S. Ridgely, "The Cosmic Voyage in Charles Sorel's *Francion,*" *Modern Philology,* new series 65 (1967): 1–8;

Maria Alzira Seixo, *Le Parcours du plaisir: Francion de Charles Sorel* (Paris: Centre Culturel Portugais, 1985);

Jean Serroy, *Roman et réalité: Les Histoires comiques au XVIIe siècle* (Paris: Minard, 1981), pp. 93–205, 294–319;

Serroy, "D'un roman à métamorphoses: La Composition du *Francion* de Charles Sorel," *Baroque,* 6 (1973): 97–103;

Andrew G. Suozzo Jr., *The Comic Novels of Charles Sorel: A Study of Structure, Characterization, and Disguise* (Lexington, Ky.: French Forum, 1982);

Gabrielle Verdier, *Charles Sorel* (Boston: Twayne, 1984).

Papers:

The most important collections of Charles Sorel's papers are at the Bibliothèque Nationale, and the Bibliothèque de l'Arsenal, both in Paris.

Honoré d'Urfé

(10 February 1567 – 1 June 1625)

Jean-Pierre van Elslande
University of Neuchâtel, Switzerland

BOOKS: *Les Epistres morales* (Lyon: J. Roussin, 1598; revised and enlarged edition, Paris: J. Micard, 1603; revised and enlarged edition, Paris: J. Micard, 1608);

Le Sireine (Paris: J. Micard, 1606; revised and enlarged, 1618)–first edition is lost; 1618 edition includes "Paraphrases sur les Cantiques de Salomon";

L'Astrée, 4 volumes (Paris: T. du Bray, 1607–1627); translated by John Davies as *Astrea,* 3 volumes (London: Printed by W.W. for Humphrey Moseley, Thomas Dring, and Henry Herringman, 1657–1658);

La Sylvanire, ou La Morte-vive, fable bocagère (Paris: R. Fouet, 1627).

Editions: *L'Astrée,* 5 volumes, edited by Hugues Vaganay (Lyon: P. Masson, 1925–1928);

L'Astrée, abridged by Gérard Genette (Paris: Union Générale d'Editions, 1964);

Les Epistres morales et amoureuses (Geneva: Slatkine, 1973);

L'Astrée, abridged by Jean Lafond (Paris: Gallimard, 1984);

La Sylvanire, edited by Laurence Giavarini (Toulouse: Société de Littératures Classiques / Paris: H. Champion, 2001).

OTHER: *La Savoysiade* [excerpt], in *Les Délices de la poésie françoise, ou Recueil des plus beaux vers de ce temps,* edited by François de Rosset (Paris: T. du Bray, 1618).

Honoré d'Urfé (engraving after a portrait by Sir Anthony Van Dyck; from Odon Claude Reure, La Vie et les oeuvres de Honoré d'Urfé, *1910; Thomas Cooper Library, University of South Carolina)*

Honoré d'Urfé wrote only one novel, but he is still considered one of the most important novelists of the seventeenth century. He is the author of *L'Astrée* (1607–1627; translated as *Astrea,* 1657–1658), a vast novel of several thousand pages, which had considerable influence throughout the century and beyond. Later admirers included Jean-Jacques Rousseau, who knew the novel quite well. The work, composed over a period of approximately twenty years, lastingly marked sensibilities, established fashion, and captured the imagination of countless readers. The novel touches on many subjects, including love, friendship, ambition, war, tyranny, and the origin of the French people. A vast learnedness permeates the entire story, which is replete with diverse philosophical theories and multiple historical references. *L'Astrée* also made its mark on language and style, and d'Urfé displays great virtuosity in holding the reader's attention throughout the considerable length of the novel.

Honoré d'Urfé was born in Marseille on 10 February 1567 and spent his childhood at Bastie-d'Urfé, the family's château in Forez, near Lyon. He came from an old aristocratic French family, whose members included officers in the king's service, diplomats, and high-ranking members of the military. His grandfather, Claude d'Urfé, held the office of *gouverneur* (governor) of the dauphin and tutor of Henri II's children, after having been François I's ambassador to the Holy See in Rome. Greatly influenced by Italian Renaissance culture, Claude d'Urfé had the Bastie remodeled according to Italian tastes, and in it he assembled many rare works. The beauty of the château and the richness of its library, which included historical and moral works, exerted a lasting influence on his grandson Honoré. As an adolescent, Honoré enrolled in the Jesuit school at Tournon, where he undertook a thorough study of the classics, thus completing his already considerable cultural education.

At this time, however, members of the aristocracy were also expected to learn the art of soldiering. Honoré d'Urfé was given the opportunity to serve when civil unrest was unfolding across France and in the Forez region. He was twenty-two when he took up arms and joined those who refused to see the Protestant Henri of Bourbon become king of France, in spite of his rightful claim, according to the rules of dynastic succession, to succeed the Catholic Henri III. This episode was one of the bloodiest of the religious wars that engulfed France beginning in 1560. D'Urfé fought at Saint-Etienne, where he commanded a company in charge of defending the city against Protestant troops and Catholic legitimists who supported Henri IV's claim to the throne. Finally thrown in prison in 1595, d'Urfé there composed the first book of his *Les Epistres morales* (Moral Epistles, 1598).

This work is presented as a collection of letters to a friend named Agathon and follows the classical model established by the Roman author Lucius Annaeus Seneca in his writings to Lucilius. The tone is one of painful reflection on death, war, and suffering. During the civil wars D'Urfé had lost dear friends and family, notably one of his brothers, and he had seen the collapse of his party. He had known treason and sickness. Thus, his meditating on the cruelty of Fortune and the necessity of hardening the soul to adversity is hardly surprising. His praise of friendship and courage under trial is inspired by Stoicism.

Once released from prison d'Urfé retired to a little château on his lands at Senoy. There, between 1596 and 1599, he added a second book to *Les Epistres morales* and began writing the heroic poem *La Savoysiade,* the epic story of the House of Savoie (partially published in the anthology *Les Délices de la poésie françoise, ou Recueil des plus beaux vers de ce temps* in 1618). He also composed religious poems and the

pastoral poem *Le Sireine* (Sirein, second edition published 1606 [first edition lost]). The second book of *Les Epistres morales,* published in 1603, includes reflections on human passions, moral greatness, and the serenity of wisdom, as well as ruminations on perfect love and religion. *La Savoysiade* is an epic celebrating the military feats of Bérold, the legendary founder of Savoie, and related exploits of great Savoyard families. Though the text was completed before d'Urfé's death, it was never published in its entirety during his lifetime. The religious poems are paraphrases of the Song of Songs and the Psalms and bear witness to the solid religious education d'Urfé received at Tournon. The poem *Le Sireine* tells the love story of the shepherd Sireine and the shepherdess Diane in three parts—the Departure, the Absence, and the Return. Sireine must leave Diane to go and guard the faraway flocks of his master. Diane sends notice to him to return, because during his absence her hand has been promised to Délio, a rich shepherd. Sireine returns too late: Diane is married to Délio and can no longer see him. One may perhaps read *Le Sireine* as a poetic transposition of a sad episode from d'Urfé's youth. As the story goes, the young d'Urfé was madly in love with his future sister-in-law, Diane de Chateaumorand, who was promised to his older brother, Anne d'Urfé. Hoping to cure young d'Urfé of his troublesome passion, the family sent him away, but in vain. Whatever the case, the story told in *Le Sireine* seems to be equally inspired by a Spanish novel, *Diana* (1559?), written by Jorge de Montemayor, a text that d'Urfé, fluent in Spanish, knew quite well. Above all, the pastoral framework of *Le Sireine,* like the love story it develops, is a prelude to *L'Astrée.*

The conception of *L'Astrée* dates from 1587 to 1590, but the first part of the novel was not published until 1607. This first part consisted of twelve books and was followed in 1610 by a second part, also divided into twelve books. In 1619 a third part followed, again in twelve books. The lengthy intervals between the publication of each section are explained by d'Urfé's "part-time" status as a writer. Even to call him a writer may be going too far, since at the time, writing was not a professional activity per se, especially not for a gentleman. D'Urfé himself considered writing a pastime, something he could do when his obligations as a gentleman left him enough moments of leisure. Between writing the successive books of *L'Astrée,* he participated in diplomatic missions, negotiated alliances, raised troops, and was busy with politics and travel. D'Urfé's focus on other aspects of his life explains why *L'Astrée* remained incomplete at his death in 1625, with only the first four books of the fourth part having been written. His secretary, Balth-

The d'Urfé family home, Château de la Bastie, in Forez, near Lyon

azar Baro, was the person who undertook to publish, in 1627, the eight missing books of the fourth part of the novel, as well as the twelve books of the fifth part, based on notes and rough drafts left by d'Urfé.

D'Urfé's interest in philosophy, history, ethics, and theology is clearly present in *L'Astrée*. The five thousand pages of the novel constitute a veritable tome of knowledge. These subjects also play a decisive role in the definition of a code of behavior called *politesse* (refined manners), which aristocratic society eventually claimed more and more as its own, notably during the reign of Louis XIII. D'Urfé's interest in philosophy also impacted his writing style: his prose is supple, flowing, and copious. Notably, the vocabulary he uses to describe the passion of love is extremely rich and precise in its nuanced portrayal of sentiment. His descriptions of the countryside and of paintings are powerfully evocative.

The novel takes place in Forez, home of a pastoral society whose members are descendants of gentlemen and ladies who had decided to dress as shepherds in order to live far from the troubled world of the court and cities. The shepherds and shepherdesses of *L'Astrée* are not in the least country bumpkins, and their clothing reflects a choice of lifestyle based on the rejection of ambition and the sharing of common values. They are on the best of terms with the nymph Amasis and her daughter Galathée, who rule over the region, and their aristocratic education enables them to welcome with the proper decorum the chevaliers (knights), gentlemen, and ladies who pass through their land.

D'Urfé's choice of Forez as the backdrop for the novel is significant. Since the time of Virgil the pastoral genre traditionally had been set in Sicily or Greece, and in choosing a French locale, d'Urfé was therefore innovative. As he explains at the beginning of the novel, he wished to pay homage to his native province. But the gesture also had political and cultural implications. While conforming to a literary tradition, d'Urfé also moved away from it, and by setting his pastoral on national soil, he placed *L'Astrée* in the tradition of the French medieval romans (romances) such as *Lancelot* and the Renaissance French translations and continuations of the Spanish prose romance of chivalry *Amadis* (earliest extant version published 1508).

The era of the action of *L'Astrée* confirms its political dimensions. The characters of *L'Astrée* live during the fifth century A.D., a setting that permits d'Urfé to evoke at length the historical and mythical origins of Gaul, shared among the Romans, Franks, Burgundians, and Visigoths. In the novel the Forez of the shepherds miraculously escapes wars fought by other groups of people. Forez in effect is a peaceful enclave within a violent world. In spite of the Romans' domination and their influence in the region, the ancient Druidic religion continues to be celebrated in its purity, under the leadership of the great Druid Adamas. Elements of Roman religion are eventually added, but without troubling the general peace of the region. This enclave is not, however, closed in upon itself. People from far and wide come to Forez to share the peaceful existence of the shepherds who live in hamlets along the shore of the Lignon River. Once there these travelers from far away recount their adventures–the perils endured and the dangers of the voyage; they denounce the ravages of the wars raging elsewhere, the depraved morals of the courts of the Orient and the Occident, and the ferocity of barbarous kings, so that Forez becomes a great echo chamber where the noise of the outside world comes to resonate.

The novel also includes many stories inserted into the primary narrative. They are told by those who come to Forez and sometimes decide to live in the company of the shepherds and there recount their tumultuous adventures. These stories always find eager listeners who beg the storyteller not to omit any detail, and they become the object of renewed discussion that can last an entire day. The art of conversation thus permits rich and equal exchanges among characters of diverse backgrounds. The pastoral society as d'Urfé portrays it is a model of refined civility and thus both responds to and encourages practices developing in aristocratic Parisian salons at the beginning of the seventeenth century, especially those of the famous Hôtel de Rambouillet. To these salons, *L'Astrée,* which located values of sociability in the historical and mythical origins of the French kingdom, indirectly offered both a model and a validation.

But above all, in making fifth-century Forez the ancestor of modern France and by depicting it as a veritable crucible in which diverse traditions mix, thanks to the civilizing virtue of conversation, d'Urfé assigns to early-seventeenth-century France an important political and cultural role. The task of modern France is to bring about the just synthesis of diverse cultural elements. To undertake such a synthesis, modern France takes recourse in a prestigious tool–the French language.

The great variety of sources, both ancient and modern, d'Urfé drew upon to write *L'Astrée* is also part of this synthesizing effort. Virgil's *Eclogues* (42–37 B.C.) provides the pastoral frame and the shepherd characters. Works by Greek writers–Heliodorus's *Aethiopica* (third century B.C.), Longus's *Daphnis and Chloe* (third century A.D.), and Achilles Tatius's prose romance *Clitophon and Leucippe* (second century A.D.)–were the models for many characteristic episodes and narrative techniques. The disguises and the scenes of recognition, the narratives inserted within the primary narrative, and the virtuoso descriptions of works of art owe much to this tradition. As for the contemporary sources of *L'Astrée,* they also reveal a deliberate synthesis. D'Urfé's excellent knowledge of Italian and Spanish enabled him to read the works of authors whose style and ideas he then perfectly assimilated. Montemayor's *Diana,* Miguel de Cervantes's *Galatea* (1585), and Spanish pastoral novels thus inspired many developments in *L'Astrée,* including themes of jealousy and rivalry and philosophical discussions about the true nature of love. Among Italian works Jacopo Sannazzaro's *Arcadia* (1504), the first pastoral romance, Torquato Tasso's *Aminta* (first performed 1573; published 1581), the first pastoral drama, and Battista Guarini's *Il Pastor Fido* (The Faithful Shepherd, published 1590; first performed 1595), another pastoral drama, offered a nuanced analysis of love that was further refined by d'Urfé. Added to this diverse collection of foreign sources was the French literary tradition exemplified by Marguerite de Navarre's *L'Heptaméron* (Seven Days, written in the 1540s; published in its entirety 1559), tales told on a journey; the French versions of *Amadis;* and the novels of the Middle Ages. This extensive list of influences demonstrates how a modern critic such as Gérard Genette can write that *L'Astrée* constitutes "l'étroit goulet par où tout l'ancien se déverse dans le moderne" (the narrow neck through which everything ancient flows into the modern).

L'Astrée, however, in spite of its diverse sources and the proliferation of framed narratives, is a highly structured novel that never allows the reader's attention to wander. The principal intrigue concerns the shepherd Céladon and the shepherdess Astrée. Although in love, they are prevented by their families' rivalry from openly declaring their feelings. Astrée thus asks Céladon to pretend to love another in order to turn suspicion away from themselves. But Astrée allows herself to be taken in by a jealous shepherd who leads her to think that in feigning love for another, Céladon has in fact fallen in love. Furious, Astrée unjustly sends Céladon away and orders him never again to appear before her unless she commands him to. Mortified, the shepherd complies, tries in vain to kill himself, and seeks refuge in a cave deep in the forest. Astrée, on the other hand, once she discovers she has been misled, is plunged into deep regret, worsened by her belief that she is responsible for Céladon's death. The novel opens on this episode, leaving the reader to wonder whether Astrée and Céladon will ever be reunited, and if so, how. The unfolding of the ensuing story is in large part orga-

Page from the manuscript for d'Urfé's epic poem La Savoysiade, *which he began around 1596–1599*
(Bibliothèque Nationale, Paris)

Diane de Chateaumorand, whose marriage to d'Urfé's older brother is said to have inspired the story of lost love in d'Urfé's pastoral poem Le Sireine *(from Odon Claude Reure,* La Vie et les Œuvres de Honoré d'Urfé, *1910; Thomas Cooper Library, University of South Carolina)*

nized in such a way as to let the reader know that these questions will be answered in due time.

In addition, the many characters the reader encounters throughout the book are linked, in one way or another, to this initial narrative, either by taking part in Astrée and Céladon's pain, in debating what love is, or in recounting their own stories, which contribute to the coherence of the novel in their likeness to or contrast with the hero's own drama. The couple of Céladon and Astrée is thus repeated in the couples Silvandre and Diane, Hylas and Stelle, and Tircis and Laonice. Silvandre's idealized vision of love is opposed to Hylas's sensual love; Céladon adopts a position of compromise: he religiously adores Astrée to the point of worshiping her image, without renouncing sensuality. Stelle boasts of inconstancy, while Diane insists on uncompromising fidelity between lovers. Tircis's idea of love is close to Silvandre's idealized version. Tircis is equally close to Diane, because both are in similar situations: Tircis is insensible to the charms of Laonice because he is still

mourning the death of Cléon, whom he had loved, and Diane does not respond to Silvandre's advances because she, too, is mourning the death of a lover. The parallelism that engages the reader to connect the characters is reinforced by the similarity in the characters' circumstances: just as Tircis ends by giving up his attachment to Cléon and yielding to the charms of Laonice, Diane finally returns Silvandre's love after having put the past behind her. A dense network of relations is thus interwoven throughout the story, and the characters' evolution depends on this elaborate plan.

Nonetheless, these games of symmetry and contrast are not such that they obscure the particularities of each shepherd's story. Tircis and Silvandre share the same idea of love, but they are not faced with the same set of circumstances. Likewise, if Astrée and Diane are alike on certain points, their temperaments are not. Consequently, dialogue among the many protagonists remains possible, and the general reflection on love that runs throughout the text is heavily nuanced. Between the extreme positions of Silvandre and Hylas runs a gamut of feelings described at length page after page. Astrée and Céladon occupy a median position, which makes them the principal couple of the novel. Each character thus incarnates a certain idea of love that is illustrated throughout the main story by his or her actions and gestures. In turn, the retrospective secondary stories give the shepherd audience something upon which to reflect. When a character recounts his or her life to the other characters, the audience offers a wealth of commentary in order to extract a moral lesson from the story. In *L'Astrée* fiction often adopts a philosophical guise.

In fact, Silvandre's definition of love is clearly inspired by Neoplatonism. Physical beauty is a reflection of divine beauty, which itself is identified with goodness. The lover must thus adore the beloved on a spiritual plane in order that his passion may raise his soul toward the supreme good. Themes laid out in Italian Renaissance works composed by Marsilus Ficinus, Pico de la Mirandola, and Leo Hebreus are taken up by the figure of the shepherd, who sets forth in fiction a doctrine familiar to readers of the time. Thus, certain traits that today may appear conventional help make characters more coherent and believable. For example, if Astrée and Diane are described as having perfect beauty, if Céladon and Silvandre celebrate their lovers' charms in many ways, the reason is that the love each inspires in the other is divine.

Nevertheless, to extract from *L'Astrée* a simple philosophy of love is impossible. The shepherd Hylas contradicts Silvandre—in his eyes, beauty and ugliness are but a relative opinion that varies according to country and culture. Thus, the perception of the lover is what determines the beauty of the beloved and not some superior quality reflected by the body. What is required is to live in the moment and to enjoy the pleasures of life without regret. Inconstancy in love is legitimate, since the body reflects nothing of a superior and eternal reality but rather is a vehicle of pleasure necessarily ephemeral. Hylas is the mouthpiece for a libertine point of view that follows the currents of skepticism and Epicureanism at the same time and announces, in certain regards, Don Juan's position. Hylas openly debates these ideas at length with Silvandre during the discussions of the shepherds and the shepherdesses.

But *L'Astrée* is above all a novel, not a philosophical treatise. Consequently, the diverse theories expounded in it are often complicated by the characters' situations. For example, Céladon cross-dresses in order to approach Astrée without violating her command. He lives at the side of his shepherdess, even shares her bed, and goes so far as to exchange clothes with her. Both play parts in a love story: Céladon dressed as a girl plays the "mistress," and Astrée plays the "male servant." What can the reader make of this episode? Some critics interpret it in an idealist sense that corresponds to Silvandre's theories. Maxime Gaume thus sees Céladon's disguise as an allusion to the Platonic myth of the Androgynes: the lover in this instance is "en quête de sa moitié" (in search of his half) and seeks to reconstitute "l'union qui est le vrai amour" (the union that is true love). In permitting him to be at once man and woman, his disguise symbolically realizes the fusion of masculine and feminine principles, to which he aspires in courting Astrée. For his part Marc Fumaroli thinks that Céladon in disguising himself as a girl learns to renounce what is too harshly virile in himself. From this perspective his proximity to Astrée becomes a sort of test. If he succeeds in playing his feminine role, he will prove his capacity to master his instincts and to rise above them. Astrée will thus be able to overcome "ce qu'il y avait de menaçant pour elle dans la virilité de Céladon" (that which she finds menacing in Céladon's virility) and convince herself that "il y avait en elle assez de volonté virile, en lui de douceur féminine, pour qu'ils puissent former le couple androgynique parfait" (there is enough virile will in herself, and in him enough feminine sweetness, for both to form a perfect androgynous couple).

But certain critics also insist on the erotic dimension of the situation. According to them, the cross-dressing, the exchange of clothes, the sharing of the same bed, all have an erotic aspect. The reader is indeed troubled

Title page for a later edition of the first part (1607) of d'Urfé's influential pastoral novel (from the 1966 facsimile edition)

that Astrée does not recognize Céladon under his clothing and that she takes pleasure in letting herself be undressed by a girl who reminds her of her lover. As for Céladon, if he succeeds so well in playing his role, it is because he explores with full abandon the most troubling aspects of sexuality. For Jacques Ehrmann, the episode opens a parenthesis in the novel in which "toute anomalie est normale, où toute anormalité est naturelle, où valeurs et contre-valeurs amoureuses et sexuelles se correspondent pour s'annuler, s'annulent pour se réaffirmer" (all anomaly is normal, where all abnormality is natural, where values and countervalues of love and sexuality correspond in order to annul each other, and annul each other in order to reaffirm each other).

Likewise, according to Louise Horowitz, "In *L'Astrée,* characters simultaneously love heterosexually and homosexually (within the same episode), reflecting the freest moves of the imagination: the author's, the characters', our own." Genette aptly summarizes the ambiguity of the work in revealing in *L'Astrée* "une contradiction très sensible entre un idéal spirituel cent fois proclamé qui vise à la sublimation totale de l'instinct amoureux, et une conduite réelle, au moins chez le couple principal, qui semble traiter cet idéal comme un obstacle aux satisfactions immédiates du désir, comme un prétexte aux travestissements les plus subtils et aux variations les plus complaisantes de ce désir, et donc comme un instrument non de perfection spirituelle, mais de raffinement érotique" (a marked contradiction between a spiritual ideal constantly reaffirmed that aims at the total sublimation of amorous instinct and a real-life behavior, at least by the principal couple, that seems to treat this ideal as an obstacle to the immediate satisfaction of desire, as a pretext to the most subtle disguises and the most obliging variations of this desire, and thus as an instrument not of spiritual perfection, but of erotic refinement).

When he died on 1 June 1625 at the battle of the Valteline, Honoré d'Urfé left an unfinished work, but one that had considerable influence. *L'Astrée* established a long-held ideal norm concerning "politesse mondaine" (fashionable politeness) and gallant conversation. The novel also had a lasting impact on literary production. Several dozen pastoral dramas were staged in theaters during the years that followed the publication of the five parts of *L'Astrée*. Before his death d'Urfé himself composed a stage adaptation of the story of Silvandre, an episode from the fourth book of *L'Astrée*. The play was published in 1627, and the playwright Jean Mairet, taking up the subject, staged his own play, *La Sylvanire,* in 1631.

L'Astrée exerted considerable influence on later novels. Although the long narratives of Marin LeRoy de Gomberville, Gautier de Costes de La Calprenède, and Madeleine de Scudéry abandon the pastoral aspect, they adopt the narrative technique of *L'Astrée*—retrospective stories inserted into the primary narrative, the nuanced analysis of the sentiments of love, and the idealization of the protagonists. Until 1660 *L'Astrée* remained an indispensable resource, to the point that romance novels were commonly called "Astrées." After this date the influence of *L'Astrée* on the composition of the novel lessened. The novel had its detractors, notably among "realist" novelists who, like Charles Sorel, denounced its conventional character and lack of believability. But many authors, among them Marie de Rabutin-Chantal, marquise de Sévigné, and Jean de La Fontaine, still confessed their admiration for the work, which has now taken its rightful place in the French canon.

Bibliography:

Claude Longeon, *Les Ecrivains foréziens du XVIe siècle: Répertoire bio-bibliographique* (Saint-Etienne: Centre d'Etudes Foréziennes, 1970).

Biography:

Odon Claude Reure, *La Vie et les œuvres de Honoré d'Urfé* (Paris: Plon-Nourrit, 1910).

References:

Elisabeth Aragon, "Conformité et déviance dans *L'Astrée* d'Honoré d'Urfé," *Cahiers de Littérature du XVIIe Siècle,* 1 (1979): 21–39;

Madeleine Bertaud, *"L'Astrée" et "Polexandre": Du roman pastoral au roman héroïque* (Geneva: Droz, 1986);

Daniel Chouinard, "*L'Astrée* et la rhétorique: L'Adaptation romanesque du genre judiciaire," *Papers on French Seventeenth-Century Literature,* second series 10 (1978): 41–56;

Jacques Ehrmann, *Un Paradis désespéré: L'Amour et l'illusion dans "L'Astrée"* (New Haven: Yale University Press, 1963);

Marc Fumaroli, "Le Retour d'Astrée," in *Précis de littérature française du XVIIe siècle,* edited by Jean Mesnard (Paris: Presses Universitaires de France, 1990), pp. 47–64;

Maxime Gaume, *Les Inspirations et les sources de l'œuvre d'Honoré d'Urfé* (Saint-Etienne: Centre d'Etudes Foréziennes, 1977);

Gérard Genette, "Le Serpent dans la bergerie," in his *Figures, I* (Paris: Seuil, 1966), pp. 109–122;

Mitchell Greenberg, "*L'Astrée* and Androgyny," *Cahiers du dix-septième,* 1 (Spring 1987): 169–178;

Greenberg, "*L'Astrée,* Classicism, and the Illusion of Modernity," *Continuum,* 2 (1990): 3–25;

Laurence A. Gregorio, "Implications of the Love Debate in *L'Astrée*," *French Review: Journal of the American Association of Teachers of French,* new series 56 (October 1992): 31–39;

Gregorio, *The Pastoral Masquerade: Disguise and Identity in "L'Astrée,"* Stanford French and Italian Studies, no. 73 (Saratoga, Calif.: Anma Libri, 1992);

Jacques Grieder, "Le Rôle de la religion dans la société de *L'Astrée*," *XVIIe Siècle,* 93 (1972): 3–12;

James Hembree, *Subjectivity and the Signs of Love: Discourse, Desire, and the Emergence of Modernity in Honoré d'Urfé's "L'Astrée"* (New York: Peter Lang, 1997);

Eglal Henein, *La Fontaine de la Vérité d'amour, ou Les promesses de bonheur dans "L'Astrée" d'Honoré d'Urfé* (Paris: Klincksieck, 1999);

Henein, "Fortune des chevaliers, fortune des bergers," *Cahiers du dix-septième,* 6 (Fall 1992): 1–12;

Henein, *Protée romancier: Les Déguisements dans "L'Astrée" d'Honoré d'Urfé* (Fasano, Italy: Schena / Paris: Nizet, 1996);

Louise Horowitz, *Honoré d'Urfé*, Twayne's World Authors Series, no. 698 (Boston: Twayne, 1984);

Horowitz, "1619–Pastoral Fiction," in *A New History of French Literature*, edited by Denis Hollier (Cambridge, Mass.: Harvard University Press, 1989), pp. 258–262;

Daniel Jourlait, "La Mythologie dans *L'Astrée*," *Esprit Créateur*, second series 16 (Summer 1976): 125–137;

Servais Kevorkian, *Thématique de "L'Astrée" d'Honoré d'Urfé* (Paris: H. Champion, 1991);

Maurice Laugaa, "Structures ou personnages dans *L'Astrée*," *Etudes françaises*, 2 (1966): 3–27;

Anne Sancier-Château, *Une Esthétique nouvelle: Honoré d'Urfé, correcteur de "L'Astrée"* (Geneva: Droz, 1995);

Jean-Pierre van Elslande, *L'Imaginaire pastoral du XVIIe siècle: 1600–1650* (Paris: Presses Universitaires de France, 1999);

Christian Wentzlaff-Eggebert, "Structures narratives de la pastorale dans *L'Astrée*," *Cahiers de l'Association Internationale des Etudes Françaises*, 39 (May 1987): 63–78;

Kathleen Wine, "*L'Astrée*'s Landscapes and the Poetics of Baroque Fiction," *Symposium*, second series 40 (Summer 1986): 141–153;

Wine, *Forgotten Virgo: Humanism and Absolutism in Honoré d'Urfé's "L'Astrée*," Travaux du Grand Siècle, no. 15 (Geneva: Droz, 2000);

Frances A. Yates, *Astrea: The Imperial Theme in the Sixteenth Century* (London: Routledge & Kegan Paul, 1975);

Bernard Yon, "Composition dans L'Astrée, composition de *L'Astrée*," *Papers on French Seventeenth-Century Literature*, second series 10 (1978): 9–27;

Yon, "Sens et valeur de la symbolique pastorale dans *L'Astrée*," in *Le Genre pastoral en Europe du XVe au XVIIe siècle*, edited by Claude Longeon (Saint-Etienne: Publications de l'Université de Saint-Etienne, 1980), pp. 199–205;

Alexandre Zotos, "L'Univers pastoral dans *L'Astrée*," *Travaux de Littérature*, 7 (1994): 91–101.

Papers:

Honoré d'Urfé's manuscripts can be found at the Bibliothèque Nationale as well as in the Bibliothèque de l'Arsenal, both in Paris. The State Archives of Torino, Italy, hold a manuscript of *La Savoysiade*. Lesser manuscripts and autograph letters are to be found at the Archives de Chateaumorand, in Saint-Martin d'Estreaux, France.

Claude Favre de Vaugelas

(5? January 1585 – February 1650)

Wendy Ayres-Bennett
New Hall, Cambridge University

BOOKS: *Remarques sur la langue françoise, utiles à ceux qui veulent bien parler et bien escrire* (Paris: Veuve de J. Camusat et P. Le Petit, 1647);

Nouvelles Remarques de M. de Vaugelas sur la langue françoise; Ouvrage posthume, avec des observations de M***** [Louis-Augustin Alemand], Avocat au Parlement (Paris: G. Desprez, 1690).

Edition: *Remarques sur la langue françoise: Fac-similé de l'édition originale,* edited, with an introduction, by Jeanne Streicher (Paris: Droz, 1934; reprinted, Geneva: Slatkine, 1970).

TRANSLATIONS: Cristóbal de Fonseca, *Les Sermons de Fonseque sur tous les Evangiles du Caresme, avec une Paraphrase perpetuelle sur toutes les parties des Evangiles, traduits d'Espagnol en François par C.F.D.V. Œuvre remplie de Conceptions nouvelles, doctes, curieuses et devotes, non seulement à l'usage des Predicateurs, et des doctes, mais de toutes personnes pieuses* (Paris: R. Thierry et E. Foucault, 1615);

Quintus Curtius Rufus, *Quinte Curce, De la vie et des actions d'Alexandre le Grand, de la traduction de Monsieur de Vaugelas, avec les supplémens de Jean Freinshemius sur Quinte Curce, traduits par Pierre Du Ryer,* edited by Valentin Conrart and Jean Chapelain (Paris: A. Courbé, 1653; completely revised and edited by Olivier Patru, 1659).

Claude Favre de Vaugelas (Musée National du Château Versailles)

Claude Favre de Vaugelas, grammarian, translator and member of the French Academy, is best known for his *Remarques sur la langue françoise, utiles à ceux qui veulent bien parler et bien escrire* (Observations on the French Language, Useful for Those Who Wish to Speak and Write Well, 1647), a collection of more than five hundred observations promoting good usage of the French language. Viewed as a kind of "applied grammar," Vaugelas's translation of Quintus Curtius Rufus's *Life of Alexander* was deemed a model of good prose style for a hundred years after he first started working on it.

Vaugelas was born in Meximieux, probably on 5 January 1585, the second of eleven children. He came from a well-established family of magistrates and officers to the counts and dukes of Savoy, who had lived in Bourg, according to Samuel Guichenon's *Histoire de Bresse et de Bugey* (1650), at least since the end of the fourteenth century. Vaugelas's father, Antoine Favre, was a celebrated jurisconsult, author not only of many legal works but also of a tragedy and religious and moral verse.

Vaugelas's early education was probably conducted by the Jesuits in Chambéry and possibly at the Collège Chappuisien at Annecy, but his later education, particularly regarding matters of the law, was supervised by his father. In 1599 Favre took his two eldest sons with him to Italy, where Vaugelas spent two years, gaining a thorough knowledge of the Italian language and culture and even composing verse in Italian. The party left Rome in July 1601 and returned briefly to Savoy before embarking in December 1601 on a journey to Paris, where Vaugelas completed his education before returning home once again in the summer of the following year.

Relatively little is known of the next five years of his life, spent in his native Savoy, although a letter of condolence written in July 1606 by Vaugelas to his aunt, described by François Mugnier in *Histoire et correspondance du premier président Favre* (1902–1905) as "un modèle de courtoisie et de délicatesse" (a model of politeness and delicacy) already displays a concern for finding the mot juste. (See also Jeanne Streicher's introduction to the 1970 facsimile edition of *Remarques sur la langue françoise*.) Probably during this period Vaugelas became increasingly aware of the peculiarities of the French language: he learned Spanish and perhaps heard other European languages in his father's house, where foreign students lodged. Also important in this period was the founding of the Académie Florimontane by Favre and François de Sales in the winter of 1606–1607. It was modeled on the Italian academies and may in some ways be viewed as a forerunner of the Académie Française (French Academy), having forty members and the duc de Nemours as its protector. While it boasted an ambitious program of study—including theology, philosophy, rhetoric, cosmography, geometry, and arithmetic—the Académie Florimontane also claimed to treat matters of style, especially in relation to French).

Around this period the question of Vaugelas's career arose. The shy, nervous, and rather gullible character described by Paul Pellisson in his *Histoire de l'Académie Française* (1653; edited by Charles-Louis Livet, 1858) was obviously unsuited for the law, and his father therefore arranged for him to go into the service of Henri de Savoie, duc de Nemours, in Paris from 1607.

Documents relating to Vaugelas's first years in Paris are scarce, but, according to the preface to *Remarques sur la langue françoise,* Vaugelas met Jacques Davy Du Perron early on and gathered with other learned men and authors at his house. From about 1622 on Nicolas Coëffeteau held a sort of academy in Paris, where men such as François de Malherbe, Honorat de Bueil, Seigneur de Racan, Théophile de Viau,

Nicolas Faret, and Vaugelas gathered to discuss points of language.

Vaugelas's French translation of the Lenten sermons of the Spanish preacher Fonseca dates from these early years in Paris. The translation was published in 1615 as *Les Sermons de Fonseque sur tous les Evangiles du Caresme, avec une Paraphrase perpetuelle sur toutes les parties des Evangiles* (The Sermons of Fonseca on All the Gospel Readings for Lent, with a Running Paraphrase of All the Gospel Passages). Because of his good command of Spanish, Vaugelas had visited Spain in 1612 as interpreter for the duc de Mayenne, who was negotiating the marriage of King Louis XIII with Anne d'Autriche, and Vaugelas might have heard Fonseca preach in person. Fonseca was a popular preacher of the period, and Vaugelas might have been encouraged to undertake the translation by his family friend, de Sales. The translation seems to have received little attention, since it is generally not listed among Vaugelas's works by either his contemporaries or later commentators. The use of French in the translation differs in several ways from that recommended later by Vaugelas himself in *Remarques sur la langue françoise* and is in many ways typical of usage of the first decades of the seventeenth century. There are morphological examples of this usage in forms such as the periphrastic present continuous (*je vais reconoissant*) and the contracted forms of the future and conditional of certain verbs (*ils ne lairront [laisseront] pas);* syntactic examples in the nonuse of the article (*ce n'est pas merveilles, que*) and in agreement patterns; lexical examples, such as the usage of *ains* to mean *but* after a negative; and orthographic examples such as the spelling of *avecques*. In the 1615 translation Vaugelas's sentences are frequently long and rather contorted in syntax, with the occasional running together of two or more sentences from the Spanish original. In this period Vaugelas appears to have been influenced particularly by the translation method of Coëffeteau, who tended to elaborate and expand on the original text, while not diverging from the source text to nearly the same extent as Nicolas Perrot d'Ablancourt, who was subsequently to influence Vaugelas in his translation of Quintus Curtius Rufus.

In 1616 the duc de Nemours joined forces with the Spanish, declaring war on the duc de Savoie, who was helped by Louis XIII. While Vaugelas seems to have remained loyal to the duc de Nemours, the awkwardness of the situation might have encouraged Favre to attach his son to the king's household, obtaining for him in the winter of 1618–1619 a position as Gentilhomme entretenu de la Maison du Roy de France, with a pension of 2,000 livres.

From about 1620 on Vaugelas worked on his translation of Quintus Curtius Rufus's *Life of Alexander,* a task that occupied him for the rest of his life. The arts of grammar and translation were viewed as complementary in the seventeenth century, as is indicated by Malherbe's refusal to produce a grammar of French, referring his friends instead to his translations, which he viewed as the ideal illustration of his ideas on good French usage. Thus it was that Vaugelas appears to have spent some thirty years engaged in the twin occupations of writing *Remarques sur la langue françoise* and of refining and polishing his translation of the *Life of Alexander.* By this time Vaugelas was a regular attendee of the Parisian salons, notably that of the Hôtel de Rambouillet, where he no doubt collected data for *Remarques sur la langue françoise* and became a respected figure and authority on French usage, despite his provincial upbringing and, according to Vincent Voiture, his Savoyard accent. Vaugelas numbered among his friends several of the literary figures of the day, including Coëffeteau, Voiture, Faret, Jean Chapelain, Valentin Conrart, and Jean-Louis Guez de Balzac.

With the death of de Sales in 1622 and of his father two years later, Vaugelas lost the support of these two great men. His pension was apparently badly paid, and Vaugelas found himself in financial difficulty. In 1626 his friends secured for him a full-time position in the household of Gaston d'Orléans, where he later became chamberlain. This must have seemed an opportunity for Vaugelas since the king was ill and without children, but Gaston d'Orléans's fortune changed; when the king stripped him of the command of the siege of La Rochelle, replacing him with the duc de Richelieu, Orléans left France in rebellion, loyally followed, according to Pellisson, by Vaugelas. This loyalty apparently led to Vaugelas's financial ruin, since Richelieu stopped paying his pension; his salary was irregularly paid; and he was forced to sell his barony of Péroges.

There is no record of when Vaugelas finally left the service of Orléans, but it may have been in 1634, when the latter fled to France, abandoning most of his servants. What is certain is that Vaugelas was made a member of the French Academy in that year and that three years later he presented the academy with his observations on the French language, possibly in the form that is recorded in the Arsenal manuscript (the only surviving manuscript of *Remarques sur la langue françoise,* now at the Bibliothèque de l'Arsenal in Paris). Before Vaugelas's pension was reestablished in 1639, when he began work on the dictionary for the French Academy, he was forced to resort to various schemes to make money, some of them of a rather dubious nature (see Streicher's introduction to the 1934 facsimile edition of *Remarques sur la langue françoise*). In his *Histoire et recherches des antiquités de la ville de Paris* (History and Research on the Antiquities of the City of Paris, 1724) Henri Sauval recounts that Vaugelas might have been involved in starting a lottery in 1644, a project that was destined to fail.

Progress on the French Academy dictionary, projected as a mission of the academy in its statutes, had been slow, and by 1639 Richelieu was becoming impatient. Chapelain proposed to Richelieu that Vaugelas should be put in charge of the compilation of the dictionary and his pension reinstated. Richelieu agreed to this plan, and in a letter to Balzac dated 30 January 1639 Chapelain records Vaugelas's delight. Vaugelas devoted the rest of his life to work on the dictionary, but his perfectionist nature meant that only a small part of the work had been completed by the time he died in February 1650. In his history of the French Academy, Pellisson lists the writers that the academy proposed to consider for the compilation of the dictionary, several of whom—such as Coëffeteau, Du Perron, Malherbe, and Guillaume du Vair—are also cited or referred to quite extensively in *Remarques sur la langue françoise.*

Once again Vaugelas's pension was not regularly paid, and he faced more financial problems. He went to live at the Hôtel de Soissons as tutor to the sons of Prince Thomas de Savoie-Carignan, one of whom was dumb and the other of whom stammered. The end of Vaugelas's life was unhappy—he was dogged by illness and fear of his creditors—despite the publication in 1647 of *Remarques sur la langue françoise.* The book is a collection of randomly ordered observations on the finer points of doubtful French usage. Vaugelas's guiding principle is "le bon usage" (good usage), which he defines in elitist terms as the usage of "la plus saine partie" (the soundest part) of the speakers at the royal court and of the "soundest" part of the authors of the day. While in principle Vaugelas claims to resolve matters of doubt by referring to "le bon usage," in practice other criteria—such as etymology, regularity, euphony, and analogy (defined as a type of general usage applied to doubtful cases)—are sometimes invoked to determine the preferred usage. Usage is said always to take precedence over "raison" (reason), although Vaugelas is conscious that many French constructions are "raisonnable" in the sense that they conform to regular patterns. Three qualities of good usage are particularly cherished—purity, clarity, and the appropriate choice of word or expression. Ambiguity leading to hesitation on the part of the listener or reader is abhorred, so that proximity of related terms, linearity, and explicitness of syntactic construction are promoted, and new words are discouraged.

Remarques sur la langue françoise was in general extremely well received in the seventeenth century, going through more than twenty editions in the period up to 1738. Well-known anecdotes confirm the reputation of Vaugelas's observations: between 1652 and 1659 Pierre Corneille is said to have revised his earlier plays to bring the usage in line with that recommended by Vaugelas, and Jean Racine took a copy of the work with him to Uzès so that his usage should not be corrupted by provincial speech. In *Les Femmes Savantes* (The Learned Ladies, 1672) Molière could use the expression "parler Vaugelas" (to speak Vaugelas), confident that his audience would understand the allusion. Some subsequent editions of *Remarques sur la langue françoise* featured the annotations and comments of other writers, such as Olivier Patru and Thomas Corneille, and, most notably, of the French Academy in 1704. Moreover, several writers adopted Vaugelas's format and produced new collections of observations on the French language, among which those by Dominique Bouhours and Gilles Ménage are worthy of particular mention (see especially Streicher, *Commentaires sur les Remarques de Vaugelas*, 1936). The success of Vaugelas's book must in part be attributed to the fact that his observations responded to the contemporary need, especially for the upwardly mobile, for a means of acquiring the language of the *honnête homme* (gentleman), since a good command of language and conversational skills was an essential prerequisite for succeeding in the polite society of the day.

Vaugelas died in February 1650 of a stomach abscess and was buried on 27 February in the Church of Saint-Eustache in Paris. His papers were seized by his creditors and only returned to the French Academy in May of the following year. Two works were published posthumously. Vaugelas spent about thirty years constantly rewriting and polishing his translation of Quintus Curtius Rufus's *Life of Alexander,* but he was unable to decide on its publication before his death, so no definitive version from his hand remains; there is no extant manuscript of the work. In his preface to the published translation, *Quinte Curce, De la vie et des actions d'Alexandre le Grand* (1653), Pierre Du Ryer writes that the editors of the first edition, Conrart and Chapelain, were faced with three different copies of Vaugelas's text, one of which was marked as having been revised following the 1646 publication of Perrot d'Ablancourt's translation of Arrian's life of Alexander, but which was full of variants and in parts illegible. The second edition, dated 1655, was based on the same manuscript. In 1659,

REMARQVES
S V R L A
LANGVE FRANÇOISE
VTILES A CEVX QVI VEVLENT
BIEN PARLER ET BIEN ESCRIRE.

A PARIS,
Chez la Veuue IEAN CAMVSAT,
ET
PIERRE LE PETIT, Imprimeur & Libraire
ordinaire du Roy, ruë Sainct Iacques,
à la Toison d'Or.

M. DC. XLVII.
AVEC PRIVILEGE DV ROY.

Title page for Vaugelas's collection of observations on proper usage of the French language, published in 1647 (Bibliothèque Nationale, Paris)

however, a third, completely new edition of Vaugelas's translation appeared, edited by Patru and based on a single new manuscript described as "beaucoup plus nette, & . . . celle à laquelle l'Auteur vouloit s'arrester" (much clearer, and . . . the one on which the author wished to settle) and said to have been discovered in the intervening period. Du Ryer notes, however, that there were passages not finalized in this manuscript and that Patru had to intervene actively in order to produce a text suitable for publication.

Vaugelas was principally influenced by Coëffeteau's style of translation when he began working on the *Life of Alexander* in the 1620s. Probably by the 1630s parts of Vaugelas's translation were being read out in the salons, and its publication was being viewed with great anticipation. In a 1636 letter Balzac praises the translation in glowing terms: "Tout cela me semble si François et si naturel, qu'il est impossible d'y remarquer une seule ligne qui sente l'original Latin, & où le premier Autheur ait de l'advantage sur le second. L'Alexandre de Philippe estoit invincible, & celuy de Vaugelas est inimitable" (It all seems so French and so natural, that it is impossible to find a single line in which one detects the Latin original, and where the first author has the advantage over the second. Alexander, son of Philippe, was invincible, and Vaugelas's Alexander is inimitable). In the following year, however, the first of Perrot d'Ablancourt's eleven translations of the life of Alexander was published, and he was admitted to the French Academy; on Vaugelas's own admission, this occasioned a complete revision of his own translation. While Vaugelas never entirely freed himself from Coëffeteau's influence nor totally adopted Perrot d'Ablancourt's translation methods, he was clearly influenced by the trend toward greater freedom of translation favored by Perrot d'Ablancourt. Apart from this general influence, Perrot d'Ablancourt's influence in terms of word choice and construction can be identified, and, indeed, in the inclusion of directly borrowed details and short passages that have no counterpart in the Quintus Curtius Rufus's Latin original.

Vaugelas's translation was a great publishing success, going through even more editions than *Remarques sur la langue françoise* (there were more than forty editions of the translation before 1850). That the translation was deemed a model of good prose style is indicated by the fact that as late as 1719–1720 the French Academy decided to carry out a detailed and meticulous commentary on the linguistic usage in the translation.

Vaugelas's second posthumous work, *Nouvelles Remarques de M. de Vaugelas sur la langue françoise,* published in 1690 by Louis-Augustin Alemand, is not essentially a new collection of observations, as Alemand claims, but is rather comprised for the most part of observations taken word for word from the Arsenal manuscript, which Vaugelas chose not to publish in 1647 (there are thirty-one other observations in the 1690 collection). Although Vaugelas's work is now little read, his influence on the establishment of standard French and on the production of observations and usage-based grammars of French has been profound and is, indeed, still evident today.

References:

Wendy Ayres-Bennett, "A Study in the Genesis of Vaugelas's *Remarques sur la langue françoise:* The Arsenal Manuscript," *French Studies,* 37 (1983): 17–34;

Ayres-Bennett, *Vaugelas and the Development of the French Language* (London: Modern Humanities Research Association, 1987);

Ayres-Bennett and Philippe Caron, eds., *Les Remarques de l'Académie Française sur le Quinte-Curce de Vaugelas, 1719–1720* (Paris: Presses de l'Ecole Normale Supérieure, 1996);

Samuel Guichenon, *Histoire de Bresse et de Bugey,* 4 parts (Lyon: J.-A. Huguetan et M.-A. Ravaud, 1650);

Zygmunt Marzys, *Claude Favre de Vaugelas, La Préface des "Remarques sur la langue françoise"* (Neuchâtel: Faculté des Lettres / Geneva: Droz, 1984);

François Mugnier, *Histoire et correspondance du premier président Favre,* 3 volumes (Chambéry: Veuve Ménard, 1902–1905);

Paul Pellisson and Pierre-Joseph Thoulier d'Olivet, *Histoire de l'Académie Française,* 2 volumes, edited by Charles-Louis Livet, (Paris: Didier, 1858);

Henri Sauval, *Histoire et recherches des antiquités de la ville de Paris,* 3 volumes (Paris: C. Moette, 1724);

Jeanne Streicher, introduction to Vaugelas, *Remarques sur la langue françoise: Fac simile de l'édition originale,* edited by Streicher (Paris: Droz, 1934; reprinted, Geneva: Slatkine, 1970);

Streicher, ed., *Commentaires sur les Remarques de Vaugelas par La Mothe le Vayer, Scipion Dupleix, Ménage, Bouhours, Conrart, Chapelain, Patru, Thomas Corneille, Cassagne, Andry de Boisregard et l'Académie Française,* 2 volumes (Paris: Droz, 1936).

Papers:

The only surviving manuscript of Claude Favre de Vaugelas's *Remarques sur la langue françoise* is in the Bibliothèque de l'Arsenal in Paris (3105). This manuscript differs significantly, however, from the published version, notably in its broadly alphabetical presentation of the material and in its more detailed and open criticism of François de Malherbe's use of French. Papers and letters by Vaugelas may be found in the Bibliothèque Nationale in Paris. Annotated copies of *Remarques sur la langue françoise* are in the Bibliothèque de l'Arsenal and the Bibliothèque Mazarine in Paris. The manuscript of the Académie Française's observations of Vaugelas's translation of Quintus Curtius Rufus's *Life of Alexander* is in the Archives of the Institut de France, L'Académie Française, Paris.

Madame de Villedieu
(Marie-Catherine Desjardins)
(1640? – 1683)

Donna Kuizenga
University of Vermont

BOOKS: *Récit en prose et en vers de la Farce des Précieuses* (Paris: G. de Luyne, 1659; authorized edition, Paris: C. Barbin, 1660);

Alcidamie, 2 volumes (Paris: C. Barbin, 1661);

Recueil de poésies de Mademoiselle Desjardins (Paris: C. Barbin, 1662); enlarged as *Recueil de poésies de Mademoiselle Desjardins, augmenté de plusieurs pièces et lettres en cette dernière édition* (Paris: C. Barbin, 1664);

Le Carousel de Monseigneur le Daufin à Mademoiselle de Montausier (Paris: Mille de Beaujeu, 1662);

Manlius (Paris: C. Barbin, 1662);

Lisandre (Paris: C. Barbin, 1663);

Nitetis (Paris: C. Barbin, 1664);

Œuvres de Mademoiselle Des Jardins (Paris: G. Quinet, 1664; enlarged, 1664)–comprises *Recueil de poésies, Lettres diverses, Le Carousel de Monseigneur le Dauphin, Manlius, Nitetis,* and *Le Favory; Le Favory* translated by Perry Gethner as *The Favorite Minister* in *The Lunatic Lover and Other Plays by French Women of the 17th and 18th Centuries,* edited and translated by Gethner (Portsmouth, N.H.: Heinemann, 1994), pp. 27–88;

Anaxandre (Paris: J. Ribou, 1667);

Relation d'une Reveue des troupes de l'Amour [bound with *Jaloux par force et le bonheur des femmes qui ont des maris jaloux,* by Jean Donneau de Visé, and *La Chambre de justice de l'amour,* attributed to Louis La Laboureur] (Fribourg: P. Bontemps, 1668);

Carmente (Paris: C. Barbin, 1668);

Lettres et Billets Galants (Paris: C. Barbin, 1668);

Recueil de quelques lettres, ou Relations galantes (Paris: C. Barbin, 1668);

Nouveau Recueil de quelques pièces galantes (Paris: Jean Ribou, 1669);

Cléonice, ou Le Roman galant (Paris: C. Barbin, 1669);

Le Journal Amoureux, 6 volumes, parts 1, 2, 5, and 6 by Villedieu (Paris: C. Barbin, 1669–1671); translated as *Loves Journal: A Romance, Made of the Court*

Marie-Catherine Desjardins, Madame de Villedieu (from the frontispiece for the 1664 edition of her works; Bibliothèque Nationale, Paris)

of Henry the II. of France (London: Printed by Thomas Ratcliff and Mary Daniel, 1671);

Fables, ou Histoires allégoriques (Paris: C. Barbin, 1670);

Annales galantes, 2 volumes, anonymous (Paris: C. Barbin, 1670);

Les Amours des Grands Hommes, 4 volumes (Paris: C. Barbin, 1671); translated as *The Amours of Solon. Socrates. Julius Caesar. Cato of Utica. D'Andelot. Bussy d'Amboyse* (London: Printed for Henry Herringman and John Starkey, 1673);

Les Exiléz de la Cour d'Auguste, 6 volumes (Paris: C. Barbin, 1672–1673); translated as *The Unfortunate Heroes, or The Adventures of Ten Famous Men, viz, Ovid, Lentullus, Hortensius, Herennius, Cepion, Horace, Virgil, Cornelius Gallus, Crassus, Agrippa, Banished from the Court of Augustus Caesar: In Ten Novels* (London: Printed by T.N. for Henry Herringman, 1679);

Mémoires de la vie de Henriette-Sylvie de Molière, 6 volumes, anonymous (Paris: C. Barbin, 1672–1674); translated as *The Memoires of the Life, and Rare Adventures of Henrietta Silvia Moliere*, 2 volumes (volume 1, London: Printed for William Crook, 1672; volume 2, London: Printed by J.C. for W. Crooke, 1677);

Les Galanteries Grenadines, 2 volumes (Paris: C. Barbin, 1673);

Les Nouvelles Afriquaines (Paris: C. Barbin, 1673);

Œuvres mêlées (Rouen: Macherel, 1674)–includes *Le Portefeuille*;

Les Désordres de l'Amour (Paris: C. Barbin, 1675); translated as *The Disorders of Love: Truly Expressed in the Unfortunate Amours of Givry with Mademoiselle de Guise* (London: Printed for James Magnes and Richard Bentley, 1677);

Portrait des foiblesses humaines (Paris: C. Barbin, 1685);

Annales galantes de Grèce, 2 volumes (Paris: C. Barbin, 1687).

Editions and Collections: *Récit en prose et en vers de la Farce des Précieuses* (Geneva: Slatkine, 1969);

Les Désordres de l'Amour, edited by Micheline Cuénin, Textes Littéraires Français, volume 174 (Geneva: Droz, 1970);

Œuvres complètes, 3 volumes (Geneva: Slatkine, 1971);

Le Récit de la farce des Précieuses, in *Les Précieuses ridicules: Documents contemporains, lexique du vocabulaire précieux*, edited by Cuénin, Textes Littéraires Français, volume 200 (Geneva: Droz / Paris: Minard, 1973), pp. 103–122;

Lettres et billets galants, edited by Cuénin (N.p.: Société d'Etude du XVIIe Siècle, 1975);

Mémoires de la vie de Henriette-Sylvie de Molière, edited by Cuénin (Tours: Editions de l'Université François-Rabelais, 1977);

Annales galantes, edited by René Godenne (Geneva: Slatkine, 1979);

Cléonice, ou Le Roman galant, edited by Godenne (Geneva: Slatkine, 1979);

Le Portefeuille, edited by Jean-Paul Homand and Marie-Thérèse Hipp (Exeter: University of Exeter, 1979);

Les Désordres de l'amour, edited by Arthur Flannigan (Washington, D.C.: University Press of America, 1982);

Le Favori, in *Femmes dramaturges en France (1650–1750)*, edited by Perry Gethner (Paris & Seattle: Papers in French Seventeenth Century Literature, 1993), pp. 69–126;

Lettres et billets galants, in *Lettres d'amour du XVIIe siècle*, edited by Jean Rohou (Paris: Seuil, 1994), pp. 9–101;

Selected Writings of Madame de Villedieu, edited by Nancy Deighton Klein (New York: Peter Lang, 1995)–comprises *Jouissance, Manilus, Lisandre*, and selections from *Fables, ou Histoires allégoriques* and *Les Amours des grands hommes*.

Edition in English: *Mémoires de la vie de Henriette-Sylvie de Molière* [selections], translated by Donna Kuizenga and Francis Assaf, in *Writings by Pre-Revolutionary French Women*, edited by Anne R. Larsen and Colette H. Winn (New York: Garland, 2000), pp. 361–376.

PLAY PRODUCTIONS: *Manlius Torquatus*, Paris, Hôtel de Bourgogne, April 1662;

Nitetis, Paris, Hôtel de Bourgogne, April 1663;

Le Favory, Paris, Théâtre du Palais-Royal, 24 April 1665.

OTHER: "Etre dans une maison charmante et solitaire," in *Les Muses illustres*, edited by François Colletet *fils* (Paris: P. David et L. Champhoudry, 1658), p. 288;

Recüeil des portraits et éloges en vers et en prose dedié à Son Altesse Royale Mademoiselle, by Anne-Marie-Louise-Henriette d'Orléans, Mademoiselle de Montpensier, and others; contributions by Villedieu (Paris: C. de Sercy et C. Barbin, 1659), pp. 265, 436, 444;

Poésies choisies de MM. Corneille, Boisrobert, de Marigny, Desmarests, Gombault . . . et plusieurs autres: Cinquième partie, edited by Charles de Sercy, contributions by Desjardins (Paris: C. de Sercy, 1660), pp. 55–67.

Madame de Villedieu was a prolific writer who not only played an important role in the evolution of the early modern novel in France but also wrote poetry and plays as well as being the first woman playwright in France to have one of her works produced by a professional theater company. She was one of the few French women who earned her living by writing. Villedieu practiced many genres, both following popular taste and innovating. Among her innovations are the first-person pseudo-autobiographical novel, an early epistolary novel, and the "gallant" tale, focusing on the partially or wholly fictional love affairs of historical personages. This latter genre provides an alternative to official history, one that asks readers to take a second look at the kinds of relationships and motivations that determine the behavior of famous historical figures; through this genre she suggested that women play a significant role in shaping the course of history. Her pseudo-autobiographical *Mémoires de la vie de Henriette-Sylvie de Molière* (1672–1674; translated as *The Memoires of the Life, and Rare Adventures of Henrietta Silvia Moliere,* 1672, 1677) offers the reader the image of a nonconformist and enterprising woman protagonist. Villedieu was widely read in her own time and through much of the eighteenth century. Her role in the evolution of the novel is now attracting renewed attention from modern critics.

Establishing a fully reliable bibliography of first editions of Villedieu's works is difficult. Because of her popularity, spurious works were attributed to her both during her life and after her death. The scholar Micheline Cuénin has done the most extensive and authoritative research on Villedieu's bibliography. Likewise, scholarly knowledge of Villedieu's life includes significant gaps. Following initial research by Bruce Morissette, Cuénin's extensive archival research is the most definitive and authoritative source today for Villedieu's biography. Beyond the documents examined by Cuénin, one of the more detailed firsthand accounts of Villedieu's life is found in Gédéon Tallemant des Réaux's *Historiettes* (completed circa 1659; published 1834; translated as *Miniature Portraits,* 1925). How Tallemant's negative view of Villedieu inflects his narrative cannot be evaluated precisely. Other contemporary accounts are of varying degrees of reliability and present a variety of views of the author.

Until 1668–1669 Marie-Catherine Desjardins's works appeared under that name. After this date, however, she adopted the name Madame de Villedieu, and the rest of her writings appeared under that name. Even before this time she had in fact been using the name Villedieu, although not on her publications. The source of the name was her beloved, Antoine de Boësset, known beginning in 1648 as the sieur de Villedieu. Desjardins took his name, although they were never married.

The parents of Marie-Catherine Desjardins, who was almost certainly born in 1640, were from the lower ranks of the provincial nobility. They were introduced thanks to their common protectors, Henri, duc de Rohan-Montbazon, and his wife. After the marriage, the duke found a post for Marie-Catherine's father, and the family moved to Alençon, the city in which Marie-Catherine, the family's second child, spent her early years. Nothing is known about her childhood. In 1655, however, she met a cousin at a family baptism and secretly promised to marry him. When her father discovered this secret engagement, he took legal action to break it off. Shortly afterward, Marie-Catherine's mother was legally separated from her husband. She moved to Paris with her two daughters and soon obtained control of her own financial assets. Evidence suggests that at about this time, Marie-Catherine made her first efforts as a writer. In Paris her mother renewed old acquaintances and alliances in an effort to obtain necessary protection, and in this way Marie-Catherine made her first acquaintances among those people who were to become her friends and protectors. She remained well connected to members of both the nobility and the upper bourgeoisie during her entire career.

About 1658 Desjardins met Boësset, son of well-known court musicians. Boësset, whose father left him solid financial resources, was destined for a military career and was attached to the Picardy regiment. Desjardins fell in love at first sight, and her 1659 sonnet "Jouissance" (Pleasure) has traditionally been considered to be a reflection on that passion. The sonnet is the initial source of Desjardins's literary fame and attracted as much criticism as it did praise because its erotic subject matter was not considered suitable for a young woman. Although probably not her first work, "Jouissance," with its evocation of sexual pleasure, was soon widely circulated in manuscript and brought Desjardins a degree of literary success mixed with hints of notoriety. Cuénin, however, considers suspect the authenticity of the ten other poems published along with "Jouissance" in the 1660 *Poésies choisies de MM. Corneille, Boisrobert, de Marigny, Desmarests, Gombault . . . et plusieurs autres: Cinquième partie* (Selected Poems of MM. Corneille, Boisrobert, de Marigny, Desmarests, Gombault . . . and Several Others: Fifth Part), edited by Charles de Sercy.

The first performance of Molière's play *Les Précieuses ridicules* (The High-Brow Ladies) took place on 18 November 1659 and then was performed again on 2 December. The play was a great success, and the public was extremely curious about it. In these circumstances, at the request of a friend and protector, Desjardins wrote the *Récit en prose et en vers de la Farce des Précieuses* (Account in Prose and in Verse of the Farce of the High-Brow Ladies, 1659). This secondhand account of the play was widely circulated and published in an incorrect and unauthorized edition. In order to get a proper edition published, Desjardins entered into a professional relationship with the publisher Claude Barbin, the man who published so much of the fashionable literature of the latter part of the seventeenth century. This publication marked the beginning of a sometimes troubled collaboration that continued throughout Desjardins's career. The authorized version of her account was published by Barbin in 1660. The publication of the poems in de Sercy's collection and the appearance of the *Récit en prose et en vers de la Farce des Précieuses* marked the beginning of Desjardins's success as a writer. At the same time, de Sercy included some of Desjardins's verbal portraits in a revised and expanded edition of the collection of portraits composed by Louis

XIII's niece, Louise d'Orléans, duchesse de Montpensier (known as la Grande Mademoiselle), and her entourage. Desjardins's portraits appear in the *Recüeil des portraits et éloges en vers et en prose dedié à Son Altesse Royale Mademoiselle* (Collection of Portraits and Praise in Verse and in Prose, Dedicated to Her Royal Highness Mademoiselle) of 1659.

At some point during these early years in Paris, Desjardins began living *sous sa bonne foi,* meaning that although she was still a minor, she was considered independent of her parents and able to act on her own without their consent. This emancipation might well have been motivated by her family's financial difficulties and her intention to make her own way in Paris. As her reaction to the unauthorized version of the *Récit en prose et en vers de la Farce des Précieuses* shows, Desjardins was already concerned with managing her literary reputation. The first two volumes of a novel, *Alcidamie,* were published by Barbin in 1661, but the rest never appeared, either because the public was no longer interested in long novels or because the story alluded, indiscreetly, to well-placed members of society. Desjardins then put together a collection of her poetry, the *Recueil de poésies de Mademoiselle Desjardins* (Anthology of Poems by Mademoiselle Desjardins, 1662), including both verses that had been published earlier and other pieces that had circulated in manuscript. The success of this volume led her to publish an augmented edition in 1664.

Known principally as a poet dealing with amorous subject matter, Desjardins at this point in her career turned her attention to the theater, and in 1662 her tragicomedy *Manlius Torquatus* (published later that year as *Manlius*) was performed by the actors of the Hôtel de Bourgogne. This production made Desjardins both the first woman playwright in France to have her work produced by a professional theater company and the first to have her work reviewed in the press. The play was at least reasonably successful and attracted a good deal of attention both because of the sex of the author and because of the way in which Desjardins had modified the material she had taken from Roman history. The theoretician of theater François Hédelin, abbé d'Aubignac, a critic of Pierre Corneille, used Desjardins's play as an example, positive or negative, in contemporary quarrels about theatrical aesthetics. That same year, seeking favor and protection, Desjardins published *Le Carousel de Monseigneur le Daufin à Mademoiselle de Montausier* (The Dauphin's Carousel, offered to mademoiselle de Montausier), a fantasy in verse and in prose, presenting a flattering picture of the young dauphin and of festivities sponsored by King Louis XIV. Again the work was a success, and Desjardins was invited to recite some of the verses in public.

During the same period, the relationship between Desjardins and Boësset took its first important turn. According to Tallemant, whose perspective on Desjardins is extremely critical, Boësset was locked out of his house when he returned late one night; as a result, he sought refuge in Desjardins's room, refuge she accorded him. She, meanwhile, went to sleep with her sister. The next day Boësset fell ill and was forced to remain in Desjardins's room. She cared for him during his illness; he promised marriage; and they lived together rather openly for three months. Boësset, however, soon became unfaithful. Cuénin's study of legal documents suggests that Boësset's behavior may also have been motivated by his knowing that Desjardins's family was having increasing financial difficulties, a circumstance that made her a bad marriage partner. Intent on furthering his military career, Boësset had Desjardins affirm in 1663 that he had never promised to marry her.

Desjardins continued to devote attention to the theater, composing a second play, *Nitétis* (published 1664), with a subject taken not from Roman history but from the popular novel by Madeleine de Scudéry, *Le Grand Cyrus* (1649–1653). *Nitétis* was also put on by the actors of the Hôtel de Bourgogne in 1663 but was, by all accounts, a failure. Desjardins then turned to Molière and his company, which in early 1664 began rehearsals for her third play, the tragicomedy *Le Favory* (published in the enlarged edition of the *Œuvres de Mademoiselle Desjardins* [Works of Mademoiselle Desjardins, 1664]; translated as *The Favorite Minister,* 1994). According to Tallemant, upon learning that Boësset had left for Paris to rejoin his regiment, Desjardins borrowed money from Molière in order to follow her beloved to Provence. On 21 June 1664 a second promise of marriage was made, this time in the presence of a notary. Boësset then sailed, and Desjardins apparently remained in Provence.

When Boësset returned, he put off the marriage, and Desjardins eventually returned to Paris, where she was again in contact with Molière, and new rehearsals of *Le Favory* began in the spring of 1665. According to Tallemant, when the play was advertised, Desjardins insisted that her name no longer be listed as Mademoiselle Desjardins, the name under which she had earned her literary reputation, but rather as Madame de Villedieu. Molière refused, saying that using Madame de Villedieu would cause confusion, but he indicated that in everything save the advertisements for the play, he would call her Madame de Villedieu, as she wished. *Le Favory* was performed by Molière's company on 24 April 1665, enjoying a modest success. Molière then chose it for performance at Versailles on 13 June 1665 as part of one of the king's royal entertainments. Jean-

Baptiste Lully composed some music for the play, and Molière wrote a prologue, now lost. *Le Favory* is the first play by a woman to be used in a command performance before the king. Desjardins's own account of the performance is found in the collection *Nouveau Recueil de quelques pièces galantes* (1669). Although her name was regularly included in lists of playwrights in treatises on the theater up until the end of the seventeenth century, Desjardins did not write another play after *Le Favory*, and she now turned her attention to the emerging genre of the novel, the domain in which she made her most significant literary achievements.

On 5 February 1667 Boësset had Desjardins sign a document freeing him from his promises of marriage. In short succession, he then married and left for battle in the recently declared War of Devolution. Despite the second renunciation, Desjardins used the name Madame de Villedieu during her travels in Holland and other Low Countries, a voyage beginning in March 1667. The explicit motive for her trip was the need to settle some legal matters, but scholars speculate that her recent rupture with Boësset also motivated her departure. In Brussels, the émigré community offered Villedieu a warm reception, and at The Hague she met the erudite Constantjn Huygens. Her short fiction *Anaxandre* (published under the name Desjardins) appeared in 1667. Villedieu continued to suffer from financial difficulties and apparently from health difficulties as well, spending some time at Spa in 1668.

During a brief return visit to Paris to seek additional funding for his military activities, Boësset apparently gave or sold Villedieu's love letters to her publisher, Barbin. Barbin was eager to publish them and finally reached Villedieu in Holland. Her refusal to allow publication was categorical, but in the end all that she obtained was the removal of her name from the title page and a decrease in the number of copies printed. Villedieu never had the opportunity to avenge this betrayal of trust, because Boësset was killed in 1668 at the siege of Lille, while Villedieu was at Spa. The *Lettres et Billets Galants* (Letters and Gallant Notes) of 1668 chronicle Villedieu's unhappy love for Boësset. During this period, Villedieu remained outside of France, perhaps staying with Marie de Longueville, duchesse de Nemours, to whom she had dedicated her pastoral novel *Carmente* (1668). At this time Villedieu probably also wrote *Relation d'une Reveue des troupes de l'Amour* (Account of the Review of Love's Troops, 1668), although there is some question about the attribution of this work.

She might also have composed *Cléonice, ou Le Roman galant* (Cléonice, or the Gallant Novel) at this time, although it did not appear until 1669. It was the first of her published works to carry the name Madame

DESORDRES
DE L'AMOUR.
Par M. DE VILLEDIEV.
TOME III.

A PARIS,
Chez CLAVDE BARBIN, au Palais, sur le second Perron de la Sainte Chapelle.

M. DC. LXXV.
AVEC PRIVILEGE DV ROY.

Title page for the third volume in Villedieu's 1675 collection of stories depicting the disorder caused by passion (from the 1970 edition of Desordres de l'amour)

de Villedieu, although she had already been using that name in other contexts. She maintained excellent relations with the Boësset family after Antoine's death, and they made no known objections to her use of the name or to her signing her name as Marie-Catherine Desjardins, widow of Villedieu. After Boësset's death in 1668, Villedieu used this name in her literary dealings as well as her life.

Upon her return to Paris, Villedieu faced severe financial difficulties, continued to seek a royal pension, and gave both *Cléonice* and her correspondence from Holland and other Low Countries, the *Recueil de quelques lettres, ou Relations galantes* (Collection of Several Letters, or Gallant Accounts, 1668), to Barbin for publication. Villedieu also collected many of her earlier poems and some occasional pieces, publishing the *Nouveau Recueil de quelques pièces galantes* in 1669. At the beginning of *Cléonice*, published the same year,

Villedieu underlines her creation of a new genre, the gallant novel or *roman galante,* with a new respect for verisimilitude that distinguishes it from the longer heroic works, which had enjoyed great popularity.

The period extending from 1669 to 1672 was productive for Villedieu. Multiple works by her were published, almost all of them novels. This period was one of intense, almost frenetic writing on Villedieu's part, each work intended to follow on the success of a previous one. Her financial situation probably made the rapid pace of her writing necessary, and it might have been Barbin, encouraged by the success of *Carmente,* who pushed her toward the genre of the novel. Possibly also, as Faith E. Beasley has suggested in her "Apprentices and Collaborators: Villedieu's Worldly Readers," Villedieu's move to the novel might have been motivated by her understanding of the increased power of the worldly, rather than academic, public in cultural matters. Her position was thus a modernist one, allying her intellectually with those who formed one side of the *Querelle des anciens et des modernes* (Quarrel of the Ancients and the Moderns).

In 1669 Barbin asked Villedieu to rewrite a manuscript he owned called the "Journal Amoureux" (published as *Le Journal Amoureux,* 1669–1671; translated as *Loves Journal: A Romance, Made of the Court of Henry the II. of France,* 1671). She reworked the first and second parts of the text. However, there were difficulties with the original author, who subsequently published third and fourth parts. Villedieu disavows these sections in her preface to a second edition in 1671. This edition provides clear demonstration of Villedieu's concern with the management of her public image as a writer. In it she not only dissociates herself from the lascivious third and fourth parts of *Le Journal Amoureux* but also provides a catalogue of her own works through 1671, in order to eliminate spurious attributions. The fifth and sixth parts, which Villedieu wrote, appeared in 1671 as well.

At the same time he was having Villedieu rewrite *Le Journal Amoureux,* Barbin took out a "privilege" (copyright) for a second series, called the *Annales galantes;* the four parts of this text appeared anonymously in 1670. This anonymity might well have been transparent and might have been motivated by the social criticism included in the text. Both the *Annales galantes* and *Le Journal Amoureux* played an important role in the development of prose fiction, and Villedieu is credited by the historian Pierre Bayle with the invention of the gallant tale, which replaced the long sentimental novels that had been fashionable. The frame for the stories that make up the "days" of *Le Journal Amoureux* is French history, but the characters are motivated almost solely by

love, and it is in their passions that the reader finds the motivation for historical events.

In the preface to the *Annales galantes,* Villedieu gives readers a clear picture of her intentions. Official history leaves out important aspects of the events it portrays, Villedieu writes. By adding information that official history omits, providing the speeches personages should have made, and giving them personal and often amorous motivations for their public actions, Villedieu subverts official history and provides a critique of it, suggesting that the great deeds are not motivated by principle or politics but rather by emotion. Villedieu suggests in this way that history is not one official story, but rather multiple and contingent stories; thus, she creates a version of history in which women may play as important a role as men. *Les Amours des Grands Hommes* (translated as *The Amours of Solon. Socrates. Julius Caesar. Cato of Utica. D'Andelot. Bussy d'Amboyse,* 1673) was published the same year, 1671, as were the continuations of *Le Journal Amoureux.*

Villedieu had presented the king with an ornate manuscript of a work in verse, and she published the text in 1670 as *Fables, ou Histoires allégoriques* (Fables, or Allegorical Stories). Villedieu's motivation for the publication might have been to remind the king of her gift, and Barbin's might have been a desire to profit from the recent success of Jean de La Fontaine's *Fables* (1668). In short succession, more of her important works followed. Parts 1 through 4 of *Les Exiléz de la Cour d'Auguste* (translated as *The Unfortunate Heroes, or The Adventures of Ten Famous Men, viz, Ovid, Lentullus, Hortensius, Herennius, Cepion, Horace, Virgil, Cornelius Gallus, Crassus, Agrippa, Banished from the Court of Augustus Caesar: In Ten Novels,* 1679) appeared in 1672, with parts 5 and 6 following in 1673. The *Exiléz,* like *Les Amours des Grands Hommes,* continued Villedieu's rewriting of historical material.

The first four parts of the pseudo-autobiographical *Mémoires de la vie de Henriette-Sylvie de Molière* date from 1672, the last two parts from 1674. This work is one of Villedieu's most important, inaugurating as it does the genre of fictional memoirs. The text, which has many picaresque elements, skillfully mixes real events from the author's life with fictional adventures, creating a first-person tale of an independent and enterprising woman. Its tropes of identity and disguise undermine conventional notions of gender and present the complexities of creating an authoritative female narrative voice in early modern France. In 1673 both *Les Galanteries Grenadines* and *Les Nouvelles Afriquaines* were published. The stories in *Les Galanteries Grenadines* are set at the time of the fall of Grenada in the fifteenth century and exploit the seventeenth-century interest in Spain and its past. *Les Nouvelles Afriquaines,* on the other hand, uses another exotic location, but contemporary historical events as their frame. Villedieu was responding to a wave of interest in northern Africa.

Villedieu apparently entered a convent for a period in 1672, leaving in 1673, after which she reportedly lived a more retired life. Her production also slowed considerably. These facts are almost all that is known about Villedieu's life during this period of intense literary activity. The last works to appear during her lifetime were the *Œuvres mêlées* (Diverse Works, 1674), which picked up a variety of earlier pieces but also included an important new work, the short epistolary novel *Le Portefeuille* (The Pocketbook), and her collection of three short stories, *Les Désordres de l'Amour* (1675; translated as *The Disorders of Love: Truly Expressed in the Unfortunate Amours of Givry with Mademoiselle de Guise,* 1677). This last work is often considered to reveal Villedieu's new and more sober vision of love. It portrays the political disorder sown by passion and its manipulation. Critics also consider this text to be the one in which Villedieu brings her conception of historical fiction to fruition.

In 1676 Villedieu finally received the royal pension she had so long sought; she was, in fact, one of only two women writers to receive royal support in the seventeenth century. In 1677 Villedieu married Claude-Nicolas de Chaste, and in 1678 she gave birth to a son, Louis de Chaste. The marriage remained secret, however, probably because Claude-Nicolas had to be released from religious orders he had taken. That year he was appointed governor of the Invalides but died before he could take the position. Louis XIV gave both the position and a pension to the infant, and Villedieu, now Madame de Chaste, was also able to obtain her husband's inheritance from his father. She then retired with her son to a property at Clinchemire, where her mother, sister, and brother were living. Villedieu remained there until her death in 1683.

Two works appeared posthumously, *Portrait des foiblesses humaines* (Portrait of Human Weaknesses, 1685) and *Annales galantes de Grèce* (Gallant Annals of Greece, 1687). No one knows whether Villedieu had intended to publish these writings or whether that decision was made solely by her publisher, Barbin, who gained possession of her manuscripts at the time of her death. The four tales that make up the *Portrait des foiblesses humaines* reflect an interest in moral instruction on the author's part, suggesting a date of composition at or after the 1675 *Désordres de l'Amour.* The portraits of human weaknesses are intended as an admonition to those subject to the vices portrayed and an inducement to moral improvement. The *Annales galantes de Grèce,* on the other hand, are almost certainly intended to exploit the success of the *Annales galantes.* No one knows with certainty when the work was composed or why

Villedieu chose not to publish it, although some scholars speculate that its materials might have been incompatible with the more sober outlook of her latter years.

Villedieu's success in her own time was considerable. She was widely known and both praised for her skill as a writer and derided as an immoral woman whose work was of slight value. The degree of her popularity is indicated by the publication of three editions of her collected works, augmented by many false attributions, between 1702 and 1741. Two pirated editions appeared during the same period. Like the works of many of the women writers of the later seventeenth century, Villedieu's continued to be read during the eighteenth century. As Joan DeJean has demonstrated in the final chapter of her *Tender Geographies* (1991), the works of many women writers, including Villedieu's, disappeared from view as the canon of French literature was formed after the French Revolution. As a consequence, only in the latter part of the twentieth century did interest in Villedieu's works begin to extend beyond that of a few specialists. Until that time, scholars often read Villedieu's works almost exclusively as being unmediated reflections of her own life and experiences. This approach is particularly attractive in Villedieu's case, precisely because there are such gaps in knowledge of her life. While this approach continues to be practiced, beginning in the 1980s a new generation of scholars has suggested that while elements of Villedieu's experience are certainly reflected in her works, to assume that the works are merely a reflection of her life is erroneous, when in fact their intentionally literary nature makes the relation between life and work a much more complex and subtle one. This approach has allowed scholars to emphasize Villedieu's important and innovative role in the evolution of the novel during the early modern period.

References:

Francis Assaf, "Madame de Villedieu et le picaresque au féminin: Les Mémoires de la vie d'Henriette-Sylvie de Molière (1617–1674)," in *L'Image du souverain dans le théâtre de 1600 à 1650; Maximes; Madame de Villedieu: Actes de Wake Forest,* edited by Milorad R. Margitic and Byron R. Wells (Paris, Seattle & Tübingen: Papers on French Seventeenth Century Literature, 1987), pp. 361–377;

Pierre Bayle, "Jardins, Marie-Catherine des," *Dictionnaire historique et critique,* 16 volumes (Paris: France-Expansion, 1973), VIII: 331–333;

Faith E. Beasley, "Apprentices and Collaborators: Villedieu's Worldly Readers," in *A Labor of Love: Critical Reflections on the Writings of Marie-Catherine Desjardins (Madame de Villedieu)* (Madison, N.J.: Fairleigh Dickinson University Press / London:

Associated University Presses, 2000), pp. 177–202;

Micheline Cuénin, "Madame de Villedieu: Bibliographie," *Répertoire analytique de la littérature française*, 2 (January/February 1971): 7–26;

Cuénin, "Marie-Catherine Desjardins, Madame de Villedieu: Mise au point biographique," *Répertoire analytique de la littérature française*, 1 (November/December 1970): 7–39;

Cuénin, *Roman et société sous Louis XIV: Madame de Villedieu (Marie-Catherine Desjardins 1640–1683)*, 2 volumes (Paris: H. Champion, 1979);

Joan E. DeJean, *Tender Geographies: Women and the Origins of the Novel in France* (New York: Columbia University Press, 1991);

René Démoris, "Madame de Villedieu–Histoire de femme," in *L'Image du souverain dans le théâtre de 1600 à 1650; Maximes; Madame de Villedieu: Actes de Wake Forest*, edited by Margitic and Wells (Paris, Seattle & Tübingen: Papers on French Seventeenth Century Literature, 1987), pp. 286–319;

Henriette Goldwyn, "Manlius–L'Héroïsme in verse," in *L'Image du souverain dans le théâtre de 1600 à 1650; Maximes; Madame de Villedieu: Actes de Wake Forest*, edited by Margitic and Wells (Paris, Seattle & Tübingen: Papers on French Seventeenth Century Literature, 1987), pp. 421–437;

Marie-Thérèse Hipp, "Fiction et réalité dans les *Mémoires de la vie de Henriette-Sylvie de Molière* de Madame de Villedieu," *Dix-Septième Siècle*, 94–95 (1971): 93–117;

Hipp, *Mythes et réalités, enquête sur le roman et les mémoires, 1660–1700* (Paris: Klincksieck, 1976);

Donna Kuizenga, "*Ce rusé d'Amour:* Les Ruses des *Annales galantes*," in *Ecriture de la ruse*, edited by Elzbieta Grodek (Amsterdam & Atlanta: Rodopi, 2000), pp. 319–333;

Kuizenga, "'La Lecture d'une si ennuyeuse histoire': Topoï de la lecture et du livre dans les *Mémoires de la vie de Henriette-Sylvie de Molière*," in *L'Epreuve du lecteur: Livres et lectures dans le roman d'Ancien Régime: Actes du VIIIe colloque de la Société d'analyse de la topique romanesque, Louvain, Anvers, 19–21 mai 1994*, edited by Jan Herman and Paul Pelckmans (Louvain & Paris: Editions Peeters, 1995), pp. 120–128;

Kuizenga, "The Play of Pleasure and the Pleasure of Play in the *Mémoires de la vie de Henriette-Sylvie de Molière*," in *A Labor of Love: Critical Reflections on the Writings of Marie-Catherine Desjardins (Madame de Villedieu)*, edited by Lalande (Madison, N.J.: Fairleigh Dickinson University Press / London: Associated University Presses, 2000), pp. 147–161;

Brucc Morrissette, *The Life and Works of Marie-Catherine Desjardins (Mme. de Villedieu), 1632–1683*, Washington University Studies in Language and Literature, no. 17 (St. Louis: Washington University Press, 1947);

Domna Stanton, "The Demystification of History and Fiction in *Les Annales galantes*," in *L'Image du souverain dans le théâtre de 1600 à 1650; Maximes; Madame de Villedieu: Actes de Wake Forest*, edited by Margitic and Wells (Paris, Seattle & Tübingen: Papers on French Seventeenth Century Literature, 1987), pp. 339–360;

Mary Elizabeth Storer, "Bibliographical Note on Mme de Villedieu (Mlle Desjardins)," *Modern Language Notes*, 62 (1947): 413–418;

Gédéon Tallemant des Réaux, *Historiettes*, 2 volumes, edited by Antoine Adam, Bibliothèque de la Pléiade, nos. 142 and 151 (Paris: Gallimard, 1960, 1961), II: 900–909;

Gabrielle Verdier, "Madame de Villedieu and the Critics: Toward a Brighter Future," in *L'Image du souverain dans le théâtre de 1600 à 1650; Maximes; Madame de Villedieu: Actes de Wake Forest*, edited by Margitic and Wells (Paris, Seattle & Tübingen: Papers on French Seventeenth Century Literature, 1987), pp. 323–338.

Appendix

Lyric Poetry of the Seventeenth Century

Lyric Poetry

Robert Corum
Kansas State University

The seventeenth century in France was long considered a period in which lyric poetry was an inferior genre, practiced for the most part by second-rate writers who, through ignorance or accident of birth date, failed to adhere to the classical principles espoused by such hallowed masters associated with the reign of King Louis XIV as Jean Racine, Jean de La Fontaine, Molière, and Nicolas Boileau-Despréaux. Although classical writers and critics recognized the historical importance of François de Malherbe (1555–1623) as an influential innovator as French poetry moved away from the principles of the Pléiade, poets such as Théophile de Viau (1590–1626), Antoine Girard de Saint-Amant (1594–1661), Tristan L'Hermite (1601–1655), and Jean de La Ceppède (1548–1623)–now celebrated–were scorned and ignored throughout the latter part of the seventeenth century, the eighteenth century, and well into the nineteenth century. In his *Histoire de la littérature* (1894) the famous nineteenth-century French critic Gustave Lanson branded these poets "attardés" (laggards, old-fashioned) and "égarés" (lost, astray). Clearly, they did not receive the respect that they deserved as artists of the first rank. Only in the twentieth century, with the serious reevaluation and consequent rehabilitation of the poets of the "premier dix-septième siècle" (the first seventeenth century), have these writers gained acceptance, then renown, in French literary studies.

The classical prejudice evident in Boileau's almost wholesale condemnation of the lyric poets of the first part of the seventeenth century tended to emphasize order, logic, adherence to certain standards of good taste, clarity of expression, and a strong moral element in the works that it approved. Poets such as Théophile and Saint-Amant were for the most part conscious of their autonomy as independent artists, as "modern" writers who broke from tradition and set a new direction in French lyric poetry. The classicists and their apologists in subsequent centuries judged these poets as excessively individualistic–even idiosyncratic–writers, whose incoherent, disordered poetry breached all standards of good taste and decorum. They cited the "basse morale" (base immorality) of such poets as Saint-Amant and the freethinking libertinism of Théophile as signal examples of this aberrant branch of French poetry. This anachronistic view accentuates the perceived failure of these poets to conform to standards that became widespread after their deaths. Malherbe, who worked early in the century to purify the French language and regularize French poetry, was given a place of honor among this group, precisely because he appeared to facilitate the triumph of classicism during the second half of the century. The rest of these poets, who appeared to oppose Malherbe's reforms and claimed a modicum of independence from proscribed rules, were judged as obstructionists who stood in the way of "progress" toward the artistic apogee of Louis XIV's reign.

The traditional commentators failed to appreciate this poetry on its own terms. More recent scholarly work has discovered principles of composition unrecognized by the classical critics. Poems based on structural principles other than classical logic and causality–such as association, enumeration, serial order, allusive narrative patterns, and the order of established devotional exercises, for example–inform many of the lyric poems of the early seventeenth century. In addition to structural patterns, baroque poetry often relies on networks of allied images that converge around themes. For many years general stylistic categories have been used to delineate the baroque period and to distinguish it from the classical. These elements include the poet's desire to surprise or shock readers and to impress them with his ingenuity and talent, perhaps by resorting to the grotesque or the macabre. The notion of trompe l'oeil in the plastic arts, which in literature became an express desire to deceive the reader, has also been identified as a hallmark of the baroque style. Also manifested in the poems of the period are the concepts of metamorphosis and instability and a taste for movement and for the ephemeral, which are rendered by images such as wind, water, clouds, snow, smoke, lightning, and thunder. The poems exhibit a penchant for hyperbole–a willful desire to exaggerate, to speak in

François de Malherbe (posthumous 1658 engraving;
from Roselyne de Ayala and Jean-Pierre Guéno,
Belles Lettres, *2001)*

superlatives. There is also a tendency toward theatricality and surface appearance.

Although imprecise, a contrast between the major descriptive categories of classicism and the baroque serves to allow some general insight into the two styles. Whereas reliance on reason is the linchpin of any definition of classicism, a bias toward the imagination–the unusual and the fantastic–obtains in the lyric French poetry of the first half of the seventeenth century. Sometimes far-fetched metaphors characterize this orientation. Based on understatement–"dire le moins pour faire entendre le plus" (say the least in order to suggest the most)–the reserved, sober, classical style finds its counterpart in the baroque taste for hyperbole and exaggeration. The relative complexity of baroque art contrasts with the search for simplicity among the classical writers. Other binary oppositions–stability/instability, symmetry/asymmetry, and verbosity/concision–have been used to distinguish the two prime movements of seventeenth-century French literature. The baroque lyric poets wished to create a palpable effect–to impress or surprise by recourse to paradox, antithesis, ingenuity, and drama–in order to disrupt the expectations of readers who were perhaps too complacent and too accustomed to the ordinary.

The best-known lyric poet of the period is Malherbe, one of the few poets of the early seventeenth

century praised by Boileau in his influential *Art poétique* (1674): "Enfin Malherbe vint, et le premier en France, / Fit sentir dans les vers une juste cadence" (Finally Malherbe appeared, the first in France to fashion rhythmic verse). Malherbe was hailed by seventeenth-, eighteenth-, nineteenth-, and even twentieth-century critics as an early exponent of the rationalist movement that reached its apogee under Louis XIV after 1660. In this traditional view Malherbe is regarded as the main proponent of early prescriptive rules in lyric poetry, echoing the injunctions and style of Horace and Seneca the Younger as well as the neoclassical sixteenth-century Italian critics. Malherbe attempted to "purify" French poetry, to free it from the stylistic excesses of the Pléiade poets. His doctrine, which is limited in written form to his marginal notes in his personal editions of the work of the Pléiade poet Philippe Desportes, aimed to subvert the principal tenets of the Pléiade's recommendations for a complete reform of French poetry, which had been enunciated in Joachim Du Bellay's *Défense et illustration de la langue francaise* (Defense and Illustration of the French Language, 1549). Malherbe rejected Du Bellay's insistence on enriching–that is, expanding–poetic vocabulary, wishing instead to ban most of the Pléiade's advice to exploit neologisms, compound words, technical terms, colloquialisms, and archaisms as a means of enhancing the expressiveness of French poetry. Malherbe rejected all sources of poetic obscurity: abstruse mythological allusions, syntactical inversions, and illogical transitions. His recommendations concerning prosody held sway throughout the seventeenth, eighteenth, and early nineteenth centuries, when the Romantic movement and its followers began to rebel against the old Malherbian rules. His ambition to create a pure, concise, clear, and logical poetic language has marked the French language to this day.

Malherbe thus moved away from the Pléiade's belief in freewheeling inspiration to a slower, more rational, more intellectual concept of poetry. His poetic output is limited to a mere four thousand lines, reflecting this emphasis on care and deliberation. Most of his work is poetry of circumstance, written on the command of royal patrons such as Henri IV, Cardinal Richelieu, and Louis XIII. An early work is the devotional poem "Les Larmes de Saint Pierre" (The Tears of St. Peter, 1587). Notable as well are poems dedicated to noble patrons, "A la Reine sur sa bienvenue" (To the Queen on her welcome), "Pour le roi allant en Limousin" (For the King en Route to Limousin, 1610), and "Ode a la Reine sur l'heureux succès de sa régence" (Ode to the Queen on the Happy Success of her Regency, 1610). Other often-anthologized poems are the Senecan "Consolation à M. Du Périer, sur la mort de sa fille" (Consolation for M. du Périer, on the Death of his Daughter, 1598) and an intensely personal poem, written near the end of his life, "Sonnet sur la mort de son fils" (Sonnet on the Death of his Son, 1627). Malherbe's lines impress the reader with their stoical sense of calm, elevated style, and moral tone. While many nineteenth- and twentieth-century critics have emphasized the logical structure, precise versification, and rhetorical richness of Malherbe's work, recent critics such as David Rubin also see a "higher hidden" order based on mythical allusions, metaphors, themes, and logical structural connections. Other commentators have challenged the traditional view concerning Malherbe's influence on the literary production that followed.

Malherbe's sober stoicism and methodical versification are evident in the "Consolation à M. Du Périer, sur la mort de sa fille." The speaker, in effect, chides the grieving father, citing the ubiquity of death, the danger of excessive grief, and the irrelevance of the length of one's life. Like Seneca in his *Epistulae morales* (circa first century A.D.), the speaker alludes to mythological and historical exemplars illustrating great losses. Malherbe concludes with references to his own loss of two sons, which he has overcome with stoic resolve—submission to God's will and Christian resignation to the rigors of death. The poem displays the qualities most often associated with Malherbe: rationality, stoical determination, and a sober formal structure.

A sonnet composed at the end of his life reveals another aspect of Malherbe's work. In 1627 one of Malherbe's sons was killed in a fight with two other young men. There were conflicting versions of what actually occurred. According to one account, Malherbe's son was killed in an ambush, and one of the murderers was Jewish. Although "Sonnet sur le mort de son fils" is full of the emotional pain occasioned by his son's untimely death, the poet's impassioned plea to God for justice is nonetheless based on a logical, though daring, analogy between Malherbe's son and the Son of God. The argument of the appeal was based on the age-old belief that the Jews were the killers of Christ. Malherbe's speaker in the poem admits that "par la raison / Le trouble de âme étant sans guérison" (even reason cannot cure the pain in my soul), thus counteracting the resigned submission of "Consolation à M. Du Périer." Malherbe's use of overstatement in the poem—if one follows the analogy, the speaker falls into the same category as God—aligns him with the baroque movement, with its reliance on hyperbole and conflation.

Malherbe's influence on French lyric poetry has been castigated as negative, leading to the virtual disappearance of lyric poetry in the second half of the seventeenth century and its reappearance only with the development of the Romantic movement in the early nineteenth century. His influence on the evolution of the French language, however, remains decisive. Perhaps more than anyone else, Malherbe propagated the fundamental belief that expression in French is supremely clear and lucid. Every French child knows Antoine de Rivarol's famous dictum: "ce qui n'est pas clair n'est pas français" (what is not clear is not French). Modern French is remarkably close to the language of the seventeenth century, proof that Malherbe's reforms profoundly affected the historical evolution of the language.

Seventeenth-century lyric poetry in France includes a large body of work inspired by the renewed spirit of the Catholic Church after the Council of Trent (1643–1655) enacted reforms designed to counteract the inroads of the Reformation. The Counter-Reformation inspired a huge outpouring of paraphrases from the Bible, poetic translations of the Psalms, and poems of all genres devoted to pious subjects, meditations, and individual spiritual exercises. Meditative poetry focuses on the contemplation of man's fall and what awaits him after death. These meditations then shift to reflections on the life of Christ and on his role as redeemer of the truly penitent sinner.

The best known of the many devotional poets is the Marseille-born Jean de La Ceppède. His greatest work is *Les Théorèmes sur le sacré mystère de notre rédempteur* (Theorems on the Sacred Mystery of Our Redeemer, 1613–1621), a long series of sonnets representing diverse intellectual and spiritual currents that were present in France at the end of the sixteenth century. In his attempts to reconcile the sacred and the profane, the intimacy of individual devotional exercises accompanies a desire for public display. Full of mysticism and profound insights into the nature of the spiritual, *Les Théorèmes sur le sacré mystère de notre rédempteur* depicts man's wish to plumb the mysteries of his nature. La Ceppède pursued the paradoxical mission of the religious poet: to express and articulate the ineffable. Fundamental to La Ceppède's approach is his belief that each of God's creations has a profound meaning that the poet-priest is able to decipher. The result is a coherent universe made comprehensible through the mystical élan of the poet.

Les Théorèmes sur le sacré mystère de notre rédempteur is based on the tripartite devotional exercise comprising the composition, or sensual evocation, of an episode from the life of Christ; the intellectual analysis of the meaning of the episode; and an emotional prayer in which the penitent asks for God's further guidance. Although it is impossible to reduce the entire work to this model, these three modes lend the sonnets their remarkable variety, vivid images, realism, and power to move the reader. The brisk interplay between the intellectual and the sensual—and their fusion—makes these sonnets a monument in French literature. Like many of the lyric poets of this period, La Ceppède received critical acclaim only centuries after his death, when commentators rediscovered him in the early twentieth century.

To express the ineffable was the goal of another devotional poet from southern France, César de Nostredame (1553–1623). Son of the famous mystic and supposed prophet Michel Nostradamus, Nostredame was also a musician and painter who, like many before him, combined the expressiveness of these arts in his attempts to stir his readers to the height of spiritual fervor. Nostredame exploited the emphasis placed on the sense of sight—the visibility of the object of contemplation—in the devotional exercise, whether it was the cross, a biblical scene, or the spectacle of death. His poems are full of allusions to the art of painting, and there is a "pictorial" aspect to his poetry characteristic of the notion of poetry as a *peinture parlante* (painting that speaks) that was popular in the period. A remarkable poem illustrating this technique is "Le Portrait ou image du Sauveur" (The Portrait or Image of the Savior, 1606), which describes in minute detail the face of Christ. Nostredame's poems include *Dymas, ou le bon larron* (Dymas, or the Good Thief, 1606), *Les Perles, ou les larmes de la Sainte Magdeleine* (The Pearls, or the Tears of Saint Madeleine, 1606), and *La Marie dolente* (The Grieving Mary, 1608).

The long neglect that seventeenth-century French lyric poetry suffered has allowed modern critics to discover La Ceppède and Nostredame. Another such poet is Abraham de Vermeil (1555–1620). His poems were first published in 1600 and republished in 1602 and 1607. Aside from occasional poems composed for noble patrons and devotional poems, Vermeil's best-known works are love sonnets in the Petrarchan mode. Petrarchist imagery, with its focus on love's heartaches and pleasures, freighted with such opposing images as fire and ice, lightness and darkness, freedom and servitude, fidelity and infidelity, jealousy and serenity, was widely exploited in the lyric poetry of the period. Like those of Petrarch, Vermeil's love sonnets form a cycle that traces the various stages of love: its beginnings, inevitability, anguish, and pleasures, all of which conspire to destroy the emotional equilibrium of the suffering speaker. Despite the fact that the poem constitutes a work of art that may or may not be a real experience in the life of the poet, the reader is impressed with the apparent sincerity of Vermeil's work; the poems seem to reflect the genuine feelings of the poet behind the speaker. He rarely mentions happiness; rather, love is depicted as a tyrannical, malignant, and destructive force. The speaker's feelings run the gamut from ten-

derness to threatened violence toward the love object, but he cannot resist the all-powerful might of his bond. There is no ultimate resolution to the conflict between sexual desire, the irrational, and reason.

A typical Vermeil sonnet is "Je m'embarque joyeux, et ma voile pompeuse" (I embark full of joy, and my proud sail, 1600). This figurative ocean voyage has an auspicious start, but an oncoming tempest wrecks and sinks the ship, drowning the unfortunate speaker. The violence of the images evokes the emotional anguish the forlorn lover suffers. His rejection is likened to the horrible pain of death by drowning. The enumeration of verbs in the final lines suggests the stages in this untimely demise. The speaker's four clear stages in his nautical experience delineate the development of his emotional experience: first, he rejoices in the blue sky and sea; second, he espies the oncoming clouds, thunder, and lightning that menace the ship; third, huge waves buffet the vessel, ripping the masts from the decks; finally, death comes. The protean metamorphosis of the sea is a reflection of the speaker's tortured psyche.

Another sonnet by Vermeil, "Belle, je sers vos yeux et vos cheveux dorés" (Beautiful lady, I serve your eyes and your golden hair), addresses the love object directly, wittily playing on the notion of liberty and servitude. The speaker surveys the vast panorama of nature, observing lambs, flies, cattle, dogs, horses, and finally, on an incongruous note, jailed prisoners. He emphasizes that, although seemingly they must ceaselessly labor under the dictates of a cruel destiny, they are more fortunate than he, since they at least on occasion have the luxury of respite and repose, while he must ceaselessly submit to the eyes and the hair of his beloved. The miserable creatures he has commented upon at least have the right to live, while he is doomed to die in chains. Again, the profound torments of love are expressed in a typically baroque—that is, indirect—way. In the final *pointe* the speaker seems to reverse the idea developed in the poem that he is in greater torment than animals, convicts, and even insects.

This sonnet employs a form that Vermeil's contemporary lyric poets also used to great effect. In his "Le Matin" (The Morning, 1621) Théophile employs the same technique but concludes on a more optimistic note, casting his gaze over a natural landscape in which creatures must endlessly labor to survive. In Théophile's poem, however, the speaker and his lover enjoy a privileged status as god-like observers, not participants, in the daily toils that nature requires of its creatures. Both poems illustrate the role of nature in the lyric poetry of the period. It is more often used as a backdrop accentuating major themes. Nature is instrumental, not essential.

Manuscript for two sonnets by Malherbe, 1608 (Bibliothèque Nationale, Paris)

Saint-Amant stands as one of the major lyric poets of the seventeenth century. Called the "bon gros" (big fat) Saint-Amant, he was a bon vivant whose work varied greatly over a long career. Like many of the other lyric poets of the first half of the century, Saint-Amant was roundly criticized by Boileau, who in his *Art poétique* mocked the poet's poverty in his last days. Largely forgotten in the eighteenth century, Saint-Amant was rehabilitated in the nineteenth, praised in a collection of biographical and critical sketches by Théophile Gautier titled *Les Grotesques* (1844). Yet, the title of the book indicates the classical prejudices of even the most sympathetic critics. Twentieth-century criticism acknowledged Saint-Amant's prominent place among the great French lyric poets.

Traditional descriptions depict Saint-Amant as a drunk, joyously scrawling his poems on tavern walls. He often refers to his many travels in his poetry, describing the Canary Islands, the Alps, Rome, and Poland in his entertaining verse. Saint-Amant proclaimed the freedom of his inspiration throughout his career, proudly citing his natural verve and talent. Generations of commentators have seen his work as disordered and fragmented, calling him a careless, naive poet. The truth is that he was highly conscious of his art, with its complex mythological allusions, rhetorical stance of the speaker, and poetic structures based on association rather than logic, as dictated by Malherbe. Saint-Amant's versification is conservative, adhering to the Malherbian strictures so widespread throughout the century. Saint-Amant was inspired by several models, most notably Ovid among the ancients, as well as the French writers of the Renaissance–Clément Marot, Rabelais, and the Pléiade–yet the Italian and Spanish influence predominated. The mark of Spanish poet Góngora and his *Soledades* (Solitudes, 1613) can be seen especially in Saint-Amant's nature poems.

Saint-Amant himself was never too timid to boast of his own talents in his poetry, particularly in the art of description. His evocative tableaux of natural spectacles, depicted with great enthusiasm and verve, are perhaps most apparent in his best-known poem, "La Solitude" (1623), his noble "coup d'essai" (first try). The many editions of the poem are proof of its huge success, with many imitators throughout the century. Derivative of the Spanish *soledad,* the poem represents the speaker's solitary walk, reflections, and descriptions of a natural locale far from normal human contact. The work consists of a series of tableaux, each representing a description of natural or man-made objects. Featuring mythological deities and products of the supernatural, nature is depicted in the speaker's reactions as permanent yet in constant flux, a source of quasi-religious mystery. His references to other men are couched in contrasting terms, stressing their impermanence, inferiority, and vain pretensions.

Although "La Solitude" is often cited as an expression of pre-Romantic feeling for nature, the speaker's role in poetically recreating nature downgrades pure nature's intrinsic value. The "nature" personally conceived and represented by the speaker is a constantly changing, fabulous place, where other mortals have no real place. This "second" nature possesses clear superiority over the natural reality that everyone can experience. The speaker's control of nature–his ability to witness and absorb its beauty and to re-create nature in his words–places him on a quasi-divine level. His complete, almost magical, mastery of his environment contributes to his glorification. Most importantly, he includes in this exaltation the person to whom the poem is addressed, his patron, whose brilliant company surpasses even that of the poet's own muse, and who is privileged to share, as the dedicatee, this fantastical re-creation of nature. The poem can be considered an exercise in self-acclaim and even advertisement, for the speaker praises his own wondrous superiority as well as his patron's. It is a "coup d'essai" composed by a young, confident writer who, rather than boasting directly of his artistic prowess, rather expresses it in the many layers of the poem.

A similar poem is "Le Contemplateur" (1628), which presents the speaker's complex reactions to the natural features of Belle-Ile, an island off the coast of Normandy. Many critics have taken a biographical approach to this poem, emphasizing the sincerity or, indeed, the insincerity of the Protestant-born Saint-Amant's conversion to Catholicism in the 1620s. Addressed to Philippe Cospéan, the bishop of Nantes, the poem illustrates the speaker's activities and solitary meditations on a wide range of subjects. He discloses his loyalty to the French crown, his reverence for God and for Cospéan, and his broad interest in natural and scientific wonders. The religious orientation of many of the speaker's reactions conforms to the status and rank of his intended audience; clearly, he wishes to impress upon Cospéan the sincerity of his faith in God and the Catholic Church. Preoccupied with immortality, the speaker intimates the existence of a literal immortality through the love of God as well as a figurative immortality attained through the preeminence of his own art. Despite his protestations of faith in the Church, he indicates that his primary concern is for the latter kind of immortality. In this respect, then, Saint-Amant continues one of the primary themes of "La Solitude," self-promotion. The work stands as an example of the speaker's imagination, talent, faith, and loyalty. His reactions to natural phenomena are the means that allow him to advertise his talents:

Je ferai briller mes pensées,
Et crois que les plus grands censeurs
Les verront si bien agencées,
Qu'ils en goûteront les douceurs.

(I will make my thoughts shine,
And I believe that even the most severe critics
Will see them as so ordered,
That they will fully appreciate all my thoughts.)

The order that Saint-Amant boasts of in "Le Contemplateur" can also be seen in another nature poem, "La Pluie" (The Rain, 1624). Presenting a specific natural event rather than a panorama of nature, as in "Le Contemplateur" and "La Solitude," the work transports the reader to the country estate belonging to Jean-François Payen, the poet's friend and patron when "La Pluie" was composed. The poem opens with a description of the countryside parched by a long drought. A threatening sky appears, followed by a sudden downpour, beneficial in particular to the grapevines. The speaker's feelings of immense joy are set off against those of the peasants who till the soil. In effect, the speaker and his addressee stay on the periphery, observing the shower and the reactions of others who appear to exist within nature—the peasants, farm animals, a solitary pilgrim, and so forth. From this scheme a hierarchy suggests itself: the speaker and his patron enjoy a privileged status, whereas the rest of nature is downgraded. Its value consists primarily in the production of wine, which, of course, is to be consumed by Payen and his guest.

In true baroque style, "La Pluie" paradoxically reverses a series of traditional associations and meanings. The poem can be seen as a reversal of the biblical story of the Deluge: in this case divine wrath becomes a long period of dry sterility, and mercy and forgiveness take the form of a kind of "deluge," which grants renewed life to a dry and dying earth. Reinforcing these reversals are such details as the ominous, black rain clouds, which augur God's blessings; the peasants, who run away from the drenching object of their joy rather than toward it; and the abundance of water, which means that the speaker will not have to drink it. The divine libation, wine, will come from this blessing.

Despite the hierarchical view of nature in "La Pluie," in which the gods, the speaker, and Payen occupy roughly equivalent levels, while the humans, the animals, indeed all of nature, exist on a lower level, the poem constantly interweaves the noble style, the burlesque, and the realistic. Since the high, middle, and low styles in seventeenth-century French literature corresponded to certain classes of people or to certain types of actions, their intermingling in a single poem suggests and confirms the principal theme. Hierarchies

do exist in nature and among men, yet the marvelous arrival of the rain has created a renewed union among all levels of being. Both separately and equally real, the physical and the spiritual join together in this work to form a single entity. The enmity of the gods, made manifest in the sterilizing drought, has given way to a new period of harmony, fertility, and peace.

Saint-Amant's cycle of four seasonal sonnets has enjoyed much critical attention. Reflecting the various travels of the peripatetic poet, each sonnet depicts its respective season in a different locale: "Le Printemps aux environs de Paris" (Spring on the outskirts of Paris, 1649), "L'Eté de Rome" (Summer in Rome, 1643), "L'Automne des Canaries" (Autumn in the Canaries, 1649), and "L'Hiver des Alpes" (Winter in the Alps, 1649). The last poem describes a richly beautiful Alpine scene, evidently taken from Saint-Amant's experiences as he was traversing the Alps in mid winter. The beauty of the sun's reflections on the ice and snow is the subject of the first quatrain. Personification continues in the second quatrain, and the poem concludes with the speaker's profound pleasure in contemplating this beautiful—and healthful—locale. An image of the dazzling colors and light reflecting off the speaker's own eyes suggests an almost Romantic kind of aesthetic and psychic interpenetration between the speaker and the natural scene that he describes.

In the first tercet the speaker expands on the reasons why he takes such delight in the Alpine winter's beauties. As in many of Saint-Amant's other poems, paradox is a prime technique: the speaker's affection for the winter cold is a reversal of expectations, since the season is traditionally associated with old age and death in the literature of the time. Besides lending great beauty to the landscape, the snow takes on another function. It becomes a kind of deceptive cloak concealing the earth's true, sinful nature. The speaker's affection for winter goes beyond mere aesthetic pleasure; moral qualities come significantly into play in this stanza. The sonnet takes yet another tack in the concluding tercet. The consequences of the images of costume and concealment predominate here. The deceptive appearance of beautiful innocence and seeming virtue that the winter lends to the earth deludes even the mighty Jupiter, who showers divine mercy on the globe in the form of a refusal to cast punishing thunderbolts and lightning flashes on a sinful world. Again, the conclusion is paradoxical: Jupiter's clemency occurs during a season normally associated with the inclemency of the weather. What began as a paean to the beauties of a wintry mountain scene becomes in the last tercet a mythical explanation for an empirical meteorological phenomenon. Thunder and lightning do indeed occur extremely infrequently in the winter. The speaker

Decorated title page and title page for Jean de La Ceppède's long sonnet sequence on the various intellectual and spiritual currents present in late-sixteenth-century France (Musée Arbaud, Aix-en-Provence)

thus relies on his imagination, erudition, and observation to explore a scientific problem concerning the absence of thunder in winter. His fanciful answer can only delight the unsuspecting reader.

What critics now call *libertinage* played an important role in the French lyric poetry of the seventeenth century. A manifestation of the skeptical spirit that grew out of the Renaissance, the *libertins* questioned the traditional values and beliefs related to religion as well as morality. This emphasis on applying reason to venerated articles of faith accompanied the rise of the scientific method and spirit represented by such thinkers as Copernicus, Francis Bacon, and Galileo. The best-known poet associated with libertinage is Théophile. In 1619 he was exiled for one year, on the order of the king, for having written verses "indignes d'un chrétien" (unworthy of a Christian). Dubbed "le chef de la bande athéiste" (the leader of the atheist gang) and "le roi des libertins" (the king of the libertines) by the influential cleric Father François Garasse, in 1623 Théophile was accused of impiety and immorality, put on trial, and

condemned to the stake for the crime of "lèse-majesté divine" (treason against God). The poet fled but was arrested and imprisoned in Paris for two years. His most heartfelt poems were composed in his wretched prison cell. In 1625 he was released and banished for life from France. His once robust health ruined after two years of misery, Théophile died one year later.

Despite these persecutions, during his lifetime Théophile was recognized as a preeminent French poet. His work bears some influence of Malherbe's reforms, without rejecting outright the heritage of Pierre de Ronsard and the rest of the Pléiade. From his earliest poetic efforts he proclaimed his independence and autonomy as an innovator, a "modern" poet. Théophile's refusal to imitate his predecessors and belief that the poet should be guided by his own natural talents can be seen in "Elégie à une dame" (Elegy to a Lady). The poem functions as a preface to the 1621 edition of his works, a kind of personal *art poétique* promulgating the author's thoughts on the contemporary social and professional status of the poet, including a criticism of the methods and procedures of other poets, a definition of Théophile's own artistic manner, and, of course, an invitation to read and reflect on the selections in the edition. The apparently disjointed nature of his art, attributed to his libertine philosophy and a lack of discipline and self-restraint, prompted the poet to defend his work. Individual choice and predilection lie at the basis of Théophile's poetics.

A key line in the poem reads "La règle me deplaît, j'écris confusément" (I detest rules, I write confusedly). The adverb "confusément" in this line is difficult to translate since it comprehends several concepts. On the surface it simply carries the meaning of its closest English equivalent, "confusedly," which appears to confirm and admit the accusations of the classical critics that his poetry, like most of the lyric poetry of the period, was devoid of unity and coherence, that its overall disorder and "confusion" made it incomprehensible and, in the end, worthless. Théophile, however, is using an indirect—a baroque—device here. If one takes into account the original Latin meaning of this word (it is derived from the past participle of *confundere,* to pour together), the speaker intimates that his work is a skillful amalgamation of diverse parts, a clever "blend" of disparate elements that form a unified and pleasing ensemble. This indeed is the case in Théophile's poetry.

The charge of incoherence and discontinuity in Théophile's work—that it presents an undisciplined and immoral freethinker's ideology pointing to man's alienation in a godless universe—has been challenged by many twentieth-century critics. In fact, the apparent discontinuities in his complex poems are intended to challenge the reader. Théophile was aware that his text demanded a responsive and sensitive reader, capable of discerning cohesive patterns within an apparently incoherent structure. Just as Théophile wished to liberate himself from the tutelage of prior poets, he asked that his readers exercise the same free thought.

The poetry of love occupies the major portion of Théophile's output. Even his earliest poetic efforts, which were immediately recognized as those of an outstanding talent, impress the reader with their capacity to express the sensuality of love. The large number of editions of his poetry in the seventeenth century, including the second half of the century, demonstrate the popular acclaim that Théophile enjoyed among his contemporaries. Boileau's sweeping pronouncements condemning the irregularity and "aberrations" of the baroque poet greatly influenced the opinions of later generations. Now, however, Théophile is one of the most appreciated and studied poets of the period. Like Saint-Amant, Théophile's feeling for nature plays a large role in his work. The fusion of sensual love and

nature in his best-known poem, "La Solitude" (1621), is worthy of note.

The setting of "La Solitude" is the *locus amoenus* (pleasant place) so dear to many writers of Théophile's time. It is an enchanted, mysterious, remote locale in nature, a place of privilege where the lovers will meet and consummate their love. The transcendence of this tryst is reinforced by the remarkable sonorities in the verse, full of internal rhymes, assonance, alliteration, and a striking variety of rhetorical devices. The seeming perfection of this natural locale is subverted by an implicit undercurrent of violence, made manifest for the most part in the many mythological allusions. The violence announces the possible conflict between the self and the other that is to come later in the work. Two transitional stanzas, in which the speaker speaks directly to the natural locale, augur the coming of his beloved, Corinne.

The remainder of "La Solitude" is for the most part a long and complex address to Corinne, in which the speaker first describes her feminine charms in conventional terms. The sensuality of the speech is telling. Three stanzas depart from direct address, when, in an aside, the speaker self-consciously expresses his possible inability to convey to the reader the depth of this transcendent beauty in his art. In order to accomplish this formidable task, he assimilates Corinne to the natural setting in which she was initially framed. He exploits a favorite baroque image, that of Narcissus contemplating himself in the smooth surface of a pond, to enhance the interpenetration of flesh and nature. The fluid, impalpable reflection of Corinne's face on the water accentuates the fragility of her presence and the fleeting nature of the other, who must confront the speaker's attempts to appropriate her being. Liquid and flesh melt together to become one in a synesthetic concord:

Prête-moi ton sein pour y boire
Des odeurs qui m'embameront,
Ainsi mes sens se pâmeront
Dans les lacs de tes bras d'ivoire.

Je baignerai mes mains folâtres
Dans les ondes de tes cheveux,
Et ta beauté prendra les voeux
De mes oeillades idolâtres.

(Give me your breast, so that I can drink in
Aromas that will enrapture me,
And my senses will collapse
In the lakes of your ivory arms.

I will bathe my thrilled hands
In the waves of your hair,
And your beauty will acquiesce to the wishes
Of my worshipful glances.)

Frontispiece to the 1653 edition of Antoine Girard de Saint-Amant's Moyse sauvé, idylle héroïque
(engraving by Abraham Bosse; Archives de l'Institut de France)

The esoteric aspect of this declaration of love and fervent desire changes in the final four stanzas of the poem, as the speaker focuses more and more closely on the human reactions of Corinne as she hears his supplications. The speaker's lustfulness relies on one of the fundamental motifs of the poem, that this *locus amoenus* remains a hidden, secret place, far from prying eyes. The poem thus ends with a conventional reference to the law of discretion in love. The resolution of this tryst appears to be certain, but the speaker keeps his "promise" to Corinne, since the reader will never know for sure exactly what he and she did "Dans ce val solitaire et sombre" (In this solitary and dark place). Despite his apparently submissive entreaties, the speaker maintains constant control in the poem. He molds a fantastic, mythic scene that serves as an appropriate background to the apparently transcendent activities that will occur there. In effect, the entire poem is an elaborate exercise in magical transformation: the banal, secret meeting of illicit lovers becomes a poetic, mythologized encounter between two extraordinary, even god-like, individuals.

Another of Théophile's frequently anthologized love-nature poems is "Le Matin" (The Morning, 1621).

Based on a conventional medieval lyric form called the *aube* (dawn), in which illicit lovers must separate at dawn after a night spent together, far from the gaze of others, Théophile's baroque lyric inverts this pattern, allowing the privileged couple to remain together and to rejoice in the natural beauties that surround them. The stark contrasts drawn between the speaker and his beloved and the rest of nature's creatures, including other men, recalls Vermeil's sonnet "Belle, je sers vos yeux et vos cheveux dorés." The first section of the poem describes the coming of the dawn. As in "La Solitude," Théophile uses synesthesia, personification, allusions to myth, and hyperbole to create remarkable images of the rising sun:

L'aurore, sur le front du jour,
Sème l'azur, l'or et l'ivoire,
Et le soleil, lassé de boire,
Commence son oblique tour.

Ses chevaux, au sortir de l'onde,
De flamme et de clarté couverts,
La bouche et les naseaux ouverts,
Ronflent la lumière du monde.

(The dawn, on the day's brow,
Sows azure, gold, and ivory,
And the sun, weary of drinking,
Begins her oblique tour.

Her horses, on arising from the waves,
Covered with flame and fire,
Mouth and nostrils flaring,
Bellow the light of the world.)

There follows a series of stanzas enumerating the various creatures that greet the dawn and begin their work-laden day. The animals, birds, and insects who must begin their day precede the human domain, where various individuals awaken, weary, to commence their own lives. The coming day is described as a negative force that disrupts and troubles the calm and peace of the night. Among the unfortunate souls who must abandon the blessed realm of dreams and sleep is Alidor, in search of his beloved Iris, whose oneiric presence deceived the sleeping Alidor into thinking that she was actually present with him. His "doux sommeil" (sweet sleep) dissipates just as the calm, the shadows, and the silence of the night disappear before the oncoming sun. Like their master, the farm animals "Tremblent de voir la lumière" (Tremble on seeing the light). In the concluding two stanzas of the poem the speaker brings the reader back to his own domain, which he shares with his beloved Philis. For this privileged couple the coming day will not dispel the happiness and pleasure that they have enjoyed during the night. Rather than beginning a day of toil, which is the lot of the rest of nature, Philis and the speaker are free to commence a casual garden stroll. Here he will engage in a time-honored lover's pastime: comparing the beauty of the flowers to Philis's feminine charms. This conceit recalls the love poetry of the previous century, most notably that of Ronsard and the Pléiade, which Théophile admired and imitated. Thus, the blessed couple, separate from and superior to the nature around them, are exempt from the normal quotidian struggle for existence. They can devote themselves to the pursuit of love and contentment.

Théophile's genius went well beyond the realm of nature and love. Certain of his poems express an almost existential anguish, echoing, perhaps, the many trials and troubles in his life as well as his *libertin* thought. A remarkable poem in this vein is an ode, "Un corbeau devant moi croasse" (A raven before me caws). Théophile composed the poem most likely in 1620, a period of great stress in his life immediately after his 1619 exile and during his forced service to Charles d'Albert, duc de Luynes, whom he detested. Whereas in "La Solitude" and "Le Matin," in which the ongoing situation of the poems is readily apparent—the experi-

ence of two lovers ensconced in a natural locale—in the ode, reference to reality is more difficult to discern. The poem revolves around the hallucinatory visions of the speaker, who takes an almost surreal voyage into the subconscious. Comprised of two decasyllabic *dizains* (ten-line stanzas), the poem has two parts: in the first the speaker, on horseback, observes what appear to be strange manifestations of the supernatural, which become more and more fantastic as he enumerates them: a cawing crow, the sun passing behind a cloud, and then, bizarrely enough, two weasels and two foxes—animals traditionally associated with guile, evil, and the subterranean. When these creatures cross his path, his horse stumbles; his valet has an attack of epilepsy; and, like a kind of celestial punctuation, thunder cracks. An apparition materializes before the speaker's stricken eyes. At this point the reader is plunged into the fantastic: Charon, transporter of souls across the river Styx, calls out to the stunned speaker. The earth appears to open up under his feet. The second stanza offers a series of visions that seem to loom straight from hell:

Ce ruisseau remonte en sa source;
Un boeuf gravit sur un clocher;
Le sang coule de ce rocher;
Un aspic s'accouple d'une ourse;
Sur le haut d'une vieille tour
Un serpent déchire un vautour;
Le feu brûle dedans la glace,
Le soleil est devenu noir;
Je vois la lune qui va choir;
Cet arbre est sorti de sa place.

(This stream ascends to it source;
A bull climbs on a steeple;
Blood flows from this rock,
A viper couples with a bear;
On the top of an old tower
A snake tears a vulture;
Fire burns in ice,
The sun has blackened;
I see the moon as it begins to fall;
This tree has moved from its place.)

These mad dreams depict a descent into hell, where natural laws have been contravened. It is an apocalyptic fantasy (the final lines echo the biblical Apocalypse) foretelling the end of all things, the triumph of evil over man and, symbolically, the positive forces of nature and natural order. The paratactic developmental structure of the poem, which enumerates without elaborating on the possible significance of the descriptions and occurrences, bolsters the atmosphere of horror and terror. Though characteristic of baroque lyric poetry, the bizarre images in the poem met with profound disapproval among the classically biased critics who followed

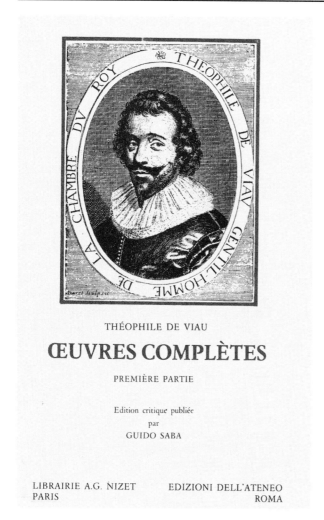

THÉOPHILE DE VIAU

ŒUVRES COMPLÈTES

PREMIÈRE PARTIE

Edition critique publiée
par
GUIDO SABA

LIBRAIRIE A.G. NIZET   EDIZIONI DELL'ATENEO
PARIS   ROMA

*Théophile de Viau (engraving by Pierre Daret;
Bibliothèque Nationale, Paris)*

Théophile. They saw only a parade of disgusting, outlandish poetic figures betraying the dismal taste and sensibilities of a disgraced "égaré" (lost one) such as Théophile, a writer who, content to remain faithful to his own muse, forswore the salutary influence of Malherbe, who had preached adherence to reason and regularity in poetry. Théophile's attempt to express poetically these subconscious hallucinations were for the classicists mere self-indulgent nonsense.

Another lyric poet of the early seventeenth century who shared Théophile's liberated views was Tristan L'Hermite. Known in his lifetime more for his plays than his poetry, Tristan was never mentioned in Boileau's condemnations of early-seventeenth-century poets. Tristan's poetry reveals three major influences, those of Malherbe, Théophile, and the Italian poet Giambattista Marino. Malherbe passed on to Tristan the various poetic forms that he used most frequently, as well as his generic and stylistic variety. Tristan's

poetry displays virtuosity and ingenuity and a willingness to dazzle and surprise the reader that are characteristic of Marino and Théophile. Yet, Tristan's work is so diverse that critics have had difficulty classifying him. The author of an *Office de la Vierge* (Office of the Virgin, 1646) and, conversely, a fast friend of the renowned libertine skeptic Cyrano de Bergerac, Tristan was above all careful to preserve his artistic independence. In the editions of his poetry many genres and styles are intermingled. Indeed, he mixes the poems of youth with the work of later years in the same volume, making his poems virtually impossible to date. His work seems to oscillate between opposite poles: depictions of untamed nature and delicately designed gardens, peaceful ponds and the fury of the sea, the clear light of the day and the somber obscurity of the night, skepticism and religious faith, dreams of death and the exuberance of youthful passion.

Tristan's most-read poem is probably "Le Promenoir des deux amants" (The Two Lovers' Stroll, 1633). Made famous for the quatrains that Claude Debussy set to music, the poem, like the solitudes of Saint-Amant and Théophile, depicts a *locus amoenus,* an ideal natural trysting place far from the ills and travails of other men and their civilized salons and courts. Full of ingenious Marinistic conceits, mythological allusions, and sometimes far-fetched descriptions, the poem is a wonderful example of the poetry of the period. The speaker's lover, Climène, displays the conventional features of feminine beauty inherited from antiquity (rosy cheeks, alabaster skin, golden hair, perfumed breath, and so forth), yet her assimilation with the natural locale and the concomitant anthropomorphizing of the locus reinforce the novelty of the piece. Entering more and more into the spirit of the locale as the poem develops, the two lovers appear to become one with the setting. As Claude K. Abraham has said, here the reader sees an example of the notion that "le paysage est un état d'âme" (the countryside is a state of the soul). In effect the characters dissolve into the natural tableau. The concluding stanzas illustrate the esotericism of the poem:

J'aurais plus de bonne fortune,
Caressé d'un jeune Soleil
Que celui qui dans le sommeil
Reçut les faveurs de la Lune.

Climène ce baiser m'enivre,
Cet autre me rend tout transi,
Si je ne meurs de celui-ci
Je ne suis pas digne de vivre.

(I would have greater fortune,
Caressed by a young sun [Climène]

Than he who received the moon's favors
As he slept. [the mythological Endymion]

Climène, this kiss transports me,
This one paralyzes me.
If I don't die from this one,
I do not deserve to live.)

The personal side of Tristan's poetry can be clearly seen in "La Mer" (The Sea, 1628). Because of its protean nature, water appealed particularly to the lyric poets of the period as a source of imagery. Here the sea exhibits its diverse moods as the speaker contemplates its transformations, which appear to reflect his own emotional state. The poem was occasioned by the death of a close friend of the poet in an engagement during the siege of the Ile de Ré directed by Gaston d'Orléans. As with Saint-Amant's "La Solitude," on first impression "La Mer" seems to be a series of unlinked descriptive tableaux, but the various scenes of the ever-changing sea are brought together through a network of recurring images, structures, mythological allusions, and metaphors. The work addresses Gaston, and in the conclusion the speaker, consoled by the sea's beauty and constant transformations, looks to a bright future in which the king's brother will accomplish glorious feats of arms. Hope and optimism displace grief and despair. This interpenetration between the microcosm and the macrocosm recalls not only a Renaissance preoccupation but also anticipates the works of the nineteenth-century Romantic movement, in which peace and solace are found within the beauties and wonder of nature. A long description of the changing sea leads to the depiction of a violent storm, which exteriorizes and concretizes the speaker-poet's pain. The tempest objectifies the depths of the speaker's sorrow, and like the "pilote désespéré" (desperate pilot) who "Ne reconnaît plus les étoiles, / Et ne tient plus le gouvernail" (Can no longer pinpoint the stars, / And can no longer control the rudder), he is in danger of losing all sense of direction. But the sudden return to calm restores the speaker-pilot's emotional and mental equilibrium. The entire seascape can thus be seen as an elaborate metaphor, with the sea reflecting the innermost feelings that the poet must confront in order to purge himself of emotional instability. Nature not only consoles man but also forces him to face and triumph over the inner forces that threaten to crush him.

A Tristan sonnet famous for its antitheses and paradoxes is "La Belle Esclave maure" (The Beautiful Moorish Slave). Imitated from Marino, the poem displays baroque taste at its extreme:

Beau monstre de nature, il est vrai, ton visage
Est noir au dernier point, mais beau parfaitement:

Title page for the third edition of Théophile's works, published in 1623, the same year that he was tried and convicted for "treason against God" (Bibliothèque Nationale, Paris)

Et l'ébène poli qui te sert d'ornement
Sur le plus blanc ivoire emporte l'avantage.

O merveille divine inconnue à notre âge
Qu'un objet ténébreux luise si clairement!
Et qu'un charbon éteint brûle si vivement
Que ceux qui de la flamme entretient l'usage!

Entre ces noires mains, je mets ma liberté;
Moi qui fus invincible à toute autre beauté,
Une Maure m'embrase, une esclave me dompte.

Mais cache-toi, Soleil, toi qui viens de ces lieux
D'où cet astre est venu, qui porte pour ta honte
La nuit sur son visage et le jour dans ses yeux.

(Beautiful monster of nature, it's true, your face
Is black to the extreme, but perfectly beautiful:
And the polished ebony with which you adorn yourself
Is superior to the whitest ivory.

O divine miracle unknown to our age
That such a dark object can shine so clearly!

Tristan L'Hermite (portrait by Desrochers;
Bibliothèque Nationale, Paris)

And that a charred coal can burn more brightly
Than those consumed in flames!

Between these black hands I place my liberty;
I, who was unconquerable by any other beauty,
A Moor enflames me, a slave enslaves me.

Hide, Sun, you who come from those places
Whence this star has come, who bears, much to your
    shame,
Night on her face and day in her eyes.)

The complete inversion of the traditional features of
feminine beauty forces the reader to challenge a fundamental received belief, that womanly charm must
be associated with white, blond, pink, and blue. The
oxymoron that opens the poem signals the paradoxical nature of the piece, surprising readers by presenting them with a proposition that contradicts the laws
of nature. Based on the conventional motif of the *belle
matineuse* (morning beauty) that is also seen in Théophile's "Le Matin," the sonnet reflects Tristan's penchant for stretching the limits of the lyric manner of
the period.

Tristan's effort to upset the reader's expectations
is indeed typical of baroque lyric poetry. Commentators have demonstrated that the French poets of the
early seventeenth century aimed above all to redefine
inherited aesthetic systems. These poets wished to
"deautomatize" the reader's reactions, to offer new
poems based on the old schemes, and to create a new
audience capable of assimilating these artistic innovations. One way of achieving this goal was to subvert
long-established poetic genres. Since an author can
narrow interpretative possibilities by focusing on a
particular genre, a poet, by mixing generic signs, may
disrupt the reader's expectations and thereby create
new meanings. One such genre was the ancient "consolation." This literature of bereavement was meant to
comfort the grieving addressee and to offer moral precepts intended to demonstrate that inevitable, natural
death must be borne with patience, resignation, and
faith. The best-known consolation in seventeenth-century
French poetry is Malherbe's "Consolation à M. du
Périer, sur la mort de sa fille." In it Malherbe strictly
follows the generic parameters inherited from the stoic
Roman writer Seneca. Since Malherbe assumed that
his readers would be aware of the generic assumptions
inherent in the consolation, their expectations were
not disrupted. Thus, Malherbe's intention in this particular poem was not to inject generic innovation into
the poetic enterprise.

Most of Malherbe's other consolations exhibit
the same bent, but several, nonetheless, modulate
genre by inserting and thus evoking other genres. In
consolations addressed to young widows, Malherbe
suggests that new love may give solace to the
bereaved. Accompanying this idea is the admonition
to hearken to the passage of time because youth and
beauty are fleeting, thus modulating to another genre
quite different from the consolation, the "carpe diem"
poem. The gradual infiltration of carpe-diem motifs
into the consolation is expanded in Tristan's "Consolation à Idalie, sur la mort d'un parent" (Consolation
for Idalie, on the Death of a Parent). The speaker is
not so audacious as to offer his own affections to the
stricken lady, which is a logical step, given the nature
of the carpe-diem genre. The opening stanzas of the
poem proffer the typical commonplaces about the
inevitability of death–that all people are subject to its
rigors despite their worth and that it is self-indulgent
to grieve excessively because to do so is to ignore the
blessings of those who remain. True to the consolation, the speaker emphasizes the brevity of Idalie's
own life. Despite the distressing impermanence of
Idalie's life, the speaker offers the gift of immortality
based on the eternal merit of his poetic art. In a
time-honored device belonging to the carpe-diem
genre, the speaker suggests an exchange: he will grant
eternal "life" to the lady in his poetry, while she in
turn will acquiesce to his amorous advances. Having
abandoned the conventional consolation at this point
in the poem, the speaker in the final lines clearly

expresses his desire to gather rosebuds while he and Idalie may.

Not surprisingly, perhaps, a consolation by the professed freethinker Théophile displays the highest degree of innovation. Although the title of the poem, "A Monsieur de L., sur la mort de son père" (To Mr. de L., on the Death of His Father, 1621), immediately signals the consolation, the opening lines abruptly upset the reader's expectations. The speaker's brusque imperatives are alien to the genre, immediately disrupting the intimate communication between addressee and speaker that are basic to the consolation. The speaker's desire to commune with nature recalls other genres: the solitude and, with its reference to the dawn, the *belle matineuse*. Subsequent stanzas allude to a violent storm and long winter rains that prevented the addressee from "arriving," which can be interpreted as reaching an emotional resolution as well as a geographical destination. The poem thus turns obliquely to the subject of consolation by reference to natural events. The newly arrived "Soleil qui luit" (shining sun) signals a new beginning, recovery from past grief, and a bright future. Théophile uses the conventional motifs of the solitude—nature's beauty and effervescence, inspiration in solitary meditation, and pastoral sensuality—to create a decidedly unconventional consolation. There follows a sudden dialectical shift from the sun's warmth to the frigidity of death. The hideousness of death, while common to the solitude, was often linked to the consolation. These verses lead to a series of death-related themes familiar in the consolation: death is all-powerful; no one is immune to its rigors; the addressee, too, will meet death; his dead father, unaware of his son's grief, has passed on to inexorable oblivion. In the final section of the poem the speaker moves on to apocalyptic visions that recall neither the consolation nor the carpe-diem genre but rather the solitude, particularly Saint-Amant's "Le Contemplateur," which in turn shares elements with the contemporary devotional lyric as practiced by such artists as La Ceppède. Théophile's consolation thus emerges as a curious hybrid that incorporates or alludes to four lyric genres: the solitude, the carpe-diem poem, the religious meditation, and, of course, the consolation.

The French classicists dictated that poetic genres should be pure, that the mixing of genres betrayed a defective poetic aesthetic interested only in empty display and frivolous surprises. The baroque lyric poets clearly saw things differently and did not hesitate to experiment with generic modulation in order to create not only new texts but also new audiences as well. A new poetic generation's quest for innovation, for liberation from the preceding Pléiade generation, explains

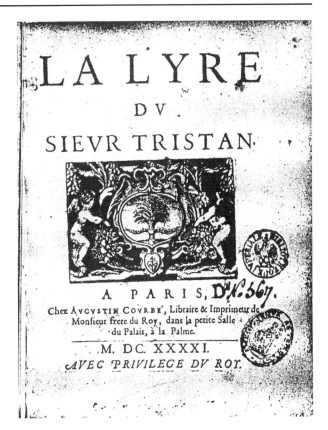

Title page for the 1641 collection of Tristan's poetry that includes his sonnet "La Belle Esclave maure" (The Beautiful Moorish Slave; Bibliothèque Nationale, Paris)

the generic "instability" seen in the lyric genre of the consolation. Tristan and Théophile in particular viewed their poetic tradition as ripe for subversion.

Seventeenth-century French lyric poetry has sometimes been dubbed "post-Renaissance," "preclassical," or even "pre-Romantic." After long years of neglect, scorn, and persistent misconceptions, this body of work is now judged on its own terms. The lyric poets of this period saw themselves as innovators and pioneers who devoted themselves to creating an art that was rooted in the past but that also staked out new taxonomies and new directions.

Selected Works of Lyric Poetry:
Jean de La Ceppède, *Les Théorèmes . . . sur le sacré mystère de nostre rédemption . . .* (Toulouse: Colomiez, 1613–1621);

François de Malherbe, *Œuvres* (Paris: C. Chappellain, 1630);

César de Nostredame, *Dymas, ou le bon larron* (Toulouse: Colomiez, 1606);

Nostredame, *La Marie dolente* (Toulouse: Colomiez, 1608);

Nostredame, *Les Perles, ou les larmes de la Sainte Magdeleine* (Toulouse: Colomiez, 1606);

Nostredame, *Pièces héroïques et diverses poésies* (Toulouse: Colomiez, 1608);

Antoine Girard de Saint-Amant, *Dernier recueil de diverses poésies* (Paris: A. de Sommaville, 1658);

Saint-Amant, *Moyse sauvé, idylle héroïque* (Paris: A. Courbé, 1653);

Saint-Amant, *Œuvres* (Paris: Printed by R. Estienne for F. Pomeray & T. Quinet, 1629; enlarged, Rouen: J. Boulley, 1642);

Théophile de Viau, *Œuvres* (Paris: J. Quesnel, 1621; revised and enlarged, Paris: J. Quesnel, 1623; revised and enlarged, Paris: P. Billaine & J. Quesnel, 1626);

Tristan L'Hermite, *Les Amours* (Paris: P. Billaine & A. Courbé, 1638);

Tristan, *La Lyre* (Paris: A. Courbé, 1641);

Tristan, *L'Office de la Sainte Vierge* (Paris: P. des-Hayes, 1646);

Tristan, *Les Plaintes d'Acante et autres oeuvres* (Paris: P. Billaine, 1634);

Tristan, *Les Vers héroïques* (Paris: J. B. Loyson & N. Portier, 1648).

References:

Claude K. Abraham, *Enfin Malherbe: The Influence of Malherbe on French Lyric Prosody, 1605–1674* (Lexington: University Press of Kentucky, 1971);

Abraham, *Tristan L'Hermite* (Boston: Twayne, 1980);

Antoine Adam, *Histoire de la littérature française au XVIIe siècle,* 5 volumes (Paris: Domat, 1948–1956);

Adam, *Théophile de Viau et la libre pensée française en 1620* (Paris: Droz, 1935);

Roselyne de Ayala and Jean-Pierre Guéno, *Belles Lettres: Manuscripts by the Masters of French Literature,* translated by John Goodman (New York: Abrams, 2001);

Ferdinand Brunetière, *Histoire de la littérature française classique,* 4 volumes (Paris: C. Delagrave, 1904–1917);

Ferdinand Brunot, *La doctrine de Malherbe d'après son commentaire sur Desportes* (Paris: G. Masson, 1891);

Imbrie Buffum, *Studies in the Baroque from Montaigne to Rotrou* (New Haven: Yale University Press, 1957);

Terence C. Cave, *Devotional Poetry in France, ca. 1570–1613* (Cambridge: Cambridge University Press, 1969);

Paul A. Chilton, *The Poetry of Jean de La Ceppède: A Study in Text and Context* (Oxford: Oxford University Press, 1977);

Robert Corum, *Other Worlds and Other Seas: Art and Vision in Saint-Amant's Nature Poetry* (Lexington: French Forum, 1979);

Lance K. Donaldson-Evans, *Poésie et meditation chez Jean de La Ceppède* (Geneva: Droz, 1969);

Edwin M. Duval, *Poesis and poetic tradition in the early works of Saint-Amant: Four Essays in Contextual Reading* (York, S.C.: French Literature Publications, 1981);

René Fromilhague, *Malherbe, technique et création poétique* (Paris: A. Colin, 1954);

Julien Goeury, *L'autopsie et le théorème: Poétique des Théorèmes spirtiruels (1613–1622) de Jean de La Ceppède* (Paris: H. Champion, 2001);

Françoise Gourier, *Etude des oeuvres poétiques de Saint-Amant* (Geneva: Droz, 1961);

Roger Guichemerre, *Quatre poètes du XVIIe siècle: Malherbe, Tristan L'Hermite, Saint-Amant, Boileau* (Paris: SEDES, 1991);

Henri Lafay, *La Poésie française du premier XVIIe siècle (1598–1630): Esquisse pour un tableau* (Paris: Nizet, 1975);

Jean Lagny, *Le Poète Saint-Amant, 1594–1661: Essai sur sa vie et ses oeuvres* (Paris: Nizet, 1964);

John D. Lyons, *The Listening Voice: An Essay on the Rhetoric of Saint-Amant* (Lexington, Ky.: French Forum, 1982);

Odette de Mourgues, *Metaphysical, Baroque & Précieux Poetry* (Oxford: Clarendon Press, 1953);

Yvette Quenot, *Jean de La Ceppède* (Paris: Memini, 1998);

Quenot, *Les lectures de La Ceppède* (Geneva: Droz, 1986);

Christopher D. Rolfe, *Saint-Amant and the Theory of "Ut Pictura Poesis"* (London: Modern Humanities Research Association, 1972);

Jean Rousset, *La Littérature de l'âge baroque en France: Circé et le paon* (Paris: J. Corti, 1953);

David Lee Rubin, *Higher, Hidden Order: Design and Meaning in the Odes of Malherbe* (Chapel Hill: University of North Carolina Press, 1972);

Rubin, *The Knot of Artifice: A Poetic of the French Lyric in the Early 17th Century* (Columbus: Ohio State University Press, 1981);

Rubin, ed., *La Poésie française du premier 17e siècle: Textes et contextes* (Tübingen: G. Narr, 1986);

Rubin and Mary B. McKinley, eds., *Convergences: Rhetoric and Poetic in Seventeenth-Century France* (Columbus: Ohio State University Press, 1989);

Guido Saba, *Fortunes et infortunes de Théophile de Viau: histoire de la critique* (Paris: C. Klincksieck, 1997);

Saba, *Théophile de Viau: un poète rebelle* (Paris: Presses universitaires de France, 1999);

James C. Shepard, *Mannerism and Baroque in Seventeenth-Century French Poetry: the example of Tristan L'Hermite* (Chapel Hill: University of North Carolina Press, 2001).

Books for Further Reading

Adam, Antoine. *Histoire de la littérature française au dix-septième siècle,* 3 volumes. Paris: Albin Michel, 1997.

Baldner, Ralph Willis. *Bibliography of Seventeenth-Century French Prose Fiction.* New York: Printed for the Index Committee of the Modern Language Association of America by the Columbia University Press, 1967.

Beugnot, Bernard. *Les muses classiques: Essai de bibliographie rhétorique et poétique, 1616–1716.* Paris: Klincksieck, 1996.

Boilève-Guerlet, Annick. *Le genre romanesque: Des théories de la Renaissance italienne aux réflexions du XVIIe siècle français.* Santiago de Compostella: Servicio de Publicacions e intercambio cientifico, 1993.

Burke, Peter. *The Fabrication of Louis XIV.* New Haven: Yale University Press, 1992.

Bury, Emmanuel. *Littérature et politesse: L'Invention de l'honnête homme 1580–1750.* Paris: Presses Universitaires de France, 1996.

Church, William F. *Richelieu and Reason of State.* Princeton: Princeton University Press, 1972.

Cioranescu, Alexandre. *Bibliographie de la littérature française du dix-septième siècle,* 3 volumes. Paris: CNRS, 1965–1966.

Cornette, Joël. *Les années cardinales: Chronique de la France, 1599–1652.* Paris: Sedes, 2000.

Cornette. *Chronique du règne de Louis XIV.* Paris: Sedes, 1997.

Davidson, Hugh. *Audience, Words and Art: Studies in Seventeenth-Century French Rhetoric.* Columbus: Ohio State University Press, 1965.

Foucault, Michel. *Folie et déraison: Histoire de la folie à l'âge classique.* Paris: Plon, 1961. Translated by Richard Howard as *Madness and Civilization: A History of Insanity in the Age of Reason.* New York: Pantheon, 1965.

Foucault. *Les mots et les choses.* Paris: Gallimard, 1966.

Fumaroli, Marc. *L'âge de l'éloquence: Rhétorique et "res literaria" de la Renaissance au seuil de l'époque classique.* Paris: Albin Michel, 1994.

Godenne, René. *Histoire de la nouvelle française aux XVIIe et XVIIIe siècles.* Geneva: Droz, 1970.

Harth, Erica. *Cartesian Women: Versions and Subversions of Rational Discourse in the Old Regime.* Ithaca, N.Y.: Cornell University Press, 1992.

Harth. *Ideology and Culture in Seventeenth-Century France.* Ithaca, N.Y.: Cornell University Press, 1983.

Hipp, Marie-Thérèse. *Mythes et réalités: Enquête sur le roman et les mémoires 1600–1700.* Paris: Klincksieck, 1976.

Kettering, Sharon. *French Society, 1589 to 1715.* Harlow, U.K.: Prentice Hall, 2001.

Kolakowski, Leslek. *Chrétiens sans église: La conscience religieuse et le lien confessionnel au XVIIe siècle,* translated by Anna Posner. Paris: Gallimard, 1969.

Kors, Alan Charles. *Atheism in France, 1650–1729.* Princeton: Princeton University Press, 1990.

Lancaster, Henry Carrington. *A History of French Dramatic Literature in the Seventeenth Century,* 5 volumes. Baltimore: Johns Hopkins University Press / Paris: Presses Universitaires de France, 1929–1942.

Laplanche, François. *L'écriture, le sacré et l'histoire: Erudits et politiques protestants devant la Bible en France au XVIIe siècle.* Amsterdam: APA-Holland University Press, 1986.

Lever, Maurice. *La fiction narrative en prose au XVIIe siècle: Répertoire bibliographique du genre romanesque en France (1660–1700).* Paris: CNRS, 1976.

Lever. *Romanciers du Grand Siècle,* revised and enlarged edition. Paris: Fayard, 1996.

Lougee, Carolyn. *Le Paradis des femmes: Women and Social Stratification in Seventeenth-Century France.* Princeton: Princeton University Press, 1976.

Lough, John. *France Observed in the Seventeenth Century by British Travellers.* Stocksfield, U.K. & Boston: Oriel Press, 1984.

Lough. *Paris Theater Audiences in the Seventeenth and Eighteenth Centuries.* London: Oxford University Press, 1957.

Lough. *Writers and Public in France: From the Middle Ages to the Present Day.* Oxford & New York: Clarendon Press, 1978.

Lyons, John D. *Exemplum: The Rhetoric of Example in Early Modern France and Italy.* Princeton: Princeton University Press, 1989.

Lyons. *Kingdom of Disorder: The Theory of Tragedy in Classical France.* West Lafayette, Ind.: Purdue University Press, 1999.

Maclean, Ian. *Woman Triumphant: Feminism in French Literature, 1610–1652.* Oxford: Clarendon Press, 1977.

Mandrou, Robert. *From Humanism to Science, 1480 to 1700,* translated by Brian Pearce. Hassocks, U.K.: Harvester Press, 1979.

Martin, Henri-Jean. *Livre, pouvoirs et société à Paris au 17e siècle.* Geneva: Droz, 1969. Translated by David Gerard as *Print, Power and People in Seventeenth-Century France.* Metuchen, N.J. & London: Scarecrow Press, 1993.

Merlin, Hélène. *Public et littérature en France au XVIIe siècle.* Paris: Les Belles Lettres, 1994.

Mesnard, Jean. *La culture du XVIIe siècle: Enquêtes et synthèses.* Paris: Presses Universitaires de France, 1992.

Mesnard, ed. *Précis de littérature française du XVIIe siècle,* with the collaboration of Fumaroli. Paris: Presses Universitaires de France, 1990.

Phillips, Henry. *Church and Culture in Seventeenth-Century France.* New York & London: Cambridge University Press, 1997.

Phillips. *The Theater and Its Critics in Seventeenth-Century France.* Oxford & New York: Oxford University Press, 1980.

Ranum, Orest. *Artisans of Glory: Writers and Historical Thought in Seventeenth-Century France.* Chapel Hill: University of North Carolina Press, 1980.

Ranum. *The Fronde: A French Revolution 1648–1652.* New York: Norton, 1993.

Ranum. *Paris in the Age of Absolutism.* New York: Wiley, 1968.

Schérer, Jacques. *La dramaturgie classique en France.* Paris: Nizet, 1950.

Showalter, English. *The Evolution of the French Novel, 1641–1782.* Princeton: Princeton University Press, 1972.

Solomon, Howard. *Public Welfare, Science and Propaganda in Seventeenth-Century France.* Princeton: Princeton University Press, 1972.

Stankiewicz, W. J. *Politics and Religion in Seventeenth-Century France.* Berkeley: University of California Press, 1960.

Thirouin, Laurent. *L'aveuglement salutaire· Le Réquisitoire contre le théâtre dans la France classique.* Paris: Champion, 1997.

Thuau, Etienne. *Raison d'Etat et pensée politique à l'époque de Richelieu.* Paris: Colin, 1966.

Timmermans, Linda. *L'accès des femmes à la culture (1598–1715): Un débat d'idées de Saint François de Sales à la marquise de Lambert.* Paris: Champion, 1993.

Tocanne, Bernard. *L'idée de nature en France dans la seconde moitié du XVIIe siècle: Contribution à l'histoire de la pensée classique.* Paris: Klincksieck, 1978.

Truchet, Jacques, ed. *Le XVIIe siècle: Diversité et cohérence.* Paris: Berger-Levrault, 1992.

Zuber, Roger. *Le Classicisme: Histoire de la littérature française,* with the collaboration of Micheline Cuénin. Paris: Flammarion, 1998.

Zuber. *La Littérature française du XVIIe siècle classique.* Paris: Presses Universitaires de France, 1993.

Contributors

Wendy Ayres-Bennett . . . . *New Hall, Cambridge University*

Mark Bannister . . . . *Oxford Brookes University*

Faith E. Beasley . . . . *Dartmouth College*

Christian Biet . . . . *Université Paris X–Nanterre, France*

Jean-Vincent Blanchard . . . . *Swarthmore College*

Thomas M. Carr Jr. . . . . *University of Nebraska–Lincoln*

Mark A. Cohen . . . . *Bard College*

Robert Corum . . . . *Kansas State University*

Jean-Pierre van Elslande . . . . *University of Neuchâtel, Switzerland*

Perry Gethner . . . . *Oklahoma State University*

Elizabeth C. Goldsmith . . . . *Boston University*

Eglal Henein . . . . *Tufts University*

Olivier Jouslin . . . . *Université Paris IV–Sorbonne*

Erec R. Koch . . . . *Tulane University*

Donna Kuizenga . . . . *University of Vermont*

John D. Lyons . . . . *University of Virginia*

Georges May . . . . *Yale University*

Gita May . . . . *Columbia University*

Craig Moyes . . . . *King's College London*

Buford Norman . . . . *University of South Carolina*

Jeffrey N. Peters . . . . *University of Kentucky*

Jeremy Sabol . . . . *Yale University*

Allison Stedman . . . . *Bucknell University*

Malina Stefanovska . . . . *University of California, Los Angeles*

Michael Taormina . . . . *Columbia University*

David Wetsel . . . . *Arizona State University*

Abby E. Zanger . . . . *Yale University*

Jeanne Morgan Zarucchi . . . . *University of Missouri–St. Louis*

Cumulative Index

Dictionary of Literary Biography, Volumes 1-268
Dictionary of Literary Biography Yearbook, 1980-2001
Dictionary of Literary Biography Documentary Series, Volumes 1-19
Concise Dictionary of American Literary Biography, Volumes 1-7
Concise Dictionary of British Literary Biography, Volumes 1-8
Concise Dictionary of World Literary Biography, Volumes 1-4

Cumulative Index

DLB before number: *Dictionary of Literary Biography,* Volumes 1-268
Y before number: *Dictionary of Literary Biography Yearbook,* 1980-2001
DS before number: *Dictionary of Literary Biography Documentary Series,* Volumes 1-19
CDALB before number: *Concise Dictionary of American Literary Biography,* Volumes 1-7
CDBLB before number: *Concise Dictionary of British Literary Biography,* Volumes 1-8
CDWLB before number: *Concise Dictionary of World Literary Biography,* Volumes 1-4

Cumulative Index

Peck, Harry Thurston 1856-1914..... DLB-71, 91

Peden, William 1913-1999 .... DLB-234

Peele, George 1556-1596 .... DLB-62, 167

Pegler, Westbrook 1894-1969 ....DLB-171

Péguy, Charles Pierre 1873-1914 .... DLB-258

Pekić, Borislav 1930-1992... DLB-181; CDWLB-4

Pellegrini and Cudahy DLB-46

Pelletier, Aimé (see Vac, Bertrand)

Pelletier, Francine 1959- DLB-251

Pemberton, Sir Max 1863-1950 .... DLB-70

de la Peña, Terri 1947- DLB-209

Penfield, Edward 1866-1925.......... DLB-188

Penguin Books [U.K.].............. DLB-112

Penguin Books [U.S.] DLB-46

Penn Publishing Company............ DLB-49

Penn, William 1644-1718 .... DLB-24

Penna, Sandro 1906-1977 .... DLB-114

Pennell, Joseph 1857-1926............ DLB-188

Penner, Jonathan 1940- Y-83

Pennington, Lee 1939- Y-82

Penton, Brian 1904-1951 .... DLB-260

Pepys, Samuel
    1633-1703........ DLB-101, 213; CDBLB-2

Percy, Thomas 1729-1811 .... DLB-104

Percy, Walker 1916-1990......DLB-2; Y-80, Y-90

Percy, William 1575-1648.............DLB-172

Perec, Georges 1936-1982 .... DLB-83

Perelman, Bob 1947- DLB-193

Perelman, S. J. 1904-1979 .... DLB-11, 44

Perez, Raymundo "Tigre" 1946- DLB-122

Peri Rossi, Cristina 1941- DLB-145

Perkins, Eugene 1932- DLB-41

Perkoff, Stuart Z. 1930-1974........... DLB-16

Perley, Moses Henry 1804-1862 .... DLB-99

Permabooks DLB-46

Perovsky, Aleksei Alekseevich
    (Antonii Pogorel'sky) 1787-1836..... DLB-198

Perrault, Charles 1628-1703 .... DLB-268

Perri, Henry 1561-1617 .... DLB-236

Perrin, Alice 1867-1934.............. DLB-156

Perry, Bliss 1860-1954 .... DLB-71

Perry, Eleanor 1915-1981............. DLB-44

Perry, Henry (see Perri, Henry)

Perry, Matthew 1794-1858 .... DLB-183

Perry, Sampson 1747-1823 .... DLB-158

Perse, Saint-John 1887-1975 .... DLB-258

Persius A.D. 34-A.D. 62 .... DLB-211

Perutz, Leo 1882-1957 .... DLB-81

Pesetsky, Bette 1932- DLB-130

Pestalozzi, Johann Heinrich 1746-1827 .... DLB-94

Peter, Laurence J. 1919-1990 .... DLB-53

Peter of Spain circa 1205-1277 .... DLB-115

Peterkin, Julia 1880-1961 .... DLB-9

Peters, Lenrie 1932- DLB-117

Peters, Robert 1924- DLB-105

"Foreword to *Ludwig of Baviria*" DLB-105

Petersham, Maud 1889-1971 and
    Petersham, Miska 1888-1960........ DLB-22

Peterson, Charles Jacobs 1819-1887 ..... DLB-79

Peterson, Len 1917- DLB-88

Peterson, Levi S. 1933- DLB-206

Peterson, Louis 1922-1998 .... DLB-76

Peterson, T. B., and Brothers DLB-49

Petitclair, Pierre 1813-1860............ DLB-99

Petrescu, Camil 1894-1957 .... DLB-220

Petronius circa A.D. 20-A.D. 66
    .... DLB-211; CDWLB-1

Petrov, Aleksandar 1938- DLB-181

Petrov, Gavriil 1730-1801............. DLB-150

Petrov, Valeri 1920- DLB-181

Petrov, Vasilii Petrovich 1736-1799 ..... DLB-150

Petrović, Rastko
    1898-1949 ....DLB-147; CDWLB-4

Petruslied circa 854? DLB-148

Petry, Ann 1908-1997................ DLB-76

Pettie, George circa 1548-1589........ DLB-136

Peyton, K. M. 1929- DLB-161

Pfaffe Konrad flourished circa 1172 .... DLB-148

Pfaffe Lamprecht flourished circa 1150 .. DLB-148

Pfeiffer, Emily 1827-1890 .... DLB-199

Pforzheimer, Carl H. 1879-1957 .... DLB-140

Phaedrus circa 18 B.C.-circa A.D. 50 .... DLB-211

Phaer, Thomas 1510?-1560 .... DLB-167

Phaidon Press Limited DLB-112

Pharr, Robert Deane 1916-1992 .... DLB-33

Phelps, Elizabeth Stuart 1815-1852..... DLB-202

Phelps, Elizabeth Stuart 1844-1911... DLB-74, 221

Philander von der Linde
    (see Mencke, Johann Burckhard)

Philby, H. St. John B. 1885-1960 ...... DLB-195

Philip, Marlene Nourbese 1947- DLB-157

Philippe, Charles-Louis 1874-1909 ...... DLB-65

Philips, John 1676-1708............. DLB-95

Philips, Katherine 1632-1664 .... DLB-131

Phillipps, Sir Thomas 1792-1872....... DLB-184

Phillips, Caryl 1958- DLB-157

Phillips, David Graham 1867-1911..... DLB-9, 12

Phillips, Jayne Anne 1952- Y-80

Phillips, Robert 1938- DLB-105

"Finding, Losing, Reclaiming: A Note
    on My Poems"................. DLB-105

Phillips, Sampson and Company DLB-49

Phillips, Stephen 1864-1915 .... DLB-10

Phillips, Ulrich B. 1877-1934........... DLB-17

Phillips, Wendell 1811-1884.......... DLB-235

Phillips, Willard 1784-1873............ DLB-59

Phillips, William 1907- DLB-137

Phillpotts, Adelaide Eden (Adelaide Ross)
    1896-1993 .... DLB-191

Phillpotts, Eden 1862-1960...DLB-10, 70, 135, 153

Philo circa 20-15 B.C.-circa A.D. 50......DLB-176

Philosophical Library DLB-46

Phinney, Elihu [publishing house] DLB-49

Phoenix, John (see Derby, George Horatio)

PHYLON (Fourth Quarter, 1950),
    The Negro in Literature:
    The Current Scene................ DLB-76

Physiologus circa 1070-circa 1150 .... DLB-148

Piccolo, Lucio 1903-1969 .... DLB-114

Pickard, Tom 1946- DLB-40

Pickering, William [publishing house] ... DLB-106

Pickthall, Marjorie 1883-1922 .... DLB-92

Pictorial Printing Company DLB-49

Pielmeier, John 1949- DLB-266

Piercy, Marge 1936- DLB-120, 227

Pierro, Albino 1916- DLB-128

Pignotti, Lamberto 1926- DLB-128

Pike, Albert 1809-1891............... DLB-74

Pike, Zebulon Montgomery
    1779-1813.................. DLB-183

Pillat, Ion 1891-1945 .... DLB-220

Pilon, Jean-Guy 1930- DLB-60

Pinckney, Eliza Lucas 1722-1793 .... DLB-200

Pinckney, Josephine 1895-1957 .... DLB-6

Pindar circa 518 B.C.-circa 438 B.C.
    ....DLB-176; CDWLB-1

Pindar, Peter (see Wolcot, John)

Pineda, Cecile 1942- DLB-209

Pinero, Arthur Wing 1855-1934......... DLB-10

Piñero, Miguel 1946-1988 .... DLB-266

Pinget, Robert 1919-1997.............. DLB-83

Pinkney, Edward Coote 1802-1828 ..... DLB-248

Pinnacle Books...................... DLB-46

Piñon, Nélida 1935- DLB-145

Pinsky, Robert 1940- Y-82

Robert Pinsky Reappointed Poet Laureate.... Y-98

Pinter, Harold 1930- DLB-13; CDBLB-8

Piontek, Heinz 1925- DLB-75

Piozzi, Hester Lynch [Thrale]
    1741-1821..................DLB-104, 142

Piper, H. Beam 1904-1964 .... DLB-8

Piper, Watty........................ DLB-22

Pirandello, Luigi 1868-1936........... DLB-264

Pirckheimer, Caritas 1467-1532 ....DLB-179

Pirckheimer, Willibald 1470-1530 ....DLB-179

Pisar, Samuel 1929- Y-83

Pisemsky, Aleksai Feofilaktovich
    1821-1881 .... DLB-238

Pitkin, Timothy 1766-1847............ DLB-30

The Pitt Poetry Series: Poetry Publishing
    Today Y-85

Pitter, Ruth 1897- DLB-20

Pix, Mary 1666-1709 .... DLB-80

Pixerécourt, René Charles Guilbert de
    1773-1844.................... DLB-192

Plaatje, Sol T. 1876-1932 .... DLB-125, 225

Plante, David 1940- Y-83

Platen, August von 1796-1835 .... DLB-90

W

Cumulative Index

ISBN 0-7876-6012-4

9 780787 660123

90000